APPLIED MATHEMATICS
FOR BUSINESS, ECONOMICS,
AND THE SOCIAL SCIENCES

FRANK S. BUDNICK

University of Rhode Island

APPLIED
MATHEMATICS

FOR BUSINESS, ECONOMICS,
AND THE SOCIAL SCIENCES

McGRAW-HILL BOOK COMPANY

New York   St. Louis   San Francisco   Auckland   Bogotá
Düsseldorf   Johannesburg   London   Madrid   Mexico
Montreal   New Delhi   Panama   Paris
São Paulo   Singapore   Sydney   Tokyo   Toronto

CHAPTER PHOTO CREDITS

O. Chris Maynard—Magnum; 1. Werner Bischof—Magnum; 2. Mary Alice McAlpin—
Nancy Palmer; 3. Burk Vzzle—Magnum; 4. American Museum of Natural History;
5. U.S. Department of Agriculture; 6. Bruce Thomas—Nancy Palmer; 7. Tektronix
Corporation; 8. IBM Corporation; 9. Cornell Capa—Magnum; 10. Burk Vzzle—
Magnum; 11. Harald Sund—Nancy Palmer; 12. Reflejo—Nancy Palmer; 13. Bruce
Davidson—Magnum; 14. David A. Rahm—McGraw-Hill; 15. Bruce Davidson—
Magnum; 16. Ken Kennedy—Nancy Palmer.

Library of Congress Cataloging in Publication Data

Budnick, Frank S
    Applied mathematics for business, economics, and the
social sciences.

    Includes index.
    1. Business mathematics. I. Title.
HF5691.B88   513'.93   78-31948
ISBN 0-07-008851-9

APPLIED MATHEMATICS
FOR BUSINESS, ECONOMICS,
AND THE SOCIAL SCIENCES

1234567890 DODO 7832109

This book was set in Bodoni by Progressive Typographers.
The editors were Charles E. Stewart and Stephen Wagley;
the designer was Nicholas Krenitsky;
the production supervisor was Dominick Petrellese.
The drawings were done by Fine Line Illustrations, Inc.
R. R. Donnelley & Sons Company was printer and binder.

TO JANE, WITH LOVE

APPLICATIONS*

* Explicitly labeled in the text.

APPLICATIONS

INTRODUCTION Mathematics is an integral part of the education of students in business, economics, and the social sciences. There is increasingly a desire to improve the level of quantitative sophistication possessed by graduates in these types of programs. The objective is not to make mathematicians of these students, but to make them as comfortable as possible in an environment which increasingly makes use of quantitative analysis and the computer. Students are discovering that they must integrate mathematics, statistical analysis, and the computer in both required and elective courses within their programs. Furthermore, organizations are becoming more effective users of quantitative tools and the computer. Decision makers will be better equipped to operate within this type of environment if they are familiar with the more commonly used types of quantitative analyses and the technology of the computer. Such familarity can assist them in being better "critics" and "users" of these tools, and hopefully, better decision makers.

DESIGN OF BOOK This book is an applied mathematics book for students in business, economics, and the social sciences. It provides a comprehensive treatment of selected topics in both finite mathematics and calculus. Although intended principally for students in business and economics, the book is appropriate for students in the social sciences. Designed primarily for a two-term course, the book can be adapted easily for a one-term course. It is appropriate for use in both two-year schools and four-year schools, as well as at the "foundation" level for graduate programs which require some mathematics background. M.B.A. and M.P.A. programs are typical graduate programs having this type of requirement.

Suggested course structures follow. For a two-term course, Term 1 would cover Chapters 0 to 9, while Term 2 would cover Chapters 10 to 16.

The first term is primarily a course in finite mathematics. Using Chapters 2 to 6 and 8 as a suggested core, Chapters 0, 1, 7, and 9 may be included depending upon the needs of students and the interest of the instructor. Chapters 0 and 1 should be included when students require a review of algebra and an introduction to set theory. Chapter 7 may be covered where a more complete coverage of linear programming is desired. Chapter 9 will probably be required for students in business and economics.

The second term is primarily an applied calculus course. Complete coverage of Chapters 10 to 15 is recommended; however, certain material may be excluded depending upon the needs and abilities of students.

The following are some suggested course structures for one-term courses:

A. Emphasis on Calculus A one-term course with emphasis on calculus would have a suggested core consisting of Chapter 2, Sections 5.1 to 5.2, and Chapters 10 to 15. Where students require a review of algebra and an introduction to set theory, Chapters 0 and 1 should be included.

B. Emphasis on Finite Mathematics A one-term course with emphasis on finite mathematics would select from among Chapters 0 to 9 and 16. Chapters may be included or excluded for the same reasons mentioned in the discussion of Term 1 of the two-term structure.

C. Combination of Finite Mathematics and Calculus A one-term course emphasizing both areas might have a variety of structures. A suggestion is that this type of course have a core which includes Chapters 2 to 5, 10 to 13, and 15. To this core may be added other chapters which expand the coverage of either area or both.

Specific features of this book are

1 **A level of presentation which carefully develops and reinforces topics.**

2 **A style which appeals to the intuition of students and provides a great deal of visual reinforcement (almost 250 figures).**

3 **An applied orientation which motivates students and provides a sense of purpose for studying mathematics (see table on pages xv to xviii indicating number and breadth of applications).**

4 **An approach which first develops the mathematical concept and then reinforces with applications.**

5 **An approach which minimizes the use of rigorous mathematical proofs. Proofs are included at the end of selected chapters for interested persons.**

6 Special aids which address the most universal shortcoming of students entering this type of course: weak algebra skills. These aids include an optional chapter (Chapter 0) which reviews key algebra principles. A chapter pretest allows the student and instructor to identify areas requiring special attention. In addition, "Algebra Flashbacks" are used throughout the book to assist the student in the recall of key rules or concepts. The flashback usually consists of a restatement of a rule or concept with a reference to the appropriate section in Chapter 0.

7 Notes to students which provide them with special insights.

8 "Points for Thought and Discussion" which allow students to pause for a moment and reconsider a concept or example from a different perspective. Their purpose is to reinforce and extend the student's understanding.

9 A multitude of other learning aids including

almost 450 solved examples

a wealth of exercises (1761)

chapter tests

chapter objectives

end of chapter checklists

lists of key terms and concepts

summary lists of important formulas

10 An instructors manual which contains

answers for all exercises and tests

suggestions for different course structures

prototype examples for new applications

transparency masters for selected figures

a bank of questions for constructing quizzes and tests

Although applications are presented throughout the book, Chapters 5 and 13 are devoted entirely to applications. The intent is that instructors cover as many applications in these chapters as they feel appropriate for their students. Chapter 14 (Classical Optimizations: Functions of Several Variables) is optional and not a prerequisite for Chapter 15 (Integral Calculus). Chapter 9 (Mathematics of Finance) has no prerequisite chapter. Except for the last part of Sec. 16.5, Chapter 16 (Introduction to Probability Theory) has no prerequisite chapters.

Some exercises in the book are considered to be of a high level of difficulty. These are preceded by an asterisk (*).

ACKNOWLEDGMENTS I wish to express my sincere appreciation to the many persons who have contributed either directly or indirectly to this project. These include: my students who endured the class testing of the manuscript and who provided valuable feedback and suggestions for improvements; Richard R. Weeks and Warren F. Rogers, both of the University of Rhode Island, who provided me with administrative support and allowed minimal distractions during the course of the project.

I wish to thank Professor Howard T. Bell, Shippensburg State College; Professor Robert I. Canavan, Monmouth College; Professor H. Howard Frisinger, Colorado State University; Professor Edward L. Keller, California State University; Dr. Marvin Rothstein, University of Connecticut; Professor Charles Sinclair, Portland State University; Professor Martin K. Starr, Columbia University; Professor Dale E. Walston, University of Texas; and Professor Robert A. Yawin, Springfield Technical Community College for reviewing the manuscript at various stages along the way. Their comments proved extremely helpful in rewriting.

A very special thanks goes to Professor Susan E. Potter, Rhode Island Junior College, who stayed with the project from start to finish and helped me clean up those initial "rough" drafts of chapters. Also, to Professor Terry D. Shaw, University of Texas at Austin, who provided excellent feedback for rewriting the calculus chapters.

I want to thank the people at McGraw-Hill with whom I worked directly. These persons include Donald E. Chatham, Charles E. Stewart, Stephen Wagley, and Nicholas Krenitsky. They provided the kind of support that an author truly appreciates.

I also wish to thank: Françoise Boulanger, Mary Howard, Mary Tafuri, Cathy Hebert, and Joseph Slott for their assistance in developing problems and solution sets; Sue E. Rubinsky, Jean Parrish, and Edith Williams for typing the manuscript and the Instructor's Manual; and Diane Marcotte for her assistance in preparing copies of chapters for classroom testing.

I also wish to make a special acknowledgment to Dr. Rudolph P. Lamone, University of Maryland, who has had an important influence on my career.

I also wish to thank my parents, Mr. and Mrs. Willard L. Budnick, for their continued support and encouragement during this endeavor as well as all others.

And last, but certainly not least, I want to thank my family—Jane, Chris, Scott, and (newly arrived) Kerry—for their patience, understanding, encouragement, and love. They allowed me the necessary solitude of "my lonely writer's garret," but they regularly liberated me whenever I needed reminding that I am (first and foremost) a father and a husband.

Frank S. Budnick

As we begin our study of mathematics in this book, you may need to review certain concepts, properties, or rules of algebra. This chapter provides a brief review of the elements of algebra which the author believes
are important in studying the following material. You should take time
to test your understanding of these algebraic concepts by taking the
Chapter Pretest.

CHAPTER PRETEST

*Corresponding
Section
in Chapter*

1 $-[-(-16) + 10] =$ (0.1)

2 $|-10| =$ (0.1)

3 $35 - (-20) + (-15) =$ (0.1)

4 $\dfrac{(-3)(-4)(-6)}{(-12)(-1)} =$ (0.1)

5 $[(x^3)^2]^3 =$ (0.2)

6 $(\frac{1}{2})^{-2} =$ (0.2)

7 $x^5/x^3 =$ (0.2)

8 $(4x - 2y + z) - (-3x + 4y - 2z) =$ (0.2)

2

9 $\dfrac{2x^2(3x^3)}{(-2x^2)^2} =$ (0.2)

10 Factor $2a^3b^2c + 4a^2bc^2$. (0.3)

11 Factor $x^2 - 4$. (0.3)

12 Factor $x^2 - 5x + 4$. (0.3)

13 $\frac{1}{5} + \frac{2}{15} - \frac{1}{6} =$ (0.4)

14 $\dfrac{a}{b}\dfrac{b}{c} =$ (0.4)

15 $\dfrac{2x^2}{3} \div \dfrac{4x^3}{9} =$ (0.4)

16 $x^{1/2}x^{4/3} =$ (0.5)

17 $\sqrt[3]{a^2b}\,\sqrt[3]{ab^2} =$ (0.5)

18 $3\sqrt{2} - 2\sqrt{8} =$ (0.5)

19 $\sqrt{\dfrac{4a^2}{9}} =$ (0.5)

20 Express $\sqrt{x}$ using a fractional exponent. (0.5)

21 Express $x^{2/3}$ in radical form. (0.5)

22 Determine the roots of the equation

$$x - 4 = 2x - 6$$ (0.6)

23 Determine the roots of the equation

$$3x = 3x + 10$$ (0.6)

24 Determine the roots of the equation

$$x^2 - 4 = 0$$ (0.6)

25 Determine the roots of the equation

$$x^2 - 6x + 9 = 0$$ (0.6)

ANSWERS FOR PRETEST

1 -26; **2** 10; **3** 40; **4** -6; **5** x^{18}; **6** 4; **7** x^2; **8** $7x - 6y + 3z$; **9** $\dfrac{3x}{2}$;

10 $2a^2bc(ab + 2c)$; **11** $(x + 2)(x - 2)$; **12** $(x - 4)(x - 1)$; **13** $\frac{1}{6}$; **14** $\dfrac{a}{c}$;

15 $\dfrac{3}{2x}$; **16** $x^{11/6}$; **17** ab; **18** $-\sqrt{2}$; **19** $\dfrac{2a}{3}$; **20** $x^{1/2}$; **21** $\sqrt[3]{x^2}$; **22** 2;

23 no roots; **24** $+2, -2$; **25** 3.

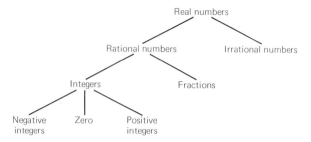

FIGURE 0.1

THE REAL NUMBER SYSTEM 0.1

In this section we discuss real numbers and some of their basic properties.

Real Numbers

In this book we will be concerned with *real numbers* only. Refer to Fig. 0.1. The real number system consists of rational numbers and irrational numbers. *Rational numbers* are those numbers which can be expressed as the *ratio*, or quotient, of two integers with the divisor being a nonzero integer. Thus, a rational number is a number which *can* be expressed in the form a/b where a and b are integers and b does not equal 0 (stated $b \neq 0$). The numbers $\frac{1}{5}$, $-\frac{2}{7}$, $\frac{23}{455}$, and $137/(-750)$ are all examples of rational numbers.

Because any integer a can be written in the form of the quotient $a/1$, all integers are also rational numbers. Examples include $-5 = -5/1$ and $54 = 54/1$. Zero is also considered to be an integer (neither negative nor positive), and it can be written in the quotient form $0/b = 0$, $b \neq 0$.

Irrational numbers are real numbers which cannot be expressed as the ratio of two integers. Numbers such as $\pi = 3.14159265 \cdots$ (which is the ratio of the circumference of a circle to its diameter), $\sqrt{2} = 1.4142 \cdots$, $\sqrt{3} = 1.7321 \cdots$, and $\sqrt{5} = 2.2361 \cdots$ are all examples of irrational numbers.

The set of real numbers can be represented using a *number line* (see Fig. 0.2). The number line has a zero point, often called the *origin*, which is used to represent the real number 0. Each and every point on the number line corresponds to a real number. The correspondence is that the real number represented by a point equals the *directed distance* traveled in moving from the origin to that point. Movements from left to right along the number line are considered to be in a *positive* direction. Thus, points to the right of the origin correspond to positive real numbers whereas points to the left correspond to negative real numbers. Note that for each and every real number there corresponds a unique point on the number line.

FIGURE 0.2

The *inequality symbol* $>$ or $<$ is used to indicate that two numbers are not equal. When the inequality symbol is placed between two numbers, it "opens" in the direction of the larger number. Given two real numbers a and b, the notation $a > b$ is read "a is greater than b." The statement $a > b$ implies that on the real number line a is located to the right of b.

Rules of Signs

The following rules of signs are very useful in combining signed numbers.

RULE 1
If a is a real number, $-(+a) = -a$.

RULE 2
If a is a real number, $-(-a) = a$.

Example 0.1
(a) $-(+5) = -5$, or -5 is the negative of $+5$.
(b) $-(-8) = 8$, or 8 is the negative of -8.

RULE 3
If the sign immediately preceding a set of parentheses is positive, the parentheses may be removed provided the signs on all terms inside the parentheses are kept the same.

Example 0.2
(a) $+(10 - 5 + 8) = 10 - 5 + 8$
(b) $+(-5 + 16) = -5 + 16$

RULE 4
If the sign immediately preceding a set of parentheses is negative, the parentheses may be removed provided the signs on all terms inside the parentheses are changed.

Example 0.3
(a) $-(10 - 6) = -10 + 6$
(b) $-(3 - 7 + 10) = -3 + 7 - 10$

RULE 5
If the sequence of signs immediately preceding a number contains an even number of minus signs, then the ultimate sign of the number is positive.

RULE 6
If the sequence of signs immediately preceding a number contains an odd number of minus signs, then the ultimate sign of the number is negative.

(a) $-[+(-10)] = 10$ since there is an even number (2) of minus signs. **Example 0.4**
(b) $-[-(-15)] = -15$ since there is an odd number (3) of minus signs.

Absolute Value

The *absolute value* of a real number is the magnitude or size of the number without the sign. The notation $|a|$ denotes the absolute value of a.

DEFINITION
For any real number a,

$$|a| = \begin{cases} a & \text{if } a \text{ is positive or zero} \\ -a & \text{if } a \text{ is negative} \end{cases}$$

The absolute value of the number $+5$ is $|+5| = 5$. The absolute value of -20 is $|-20| = 20$. The absolute value of 0 is $|0| = 0$. **Example 0.5**

Addition of Real Numbers

The following rules apply when real numbers are added.

RULE 7
If a and b are real numbers having the same sign, then the sum of a and b is found by adding their absolute values and applying the common sign to the result.

(a) $(+9) + (+7) = +(|+9| + |+7|)$ **Example 0.6**
$\qquad\qquad\quad = +(9 + 7)$
$\qquad\qquad\quad = 16$

(b) $(-23) + (-17) = -(|-23| + |-17|)$
$$= -(23 + 17)$$
$$= -40$$

RULE 8
If a and b are real numbers having opposite signs, then the sum of a and b is found by determining the absolute value of each number, subtracting the smaller absolute value from the larger, and applying to the result the sign of the number having the larger absolute value.

Example 0.7

(a) For $(+15) + (-25)$, $|+15| = 15$ and $|-25| = 25$. Therefore,
$$(+15) + (-25) = -(25 - 15)$$
$$= -(10)$$
$$= -10$$

(b) For $(-12) + (+18)$, $|-12| = 12$ and $|+18| = 18$. Therefore,
$$(-12) + (+18) = +(18 - 12) = 6$$

The following four properties apply to the addition of real numbers.

PROPERTY 0.1: COMMUTATIVE LAW FOR ADDITION
Given any two real numbers a and b, the order in which a and b are added does not affect their sum. Stated mathematically,
$$a + b = b + a$$

PROPERTY 0.2: ASSOCIATIVE LAW FOR ADDITION
If a, b, and c are real numbers, then
$$(a + b) + c = a + (b + c)$$

Example 0.8

The sum $(+7) + (-15) + (11)$ can be determined as
$$[(+7) + (-15)] + (11) = (-8) + (11)$$
$$= 3$$
or
$$(+7) + [(-15) + (11)] = (+7) + (-4)$$
$$= 3$$

PROPERTY 0.3: ADDITIVE-IDENTITY LAW
If a is a real number, the sum of a and 0 equals a, or $a + 0 = 0 + a = a$.

PROPERTY 0.4: ADDITIVE-INVERSE LAW
For any real number a there corresponds a unique
real number $-a$ which has the property that

$$a + (-a) = (-a) + a = 0$$

The number $-a$ is called the *additive inverse* of a.

(a) The additive inverse of $+15$ is -15.
(b) The additive inverse of -6 is 6.

**Example
0.9**

Subtraction of Real Numbers

The subtraction operation can be thought of in a variety of different ways. One method is to convert subtraction problems into addition problems by using the following rule.

RULE 9
Subtracting the real number b from the real number
a is the same as adding a and the additive inverse of b.
To state it mathematically,

$$(a) - (b) = (a) + (-b)$$

(a) $(10) - (6) = (10) + (-6)$
$\qquad\qquad = 4$
(b) $(-6) - (10) = (-6) + (-10)$
$\qquad\qquad\quad = -16$
(c) $(12) - (-5) = (12) + (+5)$
$\qquad\qquad\quad = 17$

**Example
0.10**

Multiplication and Division of Real Numbers

The following rules of signs apply in multiplying and dividing two real numbers.

RULE 10
If two real numbers a and b have the same
sign, the sign of their product is positive.

RULE 11
If two real numbers a and b have opposite
signs, the sign of their product is negative.

RULE 12

If two real numbers a and b have the same sign, the sign of a/b or b/a is positive.

RULE 13

If two real numbers a and b have opposite signs, the sign of a/b or b/a is negative.

Example 0.11

(a) $(+5)(+10) = 50$
(b) $(-6)(-4) = 24$
(c) $(3)(-5) = -15$
(d) $(+10)/(+5) = 2$
(e) $(-125)/(-5) = 25$
(f) $(240)/(-20) = -12$

The following five properties apply to the multiplication of real numbers.

PROPERTY 0.5: COMMUTATIVE LAW FOR MULTIPLICATION

Given two real numbers a and b, the order in which they are multiplied does not affect their product. Stated mathematically,

$$a \cdot b = b \cdot a$$

PROPERTY 0.6: ASSOCIATIVE LAW FOR MULTIPLICATION

If a, b, and c are real numbers,

$$(a \cdot b) \cdot c = a \cdot (b \cdot c)$$

Example 0.12

(a) $(25)(4)(-10) = [(25)(4)](-10)$
$= (100)(-10)$
$= -1,000$

Similarly,

$$(25)(4)(-10) = (25)[(4)(-10)]$$
$$= 25(-40)$$
$$= -1,000$$

PROPERTY 0.7: DISTRIBUTIVE LAW
If a, b, and c are real numbers,

$$a(b + c) = a \cdot b + a \cdot c$$

(a) $8(6 - 3) = (8)(6) + (8)(-3)$
$\qquad = 48 - 24$
$\qquad = 24$
(b) $(-7)[(a) + (-b)] = (-7)(a) + (-7)(-b)$
$\qquad\qquad\qquad = -7a + 7b$

**Example
0.13**

PROPERTY 0.8: MULTIPLICATIVE-
IDENTITY LAW
If a is a real number,

$$(a)(1) = (1)(a) = a$$

PROPERTY 0.9: MULTIPLICATIVE-
INVERSE LAW
For any nonzero real number a, there corresponds a
unique real number $1/a$ which has the property that

$$a \left(\frac{1}{a}\right) = \left(\frac{1}{a}\right) a = 1$$

The number $1/a$ is called the *multiplicative inverse*,
or *reciprocal*, of a.

(a) The multiplicative inverse of 8 is $\frac{1}{8}$.
(b) The multiplicative inverse of -10 is $-\frac{1}{10}$.

**Example
0.14**

The following rule is helpful when more than two numbers are multiplied.

RULE 14
If three or more signed numbers are multiplied, the
sign of the product is negative if the number of nega-
tive terms is odd. If the number of negative terms is
even, the sign of the product is positive.

(a) $(-2)(1)(-15) = 30$. The sign is positive since the product includes
two negative terms.

**Example
0.15**

(*b*) $(-3)(-5)(-1)(-5)(-2) = -150$. The sign is negative since the product includes five negative terms.

Follow-up Exercises

In Exercises 0.1 to 0.10, simplify the expression.

0.1 $-(+6)$ **0.2** $-(-10)$

0.3 $+(-5)$ **0.4** $+(-9)$

0.5 $-[-(+20)]$ **0.6** $+[+(-25)]$

0.7 $-[-(-6)]$ **0.8** $-[-(-4)]$

0.9 $-(a - b - c)$ **0.10** $-[-a + b - c]$

In Exercises 0.11 to 0.16, simplify the expression.

0.11 $|-100|$ **0.12** $|25|$

0.13 $|5| + |-6|$ **0.14** $|-(-50)|$

0.15 $|-[-(-8)]|$ **0.16** $|-(+30)|$

In Exercises 0.17 to 0.26, find the sum.

0.17 $(+10) + (-5)$ **0.18** $(+17) + (-8)$

0.19 $(-8) + (-3)$ **0.20** $(-6) + (-7)$

0.21 $(-2) + (5)$ **0.22** $(-18) + (+14)$

0.23 $(-2) + (+6) + (-4)$ **0.24** $(-7) + (-3) + (+9)$

0.25 $(+23) + (-8) + (6)$ **0.26** $(-4) + (-7) + (-4)$

In Exercises 0.27 to 0.32, perform the indicated subtraction.

0.27 $(+6) - (+7)$ **0.28** $(+15) - (-8)$

0.29 $(-9) - (+6)$ **0.30** $(-12) - (+18)$

0.31 $(-10) - (-15)$ **0.32** $(-18) - (+18)$

In Exercises 0.33 to 0.40, perform the indicated operations.

0.33 $(-10) + (-4) - (-15)$ **0.34** $(-6) - (-8) + (-9)$

0.35 $(-10) - (+10) + (-10)$ **0.36** $(-12) + (-4) - (+10)$

0.37 $(+7) - (-15) + (+6)$ **0.38** $(-7) + (-7) - (-14)$

0.39 $(8) - (-5) + (-6)$ **0.40** $(10) - (8) - (-3)$

In Exercises 0.41 to 0.52, perform the indicated operations.

0.41 $(-10)(-2.5)$ **0.42** $(-7)(+3.5)$

0.43 $(-2)(-4)(1)(-3)$ **0.44** $(-3)(-2)(-6)$

0.45 $(-9)(-0.5)(2)(6)$ **0.46** $(-2)(-2)(-2)(-2)$

0.47 $(-12)/(-1.5)$ **0.48** $(-18)/(+6)$

0.49 $\dfrac{(-8)(-2)}{-4}$ **0.50** $\dfrac{(3)(-4)(-5)}{-6}$

0.51 $\dfrac{(-2)(-4)(-.5)(-6)}{(-3)(-8)}$ **0.52** $\dfrac{(1.5)(-3)(2)(-4)}{(-1)(-6)(0.5)}$

Positive Integer Exponents

When a real number a is multiplied times itself, we denote this product as $a \cdot a$ or aa. If the same number is multiplied times itself 5 times, the product is denoted by $aaaaa$. A shorthand notation which can be used to express these products is

$$aa = a^2$$

and $$aaaaa = a^5$$

The number written above and to the right of a is called an *exponent*. The exponent indicates the number of times a occurs as a factor.

DEFINITION
If n is a positive integer and a is any real number,

$$a^n = \underbrace{a \cdot a \cdot a \cdots a}_{n \text{ factors}}$$

The term a^n can be verbalized as "a raised to the nth power" where a is considered the *base* and n is the exponent or *power*.

(*a*) $(-2)(-2)(-2)(-2)(-2)(-2) = (-2)^6$ **Example**
(*b*) $(5)(5)(5) = (5)^3$ **0.16**
(*c*) $(3)^4 = (3)(3)(3)(3)$
(*d*) $(-5)(-5)(4)(4)(4) = (-5)^2(4)^3$
(*e*) $aaaabbb = a^4b^3$
(*f*) $aa/(bbbb) = a^2/b^4$

The following four rules of exponents apply when a and b are any real numbers and m and n are positive integers.

RULE 15
To find the product of two powers of the same base, raise the base to a power equal to the sum of the two exponents. Mathematically, this is denoted as

$$a^m \cdot a^n = a^{m+n}$$

(*a*) $(a^3)(a^4) = a^{3+4} = a^7$ **Example**
(*b*) $(a^5)(a) = a^{5+1} = a^6$ **0.17**
(*c*) $(-2)^3(-2)^2 = (-2)^5$
(*d*) $(2)(2)^3(2)^5 = (2^{1+3})(2^5)$
           $= 2^{4+5}$
           $= 2^9$

Note that for *more than* two factors having the same base, the product is found by adding the exponents for all terms.

RULE 16
To raise the mth power of a to the nth power, raise the base a to a power equal to the product of the two exponents. Mathematically, this is denoted by

$$(a^m)^n = a^{mn}$$

Example 0.18

(a) $(a^2)^3 = a^{2 \cdot 3} = a^6$
(b) $[(3)^2]^4 = (3)^{2 \cdot 4} = (3)^8$
(c) $[(-1)^3]^5 = (-1)^{3 \cdot 5} = (-1)^{15} = -1$
(d) $(x^5)^4 = x^{20}$

RULE 17
To find the nth power of the product of two factors, find the product of each factor raised to the nth power. Mathematically, this is denoted by

$$(ab)^n = a^n b^n$$

Example 0.19

(a) $(ab)^4 = a^4 b^4$
(b) $(2x)^3 = (2)^3(x)^3 = 8x^3$
(c) $(4 \cdot 5)^2 = (4)^2(5)^2 = (16)(25) = 400$

The following definition will be important in dealing with the next rule of exponents.

DEFINITION
If n is a positive integer and $a \neq 0$,

$$a^{-n} = \frac{1}{a^n}$$

Example 0.20

(a) $a^{-2} = 1/a^2$
(b) $x^{-5} = 1/x^5$
(c) $(2)^{-3} = 1/(2)^3 = \frac{1}{8}$

RULE 18
To find the quotient of two powers of the same base, raise the common base to a power equal to the exponent of the numerator minus the

exponent of the denominator. Mathematically, this is denoted by

$$\frac{a^m}{a^n} = a^{m-n}$$

where $a \neq 0$.

Example 0.21

(a) $\dfrac{a^6}{a^3} = a^{6-3} = a^3$

(b) $\dfrac{x^2}{x^4} = x^{2-4} = x^{-2}$

According to the last definition, this answer can be rewritten as

$$x^{-2} = \frac{1}{x^2}$$

(c) $\dfrac{(2)^3}{(2)^7} = (2)^{3-7} = (2)^{-4} = \dfrac{1}{(2)^4} = \dfrac{1}{16}$

DEFINITION
If a is real and not equal to 0, $a^0 = 1$.

This definition can be verified by using Rule 18. If we concede that any nonzero quantity divided by itself equals 1, then $a^m/a^m = 1$. However, according to Rule 18,

$$\frac{a^m}{a^m} = a^{m-m} = a^0$$

Therefore, $\qquad\qquad a^0 = 1$

Example 0.22

(a) $(10)^0 = 1$
(b) $(4x)^0 = 1, x \neq 0$
(c) $-5y^0 = -5(1) = -5, y \neq 0$

Follow-up Exercises

In Exercises 0.53 to 0.60, express the indicated operations using exponents.

0.53 $(5)(5)(5)(5)$
0.54 $(-1)(-1)(-1)(-1)(-1)(-1)(-1)$
0.55 $(3)(3)(-2)(-2)(-2)$ **0.56** $(7)(7)(7)/[(3)(3)]$
0.57 $(-x)(-x)(-x)$ **0.58** $aaa/(bb)$
0.59 $aabbbcc$ **0.60** $xxyyyy/(zzz)$

In Exercises 0.61 to 0.74, perform the indicated operations.

0.61 $(2)^3(2)^4$ **0.62** $(3)^3(3)^2$

0.63 x^3x^5

0.64 yy^4y^3

0.65 $x^2y^3x^3y$

0.66 aa^3a^2a

0.67 $(x^2)^3$

0.68 $(a^2)^5$

0.69 $(x^3)^2(x^2)^4$

0.70 $a^3(a^3)^4$

0.71 $[(a^2)^3]^2$

0.72 $[(-1)^4]^3$

0.73 $(3x^2)^3$

0.74 $(5a^3)^2$

In Exercises 0.75 to 0.78, rewrite the expression, using positive exponents.

0.75 a^{-4}

0.76 $(xy)^{-2}$

0.77 $(\frac{1}{2})^{-3}$

0.78 x^{-1}

In Exercises 0.79 to 0.86 perform the indicated operation.

0.79 x^3/x

0.80 m^7/m^4

0.81 $(2)^5/(2)^8$

0.82 x^6/x^6

0.83 $(3)^4/(3)^3$

0.84 $(2x^2)^2/(2x^2)$

0.85 $(xy)^0$

0.86 $-(25x^0)^2$

Polynomial Expressions

In this section we will discuss some important definitions and terminology. First, *constants* are quantities which do not change in value. A constant may be represented by a letter or by the real number which equals the constant. For example, 5 is a constant, as is the letter b if $b = -20$. *Variables* are quantities whose value may change. These are usually represented by letters. For example, the letter t may be used to represent the temperature each hour in a particular city measured on either the Fahrenheit or Celsius scale. The value of t is likely to be different each hour.

An *algebraic expression* is a collection of constants and variables connected by a series of additions, subtractions, multiplications, divisions, radical signs, and parentheses or other grouping symbols. For example,

$$5x^2y - 10x^3 + 75$$

is an algebraic expression. This algebraic expression consists of the three *terms* $5x^2y$, $10x^3$, and 75. A term consists of either a single number or the product of a number and powers of one or more variables. The term $5x^2y$ consists of the factors 5, x^2, and y. The constant factor 5 is referred to as the *coefficient* of the term. In this book, *coefficient* will always refer to a constant which is a factor in a term. For instance, 10 is the coefficient on the term $10x^3$. The term 75 in the algebraic expression contains no variables and is referred to as a *constant term*.

A *polynomial* is the sum of one or more terms, with the following restrictions:

The terms of a polynomial consist of a number or the product of a number and *positive integer* powers of one or more variables. As you will see later, this definition excludes terms which have variables under a radical sign and any terms which have variables in the denominator.

A polynomial consisting of one term is called a *monomial*. A polynomial consisting of two terms is called a *binomial*. A polynomial consisting of three terms is called a *trinomial*. Polynomials consisting of more than three terms are referred to simply as polynomials.

(a) The algebraic expression 25 is a polynomial having one term; thus it is called a monomial.

(b) The algebraic expression $5x^2 - 2x + 1$ is a polynomial consisting of three terms; thus it is referred to as a trinomial.

(c) The algebraic expression $2x^2y/z$ is not a polynomial because the variable z appears in the denominator of the term.

(d) The algebraic expression $\sqrt{x}$ is not a polynomial because the variable appears under a radical.

(e) The algebraic expression $x^5 - 2x^4 - x^3 + 2x^2 + x + 9$ is a polynomial consisting of six terms.

Example 0.23

The *degree of a term* is the sum of the exponents on the variables contained in the term. For a term involving one variable, the degree is simply the exponent of the variable. The degree of the term $5x^3$ is 3 since the exponent is 3. The degree of the term $5x^2y^3z$ is 6 since the sum of the exponents of x, y, and z equals 6. The degree of a constant term is 0. To illustrate, the term -20 can be written in the equivalent form $-20x^0$. Thus, the degree of the term equals 0.

In addition to the categorization of terms by degree, polynomials may be classified by their degree. The *degree of a polynomial* is defined as the degree of the term of highest degree in the polynomial.

(a) The polynomial $2x^3 - 4x^2 + x - 10$ has terms of degree 3, 2, 1, and 0, respectively. Therefore, the degree of the polynomial is 3.

(b) The polynomial $4x^2y^3 - 6xy^5 + 2xy$ has terms of degree 5, 6, and 2, respectively. Thus the degree of the polynomial is 6.

Example 0.24

Addition and Subtraction of Polynomials

Throughout this book all letters used in algebraic expressions will represent unspecified real numbers. Thus each term in a polynomial can be considered real-valued. And, all the rules and properties of addition, subtraction, multiplication, and division presented in Sec. 0.1 apply to polynomials.

There is an important difference between adding and subtracting polynomials and adding and subtracting *specified* real numbers. That difference is that polynomials contain real numbers represented by letters. Thus, the result of adding or subtracting polynomials cannot generally be stated in the form of a single real number; in fact, generally the result will be stated as an expression in which the terms contain variables.

In adding and subtracting polynomials, we combine *like terms*. Like terms are terms which involve the same variables raised to the same powers. The terms $3x$ and $-4x$ are considered to be like terms because each involves the variable x raised (implicitly) to the first power. The fact that their coefficients (3 and -4) are different has no bearing on whether the two terms are like terms. Any real constants are considered to be like terms. The constants -5 and 18 can be envisioned as having the form $-5x^0$ and $18x^0$, which qualifies them as being like terms.

Example 0.25

(a) The terms $3y^2$ and $-10y^2$ are like terms since both have the variable y raised to the second power.

(b) The terms $10x$ and $5x^2$ are *not* like terms. Each involves the variable x, but they are raised to different powers.

(c) The terms $3x^2y$ and $8yx^2$ are like terms since they involve the same variables raised to the same powers. The fact that the variables are not expressed in the same order is not important. *The standard practice, though, is to arrange the variables of like terms in the same order, which is usually alphabetical.*

(d) The terms $7x^2y$ and $-2xy^2$ are not like terms. They involve the same variables, but the exponents are different for the variables.

When polynomials are added or subtracted, like terms may be combined in a simpler form. For example, the like terms $4x$ and $3x$ may be added, with the sum expressed in the equivalent form $7x$. The distributive law (Property 0.7) allows us to combine these terms. To illustrate,

$$4x + 3x = (4 + 3)x$$
$$= 7x$$

Similarly,

$$5xy^2 - 2xy^2 + 6xy^2 = [5 + (-2) + 6]xy^2$$
$$= 9xy^2$$

Terms which are not like terms cannot be combined into a simpler form. It is the old "apples and oranges" problem. The sum $5x + 2y$ cannot be written in a simpler form.

To add or subtract polynomials, like terms should be identified and combined. Unlike terms are added or subtracted as indicated. The following examples illustrate this process.

Example 0.26

$$(2x^2 - 5x + 10) + (4x^2 + 3x - 5) = 2x^2 - 5x + 10 + 4x^2 + 3x - 5$$
$$= 2x^2 + 4x^2 - 5x + 3x + 10 - 5$$
$$= (2 + 4)x^2 + (-5 + 3)x + 5$$
$$= 6x^2 - 2x + 5$$

As you become more skilled with this process, you will perform some of the intermediate steps mentally.

Example 0.27

$$(5x^2y + 2xy^2 - 4y^3) + (-3x^2y + y^3 - 10)$$
$$= 5x^2y + 2xy^2 - 4y^3 - 3x^2y + y^3 - 10$$
$$= 5x^2y - 3x^2y + 2xy^2 - 4y^3 + y^3 - 10$$
$$= (5 - 3)x^2y + 2xy^2 + (-4 + 1)y^3 - 10$$
$$= 2x^2y + 2xy^2 - 3y^3 - 10$$

$$(3x^2 + 2x - 5) - (6x^2 + x - 16) = (3x^2 + 2x - 5) + (-6x^2 - x + 16)$$
$$= 3x^2 + 2x - 5 - 6x^2 - x + 16$$
$$= 3x^2 - 6x^2 + 2x - x - 5 + 16$$
$$= -3x^2 + x + 11$$

Example 0.28

NOTE

In the subtraction of these two polynomials, the problem was converted into an addition problem by adding the negative of the second polynomial to the first polynomial. In practice, it is easier to think of subtraction in terms of Rule 4 (see Sec. 0.1). This rule suggests that subtraction of a polynomial can be envisioned as removing parentheses which are preceded by a minus sign.

$$(4x^2y - 2xy^2 + 2x - y) - (3x^2y + 5xy^2 - 4x + y)$$
$$= 4x^2y - 2xy^2 + 2x - y - 3x^2y - 5xy^2 + 4x - y$$
$$= 4x^2y - 3x^2y - 2xy^2 - 5xy^2 + 2x + 4x - y - y$$
$$= x^2y - 7xy^2 + 6x - 2y$$

Example 0.29

$$(a + 2b) - (4a - 3b) + (5a + 4b) = a + 2b - 4a + 3b + 5a + 4b$$
$$= a - 4a + 5a + 2b + 3b + 4b$$
$$= 2a + 9b$$

Example 0.30

Multiplication of Polynomials

As mentioned earlier, all the rules and properties of multiplication for real numbers apply when polynomials are multiplied. We will discuss two different multiplication situations: (1) multiplication of two monomials and (2) multiplication of two polynomials.

RULE 19

To multiply two monomials, multiply their coefficients and multiply the variable terms using the rules of exponents.

(a) $(2x)(3x) = (2)(3)xx$
$\qquad = 6x^2$
(b) $(5x^2)(-2x^3) = (5)(-2)x^2x^3$
$\qquad\quad = -10x^5$
(c) $(3ab^2)(6a^3b) = (3)(6)aa^3b^2b$
$\qquad\quad = 18a^4b^3$
(d) $(mn^2)(4m^2n^3)(-3m^3n) = -12m^6n^6$

Example 0.31

RULE 20
To multiply two polynomials, multiply *each* term of one polynomial by *every* term of the other polynomial.

Example 0.32

Multiplication of a monomial times a polynomial requires the use of the distributive law. To illustrate,

$$(2)(4x - 2y) = (2)(4x) + (2)(-2y)$$
$$= 8x - 4y$$

Another illustration is

$$4x^2y(x^2 + 2x - 1) = 4x^2y(x^2) + (4x^2y)(2x) + (4x^2y)(-1)$$
$$= 4x^4y + 8x^3y - 4x^2y$$

Example 0.33

Multiplication of two polynomials also requires the use of the distributive law. For example,

$$(2x - 6)(4x + 7) = (2x)(4x + 7) + (-6)(4x + 7)$$
$$= 8x^2 + 14x - 24x - 42$$

By combining like terms, the product is simplified to equal

$$8x^2 - 10x - 42$$

Similarly,

$$(5x^2 - 2x)(x^3 + 2x^2 - 5x)$$
$$= (5x^2)(x^3 + 2x^2 - 5x) + (-2x)(x^3 + 2x^2 - 5x)$$
$$= 5x^5 + 10x^4 - 25x^3 - 2x^4 - 4x^3 + 10x^2$$
$$= 5x^5 + 8x^4 - 29x^3 + 10x^2$$

Division of Polynomials

Polynomials may also be divided. The only type of polynomial division *explicitly* required in this book will be the division of a polynomial by a monomial. When the division of two polynomials is required in this book, the quotient can be found by simplifying the factored forms of the two polynomials. You will become acquainted with the factoring of polynomials in the next section.

RULE 21
To divide a monomial by a monomial, divide the coefficients of each monomial and divide the variables using the appropriate rule(s) of exponents.

(a) $\dfrac{12x^5}{3x^2} = \left(\dfrac{12}{3}\right)\left(\dfrac{x^5}{x^2}\right) = 4x^{5-2} = 4x^3$

(b) $\dfrac{-8x^3y^2}{2xy^2} = \left(\dfrac{-8}{2}\right)\left(\dfrac{x^3}{x}\right)\left(\dfrac{y^2}{y^2}\right) = -4x^{3-1}y^{2-2}$

$$= -4x^2(1)$$
$$= -4x^2$$

**Example
0.34**

Many people actually divide by "canceling" equal factors of the numerator and denominator. This is done rather than formally applying the appropriate exponent rule. To illustrate, Example 0.34*a* would be solved as follows:

$$\frac{12x^5}{3x^2} = \frac{(4)(\cancel{3})\cancel{x}\cancel{x}xxx}{\cancel{3}\cancel{x}\cancel{x}}$$
$$= 4x^3$$

Part *b* of that example would be performed as

$$\frac{-8x^3y^2}{2xy^2} = \frac{(-4)(\cancel{2})\cancel{x}xx\cancel{y}\cancel{y}}{(\cancel{2})\cancel{x}\cancel{y}\cancel{y}}$$
$$= -4x^2$$

Using the same approach, we find

$$\frac{36a^2bc^3}{2ac^5} = \frac{(18)(2)aabccc}{(2)acccccc}$$
$$= \frac{18ab}{c^2}$$

RULE 22
To divide a polynomial by a monomial, divide each term of the polynomial by the monomial and algebraically sum the individual quotients.

(a) $\dfrac{4x^3 - 8x^2 + 6x}{2x} = \dfrac{4x^3}{2x} - \dfrac{8x^2}{2x} + \dfrac{6x}{2x}$

$$= 2x^2 - 4x + 3$$

(b) $\dfrac{24a^4b^5 + 18a^2b^3}{-3a^2b^4} = \dfrac{24a^4b^5}{-3a^2b^4} + \dfrac{18a^2b^3}{-3a^2b^4}$

$$= -8a^2b - \frac{6}{b}$$

**Example
0.35**

NOTE
You can always check your answer in division by multiplying the answer times the divisor. If your answer is correct, this product should equal the dividend.

We can check the answer to Example 0.35a by multiplying as follows:

$$(2x)(2x^2 - 4x + 3) = 4x^3 - 8x^2 + 6x$$

which is the dividend in the original problem.

Follow-up Exercises

In Exercises 0.87 to 0.94, determine whether the algebraic expression is a polynomial. If it is a polynomial, determine its degree. If it is not a polynomial, indicate why not.

0.87 $\frac{1}{2}$ **0.88** a

0.89 $x^3 - 1$ **0.90** $\sqrt{x^2 y}$

0.91 $x^3 y^2 - 5x^4 y + 10x^6$ **0.92** $(x^2 - 2x + 1)/x$

0.93 $x^{1/2} - 2x + 5$ **0.94** $a^5 b^3 - a^4 b^5 + 10a^7$

In Exercises 0.95 to 0.104, perform the indicated operations.

0.95 $10x + 3x$ **0.96** $5a + (-2a)$

0.97 $5x^2 - 4x^2 + 2x^2$ **0.98** $7y^3 - 3y^3 + (-4y^3)$

0.99 $(5y^3 - 2y^2 + y) + (4y^2 - 5y)$

0.100 $(2m^2 - 3m) + (4m^2 + 2m) - (m^2 + 6)$

0.101 $(40x^3 y^2 - 25xy^3) - (15x^3 y^2)$

0.102 $abc - cab - 4bac$

0.103 $(x - 2y) - (2x - 3y) + (x - y)$

0.104 $(7a - 2b) - (2b + 3c) - (2a - 4c)$

In Exercises 0.105 to 0.118, determine the product.

0.105 $(-5x)(4x^2)$ **0.106** $(7x^3)(3xy^2)$

0.107 $(3x^2)(2x)(-4x^3)$ **0.108** $(a^2)(4a^5)(-2a^3)$

0.109 $5x(x - 10)$ **0.110** $(-2x^2)(x^2 - y)$

0.111 $2a(a^2 - 2a + 5)$ **0.112** $x^2 y(x^2 - 2xy + y^2)$

0.113 $(x - 5)(x + 6)$ **0.114** $(a + b)(a + b)$

0.115 $(2x - 3)(2x - 3)$ **0.116** $(a - b)(a - b)$

0.117 $(x + 4)(x - 4)$ **0.118** $(x - 2)(x^2 - 4x + 4)$

In Exercises 0.119 to 0.128, determine the quotient.

0.119 $21x^5/(3x)$ **0.120** $16x^2 y^3/(4xy^2)$

0.121 $10a^4 b^2/(5ab^2)$ **0.122** $-9xy^2/(3xy^3)$

0.123 $25a^2 bc^3/(5ab^2 c^4)$ **0.124** $(15x^2 - 24x)/(3x)$

0.125 $(4x^3 y - 2x^2 y + 8xy)/(2x)$ **0.126** $(12a^3 - 9a^2 + 6a)/(-3a)$

0.127 $(3x^2 yz^3 - 4xy^2 z)/(-xyz)$ **0.128** $(4x^6 + 6x^3 - 8x^2)/(2x)$

0.3   ## FACTORING

In this section we discuss *factoring* of polynomials. To factor a polynomial means to express it as the product of two or more other polynomials. Recall that the distributive law in Sec. 0.1 was expressed as

$$a(b + c) = a \cdot b + a \cdot c$$

The binomial on the right of the equals sign can be expressed as the product of the polynomials a and $b + c$. These two polynomials are considered the factors of the expression $a \cdot b + a \cdot c$. With multiplication of polynomials, we are given the factors and must find the product. With factoring we are given the product and must determine the polynomials which, when multiplied, will yield the product. Factoring is frequently more difficult than multiplication. However, a good understanding of the multiplication of polynomials will be a great help in factoring.

Monomial Factors

The distributive law represents an example of monomial factors. That is,

$$ab + ac = a(b + c)$$

indicates that the two terms on the left side of the equals sign contain a common factor a. The common factor a may represent any monomial. For example, the polynomial $2x + 2y$ can be rewritten in the *factored form* $2(x + y)$ since each term has a common factor of 2.

(a) The terms of the polynomial $x^3 - x^2 + x$ have a common factor x. We can rewrite the polynomial as

$$x^3 - x^2 + x = x(x^2 - x + 1)$$

(b) The terms of the polynomial $9a^5 - 27a^3 + 3a^6$ have a common factor of $3a^3$. Factoring $3a^3$ from each term, we get

$$9a^5 - 27a^3 + 3a^6 = 3a^3(3a^2 - 9 + a^3)$$

(c) The terms of the polynomial $6x^2y^3 - 10xy^2$ have a common factor $2xy^2$. Factoring $2xy^2$ from each term, we obtain

$$6x^2y^3 - 10xy^2 = 2xy^2(3xy - 5)$$

**Example
0.36**

NOTE
The process of factoring a common factor from each term in a polynomial requires division of each term in the polynomial by the common factor. The factor $3xy - 5$ in the last example is obtained by dividing $6x^2y^3 - 10xy^2$ by the common factor $2xy^2$. At first, you may formally perform this division. However, as you become more skilled at factoring, probably you will perform such divisions mentally.

There is an important check on the factoring process. To determine whether your factors are correct, multiply them. Their product should equal the original polynomial.

We are usually interested in factoring polynomials *completely*. That means simply that the factors themselves cannot be factored any further. The polynomial

$$8x + 8y = 2(4x + 4y)$$

has not been factored completely since we can factor a 4 from each term in the second factor. The polynomial is factored completely when it is expressed in the form $8(x + y)$.

Similarly, the equation

$$x^3y^2 + x^4y^3 = xy(x^2y + x^3y^2)$$

is a polynomial which is not factored completely. We can still factor x^2y from each term in the second factor. The polynomial is completely factored when it is written as $x^3y^2(1 + xy)$.

Our goal in monomial factoring is usually to identify the *largest* common monomial. The largest common monomial factor is the one containing the largest common numerical factor and the highest powers of variables common to all terms.

Factoring Quadratic Polynomials

A second-degree polynomial is often referred to as a *quadratic* polynomial. We will see these types of polynomials frequently, and factoring them will be important. Specifically, we will be interested in expressing quadratic polynomials, if possible, as the product of two first-degree polynomials. The factoring process often involves trial and error. Sometimes it is easy; at other times it can be frustrating. The following cases will help you.

Case 1
$x^2 + (a + b)x + ab = (x + a)(x + b)$

Consider the product $(x + a)(x + b)$. Multiplying these two binomials, we get

$$(x + a)(x + b) = x^2 + ax + bx + ab$$
$$= x^2 + (a + b)x + ab$$

The result of the multiplication is a trinomial having an x^2 term, an x term, and a constant term. Note the coefficients of each term of the trinomial. The x^2 term has a coefficient equal to 1; the x term has a coefficient $a + b$, which is equal to the sum of the constants contained in the *binomial factors*; and the constant term ab is the product of the two constants contained in the binomial factors. In factoring a trinomial of this form, the objective is to determine the values of a and b which generate the coefficient of x, or the middle term of the polynomial, and the constant term.

**Example
0.37**

Determine the factors of $x^2 - 5x + 6$.

Solution

We are seeking values for a and b such that

$$(x + a)(x + b) = x^2 - 5x + 6$$

The coefficient of the middle term is -5. From our previous discussion, the values of a and b must be such that $a + b = -5$. And, the third term in the trinomial equals 6, suggesting that $ab = 6$. Using a trial-

and-error approach, you should conclude that the values satisfying these two conditions are -2 and -3. It makes no difference which of these two values we assign to a and b. The binomial factors are $(x - 2)(x - 3)$, or $(x - 3)(x - 2)$. Again, multiplying the factors provides a check on your answer.

Determine the factors of $m^2 + 4m - 21$.

Example 0.38

Solution

We are seeking values for a and b such that

$$(m + a)(m + b) = m^2 + 4m - 21$$

Our earlier discussions suggest that the relationships between a and b are

$$a + b = 4$$

and

$$ab = -21$$

Using a trial-and-error approach, verify that the two values satisfying these conditions are $+7$ and -3. Therefore,

$$(m + 7)(m - 3) = m^2 + 4m - 21$$

Case 2
$acx^2 + (ad + bc)x + bd = (ax + b)(cx + d)$

Consider the product

$$(ax + b)(cx + d) = acx^2 + (ad + bc)x + bd$$

Assuming that a and c are integers, both of which are not equal to 1, the product is a trinomial which differs from Case 1 in that the coefficient of the term x^2 equals an integer other than 1. When a trinomial has an integer coefficient other than 1 on the x^2 term, the binomial factors contain four constants which must be identified. The coefficient of the x^2 term equals the product of a and c, the coefficient of the x term equals $ad + bc$, and the third term equals the product bd. Identifying the values of the four constants which satisfy these conditions is more difficult than with Case 1.

Determine the factors of $6x^2 - 25x + 25$.

Example 0.39

Solution

We are seeking values of a, b, c, and d such that

$$6x^2 - 25x + 25 = (ax + b)(cx + d)$$

Looking at the coefficients of the trinomial, the conditions which must be satisfied are

$$ac = 6$$
$$ad + bc = -25$$

and

$$bd = 25$$

Verify that the values $a = 3$, $b = -5$, $c = 2$, and $d = -5$ satisfy the conditions. And,

$$(3x - 5)(2x - 5) = 6x^2 - 25x + 25$$

Example 0.40

Factor the trinomial $-8m^2 + 38m - 35$.

Solution

$$-8m^2 + 38m - 35 = (am + b)(cm + d)$$

when
$$ac = -8$$
$$ad + bc = +38$$
and
$$bd = -35$$

Verify that the values $a = -2$, $b = 7$, $c = 4$, and $d = -5$ satisfy the conditions and that

$$(-2x + 7)(4x - 5) = -8x^2 + 38x - 35$$

Example 0.41

Factor the trinomial $12x^2 - 27x + 6$.

Solution

The first step in factoring is to look for any common monomial factors. In this example, we can factor 3 from each term of the trinomial, or

$$12x^2 - 27x + 6 = 3(4x^2 - 9x + 2)$$

The next step is to determine if the trinomial *factor* can be factored. If so,

$$ac = 4$$
$$ad + bc = -9$$
and
$$bd = 2$$

Values satisfying these conditions are $a = 1$, $b = -2$, $c = 4$, and $d = -1$. Thus,

$$12x^2 - 27x + 6 = 3(x - 2)(4x - 1)$$

Example 0.42

Factor the trinomial $4m^2 - m + 1$.

Solution

$$4m^2 - m + 1 = (am + b)(cm + d)$$
When
$$ac = 4$$
$$ad + bc = -1$$
and
$$bd = 1$$

There is no set of integer values which satisfies these conditions. Thus, the trinomial cannot be factored.

Case 3
$x^2 - a^2 = (x + a)(x - a)$

This case involves factoring the *difference between perfect squares*. The binomial to be factored is the difference between the squares of two quantities, x and a. This binomial can be factored as the product of the *sum* and *difference* of x and a.

Determine the factors of $x^2 - 9$.

Example 0.43

Solution

$$x^2 - 9 = (x)^2 - (3)^2$$
$$= (x + 3)(x - 3)$$

Determine the factors of $16x^4 - 81$.

Example 0.44

Solution

$$16x^4 - 81 = (4x^2)^2 - (9)^2$$
$$= (4x^2 + 9)(4x^2 - 9)$$

However, the binomial $4x^2 - 9$ is the difference between two squares. Thus,

$$16x^4 - 81 = (4x^2 + 9)(2x + 3)(2x - 3)$$

Other Special Forms

The following rules of factoring are used less frequently in the book.

Case 4
$a^3 - b^3 = (a - b)(a^2 + ab + b^2)$

This case involves factoring the difference between two cubes.

(a) $x^3 - 1 = (x)^3 - (1)^3$
    $= (x - 1)(x^2 + x + 1)$
(b) $8x^3 - 64 = (2x)^3 - (4)^3$
    $= (2x - 4)(4x^2 + 8x + 16)$
(c) $m^3 - n^3 = (m - n)(m^2 + mn + n^2)$

Example 0.45

Case 5
$a^3 + b^3 = (a + b)(a^2 - ab + b^2)$

This case involves factoring the sum of two cubes.

(a) $x^3 + 8 = (x)^3 + (2)^3$
    $= (x + 2)(x^2 - 2x + 4)$
(b) $27y^3 + 64 = (3y)^3 + (4)^3$
    $= (3y + 4)(9y^2 - 12y + 16)$

Example 0.46

Follow-up Exercises

Completely factor (if possible) the polynomials in the following exercises. Do not forget to check your answers!

0.129 $2ax - 8a^3$
0.130 $21m^2 - 7mn$
0.131 $4x^3y - 6xy^3 + 8x^2y^2$
0.132 $65a^3b^2 - 13a^2b^3$
0.133 $9a^3 - 15a^2 - 27a$
0.134 $x^2 - 8x + 12$
0.135 $x^2 + x + 3$
0.136 $x^2 + 7x + 12$
0.137 $p^2 + 9p - 36$
0.138 $x^2 - 2x - 15$
0.139 $r^2 - 21r - 22$
0.140 $x^2 - 16x + 48$
0.141 $x^5 + y^5$
0.142 $9x^2 + 12x + 4$
0.143 $6m^2 - 19m + 3$
0.144 $2x^2 - 7x - 4$
0.145 $8x^2 - 2x - 3$
0.146 $2x^3 + 4x^2 - 42x$
0.147 $x^4 - 81$
0.148 $100x^2 - 225$
0.149 $81x^4 - 625$
0.150 $10x^2 + 13x - 3$
0.151 $x^2 + 4$
0.152 $27 - 8m^3$
0.153 $1 + 8x^3$
0.154 $a^3 - 125$
0.155 $x^4 - x^3 - 2x^2$
0.156 $4x^6 - 4x^2$

0.4   FRACTIONS

Fractions, or *rational numbers*, constitute an important part of the real number system. Up until now we have "integerized" our discussions, pretty much ignoring fractions. Even though the algebra of fractions conforms with all the rules and properties of real numbers, the arithmetic of fractions requires special considerations.

Some Basic Properties

If a and b are integers and $b \neq 0$, then a/b is called a *fraction*. Expressions such as $\frac{1}{5}$, $-\frac{2}{7}$, and $(-20)/(-75)$ are all examples of fractions. We will also be concerned with fractions a/b where a and/or b is an algebraic expression representing integers. Examples of such expressions are

$$\frac{x}{5} \qquad \frac{x}{2y - 5} \qquad \text{and} \qquad \frac{x^2 - 9}{x + 3}$$

DEFINITION
Assuming that $b \neq 0$ and $d \neq 0$, two fractions a/b and c/d are equivalent if and only if $ad = bc$. That is, $a/b = c/d$ if and only if $ad = bc$.

Example 0.47
(a) $\frac{2}{5} = \frac{4}{10}$ since $(2)(10) = (5)(4)$.
(b) $\frac{5}{8} \neq \frac{25}{45}$ since $(5)(45) \neq (8)(25)$
     or, $225 \neq 200$
(c) $\frac{13}{65} = \frac{1}{5}$ since $(5)(13) = (1)(65)$.
(d) For $x \neq 1$, $3/(x - 1) = 3x/(x^2 - x)$ since $(3)(x^2 - x) = (x - 1)(3x)$,
     or $3x^2 - 3x = 3x^2 - 3x$.

DEFINITION
If a, b, and x are integers, then

$$\frac{a}{b} = \frac{ax}{bx}$$

This definition suggests that a common factor may be introduced to or removed from *both* the numerator and denominator of a fraction and the value of the fraction will remain unchanged. This can be proved easily by applying the previous definition:

$$\frac{a}{b} = \frac{ax}{bx} \qquad \text{since} \qquad (a)(bx) = (b)(ax)$$

When all common factors have been removed from the numerator and denominator of a fraction, it is said to be stated in *simplest*, or *lowest*, *terms*. For instance, the fraction $\frac{10}{100}$ is not stated in simplest terms because there are common factors in the numerator and denominator. Thus

$$\frac{10}{100} = \frac{10(1)}{10(10)} = \frac{1}{10}$$

which is the simplest form of the fraction.

Similarly, the fraction $(x - 1)/(x^2 - 1)$ is not stated in simplest terms because

$$\frac{(x - 1)}{(x^2 - 1)} = \frac{(1)(x - 1)}{(x + 1)(x - 1)} = \frac{1}{x + 1}$$

The process resulting in the elimination of common factors is commonly referred to as *cancellation*.

This last definition also allows us to generate equivalent fractions.

Determine a fraction having a denominator of 15 which is equivalent to the fraction $\frac{7}{3}$.

Example 0.48

If we introduce a factor of 5 in both the numerator and denominator of the fraction $\frac{7}{3}$, we get the equivalent fraction

Solution

$$\frac{(7)(5)}{(3)(5)} = \frac{35}{15}$$

Checking, $(15)(7)(5) = (3)(5)(35)$, or $525 = 525$, and the two fractions are equivalent.

Determine a fraction having a denominator of 3 which is equivalent to the fraction $\frac{24}{18}$.

Example 0.49

Since $\frac{24}{18} = (4)(6)/[(3)(6)]$, the common factor of 6 can be removed, so

Solution

that

$$\frac{24}{18} = \frac{(4)(6)}{(3)(6)} = \frac{4}{3}$$

If you know how to *solve* equations, an alternative procedure is to state that if there is an equivalent fraction, then the numerator a will satisfy the equation $\frac{24}{18} = a/3$. Applying our definition of equivalent fractions,

$$\frac{24}{18} = \frac{a}{3} \qquad \text{when} \qquad (3)(24) = (18)(a)$$

or when $\qquad\qquad \frac{72}{18} = a \qquad \text{or} \qquad 4 = a$

A fraction can be thought of as containing three signs: a sign on the overall fraction and signs for the numerator and denominator. An equivalent fraction is obtained *if any two of the three signs are changed.* For example,

$$+\frac{+3}{+4} = +\frac{-3}{-4} = -\frac{+3}{-4} = -\frac{-3}{+4}$$

The standard practice in writing fractions is to avoid the use of minus signs in the denominator. A fraction $5/(-8)$ would have a preferred form of $-\frac{5}{8}$ or $-5/8$. Naturally we cannot remove minus signs from the denominators of fractions such as $1/(x-4)$.

Addition and Subtraction of Fractions

RULE 23
If two fractions have the same denominator, their sum (difference) is found by adding (subtracting) their numerators and placing the result over the common denominator.

Example 0.50

(a) $\dfrac{3}{7} + \dfrac{2}{7} = \dfrac{3+2}{7} = \dfrac{5}{7}$

(b) $\dfrac{7}{8} - \dfrac{4}{8} = \dfrac{7-4}{8} = \dfrac{3}{8}$

Fractions having different denominators require special attention before they are added or subtracted.

RULE 24
To add (subtract) two fractions which have different denominators, restate the fractions as equivalent frac-

tions having the same denominator. The sum (difference) is then found by applying Rule 23.

In applying Rule 24, any common denominator may be identified when the equivalent fractions are found. However, the usual practice is to identify the *least common multiple* (lcm) of the denominators or the *least common denominator* (lcd).

The procedure for finding the least common denominator is as follows:

1 Write each denominator in a completely factored form.

2 The lcd is a product of the factors. To form the lcd, each distinct factor is included the greatest number of times it appears in *any* one of the denominators.

To find the lcd for the fractions $\frac{5}{8}$ and $\frac{3}{20}$, each denominator is factored completely:

Example 0.51

$$8 = 8 \cdot 1 = 4 \cdot 2 \cdot 1 = 2 \cdot 2 \cdot 2 \cdot 1$$
$$20 = 20 \cdot 1 = 10 \cdot 2 \cdot 1 = 5 \cdot 2 \cdot 2 \cdot 1$$

These denominators are factored completely since each of the factors can be expressed only as the product of itself and 1 (assuming we are seeking integer-valued factors). Such factors are called *prime factors*.

In forming the lcd, each distinct prime factor is included the greatest number of times it appears in any one denominator. The distinct prime factors are 2, 5, and 1. Thus,

$$\text{lcd} = 2 \cdot 2 \cdot 2 \cdot 5 \cdot 1$$
$$= 40$$

Determine the sum $\frac{5}{8} + \frac{3}{20}$.

Example 0.52

Solution

Having identified the lcd in Example 0.51, we must restate each fraction with the common denominator 40. Restating the fractions and applying Rule 23, we get

$$\frac{5}{8} + \frac{3}{20} = \frac{5 \cdot 5}{8 \cdot 5} + \frac{3 \cdot 2}{20 \cdot 2} = \frac{25}{40} + \frac{6}{40}$$
$$= \frac{25 + 6}{40} = \frac{31}{40}$$

Determine the difference $3/(4x) - 5/(6x^2)$.

Example 0.53

Solution

Factoring each denominator, we obtain

$$4x = 4 \cdot x \cdot 1 = 2 \cdot 2 \cdot x \cdot 1$$
$$6x^2 = 6 \cdot x \cdot x \cdot 1 = 3 \cdot 2 \cdot x \cdot x \cdot 1$$

The distinct factors of these denominators are 2, 3, x, and 1, and

$$\text{lcd} = 2 \cdot 2 \cdot 3 \cdot x \cdot x \cdot 1$$
$$= 12x^2$$

Restating the fractions in terms of the lcd and subtracting, we get

$$\frac{3}{4x} - \frac{5}{6x^2} = \frac{3 \cdot 3x}{4x \cdot 3x} - \frac{5 \cdot 2}{6x^2 \cdot 2}$$

$$= \frac{9x}{12x^2} - \frac{10}{12x^2}$$

$$= \frac{9x - 10}{12x^2}$$

Example 0.54 Find the algebraic sum $3/(x - 1) - 5x/(x + 1) + x/(x^2 - 1)$.

Solution The factored forms of the three denominators are

$$x - 1 = (x - 1) \cdot 1$$
$$x + 1 = (x + 1) \cdot 1$$
$$x^2 - 1 = (x + 1)(x - 1) \cdot 1$$

Thus,

$$\text{lcd} = (x + 1)(x - 1) \cdot 1 = (x^2 - 1)$$

Restating the three fractions, we get

$$\frac{3}{x - 1} - \frac{5x}{x + 1} + \frac{x^2}{x^2 - 1} = \frac{3 \cdot (x + 1)}{(x - 1) \cdot (x + 1)} - \frac{5x(x - 1)}{(x + 1)(x - 1)} + \frac{x^2}{x^2 - 1}$$

$$= \frac{3(x + 1) - 5x(x - 1) + x^2}{x^2 - 1}$$

$$= \frac{3x + 3 - 5x^2 + 5x + x^2}{x^2 - 1}$$

$$= \frac{-4x^2 + 8x + 3}{x^2 - 1}$$

Multiplication and Division

RULE 25
The product of two or more fractions is found by dividing the product of their numerators by the product of their denominators. That is,

$$\frac{a}{b} \frac{c}{d} = \frac{ac}{bd}$$

Example 0.55 (a) $\dfrac{3}{5} \dfrac{2}{7} = \dfrac{(3)(2)}{(5)(7)} = \dfrac{6}{35}$

(b) $\dfrac{15}{x} \dfrac{x^2}{3} = \dfrac{15x^2}{3x} = \dfrac{5x}{1} = 5x$

(c) $\dfrac{x-1}{10} \dfrac{15}{x^2-1} = \dfrac{(15)(x-1)}{(10)(x-1)(x+1)} = \dfrac{3}{2(x+1)}$

RULE 26
The quotient of two fractions can be determined by inverting the divisor fraction and multiplying by the dividend fraction. That is,

$$\frac{a/b}{c/d} = \frac{a}{b}\frac{d}{c} = \frac{ad}{bc}$$

(a) $\dfrac{-\frac{5}{12}}{\frac{3}{4}} = \left(-\dfrac{5}{12}\right)\left(\dfrac{4}{3}\right) = -\dfrac{20}{36} = -\dfrac{5}{9}$

(b) $\dfrac{\frac{4}{10}}{2} = \dfrac{\frac{4}{10}}{2/1} = \left(\dfrac{4}{10}\right)\left(\dfrac{1}{2}\right) = \dfrac{4}{20} = \dfrac{1}{5}$

(c) $\dfrac{3x^2/4}{9x/2} = \dfrac{3x^2}{4}\dfrac{2}{9x} = \dfrac{6x^2}{36x} = \dfrac{x}{6}$

Example 0.56

Rule 26 requires that the fractions which are being divided be *simple fractions*. The quotient

$$\frac{1-\frac{5}{8}}{\frac{1}{2}-4}$$

requires that the numerator and denominator be expressed as simple fractions prior to dividing. Therefore,

$$\frac{1-\frac{5}{8}}{\frac{1}{2}-4} = \frac{\frac{1}{1}-\frac{5}{8}}{\frac{1}{2}-\frac{4}{1}}$$

$$= \frac{\frac{8}{8}-\frac{5}{8}}{\frac{1}{2}-\frac{8}{2}} = \frac{3/8}{-7/2}$$

$$= \frac{3}{8}\left(-\frac{2}{7}\right) = -\frac{3}{28}$$

$$\frac{1-2/x}{4/x} = \frac{x/x - 2/x}{4/x}$$

$$= \frac{(x-2)/x}{4/x}$$

$$= \frac{x-2}{x}\frac{x}{4} = \frac{x-2}{4}$$

Example 0.57

Follow-up Exercises

In Exercises 0.157 to 0.162, determine whether the fractions are equivalent.

0.157 $\frac{7}{3}$, $\frac{28}{12}$ **0.158** $\frac{3}{7}$, $\frac{15}{30}$

0.159 $-\frac{6}{13}$, $-\frac{30}{55}$ **0.160** $3x/5$, $48x^3/(80x^2)$

0.161 $(x - 1)/5$, $2(x^2 - 1)/[10(x + 1)]$

0.162 $15m^3/(4n)$, $90m^5/(24m^2n)$

In Exercises 0.163 to 0.168, state each fraction in its lowest terms.

0.163 $\frac{28}{12}$ **0.164** $\frac{140}{76}$

0.165 $4x^2/(20x^5)$ **0.166** $64m^3n^2/(4mn^3)$

0.167 $x^3y^4z/(x^2yz^3)$ **0.168** $216a/(24a^3)$

In Exercises 0.169 to 0.174, determine the equivalent fractions.

0.164 $\dfrac{5}{4} = \dfrac{}{96}$ **0.170** $\dfrac{3}{8} = \dfrac{}{120}$

0.171 $\dfrac{10}{3x} = \dfrac{}{12x^2}$ **0.172** $\dfrac{5m}{2n^2} = \dfrac{}{6mn^3}$

0.173 $\dfrac{4}{7} = \dfrac{}{35xy}$ **0.174** $\dfrac{10}{x} = \dfrac{}{x^2 - x}$

In Exercises 0.175 to 0.196, perform the indicated operations.

0.175 $\frac{1}{5} + \frac{5}{30}$ **0.176** $\frac{2}{7} - \frac{4}{21}$

0.177 $\frac{1}{3} - \frac{5}{8} + \frac{5}{12}$ **0.178** $\frac{4}{25} - \frac{3}{10} + \frac{7}{5}$

0.179 $\dfrac{1}{x} - \dfrac{2}{x^2}$ **0.180** $\dfrac{5}{2a} + \dfrac{6}{a^3}$

0.181 $\dfrac{5x}{x^2 - 4} + \dfrac{x}{x - 2}$ **0.182** $\dfrac{5}{1} + \dfrac{1}{x}$

0.183 $\dfrac{10}{1} - \dfrac{2}{x^2}$ **0.184** $\dfrac{4}{a} + \dfrac{3}{2ab}$

0.185 $\dfrac{3a}{a + 1} - \dfrac{5}{a^2 + 2a + 1}$ **0.186** $\frac{3}{11}$ $\frac{33}{6}$

0.187 $(\frac{1}{5})(\frac{10}{3})(-\frac{9}{2})$ **0.188** $\left(\dfrac{1}{x}\right)\left(\dfrac{2x^3}{3}\right)\left(\dfrac{6}{5}\right)$

0.189 $\left(\dfrac{ab}{c}\right)\left(\dfrac{c^2}{3a^2b}\right)\left(\dfrac{1}{abc}\right)$ **0.190** $\left(\dfrac{5}{x - 4}\right)\left(\dfrac{x^2 - 16}{10}\right)\left(\dfrac{x + 4}{2}\right)$

0.191 $\frac{7}{27} \div \frac{5}{9}$ **0.192** $3x^2/5 \div x/5$

0.193 $a^2b/(5c) \div 3c^2/(10ab)$ **0.194** $abc/8 \div 3a^2b/4$

0.195 $\dfrac{x - 1}{x^2 - 5x - 4} \div \dfrac{x - 1}{x - 4}$ **0.196** $\dfrac{1 - 2/(3x)}{3/x + 4}$

0.5 # EXPONENTS AND RADICALS

In Sec. 0.2 we discussed the following four rules of exponents:

Rule 15: $a^m \cdot a^n = a^{m+n}$

Rule 16: $(a^m)^n = a^{mn}$

Rule 17: $(ab)^n = a^n b^n$

Rule 18: $\dfrac{a^m}{a^n} = a^{m-n} \qquad a \neq 0$

In addition, we provided the definition

$$a^{-n} = \frac{1}{a^n} \qquad a \neq 0$$

These rules and the definition were stated as applying when m and n were integers. At that point in our discussion, the restriction to integers was convenient. However, these rules are equally valid when m and n are real numbers.

Fractional Exponents

With exponents not restricted to integers occasionally we will need to deal with fractional exponents. We studied how to combine fractions in the last section. Example 0.58 illustrates the application of the rules of exponents when the exponents are fractions.

$(a)\ \ x^{1/2} \cdot x^{1/2} = x^{1/2+1/2} = x$	$(e)\ \ (2x^{1/4})^4 = (2)^4(x^{1/4})^4$
$(b)\ \ x^{3/2} \cdot x^{1/3} = x^{3/2+1/3}$	$\qquad = 16x$
$\qquad = x^{9/6+2/6}$	$(f)\ \ x^{3/4}/x^{1/2} = x^{3/4-1/2}$
$\qquad = x^{11/6}$	$\qquad = x^{3/4-2/4} = x^{1/4}$
$(c)\ \ (x^{1/2})^4 = x^{(1/2)(4)} = x^2$	$(g)\ \ x^{5/8}/x^{3/4} = x^{5/8-3/4}$
$(d)\ \ (x^{2/3})^{-3} = x^{(2/3)(-3)}$	$\qquad = x^{5/8-6/8}$
$\qquad = x^{-2} = 1/x^2$	$\qquad = x^{-1/8} = 1/x^{1/8}$

Example 0.58

Radicals

Frequently we need to determine the value of x which satisfies an equation of the form

$$x^n = a$$

For example, what values of x satisfy these equations?

$$x^2 = 4 \qquad x^3 = 8 \qquad x^4 = 81$$

In the first equation, we want to determine the value x which, when multiplied times itself, yields a product equal to 4. You should conclude that values of $+2$ and -2 satisfy the equation, i.e., make the left and right sides of the equation equal. Similarly, the second equation seeks the value of x which, when cubed, generates a product of 8. A value of $+2$ satisfies this equation. Verify that $+3$ and -3 satisfy the third equation.

DEFINITION
If $a^n = b$, a is called the nth root of b.

The nth root of b is denoted by $\sqrt[n]{b}$, where the symbol $\sqrt{\ \ }$ is the *radical sign*, n is the *index* on the radical sign, and b is the *radicand*. Thus, we can state

---

If $a^n = b$, then $a = \sqrt[n]{b}$

Referring to the three previous equations,

$$\text{If } x^2 = 4 \qquad x = \sqrt[2]{4} = \sqrt{4}$$

where x is said to equal the *square root* of 4. If no index appears with the radical sign, the index is implicitly equal to 2.

For the second equation we can state

$$\text{If } x^3 = 8 \qquad x = \sqrt[3]{8}$$

where x is said to equal the *cube root* of 8. And, for the third equation,

$$\text{If } x^4 = 81 \qquad x = \sqrt[4]{81}$$

where x is said to equal the *fourth root* of 81.

As we have seen with these equations, there may exist more than one nth root of a real number. We usually will be interested in just one of these roots—the *principal nth root*. Given $\sqrt[n]{b}$,

1. If b is positive, the principal nth root is positive.

2. If b is negative and n is odd, the principal nth root is negative.

The following examples indicate the principal nth root.

Example 0.59

(a) $\sqrt{9} = 3$

(b) $\sqrt[3]{-27} = -3$

(c) $\sqrt[5]{32} = 2$

(d) $\sqrt[5]{-243} = -3$

The following rules apply to computations involving radicals.

RULE 27
To add or subtract radicals, the radicals must have the same index and the same radicand.

According to Rule 27,

$$a\sqrt[n]{x} + b\sqrt[n]{x} = (a + b)\sqrt[n]{x}$$

Example 0.60

(a) $\sqrt{3} + \sqrt{3} = 2\sqrt{3}$

(b) $\sqrt[3]{a} - 3\sqrt[3]{a} + 5\sqrt[3]{a} = 3\sqrt[3]{a}$

(c) $\sqrt{x} + \sqrt[3]{x}$ cannot be simplified because the indices on the radicals are different.

(d) $\sqrt[4]{x^3} + \sqrt[4]{x^2}$ cannot be simplified because the radicands are not equal.

RULE 28

$$\sqrt[n]{ab} = \sqrt[n]{a}\sqrt[n]{b}$$

(a) $\sqrt{32} = \sqrt{(16)(2)} = \sqrt{16}\sqrt{2} = 4\sqrt{2}$

(b) $\sqrt[3]{128} = \sqrt[3]{(64)(2)} = \sqrt[3]{64}\sqrt[3]{2} = 4\sqrt[3]{2}$

(c) $\sqrt{x^3} = \sqrt{x^2 \cdot x} = \sqrt{x^2}\sqrt{x} = x\sqrt{x}, x \geq 0.$

Example 0.61

RULE 29

$$\sqrt[n]{\frac{a}{b}} = \frac{\sqrt[n]{a}}{\sqrt[n]{b}} \quad \text{for } b \neq 0$$

(a) $\sqrt{\frac{4}{9}} = \sqrt{4}/\sqrt{9} = \frac{2}{3}$

(b) $\sqrt[3]{\frac{27}{64}} = \sqrt[3]{27}/\sqrt[3]{64} = \frac{3}{4}$

(c) $\sqrt[3]{(-1)/125} = \sqrt[3]{-1}/\sqrt[3]{125} = -1/5$

Example 0.62

Radicals and Fractional Exponents

The following definition provides a very important relationship between radicals and fractional exponents.

DEFINITION

$$b^{m/n} = (\sqrt[n]{b})^m = \sqrt[n]{b^m}$$

(a) $x^{1/2} = \sqrt{x}$

(b) $x^{1/3} = \sqrt[3]{x}$

(c) $x^{1/n} = \sqrt[n]{x}$

(d) $(64)^{2/3} = \sqrt[3]{(64)^2} = (\sqrt[3]{64})^2 = 4^2 = 16$

(e) $(49)^{-1/2} = 1/(49)^{1/2} = 1/\sqrt{49} = \frac{1}{7}$

Example 0.63

Follow-up Exercises

In Exercises 0.197 to 0.206, perform the indicated operations.

0.197 $a^{3/2} \cdot a^{4/3}$

0.198 $b^{1/6} \cdot b^{1/4}$

0.199 $x^{1/3} \cdot x^{2/5} \cdot x^{3/10}$

0.200 $(x^{1/2})^{2/3}$

0.201 $(a^{3/2})^{5/6}$

0.202 $(2x^{3/4})^4$

0.203 $(-3x^{2/3})^3$

0.204 $x^{5/2}/x^{1/2}$

0.205 $a^{3/2}/a^{1/6}$

0.206 $(x^4y^2)^{1/2}$

In Exercises 0.207 to 0.214, determine the principal nth root.

0.207 $\sqrt{625}$

0.208 $\sqrt[4]{625}$

0.209 $\sqrt[3]{-a^3}$

0.210 $\sqrt[5]{-1}$

0.211 $\sqrt[3]{-8x^6}$

0.212 $\sqrt[3]{27a^9}$

0.213 $\sqrt{144x^6}$

0.214 $\sqrt[3]{-64x^3y^6}$

In Exercises 0.215 to 0.226, simplify the radical expressions.

0.215 $2\sqrt{7} + 3\sqrt{7}$

0.216 $5\sqrt{x} - 3\sqrt{x}$

0.217 $\sqrt{32} + 3\sqrt{2}$

0.218 $2\sqrt{45} - 2\sqrt{5}$

0.219 $4\sqrt{x} - \sqrt{x^3}$

0.220 $\sqrt{20} - 2\sqrt{5} + 3\sqrt{45}$

0.221 $\sqrt{2}\sqrt{8}$

0.222 $\sqrt[3]{5}\sqrt[3]{10}\sqrt[3]{5}$

0.223 $\sqrt{\frac{64}{9}}$

0.224 $\sqrt[3]{-\frac{1}{27}}$

0.225 $\sqrt{625x^2/(49y^4)}$

0.226 $\sqrt[4]{1/(81a^8)}$

In Exercises 0.227 to 0.234, express the term in radical form.

0.227 $x^{2/3}$

0.228 $x^{1/5}$

0.229 $(ab)^{3/5}$

0.230 $(xy)^{3/4}$

0.231 $x^{-1/2}$

0.232 $a^{-2/3}$

0.233 $(8)^{-1/3}$

0.234 $(32)^{-1/5}$

In Exercises 0.235 to 0.242, express the term using fractional exponents.

0.235 $\sqrt{45x}$

0.236 $\sqrt[3]{a^2}$

0.237 $\sqrt[4]{x^3}$

0.238 $\sqrt{xy}$

0.239 $\sqrt[3]{x^5}$

0.240 $\sqrt[5]{(ab)^3}$

0.241 $\sqrt{x^4}$

0.242 $\sqrt[3]{(-1)^9}$

0.6   EQUATIONS

We will work continually with equations in this book. It is absolutely essential that you understand the meaning of equations and their algebraic properties.

Equations and Their Properties

An *equation* is a shorthand way of stating that two algebraic expressions are *equal*. We can distinguish three types of equations. An *identity* is an equation which is true for all values of the letters or variables. An example of an identity is the equation

$$6x + 12 = \frac{12x + 24}{2}$$

Another example is

$$5(x + y) = 5x + 5y$$

For both these equations, any values that are assigned to the variables will make both sides of the equation equal.

A *conditional equation* is true for only a limited number of values of the variables. For example, the equation

$$x + 3 = 5$$

is true only when x equals 2.

A *false statement* is an equation which is never true. That is, there are no values of the variables which make the two sides of the equation equal. An example is the equation

$$x = x + 5$$

We indicate that the two sides are not equal by using the symbol $\neq$; for this example,

$$x \neq x + 5$$

If an equation contains one variable, any value of the variable which makes the equation true is called a *root* of the equation. We say that roots are values which *satisfy* the equation. "Solving an equation" refers to the process of finding the roots of the equation, if they exist.

We will regularly need to manipulate or rearrange equations. Thus we will need to know the proper means of manipulation. The following rules indicate allowable operations.

RULE 30
The same real number can be added to both sides of an equation.

Rule 30 is called the *addition property of equality*. It states that if $a = b$, then $a + c = b + c$. For the equation

$$x + 3 = 5$$

-3 can be added to both sides, resulting in

$$x + 3 + (-3) = 5 + (-3)$$
or
$$x = 2$$

Many of you operationalize Rule 30 by recognizing that a term may be transferred, or transposed, from one side of an equation to another as long as its sign is changed.

RULE 31
Both sides of an equation may be multiplied or divided by any nonzero constant.

Given the equation $2x = 24$, both sides of the equation may be divided by 2 to yield the equation $x = 12$. Equivalently, both sides could have been multiplied by $\frac{1}{2}$. Similarly, both sides of the equation

$$\frac{x}{5} = 6$$

may be multiplied by 5 to yield the equation $x = 30$.

Rules 30 and 31 lead to the creation of *equivalent equations*. Equivalent equations are equations which have the same roots.

Other operations may be required at times, but they may *not* result in equivalent equations. The following three rules indicate such operations.

RULE 32
Both sides of an equation may be multiplied by a quantity which involves variables.

To illustrate, the equation

$$\frac{x}{x + 3} = \frac{5}{x + 3}$$

may be multiplied on both sides by the quantity $x + 3$. The result is the equivalent equation

$$x = 5$$

This rule, however, can lead to the identification of roots which are not roots to the original equation. Such roots are often referred to as *extraneous roots*.

Example 0.64

Consider the equation

$$\frac{2x}{x - 4} = \frac{8}{x - 4}$$

Multiplying both sides of the equation by $x - 4$ yields the equation $2x = 8$. The root of this equation is $x = 4$. However, a value of $x = 4$ does not satisfy the original equation. Thus, the equations $2x/(x - 4) = 8/(x - 4)$ and $2x = 8$ are not equivalent because they do not have the same roots.

RULE 33
Both sides of an equation may be squared.

Consider the equation

$$\sqrt{x - 1} = 4$$

Squaring both sides of the equation yields

$$x - 1 = 16$$

or

$$x = 17$$

This rule may also lead to extraneous roots, although it does not in this example.

RULE 34
Both sides of an equation may be divided by an expression which involves variables provided the expression is not equal to 0.

Consider the equation

$$x(x - 5) = 0$$

If we divide both sides of the equation by $x - 5$, the result is

$$x = 0$$

This is a root of the original equation, but so is $x = 5$. Applying Rule 34 can lead to equations which do not have all the roots contained in the original equation, or equations which are not equivalent to the original equations.

Solving First-Degree Equations

The procedure used for solving equations depends upon the nature of the equation. Let's consider first-degree equations which involve one variable. The following equations are examples.

$$3x = 2x - 5$$
$$5x - 4 = 12 + x$$

Solving equations of this form is relatively easy. By using appropriate rules of manipulation, the approach is simply to isolate the variable on one side of the equation and all constants on the other side of the equation.

Solve the two first-degree equations given previously.

Example 0.65

Solution

For the equation $3x = 2x - 5$, we can add $-2x$ to both sides to get

$$3x + (-2x) = 2x - 5 + (-2x)$$
or
$$x = -5$$

The only value of x which satisfies this equation is -5.

For the equation $5x - 4 = 12 + x$, we can add $-x$ and 4 to both sides, getting

$$5x - 4 + 4 + (-x) = 12 + x + 4 + (-x)$$
$$5x - x = 12 + 4$$
or
$$4x = 16$$

Dividing both sides by 4 (or multiplying by $\frac{1}{4}$) gives us the root of the equation:

$$x = 4$$

NOTE

A quick and convenient check of your answer(s) is to substitute it (them) into the *original* equation to see if it is satisfied. Use this check. It will help protect you against careless arithmetic errors.

Solving Second-Degree Equations

A second-degree equation involving the variable x is stated, or can be rearranged, in the form

$$ax^2 + bx + c = 0$$

where a, b, and c are constants with the added provision that $a \neq 0$. If a equals zero, the x^2 term disappears and the equation is no longer of degree 2. Examples of second-degree equations are

$$6x^2 - 2x + 1 = 0$$
$$3x^2 = 12$$
$$2x^2 - 1 = 5x + 9$$

Second-degree equations are usually called *quadratic equations*. A quadratic equation (excluding an identity) can have no real roots, one real root, or two real roots. A number of different procedures can be used to determine the roots of a quadratic equation. We will discuss two of them. The first step, in either case, is to rewrite the equation in the form $ax^2 + bx + c = 0$.

Factoring Method If the left side of the quadratic equation can be factored, the roots can be identified very easily. Consider the quadratic equation

$$x^2 - 4x = 0$$

The left side of the equation can be factored, resulting in

$$x(x - 4) = 0$$

The factored form of the equation suggests that the product of the two terms equals 0. The product will equal 0 if either of the two factors equals 0. For this equation the first factor is 0 when $x = 0$, and the second factor is 0 when $x = 4$. Thus, the two roots are 0 and 4.

Example 0.66   Determine the roots of the equation

$$x^2 + 6x + 9 = 0$$

Solution   The left side of the equation can be factored such that

$$(x + 3)(x + 3) = 0$$

Setting each factor equal to 0, we find that there is one root to the equation, and it occurs when $x = -3$.

Quadratic Formula When the quadratic expression cannot be factored, or if you are unable to identify the factors, you can apply the *quadratic formula*. The quadratic formula will allow you to identify all roots of an equation of the form

$$ax^2 + bx + c = 0$$

The quadratic formula is

$$x = \frac{-b \pm \sqrt{b^2 - 4ac}}{2a}$$

The following examples illustrate the use of the formula.

Two Roots Given the quadratic equation $x^2 - 2x - 48 = 0$, the coefficients are $a = 1$, $b = -2$, and $c = -48$. By substituting these into the quadratic formula, the roots of the equation are computed as

Example 0.67

$$x = \frac{-(-2) \pm \sqrt{(-2)^2 - 4(1)(-48)}}{2(1)}$$
$$= \frac{2 \pm \sqrt{4 + 192}}{2}$$
$$= \frac{2 \pm \sqrt{196}}{2}$$
$$= \frac{2 \pm 14}{2}$$

Using the plus sign, we get

$$x = \tfrac{16}{2} = 8$$

Using the minus sign, we obtain

$$x = -\tfrac{12}{2} = -6$$

Thus, there are two values of x which satisfy the quadratic equation.

One Root Consider the quadratic equation $x^2 - 6x + 9 = 0$. With $a = 1$, $b = -6$, and $c = 9$,

Example 0.68

$$x = \frac{-(-6) \pm \sqrt{(-6)^2 - 4(1)(9)}}{2(1)}$$
$$= \frac{6 \pm \sqrt{36 - 36}}{2}$$
$$= \frac{6 \pm 0}{2}$$

Using both the plus and the minus sign, the one root to the equation is found to be $x = 3$.

Example 0.69 Given the quadratic equation $2x^2 + 4x + 8 = 0$, we know that $a = 2$, $b = 4$, and $c = 8$. Applying the quadratic formula yields

$$x = \frac{-4 \pm \sqrt{(4)^2 - 4(2)(8)}}{2(2)}$$

$$= \frac{-4 \pm \sqrt{16 - 64}}{4}$$

$$= \frac{-4 \pm \sqrt{-48}}{4}$$

Because the square root of -48 is not a real number, there are no real roots for the equation.

The expression under the radical of the quadratic formula, $b^2 - 4ac$, is called the *discriminant*. The value of the discriminant holds the key to which of the three cases you are dealing with when finding the roots to a quadratic equation.

In summary,

1 If $b^2 - 4ac > 0$, there will be two real roots.

2 If $b^2 - 4ac = 0$, there will be one real root.

3 If $b^2 - 4ac < 0$, there will be no real roots.

Although the quadratic formula may seem a little overwhelming at first, it is extremely useful and worth committing to memory or putting in a place where you can retrieve it.

Follow-up Exercises

Find (if possible) roots to the following equations.

0.243 $4x = 3x + 6$

0.244 $-2x + 8 = 2x - 4$

0.245 $5y = 10y - 30$

0.246 $4(y - 3) = y + 9$

0.247 $6x + 20 = 40 + 8x$

0.248 $15x - 4(2x + 14) = 0$

0.249 $-3y - 5(y + 4) = 4$

0.250 $3(x - 4) + 2(2x + 1) = 11$

0.251 $30x + 50(x - 6) = -20$

0.252 $4(5 - x) + 2x - 10 = -2x + 10$

0.253 $x^2 - 36 = 0$

0.254 $x^2 + 14x + 49 = 0$

0.255 $x^2 - 5x + 4 = 0$

0.256 $4x^2 + 2x - 30 = 0$

0.257 $7x^2 - 70 = 21x$

0.258 $2x^2 + 3x - 10 = x^2 + 6x + 30$

0.259 $-6x^2 + 4x - 10 = 0$

0.260 $-5x^2 + 10x - 20 = 0$

0.261 $5x^2 - 17.5x - 10 = 0$

0.262 $x^2 + 64 = 0$

0.263 $8x^2 + 2x - 15 = 0$

0.264 $-x^2 - 2x + 35 = 0$

CHAPTER CHECKLIST

If you have read all sections, you should

Understand the different components which make up the *real* _____
number system

Understand the arithmetic of *real numbers* _____

Understand *exponents* and their properties _____

Understand how to add, subtract, multiply, and divide *polynomials* _____

Be able to factor common *monomial* factors from polynomials _____

Be able to factor *quadratic* polynomials _____

Understand how to add, subtract, multiply, and divide *fractions* _____

Understand *radicals* and basic properties of radicals _____

Understand the equivalence between radicals and fractional expo- _____
nents

Understand the allowable operations which can be performed on _____
equations

Be able to solve first- and second-degree equations which are stated in _____
terms of one variable

CHAPTER TEST

Section

1 $-[-(-10)] =$ (0.1)

2 $|45 - 55| =$ (0.1)

3 $20 + (-15) - (-9) =$ (0.1)

4 $\dfrac{(-2)(-3)(-5)}{(-4)(-2.5)} =$ (0.1)

5 $[(4x^2)^2]^2 =$ (0.2)

6 $(\frac{1}{3})^{-3} =$ (0.2)

7 $m^4/m^7 =$ (0.2)

8 $(6a - 4b + c) - (-2a + 3b - 2c) + (-2b - 4c) =$ (0.2)

9 $\dfrac{(5x^2)(2x^3)(-x^4)}{-5x^6} =$ (0.2)

10 Factor $6x^4y^3 - 3x^3y^4 + 15x^5y^5$.   (0.3)

11 Factor $x^4 - \frac{1}{16}$.   (0.3)

12 Factor $x^2 + 5x - 36$.   (0.3)

13 $\frac{3}{8} - \frac{2}{3} + \frac{1}{6} =$ (0.4)

14 $\left(-\dfrac{a}{5}\right)\left(-\dfrac{2b}{ac}\right)\left(\dfrac{a}{c}\right) =$ (0.4)

15 $ab/c \div ac/b =$ (0.4)

16 $\dfrac{x - 3}{3x} \div \dfrac{x^2 - x - 6}{6x^2} =$ (0.4)

17 $a^{4/3} \cdot a^{1/5} \cdot a^{2/15} =$ (0.5)

18 $2\sqrt{3} - 4\sqrt{12} + 5\sqrt{27} =$ (0.5)

19 $\sqrt[3]{\dfrac{27a^6b^3}{c^9}} =$ (0.5)

20 Rewrite $\sqrt[5]{x^3}$, using a fractional exponent. (0.5)

21 Rewrite $x^{-1/4}$ in radical form. (0.5)

22 Determine the roots of $3x = 3x - 10$. (0.6)

23 Determine the roots of $-4x + 2(x - 5) = 3x + 10$. (0.6)

24 Determine the roots of $x^2 - 7x + 12 = 0$. (0.6)

25 Determine the roots of $4x^2 - 5x + 10 = 0$. (0.6)

1

CHAPTER OBJECTIVES **After reading this chapter you should understand the notion of a set, the properties of sets, and the notation of sets; you should be familiar with the graphical or pictorial representation of sets; you should understand the algebra of sets; and you should be familiar with some applications of set theory and the logic of sets.**

We frequently refer to "sets" of things in our daily lives, such as sets of tennis, sets of dishes, sets of agreements, and even social sets such as the jet set. The concept of a set can also be very useful in a mathematical sense.

In this chapter we will discuss set theory. Specifically, we will examine the nature of sets, the algebra of sets, and areas of application of set theory.

SETS DEFINED   1.1

Sets

A *set* is a collection of objects. The objects which belong to a set are called *elements* of the set. Reasons for membership in a set may be obvious—some common property shared by the elements. In some sets, the commonality among elements may be less obvious and in fact may be only their membership in the same set. For a set to be *well defined* and thus a mathematical set, it must be possible to determine whether any object is an element of the set. Examples of sets include the following:

The set of real numbers

The set of negative integers

The set of students enrolled in a course at a given time

The set of governors of each state in the United States

The set of products sold by a company

The set of events in the summer Olympics

The set of males over 21 years of age who live in New York City

The set of NBA players who average over 20 points and over 12 rebounds per game in a given season

Sets are usually defined in one of two ways. One method is enumeration. The *enumeration method* simply lists all elements in a set. If we designate a set by a capital letter, we might define the set of positive odd integers having a value less than 10 as

$$O = \{1, 3, 5, 7, 9\}$$

Note the use of *braces* to group the elements or members of the set O. As another example of the enumeration method, consider the set A of major United States automobile manufacturers, or

$$A = \{\text{General Motors, Ford, Chrysler, American Motors}\}$$

The enumeration method is convenient when the number of elements in a set is small or when it is not easy or possible to articulate a property defining membership in the set. However, this method is impractical when the number of elements in a set is large. Can you imagine enumerating members of the set which includes all positive integers? An alternative approach to defining sets is the *descriptive property method*. With this approach, the set is defined by stating the property required for membership in the set. The set defined in the first example of the enumeration method can be redefined as

$$O = \{x | x \text{ is a positive odd integer less than 10}\}$$

Verbally, the translation of this equation is "O is a set consisting of all elements x 'such that' (the vertical line) x is a positive odd integer having a value less than 10." The x to the left of the vertical line indicates the general notation for an element of the set; the expression to the right of the vertical line states the condition(s) required of an element for membership in the set.

Another example would be the specification of the set consisting of all positive integers. The set can be specified by the descriptive property approach as

$$I = \{x \,|\, x \text{ is a positive integer}\}$$

We can further distinguish sets on the basis of the number of elements they contain. *Finite sets* are sets which contain a definite number of elements. Sets O and A, mentioned before, are finite sets. *Infinite sets* are sets which contain an unlimited number of elements. Set I is an infinite set.

To indicate that an object e is a member of a set S, we use the notation

$$e \in S \tag{1.1}$$

Verbally, this notation translates as "e is a member of the set S." Again referring to the previously defined sets, we can make the following statements regarding set membership:

$$1 \in O$$
$$\text{Ford} \in A$$
$$4 \in I$$

The notation $e \notin S$ means that an object e is not a member of set S.

You must be very careful how you define sets. An element of a set should be enumerated, for purposes of defining the set, only once. Listing an element more than once will not change the set, but may be misleading when the number of elements in the set is to be determined. As an example, if the following scores were earned on the first test in a class of 10 students

Scores: 90, 80, 95, 80, 75, 60, 80, 70, 60, 100

the set A, which consists of the scores earned on the test, would be defined as

$$A = \{60, 70, 75, 80, 90, 95, 100\}$$

Police records indicate that the following business establishments were victims of the crimes of burglary or robbery within a given district during January.

Example 1.1

Date	Burglary Victim	Date	Robbery Victim
1/3	Ace Trucking Company	1/2	The Hot Furniture Company
1/5	Jones Market	1/4	First National Bank
1/9	Speedy Liquor	1/6	Speedy Liquor
1/17	Jones Market	1/13	Second National Bank
1/21	Ace Trucking Company	1/27	Speedy Liquor
1/24	High's Drugstore	1/30	High's Drugstore
1/27	Mac, Don, and Al's Hamburgers		
1/29	Jones Market		

The set of burglary victims B for the month of January is

B = {Ace Trucking Company; Jones Market; Speedy Liquor;
High's Drugstore; Mac, Don, and Al's Hamburgers}

The set of robbery victims R for the month is

R = {The Hot Furniture Company, First National Bank,
Speedy Liquor, Second National Bank, High's Drugstore}

EXERCISE
In Example 1.1 what is the set of victims V of commercial crimes for January?
Ans.: V = {Ace Trucking Company; Jones Market;
Speedy Liquor; High's Drug Store; Mac,
Don, and Al's Hamburgers; The Hot Furniture Company; First National Bank;
Second National Bank}.

The number of elements contained in a set B is denoted by $n(B)$. In Example 1.1, $n(B) = 5$ and $n(R) = 5$.

Special Sets

There are certain special sets to which we will refer frequently in discussing the algebra of sets. The *universal set* $\mathcal{U}$ is the set which contains all possible elements within a particular application under consideration.

Example 1.2
If we consider an opinion survey conducted of a random sample of residents within New York City, the universal set might be defined as the residents of New York City. A different universal set pertinent to the survey might be defined as the set of New York City residents selected randomly for the survey. Or, the set of residents actually selected and interviewed might be considered our universal set in this application.

DEFINITION
The *complement* of a set S is the set which consists of all elements in the universal set that are not members of set S. The complement of set S is denoted by S'.

Example 1.3
If set S consists of all positive integers and the universal set is defined as all integers, the complement S' consists of all negative integers and zero.

If $\mathcal{U}$ = {1, 2, 3, 4, 5, 6, 7, 8, 9, 10} and A = {1, 3, 5, 7, 9}, the comple- **Example** ment of set A contains all elements which are members of $\mathcal{U}$ but not A, **1.4** or A' = {2, 4, 6, 8, 10}.

The *empty*, or *null, set* $\varnothing$ is the set consisting of no elements. Verify for yourself that $\mathcal{U}'$ = $\varnothing$. Later in the chapter we will need to use the concept of the null set.

Another concept in set theory is the notion of a *subset. A set A is a subset of the set B if and only if every element of set A is also an element of set B.* This subset relationship is denoted by $A \subset B$, which may be read "A is a subset of B."

Given the following sets, define any subset relationships which exist. **Example**
1.5

$$A = \{1, 2, 3, 4, 5, 6, 7, 8, 9, 10\}$$
$$B = \{1, 3, 5, 7, 9\}$$
$$C = \{x | x \text{ is a real number}\}$$
$$D = \{z | z - 1 = 4\}$$

Since sets A, B, and D all contain elements which are real numbers, **Solution** each of these sets is a subset of set C, or

$$A \subset C \qquad B \subset C \qquad \text{and} \qquad D \subset C$$

Since every member of B is also a member of set A, we can state that $B \subset A$.

The only member of set D is 5. Since 5 is also a member of sets A and B we can state that

$$D \subset A \qquad \text{and} \qquad D \subset B$$

NOTE
By definition, the null set is a subset of every set. Consequently, in the previous example $\varnothing \subset A$, $\varnothing \subset B$, $\varnothing \subset C$, **and** $\varnothing \subset D$**.**

Venn Diagram Representation

A convenient way of envisioning set relationships is by using the pictorial representation of *Venn diagrams*. Venn diagrams utilize rectangular and circular areas to represent sets. Typically, a large rectangular area is used to designate the universal set, and all other sets are represented by areas inside the rectangle.

To illustrate the use of Venn diagrams, Fig. 1.1 depicts a universal set $\mathcal{U}$ within which is another set A, depicted by a circular area. In drawing Venn diagrams, there is nothing which states that the size of an area should be proportional to the size of a set. The primary value of

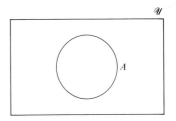

FIGURE 1.1

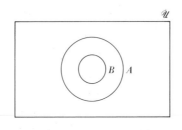

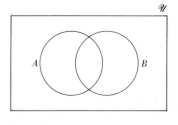

FIGURE 1.2 **FIGURE 1.3**

these figures is the information they convey about the relationships among sets. For example, if a set B is a subset of another set A, the Venn diagram representation of set B should be contained within set A. In Fig. 1.1, set A is drawn entirely within the universal set $\mathscr{U}$. In Fig. 1.2, sets A and B are both subsets within the universal set, with set B portrayed as a subset of A.

Figure 1.3 depicts a situation in which sets A and B seem to have some common elements. This is suggested by the overlap of the areas representing these two sets. From such a diagram, however, it should not be inferred that A and B actually do have elements in common. We would have to know more about A and B in order to draw such a conclusion.

Example 1.6   Given the following sets, represent them by use of a Venn diagram.

$$\mathscr{U} = \{1, 2, 3, 4, 5, 6, 7, 8, 9, 10\} \quad \text{and} \quad A = \{1, 3, 5, 7, 9\}$$

Solution   Figure 1.4 illustrates the Venn diagram representation of these sets. Note the way in which the elements of each set have been indicated. This is not necessary in a Venn diagram, but it is sometimes helpful in further analysis of a situation.

Example 1.7   In addition to the sets mentioned in Example 1.6, consider the set $B = \{1, 5, 9\}$. Draw a Venn diagram representing the three sets.

Solution   Figure 1.5 presents the Venn diagram representation.

Example 1.8   In addition to the sets mentioned in Example 1.7, consider the set $C = \{2, 4, 3, 7\}$. Draw a Venn diagram representing the four sets.

Solution   Figure 1.6 presents the Venn diagram.

Example 1.9   **Ridership Survey** Twelve families have been surveyed regarding their use of public transportation in a certain city. The two modes of public transportation in that city are bus and subway. The families were asked whether any member had used either mode during the past year. The results are summarized below.

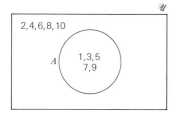

FIGURE 1.4

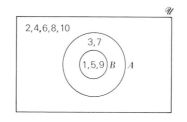

FIGURE 1.5

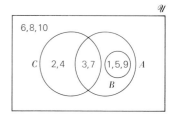

FIGURE 1.6

Family	1	2	3	4	5	6	7	8	9	10	11	12
Modes Used	B	B, S	S	B	N	S	B, S	N	B, S	B, S	N	B

Legend: B = Bus, S = Subway, N = Neither

Construct a Venn diagram which summarizes the results of the survey. Assume the universal set to include the 12 families surveyed, and utilize sets B and S to represent the set of families who have ridden buses and the set of families who have used the subway, respectively.

Solution

With sets B and S defined as indicated, the two sets must be drawn allowing for the possibility of overlap. In this survey application, the overlap identifies those families who have ridden both buses and the subway. In addition, although there was no formal identification of the set N representing those families who have ridden neither mode of transportation, those respondents are identified in Fig. 1.7 as the elements contained in $\mathscr{U}$ but not in B or S.

The complement of a set can be portrayed very nicely by Venn diagrams. In Fig. 1.8 the complement of set A is denoted by the shaded area.

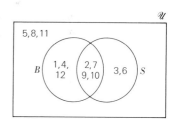

FIGURE 1.7

Follow-up Exercises

In Exercises 1.1 to 1.5, redefine the set using the descriptive property method.

1.1 $A = \{0, 2, 4, 6, 8, 10, 12, 14, 16, 18, 20\}$
1.2 $S = \{-5, +5, -4, +4, -3, +3, -2, +2, -1, +1, 0\}$
1.3 $V = \{a, e, i, o, u\}$
1.4 $S = \{0, 1, 4, 9, 16, 25, 36\}$
1.5 $C = \{1, 8, 27, 64\}$

In Exercises 1.6 to 1.10, redefine the set by enumeration.

1.6 $A = \{a | a \text{ is a negative odd integer greater than } -12\}$
1.7 $B = \{b | b \text{ is a positive integer less than 5}\}$
1.8 $C = \{c | c \text{ is the name of a day of the week}\}$
1.9 $B = \{b | \text{ when } a = 2, a + 3b = -7\}$
1.10 $M = \{m | m \text{ is the fourth power of a positive integer less than 5}\}$

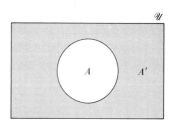

FIGURE 1.8

1.11 If $\mathcal{U}$ equals the set of real numbers and A equals the set of irrational numbers, define A'.

1.12 If $\mathcal{U}$ equals the set consisting of the months of the year and if $A = \{\text{April, May, September, November}\}$, define A'.

1.13 If $\mathcal{U} = \{1, 2, 3, 4, 5, 6, 7, 8, 9, 10\}$ and $B = \{b|b$ is a positive odd integer less than 8$\}$, define B'.

1.14 If $\mathcal{U}$ equals the set of students in a mathematics class and P is the set of students who fail the course, define P'.

1.15 If $\mathcal{U} = \{x|x$ is an integer greater than 5 but less than 15$\}$ and $S' = \{7, 9, 10, 12, 13\}$, define S.

1.16 If $\mathcal{U}$ is the set consisting of all positive integers and T' equals the set consisting of all positive even integers, define T.

1.17 If $\mathcal{U} = \{x|x$ is a positive integer less than 20$\}$, $A = \{1, 5, 9, 19\}$, $B = \{b|b$ is a positive odd integer less than 11$\}$, and $C = \{c|c$ is a positive odd integer less than 20$\}$, define all subset relationships which exist among $\mathcal{U}$, A, B, and C.

1.18 Given

$$\mathcal{U} = \{2, 4, 6, 8, 10, 12, 14, 16, 18\}$$
$$A = \{4, 8, 16\}$$
$$B = \{2, 4, 6, 8, 10\}$$

draw a Venn diagram representing the sets.

1.19 If $\mathcal{U} = \{x|x$ is a negative integer greater than $-11\}$, $A = \{a|a$ is a negative odd integer greater than $-10\}$, and $B = \{b|b$ is a negative integer greater than $-6\}$, draw a Venn diagram representing the sets.

1.20 Twenty people were surveyed regarding their attitudes about nuclear power. The results of the survey are

Person	1	2	3	4	5	6	7	8	9	10	11	12	13	14	15	16	17	18	19	20
Response	A	F	A	A	F	F	F	I	A	I	F	I	A	F	I	I	F	F	I	A

Legend: F = For, A = Against, I = Indifferent

Construct a Venn diagram which summarizes how these persons responded.

1.2   **SET OPERATIONS**

Just as there are arithmetic operations which provide the foundation for algebra, trigonometry, and other areas of study in mathematics, there is an arithmetic of set theory which allows for the development of an algebra of sets. In this section we will discuss basic set operations which provide the needed foundations.

Set Equality

Two sets A and B are said to be equal—$A = B$—if and only if every element in A is an element of B and every element of B is an element of A. Or, by using our knowledge of subsets, A and B are equal if and only if $A \subset B$ and $B \subset A$.

Given the following sets, determine whether any sets are equal.

Example 1.10

$$A = \{1, 2\}$$
$$B = \{x \,|\, (x - 1)(x - 2)(x - 3) = 0\}$$
$$C = \{1, 2, 3\}$$
$$D = \{x \,|\, x^2 - 3x + 2 = 0\}$$

To find the members of set B, recall that the product of three factors will equal zero only if any one of the factors equals zero; or, $abc = 0$ only if a or b or c equals zero. Consequently,

$$(x - 1)(x - 2)(x - 3) = 0 \quad \text{when} \quad \begin{array}{lll} x - 1 = 0 & \text{or} & x = 1 \\ x - 2 = 0 & \text{or} & x = 2 \\ x - 3 = 0 & \text{or} & x = 3 \end{array}$$

Thus, set B can be defined in an equivalent manner as $B = \{1, 2, 3\}$. And we can make the statement that set B equals set C, or $B = C$.

Before we determine the members of set D, consider the information contained in the following Algebra Flashback.

ALGEBRA FLASHBACK
Two approaches for finding the roots of an equation of the form

$$ax^2 + bx + c = 0$$

are *factoring* and use of the *quadratic formula.* The quadratic formula is

$$x = \frac{-b \pm \sqrt{b^2 - 4ac}}{2a}$$

For further discussion refer to Sec. 0.6.

Using a factoring approach, we get

$$x^2 - 3x + 2 = 0$$
$$(x - 2)(x - 1) = 0$$
or $$x = 2 \quad \text{and} \quad x = 1$$

Or, if you are unable to factor but remember the quadratic formula, $a = 1$, $b = -3$, and $c = 2$. Substituting into the quadratic formula gives

$$x = \frac{-(-3) \pm \sqrt{(-3)^2 - 4(1)(2)}}{2(1)}$$
$$= \frac{3 \pm \sqrt{1}}{2}$$
$$= \frac{3 \pm 1}{2}$$

The first root is found by using the plus sign, or $x = \frac{4}{2} = 2$. The second root is found using the minus sign, or $x = \frac{2}{2} = 1$. Thus, set D can be defined as

$$D = \{1, 2\}$$

and we can make the statement that set A equals set D, or $A = D$.

Union of Sets

The *union* of two sets is a set which consists of all elements found in either set or both sets. The union of sets A and B to form set C is denoted by

$$C = A \cup B$$

where $\cup$ is the union "operator."

Example 1.11   Given the following sets,

$$A = \{1, 2, 3, 4, 5\}$$
$$B = \{1, 3, 5, 7, 9\}$$
$$C = \{2, 4, 6, 8, 10\}$$

find

(a) $A \cup B$
(b) $A \cup C$
(c) $B \cup C$

Solution   (a) $A \cup B = \{1, 2, 3, 4, 5\} \cup \{1, 3, 5, 7, 9\}$
$\qquad\qquad\quad = \{1, 2, 3, 4, 5, 7, 9\}$
(b) $A \cup C = \{1, 2, 3, 4, 5\} \cup \{2, 4, 6, 8, 10\}$
$\qquad\qquad\quad = \{1, 2, 3, 4, 5, 6, 8, 10\}$
(c) $B \cup C = \{1, 3, 5, 7, 9\} \cup \{2, 4, 6, 8, 10\}$
$\qquad\qquad\quad = \{1, 2, 3, 4, 5, 6, 7, 8, 9, 10\}$

Example 1.12   Given the sets in Example 1.11 and that $\mathcal{U} = \{1, 2, 3, 4, 5, 6, 7, 8, 9, 10\}$, find

(a) $A' \cup B'$
(b) $B' \cup B$
(c) $C \cup B'$

Solution   (a) $A' \cup B' = \{1, 2, 3, 4, 5\}' \cup \{1, 3, 5, 7, 9\}'$
$\qquad\qquad\quad = \{6, 7, 8, 9, 10\} \cup \{2, 4, 6, 8, 10\}$
$\qquad\qquad\quad = \{2, 4, 6, 7, 8, 9, 10\}$
(b) $B' \cup B = \{1, 3, 5, 7, 9\}' \cup \{1, 3, 5, 7, 9\}$
$\qquad\qquad\quad = \{1, 2, 3, 4, 5, 6, 7, 8, 9, 10\}$
$\qquad\qquad\quad = \mathcal{U}$
(c) $C \cup B' = \{2, 4, 6, 8, 10\} \cup \{1, 3, 5, 7, 9\}'$
$\qquad\qquad\quad = \{2, 4, 6, 8, 10\} \cup \{2, 4, 6, 8, 10\}$
$\qquad\qquad\quad = \{2, 4, 6, 8, 10\}$

EXERCISE
In Example 1.9, give a verbal interpretation of $B \cup S$.
(Ans.: $B \cup S$ is a set which consists of those respondents who have ridden buses, subways, or both.

The Venn diagram representation of the union of two sets A and B is shown by the shaded area in Fig. 1.9.

Look back at Example 1.12b. Can you draw any general conclusion based upon the results? Compare the following statement with your answer.

The union of any set A and its complement results in the universal set $\mathcal{U}$

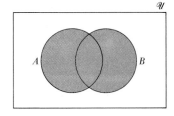

FIGURE 1.9

How did your answer compare?

Intersection of Sets

DEFINITION
The *intersection* of two sets is the set consisting of all elements which belong to *both* sets.

We can denote that the intersection of sets A and B results in the set C by

$$A \cap B = C$$

where $\cap$ is the intersection operator. The Venn diagram representation of the intersection of two sets A and B is the shaded area in Fig. 1.10. Note in the diagram that the intersection is the area *common to* the two sets.

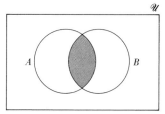

FIGURE 1.10

Referring to the sets defined in Examples 1.11 and 1.12, find

(a) $A \cap B$
(b) $A \cap C$
(c) $B \cap C$
(d) $A \cap A'$
(e) $A \cap A$
(f) $B \cap \mathcal{U}$

Example 1.13

Remembering that the set formed by the intersection of two or more sets consists of elements which are common to the original sets, we have

Solution

(a) $A \cap B = \{1, 2, 3, 4, 5\} \cap \{1, 3, 5, 7, 9\}$
$= \{1, 3, 5\}$
(b) $A \cap C = \{1, 2, 3, 4, 5\} \cap \{2, 4, 6, 8, 10\}$
$= \{2, 4\}$
(c) $B \cap C = \{1, 3, 5, 7, 9\} \cap \{2, 4, 6, 8, 10\}$
$= \varnothing$
(d) $A \cap A' = \{1, 2, 3, 4, 5\} \cap \{6, 7, 8, 9, 10\}$
$= \varnothing$
(e) $A \cap A = \{1, 2, 3, 4, 5\} \cap \{1, 2, 3, 4, 5\}$
$= \{1, 2, 3, 4, 5\}$
(f) $B \cap \mathcal{U} = \{1, 3, 5, 7, 9\} \cap \{1, 2, 3, 4, 5, 6, 7, 8, 9, 10\}$
$= \{1, 3, 5, 7, 9\}$

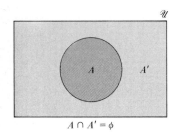

$A \cap A' = \phi$

FIGURE 1.11

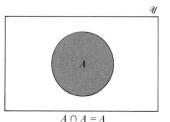

$A \cap A = A$

FIGURE 1.12

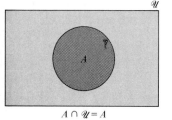

$A \cap \mathcal{U} = A$

FIGURE 1.13

Do the results in Example 1.13*d*, *e*, and *f* seem to make sense intuitively? Can you venture any conclusions from these results?

Let's speculate on some general properties of sets. See whether these are consistent with your own conclusions.

1 From Example 1.13*d*, the intersection of any set A and its complement A' is the null set. Graphically this is shown in Fig. 1.11.

2 From Example 1.13*e*, the intersection of any set A and itself is the same set A. Graphically this is shown in Fig. 1.12.

3 From Example 1.13*f*, the intersection of any set A and the universal set $\mathcal{U}$ is the set A. This is shown graphically in Fig. 1.13.

In algebra, the *associative property of addition* states that for any real numbers a, b, and c,

$$a + b + c = (a + b) + c = a + (b + c) \qquad (1.2)$$

Similarly, the associative property of multiplication states that

$$a \cdot b \cdot c = (ab) \cdot c = a \cdot (bc) \qquad (1.3)$$

A similar associative property holds for the union and intersection operations in set theory. That is,

$$A \cup B \cup C = (A \cup B) \cup C = A \cup (B \cup C) \qquad (1.4)$$
and $\quad A \cap B \cap C = (A \cap B) \cap C = A \cap (B \cap C) \qquad (1.5)$

When the union or intersection of more than two sets is to be found, these properties suggest grouping pairs of sets, finding their union or intersection, and combining this result with the remaining set(s).

Example 1.14

Continuing Example 1.13, find

(a) $A \cup B \cup C$
(b) $A \cap B \cap C$

(*a*) Grouping the first two sets, we have   **Solution**

$$
\begin{aligned}
A \cup B \cup C &= (A \cup B) \cup C \\
&= (\{1, 2, 3, 4, 5\} \cup \{1, 3, 5, 7, 9\}) \cup \{2, 4, 6, 8, 10\} \\
&= \{1, 2, 3, 4, 5, 7, 9\} \cup \{2, 4, 6, 8, 10\} \\
&= \{1, 2, 3, 4, 5, 6, 7, 8, 9, 10\}
\end{aligned}
$$

(*b*) To change the order of evaluation, let's group the last two sets. Therefore,

$$
\begin{aligned}
A \cap B \cap C &= A \cap (B \cap C) \\
&= \{1, 2, 3, 4, 5\} \cap (\{1, 3, 5, 7, 9\} \cap \{2, 4, 6, 8, 10\}) \\
&= \{1, 2, 3, 4, 5\} \cap \varnothing \\
&= \varnothing
\end{aligned}
$$

This result implies that there are no elements common to all three sets.

EXERCISE
**Re-solve Example 1.14 by grouping the sets in the
other way. That is, find $A \cup (B \cup C)$ and $(A \cap B) \cap C$
and compare with the results in Example 1.14.**

In Fig. 1.14 areas 1 through 8 represent subsets within $\mathscr{U}$. What areas   **Example**
represent   **1.15**

(*a*) $R \cup S \cup T$
(*b*) $R \cap S \cap T$

(*a*) If you remember that the *union* of sets is the set consisting of all the   **Solution**
elements which belong to any of the sets being combined, then by
observation $R \cup S \cup T$ consists of areas numbered 2, 3, 4, 5, 6, 7,
and 8. If this is not obvious, a more explicit approach might be the
following:

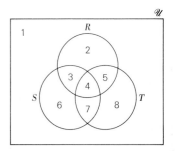

By observation, set R is represented by areas 2, 3, 4, and 5; set S
by areas 3, 4, 6, and 7; and set T by areas 4, 5, 7, and 8. Since

$$R \cup S \cup T = (R \cup S) \cup T$$

the areas representing $(R \cup S) \cup T$ are

$$[(2, 3, 4, 5) \cup (3, 4, 6, 7)] \cup (4, 5, 7, 8)$$
or $\qquad (2, 3, 4, 5, 6, 7) \cup (4, 5, 7, 8)$
or $\qquad (2, 3, 4, 5, 6, 7)$

FIGURE 1.14

(*b*) Similarly, if you remember that the intersection of sets is the set
consisting of all the elements common to all sets, then by observation $R \cap S \cap T$ is represented by area 4. The more explicit solution
would recognize that $R \cap S \cap T = (R \cap S) \cap T$, and the areas representing $(R \cap S) \cap T$ are

$$[(2, 3, 4, 5) \cap (3, 4, 6, 7)] \cap (4, 5, 7, 8)$$
or $\qquad (3, 4) \cap (4, 5, 7, 8)$
or $\qquad = (4)$

Follow-up Exercises

1.21 Given the following sets, state which, if any, are equal.

$$A = \{3, -4\}$$
$$B = \{x|(x - 3)(x + 4) = 0\}$$
$$C = \{x|x^3 + x^2 - 12x = 0\}$$
$$D = \{0, -4, -3\}$$

1.22 Given the following sets, state which, if any, are equal.

$$A = \{0, 1, -1\}$$
$$B = \{b|b^3 - b = 0\}$$
$$C = \{1, 0, -1\}$$
$$D = \{d|-d + d^3 = 0\}$$

1.23 Given the sets

$$A = \{-1, -3, -5, -7, -9\}$$
$$B = \{-1, -2, -3, -4, -5, -6, -7, -8, -9\}$$
$$C = \{-2, -4, -6, -8\}$$

find

(a) $A \cup B$ (d) $A \cap B$
(b) $A \cup C$ (e) $A \cap C$
(c) $B \cup C$ (f) $B \cap C$

1.24 If in Exercise 1.23 $\mathcal{U} = \{x|x$ is a negative integer greater than $-12\}$, find

(a) $A \cap A'$ (d) $A \cap C'$
(b) $A' \cap B'$ (e) $B' \cup A$
(c) $B' \cup C$ (f) $C' \cap A'$

1.25 Given the sets

$$A = \{0, 1, 2, 3, 4, 5, -1, -2, -3, -4, -5\}$$
$$B = \{-2, -4, 0, 2, 4\}$$
$$C = \{1, 2, 3, 4, 5\}$$

find

(a) $A \cup (B \cup C)$ (c) $(A \cap C) \cup B$
(b) $A \cap (B \cap C)$ (d) $C \cap (A \cup B)$

1.26 Given the sets

FIGURE 1.15

$$A = \{0, 5, 10, 15, 20, 25, 30, 35, 40, 45, 50\}$$
$$B = \{10, 20, 30, 40, 50, 60\}$$
$$C = \{5, 15, 25, 35, 45, 55\}$$

find

(a) $A \cap (B \cap C)$ (c) $(A \cap B) \cup C$
(b) $A \cup (B \cup C)$ (d) $A \cup (B \cap C)$

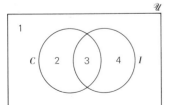

1.27 Figure 1.15 is a Venn diagram used to represent the results of a survey. Set C consists of respondents who suffered colds during the previous year, set I consists of respondents who suffered influenza (flu), and $\mathcal{U}$ represents all respondents to the survey. Give a verbal interpretation of the elements represented by the numbered areas 1 to 4.

1.28 Figure 1.16 is a Venn diagram used to represent a breakdown of student involvement in cultural and extracurricular activities at a local college. Set A consists of all students who attended an athletic event during the year, set B consists of all students who attended a concert, and set C consists of all students who attended a theater production. If $\mathcal{U}$ represents all persons attending the college during the previous year, verbally interpret the elements represented by the numbered areas 1 to 8.

1.29 *Consumer Survey* Consumers were surveyed regarding their purchases of three soft drinks during the past month. If, in Fig. 1.16, sets A, B, and C consist, respectively, of respondents who purchased soft drink brands A, B, and C, and if $\mathcal{U}$ represents all consumers surveyed, interpret the elements represented by the numbered areas 1 to 8.

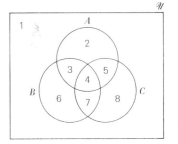

FIGURE 1.16

SAMPLE APPLICATIONS 1.3

In this section we will examine some sample scenarios which illustrate some applications of set theory. The examples and data are hypothetical, so the conclusions should not be taken too seriously. However, this should not detract from the significance of these examples; they are, indeed, very likely areas for applying the concepts of set theory.

Vitamin C Research In recent years there has been much controversy about the possible benefits of using supplemental doses of vitamin C. Claims have been made by proponents of vitamin C that supplemental doses will reduce the incidence of the common cold and influenza (flu). A test group of 1,000 persons received supplemental doses of vitamin C for a period of 1 year. During this period it was found that 300 such people had one or more colds, 100 people suffered from influenza, and 80 people suffered from both colds and influenza. Use a Venn diagram to summarize the results of this study if $\mathcal{U}$ represents all persons in the control group, C is the set of persons incurring colds, and I is the set of persons suffering from influenza during the study period. How many persons suffered from neither colds nor influenza? How many persons suffered colds and not influenza? Influenza but not colds? What conclusions can you draw regarding vitamin C and its effect on these ailments?

Example 1.16

NOTE
The number of elements contained in set B is denoted by $n(B)$. Similarly, the number of elements contained in the set $A \cap B$ is denoted by $n(A \cap B)$.

60

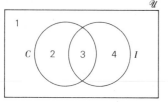

FIGURE 1.17

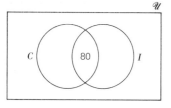

FIGURE 1.18

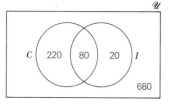

FIGURE 1.19

Given the sets which were defined, a Venn diagram representation is provided by Fig. 1.17. The Venn diagram provides the *framework* for answering the questions asked about the survey. In order to answer the questions, it is necessary to determine the number of elements in each of the four numbered areas in Fig. 1.17. Given the survey data, the only set for which we can immediately identify the number of elements is that represented by area 3, or $C \cap I$. This area represents those 80 people who incurred both colds and influenza during the test period, and this is shown in Fig. 1.18. Can you think of any way in which the number of elements contained in areas 2 and 4 could have been filled in before area 3? These areas represent the sets of people who contracted colds *only* and influenza *only*, respectively; and data on these sets are not available without some analysis. For instance, we are told that the number of people having colds during the test period was 300; however, included in this number are those who had *both* colds and influenza. Thus, to determine those who had colds only, we must subtract from the 300 the 80 who had both. Therefore 220 people had colds only. Area 4 represents the set of people who incurred influenza only. The number of people in this set is the 100 identified as having influenza minus the 80 who had both, or 20. The last set of people, represented by area 1, consists of all people who had neither colds nor influenza during the test period. This set is the complement of the union of the other three sets; it contains $1,000 - 220 - 80 - 20 = 680$ members. The numbers of members of each set are indicated in Fig. 1.19.

It is difficult to draw any conclusions about the study without having some comparative data. For example, if there had been a similar control group of 1,000 people who received no vitamin C supplement over the same period, a comparison of health histories during the test period might allow us to reach conclusions about the relative benefits of using or not using vitamin C.

**Example
1.17**

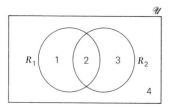

FIGURE 1.20

Voter Crossover Immediately following the famed Watergate scandal from 1972 to 1974, many voters became disillusioned with the Republican party and further disillusioned with politics in general. A public opinion research organization wanted to determine the effect that Watergate *might* have had on voters and their political preferences. Therefore, it surveyed 15,000 registered Republicans to determine how they voted during the 1972 and 1976 Presidential elections.

The survey results indicated that of the 15,000 people, 7,500 voted for the Republican candidate in 1972, 4,500 voted for the Republican candidate in 1976, and 4,000 voted for the Republican candidate in both 1972 and 1976. Figure 1.20 is a Venn diagram which summarizes the survey results; R_1 is the set of people who voted for the Republican candidate in 1972, and R_2 the set of people who voted for the Republican candidate in 1976. Determine the number of elements in each of the four subsets represented by the numbered areas 1 to 4, and interpret your answers with respect to voter behavior.

Figure 1.21 indicates the number of members in each subset. As in Example 1.16, these numbers are found by first recognizing that $n(R_1 \cap R_2) = 4{,}000$. Since R_1 contains 7,500 voters in total, the subset represented by area 1 must have 3,500 voters. Similarly, since R_2 contains 4,500 voters, the subset represented by area 3 has 500 voters. The number of people in $R_1 \cup R_2$ can be calculated as

$$n(R_1 \cup R_2) = n(R_1) + n(R_2) - n(R_1 \cap R_2)$$
$$= 7{,}500 + 4{,}500 - 4{,}000$$
$$= 8{,}000$$

Therefore the number of people in the subset represented by area 4 is

$$n(R_1 \cup R_2)' = n(\mathcal{U}) - n(R_1 \cup R_2)$$
$$= 15{,}000 - 8{,}000$$
$$= 7{,}000$$

The 3,500 members of the subset represented by area 1 are those who voted for the Republican candidate in 1972 but not in 1976. The 4,000 people represented by area 2 are those who voted for the Republican candidates in both years. The 500 people represented by area 3 voted for the Republican candidate in 1976 but not in 1972. The 7,000 persons represented by area 4 are those Republicans surveyed who did not vote for a Republican candidate during either election. This set could include those persons who (1) did not vote in either election, (2) voted for another candidate in one election and did not vote in the other election, or (3) voted for another candidate in both elections.

The following observations can be made from the survey results:

1 Of the 15,000 registered Republicans, 8,000 voted for a Republican during at least one of the two elections.

2 Of the 15,000, 7,000 did not vote for the Republican candidate during either election.

3 Of the 7,500 Republicans who voted in 1972 for the Republican candidate, 3,500 did not vote Republican in 1976. These 3,500 may indicate a loss attributable to Watergate. Can we state that this loss was caused by Watergate? What else might explain the loss of these votes?

4 The 500 persons represented by area 3 are a measure of gains to the Republican party from 1972. Where might these voters have come from?

Solution

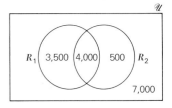

FIGURE 1.21

Cancer Research A cancer research team working with the support of the Department of Health, Education, and Welfare has gathered statistics related to the deaths of 20,000 cancer victims. Extensive data have been gathered regarding the health histories and living habits of both the victims and their relatives. Three significant variables appear to be associated with victims of cancer: regular smoking, moderate to heavy drinking, and age of 35 or more. The following data were gathered on 20,000 victims.

Example 1.18

14,500 victims regularly smoked.

12,500 victims were moderate-to-heavy drinkers of alcohol.

15,000 victims were 35 or more years of age.

11,000 victims smoked regularly and were moderate-to-heavy drinkers.

12,000 victims smoked regularly and were 35 or older.

10,000 victims were moderate-to-heavy drinkers and were 35 or older.

10,000 victims had all three characteristics.

If $\mathcal{U}$ is defined as the set of victims, S the set of victims who were regular smokers, D the set who were moderate-to-heavy drinkers, and A those who were 35 or older, construct a Venn diagram showing the numbers of members having each possible combination of these three attributes. How many victims had none of the three characteristics?

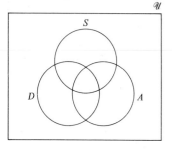

FIGURE 1.22

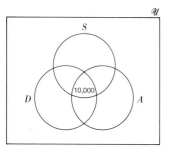

FIGURE 1.23

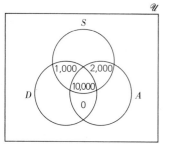

FIGURE 1.24

Solution   Since three sets of interest have been identified as being contained within $\mathcal{U}$, the Venn diagram should have the form of Fig. 1.22. Given the information pertaining to the numbers of victims having each combination of attributes, you would very likely conclude that there are far more than 20,000 cancer victims in this group. "Something must be wrong with the data—if you add the 12,500 drinkers to the 14,500 smokers, you already have 27,000 victims." This logic fails to recognize the overlap or intersection property. Many smokers also drink, not all smokers and drinkers are under 35 years of age, and so forth. So what is required is that we sift through the information to identify the eight distinct subsets of interest in the sample.

If you construct a Venn diagram, identify the eight areas, and review the information presented, you should conclude that the only area for which the number of elements is immediately obvious represents the set of victims who had all three characteristics. These 10,000 victims are denoted in Fig. 1.23. Once this one area is filled in, it becomes a matter of solving some mental equations and filling in a type of jigsaw puzzle. For example, we are told that the number of victims who were both smokers and drinkers was 11,000, or $n(S \cap D) = 11,000$. In Fig. 1.24 we can see that the set $S \cap D$ is represented by two areas. Since one of these areas represents 10,000 members, the other area must represent the remaining 1,000 elements. Using the information that $n(S \cap A) = 12,000$ and $n(D \cap A) = 10,000$, and applying the same logic, we can complete the Venn diagram to the point shown in Fig. 1.24.

To complete the Venn diagram, we need to use the information that $n(S) = 14,500$, $n(D) = 12,500$, and $n(A) = 15,000$. Since S should contain 14,500 elements, the remaining part of S must contain the other 1,500 elements. Similar reasoning should lead you to agree with the figures in the Venn diagram in Fig. 1.25. Can you verify the figure of 1,000 victims who possessed none of the attributes?

Follow-up Exercises

1.30 A survey of 500 consumers was conducted to determine their purchasing behavior regarding two leading soft drinks. It was found that during the past month 250 had purchased brand A, 200 had purchased brand B, and 100 had purchased both brand A and brand B.

(a) Construct a Venn diagram summarizing the results of the survey.
(b) How many respondents purchased A only?
(c) How many respondents purchased B only?
(d) How many respondents purchased neither A nor B?

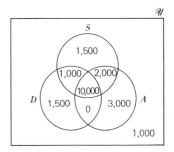

FIGURE 1.25

1.31 A survey of 1,000 people was conducted to determine the extent to which they attempt to learn the news of the day. It was found that 400 people regularly watch the news on TV, 300 people regularly listen to the news on the radio, and 275 people regularly get the news from both TV and radio.

(a) Construct a Venn diagram summarizing the results of the survey.
(b) How many of the respondents watch the news only on TV?
(c) How many listen to the news only on the radio?
(d) How many respondents do not listen to the news on either radio or TV? Describe this group of persons regarding their access to the news.

1.32 *Energy Conservation* A group of 5,000 people was surveyed regarding policies which might be enacted to conserve oil. Of the 5,000, 2,000 people said that gas rationing would be acceptable to them, 1,500 people said that a federal surtax of \$0.25 per gallon would be acceptable, and 750 people indicated that both rationing and the surtax would be acceptable.

(a) Construct a Venn diagram which summarizes the results of the survey.
(b) How many people would willingly accept gas rationing but not the surtax?
(c) How many people would willingly accept the surtax but not gas rationing?
(d) How many respondents would willingly accept neither policy?

1.33 A group of 1,000 people was asked if they had purchased three different brands of yogurt. The following data were gathered.

175 people had purchased brand A.

220 had purchased brand B.

150 had purchased brand C.

50 had purchased both A and B.

75 had purchased both A and C.

60 had purchased both B and C.

20 had purchased all three.

(a) Construct a Venn diagram which summarizes the results of the survey.

(b) How many people purchased only *A*? Only *B*? Only *C*?

(c) How many purchased *A* and *B* only?

(d) How many purchased *A* and *C* only?

(e) How many people purchased *B* and *C* only?

(f) How many had not purchased any of the three?

1.34 *Education Survey* A group of 5,000 students at a local college was asked three questions about their college experiences. Four thousand students said they were satisfied with the quality of instruction; 3,000 stated they were satisfied with the course offerings in their major field of study; 3,800 said they were satisfied generally with the total college experience (academic and nonacademic). A further breakdown indicated that 2,500 were satisfied with both the quality of instruction and the course offerings in their major; 3,200 were satisfied with both the quality of instruction and the total college experience; 2,000 were satisfied with both the course offerings and the total college experience; and 1,800 were satisfied with all three areas.

(a) Construct a Venn diagram which summarizes the results of the survey.

Determine the percentage of students:

(b) Satisfied *only* with the quality of instruction

(c) Satisfied *only* with the course offerings

(d) Satisfied *only* with the total college experience

(e) Not satisfied with any of the three areas.

1.35 *Public Transportation* The Department of Transportation surveyed 100,000 people to determine their use of different modes of public transportation during the past year. The results of the survey indicated that

25,000 had flown in airplanes.

41,000 had ridden buses.

20,000 had ridden trains.

7,000 had ridden both airplanes and buses.

9,000 had ridden both buses and trains.

8,000 had ridden both airplanes and trains.

5,000 had ridden all three modes.

Determine the percentage of respondents who

(a) Flew airplanes only

(b) Rode only airplanes *and* buses

(c) Rode only airplanes *and* trains

(d) Rode only buses *and* trains

(e) Rode buses only

(f) Did not use any of the three modes

1.36 *Criminal Justice System* The Department of Justice mailed a survey to 1,000 criminal justice system experts to determine where the most immediate needs were—the law enforcement area, the court system, or the corrections area (jails and prisons). All respondents were asked to indicate the sector(s) having the greatest needs. The numbers of experts citing the different areas of need were as follows:

625 experts cited the law enforcement area.

625 experts cited the court system.

525 experts cited the corrections area.

450 experts cited both law enforcement and the courts.

400 experts cited both the courts and corrections areas.

375 experts cited both law enforcement and corrections.

300 experts cited all three areas.

Determine the number of experts who
(*a*) Cited law enforcement only
(*b*) Cited the court system only
(*c*) Cited the corrections sector only
(*d*) Cited law enforcement and courts only
(*e*) Cited law enforcement and corrections only
(*f*) Assuming that each survey returned to the Department of Justice cited at least one of the three areas, how many surveys were not returned?

SUMMARY

This chapter has introduced the notion of sets, the algebra of sets, and some illustrative areas of application. Set theory provides a logical framework which can be very useful for envisioning relationships. There is much more that we could do with this topic. The concepts of set theory can be extended to form the foundations for the study of logic and reasoning. Our purpose has been to survey the area and to present enough of a foundation for us to be able to draw upon these concepts in later chapters. You will see the notion and notation of sets used frequently in the coming chapters.

CHAPTER CHECKLIST

If you have read all sections of this chapter, you should

Understand what constitutes a *set*　　　　　　　　　　＿＿＿＿

Understand the *enumeration* **and** *descriptive property* **methods of**　＿＿＿＿
defining sets

Understand the concept and notation of set membership　　＿＿＿＿

Understand the concepts and notation associated with the *universal*　＿＿＿＿
set, **the** *complement* **of a set, the** *empty set,* **and** *subsets*

Be able to represent sets using *Venn diagrams*　　　　　＿＿＿＿

Understand *set equality* **and the set operations of** *union* **and** *intersec-*　＿＿＿＿
tion

_____ **Be comfortable using Venn diagrams to display and interpret results of surveys**

1.4 ## KEY TERMS AND CONCEPTS

set	**empty or null set**
element	**subset**
enumeration method	**Venn diagram**
descriptive property method	**set equality**
finite versus infinite sets	**union of sets**
universal set	**intersection of sets**
complement	

ADDITIONAL EXERCISES

Exercises 1.37 to 1.43 are related to Sec. 1.1.

1.37 Redefine set A using the descriptive property method if
(a) $A = \{2, 4, 8, 16, 32, 64\}$
(b) $A = \{3, 9, 27, 81, 243\}$
(c) $A = \{-1, 4, -9, 16, -25, 36, -49, 64\}$
(d) $A = \{10, 100, 1,000, 10,000, 100,000\}$
1.38 Given

$\mathcal{U} = \{x|x$ is an integer greater than -6 but less than $+11\}$
$A = \{a|a$ is an even positive integer less than 12$\}$
$B = \{b|b$ is an odd integer greater than -4 but less than $+6\}$

(a) Define A'.
(b) Define B'.
1.39 If $\mathcal{U}$ consists of all students enrolled in courses at a university, A consists of all male students, B consists of all students aged 35 years or over, and C consists of all engineering students, (a) define the set A', (b) define the set B', and (c) define the set C'.
1.40 If $\mathcal{U}$ consists of the different total scores possible on the roll of a pair of dice and B' consists of the scores of 5, 7, and 9, define B.
1.41 If

$\mathcal{U} = \{1, 2, 3, 4, 5, 6, 7, 8, 9, 10\}$
$A = \{1, 5, 9\}$
$B = \{1, 3, 5, 7, 9\}$
$C = \{2, 4, 6, 8, 10\}$

define all subset relationships which exist for these sets.
1.42 Draw a Venn diagram representing all the sets in Exercise 1.41.
1.43 Ten residents of a city were surveyed regarding their use of public transportation in that city. They were asked whether they had ridden the subway (S), the bus (B), or neither (N) during the past year. The responses were as follows:

Resident	1	2	3	4	5	6	7	8	9	10
Response	N	N	B	B, S	S	B, S	B, S	B, S	B	S

Draw a Venn diagram which shows how each resident responded to the survey.

Exercises 1.44 to 1.47 are related to Sec. 1.2.

1.44 Given the following sets, determine if any sets are equal.

$$A = \{x \mid x^3 + 6x^2 + 9x = 0\} \qquad C = \{-3, 0\}$$
$$B = \{x \mid x^2 + 3x = 0\} \qquad D = \{-3, 0, 3\}$$

1.45 Given the sets

$$\mathcal{U} = \{x \mid x \text{ is a positive integer less than } 20\}$$
$$A = \{5, 10, 15\}$$
$$B = \{2, 4, 6, 8, 10\}$$
$$C = \{1, 5, 9, 15, 17\}$$

find
(a) $A \cap B$
(b) $A \cup B \cup C$
(c) $A' \cap B'$
(d) $A' \cup C'$
(e) $A \cap B \cap C$
(f) $A' \cup B$
(g) $A' \cap B$
(h) $(A \cap B \cap C)'$

1.46 In Fig. 1.26, the numbers represent the elements contained in the various subsets. Determine
(a) $n(A)$
(b) $n(A \cup B)$
(c) $n(A \cup B \cup C)$
(d) $n(\mathcal{U})$
(e) $n(A' \cup B)$
(f) $n(B' \cap C')$
(g) $n(B \cap C)$
(h) $n(A' \cap B' \cap C')$

1.47 *Victimization Survey* Figure 1.27 is a Venn diagram used to represent the results of a survey. Set A represents those respondents who have been victims of robbery, set B represents those respondents who have been victims of automobile theft, set C represents those respondents who have been victims of burglary, and $\mathcal{U}$ consists of all respondents. Give a verbal interpretation of the elements contained in areas 1 to 8.

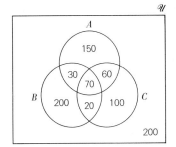

FIGURE 1.26

Exercises 1.48 to 1.49 are related to Sec. 1.3.

1.48 *Child Abuse* A survey of 500 high school seniors was conducted to determine the extent to which child abuse exists. It was found that 50 respondents recalled having been physically abused by their fathers, 60 recalled having been physically abused by their mothers, and 20 recalled having been physically abused by both parents. What percentage of respondents was
(a) Physically abused by fathers only?
(b) Physically abused by mothers only?
(c) Physically abused by both parents?
(d) Physically abused?
(e) Not physically abused?

1.49 A major TV network surveyed 50,000 viewers to determine their viewing habits during the past week. They found that

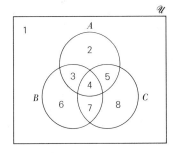

FIGURE 1.27

29,000 viewers had watched a sports event.

25,000 viewers had watched a news show.

28,000 viewers had watched a TV movie.

16,000 viewers had watched both sports and news shows.

15,000 viewers had watched both news shows and TV movies.

18,000 viewers had watched both sports shows and TV movies.

10,000 viewers had watched all three types of shows.

What percentage of viewers watched
(a) News shows only?
(b) Sports shows only?
(c) TV movies only?
(d) None of the three types of programs?

CHAPTER TEST

1 Redefine set A using the descriptive property method if

$$A = \{100, 400, 900, 1600\}$$

2 You are given the sets

$$\mathcal{U} = \{x \mid x \text{ is a positive integer less than 15}\}$$
$$A = \{1, 3, 5, 7, 9\}$$
$$B = \{2, 4, 6, 8, 10, 12, 14\}$$
$$C = \{5, 6, 7, 8, 9, 10\}$$

(a) Draw a Venn diagram representing the sets.
(b) What elements are in the set $A \cap B \cap C'$?
(c) Determine $n(A \cap B \cap C)$.
3 Given sets A, B, and C contained in $\mathcal{U}$, draw a Venn diagram shading the area(s) which correspond to
(a) $(A' \cup B)' \cap (B \cap C)'$
(b) $(A \cap B)' \cup (A \cap B \cap C)$
4 A group of 1,000 consumers was surveyed regarding their purchase of three different detergents during the past year. The results of the survey indicated that

300 people had purchased brand A.

200 had purchased brand B.

250 had purchased brand C.

50 had purchased both A and B.

75 had purchased both A and C.

60 had purchased both B and C.

25 had purchased all three brands.

(a) How many people had purchased none of the three brands?
(b) How many had purchased A only?
(c) How many had purchased B and C only?

CHAPTER OBJECTIVES After reading this chapter, you should be familiar with the concept of the cartesian product and cartesian or rectangular coordinate systems; you should understand relations and their characteristics; you should be familiar with the characteristics and notation of mathematical functions; and you should know how to sketch the graphical representation of mathematical functions.

Mathematical functions are fundamental to much of what we will do in this book. The purpose of this chapter is to develop the notion of mathematical functions. First, we will extend our knowledge of set theory by defining the *cartesian product*. This concept will be used to define a *relation*. With an understanding of these two concepts, we will concentrate on the meaning and notation of mathematical functions. Finally, we will discuss the graphical representation of mathematical functions.

THE CARTESIAN PRODUCT AND RELATIONS 2.1

Cartesian Product

The cartesian product of two sets is a set defined as follows:

DEFINITION
The *cartesian product* of the set A and the set B, written as $A \times B$, is the set consisting of all *ordered pairs* (a, b) where a is an element of set A and b is an element of set B.

The cartesian product can be represented symbolically as

$$A \times B = \{(a, b) | a \in A \text{ and } b \in B\}$$

Example 2.1

Given the sets

$$A = \{1, 2\} \quad B = \{-1, 3, 7\}$$
$$A \times B = \{(1, -1), (1, 3), (1, 7), (2, -1), (2, 3), (2, 7)\}$$

Note that each element of $A \times B$ consists of a pair of values; the first is an element of A, and the second an element of B. Each element of the set $A \times B$ is an ordered pair of elements. The order of the elements within a pair *is* significant, and the ordered pairs (1, 5) and (5, 1) are not considered the same.

Example 2.2

Considering sets A and B in Example 2.1, the cartesian product $B \times A$ is

$$B \times A = \{(-1, 1), (-1, 2), (3, 1), (3, 2), (7, 1), (7, 2)\}.$$

Note that sets $A \times B$ and $B \times A$ are not equal. Even though the sets consist of the same number of elements, the reverse *order* of the pairs makes the elements, and thus the respective sets, unequal.

Example 2.3

If $A = \{a, b\}$ and $B = \{1, -5, 10\}$, find the set $A \times B$.

Solution

$$A \times B = \{(a, 1), (a, -5), (a, 10), (b, 1), (b, -5), (b, 10)\}$$

The number of elements, i.e., ordered pairs, contained in a cartesian product depends upon the number of elements in the component sets. If A consists of m elements and B consists of n elements, $A \times B$ consists of $m \cdot n$ ordered pairs.

The cartesian product may involve sets whose elements are not real numbers. However, our attention will be focused upon sets whose elements are real numbers. Given this assumption, we can provide a visual representation of ordered pairs and thus the cartesian product. Consider the set $X = \{-4, 2\}$. The elements of this set can be represented graphically by locating them on a real number line, as in Fig. 2.1.

Also consider the set $Y = \{-2, 3\}$. The elements of this set can be represented by a real number line, as with set X. Figure 2.2 illustrates this.

FIGURE 2.1

FIGURE 2.2

The cartesian product $X \times Y$ is

$$X \times Y = \{(-4, 2), (-4, 3), (2, -2), (2, 3)\}$$

We can obtain a graphical representation of this cartesian product by rearranging the real number lines in Figs. 2.1 and 2.2. If the real number line representing the elements of set Y is rotated counterclockwise such that (1) it is perpendicular to the line representing the elements of X and (2) the two number lines intersect at their *zero points*, then the result is as shown in Fig. 2.3. The horizontal number line is called the *horizontal axis*, or the *x axis*. The vertical line is called the *vertical axis*, or the *y axis*. The two axes together are called *coordinate axes*.

To graph an ordered pair (x, y) of $X \times Y$, first draw a vertical line perpendicular to the x axis, through the point x which represents the member of X. Then draw a horizontal line perpendicular to the y axis, through the point y which represents the member of Y. The point of intersection of these two lines represents the ordered pair (x, y) which is a

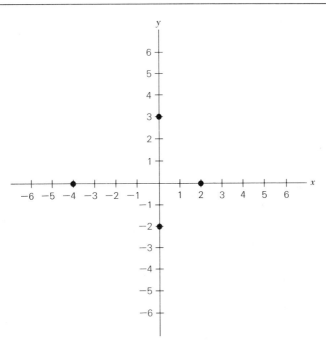

FIGURE 2.3

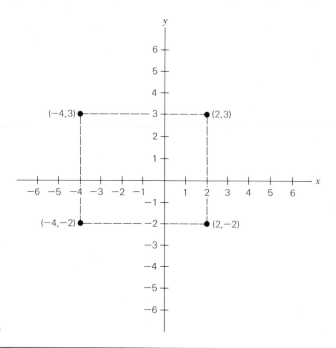

FIGURE 2.4

member of $X \times Y$. Figure 2.4 is a graphical representation of the ordered pairs of $X \times Y$ for our example.

Given that an element (x, y) of $X \times Y$ is represented by a point, the first member of the ordered pair is usually called the *x coordinate* of the point and the second member the *y coordinate* of the point. In Fig. 2.4, -4 is the x coordinate and 3 is the y coordinate of the point $(-4, 3)$.

The x and y coordinates are sometimes referred to, respectively, as the *abscissa* and *ordinate* of a point. The plane formed by the coordinate axes is often called the *cartesian plane*. The cartesian plane can be described as the graphical representation of $A \times A$ where $A = \{a | a$ is a real number$\}$. The ordered pairs (x, y) belonging to the set $A \times A$ would consist of all ordered pairs of real numbers.

The system of coordinates used in the cartesian plane is called a *cartesian*, or *rectangular*, *coordinate system*.

Any point in the cartesian plane may be assigned an ordered pair of coordinates (x, y) which describes the location of the point. To assign these values, horizontal and vertical lines should be drawn through the point. The place where the vertical line crosses the x axis is the x coordinate of the point, and where the horizontal line crosses the y axis is the y coordinate of the point. In Fig. 2.5, point (x, y) would be assigned the coordinates $(-2, 3)$.

Look at Fig. 2.5 and convince yourself that (1) the x coordinate for any point located on the y axis is 0, (2) the y coordinate for any point located on the x axis is 0, and (3) the coordinates of the point located at the intersection of the two axes are $(0, 0)$. This last point is commonly referred to as the *origin*.

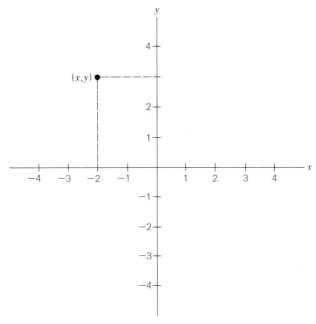

FIGURE 2.5

Relations

Although the cartesian product is an important mathematical concept, we will not often need to use it directly. We will, however, use it indirectly because of its importance in the development of other mathematical concepts such as the cartesian plane and rectangular coordinate system. The cartesian product also forms the basis for defining a *relation*.

DEFINITION
Given two sets X and Y, a *relation* between X and Y is any subset of the cartesian product $X \times Y$.

If $X = \{1, 4\}$ and $Y = \{-1, 2\}$,

$$X \times Y = \{(1, -1), (1, 2), (4, -1), (4, 2)\}$$

Each of the following sets is a relation between X and Y.

$\{(1, -1)\}$, $\{(1, 2)\}$, $\{(4, -1)\}$, $\{(4, 2)\}$, $\{(1, -1), (1, 2)\}$,
$\{(1, -1), (4, -1)\}$, $\{(1, -1), (4, 2)\}$, $\{(1, 2), (4, -1)\}$,
$\{(1, 2), (4, 2)\}$, $\{(4, -1), (4, 2)\}$, $\{(1, -1), (1, 2), (4, -1)\}$,
$\{(1, -1), (4, -1), (4, 2)\}$, $\{(1, 2), (4, -1), (4, 2)\}$,
$\{(1, -1), (1, 2), (4, 2)\}$, $\{(1, -1), (1, 2), (4, -1), (4, 2)\}$, $\varnothing$

Example 2.4

Although we will rarely need to enumerate all relations between two sets, a formula allows us to determine the total number of relations. If $X \times Y$ consists of n ordered pairs, 2^n total relations can be formed from $X \times Y$. In Example 2.4, $X \times Y$ consisted of four ordered pairs, and we enumerated $2^4 = 16$ possible relations.

Example 2.5   If $X = \{2, -3\}$ and $Y = \{1, 4, 6\}$, determine all ordered pairs (x, y) which satisfy the relation

$$R = \{(x, y)|x + y = 3\}$$

Solution   All ordered pairs (x, y) are formed by $X \times Y$. And

$$X \times Y = \{(2, 1), (2, 4), (2, 6), (-3, 1), (-3, 4), (-3, 6)\}$$

Examination of each ordered pair leads us to the conclusion that

$$R = \{(2, 1), (-3, 6)\}$$

Example 2.6   For X and Y defined as in Example 2.5, determine the relation R, where

$$R = \{(x, y)|y \geq x\}$$

Solution   Again, examination of the ordered pairs formed by $X \times Y$ leads us to conclude that

$$R = \{(2, 4), (2, 6), (-3, 1), (-3, 4), (-3, 6)\}$$

DEFINITION
The *domain D* of a relation is the set of all first components of the ordered pairs of the relation.

DEFINITION
The *range R* of a relation is the set consisting of all second components of the ordered pairs of the relation.

Example 2.7   Given the relation

$$N = \{(1, 5), (1, -2)\}$$

the domain of the relation is $D = \{1\}$, and the range of the relation is $R = \{5, -2\}$.

Given the relation

$$M = \{(1, -2), (1, 5), (2, -3), (2, 4), (2, -6)\}$$

the domain of the relation is $D = \{1, 2\}$. The range of the relation is $R = \{-6, -3, -2, 4, 5\}$.

Example 2.8

We almost always will be concerned with relations defined by equations or inequalities. The equation or inequality provides a "rule" which relates values of x and y to one another. These rules provide a convenient means for matching elements of the domain with the corresponding elements of the range.

Determine the elements of the relation

$$N = \{(x, y)|y = 4x - 5 \text{ where } x = 1, 2, 3\}$$

Example 2.9

Substituting the three values for x from the domain into the equation, we generate the following ordered pairs of the relation:

$y = 4(1) - 5 = -1$ leading to the ordered pair $(1, -1)$
$y = 4(2) - 5 = 3$ leading to the ordered pair $(2, 3)$
$y = 4(3) - 5 = 7$ leading to the ordered pair $(3, 7)$

Therefore $N = \{(1, -1), (2, 3), (3, 7)\}$. The domain of the relation is $D = \{1, 2, 3\}$ and the range is $R = \{-1, 3, 7\}$.

Let's adopt a notational convention which we will assume from now on. Unless otherwise stated, the notation

$$N = \{(x, y)|y = 4x - 5\}$$

suggests that a relation N consists of ordered pairs (x, y) which are real-valued. In addition, unless otherwise stated, the domain of a relation will consist of the entire set of real numbers.

The relation

$$M = \{(x, y)|y = x^3 - 6, 1 \leq x \leq 3\}$$

Example 2.10

consists of real-valued ordered pairs which satisfy the equation $y = x^3 - 6$. The domain of the relation is restricted to values greater than or equal to 1 but less than or equal to 3.

The relation

$$P = \{(x, y)|y = 3x + 5\}$$

Example 2.11

consists of real-valued ordered pairs which satisfy the equation $y = 3x + 5$. Since no restriction is placed on the value of x, the domain of the relation consists of all real numbers.

Our treatment of relations assumes that the elements of the range depend upon the elements of the domain. Thus, given the domain of a relation, the corresponding elements of the range can be determined.

Example 2.12

The relation M in Example 2.10 had a restricted domain. A few ordered pairs of the relation are $(1, -5)$, $(2, 2)$, and $(3, 21)$.
Confirm for yourself that if

$$D = \{x | 1 \leq x \leq 3\}$$

then the range of the relation is

$$R = \{y | -5 \leq y \leq 21\}$$

Example 2.13

The relation P in Example 2.11 had a domain consisting of all real numbers. A few ordered pairs of the relations are $(0, 5)$, $(-2, -1)$, and $(5, 20)$. Verify for yourself that if x can equal any real number, then a value of x can be selected such that y will equal any desired value. Thus

$$D = \{x | x \text{ is real}\}$$

makes the range of the relation

$$R = \{y | y \text{ is real}\}$$

Graphing Relations

The ordered pairs of a relation can be represented by points in the cartesian plane. The following examples illustrate the graphing of relations whose domains consist of either a finite or an infinite number of elements.

Example 2.14

Consider the relation

$$P = \{(x, y) | y = x, x \in \{-1, 0, 1, 2, 3, 4, 5\}\}$$

The relation can be redefined as

$$P = \{(-1, -1), (0, 0), (1, 1), (2, 2), (3, 3), (4, 4), (5, 5)\}$$

The graph of these ordered pairs, and thus of the relation P, appears in Fig. 2.6.

Example 2.15

Consider the relation

$$K = \{(x, y) | y = -2x + 4, -2 \leq x \leq 5\}$$

The domain of K consists of all real numbers greater than or equal to -2 but less than or equal to 5. The domain consists of an infinite number of elements, and enumeration of all ordered pairs of the relation would be impossible. For purposes of graphing the relation, a "sufficient" number of ordered pairs should be identified and located on the graph.

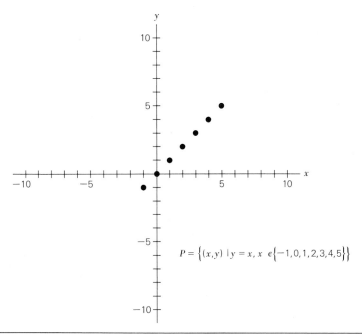

$$P = \left\{(x,y) \mid y = x, \, x \, \epsilon \{-1, 0, 1, 2, 3, 4, 5\}\right\}$$

FIGURE 2.6

The approximate graph of the relation will be found by connecting these points with a smooth line or curve.

Sample ordered pairs for K are $(-2, 8)$, $(-1, 6)$, $(0, 4)$, $(1, 2)$, $(2, 0)$, $(3, -2)$, $(4, -4)$, and $(5, -6)$. Graphing these pairs and connecting them yield the graphical representation of K in Fig. 2.7.

FIGURE 2.7

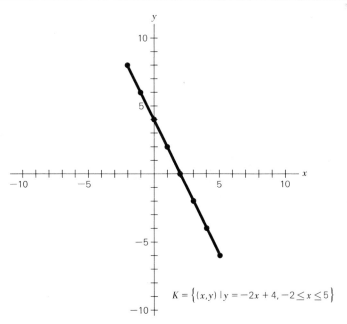

$$K = \left\{(x,y) \mid y = -2x + 4, \, -2 \le x \le 5\right\}$$

Follow-up Exercises

2.1 Given $A = \{-4, -2, 0\}$ and $B = \{1, 3, 5\}$, determine $A \times B$.

2.2 Given $M = \{a, b, c\}$ and $N = \{y, z\}$, determine $M \times N$.

2.3 Given $P = \{10, 20\}$ and $Q = \{a, b, c, d, e\}$, determine $P \times Q$.

2.4 Given $A = \{-1, 3\}$ and $B = \{-5, -3, 0, 3, 5\}$, determine $A \times B$.

2.5 Given $X = \{1, 4\}$ and $Y = \{-2, 0, 3\}$, (a) determine $X \times Y$ and (b) graph the members (x, y) of $X \times Y$.

2.6 Given $X = \{-2, 2\}$ and $Y = \{-4, 0, 4\}$, (a) determine $X \times Y$ and (b) graph the members (x, y) of $X \times Y$.

2.7 Given $A = \{-1, 2, 5\}$ and $B = \{-4, 4\}$, (a) determine $A \times B$ and (b) graph the members (x, y) of $A \times B$.

2.8 Given $M = \{-5, -3, 4\}$ and $N = \{1, 3, 5\}$, (a) determine $M \times N$ and (b) graph the members (x, y) of $M \times N$.

2.9 If $X = \{1, 2\}$ and $Y = \{-3, 3\}$, (a) determine $X \times Y$ and (b) enumerate all relations between X and Y.

2.10 If $X = \{a, b\}$ and $Y = \{x, y, z\}$, (a) determine $X \times Y$. (b) How many relations are there between X and Y?

2.11 If $X = \{1, 2, 3\}$ and $Y = \{-1, 0, 1\}$, determine all ordered pairs (x, y) which satisfy the relation $R = \{(x, y)|x + y = 2\}$.

2.12 If $X = \{-5, 0, 5\}$ and $Y = \{-10, 0, 10\}$, determine all ordered pairs (x, y) which satisfy the relation $R = \{(x, y)|x + y \leq 0\}$.

2.13 If $X = \{-3, -1, 1, 3\}$ and $Y = \{-1, 0, 1\}$, determine all ordered pairs (x, y) which satisfy the relation $R = \{(x, y)|x > y\}$.

2.14 If $X = \{5, 10, 15\}$ and $Y = \{-20, 0, 20\}$, determine all ordered pairs (x, y) which satisfy the relation $R = \{(x, y)|xy > 0\}$.

2.15 Given the relation

$$M = \{(-3, 2), (-1, 2), (5, 2), (20, 2)\}$$

(a) define the domain D and (b) define the range R.

2.16 Given the relation

$$P = \{(1, 0), (-2, 3), (-1, 2), (1, 4), (-1, 0), (3, 3)\}$$

(a) define the domain D and (b) define the range R.

2.17 Determine the elements of the relation

$$N = \{(x, y)|y = -x, x \text{ equals a positive integer greater than } 5\}$$

2.18 Determine the elements of the relation

$$P = \{(x, y)|y = x^3, x \text{ equals a negative integer greater than } -4\}$$

2.19 Graph the relation

$$M = \{(x, y)|y = -5x + 10, x = -2, 0, 2, 4, 6\}$$

2.20 Graph the relation

$$N = \{(x, y)|y = -(x)^2, x = -3, -2, -1, 0, 1, 2, 3\}$$

2.21 Graph the relation

$$Q = \{(x, y)|y = -2x, -2 \leq x \leq 4\}$$

2.22 Graph the relation

$$T = \{(x, y)|y = x^2, -3 \leq x \leq 3\}$$

As we proceed through the book, we will have a special interest in a particular class of relations called *functions*. This section will define functions, develop the notation of functions, and present examples.

Functions Defined

As indicated already, functions are a special class of relations.

DEFINITION
A *function* is a relation in which to each element in the domain D, there corresponds one and only one element in the range R.

Determine whether the relation N is a function when

$$N = \{(x, y)|y = x^2, x \in \{-1, 0, 1, 2, 3\}\}$$

**Example
2.16**

Redefining the ordered pairs of N, we get

$$N = \{(-1, 1), (0, 0), (1, 1), (2, 4), (3, 9)\}$$

Solution

Observation of these ordered pairs indicates that the relation N, described by the rule $y = x^2$, is a function over the stated domain. To each value of x in the domain, there corresponds one and only one value of y in the range.

Determine whether the relation P is a function, where

$$P = \{(x, y)|y^2 = x, x \in \{4, 9, 16\}\}$$

**Example
2.17**

The ordered pairs of P are

$$P = \{(4, 2), (4, -2), (9, 3), (9, -3), (16, 4), (16, -4)\}$$

Solution

To each member of the domain there correspond two different members of the range [for example, (4, 2) and (4, -2)]. This condition violates the definition of a function.

The Nature and Notation of Functions

Functions, as we will treat them, suggest that the value of something depends upon the values of other things. There are uncountable numbers of functional relationships in the world about us. The size of the crowds at a beach may depend upon the temperature, quantities sold of a product may depend on the price charged for the product, grades may depend upon the amount of time that a student studies, city tax rates may depend upon the level of municipal spending, and the length of a person's hair may depend upon time.

The language of mathematics is convenient for describing how variables are functionally related. Rather than using the somewhat cumbersome set notation to express functions, we use the equation

$$y = f(x) \qquad (2.1)$$

to denote a functional relationship between x and y. A verbal translation of this equation is "y equals f of x" or "y is a function of x." This equation is *not* to be interpreted as "y equals f times x." When we say that y is *a function of x*, we mean that the value of the variable y *depends upon* and is uniquely determined by the value of the variable x. The respective roles of the two variables result in the variable x being called the *independent variable* and the variable y being called the *dependent variable*. "f" is the *name* of the function or rule which allows one to determine the unique value of y, given a value for x.

Example 2.18

Suppose that you have taken a job as a salesperson. Your employer has stated that your salary will depend upon the number of units you sell each week. If we let

y = weekly salary in dollars
x = number of units sold each week

the dependency stated by your employer can be represented by the equation

$$y = f(x)$$

where f is the name of the salary function.

Although y usually represents the dependent variable, x the independent variable, and f the name of the function, *any* letter may be used to represent the dependent and independent variables and the function name. The equation

$$u = g(v)$$

is a legitimate way of representing that the value of a dependent variable u is determined by an independent variable v. And the name of the function or rule relating the two variables is g.

Suppose your employer in Example 2.18 has given you an equation for determining your weekly salary and it is

$$y = 3x + 25 \qquad (2.2)$$

The specific rule which determines y is

$$f(x) = 3x + 25$$

Given any value for x, substitution of this value into $f(x)$ will result in the corresponding value of y. For instance, if we want to compute your weekly salary when you sell 100 units, substitution of $x = 100$ into Eq. (2.2) yields

$$y = 3(100) + 25$$
$$= \$325$$

Functional notation provides an efficient way of representing this type of computation. For a function of the form $y = f(x)$, the value of y which corresponds to a value of $x = b$ can be denoted by $f(b)$.

In Eq. (2.2), the salary associated with selling 75 units can be denoted by $f(75)$. To evaluate $f(75)$, simply substitute the value $x = 75$ into Eq. (2.2) wherever the letter x appears, or

$$f(75) = 3(75) + 25$$
$$= \$250$$

Similarly, the value of y corresponding to $x = 0$ is denoted as $f(0)$ and computed as $f(0) = 3(0) + 25 = \$25$.

Given the functional relationship

$$z = h(t)$$
$$= t^2 + t - 10$$

find (a) $h(0)$, (b) $h(-5)$, (c) $h(20)$, and (d) $h(a + b)$.

Example 2.19

(a) $h(0) = (0)^2 + (0) - 10$
$\quad = -10$
(b) $h(-5) = (-5)^2 + (-5) - 10$
$\quad = 25 - 5 - 10$
$\quad = 10$
(c) $h(20) = (20)^2 + 20 - 10$
$\quad = 400 + 20 - 10$
$\quad = 410$
(d) $h(a + b) = (a + b)^2 + (a + b) - 10$
$\quad = a^2 + 2ab + b^2 + a + b - 10$
$\quad = a^2 + a + 2ab + b + b^2 - 10$

Solution

Note in d that the value assigned to t is the sum of two variables. The procedure is exactly the same as for the other three parts of the problem. Wherever t appears in the function, substitute the quantity $a + b$.

A small city police department is contemplating the purchase of an additional patrol car. Police analysts estimate the purchase cost of a fully equipped car to be \$18,000. They also have estimated an average operating cost of \$0.40 per mile. (a) Determine the mathematical function which represents the total cost C of owning and operating the car in terms of the number of miles x it is driven. (b) What are total projected costs if the car is driven 50,000 miles during its lifetime? (c) If it is driven 100,000 miles?

Example 2.20

(a) In this example, we are asked to determine the function which relates total cost C to miles driven x. The first question is: Which variable depends upon the other? A rereading of the problem and some thought about the two variables should lead you to conclude that total cost C is the dependent variable and that

$$C = f(x)$$

Solution

At this stage you may be able to write the cost function as

$$C = 0.40x + 18{,}000$$

For those who cannot write the cost function, mentally or on paper, determine the value of the dependent variable, given arbitrary values of the independent variable. Examine the respective values of the variables and see if a pattern begins to emerge. If it does, then *articulate your mental model* (or more simply, write out the function).

Let's apply this approach. What would total cost equal if the car were driven 0 miles (assuming it was purchased)? Your mental model should respond "$18,000." What would the total cost equal if the car were driven 10,000 miles? $22,000. What if it were driven 20,000 miles? $26,000. If you are having no difficulty arriving at these answers, indeed you have some mental cost model. Now is the time to express that model mathematically. The total cost of owning and operating the police car is the sum of two component costs—purchase cost and operating cost. And the type of computation you should have been making when responding to each question was to multiply the number of miles by $0.40 and add this result to the $18,000 purchase cost. Or,

$$
\begin{aligned}
C &= f(x) \\
&= \text{total operating cost} + \text{purchase cost} \\
&= (\text{operating cost per mile})(\text{number of miles}) \\
&\qquad\qquad\qquad\qquad\qquad\qquad + \text{purchase cost}
\end{aligned}
$$

or $C = 0.40x + 18{,}000$

(b) If the car is driven 50,000 miles, total costs are estimated to equal

$$
\begin{aligned}
C &= f(50{,}000) \\
&= 0.40(50{,}000) + 18{,}000 \\
&= \$38{,}000
\end{aligned}
$$

(c) Similarly, at 100,000 miles

$$
\begin{aligned}
C &= f(100{,}000) \\
&= 0.40(100{,}000) + 18{,}000 \\
&= \$58{,}000
\end{aligned}
$$

For many mathematical functions the value of a dependent variable depends upon more than one independent variable. In most real-world applications, these types of functions are the most appropriate to use. For example, stating that profit is dependent only upon the number of units sold probably oversimplifies the situation. Many variables usually interact with one another in order to determine the profit for a firm.

Bivariate functions have two independent variables. The notation

$$z = f(x, y) \tag{2.3}$$

suggests that the dependent variable z depends upon the values of the two independent variables x and y. An example of a bivariate function is

$$z = x^2 - 2xy + y^2 - 5$$

For the bivariate function

Example 2.21

$$z = x^2 - 2xy + y^2 - 5$$

find (a) $f(0, 0)$, (b) $f(10, 20)$, and (c) $f(-10, 5)$.

(a) The notation $f(0, 0)$ represents the value of the function when $x = 0$ **Solution**
and $y = 0$. Therefore

$$
\begin{aligned}
z &= f(0, 0) \\
&= 0^2 - 2(0)(0) + 0^2 - 5 \\
&= -5
\end{aligned}
$$

(b) $\begin{aligned} z &= f(10, 20) \\
&= 10^2 - 2(10)(20) + 20^2 - 5 \\
&= 100 - 400 + 400 - 5 \\
&= 95 \end{aligned}$

(c) $\begin{aligned} z &= f(-10, 5) \\
&= (-10)^2 - 2(-10)(5) + 5^2 - 5 \\
&= 100 + 100 + 25 - 5 \\
&= 220 \end{aligned}$

As the number of independent variables increases, the convention of using a different letter to represent each independent variable can become cumbersome. Consequently, a convenient way of representing multivariate functions is the use of *subscripted variables*. A general way of denoting a function where the value of a dependent variable y depends on the value of n independent variables is

$$y = f(x_1, x_2, x_3, \ldots, x_n) \tag{2.4}$$

The *subscript* is the positive integer index located to the right of and below each x. The index simply numbers the independent variables and enables you to distinguish one from another. We will frequently make use of subscripted-variable notation in this book.

Given the function

Example 2.22

$$
\begin{aligned}
y &= f(x_1, x_2, x_3, x_4) \\
&= x_1^2 - 2x_1 x_2 + x_3^2 x_4 - 25
\end{aligned}
$$

determine $f(-2, 0, 1, 4)$.

$$
\begin{aligned}
f(-2, 0, 1, 4) &= (-2)^2 - 2(-2)(0) + (1)^2(4) - 25 \\
&= 4 - 0 + 4 - 25 \\
&= -17
\end{aligned}
$$

Solution

Characterizing Mathematical Functions

There are a number of ways to characterize the nature of mathematical functions.

Refer to the definition of a function. One characteristic of mathematical functions is that for any value of the independent variable(s), there is one and only one corresponding value for the dependent variable. In the cost function of Example 2.20,

$$C = 0.40x + 18,000$$

given any value for x, there is one and only one corresponding value for cost. This characteristic does not imply, however, that two different values of the independent variable cannot yield the same value of the dependent variable. To illustrate this, y assumes a value of 12 in the function

$$y = x^2 - 4$$

when x equals either $+4$ or -4. However, given any value for x, there is one and only one corresponding value of y.

Another way to characterize functions is by the *domain* and *range* of the function. The domain of a function is the set of values which the independent variable can assume. The range is the corresponding set of values which the dependent variable can assume. The range is obviously dependent upon the domain of the function. So once the domain has been specified, the range may be defined.

Although we will rarely need to specify explicitly both the domain and range of a function, we *will* be concerned with identifying values excluded from the domain. Values excluded from the domain will include any values of the independent variable for which the function is not defined. The two exclusions we will focus upon are

1 Any values of the independent variable which result in the denominator assuming a value of 0 for a quotient function

2 Any values of the independent variable which result in no real roots of a radical

The following examples illustrate these cases.

Example 2.23

Define the domain of the function

$$u = f(v)$$

$$= \frac{1}{v^2 - 4}$$

Solution

Since this function has the form of a quotient, any values of v which make the denominator equal 0 would be excluded from the domain. The denominator equals 0 whenever $v^2 - 4 = 0$ or when v assumes a value of either $+2$ or -2. The domain of the function includes all real numbers *except* $+2$ and -2.

Example 2.24

Define the domain and range for the function

$$y = f(x)$$

$$= \sqrt{x - 5}$$

If we restrict our interest to the real (as opposed to imaginary or complex) number system—and we always will in this text—x can assume any value for which the expression under the square root sign is positive or zero. To determine these values, we solve the inequality

$$x - 5 \geq 0$$
or
$$x \geq 5$$

Thus the domain of the function includes all real numbers which are greater than or equal to 5.

We have discussed the concepts of domain and range in a purely mathematical sense. In a practical sense there may be conditions within an application which further restrict the domain and range of a function. Returning again to the patrol car example, Example 2.20, the mathematical domain of the cost function $C = 0.40x + 18,000$ includes any real value for x. However, within the context of the application we would have to restrict x from assuming negative values (there is no such thing as negative miles traveled). In addition, if the department has a policy that no patrol car will be driven over 150,000 miles, then x would be restricted to values no greater than 150,000—Who are they kidding? Planned obsolescence and above average wear and tear would do them in long before 150,000 miles. Thus the *restricted domain* of the function in this application is

$$0 \leq x \leq 150,000$$

The *restricted range* for this cost function, in light of the restrictions on x, would be

$$\$18,000 \leq C \leq \$78,000$$

assuming that the car is purchased. What would be the effect on the restricted range if a value of $x = 0$ implies a decision not to purchase the car?

As a reflection of a cultural trend in this country, United States importers can sell every bottle of liquor that they can bring into the country. The average profit per bottle is $0.50. The U.S. Department of Customs provides restrictions on the number of liters which an importer can purchase on a quarterly basis. The quota per quarter is 500,000 liters. Assume the importer purchases liter bottles only.
(a) Determine a mathematical function which relates quarterly profit to the number of bottles sold.
(b) Temporarily ignoring the nature of the application, define the mathematical domain and range for this function.
(c) In light of the nature of the application, define the restricted domain and restricted range.

Example 2.25

NOTE
The first step in any word problem is to define your variables explicitly, carefully specifying the dimen-

Solution

sions (pounds, dollars, miles per hour, etc.) of these variables.

(a) Defining the variables, let

x = number of bottles (liters) of liquor imported
y = profit per quarter in dollars

Since the profit margin per bottle is $0.50, total profit is computed by multiplying profit per bottle times the number of bottles sold. Therefore,

Profit per quarter = f(number of bottles sold)
= (profit per bottle)
(number of bottles sold per quarter)

or $\quad\quad y = f(x)$
$= 0.50x$

(b) Since $f(x)$ is defined (mathematically) for all values of x, the domain of the function includes all real numbers. And given that x *can* assume any real number, the range of the function allows y to assume any real number.

(c) In this example there are conditions which restrict the value of x to being greater than or equal to 0 (negative imports are impossible) and less than or equal to 500,000. Thus the restricted domain is $0 \leq x \leq 500,000$. Corresponding to these values, we may state that the restricted range for the function is $0 \leq y \leq \$250,000$.

Composite Functions

Occasionally we will examine mathematical functions which are composed of, or constructed from, two or more component functions. If two functions are combined to form a third function, the third function is called a *composite function*.

To illustrate, assume that the function

$$y = g(x) = 2x + 50$$

indicates that a salesperson's weekly salary y is determined by the number of units x sold each week. Suppose that an analysis has revealed that the quantity sold each week by a salesperson is dependent upon the price charged for the product. This function h is given by the rule

$$x = h(p) = 150 - 2.5p$$

where p equals the price, stated in dollars.

Thus, to compute a salesperson's salary, first we must know the selling price for the given week. This will determine the number of units expected to be sold, which can then be substituted into $g(x)$ to determine the weekly salary. For example, suppose that the price during a given week is $30. The number of units expected to be sold during the week is

$$x = h(30)$$
$$= 150 - 2.5(30)$$
$$= 150 - 75$$
$$= 75 \text{ units}$$

Since the number of units expected to be sold is known, the weekly salary is computed as

$$y = g(75)$$
$$= 2(75) + 50$$
$$= \$200$$

Since weekly salary depends upon the number of units sold each week and the number of units sold depends upon the price per unit, weekly salary can be stated directly as a function of the price per unit. Or,

$$y = f(p) = g(h(p))$$

To define this function, we substitute $h(p)$ into the function $g(x)$ wherever an x appears. That is,

$$y = f(p) = 2(150 - 2.5p) + 50$$
$$= 300 - 5p + 50$$
$$= 350 - 5p$$

The function $f(p) = g(h(p))$ is a composite function, having been formed by combining $g(x)$ and $h(p)$. Note that we can compute the expected weekly salary directly from $f(p)$ if we know the selling price for a given week. At a price of \$30,

$$y = f(30)$$
$$= 350 - 5(30)$$
$$= 350 - 150$$
$$= \$200$$

which is the same value as determined before.

If $y = g(u) = u^2 - 2u + 10$ and $u = h(x) = x + 1$, determine the composite function $y = f(x) = g(h(x))$.

Example 2.26

The composite function is found by substituting $h(x)$ into $g(u)$ wherever u appears. Or,

$$y = f(x)$$
$$= g(h(x)) = g(x + 1)$$
$$= (x + 1)^2 - 2(x + 1) + 10$$
$$= x^2 + 2x + 1 - 2x - 2 + 10$$
$$= x^2 + 9$$

Solution

If $y = g(u) = 2u^3$ and $u = h(x) = x^2 - 2x + 5$, (a) determine $g(h(2))$ and (b) determine $g(h(-3))$

Example 2.27

Solution   (a) $h(2) = (2)^2 - 2(2) + 5$
$$= 5$$
$$g(h(2)) = g(5)$$
$$= 2(5)^3$$
$$= 2(125)$$
$$= 250$$

(b) $h(-3) = (-3)^2 - 2(-3) + 5$
$$= 9 + 6 + 5$$
$$= 20$$
$$g(h(-3)) = g(20)$$
$$= 2(20)^3$$
$$= 2(8,000)$$
$$= 16,000$$

Follow-up Exercises

2.23 Determine whether the relation N is a function, where

$$N = \{(x, y)|y = 4x^2 - 10, x = -1, 1, 2, 3\}$$

2.24 Determine whether the relation P is a function, where

$$P = \{(1, 3), (2, 1), (3, 4), (5, -2), (-2, -4), (1, 0)\}$$

For the functions presented in Exercises 2.25 to 2.30, determine (a) $f(0)$, (b) $f(-2)$, (c) $f(2)$, and (d) $f(a + b)$.

2.25 $y = f(x) = 10x - 5$
2.26 $y = f(x) = -3x^2 + 10x + 1$
2.27 $y = f(x) = 20$
2.28 $y = f(x) = 4 - x^2$
2.29 $y = f(x) = 10 - 4x$
2.30 $y = f(x) = (x + 1)^2$
2.31 If $z = f(x, y) = x^2 - 4xy + 3y^2$, determine (a) $f(0, 0)$, (b) $f(-1, 1)$, and (c) $f(5, 10)$.
2.32 If $u = v(h, g) = \frac{1}{2}h^2 - 3hg + g^2 - 100$, determine (a) $v(0, 0)$, (b) $v(4, 2)$, and (c) $v(a, b)$.
2.33 If $y = f(x_1, x_2, x_3) = (x_1 - x_2 + 3x_3)^2$, determine (a) $f(1, 1, 1)$ and (b) $f(5, -5, 10)$.
2.34 If $y = f(x_1, x_2, x_3, x_4) = x_1x_2 - 2x_3x_4$, determine (a) $f(1, 10, 4, -5)$, (b) $f(2, 2, 2, 2)$, and (c) $f(a, b, c, d)$.

In Exercises 2.35 to 2.40, determine the domain of the given function.

2.35 $f(x) = \dfrac{5x^2}{16 - x^2}$ **2.36** $f(x) = \dfrac{3x - 10}{x^3 + x^2 - 6x}$

2.37 $f(x) = \sqrt{100 - x}$ **2.38** $f(x) = 4x^5 - 2x^3 + x$

2.39 $f(x) = \dfrac{\sqrt{2x - 50}}{x^2 + 2x - 15}$ **2.40** $h(v) = \dfrac{\sqrt{20 - v/2}}{v^4 - 16}$

2.41 In manufacturing a product, a firm incurs costs of two types. Fixed annual costs of $100,000 are incurred regardless of the number of units produced. In addition, each unit produced costs the firm $5. C

equals total annual cost in dollars and x equals the number of units produced during a year.

(a) Determine the function $C = f(x)$ which expresses annual cost as dependent upon the number of units produced during the year.

(b) What is $f(20,000)$? What does $f(20,000)$ represent?

(c) State the restricted domain of the function if the maximum production capacity is 50,000 units per year.

2.42 A car rental agency leases automobiles at a rate of $10 per day plus $0.20 per mile driven. y equals the cost in dollars of renting a car for one day and x equals the number of miles driven in one day.

(a) Determine the function $y = f(x)$ which expresses the daily cost of renting a car as a function of the number of miles driven in one day.

(b) What is $f(250)$? What does $f(250)$ represent?

(c) Comment on the restricted domain of this function.

2.43 Given $y = g(u) = 2u^2 + 5u - 1$ and $u = h(x) = x - 5$, determine (a) $y = g(h(x))$, (b) $g(h(0))$, and (c) $g(h(-2))$.

2.44 Given $y = g(u) = \sqrt{u^2 - 1}$ and $u = h(x) = x^2 + 5$, determine (a) $y = g(h(x))$, (b) $g(h(3))$, and (c) $g(h(0))$.

2.45 Given $y = g(u) = 10u/(u^2 - 1)$ and $u = h(x) = 5x - 10$, determine (a) $y = g(h(x))$, (b) $g(h(0))$, and (c) $g(h(4))$.

2.46 Given $y = g(u) = \sqrt{u}$ and $u = h(x) = x^2 - 50x$, determine (a) $y = g(h(x))$, (b) $g(h(50))$, and (c) $g(h(100))$.

GRAPHICAL REPRESENTATION OF FUNCTIONS

In addition to the analytical procedures we will explore in this book, we will utilize as much as possible the technique of graphical analysis.

"A Picture Is Worth . . ."

Mathematical functions which involve two or three variables can be represented graphically. This graphical portrayal brings an added dimension to the understanding of mathematical functions. You will come to appreciate the increased understanding and insight that graphs provide. Since most of the functions we examine will involve just two variables, this graphical reinforcement will be frequent.

Graphical representation requires a dimension for each variable contained in a function. Thus, two-variable functions are graphed in two dimensions, or *2-space*. Three-variable functions can be graphed in three dimensions, or *3-space*. However, it is considerably more difficult to graph in three dimensions than in two. When a function contains more than three variables, the graphical representation is lost. Unless you have some unusual sixth sense, you will not be able to conceptualize or graph in four or more dimensions.

Graphing Functions in Two Dimensions

Functions which are graphed in two dimensions are graphed on a set of rectangular coordinate axes exactly like those used to represent ele-

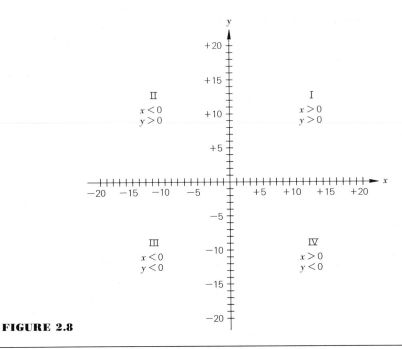

FIGURE 2.8

ments of a cartesian product. Typically the vertical axis is selected to represent the dependent variable in the function. The horizontal axis is usually selected to represent the independent variable. As shown in Fig. 2.8, the more frequent use of the letter x to represent the independent variable and y the dependent variable has led to labeling the vertical axis as the y *axis* and the horizontal axis as the x *axis*. The axes divide the cartesian plane into four subareas, or *quadrants*, denoted by the Roman numerals I to IV in Fig. 2.8.

The graphing of functions is done in exactly the same manner as graphing of relations, since functions, as we have seen, are special types of relations. To graph a mathematical function, one can simply *assume* different values for the independent variable and *compute* the corresponding value for the dependent variable. Each ordered pair of values for the two variables represents values of x and y which satisfy the function. It also specifies the coordinates of a single point which lies on the graph of the function. To *sketch* the function, determine an *adequate* number of ordered pairs of values which satisfy the function; locate their coordinates on a pair of axes. *Connect these points by a smooth curve to determine a sketch of the graph of the function.*

Example 2.28 For the function $y = f(x) = 2x - 4$, determine pairs of values which satisfy the function (i.e., make the left side of the equation equal the right side), plot the points, and sketch the approximate shape of the graph of the function.

Solution

NOTE
The most orderly way to generate the pairs of points which satisfy a function is to set up a table with one row or column containing arbitrary values for the independent variable and another containing the computed values for the dependent variable.

The first step is to arbitrarily select values for x and compute the corresponding values for y. A set of sample values is shown in Table 2.1. Next, if these values of x and y are envisioned as coordinates, the points associated with each pair of coordinates should be located. This has been done in Fig. 2.9. Once the points have been plotted, they are connected with a smooth curve, which in this case is suspiciously straight. If we wish to know how the function appears for values of x less than -4 or greater than $+4$, we should compute values of y for selected values of x within those regions of the domain.

x	-4	-3	-2	-1	0	$+1$	$+2$	$+3$	$+4$	Table
y	-12	-10	-8	-6	-4	-2	0	2	4	2.1

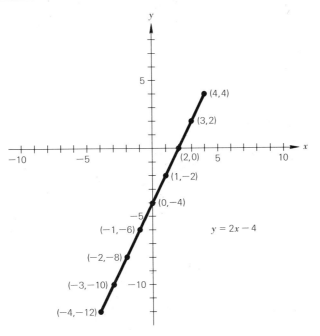

FIGURE 2.9

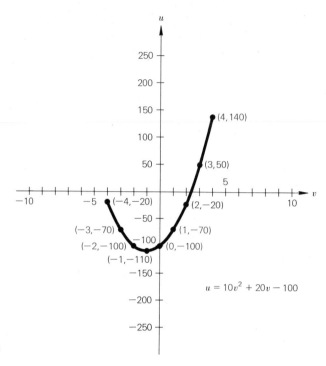

FIGURE 2.10

Example 2.29   For the function

$$u = f(v)$$
$$= 10v^2 + 20v - 100$$

determine pairs of values which satisfy the function, plot these points, and sketch the approximate shape of the function.

Solution   Sample pairs of values for u and v are shown in Table 2.2. These points are graphed in Fig. 2.10, and they have been connected to provide a sketch of the function. Note the labeling of the x axis with the independent variable v and the y axis with the dependent variable u. As opposed to the function in the previous example, this one obviously cannot be represented by a straight line.

Table 2.2	v	−4	−3	−2	−1	0	1	2	3	4
	u	−20	−70	−100	−110	−100	−70	−20	50	140

NOTE
A few points should be made regarding the graphing of functions. First, it is always useful to determine the points you want to graph prior to scaling the axes. By doing this, you determine the range of values which you wish to graph for the two variables. Once you have

determined these ranges, you can determine the appropriate scale to use on each axis. A second point is that the two axes need not be scaled the same in either units or dimensions. That is, an interval on one axis does not have to represent the same quantity as the same-sized interval on the other axis. The units on one axis may represent millions and those on the other axis single units. Examine the different scaling in Fig. 2.10. If you overlook this possibility, your graph may run beyond the boundaries of your paper. (The author has had situations during class in which graphs required points below the floor or above the ceiling.) Additionally, the unit of measurement for one variable does not have to be the same as that of the other variable. The cost function in Example 2.20 would show cost *in dollars* on one axis and miles driven on the other axis.

EXERCISE
What would be the effect on the graph in Example 2.29 if the *y* axis were scaled the same as the *x* axis? (*Ans.:* The graph (curve) would become much longer and narrower.)

In some instances, the functional relationship existing between variables is described by more than one equation. To illustrate, assume that *y* equals a salesperson's weekly salary in dollars and that *x* equals the number of units of a product sold during the week. Given that the weekly salary depends upon the number of units sold, assume that the following function applies.

Example 2.30

$$y = f(x) = \begin{cases} 2x + 50 & \text{where } 0 \le x < 40 \\ 2.25x + 75 & \text{where } x \ge 40 \end{cases}$$

If the number of units sold during a week is less than 40, the salesperson receives a base salary of $50 and a commission of $2 per unit sold. If the number of units sold during a week is 40 or more, a bonus of $25 raises the base portion of the salary to $75. In addition, the commission on *all* units increases to $2.25 per unit.

Figure 2.11 illustrates the graph of the function. Note that the graph uses quadrant I only, where *x* and *y* are both nonnegative. The sketch of the function is in two "pieces." Each piece of the graph is valid for a certain portion of the domain of the function. The open circle (○) at the end of the first segment is used to indicate that that point is *not* part of the graph. It corresponds to the break in the function at *x* = 40. The point corresponding to *x* = 40 is the first point on the second segment of the function, and this is denoted by the solid circle (●).

In this section we have been introduced to the graphical representation of mathematical functions. The procedure which has been presented must be called a "brute force" method in that it is necessary to

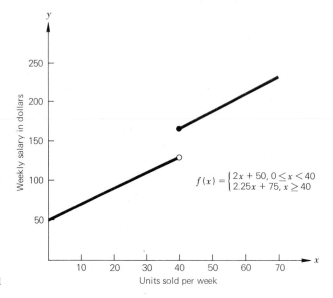

FIGURE 2.11

determine an "adequate" number of points. However, it does work! The question of how many points are adequate will be answered with experience. Throughout the text we will continue to gain knowledge about mathematical functions. You will soon come to recognize the structural differences between linear functions and the various nonlinear functions, and with this knowledge will come greater facility and ease in determining a visual or graphical counterpart.

A Graphical Characteristic of Functions

By the definition of a function, to each element in the domain there should correspond one and only one element in the range. This property allows for a simple graphical check to determine whether a relation is, in fact, a function. If a vertical line is drawn through any point in the domain, it will pass through the graph of the function at one point only. In contrast, if a vertical line passes through a curve at more than one point, the curve is not the graph of a function. The curve in Fig. 2.12 does not represent a function since the dashed vertical line passes through the curve at two points.

Follow-up Exercises

In Exercises 2.47 to 2.56, graph the indicated function.

2.47 $y = f(x) = x$ **2.48** $y = f(x) = 5x + 10$

2.49 $y = f(x) = x^2$ **2.50** $y = f(x) = -x^2$

2.51 $u = f(v) = v^2 - 4v + 10$ **2.52** $g = f(t) = t^2 + 6t + 9$

2.53 $y = f(x) = x^3$ **2.54** $y = f(x) = -x^3$

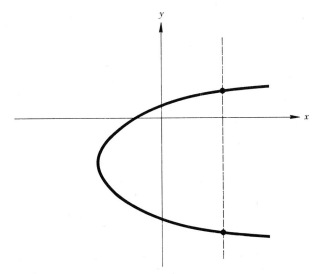

FIGURE 2.12

2.55 $y = f(x) = \begin{cases} 2x & \text{when } -5 \le x \le 5 \\ 2x + 10 & \text{when } x > 5 \end{cases}$

2.56 $y = f(x) = \begin{cases} x + 2 & \text{when } 0 \le x \le 4 \\ 10 - x & \text{when } x > 4 \end{cases}$

2.57 In Fig. 2.13 identify which graphs represent functions.

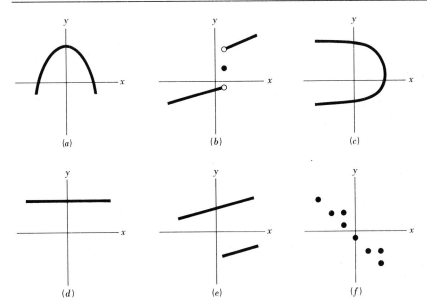

FIGURE 2.13

2.4 **SUMMARY**

This chapter has introduced mathematical functions. These will be very important to us as we go through the book. The presentation of functions later in the book will always be in terms of the notation developed in Sec. 2.2. It is important that you be comfortable with this notation and also with the procedures of graphing functions.

CHAPTER CHECKLIST

If you have read all sections of this chapter, you should

_____ Understand *cartesian products*—how to determine them and how to graph their members

_____ Understand *rectangular coordinate systems*

_____ Understand what a *relation* is

_____ Know the meaning of and how to determine the *domain* and *range* of a relation

_____ Know the definition of a *function*

_____ Be comfortable with the notation of functions

_____ Know how to determine the domain of a function

_____ Know how to sketch the approximate shape of the graph of a function

_____ Understand *composite* functions

KEY TERMS AND CONCEPTS

cartesian product	function
ordered pair	dependent variable
coordinate axes	independent variable
x axis	subscripted variable
y axis	restricted domain
cartesian plane	restricted range
rectangular coordinate system	2-space
relation	3-space
domain	quadrant
range	composite function

ADDITIONAL EXERCISES

Exercises 2.58 to 2.71 are related to Sec. 2.1.

For Exercises 2.58 to 2.59, determine $X \times Y$.

2.58 $X = \{-3, 3\}$ and $Y = \{2, 4, 0, -3, 6\}$

2.59 $X = \{a, b, c, d, e, f\}$ and $Y = \{x, y, z\}$

2.60 Given $A = \{a, b, c\}$ and $B = \{x, y\}$, (a) determine $A \times B$. (b) How many relations are there between A and B?

2.61 If $X = \{-2, 3, -1, 4\}$ and $Y = \{-4, -2, 5, 10\}$, determine all ordered pairs (x, y) which satisfy the relation

$$S = \{(x, y) | x/y > 0\}$$

2.62 Given the relation

$B = \{(x, y) | y = x^2 - 4x + 1$, where x equals

a positive integer less than 6}

(a) determine the elements of the relation and (b) define the domain and range of the relation.

2.63 Given the relation

$F = \{(x, y) | y = (x + 1)^3$, where x equals a

negative odd integer greater than -6}

(a) determine the elements of the relation and (b) define the domain and range of the relation.

2.64 Graph the relation B in Exercise 2.62.

2.65 Graph the relation F in Exercise 2.63.

Exercises 2.66 to 2.76 are related to Sec. 2.2.

2.66 Determine whether the relation P is a function if

$$P = \{(x, y) | y = \sqrt{x}, x \in \{0, 4, 9, 16, 25, 36\}\}$$

2.67 Determine whether the relation V is a function if

$$V = \{(1, -1), (2, -2), (3, -3), (2, 4), (4, -4), (5, -5)\}$$

For the functions presented in Exercises 2.68 to 2.69, determine $f(-1)$, $f(5)$, and $f(a - b)$.

2.68 $y = f(x) = 100$ **2.69** $y = f(x) = (x - 4)^2$

2.70 If $z = f(x, y) = (x^2 - y^2)/(2xy)$, determine (a) $f(1, 1)$, (b) $f(-2, 4)$, and (c) $f(10, 5)$.

2.71 If $y = f(x_1, x_2, x_3, x_4) = (2x_1 - 3x_2x_3^2 - x_4)^2$, determine (a) $f(1, 1, 1, 1)$, (b) $f(2, 0, 10, 4)$, and (c) $f(a, 0, 0, b)$.

In Exercises 2.72 to 2.74, determine the domain of the given function.

2.72 $f(x) = \sqrt{x^2 - 100}$ **2.73** $f(x) = (2x^2 - 10)/(x^2 - 8/x)$

2.74 $f(x) = \sqrt{4 - x}/(x - 10)$

For Exercises 2.75 and 2.76, determine $g(h(x))$, $g(h(0))$, and $g(h(-1))$.

2.75 $y = g(u) = u^3$ and $u = h(x) = -x^2 + 3$

2.76 $y = g(u) = \sqrt{5u - 10}$ and $u = h(x) = x^2 - 10x$

Exercises 2.77 to 2.80 are related to Sec. 2.3.

In Exercises 2.77 to 2.80, graph the function.

2.77 $y = f(x) = |x|$ **2.78** $y = f(x) = (x + 1)^2$

2.79 $y = f(x) = \begin{cases} x & \text{when } 0 \leq x < 5 \\ -x & \text{when } x \geq 5 \end{cases}$

2.80 $y = f(x) = \begin{cases} x^2 & \text{when } x < 0 \\ -x^2 & \text{when } x > 0 \\ 5 & \text{when } x = 0 \end{cases}$

CHAPTER TEST

1 Define (a) a relation and (b) a function.

2 You are given the relation

$N = \{(x, y) | y = |x^2 - 4|,$ where x is an integer *and* $-2 \leq x \leq 2\}$

(a) Determine the elements of the relation.
(b) Define the domain and range of the relation.
(c) Graph the relation.

3 Determine whether the relation Q is a function if

$Q = \{(x, y) | y = |x|, x = -3, -2, -1, 0, 1, 2, 3\}$

4 Given $u = g(v) = v^2 + 20v - 10$, determine (a) $g(0)$, (b) $g(5)$, and (c) $g(x + 1)$.

5 Determine the domain of the function $f(x) = \sqrt{6 - x}/x$.

6 Sketch the function

$$y = f(x) = \begin{cases} 10 - 2x & \text{when } -5 \leq x < 0 \\ -2x & \text{when } 0 \leq x \leq 5 \end{cases}$$

7 A salesperson is paid weekly on a commission basis. The commission on each unit sold is $5. If weekly sales are 20 units or more, a bonus of $25 is earned. If y equals the weekly salary in dollars and x equals the number of units sold during the week, determine the function $y = f(x)$. (*Hint:* The function will be defined in two parts.)

8 If $y = g(u) = u^2/(u + 5)$ and $u = h(x) = x - 9$, determine (a) $g(h(x))$ and (b) $g(h(-4))$.

CHAPTER OBJECTIVES After reading this chapter, you should be able to distinguish linear equations from nonlinear equations; you should understand the meaning of solution sets to linear equations; you should be familiar with the algebraic properties of linear equations; you should be familiar with the graphical properties of linear equations and be able to graph linear equations in two dimensions; and you should have some familiarity with applications of linear equations.

When you consider all the areas of study within mathematics, it is possible to distinguish between two major *subsets*—linear mathematics and nonlinear mathematics. In this book we will distinguish between the two areas, and we will spend a good portion of our time examining areas of study within each. In this chapter we begin a discussion of linear mathematics which will be continued in the following five chapters.

Linear mathematics is significant for a number of reasons:

1 Many of the real-world phenomena which we might be interested in representing mathematically either are linear or can be approximated reasonably well by using linear relationships. As a result, linear mathematics is widely used.

2 Given that some method of mathematical analysis, i.e., finding a solution, is needed, the analysis of linear relationships is generally easier than for nonlinear relationships.

3 The methods used in nonlinear mathematics are often similar to, or extensions of, those used in linear mathematics. Consequently, having a good understanding of linear mathematics is likely to be of considerable benefit in the study of nonlinear mathematics.

The purposes of this chapter are:

To acquaint us thoroughly with the algebraic and graphical characteristics of linear equations

To provide the tools which will enable us to determine the equation representing a linear relationship

To acquaint us with a variety of applications of linear equations

3.1 CHARACTERISTICS OF LINEAR EQUATIONS

General Form

DEFINITION
A linear equation involving two variables x and y has the standard form

$$ax + by = c \qquad (3.1)$$

where a, b, and c are real numbers *and* a and b cannot both equal zero.

Notice that the exponents (powers) are (implicitly) 1 for each variable in a linear equation. The presence of terms having exponents other than 1 (for example, x^2) would exclude an equation from being considered linear. The presence of terms involving a product of the two variables (for example, $2xy$) would also exclude an equation from being considered linear.

The following are all examples of linear equations involving two variables:

	a	b	c
$2x + 5y = -5$	2	5	-5
$-x + \frac{1}{2}y = 0$	-1	$\frac{1}{2}$	0
$x/3 = 25$	$\frac{1}{3}$	0	25
(*Note:* $x/3 = \frac{1}{3}x$.)			
$2s - 4t = -\frac{1}{2}$	2	-4	$-\frac{1}{2}$

(*Note:* The variables may be different from x and y.)

The following are examples of equations which are not linear. Can you explain why?

$$2x + 3xy - 4y = 10$$
$$x + y^2 = 6$$
$$\sqrt{u} + \sqrt{v} = -10$$

In attempting to identify the form of an equation (linear versus non-linear), an equation is linear if it *can be* written in the form of Eq. (3.1). A quick glance at the equation

$$2x = \frac{5x - 2y}{4} + 10$$

might lead to the false conclusion that it is not linear. However, multiplying both sides of the equation by 4 and moving all variables to the left-hand side yields $3x + 2y = 40$, which is in the form of Eq. (3.1).

DEFINITION
A linear equation involving n variables x_1, $x_2, x_3, \ldots, x_n$ has the general form

$$a_1x_1 + a_2x_2 + a_3x_3 + \cdots + a_nx_n = b \quad (3.2)$$

where $a_1, a_2, a_3, \ldots, a_n$ and b are real numbers and *not all* $a_1, a_2, a_3, \ldots, a_n$ equal zero.

We will spend much of our time in this book discussing equations and mathematical functions that involve two variables. Aside from the fact that the arithmetic is a little easier, another important reason for concentrating on the two-variable situation is that these functions can be graphed to provide a visual frame of reference. Equation (3.2), however, generalizes the definition of a linear equation for those instances in which we venture beyond two variables.

Representation Using Linear Equations

Given a linear equation involving two variables, there is often an interest in determining the values for the two variables which satisfy the equation. The set of all possible ordered pairs (x, y) which satisfy the equation $ax + by = c$ may be thought of as the *solution set* for the equation. The solution set S may be defined by using set notation:

$$S = \{(x, y) | ax + by = c\} \quad (3.3)$$

Verbally, this equation states that the solution set S consists of elements (x, y) such that $ax + by = c$. For any linear equation, S is an infinite set; that is, *there are an infinite number of pairs of values (x, y) which satisfy any linear equation involving two variables.*†

To determine any pair of values which satisfy a linear equation, as-

† That (x, y) notation looks suspiciously like coordinate notation! Graphical representation will follow in Sec. 3.2.

sume *any* value for one of the variables, substitute this value into the equation, and solve for the corresponding value of the other variable.

Example 3.1

You are given the equation

$$2x + 4y = 16$$

(a) Determine *any* pair of values which satisfies the equation.

(b) Determine the pair of values which satisfies the equation when $x = -2$.

(c) Determine the pair of values which satisfies the equation when $y = 0$.

Solution

(a) According to the procedure specified, we might let $x = 0$. Substituting this value into the equation, we get

$$2(0) + 4y = 16$$

or

$$4y = 16$$

and

$$y = 4$$

Thus, one pair of values satisfying the equation is $x = 0$ and $y = 4$, or $(0, 4)$.

(b) Substituting $x = -2$ into the equation, we have

$$2(-2) + 4y = 16$$
$$4y = 20$$

and

$$y = 5$$

When $x = -2$, the pair of values satisfying the equation is $x = -2$ and $y = 5$, or $(-2, 5)$.

(c) Substituting $y = 0$ into the equation gives

$$2x + 4(0) = 16$$
$$2x = 16$$

and

$$x = 8$$

When $y = 0$, the pair of values satisfying the equation is $(8, 0)$. If $S = \{(x, y)|2x + 4y = 16\}$, we can make the statement that

$$\{(0, 4), (-2, 5), (8, 0)\} \subset S$$

Example 3.2

Product Mix A company manufactures two different products. For the coming week 120 hours of labor are available for manufacturing the two products. Work-hours can be allocated for production of either product. In addition, since both products generate a good profit, management is interested in using all 120 hours during the week. Each unit produced of product A requires 3 hours of labor and each unit of product B requires 2.5 hours.

(a) Define an equation which states that total work-hours used for producing x units of product A and y units of product B equal 120.

(b) How many units of product A can be produced if 30 units of product B are produced?

(c) If management decides to produce one product only, what is the maximum quantity which can be produced of product A? The maximum of product B?

(a) From the statement of Example 3.2a we can define our variables as **Solution**
follows:

$$x = \text{number of units produced of product } A$$
$$y = \text{number of units produced of product } B$$

The equation we desire has the following structure.

Total hours used in producing products A and B = 120   (3.4)

What we need, then, is the expression for the left-hand side of the
equation.

NOTE

**Remember the discussion of mental models in Chap. 2? You may well
have a mental model for the left side of this equation—it is simply a
matter of recognizing its form and stating it. Try it by asking yourself
how many hours would be used if you produced 1 unit of each product? 2 units of each? 10 units of product A and 20 of product B? Look
back at the definitions of x and y and state the model that allows you to
answer these questions.**

As you reason through the structure of the left side of Eq. (3.4), the
final equation might evolve as follows:

$$\begin{array}{c} \text{Total hours used} \\ \text{in producing} \\ \text{product } A \end{array} + \begin{array}{c} \text{total hours} \\ \text{used in producing} \\ \text{product } B \end{array} = 120 \qquad (3.5)$$

Since the total hours required to produce either product equals
hours required per unit produced times number of units produced,
Eq. (3.5) reduces to

$$3x + 2.5y = 120 \qquad (3.6)$$

Is that the answer you reached?

(b) If 30 units of product B is produced, then $y = 30$. Therefore

$$3x + 2.5(30) = 120$$
$$3x = 45$$
$$x = 15 \text{ units}$$

A pair of values satisfying Eq. (3.6) is (15, 30). In other words, *one
combination* of the two products which will fully utilize the 120 hours
is 15 units of product A and 30 units of product B.

(c) If management decides to produce product A only, no units of product B are produced, or $y = 0$. If $y = 0$,

$$3x + 2.5(0) = 120$$
$$3x = 120$$
$$x = 40$$

Therefore 40 is the maximum number of units of product A which
can be produced using the 120 hours available.

If management decides to produce product B only, $x = 0$ and

$$3(0) + 2.5y = 120$$

or $\qquad\qquad y = 48 \text{ units}$

Example 3.3 We stated earlier that there are an infinite number of pairs of values (x, y) which satisfy any linear equation. In Example 3.2, are there any members of S which might not be realistic in terms of what the equation represents?

Solution In the example, x and y represent the number of units produced of the two products. Since we can never have *negative* production, we are not interested in negative values of x and y. There are negative values which satisfy Eq. (3.5). For instance, if $y = 60$, then

$$3x + 2.5(60) = 120$$
$$3x = -30$$
$$x = -10$$

In addition to negative values, it is possible to have decimal or fractional values for x and y. For example, if $y = 40$,

$$3x + 2.5(40) = 120$$
$$3x = 20$$
$$x = 6\tfrac{2}{3}$$

Given all the pairs of *nonnegative* values for x and y which satisfy Eq. (3.6), we may or may not desire only *integer* values. Can you suggest a situation where only integer values would be permitted? How about a situation in which noninteger values would be allowed?

Generalizing for *n*-Variable Linear Equations

Given a linear equation involving n variables, as defined by Eq. (3.2), the solution set S can be specified as

$$S = \{(x_1, x_2, x_3, \ldots, x_n)|a_1x_1 + a_2x_2 + a_3x_3 + \cdots + a_nx_n = b\} \quad (3.7)$$

As with the two-variable case, there are an infinite number of elements in the solution set. An element in S is represented by a collection of values $(x_1, x_2, x_3, \ldots, x_n)$, one for each of the n variables in the equation. One way of identifying specific elements in S is to assume values for $n - 1$ of the variables, substitute these into the equation, and solve for the value of the remaining variable.

Example 3.4 You are given the equation

$$2x_1 + 3x_2 - x_3 + x_4 = 16$$

(*a*) Determine one set of values for $x_1, x_2, x_3,$ and x_4 which satisfies the equation.

(b) What values satisfy the equation when $x_1 = 2$, $x_2 = -1$, and $x_3 = 0$?

(c) Determine all members of the solution set which have values of 0 for three of the four variables.

Solution

(a) Let's assume that $x_1 = x_2 = x_3 = 1$ and substitute these into the equation:

$$2(1) + 3(1) - (1) + x_4 = 16$$

or

$$x_4 = 12$$

Therefore one element of the solution set is $x_1 = 1$, $x_2 = 1$, $x_3 = 1$, and $x_4 = 12$, or (1, 1, 1, 12).

(b) Substituting the given values into the equation yields

$$2(2) + 3(-1) - (0) + x_4 = 16$$

or

$$x_4 = 15$$

The corresponding element of the solution set is $(2, -1, 0, 15)$.

(c) If $x_1 = x_2 = x_3 = 0$, then

$$2(0) + 3(0) - (0) + x_4 = 16$$

or

$$x_4 = 16$$

If $x_1 = x_2 = x_4 = 0$,

$$2(0) + 3(0) - x_3 + 0 = 16$$

or

$$x_3 = -16$$

If $x_1 = x_3 = x_4 = 0$, then

$$2(0) + 3x_2 - 0 + 0 = 16$$

or

$$3x_2 = 16$$

and

$$x_2 = \tfrac{16}{3}$$

If $x_2 = x_3 = x_4 = 0$,

$$2x_1 + 3(0) - 0 + 0 = 16$$

or

$$2x_1 = 16$$

and

$$x_1 = 8$$

Therefore, the elements of the solution set which have three of the four variables equaling 0 are $(0, 0, 0, 16)$, $(0, 0, -16, 0)$, $(0, \tfrac{16}{3}, 0, 0)$, and $(8, 0, 0, 0)$.

Follow-up Exercises

Determine whether the following equations are (or can be shown to be) linear.

3.1 $-3y = 0$

3.2 $\sqrt{2}x + 6y = \sqrt{7}$

3.3 $\sqrt{x + y} = \sqrt{6}$

3.4 $-x^2 + y = 4$

3.5 $\dfrac{x + y}{4} - \dfrac{y}{2} = 3y - x$

3.6 $x_1 + 2x_2 = 13x_3$

3.7 Use set notation to specify membership in the solution set P for the equation $-3s + 5t = -15$.

3.8 For the equation $5x - 4y = 60$, (a) define a pair of values which satisfies the equation. (b) What pair of values satisfies the equation when $x = -4$? When $y = 0$? When $x = 0$?

3.9 Consider the equation $6x = 90$ as a two-variable equation in the form of Eq. (3.1).

(a) What are a, b, and c?

(b) Define a pair of values for x and y which satisfies the equation.

(c) What pair of values satisfies the equation when $y = 10$?

(d) What pair satisfies the equation when $x = 5$? (Be careful.)

(e) Can you generalize a statement about the nature of the values for x and y which belong to the solution set for this equation?

3.10 Rework Example 3.2 if product A requires 2 hours per unit and product B requires 1.5 hours per unit.

3.11 You are given the equation

$$2x_1 - 7x_2 + 5x_3 = 0$$

(a) What values satisfy the equation when $x_1 = 1$ and $x_3 = 1$?

(b) Define the elements of the solution set in which the values of two variables equal 0. Do you notice the difference between this example and Example 3.4c? The right-hand side value of 0 [$b = 0$ in Eq. (3.2)] makes the difference.

3.2   GRAPHICAL CHARACTERISTICS

Graphing Two-Variable Equations

This should not come as a great surprise, but a *linear equation involving two variables has a graph which is a straight line in two dimensions*. In order to graph a linear equation involving two variables, you only need to (1) identify the coordinates of any two points which lie on the line, (2) connect the two points with a straight line, and (3) extend the straight line in both directions as far as necessary or desirable for your purposes. The coordinates of the two points are found by identifying any two members of the solution set. The graphical representation (counterpart) of each element in the solution set is a point in 2-space. The location of this point is described by coordinates (x, y) where x and y are the respective values of the two variables. For example, if the values of $x = 1$ and $y = 3$ satisfy an equation, the graphical representation of this member of the solution set is a point located at $(1, 3)$.

Example 3.5   The graph of the equation

$$2x + 4y = 16$$

is found by first identifying any two pairs of values for x and y which satisfy the equation.

NOTE

Aside from the case where the right side of the equation equals 0, the easiest points to identify (algebraically) are those found by setting one

variable equal to 0 and solving for the value of the other variable. That is, let $x = 0$ and solve for the value of y; then let $y = 0$ and solve for the value of x.

Letting $x = 0$, the corresponding value for y is 4, and letting $y = 0$ results in $x = 8$. Thus $(0, 4)$ and $(8, 0)$ are two members of the solution set, and their graphical representation is indicated by the two points in Fig. 3.1. The two points have been connected by a straight line, and the line has been extended in both directions.

Just as $(0, 4)$ and $(8, 0)$ are members of the solution set for the equation $2x + 4y = 16$, the coordinates of every point lying on the line represent other members of the solution set. How many unique points are there on the line? There are an infinite number, which is entirely consistent with our earlier statement that there are an infinite number of pairs of values for x and y which satisfy any linear equation. In summary, if there are any values of x and y that satisfy an equation, their values can be identified respectively by the coordinates of points lying on the line representing the equation. With reference to Fig. 3.1, the coordinates of any point *not* lying on the line will not satisfy the equation.

Graph the linear equation $4x - 7y = 0$.

Example 3.6

FIGURE 3.1

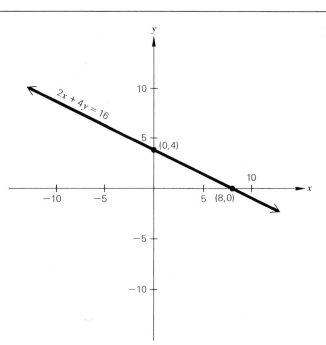

108

Solution This equation is an example of the situation where two points will not be found by setting each variable equal to 0 and solving for the remaining variable. Watch what happens! If $x = 0$,

$$4(0) - 7y = 0 \quad \text{or} \quad y = 0$$

If $y = 0$,

$$4x - 7(0) = 0 \quad \text{or} \quad x = 0$$

Both cases have yielded the same point, (0, 0). Therefore another value must be assumed for one of the variables. If $x = 7$,

$$4(7) - 7y = 0$$
$$-7y = -28$$
$$y = 4$$

Two members of the solution set, then, are (0, 0) and (7, 4). Figure 3.2 illustrates the graph of the equation.

NOTE
Any two-variable linear equation in the standard form of Eq. (3.1) having a right side equal to 0 graphs as a straight line which *passes through the origin*.

FIGURE 3.2

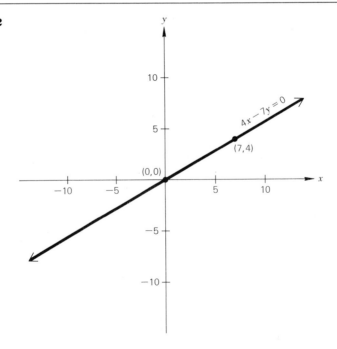

Intercepts

In describing the graphical appearance of mathematical functions, two characteristics of frequent interest are the *x intercepts* and *y intercepts* of the function. These can be described both in a visual or graphical sense and algebraically.

DEFINITION
The x intercepts of an equation are the points where the graph of the equation crosses the x axis. Algebraically, the x intercepts represent the values of x when $y = 0$.

DEFINITION
The y intercepts of an equation are the points where the graph of the equation crosses the y axis. Algebraically, the y intercepts represent the values of y when $x = 0$.

For a two-variable linear equation there exist (except for two special cases) one x intercept and one y intercept. In Fig. 3.1, the x intercept is 8, and the y intercept is 4 for the equation $2x + 4y = 16$. In Fig. 3.2, the x and y intercepts both occur at the same point, the origin. The x intercept is 0, and the y intercept is 0. Look at both figures carefully and verify that the x intercept represents the value of x when $y = 0$ and that the y intercept represents the value of y when $x = 0$.

NOTE
The procedure suggested in Example 3.5 for identifying two points essentially determines the x and y intercepts.

The next two sections cover the special cases where there is either no x intercept *or* no y intercept.

The Equation $x = k$

A linear equation of the form $ax = c$ is a special case of Eq. (3.1) where $b = 0$ or, more simply, there is no y term. Dividing both sides by a yields the simplified form

$$x = c/a$$
or $\qquad x = \text{some constant value}$

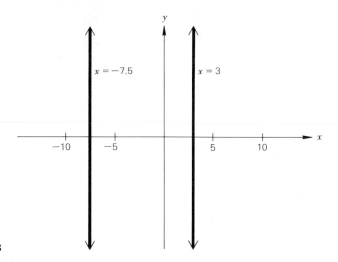

FIGURE 3.3

Let's generalize this as $x = k$, where k is a real number. This linear equation is special in the sense that $x = k$ regardless of the value of y. The variable y may assume any value as long as $x = k$. That is the only thing required by the equation. As a result, any equation of this form graphs as a vertical line crossing the x axis at $x = k$. Figure 3.3 illustrates two equations of this type. Note that for these equations there is an x intercept but *no y* intercept.

The Equation $y = k$

Similarly, a linear equation of the form $by = c$ is a special case of Eq. (3.1) where $a = 0$, i.e., where there is no x term. After both sides of the equation are divided by b, it becomes clear that the general reduced form of this case is $y = k$, where k is again a real number (or constant). This equation suggests that $y = k$ regardless of the value of x. The variable x may assume any value as long as $y = k$. Any equation of this form graphs as a horizontal line crossing the y axis at $y = k$. Figure 3.4 illustrates two such equations. Note that equations of this form have no x intercepts.

Slope

Any straight line, with the exception of vertical lines, can be characterized by its *slope*. By "slope" we mean basically the inclination of a line—whether it rises or falls as you move from left to right along the x axis—and the rate at which the line rises or falls (in other words, how steep the line is).

The slope of a line may be *positive, negative, zero,* or *undefined*. A line with a positive slope rises from left to right, or runs uphill. Another way to describe such a line is to say that the relationship between x and y is such that the value of y increases as x increases (or y decreases as x

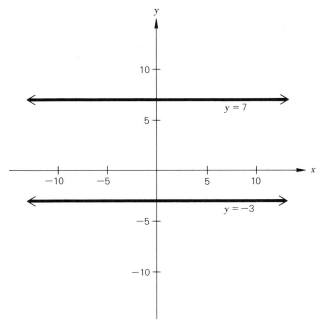

FIGURE 3.4

decreases). Line l_1 in Fig. 3.5 has a positive slope. A line having a negative slope falls from left to right, or runs downhill. To state it differently, for such a line the value of y decreases as x increases (or y increases as x decreases). This means that x and y are behaving in an *inverse* manner; that is, as one increases, the other decreases and vice versa. Line l_3 in

FIGURE 3.5

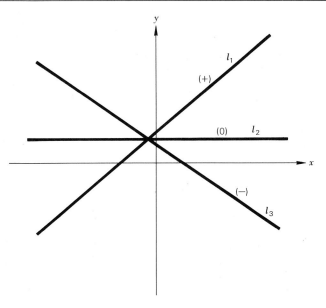

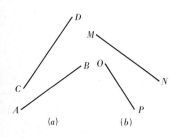

FIGURE 3.6

Fig. 3.5 has a negative slope. A line having a zero slope is perfectly horizontal. As x increases or decreases, y stays constant (our special case: $y = k$). Line l_2 has a zero slope. Vertical lines (of the form $x = k$) have a slope which is undefined.

Aside from the question of whether a line is rising or falling, there may be an interest in some measure of the relative steepness of the line. This information is provided by the *slope*. The slope tells us at what rate the value of y changes *relative to* changes in the value of x. The larger the *absolute value* (Sec. 0.1) of the slope, the steeper the angle at which the line rises or falls. In Fig. 3.6a lines AB and CD both have positive slopes, but the slope associated with CD is larger than that for AB. Similarly, in Fig. 3.6b lines MN and OP both have negative slopes, but OP would have the larger slope in an absolute value sense.

Given any two points which lie on a straight line that is not vertical, the slope can be computed as a ratio of the change in the value of y in moving from one point to the other divided by the corresponding change in the value of x, or

$$\text{Slope} = \frac{\text{change in } y}{\text{change in } x}$$

$$= \frac{\Delta y}{\Delta x}$$

where Δ (delta) means "change in." Thus Δy denotes the change in the value of y and Δx the change in the value of x. The *two-point formula* is one way of determining the slope of a straight line connecting two points.

TWO-POINT FORMULA
The slope m of the straight line connecting two points having coordinates (x_1, y_1) and (x_2, y_2), respectively, is computed as

$$m = \frac{y_2 - y_1}{x_2 - x_1} \qquad (3.8)$$

where $x_1 \neq x_2$

Figure 3.7 illustrates the computation of Δx and Δy for the line segment PQ.

Example 3.7 Compute the slope of the straight line connecting points located at (2, 4) and (5, 12).

Solution The first step in using the two-point formula is to arbitrarily identify one point as point 1 having coordinates (x_1, y_1) and the other as point 2 having coordinates (x_2, y_2). Most people who plot the points on a graph label the leftmost point as the first. However, it makes absolutely no difference. Given the location of the two points in Fig. 3.8, let's label

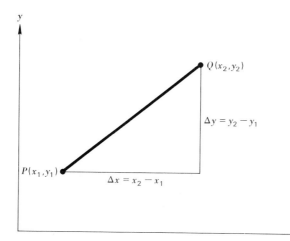

FIGURE 3.7

(5, 12) as point 1 and (2, 4) as point 2. For purposes of using Eq. (3.8),
$(x_1, y_1) = (5, 12)$ and $(x_2, y_2) = (2, 4)$. Substituting into Eq. (3.8) gives

$$m = \frac{y_2 - y_1}{x_2 - x_1}$$

$$= \frac{4 - 12}{2 - 5}$$

$$= \frac{-8}{-3}$$

$$= \frac{8}{3}$$

FIGURE 3.8

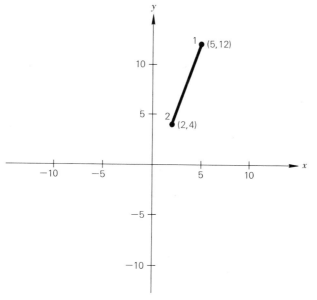

The slope of $\frac{8}{3}$ indicates that the line segment rises and that y increases at a rate of 8 units for every 3 units that x increases.

Another way of interpreting the slope is given by the following definition.

DEFINITION
The *slope* indicates the change in the value
of *y* if *x* increases by 1 unit.

According to this definition, the value of $m = \frac{8}{3}$ indicates that if x increases by 1 unit, then y will *increase* by $\frac{8}{3}$ or $2\frac{2}{3}$ units.

An important point needs to be made. *Along any straight line the slope is constant.* That is, if a line is said to have a slope of -2, the slope of the line segment connecting *any* two points on the line will always equal -2.

Example 3.8   Figure 3.1 is repeated here for the equation $2x + 4y = 16$. Determine the slope of this line.

Solution   Choosing the x and y intercepts for use in the two-point formula, we have $(x_1, y_1) = (0, 4)$ and $(x_2, y_2) = (8, 0)$. Substituting into Eq. (3.8) gives

---

FIGURE 3.1

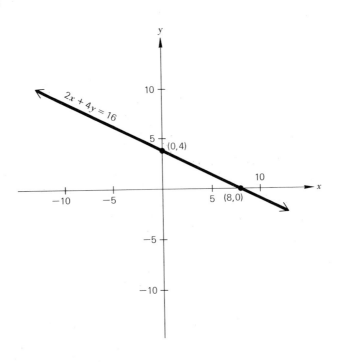

$$m = \frac{0 - 4}{8 - 0}$$

or

$$= -\tfrac{4}{8} = -\tfrac{1}{2}$$

Our conclusion is that the slope of the line representing the equation $2x + 4y = 16$ is $-\tfrac{1}{2}$. And as we move along the line, y *decreases* 0.5 unit for each unit that x increases.

We have already seen that the slope of a linear equation having the form $y = k$ is 0. For a horizontal line, the value of y is always the same, and the numerator of the two-point formula $y_2 - y_1$ always equals 0. We also examined the other special case of a linear equation, $x = k$. We verified that any linear equation having this form graphs as a vertical line crossing the x axis at $x = k$. *The slope of any vertical line is undefined.* This can be verified by using the two-point formula to determine the slope of the line represented by $x = 5$. Choosing two points arbitrarily which satisfy this equation, let $(x_1, y_1) = (5, 0)$ and $(x_2, y_2) = (5, -1)$. Substituting into Eq. (3.8) gives

Example 3.9

$$m = \frac{-1 - 0}{5 - 5}$$

$$= \frac{-1}{0}$$

which is not defined.

Follow-up Exercises

For each of the following linear equations, identify the x and y intercepts if they exist.

3.12 $4x - 3y = 24$
3.13 $-2x - 6y = 33$
3.14 $-x - 4y = -8$
3.15 $25x = 150$
3.16 $-6y = 72$
3.17 $x + y = 0$
3.18 $x - 5 = (x + 2y)/3$

For exercises 3.19 to 3.24, graph each of the linear equations.

3.19 $2x - 2y = 10$
3.20 $-4x - 6y = -24$
3.21 $2x + 3y = 12$
3.22 $3x = (x - y)/2$
3.23 $4x = (x - 11)/3$
3.24 $-2y = 4$

3.25 What algebraic justification is there for the equations in Exercises 3.20 and 3.21 having the same graphical appearance?

3.26 What is the equation for the x axis? The y axis?

3.27 Recompute the slope in Example 3.7 and verify that the answer is the same if the points are labeled as $(x_1, y_1) = (2, 4)$ and $(x_2, y_2) = (5, 12)$.

3.28 Find the slope of the line segment connecting points $(-2, 12)$ and $(4, -12)$.

3.29 Find the slope of the line segment connecting points $(5, 3)$ and $(-2, 3)$.

3.30 Find the slope of the line segment connecting points $(5, -6)$ and $(5, 0)$.

3.31 Compute and verbally interpret the meaning of the slope of the line representing the equation $-6x + 2y = 15$.

3.32 Compute and verbally interpret the meaning of the slope of the line representing the equation $x + 4y = 0$.

3.33 Find the expression for the slope of the line segment connecting the two points (a, b) and (c, d).

3.34 Rework Exercise 3.33 for the points (r, t) and (r, s).

3.3   SLOPE-INTERCEPT FORM

From a Different Vantage Point

In this section we discuss another form of expressing linear equations. In Sec. 3.1 we stated the general form of a two-variable linear equation as

$$ax + by = c \tag{3.1}$$

Solving Eq. (3.1) for the variable y, we get

$$by = c - ax$$

or

$$y = \frac{c}{b} - \frac{ax}{b} \tag{3.9}$$

For any linear equation the terms c/b and $-a/b$ on the right side of Eq. (3.9) have special significance. The term c/b represents the y intercept for the equation, and $-a/b$ represents the slope of the equation. This information is obtained from any linear equation of the form of Eq. (3.1) if it can be solved for y.

The form of Eq. (3.9) is called the *slope-intercept form* of a linear equation. Equation (3.9) can be generalized in a simpler form as

$$y = mx + i \tag{3.10}$$

where m represents the slope of the equation and i equals the y intercept. There could be some temporary confusion here in going from Eq. (3.9) to Eq. (3.10), so look closely at the structure of the right side of Eq. (3.10). In solving any linear equation for y, the *slope* is represented by the constant (sign included) which is being multiplied times x. And, the y intercept is the isolated constant (sign included) on the same side of the equation.

To illustrate this form, the equation

$$y = -5x + 10$$

is a linear equation which has a slope of -5 and a y intercept of $+10$. The equation $y = 2x/3$ is a linear equation having a slope of $+\frac{2}{3}$ and a y intercept of 0. The absence of the isolated constant implicitly suggests that $i = 0$ in Eq. (3.10).

Example 3.10   In Example 3.8 we verified that the slope of the equation $2x + 4y = 16$ is $-\frac{1}{2}$. From Fig. 3.1 we can also see that the y intercept is at $y = 4$.

Let's verify these two values by rewriting the equation in the slope-intercept form:

$$2x + 4y = 16$$
$$4y = 16 - 2x$$
$$y = \frac{16 - 2x}{4}$$
$$= \frac{16}{4} - \frac{2x}{4}$$

or

$$y = 4 + (-\tfrac{1}{2}x)$$

A *coefficient* is a constant which is multiplied times a variable. The coefficient of x, and thus the slope, equals $-\tfrac{1}{2}$ in this example. The other constant term on the right side, 4, represents the y intercept.

Example 3.11

The special case of a linear equation $y = k$ is in the slope-intercept form. To realize this, you must recognize that this equation can be written in the form $y = k + 0x$. The absence of the x term on the right side implicitly suggests that $m = 0$, i.e., the slope of an equation having this form equals zero. We confirmed this in Sec. 3.2 when we discussed the graphical characteristics of this case. Note that the y intercept equals k for such equations.

Example 3.12

For the special case where $x = k$, it is impossible to solve for the slope-intercept form of the linear equation. The variable y is not a part of the equation. Our conclusion is that it is impossible to determine the slope and y intercept for equations having this form. Look back at Fig. 3.3 to see if this conclusion is consistent with our earlier findings.

Interpreting the Slope and y Intercept

In many applications of linear equations, the slope and y intercept have interpretations which are of interest. Take, for example, the salary equation

$$y = 25 + 3x$$

where y = weekly salary (in dollars)

x = number of units sold during one week

The salary equation is linear and is written in the slope-intercept form. Graphically, the equation is represented by the line in Fig. 3.9, which has a slope of $+3$ and y intercept equal to 25. Notice that this equation has been graphed only for nonnegative values of x and y. Can you suggest why this would be appropriate?

Think back to the definition of *slope*. Slope represents the change in the value of y associated with a 1-unit increase in the value of x. For this example, the slope of $+3$ means that weekly salary y increases by \$3 for each additional unit sold. The y intercept represents the value of y when $x = 0$, or the salary which would be earned if no units are sold. This is the base salary per week.

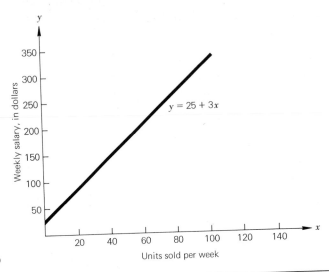

FIGURE 3.9

Example 3.13   If you refer to Example 2.20, we developed an estimated total cost function associated with owning and operating a police patrol car. The cost equation was

$$C = 0.40x + 18,000$$

where C = total cost (in dollars)
   x = number of miles driven

This equation is also in the slope-intercept form with a slope of 0.40 and y intercept of 18,000. The slope suggests that total cost increases at a rate of $0.40 for each additional mile driven. The 18,000 implies a fixed cost of $18,000 which is incurred whether or not the car is driven. Although we might speculate about what makes up this $18,000, it is likely to be mainly the purchase cost of the car. Can you think of other costs which might be a part of this $18,000? How about the cost of a lifetime maintenance policy purchased from the manufacturer or from a local garage?

Follow-up Exercises

Rewrite each equation below in the slope-intercept form and determine the slope and y intercept.

3.35 $6x + 3y = 50$

3.36 $x + 4y = 0$

3.37 $6y - 24 = 0$

3.38 $-2x - 6y = 24$

3.39 $-6x + 12 = 0$

3.40 Graph the total cost equation in Example 3.13.

3.41 Graph each of the equations in Exercises 3.35 to 3.39.

3.42 The chamber of commerce for a resort town is trying to determine how many tourists will be visiting each season over the coming years. A marketing research firm has estimated that the number of tourists can be predicted by the equation $p = 50,000 + 5,000t$, where p = number of tourists per year and t = years (measured *from* this current season)—

$t = 0$ identifies the current season, $t = 1$ is the next season, etc. Let p be the dependent variable (plotted on the vertical axis).
(a) Graph the equation.
(b) Identify the slope and y intercept (p intercept, here).
(c) Interpret the meaning of the slope and p intercept in this application.
3.43 *Think metric!* $C = \frac{5}{9}F - \frac{160}{9}$ is an equation relating temperature in Celsius units to temperature measured on the Fahrenheit scale. Let $C =$ degrees Celsius and $F =$ degrees Fahrenheit, and assume this equation is graphed with C measured on the vertical axis.
(a) Identify the slope and y intercept.
(b) Interpret the meaning of the slope and y intercept for purposes of converting from Fahrenheit to Celsius temperatures.
(c) Solve the equation for F and rework parts a and b if F is plotted on the vertical axis.

DETERMINING THE EQUATION OF A STRAIGHT LINE

3.4

In applying mathematics, usually we must begin our analysis by determining the true or approximate relationship among the variables of interest. For instance, the cost equation for the patrol car in Example 3.13 had to be derived from information available to department analysts. We will look at this preliminary stage of analysis continually as we move through the book. This is a very important stage with which you should be familiar and comfortable. A statistics course will help you further in realizing these objectives.

In this section we will see how the equation for a linear relationship can be determined. The way in which you determine the equation depends upon the information available. The following sections discuss different situations that you might encounter.

Slope and Intercept

The easiest situation is one in which you know the slope and y intercept of the line representing an equation. To determine the linear equation in this almost trivial case, simply substitute these two values into the slope-intercept form, Eq. (3.10). If you are interested in stating the equation in the standard form of Eq. (3.1), simply rearrange the terms in the slope-intercept equation.

Determine the linear equation which has a slope of -5 and a y intercept of 15.

Example 3.14

Substituting values of $m = -5$ and $i = 15$ into Eq. (3.10) gives

Solution

$$y = -5x + 15$$

Restated in the form of Eq. (3.1), an equivalent form of this equation is

$$5x + y = 15$$

Example 3.15 Determine the linear equation which has a slope of $+\frac{1}{2}$ and a y intercept equal to 0.

Solution Substituting $m = \frac{1}{2}$ and $i = 0$ into Eq. (3.10) gives

$$y = \tfrac{1}{2}x + 0$$

or
$$y = \tfrac{1}{2}x$$

In the form of Eq. (3.1), the equation can be stated as $\frac{1}{2}x - y = 0$, or even as $x - 2y = 0$.

POINT FOR THOUGHT AND DISCUSSION
Is the equation $y - \frac{1}{2}x = 0$ an equivalent form of the equation in this example? Why? Graph the two to see if they are the same.

Slope and One Point

In another situation you may know the slope of the line representing an equation and also one member of the solution set (i.e., the coordinates of one point on the line). If you consider the slope-intercept form [Eq. (3.10)], any member of the solution set should satisfy this equation. That is, we can define the values of x and y which satisfy an equation by the set S, where

$$S = \{(x, y)|y = mx + i\} \tag{3.11}$$

Now follow this carefully! In the last section we said that knowing the slope and the y intercept of an equation allows you to write out the slope-intercept equation directly. In this section we talk of knowing the slope and one point—but not the y intercept. From Eq. (3.11), any point which lies on a line should satisfy the slope-intercept equation. If we take the known slope m and the coordinates of the point which are known to satisfy the equation, substitution of these *three* values into Eq. (3.10) allows us to solve for i, the y intercept. At this stage we would have the slope m and y intercept i for the line, and the equation would follow directly. Let's illustrate this with a few examples.

Example 3.16 If the slope of a straight line is -2 and one point lying on the line is $(2, 8)$, determine the equation of the line.

Solution Substituting the slope and coordinates into Eq. (3.10), we compute the y intercept i:

$$8 = (-2)(2) + i$$

or
$$12 = i$$

Knowing that $m = -2$ and $i = 12$ leads directly to the slope-intercept equation

$$y = -2x + 12$$

And, as before, we could rewrite this equation in the equivalent form

$$2x + y = 12$$

NOTE
**You may be wondering which form of the linear equation—Eq. (3.1)
or Eq. (3.10)—is the correct one. The answer depends on what you in-
tend to do with the equation. Depending on the type of analysis to be
conducted, one of these forms may be more appropriate than the
other.**

If the slope of a straight line is zero and one point lying on the line is $(5, -30)$ determine the equation of the line.

**Example
3.17**

Substituting the zero slope and coordinates $(5, -30)$ into Eq. (3.10), we compute the y intercept i:

Solution

$$-30 = (0)(5) + i$$
or
$$-30 = i$$

Since we know that $m = 0$ and $i = -30$, the slope-intercept equation is

$$y = 0x + (-30)$$
or
$$y = -30$$

If the slope of a straight line is -1 and one point lying on the line is $(-5, 5)$, determine the equation of the line.

**Example
3.18**

Substituting as before, we get

Solution

$$5 = (-1)(-5) + i$$
$$5 = 5 + i$$
or
$$0 = i$$

With $m = -1$ and $i = 0$, the slope-intercept equation is

$$y = -x$$

or, alternatively,

$$x + y = 0$$

*If a line has a slope m_1 ($m_1 \neq 0$), the slope of any line which is perpen-
dicular to the given line has a slope equal to the negative reciprocal of*

**Example
3.19**

the given line, or $m_2 = -1/m_1$. You are given the linear equation $3x - 6y = 24$.

(a) What is the slope of the line represented by the given equation?

(b) How many different lines are perpendicular to this line?

(c) Find the equation of the line which is perpendicular to the given line *and* which passes through the point (2, 5).

Solution

(a) Restating the equation in the slope-intercept form, we have

$$-6y = 24 - 3x$$

or

$$y = -4 + \tfrac{1}{2}x$$

From this equation the slope can be seen to equal $+1/2$.

(b) An infinite number of lines would be perpendicular to any given line.

(c) Since $m_1 = \tfrac{1}{2}$, the slope of any line perpendicular to the line $3x - 6y = 24$ is

$$m_2 = -\frac{1}{\tfrac{1}{2}}$$

$$= -2$$

Thus, for the line we are concerned with, $m = -2$ and one point on the line is (2, 5). Substituting these three values into Eq. (3.10) yields

$$5 = (-2)(2) + i$$

or

$$9 = i$$

Therefore the equation of the line is

$$y = -2x + 9$$

or, alternatively,

$$2x + y = 9$$

Two Points

A more likely situation is that some data points have been gathered which lie on a line and we wish to determine the equation of the line. Assume the special case where two points (x_1, y_1) and (x_2, y_2) are known. Different approaches exist for proceeding from this starting point. Our focus has been on the slope-intercept form, and we shall continue that orientation.

Remember that given the coordinates of two points which lie on a straight line, we can determine the slope of the line by using the two-point formula [Eq. (3.8)]. As soon as we know the slope, the y intercept can be determined by using *either* of the two data points, as we did in the last section.

Example 3.20

Determine the equation of the straight line which passes through $(-4, 2)$ and the origin.

Using the two-point formula, we have

$$m = \frac{0 - 2}{0 - (-4)}$$
$$= -\frac{-2}{4}$$
$$= -\frac{1}{2}$$

Substituting $m = -\frac{1}{2}$ and the coordinates $(-4, 2)$ into Eq. (3.10) yields

$$2 = (-\tfrac{1}{2})(-4) + i$$
$$2 = 2 + i$$
$$0 = i$$

Thus, the slope-intercept form of the equation is

$$y = -\tfrac{1}{2}x$$

Let's check ourselves and solve for the y intercept i by substituting $(0, 0)$ into Eq. (3.10) as opposed to $(-4, 2)$. Doing this,

$$0 = (-\tfrac{1}{2})(0) + i$$
or
$$0 = i$$

which is consistent with our original result.

Depreciation The value of the police patrol car in Example 3.13 is expected to decrease at a linear rate over time. Figure 3.10 shows two data points on the line which represents the value V of the car over time t, where V is measured in dollars and t is measured in years from the time of purchase. The two data points indicate that the value of the car at $t = 0$ (time of purchase) is \$18,000 and its value in one year will equal \$14,500.

Example 3.21

Determine the slope-intercept equation which relates the value of the patrol car V to time t.

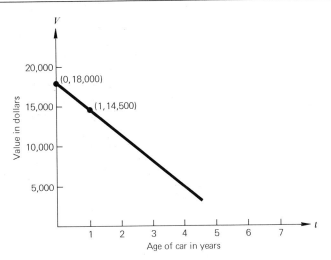

FIGURE 3.10

Solution Determining the slope by the two-point formula, we have

$$m = \frac{14{,}500 - 18{,}000}{1 - 0}$$

$$= \frac{-3{,}500}{1}$$

$$= -3{,}500$$

Substituting $m = -3{,}500$ and $(0, 18{,}000)$ into Eq. (3.10)—with V and t replacing y and x, respectively—we get

$$18{,}000 = (-3{,}500)(0) + i$$

or $\qquad 18{,}000 = i$

(That was obvious from Fig. 3.10, wasn't it?) Consequently, the slope-intercept equation is

$$V = -3{,}500t + 18{,}000$$

Example 3.22 (a) For the last example, interpret the meaning of the slope.
(b) At what point in time is the value of the car expected to equal 0?

Solution (a) The slope of $-3{,}500$ implies that with each additional year of ownership the value of the patrol car decreases by \$3,500. (The term *depreciation* is often used by accountants to describe the rate at which an asset, i.e., something of value, declines in value over time.)
(b) V will equal 0 when the line crosses the t axis (equivalent to the x intercept); algebraically, we are searching for the value of t when $V = 0$. By setting V equal to 0 in the equation developed in the last example and solving for t, we find

$$0 = -3{,}500t + 18{,}000$$
$$3{,}500t = 18{,}000$$
$$t = \frac{18{,}000}{3{,}500}$$

or $\qquad t = 5.142$ years

Follow-up Exercises

Given the information available in Exercises 3.44 to 3.56, determine the slope-intercept form of the linear equation. Also restate the equation in the standard form of Eq. (3.1).

3.44 slope $= 0$, y intercept $= -6$
3.45 slope $= -5$, y intercept $= 10$
3.46 slope $= +3$, y intercept $= 0$
3.47 slope undefined, infinite number of y intercepts
3.48 $m = +\frac{1}{4}$, $(0, 0)$ lies on the line
3.49 $m = -2.5$, $(-5, 10)$ lies on the line
3.50 m is undefined, $(3, 5)$ lies on the line
3.51 $m = 0$, $(-5, 6)$ lies on the line

3.52 (6, 3) and (4, 3) lie on the line

3.53 (4, 10) and (4, −6) lie on the line

*__3.54__ (a, b) and (c, d) lie on the line

3.55 (0, c) and (6, c) lie on the line

3.56 (a, −2) and (a, 3) lie on the line

3.57 Without graphing, determine whether the points (3, 8), (−1, 4), and (−4, 0) are all on the same straight line. (*Hint:* One approach is to find the equation of the line connecting two of the points and substitute the coordinates of the third point into the equation to see if they satisfy it.)

3.58 *Parallel lines have slopes which are equal to one another.* Find the equation of the line which passes through (6, 4) and is also parallel to the line $x + y = 0$.

3.59 Find the equation of the line which is perpendicular to the line $x + y = 0$ and passes through (6, 4).

3.60 In Exercise 3.42 the chamber of commerce was trying to forecast the number of tourists who would be visiting in the coming years. Some students from the local university have examined the problem as part of a class project. They estimated this current year's volume at 60,000 tourists, or that one data point is (0, 60,000). They have also projected that the volume next year will be 67,500 people and that the volume in the future will continue to grow at the same rate according to a linear relationship. Determine the slope-intercept equation which relates number of tourists P to years t as measured from this current year.

3.61 If F denotes degrees Fahrenheit and C denotes degrees Celsius, assume that the relationship between these two temperature scales is being graphed with F on the vertical axis. Two data points on the line relating C and F are (5, 41) and (25, 77). Using these points, determine the slope-intercept equation which allows you to transform from Celsius into Fahrenheit.

LINEAR EQUATIONS INVOLVING MORE THAN TWO VARIABLES

When linear equations involve more than two variables, the algebraic properties remain basically the same but the visual or graphical characteristics change considerably or are lost altogether.

Equations Involving Three Variables

Equations having the form

$$a_1 x_1 + a_2 x_2 + a_3 x_3 = b$$

graph as *planes* in three dimensions. The number of variables in an equation determines the number of dimensions required to graphically represent the equation. Three variables mean three dimensions. Figure 3.11 illustrates a set of three perpendicular coordinate axes which define points in *3-space*. Notice that the location or address of any point in three dimensions must be specified by its location relative to each axis. In other words, the coordinate system requires specifying locations by

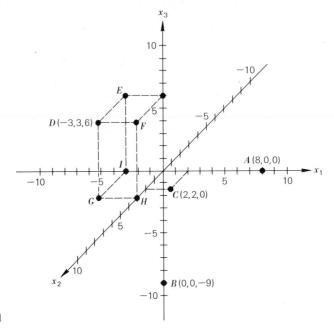

FIGURE 3.11

three-component coordinates (x_1, x_2, x_3). Points A, B, C, and D are all examples of how locations are identified by these coordinates.

EXERCISE

See if you can specify the coordinates for points E, F, G, H, and I. Can you locate points $(-2, 4, 0)$, $(+2, -2, -2)$, and $(+5, 0, -5)$?

[Ans: $E(-3, 0, 6)$, $F(0, 3, 6)$, $G(-3, 3, 0)$,
$H(0, 3, 0)$, $I(-3, 0, 0)$]

It is not so important that you actually be able to graph in three dimensions. It is more important that (1) you be aware that linear equations involving three variables graph as planes in three dimensions, (2) you know what a *plane* is, and (3) you have some feeling for how planes can be represented graphically. A plane, of course, is a flat surface like the ceiling, walls, and floor of the room in which you are currently sitting or lying. Instead of the two points needed to graph a line, three points are necessary to define a plane. The three points must not be *collinear*; that is, they must not lie on the same line. Take, for example, the equation

$$2x_1 + 4x_2 + 3x_3 = 12$$

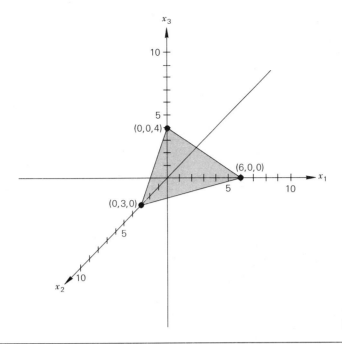

FIGURE 3.12

If we can identify three members of the solution set for this equation, they will specify the coordinates of three points lying on the plane. Three members which are identified easily are the intercepts. These are found by setting any two of the three variables equal to 0 and solving for the remaining variable. Verify that when $x_1 = x_2 = 0$, $x_3 = 4$, or $(0, 0, 4)$ is a member of the solution set. Similarly, verify that $(6, 0, 0)$ and $(0, 3, 0)$ are members of the solution set and thus are points lying on the plane representing our equation. Figure 3.12 shows these points and a portion of the plane which contains them.

When graphing equations involving two variables, we identified two points and connected them with a straight line. However, we saw that in order to represent *all* members of the solution set, the line must extend an infinite distance in each direction. The same is true with the solution set for three-variable equations. To represent all members of the solution set for the equation $2x_1 + 4x_2 + 3x_3 = 12$, the plane in Fig. 3.12 extends an infinite distance in all directions.

Graph the linear equation $x_1 = 0$ in three dimensions.

Example 3.23

In later chapters we will see that problems often involve the use of more than one equation. In a problem which involves n variables, a subset of the equations may involve fewer than n variables. Being asked to graph the above equation in 3-space suggests analysis of a three-variable problem. The given equation may be one of a group of equations which deal with x_1, x_2, and x_3.

Solution

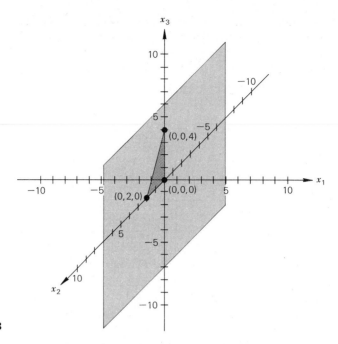

FIGURE 3.13

In order to graph the equation, we again need to identify three non-collinear points which satisfy the equation. Looking at the equation, we see that as long as $x_1 = 0$, x_2 and x_3 can equal *any* values. For example, (0, 0, 0), (0, 2, 0), and (0, 0, 4) all satisfy the equation. Figure 3.13 illustrates the graph of the equation. The equation $x_1 = 0$ graphs as a plane perpendicular to the x_1 axis and passing through $x_1 = 0$. This is referred to as the x_2x_3 *plane*.

> **Any equation of the form $x_1 = k$ graphs in 3-space as a plane perpendicular to the x_1 axis and passing through $x_1 = k$.**

> **Any equation of the form $x_j = k$, where $j = 1, 2, or\ 3$, will graph as a plane which is perpendicular to the x_j axis and crosses the x_j axis at $x_j = k$.**

Equations Involving More than Three Variables

When more than three variables exist ($n > 3$), graphing requires more than three dimensions. To the author's knowledge no one has ever provided a visual reference or graph of a linear equation in four or more dimensions. Even though we cannot envision the graphical representation of such equations, the term *hyperplane* is used to describe the geometric representation of the equation. Mathematicians would, for instance, say that the equation

$$x_1 + x_2 + x_3 + x_4 = 10$$

is represented by a hyperplane in 4-space or four dimensions. Or, in general, an equation of the form

$$a_1x_1 + a_2x_2 + \cdots + a_nx_n = b$$

where $n > 3$ would be represented by a hyperplane in *n-space*.

Follow-up Exercises

3.62 Graphically locate the points $(-2, 0, 5)$, $(1, 2, 5)$ $(0, 0, -2)$, $(4, 6, -2)$, $(-1, -1, -1)$, and $(0, 0, -5)$.

3.63 For Fig. 3.14 label the coordinates of points A through I.

3.64 For the equation $-2x_1 + x_2 + 3x_3 = 9$, where does the plane cross the x_1, x_2, and x_3 axes? Graphically sketch the plane that represents the equation.

3.65 At what points does the plane representing $2x_1 + 4x_2 = 8$ cross the x_1 axis? The x_2 axis? The x_3 axis? Sketch the plane.

3.66 Sketch the plane $6x_1 = 36$.

3.67 Sketch the plane $-x_2 = -5$.

3.68 Sketch the plane $x_3 = 4$.

FIGURE 3.14

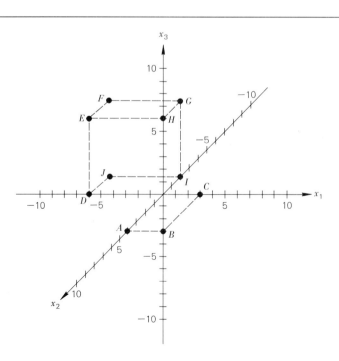

*3.69 Can you draw any general conclusions about the characteristics of planes which represent linear equations involving two of the three variables? The equation in Exercise 3.65, for instance, is an example involving x_1 and x_2 but not x_3.

3.6 ADDITIONAL APPLICATIONS

The more exposure you have to word problems, the more skilled you will become in formulating them. The following examples illustrate the formulation of linear equations for different types of applications. Study these carefully and try as many of these types of problems as you can, both at the end of this section and at the end of the chapter.

Example 3.24

Emergency Airlift The International Red Cross is making plans to airlift emergency food and medical supplies into a large South American city which has recently suffered from extensive flooding. The four items needed immediately and their respective volumes per container are shown below. The first plane to be sent into the area has a volume capacity of 6,000 cubic feet. Determine an equation whose solution set contains all possible combinations of the four items which will fill the plane to its volume capacity.

Item	Volume/Container, ft³
Blood	20
Medical supply kits	30
Food	8
Water	6

Solution

As mentioned in Chap. 2, in almost every word problem the first step is to define the unknowns or variables which are to be used. It is useful to ask yourself what decisions need to be made in the problem. If these decisions can be identified, they hold the key to defining the variables.

In this example the decision facing the Red Cross personnel deals with how many containers of each item should be sent on the first plane. Since the Red Cross wishes to ship as many supplies as possible on this first plane, they are interested in identifying the different combinations which will fill the plane to capacity (volumewise).

Verbally, the equation we are seeking should have the form

$$\text{Volume of supplies shipped} = 6,000 \text{ cubic feet}$$

We can be more specific by rewriting the equation as

$$\text{Volume of blood} + \text{volume of medical supply kits} \\ + \text{volume of food} + \text{volume of water} = 6,000$$

If we let

x_1 = number of containers of blood
x_2 = number of containers of medical supply kits

x_3 = number of containers of food

x_4 = number of containers of water

the equation can be stated in its correct mathematical form as

$$20x_1 + 30x_2 + 8x_3 + 6x_4 = 6,000$$

Verify that *each term* on the left side of the equation is formed by using the relationship

$$\frac{\text{Total volume}}{\text{of item } j} = \left(\begin{array}{c}\text{volume per container} \\ \text{of item } j\end{array}\right)\left(\begin{array}{c}\text{number of containers} \\ \text{of item } j\end{array}\right)$$

Follow-up Exercises

3.70 In a realistic sense, what are the ranges of possible values for *each* of the four variables? What are the maximum and minimum possible quantities of each item?

3.71 Assume that the plane can only carry 40,000 pounds of cargo and that the items weigh 150, 100, 60, and 70 pounds per container, respectively. State the equation whose solution set contains all combinations of the four items which will add up to equal the weight capacity of the plane.

Investment Portfolio A local university has $5 million to invest in stocks. The board of trustees has approved six different types of stocks in which the university may invest. The current prices per share for each type of stock are indicated below. Determine the equation for which the solution set includes all the different combinations of the six stocks which could be purchased for exactly $5 million.

Example 3.25

Stock	Price per Share
1	$ 35
2	60
3	125
4	100
5	500
6	250

The general form of the equation should be total dollars spent on the six stocks equals $5 million, or more specifically

Solution

Total dollars spent on stock 1 + total dollars spent on stock 2
+ · · · · + total dollars spent on stock 6 = $5 million

The basic decision to be made concerns the number of shares of each security to be purchased so as to expend the full $5 million. Therefore let's generalize our variables as

$$x_j = \text{number of shares purchased of stock } j$$

where j = 1, 2, 3, 4, 5, or 6

Using these variables, we state the equation as

$$35x_1 + 60x_2 + 125x_3 + 100x_4 + 500x_5 + 250x_6 = 5 \text{ million}$$

Note that each term on the left side of the equation has the form

Total dollars spent on stock j
$$= (\text{price per share})(\text{number of shares purchased})$$

Follow-up Exercises

3.72 In a realistic sense, what are the maximum and minimum allowable values for each variable in the equation developed above?

3.73 The expected annual dividends per share of each of the above stocks are shown below. Assume that the board of trustees desires to earn annual dividends of $500,000 from its investments. Using the same variables as in the example, develop the equation whose solution set includes all possible combinations of the six stocks which will generate annual dividends equal to $500,000.

Stock	1	2	3	4	5	6
Expected Annual Dividend	$2	$3	$5	$3.25	$50	$20

Example 3.26 **Court Scheduling** A metropolitan district court sorts its cases into three categories. Court records have enabled the court clerk to provide estimates of the average number of hours required to process each type of case. Type 1 cases average 16 hours, type 2 average 8 hours, and type 3 average 4.5 hours. For the coming month 850 hours are available in the six different courtrooms in the building. Determine an equation whose solution set includes all the different combinations of the three types of cases which would schedule the courts to their capacity.

Solution The general form of the equation should be

$$\text{Total court hours scheduled} = 850$$

Letting x_1, x_2, and x_3 equal the number of cases scheduled of Types 1, 2, and 3, respectively, the equation is

$$16x_1 + 8x_2 + 4.5x_3 = 850$$

Example 3.27 **Nutrition Planning** A dietician at a local school is planning luncheon menus. He has eight choices of items which may be served at any one meal. One concern of the dietician is meeting various nutritional requirements. Our dietician is interested in determining the various quantities of each of the eight foods which would provide exactly 45 milligrams of a required vitamin. The vitamin content of each of the eight food items is shown below. Determine the equation whose solution set satisfies this requirement.

Food Type	1	2	3	4	5	6	7	8
mg/Serving	5	7.5	3	4.5	9	10	2.5	6

Letting x_j = number of servings of food j, where $j = 1, 2, 3, 4, 5, 6, 7$, or 8, the equation is

Solution

$$5x_1 + 7.5x_2 + 3x_3 + 4.5x_4 + 9x_5 + 10x_6 + 2.5x_7 + 6x_8 = 45$$

Follow-up Exercises

3.74 In which of the last four examples should there be concern only with integer values for the variables?

3.75 A student is taking five courses and is facing the crunch of final exams. She estimates that she has 40 hours available to study. If x_j = the number of hours allocated to studying for course j, state the equation whose solution set specifies all possible allocations of time among the five courses which will exhaust the 40 hours available.

3.76 *Product-Mix* A firm produces three products. Product A requires 8 hours of production time, product B requires 5.5 hours, and product C requires 6.5 hours for each unit produced. If 600 hours are available during the coming week, determine the equation whose solution set specifies all possible amounts or quantities of the three products which can be produced using the 600 hours.

3.77 *Transportation* A manufacturer distributes its product to four different wholesalers. The monthly capacity is 34,000 units of the product. Decisions need to be made about how many units should be shipped to each of the wholesalers. Determine the equation whose solution set specifies the different quantities which might be shipped if all 34,000 units are to be distributed.

3.78 *Advertising* A national firm is beginning an advertising campaign using television, radio, and newspapers. The goal is to have 10 million people see their advertisements. Past experience indicates that for every $1,000 allocated to TV, radio, and newspaper advertising, 25,000, 18,000, and 15,000 people, respectively, will see the advertisement. The decisions that need to be made involve how much money should be allocated to each form of advertising in order to reach 10 million people. Determine the equation whose solution set specifies all the different advertising allocations which will result in the achievement of this goal.

3.79 *Agricultural Planning* An agricultural company has a goal of harvesting 500,000 bushels of soybeans during the coming year. The company has three farms available to meet this goal. Because of climate differences and other factors, the yields per acre in the different locations are 25, 23, and 27 bushels, respectively, for farms 1, 2, and 3. The decision which needs to be made concerns how many acres should be planted in soybeans at each farm in order to meet the company's goal. State the equation which allows for specifying the different possibilities for meeting the 500,000-bushel goal.

CHAPTER CHECKLIST

If you have read all sections of this chapter, you should

_____ Be able to recognize *linear equations* and distinguish them from *non-linear equations*

_____ Understand the meaning of *solution sets* for linear equations

_____ Be able to graph linear equations involving two variables

_____ Understand the concept of *slope* and its interpretation

_____ Be totally familiar with the *slope-intercept form* of a linear equation

_____ Be able to determine the equation of a straight line if given sufficient information

_____ Be familiar with the graphical representation of linear equations in three dimensions

_____ Have some difficulty in graphing linear equations involving four or more variables

_____ Be able to formulate equations which represent linear relationships in word problems or applications

KEY TERMS AND CONCEPTS

linear equation

solution set

x intercept

y intercept

slope

two-point formula

slope-intercept form
  of linear equation

coefficient

slope relationship
  for perpendicular lines

plane

3-space (three dimensions)

hyperplane

n-space

IMPORTANT FORMULAS

$$ax + by = c \tag{3.1}$$
$$a_1x_1 + a_2x_2 + a_3x_3 + \cdots + a_nx_n = b \tag{3.2}$$
$$m = \frac{y_2 - y_1}{x_2 - x_1} \tag{3.8}$$
$$y = mx + i \tag{3.10}$$

ADDITIONAL EXERCISES

Exercises 3.80 to 3.84 are related to Sec. 3.1.

In Exercises 3.80 to 3.82, determine whether the following equations are linear.

3.80 $y^2 = 3x + 7$ **3.81** $(a + b)(b - 7) = 5/a$

3.82 $5x_1 + 7x_2 = x_2/x_1$

3.83 A company manufactures two different products, A and B. Each unit of product A costs $5 to produce, and each unit of product B costs $3. The company insists that total costs be $100.

(a) Define the cost equation which states that the total cost of producing x units of product A and y units of product B equals $100.

(b) Identify a pair of values for x and y which satisfies this equation.

(c) Assuming the company has agreed to fill an order for 8 units of product A, how many units of product B should be produced if total costs are to be kept at $100?

(d) Use set notation to specify membership in the solution set P for the equation defined in part a.

3.84 Consider the equation $5x + 17y - z = 100$ as a multivariable equation in the form of Eq. (3.2).

(a) What are a_1, a_2, and a_3?

(b) If $z = 2$, identify a pair of values for x and y which satisfies the equation.

(c) If $x = 20$, find the pair of values for y and z which satisfies the equation.

(d) Use set notation to specify membership in the solution set P.

Exercises 3.85 to 3.93 are related to Sec. 3.2.

In Exercises 3.85 to 3.88, identify the x and y intercepts if they exist.

3.85 $5x = 3y$ **3.86** $-x - y = 0$

3.87 $\dfrac{3x + 17}{9} = 4y$ **3.88** $7 + 2x = 0$

For Exercises 3.89 to 3.92, graph each of the linear equations.

3.89 $x = y$ **3.90** $2y = 0$

3.91 $x + 3y = 7y/2$ **3.92** $10y - x = 7$

3.93 Find the slope of the straight line which passes through the points $(5, 7)$ and $(2, 8)$.

3.94 Find the slope of the line segment connecting points $(2, 3)$ and $(1, 4)$.

3.95 Compute the slopes of the lines represented by the equations $5y + 7x = 15$ and $12 = 2y + x$. If these linear equations were to be graphically represented, which line would be steeper?

Exercises 3.96 to 3.100 are related to Sec. 3.3.

In Exercises 3.96 to 3.99, (a) rewrite the equations in slope-intercept form, (b) identify the slope and y intercept, and (c) graph the equation.

3.96 $4x + 3y = 20$ **3.97** $x = -y$

3.98 $10x - 7 = 0$ **3.99** $3 - x = 2y/5$

3.100 A local dairy association enlists the help of a marketing research firm to predict the demand for milk. The research firm finds that the local demand for milk can be predicted by the equation $q = -3{,}000p + 4{,}200$, where p represents the price per quart (in dollars) and q represents the number of quarts purchased per week.

(a) Graph the equation.

(b) Identify the slope and y intercept.

(c) Interpret the meaning of the slope and y intercept in this application.

Exercises 3.101 to 3.106 are related to Sec. 3.4.

For Exercises 3.97 to 3.104, determine the slope-intercept form of the equation and restate the equation in the standard form of Eq. (3.1).

3.101 slope $= 1$, y intercept $= -5$

3.102 m is undefined, the line passes through $(2, 1)$

3.103 $(6, 1)$ and $(3, 9)$ lie on the line

3.104 $(2, w)$ and $(5, w)$ lie on the line

3.105 For the equation $3x - y = 7$, find the equation of the parallel line passing through the point $(2, 11)$.

3.106 In attempting to predict the demand for a particular style of shoe, a retail shoe store finds that 50 pairs are sold per week if the price per pair is $25; and when the price rises to $30 per pair, only 30 pairs are sold.

(a) If price is to be plotted on the horizontal axis, determine the slope-intercept equation of the equation for demand. Restate the equation in the standard form of Eq. (3.1).

(b) Using this equation, predict how many pairs of shoes will be sold if the price is lowered to $15.

Exercises 3.107 to 3.108 are related to Sec. 3.5.

3.107 For the equation $3x_1 - x_2 + 4x_3 = 10$, where does the plane cross the x_1, x_2, and x_3 axes? Graphically sketch the plane which represents the equation.

3.108 Sketch the plane which represents the equation $5x_2 = 25$.

Exercises 3.109 to 3.111 are related to Sec. 3.6.

3.109 A retail store sells four products. Let x_1, x_2, x_3, and x_4 represent the number of units sold, respectively, of the four products. The profits earned from each unit sold of the four products are $20, $5, $8, and $2, respectively. Target profits for the firm are $20,000.

(a) Using x_1, x_2, x_3, and x_4, define an equation which states that total profit from selling the four products equals $20,000.

(b) Give the range of values (maximum and minimum) possible for each variable in the equation developed in part a.

3.110 A woman who has recently inherited $10,000 decides to invest her inheritance in stocks. She is considering eight stocks, the prices of which are given below.

Stock	1	2	3	4	5	6	7	8
Price per Share	$12	$150	$76.50	$25	$8	$57	$200	$42

Determine the equation whose solution set contains all possible combinations of the eight stocks which can be purchased for $10,000. (Be sure to define your variables.)

3.111 *Personnel Management* The head of personnel has been given a budget allotment of $150,000 to staff an engineering department. Four types of employees are needed: senior engineers at an annual salary of $35,000 each, junior engineers at an annual salary of $20,000 each, drafters at an annual salary of $15,000 each, and secretaries at a salary of $9,000 each. Write an equation whose solution set contains the possible combinations of employees which could be hired for $150,000. (Be sure to define your variables.)

CHAPTER TEST

1 A buyer for an exclusive steak and lobster restaurant has $500 to spend for a weekly meat order. Steak can be ordered at $3 per pound and lobster can be ordered at $2.50 per pound.

(*a*) Define an equation whose solution set contains all possible combinations of steak and lobster which could be purchased for $500.

(*b*) Give a pair of values for your variables which satisfy the above equation.

2 You are given the equation $10x + 2y = 6$.

(*a*) What are the x and y intercepts, if they exist?

(*b*) Graph the equation.

3 You are given the equation $x - y = (2x + 2y)/5$.

(*a*) Rewrite it in the slope-intercept form.

(*b*) Identify the slope.

(*c*) Graph the equation.

4 Find the slope and y intercept of the line passing through the points $(10, 7)$ and $(4, 10)$.

5 A producer has a monthly supply of 500,000 pounds of steel to use as a raw material for each of four products. The steel input required for each unit of these products is 10,000, 2,000, 1,500 and 8,000 pounds, respectively. If p_1, p_2, p_3, and p_4 equal the number of units produced of each product, define the equation whose solution set includes the possible combinations of the four products which would exhaust the monthly supply of steel.

6 Determine the equation of the line which passes through the origin and which is perpendicular to the line representing $6x - 2y = 12$.

CHAPTER OBJECTIVES   After reading this chapter, you should be familiar with the characteristics of systems of linear equations; you should have a sense of the graphical characteristics of systems that involve two and three variables; you should be familiar with the different types of solution sets which can exist for a system of equations; and you should be able to determine the solution set for a system of equations by one or more methods.

INTRODUCTION   4.1

Systems of Equations

A system of equations is a set consisting of more than one equation. In many applications in business and economics we must deal with systems of equations. As such, we are often concerned with analyzing the interactions among equations. For example, in the last chapter, Example 3.24 was concerned with airlifting emergency supplies into a South American city. This equation was formulated to represent the various quantities of each item which would fill the plane to its volume capacity:

$$20x_1 + 30x_2 + 8x_3 + 6x_4 = 6{,}000$$

Exercise 3.71 introduced data concerning the weight capacity of the plane and the weight per container of each item. Your answer to that exercise should have been the equation

$$150x_1 + 100x_2 + 60x_3 + 70x_4 = 40,000$$

The solution set for this equation contains values for the four variables which represent all quantities of the various items which would fill the plane to its weight capacity of 40,000 pounds. Given these two equations, it may be profitable to determine whether there are combinations of the four items which would *simultaneously* fill the plane to both its weight and volume capacities.

The *dimensions* of a system of equations are defined as follows. If a system of equations consists of m equations and n variables, we say that this system is an "m by n" system, or that it has dimensions $(m \times n)$. A system of equations involving two equations and two variables is defined as having dimension (2×2). A system consisting of 15 equations and 10 variables is said to be a (15×10) system.

Solution Sets

In solving systems of equations, we are interested in identifying values of the variables that satisfy all equations in the system at the same time. For this reason, the group of equations that we solve is often called a *simultaneous* system of equations. For example, given the two equations

$$5x + 10y = 20$$
$$3x + 4y = 10$$

we may wish to identify whether there exist any values of x and y which satisfy both equations at the same time. Or, stated in set notation, we would want to identify the solution set S where

$$S = \{(x, y) | 5x + 10y = 20 \text{ and } 3x + 4y = 10\}$$

As you will see in this chapter, the solution set S for a system of equations may be a null set, a finite set, or an infinite set.

There are quite a few solution procedures which may be used in solving systems of simultaneous equations. Some books present five or six different ways of solving simultaneous equations. However, the most important thing is that we have the ability to solve a system, period! Therefore, we will concentrate on two different procedures. Other procedures will be presented in either examples or appendices.

In this chapter we will develop solution procedures starting with the simplest systems—two equations and two variables—emphasizing both the graphical and algebraic aspects of each situation. These procedures will be extended later in the chapter to acquaint us with how larger systems of equations are handled. We will also discuss a variety of applications of systems of equations.

Graphical Analysis

From Chap. 3 we know that a linear equation involving two variables graphs as a straight line. Thus a (2×2) system of equations is represented by two straight lines in two dimensions. In solving for the values of the two variables which satisfy *both* equations, we are graphically trying to determine if the two lines representing the equations have any points in common.

For (2×2) systems of equations three different types of solution sets might exist. Given that two lines are graphed in a plane, Fig. 4.1 illustrates the three possibilities. In Fig. 4.1*a*, the two lines intersect, or cross one another. The *coordinates* of the point of intersection (x_1, y_1) represent the solution for the equations represented by the two lines. When there is just one pair of values for the variables which satisfy the system of equations, the system is said to have a *unique solution*.

In Fig. 4.1*b*, the two lines are parallel to each other. You should remember from the last chapter that parallel lines have the same slope; and provided that they have different y intercepts, the lines have no points in common. Graphically the lines never cross one another. If a (2×2) system of equations has these characteristics, the system is said to have *no solution*. That is, there are no values for the variables which satisfy both equations. The equations in such a system are said to be *inconsistent*.

The final possibility for a (2×2) system is illustrated in Fig. 4.1*c*. In this case both equations graph as the same line, and they are considered to be *equivalent equations*. Being represented by the same line implies that both lines have the same slope *and* the same y intercept. Although this situation is relatively uncommon in an application, two equations *can* look very different from each other and still be equivalent to one another. For example, the two equations

$$-6x + 12y = -24$$
and
$$1.5x - 3y = 6$$

are equivalent. Verify that the slope and the y intercept are the same for both. Can you determine how the two equations are related?

When the situation in Fig. 4.1*c* exists, an infinite number of points

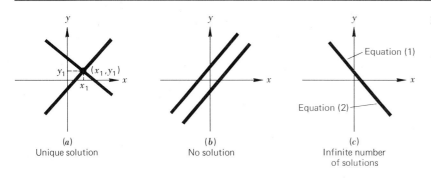

(a)	*(b)*	*(c)*
Unique solution	No solution	Infinite number of solutions

FIGURE 4.1

are common to the two lines and the system is said to have an *infinite number of solutions*.

Another way of summarizing the three cases illustrated in Fig. 4.1 is as follows:

In a (2 × 2) system of linear equations let m_1 and m_2 represent the respective slopes of the two lines and i_1 and i_2 represent the respective y intercepts.

1 There is a *unique solution* to the system if $m_1 \neq m_2$.

2 There is *no solution* to the system if $m_1 = m_2$ but $i_1 \neq i_2$.

3 There are an *infinite number of solutions* if $m_1 = m_2$ and $i_1 = i_2$.

Graphical Solutions

Graphical solution approaches are certainly valid for two-variable systems of equations. However, you must be accurate in your graphics. The following example illustrates a graphical solution.

Example 4.1 Graphically determine the solution to the system of equations

$$2x + 4y = 20 \qquad (4.1)$$
$$3x + y = 10 \qquad (4.2)$$

Solution The coordinates of the x and y intercepts are, respectively, (10, 0) and (0, 5) for Eq. (4.1). Similarly, the intercepts for Eq. (4.2) are $(\frac{10}{3}, 0)$ and (0, 10). When these are plotted in Fig. 4.2 and connected, the two lines appear to cross at (2, 4).

The problem with graphical solutions occurs when it is difficult to read the precise coordinates of the points of intersection. This is especially true when the coordinates are not integers. This is why algebraic solution procedures are generally viewed as being superior from the standpoint of identifying *exact* solutions. However, whether you use graphical or algebraic procedures, there is always a check on your answer: substitute your answer into the original equations to see if they are satisfied by the values. Substituting $x = 2$ and $y = 4$ into Eqs. (4.1) and (4.2), we get

$$2(2) + 4(4) = 20$$
or
$$20 = 20$$
and
$$3(2) + (4) = 10$$
or
$$10 = 10$$

Therefore our solution checks.

The Elimination Procedure

One popular solution method is the *elimination procedure*, which uses the operations of multiplication and addition. Given a (2 × 2) system of

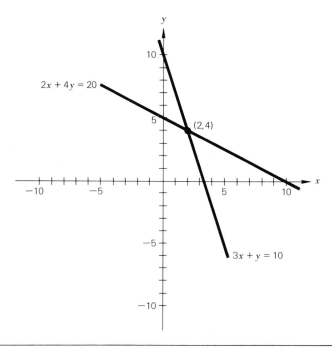

FIGURE 4.2

equations, the two equations, or multiples of the two equations, are added so as to *eliminate* one of the two variables. The resultant equation is stated in terms of the remaining variable. This equation can be solved for the remaining variable, the value of which can be substituted back into one of the original equations to solve for the value of the eliminated variable. The solution process is demonstrated in the following example, after which the procedure will be formalized.

Solve the system of equations from Example 4.1.　　　　**Example 4.2**

The original system was　　　　**Solution**

$$2x + 4y = 20 \qquad (4.1)$$
$$3x + y = 10 \qquad (4.2)$$

The objective of the elimination procedure is to eliminate one of the two variables by adding (multiples of) the equations. Confirm that adding the original equations results in the new equation

$$5x + 5y = 30$$

which still contains both variables.

Note that if we *multiply* Eq. (4.2) by -4 and *add* the resulting equation to Eq. (4.1), we get Eq. (4.3):

$$
\begin{array}{ll}
2x + 4y = 20 & (4.1) \\
-12x - 4y = -40 & (4.2a) \\
\hline
-10x = -20 & (4.3)
\end{array}
$$

Equation (4.3) contains the variable x only, and we can solve this equation to find the value of $x = 2$. Substituting this value for x into one of the original equations—let's select Eq. (4.1)—we find that

$$2(2) + 4y = 20$$
$$4y = 16$$

or

$$y = 4$$

Therefore the unique solution to the system, as we determined earlier, occurs when $x = 2$ and $y = 4$.

NOTE
It is advisable always to substitute back into one of the *original* equations to guard against careless arithmetic errors. If, for example, we had failed to multiply the right side of Eq. (4.2) by -4, the following would have occurred:

$$2x + 4y = 20 \qquad (4.1)$$
$$-12x - 4y = 10 \qquad (4.2a)$$
$$\overline{-10x \qquad\;\; = 30} \qquad (4.3)$$

and

$$x = -3$$

If we had substituted $x = -3$ *back into Eq. (4.2a)*, the value for y would have been computed as

$$-12(-3) - 4y = 10$$
$$-4y = -26$$
$$y = 6.5$$

This is not the solution to the original system. It *is* the solution to the system consisting of Eqs. (4.1) and (4.2a). Because of the multiplication error, this system is not equivalent to the original system.

   Checking your solution values in *all* the original equations is the best check on your answer.

EXERCISE
Verify that the solution is exactly the same if x is selected for elimination. To eliminate x multiply equations (4.1) and (4.2) by -3 and 2, respectively.

   The elimination procedure can be generalized as follows for a (2×2) system of equations:

1 Multiply (if necessary) the equations by constants so that the coefficients on one of the variables are the negatives of one another in the two equations.

2 Add the two resulting equations.

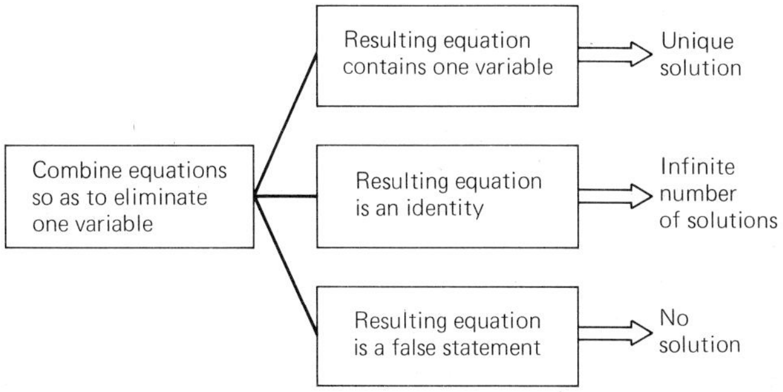

FIGURE 4.3
Elimination procedure for 2×2 systems

3 *a* **If adding the equations results in a new equation having one variable, there is a *unique solution* to the system. Solve for the value of the remaining variable, and substitute this value back into one of the original equations to determine the value of the variable that was originally eliminated.**

b **If adding the equations results in an identity, i.e., an equation that is always true, such as $0 = 0$ or $3 = 3$, the two original equations are *equivalent* to each other and there are an *infinite number of solutions* to the system.**

c **If adding the equations results in a false statement, say, $0 = 5$, the equations are *inconsistent* and there is *no solution set*.**

Solve the following system of equations by the elimination procedure. | **Example 4.3**

$$3x - 2y = 6 \qquad (4.4)$$
$$-15x + 10y = -30 \qquad (4.5)$$

Choosing x as the variable to eliminate, let's multiply Eq. (4.4) by 5 and | **Solution**
add the resulting equations:

$$
\begin{array}{rl}
15x - 10y = 30 & (4.4a) \\
-15x + 10y = -30 & (4.5) \\
\hline
0 = 0 &
\end{array}
$$

When Eqs. (4.4a) and (4.5) are added, both variables are eliminated on the left side of the equation and we are left with the identity $0 = 0$. From step 3b of the solution procedure we conclude that the two equations are equivalent and there are an infinite number of solutions. You should recall from the last chapter that members of the solution set can be identified by assuming *any* value for one of the two variables and solving for the corresponding value of the other variable.

Solve the following system of equations by the elimination procedure. | **Example 4.4**

$$6x - 12y = 24 \qquad (4.6)$$
$$-1.5x + 3y = 9 \qquad (4.7)$$

Solution

Multiplying Eq. (4.7) by 4 and adding this multiple to Eq. (4.6) yields

$$6x - 12y = 24 \qquad (4.6)$$
$$\underline{-6x + 12y = 36} \qquad (4.7a)$$
$$0 = 60$$

Since $0 \neq 60$, a false statement or inequality has resulted. Thus according to step 3c of the solution procedure, there is no solution to the system of equations.

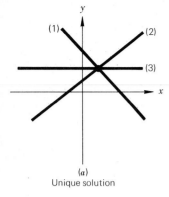

(a)
Unique solution

(m × 2) Systems

When there are more than two $(m > 2)$ equations involving two variables, each equation still graphs as a line in two dimensions. For example, Fig. 4.4 illustrates two (3×2) systems. In Fig. 4.4a the three lines all intersect at the same point, and there is a unique solution. In Fig. 4.4b there are points which are common to different pairs of lines, but there is no point common to all three, which means that there is no solution. A possible, but unlikely, situation is that the m equations are all equivalent to one another and all graph as the same line.

The solution procedure is relatively simple for these systems.

1 Take any two of the m equations and solve them simultaneously.

2 a If in step 1 there is a unique solution, substitute the values found into the remaining equations in the system. If each remaining equation is satisfied by these values, they represent a unique solution. If the values fail to satisfy *any* of the remaining equations, there is no solution to the system.

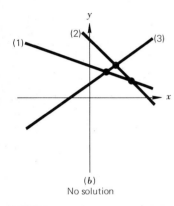

(b)
No solution

FIGURE 4.4

b If in step 1 there is no solution, there is no solution for the system.

c If in step 1 there are an infinite number of solutions, two different equations should be selected and step 1 should be repeated.

Example 4.5

Determine the solution set for the following system of equations:

$$x + 2y = 8 \qquad (4.8)$$
$$2x - 3y = -5 \qquad (4.9)$$
$$-5x + 6y = 8 \qquad (4.10)$$
$$x + y = 7 \qquad (4.11)$$

Solution

The (2×2) system consisting of Eqs. (4.8) and (4.9) is solved by multiplying Eq. (4.8) by -2 and adding it to Eq. (4.9), or

$$-2x - 4y = -16$$
$$\underline{2x - 3y = -5}$$
$$-7y = -21$$
$$y = 3$$

Substituting back into Eq. (4.8) yields

$$x + 2(3) = 8$$
or $$x = 2$$

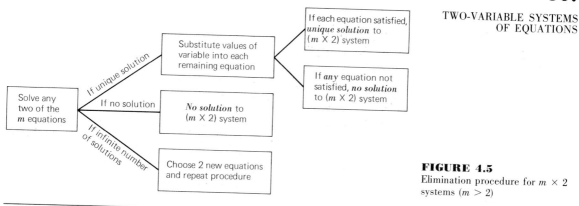

FIGURE 4.5
Elimination procedure for $m \times 2$
systems $(m > 2)$

The solution $(2, 3)$ is tested by substituting into Eq. (4.10). Since

$$-5(2) + 6(3) = 8$$

the point $(2, 3)$ satisfies the first three equations. Substituting into Eq. (4.11) gives

$$2 + 3 \neq 7$$
or
$$5 \neq 7$$

Since $(2, 3)$ does not satisfy Eq. (4.11), there is no unique solution to the system of equations. Figure 4.6 illustrates the situation.

FIGURE 4.6

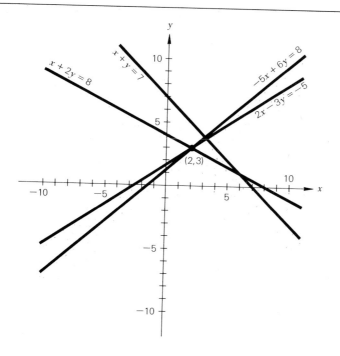

Follow-up Exercises

For the following pairs of equations draw conclusions about the type of solution set—unique, infinite, or no solution—which will exist when the systems are solved. Do this by computing the slope and y intercept for each line and comparing them.

4.1 $3x + 4y = 12$
$\quad\quad 4x + 3y = 12$

4.3 $4x + 2y = 10$
$\quad\quad 2x + y = 5$

4.5 $\quad 6x + 9y = 36$
$\quad\quad -2x - 3y = -24$

4.7 $\quad\quad\quad 2x = y - 10$
$\quad\quad 20 - 2y + 4x = 0$

4.2 $x - y = 0$
$\quad\quad x + y = 0$

4.4 $x + 2y = 12$
$\quad\quad 2y = 10 - x$

4.6 $\quad 3x - 5y = 15$
$\quad\quad -15x + 25y = -10$

4.8 $\quad x + y = 10$
$\quad\quad 2x - 2y = 20$

For each of the following systems of equations, solve graphically and check your answer.

4.9 $\quad\quad x = 4$
$\quad\quad x + y = 10$

4.11 $3x + 6y = 15$
$\quad\quad 2x - 3y = -4$

4.10 $2x - 4y = 12$
$\quad\quad x + y = 0$

4.12 $x - 2y = 8$
$\quad\quad x + 2y = -12$

4.13 Graphically verify the solution to Example 4.2.
4.14 Graphically verify the solution to Example 4.3.
4.15 Graphically verify the solution to Example 4.4.

In Exercises 4.16 to 4.23, solve by the elimination procedure.

4.16 $6x - 2y = 14$
$\quad\quad 5x + 2y = 19$

4.18 $7x + 2y = 2$
$\quad\quad 3x + 5y = -9.5$

4.20 $-4.5x + 3y = 18$
$\quad\quad 3x - 2y = 12$

4.22 $9x + 2y = +3$
$\quad\quad x - y = -7$

4.17 $x - y = 7$
$\quad\quad x + 3y = -5$

4.19 $-3x + 2y = 8$
$\quad\quad 12x - 8y = -24$

4.21 $\quad x - y = 10$
$\quad\quad -5x + 5y = -50$

4.23 $15x - 9y = 81$
$\quad\quad -5x + 3y = -27$

Solve each of the following systems of equations.

4.24 $3x - 5y = -23$
$\quad\quad x + y = 3$
$\quad\quad 6x + 2y = 2$

4.26 $\quad 20x - 5y = 10$
$\quad\quad -4x + y = -4$
$\quad\quad 2x - 0.5y = 8$

4.28 $\quad x + 5y = 13$
$\quad\quad 4x + y = -5$
$\quad\quad 3x - 2y = -12$
$\quad\quad -7x + 6y = 32$

4.30 $\quad x - 2y = 2$
$\quad\quad 5x + 2y = 34$
$\quad\quad -2x - y = -14$
$\quad\quad 3x - 7y = 4$
$\quad\quad x + y = 8$
$\quad\quad -4x + 3y = -18$

4.25 $4x - 2y = 12$
$\quad\quad x + 3y = 17$
$\quad\quad 3x + 4y = 27$

4.27 $\quad x + y = 10$
$\quad\quad 2x - 4y = -16$
$\quad\quad 3x + 7y = 41$
$\quad\quad 6x - 5y = -13$

4.29 $\quad 10x + 6y = -70$
$\quad\quad 2x - 5y = 17$
$\quad\quad 0.5x + 3y = -17$
$\quad\quad 4x - 6y = 20$

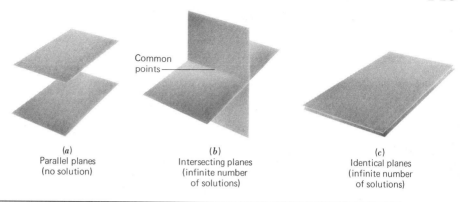

(a)
Parallel planes
(no solution)

Common points

(b)
Intersecting planes
(infinite number
of solutions)

(c)
Identical planes
(infinite number
of solutions)

FIGURE 4.7
2 × 3 systems

THREE-VARIABLE SYSTEMS 4.3

Graphical Analysis

With three variables each linear equation graphs as a *plane* in three dimensions. Again, in solving a system of three-variable equations, we are looking for any points common to the planes. Let's first consider (2 × 3) systems, or those represented by two planes. For (2 × 3) systems there cannot be a unique solution. There is no way in which two planes can intersect at only one point. Think about it! Therefore the solution sets for these systems will contain either no elements (no solution) or an infinite number of solutions. Figure 4.7 illustrates different possibilities for these types of systems.

For (*m* × 3) systems, where $m \geq 3$, it is possible to have all three types of solution sets. There can be a unique solution. Look up at a corner in the ceiling of the room. If you think of the two walls meeting in the corner and the ceiling as representing three equations, then the corner of the ceiling is the one point common to these three planes. Figure 4.8 illustrates different solution possibilities for (3 × 3) systems.

FIGURE 4.8
3 × 3 systems

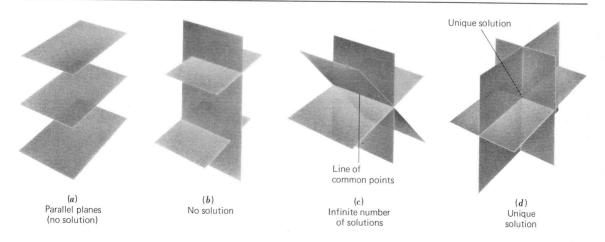

(a)
Parallel planes
(no solution)

(b)
No solution

Line of
common points

(c)
Infinite number
of solutions

Unique solution

(d)
Unique
solution

Elimination Procedure for (3 × 3) Systems

The elimination procedure for (3 × 3) systems is similar to that for
(2 × 2) systems. The aim is to start with the (3 × 3) system and to reduce this to an equivalent system having two variables and two equations. With one of the three variables eliminated, the same procedure
as used for (2 × 2) systems is employed to eliminate a second variable,
resulting in a (1 × 1) system. After you solve for the remaining variable,
its value is substituted sequentially back through the (2 × 2) system
and finally the (3 × 3) system to determine the values of the other two
variables. Figure 4.9 illustrates schematically the process. The elimination procedure for a (3 × 3) system is as follows:

**1 Add multiples of any two of the three equations in order to elimi-
nate one of the three variables. The result should be an equation involving the other two variables.**

**2 Repeat step 1 with *another* pair of the original equations, elimi-
nating the same variable as in step 1. This second pair of equations
will include *one* of the two equations used in step 1 and the equation
not used in step 1.**

**3 The results of steps 1 and 2 should be a (2 × 2) system. Use the pro-
cedure for (2 × 2) systems to determine the values for the remaining
two variables.**

**4 Substitute the values of these two variables into one of the original
equations. Solve for the value of the third variable.**

If during any phase of the elimination procedure an identity results
[see step 3*b* of the (2 × 2) procedure], then the solution set contains an
infinite number of elements. An exception to this is the case where step
1 results in an identity and step 2 a false statement. If at any stage a
false statement results [step 3*c* of the (2 × 2) procedure], then there is
no solution to the original system of equations.

FIGURE 4.9
Elimination procedure for 3 × 3
systems

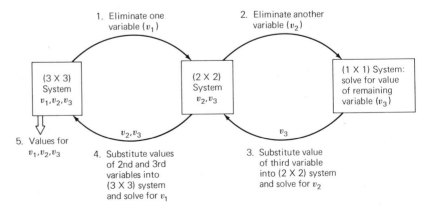

1. Eliminate one
   variable (v_1)

2. Eliminate another
   variable (v_2)

(3 × 3)
System
v_1, v_2, v_3

(2 × 2)
System
v_2, v_3

(1 × 1) System:
solve for value
of remaining
variable (v_3)

5. Values for
v_1, v_2, v_3

v_2, v_3

v_3

4. Substitute values
of 2nd and 3rd
variables into
(3 × 3) system
and solve for v_1

3. Substitute value
of third variable
into (2 × 2) system
and solve for v_2

Unique Solution Determine the solution set for the following system of equations.

Example 4.6

$$x_1 + x_2 + x_3 = 6 \tag{4.12}$$
$$2x_1 - x_2 + 3x_3 = 4 \tag{4.13}$$
$$4x_1 + 5x_2 - 10x_3 = 13 \tag{4.14}$$

Although it makes no difference which variable is eliminated first, let's eliminate x_2. If Eqs. (4.12) and (4.13) are added, the resultant Eq. (4.15) is stated in terms of x_1 and x_3:

$$\begin{array}{r} x_1 + x_2 + x_3 = 6 \\ 2x_1 - x_2 + 3x_3 = 4 \\ \hline 3x_1 \qquad + 4x_3 = 10 \end{array} \tag{4.15}$$

Multiplying Eq. (4.13) by $+5$ and adding it to Eq. (4.14) yields the new Eq. (4.16) as follows:

$$\begin{array}{r} 10x_1 - 5x_2 + 15x_3 = 20 \\ 4x_1 + 5x_2 - 10x_3 = 13 \\ \hline 14x_1 \qquad + 5x_3 = 33 \end{array} \tag{4.16}$$

Since x_2 has been eliminated, the system has been reduced to the (2×2) system

$$3x_1 + 4x_3 = 10 \tag{4.15}$$
$$14x_1 + 5x_3 = 33 \tag{4.16}$$

By proceeding as we did in Sec. 4.2, x_3 can be eliminated if we multiply Eq. (4.15) by $+5$ and Eq. (4.16) by -4. When the two equations are added, x_3 is eliminated and Eq. (4.17) is formed:

$$\begin{array}{r} 15x_1 + 20x_3 = 50 \\ -56x_1 - 20x_3 = -132 \\ \hline -41x_1 \qquad = -82 \end{array} \tag{4.17}$$

Solving Eq. (4.17) for x_1, we get $x_1 = 2$. If this value is substituted into Eq. (4.15), the value of x_3 is determined in the following manner:

$$3(2) + 4x_3 = 10$$
$$4x_3 = 4$$
$$x_3 = 1$$

Substituting the values of $x_1 = 2$ and $x_3 = 1$ into Eq. (4.12) yields

$$2 + x_2 + 1 = 6$$

or

$$x_2 = 3$$

You should verify that the solution set consists of one unique point where $x_1 = 2$, $x_2 = 3$, and $x_3 = 1$ by substituting these values into Eqs. (4.13) and (4.14).

No Solution Determine the solution set for this system of equations:

Example 4.7

$$-2x_1 + x_2 + 3x_3 = 12 \tag{4.18}$$
$$x_1 + 2x_2 + 5x_3 = 10 \tag{4.19}$$
$$6x_1 - 3x_2 - 9x_3 = 24 \tag{4.20}$$

Solution   Variable x_1 can be eliminated by multiplying Eq. (4.19) by $+2$ and adding it to Eq. (4.18) as follows:

$$\begin{array}{r} -2x_1 + x_2 + 3x_3 = 12 \\ 2x_1 + 4x_2 + 10x_3 = 20 \\ \hline 5x_2 + 13x_3 = 32 \end{array} \qquad (4.21)$$

Similarly, x_1 can be eliminated by multiplying Eq. (4.19) by -6 and adding the resulting equation to Eq. (4.20), or

$$\begin{array}{r} -6x_1 - 12x_2 - 30x_3 = -60 \\ 6x_1 - 3x_2 - 9x_3 = 24 \\ \hline -15x_2 - 39x_3 = -36 \end{array} \qquad (4.22)$$

Eliminating x_1 leaves the (2×2) system

$$\begin{array}{rr} 5x_2 + 13x_3 = & 32 \\ -15x_2 - 39x_3 = & -36 \end{array} \qquad \begin{array}{l} (4.21) \\ (4.22) \end{array}$$

To eliminate x_2, Eq. (4.21) is multiplied by $+3$ and added to Eq. (4.22), or

$$\begin{array}{rr} 15x_2 + 39x_3 = & 96 \\ -15x_2 - 39x_3 = & -36 \\ \hline 0 = & 60 \end{array} \qquad (4.23)$$

Note that Eq. (4.23) is a false statement, and this implies that there is no solution to the original system of equations.

Example 4.8   **Infinite Number of Solutions**   Determine the solution set for the system of equations

$$\begin{array}{r} x_1 + x_2 + x_3 = 20 \\ 2x_1 - 3x_2 + x_3 = -5 \\ 6x_1 - 4x_2 + 4x_3 = 30 \end{array} \qquad \begin{array}{l} (4.24) \\ (4.25) \\ (4.26) \end{array}$$

Solution   Verify that x_3 can be eliminated and Eq. (4.27) can be found by multiplying Eq. (4.24) by -1 and adding this new equation to Eq. (4.25):

$$x_1 - 4x_2 = -25 \qquad (4.27)$$

Also verify that Eq. (4.28) is formed by multiplying Eq. (4.24) by -4 and adding this to Eq. (4.26):

$$2x_1 - 8x_2 = -50 \qquad (4.28)$$

To eliminate x_1 from Eqs. (4.27) and (4.28), Eq. (4.27) may be multiplied by -2 and added to Eq. (4.28). When these operations are performed, Eq. (4.29) is an identity:

$$\begin{array}{rr} -2x_1 + 8x_2 = & 50 \\ 2x_1 - 8x_2 = & -50 \\ \hline 0 = & 0 \end{array} \qquad (4.29)$$

This is the signal that there are an infinite number of solutions to the original system.

If you are interested in determining members of the solution set, return to one of the last meaningful equations generated during the elimination procedure [Eqs. (4.27) and (4.28)] and arbitrarily assume a value for one of the variables. Given the assumed value, the corresponding value can be identified for the other variable in the equation. The corresponding value for the third variable can be found by substituting the two known values into one of the original equations.

For example, if x_1 is assumed to equal -5 in Eq. (4.27),

$$-5 - 4x_2 = -25$$
$$-4x_2 = -20$$

and
$$x_2 = 5$$

Substituting $x_1 = -5$ and $x_2 = 5$ into Eq. (4.24), we get

$$-5 + 5 + x_3 = 20$$

or
$$x_3 = 20$$

Verify that $x_1 = -5$, $x_2 = 5$, and $x_3 = 20$ satisfy Eqs. (4.25) and (4.26).

Fewer than Three Equations

In the section on graphical analysis we concluded that for a (2×3) system there is either no solution or an infinite number of solutions. The following examples illustrate how these are identified by using the elimination procedure.

Determine the solution set for the system of equations

$$-4x_1 + 6x_2 + 2x_3 = 8 \qquad (4.30)$$
$$2x_1 - 3x_2 - x_3 = -14 \qquad (4.31)$$

Example 4.9

To eliminate x_1, we multiply Eq. (4.31) by $+2$ and add to Eq. (4.30), or

Solution

$$-4x_1 + 6x_2 + 2x_3 = 8$$
$$\underline{4x_1 - 6x_2 - 2x_3 = -28}$$
$$0 = -20 \qquad (4.32)$$

This process leads to Eq. (4.32) which is a false statement, and we conclude that the original system has no solution.

Determine the solution set for the system

$$4x_1 - 2x_2 + x_3 = 10 \qquad (4.33)$$
$$-3x_1 + 2x_2 + 4x_3 = 20 \qquad (4.34)$$

Example 4.10

If Eqs. (4.33) and (4.34) are added, x_2 will be eliminated and Eq. (4.35) will result:

Solution

$$x_1 + 5x_3 = 30 \qquad (4.35)$$

Since we are left with one equation and two variables, the system cannot be reduced any further. If in a (2×3) system eliminating one variable leads to a new equation involving two variables, there are an

infinite number of solutions to the system. If you are interested in specifying different members of the solution set, you can assume an arbitrary
value for either x_1 or x_3 in Eq. (4.35) and solve for the other variable.
And, as with Example 4.8, these two values may be substituted into one
of the original equations to solve for the corresponding value of the third
variable.

If we let $x_1 = 5$ in Eq. (4.35),

$$5 + 5x_3 = 30$$
$$5x_3 = 25$$

and

$$x_3 = 5$$

By substituting these values into Eq. (4.33), the corresponding value of
x_2 is 7.5.

**Example
4.11**

Determine the solution set for the system

$$-10x_1 + 25x_2 - 15x_3 = 35 \qquad (4.36)$$
$$2x_1 - 5x_2 + 3x_3 = -7 \qquad (4.37)$$

Solution

To eliminate x_1, Eq. (4.37) is multiplied by $+5$ and added to Eq. (4.36) to
yield the equation

$$0 = 0$$

The identity implies that there are an infinite number of solutions to the
original system. To determine members of the solution set, you may assume arbitrary values for any two of the three variables in one of the
original equations and then solve for the corresponding value of the
third variable. For example, if in Eq. (4.36) x_2 and x_3 are assigned values
of 0, then

$$-10x_1 + 25(0) - 15(0) = 35$$

or

$$-10x_1 = 35$$

and

$$x_1 = -3.5$$

Thus one member of the solution set is the point $(-3.5, 0, 0)$. Verify
that this point satisfies Eq. (4.37).

More than Three Equations

For $(m \times 3)$ systems, where $m > 3$, we concluded that there may be a
unique solution, no solution, or an infinite number of solutions. Solving
by the elimination procedure is basically the same as for $(m \times 2)$
systems, where $m > 2$. The procedure is as follows:

1 Select and solve any (3×3) subset of the original system.

**2 *a* If there is a unique solution to the (3×3) system, substitute the
solution values into the remaining $m - 3$ equations to see if they are
satisfied. If they are, a unique solution has been found. If any of the remaining equations is not satisfied, there is no solution to the original
system.**

**   *b* If there is no solution to the (3×3) system, there is no solution to
the original system.**

c If there are an infinite number of solutions to the (3 × 3) system, there may be a unique system, no solution, or an infinite number of solutions to the entire (*m* × 3) system. Determining which situation exists can be complex and time-consuming; the procedures for resolving this type of situation will not be discussed here.

Determine the solution set for the system of equations

$$x_1 + x_2 + x_3 = 6 \qquad (4.38)$$
$$2x_1 - x_2 + x_3 = 7 \qquad (4.39)$$
$$2x_1 + 4x_2 - 3x_3 = 4 \qquad (4.40)$$
$$x_1 + 2x_2 + 3x_3 = 11 \qquad (4.41)$$
$$4x_1 + 2x_2 - 5x_3 = 10 \qquad (4.42)$$

Example 4.12

If the (3 × 3) subset of Eqs. (4.38) to (4.40) are solved, a unique solution is found when $x_1 = 3$, $x_2 = 1$, and $x_3 = 2$. (Verify this, if you wish.) Upon substituting these values into Eq. (4.41) we find

Solution

$$3 + 2(1) + 3(2) = 11$$

or

$$11 = 11$$

and this equation is satisfied. Substituting into Eq. (4.42), however, we find that

$$4(3) + 2(1) - 5(2) \neq 10$$

or

$$4 \neq 10$$

and consequently there is no solution to the original (5 × 3) system.

---

n-Variable Systems

With more than three variables (*n* > 3), the graphical frame of reference disappears. However, aside from the cumbersome arithmetic, the elimination procedure is a valid solution method. And the possible solution sets are similar to the cases studied for three variables. For example if *m* = *n* (the number of variables and equations are equal), it is possible to have a unique solution, an infinite number of solutions, or no solution. The indications of each of these cases are exactly the same as with (3 × 3) systems. The occurrence of a false statement at any stage indicates no solution; the occurrence of an identity implies an infinite number of solutions.

When the number of equations is less than the number of variables (*m* < *n*), there will be either no solution or an infinite number of solutions. And when the number of equations is greater than the number of variables (*m* > *n*), there may be no solution, an infinite number of solutions, or a unique solution.

The objectives, aspects of interpretation, and general nature of the elimination procedure are the same for each of these situations. However, the steps of the procedure vary slightly depending on the dimensions of the system of equations. Beyond three-variable systems manual computation procedures are impractical. Computerized solution procedures are readily available to solve larger systems for you.

Follow-up Exercises

Determine the solution set for each of the following systems of equations.

4.31
$$3x_1 + 2x_2 + x_3 = 4$$
$$6x_1 - 2x_2 + 3x_3 = 9$$
$$x_1 + x_2 + x_3 = 2$$

4.32
$$4x_1 - x_2 + 3x_3 = 14$$
$$x_1 + 3x_2 - 6x_3 = -13$$
$$2x_1 - 5x_2 + 4x_3 = 23$$

4.33
$$-x_1 + 3x_2 + x_3 = 7$$
$$3x_1 - 9x_2 - 3x_3 = 14$$
$$2x_1 + x_2 - x_3 = 12$$

4.34
$$5x_1 - 4x_2 + 6x_3 = 24$$
$$3x_1 - 3x_2 + x_3 = 54$$
$$-2x_1 + x_2 - 5x_3 = 30$$

4.35
$$5x_1 - 4x_2 + x_3 = 7$$
$$-x_1 + 8x_2 - 2x_3 = 4$$
$$x_1 - x_2 + x_3 = 5$$

4.36
$$10x_1 + 5x_2 - 15x_3 = 60$$
$$6x_1 + 4x_2 + x_3 = 48$$
$$-2x_1 - x_2 + 3x_3 = -18$$

4.37
$$4x_1 + 3x_2 - x_3 = -5$$
$$x_1 - x_2 = 10$$
$$6x_1 + 4x_2 + 7x_3 = 80$$

4.38
$$x_1 - x_2 + x_3 = 10$$
$$-6x_1 + 2x_2 - 4x_3 = 34$$
$$-4x_1 + 2x_2 - 3x_3 = 7$$

4.39 In Example 4.8 determine other members of the solution set. Specifically, determine the solution corresponding to a value of (a) $x_1 = 5$, (b) $x_2 = 0$, (c) $x_1 = 15$, (d) $x_1 = -25$.

4.40 Re-solve Example 4.7 by first eliminating x_2. See if you reach the same conclusion about the solution set.

4.41 Re-solve Example 4.8 by first eliminating x_1. See if you reach the same conclusion about the solution set.

Solve each of the following systems of equations.

4.42
$$x_1 - 2x_2 + x_3 = -10$$
$$-5x_1 + 10x_2 - 5x_3 = 50$$

4.43
$$x_1 + x_2 + x_3 = 15$$
$$-x_1 + 3x_2 + x_3 = 12$$

4.44
$$6x_1 - 3x_2 + 12x_3 = 48$$
$$-2x_1 + x_2 - 4x_3 = 20$$

4.45
$$4x_1 + 3x_2 + x_3 = 12$$
$$5x_1 - 6x_2 + 2x_3 = 25$$

4.46
$$10x_1 - 18x_2 + 12x_3 = 120$$
$$5x_1 - 9x_2 + 6x_3 = 60$$

4.47
$$x_1 + x_2 + x_3 = 1$$
$$5x_1 + 3x_2 + 6x_3 = 0$$
$$4x_1 + x_2 - x_3 = 3$$
$$2x_1 - 3x_2 + x_3 = 12$$

4.48
$$4x_1 - 2x_2 + x_3 = 8$$
$$3x_1 + x_2 - 2x_3 = 3$$
$$x_1 + x_2 + x_3 = 5$$
$$x_1 - 4x_2 + x_3 = 0$$

4.49
$$x_1 + x_2 + x_3 = 10$$
$$x_1 - x_2 + x_3 = 6$$
$$-x_1 + x_2 - 2x_3 = -9$$
$$3x_1 + x_2 - 2x_3 = 11$$
$$2x_1 + x_2 - 3x_3 = 3$$

4.50 Explain the graphics of the solution set for Example 4.9. What is happening graphically?

4.51 What are the graphical possibilities for the solution set in Example 4.10?

4.52 What solution set possibilities exist for (a) a (6×5) system of equations, (b) a (25×10) system, (c) a (6×6) system, and (d) a (100×200) system?

4.4

GAUSS-JORDAN PROCEDURE

In this section we will discuss another solution procedure which has very important value in the solution of linear programming problems

(Chap. 6). This procedure, though somewhat tedious for manual computations, is easily programmed for computer use.

The General Idea

The *Gauss-Jordan procedure* is an elimination method of sorts. The procedure begins with the original system of equations and transforms it, using row operations, into an equivalent† system from which the solution may be read directly. Figure 4.10 shows the transformation, i.e., change in form, which is desired in solving a (2×2) system. Note that as opposed to the elimination procedure, the transformed system still has dimensions of 2×2. The row operations, however, have transformed the coefficients on the variables so that only one variable remains in each equation; and the value of that variable (v_1 or v_2 in Fig. 4.10) is given by the right side of the equation.

The following row operations are at the heart of the Gauss-Jordan procedure. Given an original system of equations, the application of these operations results in an equivalent system of equations.

$$\left[\begin{array}{l} a_1 x_1 + b_1 x_2 = c_1 \\ a_2 x_1 + b_2 x_2 = c_2 \end{array}\right] \text{Original system}$$

$$\left.\begin{array}{l} \} \\ \} \end{array}\right\} \begin{array}{l} \text{Gauss-Jordan} \\ \text{transformation} \end{array}$$

$$\left[\begin{array}{l} 1\,x_1 + 0\,x_2 = v_1 \\ 0\,x_1 + 1\,x_2 = v_2 \end{array}\right] \begin{array}{l} \text{Transformed} \\ \text{system} \end{array}$$

or

$$\left[\begin{array}{rl} x_1 & = v_1 \\ x_2 & = v_2 \end{array}\right] \begin{array}{l} \{(v_1, v_2)\} \text{ is the} \\ \text{Solution set} \end{array}$$

FIGURE 4.10
Gauss-Jordan transformation for 2×2 systems

1 Both sides of an equation may be multiplied by a nonzero constant,

2 Nonzero multiples of one equation may be added to another equation.

Let's work a simple example and then generalize and streamline the procedure.

Example 4.13

Solve the following system of equations by the Gauss-Jordan elimination method:

$$2x - 3y = -7 \tag{4.43}$$
$$x + y = 4 \tag{4.44}$$

Solution

Multiplying Eq. (4.43) by $\frac{1}{2}$ makes the coefficient on the variable x become 1, resulting in the equivalent system

$$x - \tfrac{3}{2}y = -\tfrac{7}{2} \tag{4.43a}$$
$$x + y = 4 \tag{4.44}$$

The variable x can be eliminated in Eq. (4.44) if Eq. (4.43a) is multiplied by -1 and added to Eq. (4.44). This results in the equivalent system

$$x - \tfrac{3}{2}y = -\tfrac{7}{2} \tag{4.43a}$$
$$0x + \tfrac{5}{2}y = \tfrac{15}{2} \tag{4.44a}$$

By multiplying Eq. (4.44a) by $+\frac{2}{5}$, the coefficient on y becomes 1:

$$x - \tfrac{3}{2}y = -\tfrac{7}{2} \tag{4.43a}$$
$$0x + y = 3 \tag{4.44b}$$

---

† Remember that an *equivalent* system is one which has the same solution set as the original system.

Finally, the variable y can be eliminated in Eq. (4.43a) if Eq. (4.44b) is multiplied by $\frac{3}{2}$ and added to Eq. (4.43a), or

$$x + 0y = 1 \qquad (4.43b)$$
$$0x + y = 3 \qquad (4.44b)$$

There is a reason for carrying these zero coefficients through the transformation. You will see why very shortly. However, when these zero terms are dropped from Eqs. (4.43b) and (4.44b), the final system has the form

$$\begin{aligned} x &= 1 \\ y &= 3 \end{aligned}$$

which gives the solution to the system.

The Method

This procedure can be streamlined if we use a type of shorthand notation to represent the system of equations. One approach eliminates the variables and represents a system by using the variable coefficients and right-side constants only. For example, the system of equations

$$\begin{aligned} 2x + 5y &= 10 \\ 3x - 4y &= -5 \end{aligned}$$

would be written as

$$\left.\begin{array}{rr|r} 2 & 5 & 10 \\ 3 & -4 & -5 \end{array}\right.$$

The vertical line is used to separate the left and right sides of the equations.

For the general (2 × 2) system portrayed in Fig. 4.10, the Gauss-Jordan procedure would appear as in Fig. 4.11. The primary objective is to change the array of coefficients $\begin{pmatrix} a_1 & b_1 \\ a_2 & b_2 \end{pmatrix}$ into the form of $\begin{pmatrix} 1 & 0 \\ 0 & 1 \end{pmatrix}$.

In a (3 × 3) system of the form

$$\begin{aligned} a_1x_1 + b_1x_2 + c_1x_3 &= d_1 \\ a_2x_1 + b_2x_2 + c_2x_3 &= d_2 \\ a_3x_1 + b_3x_2 + c_3x_3 &= d_3 \end{aligned}$$

the Gauss-Jordan transformation would proceed as in Fig. 4.12.

Although there are variations on this procedure, and for any given problem you may be tempted to *try* a shortcut, the following procedure will always work.

1 Transform the coefficients one column at a time starting with column 1. For example, in a (2 × 2) system begin by transforming $\begin{pmatrix} a_1 \\ a_2 \end{pmatrix}$ into $\begin{pmatrix} 1 \\ 0 \end{pmatrix}$. Then transform column 2 so that it looks like $\begin{pmatrix} 0 \\ 1 \end{pmatrix}$.

FIGURE 4.11

$$\begin{array}{cc|c} a_1 & b_1 & c_1 \\ a_2 & b_2 & c_2 \end{array} \quad \text{Original system}$$

⇩ Gauss–Jordan transformation

$$\begin{array}{cc|c} 1 & 0 & v_1 \\ 0 & 1 & v_2 \end{array} \quad \text{Transformed system}$$

FIGURE 4.12

$$\begin{array}{ccc|c} a_1 & b_1 & c_1 & d_1 \\ a_2 & b_2 & c_2 & d_2 \\ a_3 & b_3 & c_3 & d_3 \end{array} \quad \text{Original system}$$

⇩ Gauss–Jordan transformation

$$\begin{array}{ccc|c} 1 & 0 & 0 & v_1 \\ 0 & 1 & 0 & v_2 \\ 0 & 0 & 1 & v_3 \end{array} \quad \text{Transformed system}$$

2 In any column transformation, first create the element which equals 1. This is done by multiplying the row (equation) in which the 1 is desired by the reciprocal of the current coefficient in that position.

3 The zeros in a column are created by first multiplying the row created in step 2 by the *negative* of the value currently in the position where the 0 is desired. This row multiple is added to the row in which the 0 is desired.

Let's illustrate this final step, since it tends to be confusing. If at some stage in the transformation process we have the following system

$$1 \quad 6 \mid 10 \qquad\qquad (1)$$
$$\textcircled{5} \quad 3 \mid 12 \qquad\qquad (2)$$

and we desire a zero where the $\textcircled{5}$ is in column 1, we can achieve this by multiplying row 1 by the negative of $\textcircled{5}$, or -5, and add this multiple of row 1 to row 2, or

$$
\begin{array}{rr|r}
-5 & -30 & -50 \\
5 & 3 & 12 \\
\hline
0 & -27 & -38
\end{array}
\qquad
\begin{array}{l}
-5 \cdot \text{row 1} \\
\text{row 2} \\
\text{new row 2 or } 2a
\end{array}
$$

The revised system would be

$$
\begin{array}{rr|r}
1 & 6 & 10 \\
0 & -27 & -38
\end{array}
\qquad
\begin{array}{l}
\text{row 1} \\
\text{row 2a}
\end{array}
$$

The following examples illustrate the procedure. After going through these carefully and trying a few problems on your own, you should feel much more comfortable with the procedure.

Solve the following system by the Gauss-Jordan method:

$$
\begin{aligned}
5x + 20y &= 25 \\
4x - 7y &= -26
\end{aligned}
$$

Example 4.14

Rewriting the system without the variables gives

Solution

$$
\begin{array}{rr|r}
5 & 20 & 25 \\
4 & -7 & -26
\end{array}
\qquad
\begin{array}{l}
R_1 \\
R_2
\end{array}
$$

Note the identification of rows 1 and 2 by R_1 and R_2. This will be convenient for summarizing the row operations.

A 1 is created in row 1 by multiplying that row by $\frac{1}{5}$, and the new system becomes

$$
\begin{array}{rr|r}
1 & 4 & 5 \\
4 & -7 & -26
\end{array}
\qquad
\begin{array}{l}
R_{1a} = \frac{1}{5}R_1 \\
R_2
\end{array}
$$

A 0 is created in row 2 by multiplying row 1 by -4 and adding this row multiple to row 2. The new system is

$$
\begin{array}{rr|r}
1 & 4 & 5 \\
0 & -23 & -46
\end{array}
\qquad
\begin{array}{l}
R_{1a} \\
R_{2a} = -4R_{1a} + R_2
\end{array}
$$

Moving to the second column, a 1 is created in row 2 by multiplying the row by $-\frac{1}{23}$. The resulting system is

$$
\begin{array}{cc|c}
1 & 4 & 5 \\
0 & 1 & 2
\end{array}
\quad
\begin{array}{l}
R_{1a} \\
R_{2b} = -\frac{1}{23}R_{2a}
\end{array}
$$

Finally, a 0 is created in the second column of row 1 by multiplying row 2 by -4 and adding this to row 1, or

$$
\begin{array}{cc|c}
1 & 0 & -3 \\
0 & 1 & 2
\end{array}
\quad
\begin{array}{l}
R_{1b} = -4R_{2b} + R_{1a} \\
R_{2b}
\end{array}
$$

Remember that embedded within this shorthand notation is a system of equations which is equivalent to the original system. This equivalent system has the form

$$
\begin{aligned}
x &= -3 \\
y &= 2
\end{aligned}
$$

which is the solution to the system.

Example 4.15

Solve the system in Example 4.6 using the Gauss-Jordan procedure.

Solution

For this example, the successive transformations will simply be listed with the corresponding row operations indicated to the right of each row.

$$
\begin{array}{ccc|c}
1 & 1 & 1 & 6 \\
2 & -1 & 3 & 4 \\
4 & 5 & -10 & 13
\end{array}
\quad
\begin{array}{l}
R_1 \\
R_2 \\
R_3
\end{array}
\qquad
\begin{array}{ccc|c}
1 & 0 & \frac{4}{3} & \frac{10}{3} \\
0 & 1 & -\frac{1}{3} & \frac{8}{3} \\
0 & 0 & -\frac{41}{3} & -\frac{41}{3}
\end{array}
\quad
\begin{array}{l}
R_{1a} \\
R_{2b} \\
R_{3b} = -R_{2b} + R_{3a}
\end{array}
$$

$$
\begin{array}{ccc|c}
1 & 1 & 1 & 6 \\
0 & -3 & 1 & -8 \\
4 & 5 & -10 & 13
\end{array}
\quad
\begin{array}{l}
R_1 \\
R_{2a} = -2R_1 + R_2 \\
R_3
\end{array}
\qquad
\begin{array}{ccc|c}
1 & 0 & \frac{4}{3} & \frac{10}{3} \\
0 & 1 & -\frac{1}{3} & \frac{8}{3} \\
0 & 0 & 1 & 1
\end{array}
\quad
\begin{array}{l}
R_{1a} \\
R_{2b} \\
R_{3c} = -\frac{3}{41}R_{3b}
\end{array}
$$

$$
\begin{array}{ccc|c}
1 & 1 & 1 & 6 \\
0 & -3 & 1 & -8 \\
0 & 1 & -14 & -11
\end{array}
\quad
\begin{array}{l}
R_1 \\
R_{2a} \\
R_{3a} = -4R_1 + R_3
\end{array}
\qquad
\begin{array}{ccc|c}
1 & 0 & \frac{4}{3} & \frac{10}{3} \\
0 & 1 & 0 & 3 \\
0 & 0 & 1 & 1
\end{array}
\quad
\begin{array}{l}
R_{1a} \\
R_{2c} = \frac{1}{3}R_{3c} + R_{2b} \\
R_{3c}
\end{array}
$$

$$
\begin{array}{ccc|c}
1 & 1 & 1 & 6 \\
0 & 1 & -\frac{1}{3} & \frac{8}{3} \\
0 & 1 & -14 & -11
\end{array}
\quad
\begin{array}{l}
R_1 \\
R_{2b} = -\frac{1}{3}R_{2a} \\
R_{3a}
\end{array}
\qquad
\begin{array}{ccc|c}
1 & 0 & 0 & 2 \\
0 & 1 & 0 & 3 \\
0 & 0 & 1 & 1
\end{array}
\quad
\begin{array}{l}
R_{1b} = -\frac{4}{3}R_{3c} + R_{1a} \\
R_{2c} \\
R_{3c}
\end{array}
$$

$$
\begin{array}{ccc|c}
1 & 0 & \frac{4}{3} & \frac{10}{3} \\
0 & 1 & -\frac{1}{3} & \frac{8}{3} \\
0 & 1 & -14 & -11
\end{array}
\quad
\begin{array}{l}
R_{1a} = -R_2 + R_1 \\
R_{2b} \\
R_{3a}
\end{array}
$$

The system has a unique solution when $x_1 = 2$, $x_2 = 3$, and $x_3 = 1$.

The Gauss-Jordan procedure works in exactly the same manner for determining the solution set for (4×4), (5×5), . . . , $(n \times n)$ systems although writer's cramp can be a problem. The indications of no solution or an infinite number of solutions are the same as with the elimination procedure. You will be asked to verify this in the Follow-up Exercises.

Follow-up Exercises

Determine the solution sets (all of which are unique) for the following systems, using the Gauss-Jordan procedure.

4.53 $\begin{aligned} 5x_1 - 3x_2 &= 8 \\ x_1 - x_2 &= 4 \end{aligned}$ **4.54** $\begin{aligned} 10x_1 + 8x_2 &= -10 \\ 3x_1 + 4x_2 &= 5 \end{aligned}$

4.55 $\begin{aligned} 3x_1 + x_2 &= 10 \\ 15x_1 - 2x_2 &= 1 \end{aligned}$ **4.56** $\begin{aligned} x_1 - x_2 &= 7 \\ 10x_1 + 20x_2 &= 10 \end{aligned}$

4.57 $\begin{aligned} 3x_1 - 5x_2 &= 4 \\ x_1 - x_2 &= 4 \end{aligned}$ **4.58** $\begin{aligned} x_1 - 3x_2 &= 3 \\ -5x_1 + 6x_2 &= -15 \end{aligned}$

4.59 $\begin{aligned} 5x_1 - 2x_2 + x_3 &= 7 \\ x_1 + x_2 + x_3 &= 0 \\ 4x_1 + 3x_2 + 5x_3 &= 1 \end{aligned}$ **4.60** $\begin{aligned} x_1 + x_2 + x_3 &= 0 \\ 3x_1 - 2x_2 + 2x_3 &= -2 \\ -4x_1 - x_2 - 3x_3 &= 0 \end{aligned}$

4.61 $\begin{aligned} 2x_1 - x_2 &= 1 \\ x_1 + 2x_2 + x_3 &= 9 \\ 5x_2 - 2x_3 &= 33 \end{aligned}$ **4.62** $\begin{aligned} 4x_1 + x_2 - x_3 &= 8 \\ x_1 + x_2 + x_3 &= 6 \\ -2x_1 + 3x_2 &= 2 \end{aligned}$

4.63 Re-solve the problem in Example 4.4 using the Gauss-Jordan method to determine how no solution is indicated for a (2×2) system.

4.64 Re-solve Example 4.3 using the Gauss-Jordan method to determine how an infinite number of solutions would be indicated for a (2×2) system.

4.65 Re-solve Example 4.7 to see how no solution is indicated by the Gauss-Jordan method for (3×3) systems.

4.66 Re-solve Example 4.8 to see how an infinite number of solutions would be indicated by the Gauss-Jordan method for (3×3) systems.

SUMMARY   4.5

In this chapter we have discussed the interactions within systems of linear equations. We have examined the graphical characteristics of solution sets for two- and three-variable systems, we have looked at the elimination procedure for solving systems of equations, and finally we examined the Gauss-Jordan procedure for solving systems of equations.

In the next chapter we will discuss applications of linear functions and systems of linear equations. Be sure that you are comfortable with the concepts presented in this and the preceding chapter before moving on.

CHAPTER CHECKLIST

If you have read all sections of this chapter, you should

Be able to characterize a system of equations by its *dimensions*   _____

Understand what is meant by the *solution set* for a system of equations   _____

Know the different types of solution sets which can exist for (2×2) _____

systems of equations and how they are distinguished from one another
graphically

_____ Know how to determine the type of solution set in a (2 × 2) system by
examining slopes and y intercepts

_____ Understand the graphics of three-variable systems of equations and
their different solution sets

_____ Understand the *elimination procedure* for solving (2 × 2) systems

_____ Understand the elimination procedure for solving (*m* × 2) systems
where $m > 2$

_____ Understand the elimination procedure for solving (2 × 3) systems

_____ Understand the elimination procedure for solving (3 × 3) systems

_____ Understand the elimination procedure for solving (*m* × 3) systems
where $m > 3$

_____ Understand the "signals" of no solution or an infinite number of solutions when using the elimination procedure

_____ Understand the *Gauss-Jordan procedure* for solving systems of equations

KEY TERMS AND CONCEPTS

system of equations	unique solution
dimensions of system of equations	no solution
solution set	infinite number of solutions
inconsistent equations	Gauss-Jordan procedure
equivalent equations	row operations
elimination procedure	

ADDITIONAL EXERCISES

Exercises 4.67 through 4.78 are related to Sec. 4.2.

For the pairs of equations in Exercises 4.67 to 4.70, draw conclusions
about the type of solution set (unique, infinite, or no solution) which will
exist when the equations are solved. Do this by computing the slope and
y intercept for each line and comparing them.

4.67 $4x - 5y = 7$
$\quad\quad x \quad\quad = 2y$

4.68 $\quad x + \quad y = 10$
$\quad\quad 2x + 2y = 20$

4.69 $y = 5x + 7$
$\quad\quad 3x - 15y = 8$

4.70 $x = \frac{5}{8}y + 1$
$\quad\quad y = \frac{8}{5}x - 2$

For each of the systems of equations in Exercises 4.71 and 4.72, solve
graphically and check your answer.

4.71 $x = y$
$\quad\quad x = -y$

4.72 $y = 10$
$\quad\quad 2x + 3y = 6$

In Exercises 4.73 to 4.76, solve by the elimination procedure.

4.73 $2x - y = 10$
$3x + y = 20$

4.74 $-x - y = 7$
$2x + 3y = 10$

4.75 $4x + 3y = 12$
$-x - y = 10$

4.76 $0.5x + 0.5y = 7$
$2x + y = 5$

For Exercises 4.77 to 4.78, solve the given systems of equations.

4.77 $x - y = 8$
$4x + 3y = 20$
$2x - y = 5$

4.78 $3x + 7y = 1$
$x - 3y = 11$
$4x + 5y = 10$
$2x + 6y = -2$

Exercises 4.79 to 4.86 are related to Sec. 4.3.

For Exercises 4.79 to 4.81, determine the solution set for each system of equations.

4.79 $2x_1 + x_2 - 2x_3 = -4$
$x_1 + 3x_2 + 5x_3 = 50$
$2x_1 - 2x_2 + 3x_3 = 19$

4.80 $x_1 + 4x_2 - x_3 = 12$
$-x_1 - x_2 + 2x_3 = -5$
$3x_1 + 2x_2 - 5x_3 = 14$

4.81 $3x_1 - 3x_2 + 3x_3 = 21$
$x_1 + x_2 - x_3 = -7$
$-5x_1 + 4x_2 + 7x_3 = 49$

In Exercises 4.82 to 4.85, solve each given system of equations.

4.82 $x_1 + x_2 - x_3 = 1$
$3x_1 + 5x_2 - x_3 = 4$

4.83 $4x_1 + 3x_2 + 2x_3 = 27$
$-2x_1 + 5x_2 - x_3 = 6$

4.84 $2x_1 - 4x_2 + x_3 = 12$
$-3x_1 + 7x_2 + 2x_3 = 12$
$x_1 + x_2 - 3x_3 = -16$

4.85 $-2x_1 + 3x_2 + x_3 = 8$
$3x_1 + x_2 - 2x_3 = 9$
$5x_1 + 2x_2 - 4x_3 = 15$
$x_1 - 4x_2 + 7x_3 = 1$

4.86 What solution set possibilities exist for (*a*) a (10×8) system, (*b*) an (8×10) system, (*c*) an (8×8) system?

4.87 What are the graphical characteristics for the solution set in Exercise 4.86?

Exercises 4.88 to 4.92 are related to Sec. 4.4.

In Exercises 4.88 to 4.90, determine the solution sets (all of which are unique) for the following systems, using the Gauss-Jordan procedure.

4.88 $-x_1 + 5x_2 = 7$
$3x_1 - x_2 = 7$

4.89 $x_1 - 4x_2 = 0$
$3x_1 + x_2 = 13$

4.90 $-x_1 + 5x_2 + 3x_3 = -7$
$2x_1 - 3x_2 + x_3 = 0$
$3x_2 - 7x_3 = 4$

In Exercises 4.91 and 4.92, use the Gauss-Jordan method to determine how nonunique solution sets are indicated for a (2×2) system.

4.91 $3x_1 + 2x_2 = 10$
$-6x_1 - 4x_2 = -20$

4.92 $3x_1 + 5x_2 = 7$
$3x_1 + 5x_2 = 8$

CHAPTER TEST

1 Solve the following system of equations graphically.

$$2x - y = 3$$
$$-x + 3y = 11$$

2 Solve the following system of equations.

$$4x - 2y = 16$$
$$-3x + y = -11$$
$$x - y = 5$$
$$x + 4y = 10$$

3 Solve the following system of equations using the elimination procedure.

$$x + y + z = 6$$
$$2x - y + z = 2$$
$$-2x + 2y - 3z = -1$$

4 Solve the following system of equations using the Gauss-Jordan procedure.

$$-3x + 2y = -4$$
$$15x - 10y = 40$$

CHAPTER OBJECTIVES After reading this chapter, you should be familiar with the structure of linear functions and a variety of applications of linear functions and systems of simultaneous equations.

In this chapter we will extend the discussion of mathematical functions presented in Chap. 2 and present a discussion of linear functions. After looking at the form and assumptions underlying these functions, we will see examples which illustrate the applications of these models in business, economics, and other areas. The remainder of the chapter will illustrate a variety of applications which involve systems of linear equations and their solution sets.

LINEAR FUNCTIONS 5.1

General Form and Assumptions

In Chap. 2 we talked about mathematical functions.

DEFINITION
A *linear function* involving one independent variable x and a dependent variable y has the general form

$$y = f(x) = ax + b \qquad (5.1)$$

You should recognize Eq. (5.1) as being the slope-intercept form of a linear equation. The parameters have been named differently, but they still represent the same characteristics. That is, a represents the slope of the line that represents the function, and b represents the y intercept.

Remember that a function having the general form $y = f(x)$ suggests that the value of the variable y depends upon the value of x. *For a linear function having the form of Eq. (5.1), a change in the value of y is directly proportional to a change in the value of x.* Or stated differently, the *rate* of change in the value of y, given a change in the value of x, is *constant*. This rate of change is represented by the slope of the function, or by the constant a in Eq. (5.1). Do you remember that the slope tells you the change expected in the value of y for a unit increase in the value of x?

The salary function in Example 2.18 was of the form

$$y = 3x + 25$$

where y was defined as weekly salary in dollars and x represented number of units sold per week. Although the terms have been rearranged on the right side of the equation, this is an example of a linear function. Graphically, the function appears as in Fig. 5.1. Note that the equation is graphed in the first quadrant only, restricting x and y to nonnegative values. Does this make sense?

DEFINITION
A linear function involving two independent variables x_1 and x_2 and a dependent variable y has the general form

$$y = f(x_1, x_2) = a_1x_1 + a_2x_2 + b \qquad (5.2)$$

where $a_1, a_2,$ and b are real-valued constants.

FIGURE 5.1

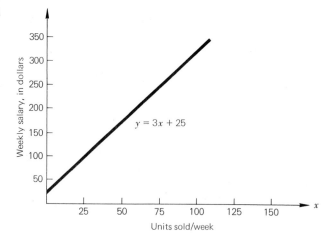

$y = 3x + 25$

Weekly salary, in dollars

Units sold/week

For a linear function of the form of Eq. (5.2) the variable y depends jointly on the values of x_1 and x_2. The value of y varies in direct proportion to changes in the values of x_1 and x_2. Specifically, if x_1 increases by 1 unit, y will change by a_1 units. And if x_2 increases by 1 unit, y will change by a_2 units.

Assume that a salesperson's salary depends on the number of units sold of each of two products. More specifically, assume that the salary function

Example 5.1

$$y = f(x_1, x_2)$$

is
$$y = 5x_1 + 3x_2 + 25$$

where y = weekly salary, x_1 = number of units sold of product A, and x_2 = number of units sold of product B. An interpretation of this salary function is that there is a base weekly salary of $25 and that commissions earned per unit sold are $5 and $3, respectively, for products A and B.

DEFINITION
A linear function involving n independent variables $x_1, x_2, \ldots, x_n$ and a dependent variable y has the general form

$$y = f(x_1, x_2, \ldots, x_n)$$
where $\quad y = a_1x_1 + a_2x_2 + \cdots + a_nx_n + b$ $\qquad$ **(5.3)**

where $a_1, a_2, \ldots, a_n$ and b are real-valued constants.

Linear Cost Functions

Organizations are concerned with *costs* because they reflect dollars flowing out of the organization. These outflows are usually to pay for salaries, raw materials, supplies, rent, heat, utilities, and so forth. As mentioned earlier, accountants and economists often define total cost in terms of two components: *Total variable cost* and *total fixed cost*. These two components must be added to determine total cost. The cost function for owning and operating the patrol car in Example 2.20 was an example of a linear cost function. The cost function

$$C(x) = 18,000 + 0.40x$$

had fixed costs of $18,000 and variable costs which varied with the number of miles driven.

Total variable costs vary with the level of output and are computed as the product of variable cost per unit of output and the level of output. In a production setting, variable cost per unit is usually composed of raw material and labor costs. In the example of the patrol car, variable cost per mile consisted of operating costs per mile such as gasoline, oil, maintenance costs, and depreciation.

Linear cost functions are very often realistic although they ignore the possibility of *economies* or *diseconomies of scale*. That is, linear cost functions imply *constant returns to scale*. Constant returns to scale imply that regardless of the number of units produced, the variable cost for each unit is always the same. This assumption ignores the possibility that the elements of the production process, laborers or machines, may become more efficient as the number of units produced increases or that buying raw materials in large quantities may result in quantity discounts which in turn may lower the variable cost per unit produced. The cost function for the patrol car assumes that operating costs per mile will be $0.40 regardless of the number of miles driven. We might expect that over the life of a piece of equipment, such as the patrol car, it will become less efficient and will require greater maintenance. If this is so, this should translate into a higher variable cost per unit. Some cost models recognize these potential "nonlinearities" by using some measure of average variable cost per unit. In other situations a set of linear cost functions might be developed, each appropriate in certain cases depending on the level of output selected.

The following example illustrates the formulation of a linear cost function.

**Example
5.2**

A firm which produces a single product is interested in determining the function that expresses annual total cost y as a function of the number of units produced x. Accountants indicate that fixed expenditures each year are $50,000. They also have estimated that raw material costs for each unit produced are $5.50, and labor costs per unit are $1.50 in the assembly department, $0.75 in the finishing room, and $1.25 in the packaging and shipping department.

The total cost function will have the form

$$y = C(x)$$
$$= \text{total variable cost} + \text{total fixed cost}$$

Total variable costs consist of the two components: raw material costs and labor costs. But labor costs can be further defined by the department in which the cost is incurred. Therefore, total cost is defined by the function

$$y = \text{total raw material cost} + \text{total labor cost} + \text{total fixed cost}$$

or $\quad y = 5.50x + (1.50x + 0.75x + 1.25x) + 50{,}000$

which simplifies to

$$y = 9x + 50{,}000$$

The 9 represents the combined variable cost per unit produced.

Linear Revenue Functions

The money which flows into an organization from either selling products or providing services is often referred to as *revenue*. The most fundamental way of computing total revenue from selling a product (or service) is

$$\text{Total revenue} = (\text{price})(\text{quantity sold})$$

An assumption in this relationship is that the selling price is the same for all units sold.

If a firm sells n products, where x_i equals the number of units sold of product i and p_i equals the price of product i, the function which allows you to compute total revenue from the n products is

$$R = p_1 x_1 + p_2 x_2 + p_3 x_3 + \cdots + p_n x_n \qquad (5.4)$$

This revenue function can be stated more concisely using *summation notation*[1] as

$$R = \sum_{i=1}^{n} p_i x_i \qquad (5.5)$$

A local car rental agency, Hurts Renta-Lemon, is trying to compete with some of the larger national firms. Realizing that many travelers are not concerned about frills such as windows, hubcaps, radios, and heaters, I. T. Hurts, owner and president of Hurts, has been recycling used cars to become part of the fleet. Hurts has also simplified the rental rate structure by charging a flat $12.50 per day for the use of a car. Total revenue for the year is a linear function of the number of car-days rented out by the agent, or if R = annual revenue and d = number of car-days rented during the year,

$$R = f(d) = 12.50d$$

Example 5.3

Linear Profit Functions

Profit for an organization is the difference between total revenue and total cost. Stated in equation form, this is

$$\text{Profit} = \text{total revenue} - \text{total cost}$$

When total revenue exceeds total cost, profit is positive. In such cases the profit may be referred to as a *net gain*, or *net profit*. When total cost exceeds total revenue, profit is negative and it may be called a *net loss*, or *deficit*.

When *both* total revenue and total cost are linear functions of the same variable(s), the composite profit function is also a linear function of the same variable(s). That is, if

$$\text{Total revenue} = R(x)$$

and
$$\text{Total cost} = C(x)$$

profit is defined as

$$P(x) = R(x) - C(x)$$

[1] If you are unfamiliar with summation notation, see Appendix B.

Example 5.4 A firm sells a single product for $65 per unit. Variable costs per unit are $20 for materials and $27.50 for labor. Annual fixed costs are $100,000. Construct the profit function stated in terms of x, the number of units produced and sold. What profit is earned if annual sales are 20,000 units?

Solution If the product sells for $65 per unit, total revenue is computed by using the function

$$R(x) = 65x$$

Is this consistent with your mental model? Similarly, total annual cost is made up of material costs, labor costs, and fixed costs:

$$C(x) = 20x + 27.50x + 100,000$$

which reduces to

$$C(x) = 47.50x + 100,000$$

(Again, check this against your mental model, if you have one.)

Thus
$$P(x) = R(x) - C(x)$$
$$= 65x - (47.50x + 100,000)$$
$$= 17.50x - 100,000$$

If the firm sells 20,000 units during the year, then

$$P(20,000) = 17.50(20,000) - 100,000$$
$$= 350,000 - 100,000$$
$$= \$250,000$$

Example 5.5 **Agricultural Planning** A corporate agricultural organization has three separate farms which are to be used during the coming year. Each farm has unique characteristics which make it most suitable for raising one crop only. Table 5.1 indicates the crop selected for planting at each farm, the annual cost of planting 1 acre of the crop, the expected revenue to be derived from each acre, the fixed costs associated with operating each farm. In addition to the fixed costs associated with operating each farm, there are annual fixed costs of $75,000 for the corporation as a whole. Determine the profit function for the three-farm operation if x_j = the number of acres planted at farm j.

Table 5.1

	Crop	Cost/Acre	Revenue/Acre	Fixed Cost
Farm 1	Soybeans	$ 900	$1,300	$150,000
Farm 2	Corn	1,100	1,650	175,000
Farm 3	Potatoes	750	1,200	125,000

Solution Total revenue comes from the sale of crops planted at each of the three farms, or

$$R(x_1, x_2, x_3) = r_1(x_1) + r_2(x_2) + r_3(x_3)$$
$$= 1,300x_1 + 1,650x_2 + 1,200x_3$$

Total costs are the sum of those at the three farms plus the corporate fixed costs, or

$$
\begin{aligned}
C(x_1, x_2, x_3) &= c_1(x_1) + c_2(x_2) + c_3(x_3) + 75{,}000 \\
&= 900x_1 + 150{,}000 + 1{,}100x_2 + 175{,}000 \\
&\quad + 750x_3 + 125{,}000 + 75{,}000 \\
&= 900x_1 + 1{,}100x_2 + 750x_3 + 525{,}000
\end{aligned}
$$

Total profit is a linear function computed as

$$
\begin{aligned}
P(x_1, x_2, x_3) &= R(x_1, x_2, x_3) - C(x_1, x_2, x_3) \\
&= 1{,}300x_1 + 1{,}650x_2 + 1{,}200x_3 - (900x_1 \\
&\quad + 1{,}100x_2 + 750x_3 + 525{,}000) \\
&= 400x_1 + 550x_2 + 450x_3 - 525{,}000
\end{aligned}
$$

Follow-up Exercises

5.1 Write out the general form of a linear function involving four independent variables.

5.2 Assume that the salesperson in Example 5.1 has a salary goal of $200 per week. If product B is not available for a given week, how many units of product A must be sold to meet the salary goal? If product A is not available, how many units must be sold of product B?

5.3 Assume in Example 5.1 that the salesperson receives a bonus when combined sales from the two products exceed 30 units. The bonus is $1.50 per unit for each unit over 30. With this incentive program, the salary function must be described by two different linear functions. What are they, and when are they valid?

5.4 For Example 5.4, how many units must be produced and sold in order to (a) earn a profit of $3 million, (b) earn zero profit (break even)?

5.5 A ski boot manufacturer produces three different types of ski boots. The table below summarizes wholesale prices, material cost per pair, and labor cost per pair. Annual fixed costs are $100,000.

	Type 1	Type 2	Type 3
Wholesale price/pair	$75	$90	$110
Material cost/pair	30	45	55
Labor cost/pair	20	25	25

(a) Determine a joint total revenue function for sales of the three styles of boots.

(b) Determine an annual total cost function for manufacturing the three styles of boots.

(c) Determine the profit function for sales of the three products.

(d) What is annual profit if the firm sells 20,000, 40,000 and 10,000 pairs, respectively, of the type 1, type 2, and type 3 boots?

5.6 For Example 5.5, the board of directors has voted on the following planting program for the coming year. Twelve hundred acres will be planted at farm 1, 1,500 at farm 2, and 1,750 at farm 3. (a) What are the expected profits for the program? (b) A summer drought has resulted in the revenue yields per acre being reduced by 25, 20, and 30 percent,

respectively, at the three farms. What is the profit expected from the
previously mentioned planting program?

5.2   ## OTHER EXAMPLES OF LINEAR FUNCTIONS

In this section we will see, by example, some other applications of linear
functions.

Example
5.6

Straight-Line Depreciation When organizations purchase
equipment, vehicles, buildings, and so forth, accountants usually allo-
cate the cost of the item over the period the item is used. For a truck
costing $10,000 and having a useful life of 5 years, accountants might al-
locate $2,000 a year as a cost of owning the truck. The cost allocated to
any given period is called *depreciation*. Accountants also keep records
of major assets and their current, or "book," value. For instance, the
value of the truck may appear on the accounting statements as $10,000
at the time of purchase, $10,000 − $2,000 = $8,000 one year from the
date of purchase, and so forth. Depreciation can also be thought of as
the amount by which the book value of an asset has decreased.

Although there are a variety of depreciation methods, one of the simplest is *straight-line depreciation*. Under this method the rate of depreciation is constant. This implies that the book value declines as a linear
function over time. If V equals the book value of an asset and t equals
time measured from the purchase date for the previously mentioned
truck,

$$V = f(t)$$
$$= \text{purchase cost} - \text{depreciation}$$

or $$= 10,000 - 2,000t$$

The graph of this function appears in Fig. 5.2

FIGURE 5.2

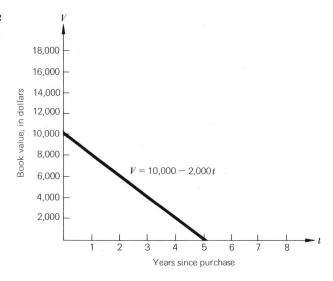

Years since purchase

Straight-Line Depreciation with Salvage Value Many assets have a *resale,* or *salvage value* even after they have served the purposes for which they were originally purchased. In such cases the cost allocated to each time period is the difference between the purchase cost and the salvage value divided by the useful life. Assume that the truck in the last example has a useful life of 5 years, after which it can be sold for $1,000. If the truck is to be depreciated on a straight-line basis, the annual depreciation will be

Example 5.7

$$\frac{\text{Purchase cost} - \text{salvage value}}{\text{Useful life (in years)}} = \frac{\$10,000 - \$1,000}{5}$$

$$= \frac{\$9,000}{5} = \$1,800$$

The function which expresses the book value V as a function of time t is

$$V = f(t) = 10,000 - 1,800t \qquad 0 \le t \le 5$$

Crime Deterrence There continues to be a debate as to whether police patrol activities have any effect on the level of crime within an area.[2] The research in this area has provided inconsistent results. Researchers generally agree that the effectiveness of patrols varies depending upon a variety of factors including the type of crime. For example, it is likely that police patrol has little effect on the incidence of shoplifting, which is more of an indoor crime. One might expect that there would be a greater effect on crimes such as automobile theft and armed robbery.

Example 5.8

A number of police departments believe that the level of serious crime is influenced by police patrol activities. One city has gathered data on crime rates while varying the number of police officers assigned to preventive patrol activities. The data indicate a linear functional relationship where

Number of serious crimes per week

$$= f \begin{pmatrix} \text{average number of police officers} \\ \text{assigned to preventive patrol} \end{pmatrix}$$

Their data indicate that with no preventive patrol activities the expected number of serious crimes is 1,250 per week. The data also indicate that the expected number of serious crimes will decrease by 2.5 for each additional police officer. This relationship is represented by the linear function

$$c = f(p) = 1,250 - 2.5p$$

where c equals the expected number of serious crimes per week and p equals the average number of officers assigned to preventive patrol.

[2] One of the more recent studies was a comprehensive experiment conducted in Kansas City.

POINTS FOR THOUGHT AND DISCUSSION
Interpret the meaning of the slope of this linear function. What does the x intercept represent in this application? Does *linearity* seem reasonable for this relationship?

Example 5.9 **Linear Demand Functions** A *demand function* is a mathematical relationship expressing the way in which the quantity demanded of an item varies with the price charged for it. The relationship between these two variables—quantity demanded and price per unit—is usually inverse. That is, as one variable increases, the other decreases. For most products, a decrease in price results in an increase in demand. The purpose of special sales is almost always to stimulate demand. If supermarkets reduced the price of filet mignon to $0.75 per pound, there would likely be a significant increase in the demand for that item. On the other hand, increases in the price of a product usually result in a decrease in the demand for it. The phrase *pricing people out of the market* refers to the customers lost as a result of price increases. If filet mignon were to suddenly triple in price with all other things such as income levels held constant, many people currently capable of purchasing it would be priced out of the market.

There are exceptions to this behavior, of course. The demand for products or services which are considered *necessities* is likely to fluctuate less with moderate changes in price. Items such as prescription medical drugs, medical services, and certain food items are examples of this class of products.

Although most demand functions are nonlinear, there are situations in which the demand relationship either is, or can be approximated by, a linear function. Figure 5.3 illustrates one such function with two sample data points (price, demand). Although most economics books measure price on the y axis and quantity demanded on the x axis, this book will adopt the convention of reversing the labeling of the axes, as illustrated in Fig. 5.3. Most view the demand relationship as having the form

$$\text{Quantity demanded} = f(\text{price per unit})$$

That is, consumers respond to price. It is not as satisfying to think of price being determined by demand. In this book we use the vertical axis to represent the dependent variable. That is the reason for the labeling in Fig. 5.3.

Verify, using the methods of the last chapter, that the demand curve in Fig. 5.3 has the form

$$q = f(p) = 47,500 - 7,500p$$

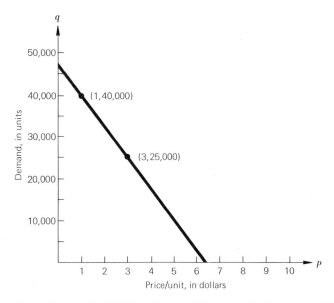

FIGURE 5.3

POINTS FOR THOUGHT AND DISCUSSION
Interpret the meaning of the y intercept in this example. Does this
seem valid? What is the interpretation of the x intercept? What is the
interpretation of the slope in this function? The restricted domain of
the function seems to be $0 \leq p \leq 6.333$. Would you be tempted to
restrict the domain any further?

Linear Supply Functions A *supply function* relates market
price to the quantities that suppliers are willing to produce and sell. The
implication of supply functions is that what is brought to the market depends upon the price people are willing to pay. As opposed to the inverse nature of price and demand in demand functions, the quantity
which suppliers are willing to provide usually varies directly with the
market price. *All other things being equal,* the higher the market price,
the more a supplier would like to produce and sell; and the lower the
price people are willing to pay, the less the incentive to produce and
sell. Assume that you own a lobster boat. All other things considered
equal, think about your incentive to take your boat and crew out if lobster is wholesaling at $0.25 per pound. Now, what if it is wholesaling at
$10 per pound?

As with demand functions, supply functions can be approximated
sometimes by using linear functions. Figure 5.4 illustrates a sample
supply function. Note that by labeling the vertical axis q, it is suggested
that

$$\text{Quantity supplied} = f(\text{market price})$$

**Example
5.10**

FIGURE 5.4

176

q

Quantity supplied

S

Market price

p

FIGURE 5.5

POINTS FOR THOUGHT AND DISCUSSION

POINTS FOR THOUGHT AND DISCUSSION
What does the *y* intercept in Fig. 5.4 suggest about the relationship between supply and demand? If the supply curve appears as in Fig. 5.5, what does the *x* intercept suggest about the relationship?

Follow-up Exercises

5.7 A piece of machinery is purchased for $50,000. Accountants have decided to use a straight-line depreciation method with the machine being fully depreciated after 8 years. Letting V equal the book value of the machine and t the age of the machine, determine the function $V = f(t)$. (Assume no salvage value.)

5.8 In Exercise 5.7 assume that the machine will have a salvage value of $6,000 at the end of 8 years. Determine the function $V = f(t)$ for this situation.

5.9 An airline claims that it is using straight-line depreciation on one of its 747s. The initial purchase cost was $5.5 million. Company records indicate that after the first year the book value of the plane was $4,950,000. After the third year the value was $3,850,000, and after the sixth year the value was $2,200,000. Assume no salvage value.
(*a*) Are they using straight-line depreciation?
(*b*) If so, what is the function $V = f(t)$?
(*c*) When will the 747 be fully depreciated?

5.10 Assume that the 747 in Exercise 5.9 has a useful life of 8 years and at this stage it can be salvaged for $750,000. Determine the function $V = f(t)$. What is the restricted domain for the function?

5.11 A metropolitan police department projects that average weekly levels of serious crime decrease in direct proportion to the number of patrol cars assigned to preventive patrol. Analysts estimate that the number of serious crimes which would occur each week with no patrol cars is 800. They also believe that the linear relationship is valid only for allocations of up to 120 patrol cars. At this level of preventive patrol, crime levels are expected to be 260 serious crimes per week. Analysts believe that any additional allocations would have no effect on the level of crime.
(*a*) Determine the linear function relating number of serious crimes to the number of patrol cars.
(*b*) Define the restricted range and domain of the function.
(*c*) What is the marginal effect of each additional patrol car for this function?

5.12 Two points (p, q) on a linear demand function are ($2.50, 20,000) and ($2.75, 18,000).
(*a*) Determine the demand function $q = f(p)$.
(*b*) What price would result in demand of 12,000 units?
(*c*) Interpret the slope of the function.
(*d*) Sketch the function.

5.13 Two points (p, q) on a linear demand function are ($50, 35,000) and ($47.50, 45,000).
(a) Determine the demand function $q = f(p)$.
(b) What price would result in demand of 60,000 units?
(c) Interpret the slope of the function.
(d) Sketch the function.

5.14 Two points (p, q) on a linear supply function are ($3, 60,000) and ($2.50, 52,000).
(a) Determine the supply function $q = f(p)$.
(b) What price would result in suppliers offering 80,000 units for sale?
(c) Interpret the slope of the function.
(d) Sketch the function.

5.15 Two points (p, q) on a linear supply function are ($12.50, 75,000) and ($15, 90,000).
(a) Determine the supply function $q = f(p)$.
(b) What price would cause suppliers to offer 50,000 units for sale?
(c) Interpret the slope of the function.
(d) Sketch the function.

5.16 *Alcoholism* Since 1960 there has been a seemingly linear increase in the percentage of the population who are alcoholics in one European country. In 1960 the percentage of the population who were alcoholics was 15.6 percent. In 1970 the percentage had risen to 21.2 percent. Let p equal the percentage of the population who are alcoholics and t represent time measured in years since 1960 ($t = 0$ for 1960).
(a) Determine the linear growth function $p = f(t)$.
(b) Interpret the meaning of the slope.
(c) If the pattern of growth continues, forecast the percentage of alcoholics in 1985. What is the forecasted percentage for 1990?

5.17 *Grade Inflation* Since 1973 there has been evidence of grade inflation at a large Midwestern university. The cumulative grade-point average for all undergraduate students was 2.42 in 1973. In 1977 the average was 2.66. Assuming the trend is linear, let g represent the cumulative grade-point average for all undergraduate students and t represent time measured in years since 1973.
(a) Determine the function $g = f(t)$.
(b) According to this function, when will the grade-point average reach 3.0?
(c) Forecast the grade-point average for 1980.
(d) Interpret the meaning of the slope in this function.

BREAK-EVEN MODELS 5.3

In this section we will discuss *break-even models*, a set of planning tools which can be, and has been, very useful in managing organizations. One significant indication of the performance of the companies is reflected by the so-called bottom line of the income statement for the firm, that is, how much profit was earned! Break-even analysis focuses upon the profitability of a firm. Of specific concern in break-even analysis is identifying the level of operation or level of output that would result in a zero profit. This level of operation or output is called the *break-even point*. The break-even point is a useful reference point in the sense that it represents the level of operation where total revenue equals total cost. Any changes from this level of operation will result in either a profit or a loss.

Break-even analysis is valuable as a planning tool when firms are contemplating expansions such as offering new products or services. Similarly, it is useful in evaluating the pros and cons of beginning a new business or venture. In every case the analysis allows for a projection of profitability.

Assumptions

Since we have been discussing linear functions, our concern is with situations in which both the total cost function and the total revenue function are linear. We will also concentrate on analysis for a single product or service.

The use of a linear total cost function implies that variable costs per unit either are constant or can be assumed to be constant. In addition, the linear cost function assumes that total variable costs depend upon the level of operation or output. It is also assumed that the fixed-cost portion of the cost function is constant over the levels of output being considered.

The linear total revenue function assumes that the selling price per unit is constant. Where the selling price is not constant, some analysts may use an average price for purposes of conducting the analysis.

Another assumption must be that price per unit is greater than variable cost per unit. Think about that for a moment. If price per unit is less than variable cost per unit, a firm will lose money on every unit produced and sold.

Break-Even Analysis

In break-even analysis the primary objective is to determine the break-even point. The break-even point may be expressed in terms of (1) volume of output, (2) total dollar sales, or possibly (3) percentage of production capacity. For example, it might be stated that a firm will break even at 100,000 units of output, when total sales equal $2.5 million or when the firm is operating at 60 percent of its plant capacity. We will focus primarily on the first of these three ways, although on occasion the expression of the break-even point in an alternative form is desirable.

The methods of performing break-even analysis are rather straightforward, and there are alternative ways of determining the break-even point. The usual approach is first to construct the total cost function $C(x)$ and the total revenue function $R(x)$, where x represents the level of output. When these functions have been identified, the break-even point may be determined by either setting $R(x)$ equal to $C(x)$ and solving for the break-even level of output x_{BE} or formulating the total profit function $P(x)$ and then setting $P(x)$ equal to 0, a procedure algebraically equivalent to the first.

The following example illustrates both approaches.

A group of engineers is interested in forming a company to produce **Example** smoke detectors. They have gone through a design stage and estimate **5.11** that variable costs per unit, including materials, labor, and marketing costs, are $22.50. Fixed costs associated with the formation, operation, and management of the company and the purchase of equipment and machinery total $250,000. They estimate that the selling price will be $30 per detector.

(a) Determine the number of smoke detectors which must be sold in order for the firm to break even on the venture.
(b) Preliminary marketing data indicate that the firm can expect to sell approximately 30,000 smoke detectors over the life of the project if they price the detectors at $30. Determine expected profits at this level of output.

(a) The total revenue function is represented by the equation **Solution**

$$R(x) = 30x$$

The total cost function is represented by the equation

$$C(x) = 22.50x + 250,000$$

The break-even condition occurs when total revenue equals total cost, or when

$$R(x) = C(x) \qquad (5.6)$$

For this problem the break-even point is computed in the following way:

or
and
$$30x = 22.50x + 250,000$$
$$7.50x = 250,000$$
$$x_{BE} = 33,333.33 \text{ units}$$

The approach which forms the profit function and sets it equal to 0 follows:

$$P(x) = R(x) - C(x)$$
$$= 30x - (22.50x + 250,000)$$
$$= 7.50x - 250,000$$

Setting $P(x)$ equal to 0, we have

or
$$7.50x = 250,000$$
$$x_{BE} = 33,333.33 \text{ units}$$

This is the same result, and our conclusion is that *given the assumed cost and price parameters (values)*, the firm must sell 33,333.33 units in order to break even.

EXERCISE
**Verify that total revenue and total costs both equal
$1,000,000 (taking rounding into account) at the
break-even point.**

(b) With sales projected at 30,000 smoke detectors,

$$P(30,000) = 7.5(30,000) - 250,000$$
$$= 225,000 - 250,000$$
$$= -25,000$$

This suggests that if all estimates hold true—price, cost, and demand—the firm can expect to lose $25,000 on the venture.

**Example
5.12** **Graphical Approach** The essence of break-even analysis is illustrated very nicely by graphical analysis. Figure 5.6a illustrates the total revenue function, Fig. 5.6b the total cost function, and Fig. 5.6c a composite graph showing both functions, for Example 5.11. Note in Fig. 5.6b that the fixed-cost component is distinguished from the variable-cost component. At *any* level of output, the darker shaded area indicates the fixed cost of $250,000. To this is added the total variable cost, which is represented by the vertical distance within the lighter area. In combination these two costs add to give you a point on the $C(x)$ line.

In Fig. 5.6c the two functions are graphed on the same set of axes. The only point where the two functions intersect represents the one level of output where total revenue and total cost are equal. This is the break-even point. Note that for all points to the left of the break-even point the cost function $C(x)$ has a value greater than the revenue function $R(x)$. For any level of output below 33.333 (1,000's) units, the vertical

FIGURE 5.6

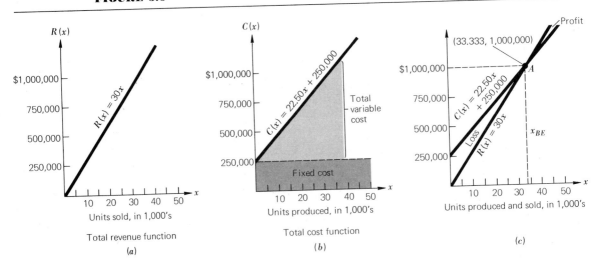

Total revenue function

(a)

Total cost function

(b)

(c)

distance separating the two functions represents the loss which would
occur. To the right of $x = 33.333$, $R(x)$ is higher than $C(x)$. And, when
total revenue exceeds total cost, a profit exists. As was true to the left of
$x = 33.333$, for levels of output greater than $x = 33.333$ the vertical distance separating $R(x)$ and $C(x)$ represents the profit.

Figure 5.7 illustrates the profit function $P(x)$ for this example. The
break-even point is identified by the x intercept. Note that to the left of
the break-even point the profit function is below the x axis, indicating a
negative profit, or loss. To the right, $P(x)$ is above the x axis, indicating a
positive profit.

An alternative way of viewing break-even analysis is in terms of profit
contribution. As long as the price per unit p exceeds the variable cost
per unit v, the sale of each unit results in a contribution to profit. The
difference between p and v is called the *profit margin*. Or, stated in
equation form,

$$\text{Profit margin} = p - v \qquad p > v$$

When there are fixed costs, the profit margin must first be allocated to
recover the fixed costs. At lower levels of output, the *total* profit contribution is typically less than fixed costs, meaning that total profit is negative (see Fig. 5.7). Only when *total* profit contribution exceeds fixed cost
will a positive profit exist. Because of this orientation—that the profit
margin per unit contributes first to recovering fixed costs after which it
contributes to profit—profit margin is often called the *contribution to
fixed cost and profit*.

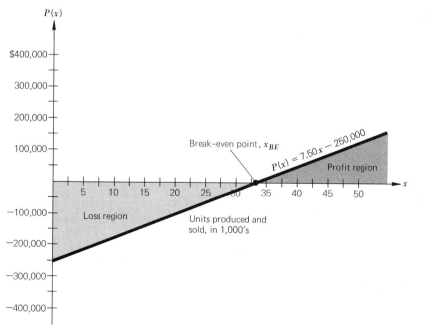

FIGURE 5.7

With this perspective in mind, the computation of the break-even point can be thought of as determining the number of units to produce and sell in order to recover the fixed costs. The calculation of the break-even point is thus

$$\text{Break-even level of output} = \frac{\text{fixed cost}}{\text{contribution to fixed cost and profit}}$$

or
$$x_{BE} = \frac{FC}{p - v}. \qquad (5.7)$$

Example 5.13

Convention Planning A professional organization is planning its annual convention to be held in San Francisco. Arrangements are being made with a large hotel in which the convention will be held. Registrants for the three-day convention will be charged a flat fee of $250 per person which includes registration fee, room, all meals, and tips. The hotel charges the organization $20,000 for the use of the facilities such as meeting rooms, ballroom, and recreational facilities. In addition, the hotel charges $145 per person for room, meals, tips, and so forth. The organization also appropriates $25 of the $250 fee to be deposited in the treasury of the national office. Determine the number of registrants necessary for the organization to cover the fixed cost of $20,000.

Solution

The contribution to fixed cost and profit is the registration cost per person less the cost per person charged by the hotel less the national organization's share per registrant, or

$$\text{Contribution per registrant} = 250 - 145 - 25$$
$$= \$80$$

Therefore, according to Eq. (5.7), the number of registrants required to cover the fixed cost is

$$x_{BE} = \frac{20,000}{80}$$
$$= 250 \text{ persons}$$

POINTS FOR THOUGHT AND DISCUSSION
What are the expected effects on the break-even point if (1) the price per unit increases (decreases), (2) the variable cost per unit increases (decreases), or (3) the fixed cost increases (decreases)?

Follow-up Exercises

5.18 A firm produces a product which sells at a price of $25 per unit. Variable costs are estimated to be $18.75 per unit, and fixed costs are $50,000.

(*a*) Determine the break-even level of output.

(*b*) Compute total cost and total revenue at the break-even point.

(*c*) What will profit equal if demand equals 7,500 units?

5.19 A firm produces a product which sells at a price of $150 per unit. Variable cost per unit is estimated at $130, and fixed costs are $250,000.

(*a*) Determine the break-even level of output.

(*b*) Compute total cost and total revenue at the break-even point.

(*c*) What will profit equal if 12,000 units are demanded?

5.20 A local charity organization is planning a chartered flight and one-week vacation to the Caribbean. The venture is a fund-raising effort. A package deal has been worked out with a commercial airline in which the charity will be charged a fixed cost of $10,000 plus $300 per person. The $300 covers the flight cost, transfers, hotel, meals, and tips. The organization is planning to price the package at $450 per person.

(*a*) Determine the number of persons necessary to break even on the venture.

(*b*) The goal of the organization is to net a profit of $10,000. How many people must participate for the goal to be realized?

5.21 The management of a local civic center is negotiating a contract with the rock and roll group The Windy City. The Windy City commands a fee of $25,000 plus 37.5 percent of gate receipts. Promoters expect to charge $8 per ticket for the performance.

(*a*) Determine the number of tickets which must be sold in order to break even.

(*b*) If the promoters hope to clear a profit of $20,000, how many tickets must be sold?

5.22 In Exercise 5.20, assume that the organization has received pledges guaranteeing that the trip will be subscribed to the capacity of 150 people. Assume the organization wished only to break even on the venture.

(*a*) What price should they charge each person?

(*b*) What price would enable the organization to realize its profit goal of $10,000?

5.23 In Exercise 5.21, assume that promoters believe that the show will be a sellout of 10,000 fanatics.

(*a*) What ticket price would allow them to break even?

(*b*) What ticket price would allow them to realize the profit goal of $20,000?

5.24 *Make or Buy Decision* Often firms face the decision as to whether it is more economical to manufacture a product or component part of some final product or to purchase the product from another manufacturer. The decision—make or buy—very often depends upon how many units are needed. If relatively few units are required, it may be cheaper to have someone else supply the item. If the number of units required is large, an investment in plant and equipment may be justified because the unit cost would be lower than your supplier charges.

Assume that a manufacturer can either purchase a needed component part from a supplier at a cost of $5 per unit or invest $18,000 in equipment and produce the item at a cost of $3.50 per unit.

(a) Determine the quantity for which total costs are equal for the *make* and *buy* alternatives.

(b) Sketch the cost functions for both the make and buy alternatives.

(c) What is the minimum cost alternative if 20,000 units are required?

(d) What is the minimum cost?

5.25 *Advertising Campaign* A firm is developing a TV advertising campaign. Development costs (fixed costs) are $100,000, and the firm must pay $10,000 per minute for television slots. The firm estimates that for each minute of advertising additional sales of $50,000 result. Of this $50,000, $37,500 is absorbed to cover the variable costs of producing the items and $10,000 must be used to pay for the minute of advertising. Any remainder is the contribution to fixed cost and profit.

(a) How many minutes of advertising are necessary to recover the development costs of the advertising campaign?

(b) If the firm uses this campaign for 60 one-minute slots, determine total revenues, total costs (production and advertising), and total profit (or loss) resulting from the campaign.

5.26 *Car Leasing* A car leasing agency purchases new cars each year for use in the agency. The cars cost $5,000 new. They are used for two years, after which they are sold for $1,800. The owner estimates that the variable costs of operating the cars, exclusive of gasoline, are $0.18 per mile. The cars are leased at a flat rate of $0.23 per mile.

(a) What is the break-even mileage for the 2-year period?

(b) What are total revenue, total cost, and total profit for the 2-year period if a car is leased for 50,000 miles?

5.27 In Exercise 5.26, it is expected that the average car will be leased for 50,000 miles during a 2-year period.

(a) What rate per mile needs to be charged in order to break even?

(b) If the dealer wishes to earn a profit of $1,000 per car over its 2-year lifetime, what rate must be charged per mile?

5.4   OTHER APPLICATIONS

In this section we will see some other applications of linear functions and simultaneous equations. Further applications are contained in the Follow-up Exercises and end-of-chapter problems.

FIGURE 5.8

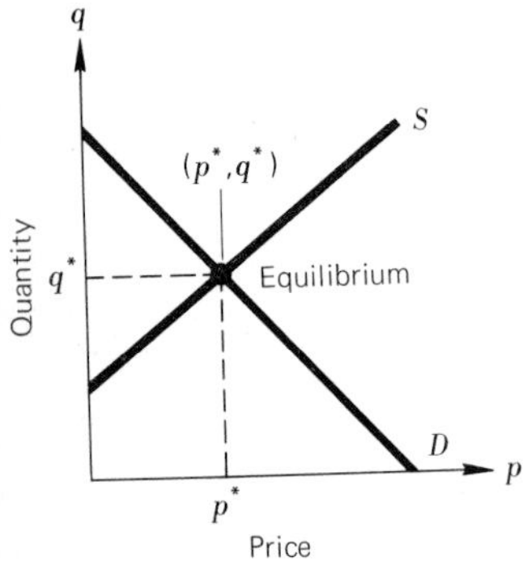

Equilibrium between Supply and Demand

In Examples 5.9 and 5.10 we discussed linear supply and demand functions. One of the concerns of economists is whether the consumers and suppliers will ever have a meeting of the minds and reach agreement about the quantities which will be supplied and purchased and the market price at which this will occur. When agreement is reached, the market is said to be in *equilibrium*. That is, at the equilibrium price the amount demanded by consumers is exactly equal to the quantity suppliers are willing to bring to the market. This equilibrium condition is defined by the coordinates of the point where the supply and demand functions intersect. Figure 5.8 illustrates this condition, where p^* is the equilibrium price and q^* is the equilibrium quantity.

**Example
5.14**

The demand function for a particular product is $q_d = 10,000 - 50p$, where p is price stated in dollars and q_d is quantity demanded in thousands of units. The supply function is $q_s = 2,000 + 30p$, where p is defined as before and q_s is the quantity supplied, in thousands of units. Determine the equilibrium price and quantity. Sketch the two functions.

Equilibrium occurs if there is a price which equates supply and demand, or when

$$q_s = q_d$$

or
$$2,000 + 30p = 10,000 - 50p$$

Solving for p, we find equilibrium occurs when

$$80p = 8,000$$

or
$$p = 100$$

At a price of $100 the quantity supplied and demanded equals 5,000 thousands, or 5 million units. Figure 5.9 illustrates the functions.

Defining Mathematical Functions

Simultaneous equations are one approach to defining mathematical functions. A linear function involving two variables has the form of Eq. (5.1), or

$$y = ax + b \qquad (5.1)$$

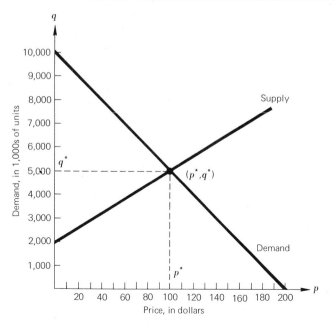

FIGURE 5.9

In order to define a linear function, values must be determined for the parameters a and b. If the coordinates of two points which lie on the function are known, the values of a and b can be determined by substituting each pair of coordinates into Eq. (5.1), forming two equations. These two equations can then be solved simultaneously to determine a and b.

Example 5.15

Using simultaneous equations, determine the linear function which contains $(4, 8)$ and $(7, -4)$.

Solution

Substituting $(4, 8)$ and $(7, -4)$ into Eq. (5.1) yields

$$8 = a(4) + b \quad \text{or} \quad 8 = 4a + b \tag{5.8}$$
$$\text{and} \quad -4 = a(7) + b \quad \text{or} \quad -4 = 7a + b \tag{5.9}$$

Multiplying Eq. (5.8) by -1 and adding to Eq. (5.9) yields

$$
\begin{aligned}
-8 &= -4a - b \\
-4 &= 7a + b \\
\hline
-12 &= 3a \\
-4 &= a
\end{aligned}
$$

or

Substituting $a = -4$ into Eq. (5.8) gives

$$8 = 4(-4) + b$$
$$24 = b$$

or

With a and b defined, the function can be specified as

$$y = f(x) = -4x + 24$$

Product-Mix Problem

A variety of applications are concerned with determining the quantities of different products which satisfy certain requirements. In the following example we are interested in determining the quantities of three products which will fully utilize production capacity.

Example 5.16

A company produces three products, each of which must be processed through three different departments. Table 5.2 summarizes the hours required per unit of each product in each department. In addition, the weekly capacities are stated for each department in terms of work-hours available. What is desired is to determine whether there are any combinations of the three products which would exhaust the weekly capacities of the three departments.

Table 5.2

	Department 1	Department 2	Department 3
Product A	2	3	4
Product B	3.5	2.5	3
Product C	3	2	2
Hours available/week	1,200	1,150	1,400

If we let x_j = number of units produced per week of product j, the conditions to be satisfied are

$$2x_1 + 3.5x_2 + 3x_3 = 1,200 \quad \text{(department 1)}$$
$$3x_1 + 2.5x_2 + 2x_3 = 1,150 \quad \text{(department 2)}$$
$$4x_1 + 3x_2 + 2x_3 = 1,400 \quad \text{(department 3)}$$

Verify that by solving these simultaneously, the solution set consists of one solution which is $x_1 = 200$, $x_2 = 100$, and $x_3 = 150$, or (200, 100, 150). This solution set implies that the product-mix of 200 units of product A, 100 units of product B, and 150 units of product C is the *only one* which will exhaust the weekly capacities in all the departments.

Emergency Airlift Revisited In Example 3.24 and at the very beginning of Chap. 4, we discussed a problem involving the airlift of emergency supplies into a South American city. Two restrictions were imposed—a volume capacity of 6,000 cubic feet and a weight capacity of 40,000 pounds. The two equations whose solution sets contain quantities of the different items which fill the plane to its respective capacities were

Example 5.17

$$20x_1 + 30x_2 + 8x_3 + 6x_4 = 6,000 \quad \text{(volume)}$$
$$150x_1 + 100x_2 + 60x_3 + 70x_4 = 40,000 \quad \text{(weight)}$$

(Refer to Example 3.24 for a definition of the variables.)

If we are interested in determining quantities of the various items which will fill the plane to *both* its volume and its weight capacities, we want the solution set for the system. Our knowledge of Chap. 4 should lead us to conclude that there is either no solution or, more likely, an infinite number of solutions. Sample solutions may be found by assuming values for two of the four variables and solving for the values of the remaining two. As an example, if $x_3 = x_4 = 0$, $x_1 = 240$, and $x_2 = 40$. One combination of items which will fill the plane to its weight and volume capacities is 240 containers of blood and 40 containers of medical supply kits. Can you generate other combinations?

Portfolio Model

A *portfolio* of stocks is simply the set of stocks owned by an investor. In selecting the portfolio for a particular investor, consideration is often given to such things as the amount of money to be invested, the attitude the investor has about risk (is he or she a risk taker?), and whether the investor is interested in long-term growth or short-run return. This type of problem is similar to the product-mix example. The products are the stocks or securities available for investment.

When people invest money, there are professionals, such as stock-brokers, who may be consulted for advice about the portfolio which best meets an individual's needs. An investor who has $50,000 to be invested has consulted with a local investment expert. After talking with the

Example 5.18

client, the investment expert determines that the client is interested in a portfolio which will have an expected annual growth in market value of 6 percent and an average risk of 10 percent. Three investments have been identified with the following growth and risk rates.

	Expected Annual Growth in Market Value	Expected Risk
Investment 1	8%	12%
Investment 2	4	9
Investment 3	6	8

To determine the portfolio, let's define x_j as the number of dollars invested in investment j. One condition which may be stated in equation form is that total dollars invested equal $50,000, or

$$x_1 + x_2 + x_3 = 50,000 \qquad (5.10)$$

The condition referring to expected annual growth in market value is a little bit more difficult to formulate than other equations we have formulated. Let's precede the formulation by looking at a simple example. Suppose that you put $100 in a bank and it earns interest of 6 percent per year. Also suppose you put $200 in another investment and it earns 12 percent interest. To determine the *average* percent return on your $300 investment, we must compute total interest and divide by the original investment, or

$$\text{Average percent return} = \frac{\text{dollars of interest earned}}{\text{dollars invested}}$$

For this example, the average annual percent return is computed as

$$\frac{0.06(100) + 0.12(200)}{100 + 200} = \frac{6 + 24}{300}$$
$$= \frac{30}{300}$$
$$= 0.10, \text{ or } 10\%$$

To compute the average percent growth in our example, we must multiply each dollar invested by the percent return on that dollar, sum these for the entire investment, and divide by the total investment, or

$$\text{Average percent growth} = \frac{0.08x_1 + 0.04x_2 + 0.06x_3}{x_1 + x_2 + x_3}$$

Since Eq. (5.10) specifies that $x_1 + x_2 + x_3 = 50,000$ and since the investor desires an average percent growth of 6 percent, we can rewrite the equation as

$$\frac{0.08x_1 + 0.04x_2 + 0.06x_3}{50,000} = 0.06$$

or, multiplying both sides of the equation by 50,000, we get

$$0.08x_1 + 0.04x_2 + 0.06x_3 = 3,000 \qquad (5.11)$$

The weighted risk condition is determined in exactly the same manner. To calculate average risk per dollar invested, each dollar must be multiplied by the risk associated with the investment of that dollar. These must be summed for all different investments and divided by the total investment. This equation can be stated in our example as

$$\frac{0.12x_1 + 0.09x_2 + 0.08x_3}{50,000} = 0.10$$

or $\qquad 0.12x_1 + 0.09x_2 + 0.08x_3 = 5,000 \qquad$ (5.12)

Verify that when Eqs. (5.10) to (5.12) are solved simultaneously, $x_1 = 20,000$, $x_2 = 20,000$, and $x_3 = 10,000$. Or, the only investment portfolio which satisfies all the investor's requirements is an investment of \$20,000 in investment 1, \$20,000 in investment 2, and \$10,000 in investment 3.

Blending Model

Some applications involve the mixing of ingredients or components to form a final blend having specific characteristics. Examples include the blending of gasoline and other petroleum products, the blending of coffee beans, and the blending of whiskeys. Very often the blending requirements and relationships are defined by linear equations or inequalities. The following example illustrates a simple application.

A coffee manufacturer is interested in blending three different types of coffee beans into a final coffee blend. The three component beans cost the manufacturer \$1.20, \$1.60, and \$1.40 per pound, respectively. The manufacturer wants to blend a batch of 40,000 pounds of coffee and has a coffee purchasing budget of \$57,600. In blending the coffee, one restriction is that the amount used of component 2 should be twice that of component 1 (the brewmaster believes this to be critical in avoiding a bitter flavor).

Example 5.19

The objective is to determine whether there is a combination of the three components which will lead to a final blend of 40,000 pounds costing \$57,600 and satisfying the blending restriction on components 1 and 2.

If x_j equals the number of pounds of component j used in the final blend, Eq. (5.13) specifies that the total blend should weigh 40,000 pounds:

$$x_1 + x_2 + x_3 = 40,000 \qquad (5.13)$$

Equation (5.14) specifies that the total cost of the three components should equal \$57,600:

$$1.20x_1 + 1.60x_2 + 1.40x_3 = 57,600 \qquad (5.14)$$

The recipe restriction is stated as

$$x_2 = 2x_1$$

or alternatively, $\qquad -2x_1 + x_2 = 0 \qquad (5.15)$

Verify that when Eqs. (5.13) to (5.15) are solved simultaneously, the solution is $x_1 = 8,000$, $x_2 = 16,000$, and $x_3 = 16,000$. The final blend will be composed of 8,000 pounds of component 1, 16,000 pounds of component 2, and 16,000 pounds of component 3.

Follow-up Exercises

5.28 Determine the equilibrium price and quantity if

$$q_d = 25,000 - 50p \quad \text{and} \quad q_s = 4,000 + 20p$$

where p is stated in dollars.

5.29 Determine the equilibrium price and quantity if

$$q_d = 100,000 - 1,500p \quad \text{and} \quad q_s = 10,000 + 3,000p$$

where p is stated in dollars.

5.30 *Income Shifts* Economists believe that if there is a general shift in income levels, demand will change at all price levels. For instance, if everyone's income increased by 10 percent, all other things remaining unchanged, at any given price level greater quantities of a product would be demanded. Tax rebates are often employed to stimulate greater demand. Similarly, it is believed that decreases in income levels will result in smaller quantities being demanded at any given price. These income shifts can be represented by a shift in the demand curve. Figure 5.10 indicates the nature of the demand curve movements. Note the changes in demand at a price p_1 for the different curves. Assume in Example 5.14 that income levels have increased such that the demand curve has shifted outward. The slope is the same, but the y intercept is 12,000 instead of 10,000. Determine the new equilibrium price and quantity.

FIGURE 5.10

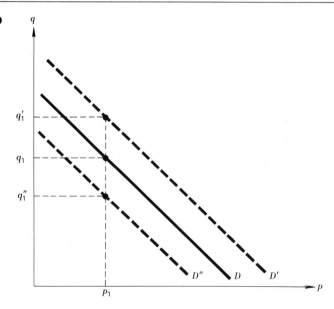

5.31 Referring to the discussion of income shifts in Exercise 5.30, assume in Exercise 5.28 that income levels have decreased sufficiently to cause a downward shift in the demand curve. The slope is the same, but the y intercept is now 17,500. Determine the new equilibrium price and quantity.

5.32 *Supply Shifts* Just as changes in income levels can cause shifts of the demand curve, there are factors which can cause shifts in supply functions. For example, severe weather conditions may lead to general shortages of crops, which may be evidenced by a *downward* shift in the supply curve. Similarly, exceptionally good years may result in a more abundant supply and an upward shift in the supply function. These shifts in the supply curve reflect the fact that when more is available, suppliers are willing to supply larger quantities at any given price. And when less is available, they are willing to supply smaller quantities at any given price.

Assume in Exercise 5.28 that poor weather conditions have resulted in a downward shift of the supply function such that it is described by

$$q_s = 500 + 20p$$

Determine the new equilibrium price and quantity.

5.33 Using simultaneous equations, determine the linear function which contains the points $(2, 6)$ and $(4, -2)$.

5.34 Using simultaneous equations, determine the linear function which contains the points $(-2, 4)$ and $(1, 10)$.

5.35 *Quadratic Functions* A quadratic function is a nonlinear function having the general form $y = ax^2 + bx + c$, where $a \neq 0$. If a, b, and c can be specified, the function is defined. Since three parameters define a quadratic function, three data points are needed to define their values. A quadratic function contains the points $(1, 8)$, $(3, 20)$, and $(-2, 5)$. Substitute these coordinates into the general quadratic equation and solve the three resulting linear equations for a, b, and c. What is the equation of the quadratic function containing these points?

5.36 A company produces three products, each of which must be processed through three different departments. Table 5.3 summarizes the hours required per unit of each product in each department. In addition, weekly capacities are stated for each department in terms of work-hours available. Determine whether there are any combinations of the three products which would exhaust the weekly capacities of the three departments.

	Department 1	Department 2	Department 3	
Product *A*	3	5	4	**Table 5.3**
Product *B*	4	3	2	
Product *C*	2	4	3	
Hours available/week	470	690	520	

5.37 *Diet-Mix Problems* A dietician is planning the menu for the evening meal at a university dining hall. Three main items will be served, each having different nutritional content. The goal is that the nutritional

Table 5.4		Vitamin 1	Vitamin 2	Vitamin 3
Food 1		5 mg	2 mg	1 mg
Food 2		3 mg	1 mg	5 mg
Food 3		2 mg	3 mg	2 mg
Minimum daily vitamin requirement		29 mg	20 mg	21 mg

content of the meal meet the minimum daily levels for three different vitamins. Table 5.4 summarizes the vitamin content *per ounce* of each food. In addition, the minimum daily levels of the three vitamins are indicated. Determine the number of ounces of each food to be included in the meal such that minimum daily vitamin levels are met for the three vitamins.

5.38 An investor has $100,000 to spend. Three investments are being considered, each having an expected annual interest rate. The interest rates are 6, 10, and 5 percent, respectively. The investor's goal is an average return of 7.5 percent in the three investments. Because of the lower risk on investment alternative 3, the investor wants the investment in this alternative to equal 60 percent of the sum of the other two alternatives. [*Hint:* $x_3 = 0.6(x_1 + x_2)$.] Determine whether there is a meaningful investment strategy which will satisfy these requirements.

5.39 A distillery is planning a production run of 60,000 gallons of a blended whiskey. Three component bourbons are mixed to form the final product. Bourbons 1, 2, and 3 cost $2, $2.50, and $1.75 per gallon, respectively. The blending recipe calls for bourbon 1 to be $2\frac{1}{2}$ times the amount of bourbon 3 in the final blend. The total cost of the component blends should equal $130,000. Determine the number of gallons of each bourbon which should be included in the final blend.

CHAPTER CHECKLIST

If you have read all sections of this chapter, you should

_____ Be familiar with the structure and characteristics of *linear functions*

_____ Understand the assumptions underlying the structure of linear functions

_____ Understand the structure of *linear cost, revenue,* and *profit functions* and the assumptions underlying these functions

_____ Be familiar with linear functions as applied to *straight-line depreciation, demand functions,* and *supply functions*

_____ Understand *break-even models,* their purpose, and the mechanics and graphics of break-even analysis

_____ Be familiar with other applications such as equilibrium conditions in supply and demand, determining equations for mathematical functions, product-mix problems, portfolio problems, and blending problems

KEY TERMS AND CONCEPTS

linear function	demand function
cost	supply function
variable cost	break-even point
fixed cost	contribution to fixed cost and
economies (diseconomies) of scale	profit
	equilibrium
revenue	product-mix
profit	portfolio
depreciation (straight-line)	blending model
salvage value	

IMPORTANT FORMULAS

$$y = f(x) = ax + b \tag{5.1}$$
$$y = f(x_1, x_2) = a_1x_1 + a_2x_2 + b \tag{5.2}$$
$$y = f(x_1, x_2, \ldots, x_n) = a_1x_1 + a_2x_2 + \cdots + a_nx_n + b \tag{5.3}$$

$$\left.\begin{array}{l} R(x) = C(x) \\ x_{\mathrm{BE}} = \dfrac{FC}{p - v} \end{array}\right\} \text{Break-even definition} \qquad \begin{array}{l}(5.6)\\[1.5em](5.7)\end{array}$$

ADDITIONAL EXERCISES

Exercises 5.40 to 5.41 are related to Sec. 5.1.

5.40 A firm sells a product for $50 per unit. Raw material costs are $22.50 per unit, labor costs are $13.50 per unit, and annual fixed costs are $70,000.

(a) Determine the profit function $P(x)$ where x equals the number of units sold.

(b) How many units would have to be sold to earn an annual profit of $35,000?

5.41 A firm produces three products which sell, respectively, for $10, $15, and $8.50. Labor requirements for each product are, respectively, 2.5, 3.5, and 2 hours per unit. Assume labor costs are $3 per hour and annual fixed costs are $50,000.

(a) Construct a joint total revenue function for the sales of the three products.

(b) Determine an annual total cost function for production of the three products.

(c) Determine the profit function for the three products.

(d) What is annual profit if 20,000, 10,000 and 30,000 units are sold, respectively, of the three products?

Exercises 5.42 to 5.46 are related to Sec. 5.2.

5.42 A city has purchased a new fire truck for $100,000. The city comptroller states that the fire truck will be depreciated by using a straight-line method. At the end of 12 years, the truck will be sold with an expected salvage value of $22,000.

(a) Determine the function $V = f(t)$ which expresses the book value of the truck V as a function of the age of the truck t.

(b) What is the book value expected to be when the truck is 6 years old?

5.43 The birthrate in a particular country has been declining linearly in recent years. In 1970 the birthrate was 25.6 births per 1,000 people. In 1978 the birthrate was 23.6 births per 1,000 people. Assume R equals the birthrate per 1,000 and t equals time measured in years since 1970 ($t = 0$ for 1970).

(a) Determine the linear birthrate function $R = f(t)$.

(b) Interpret the meaning of the slope.

(c) If the linear pattern continues, what is the expected birthrate in 1986?

(d) What is the restricted domain for this function?

5.44 Two points (p, q) on a linear demand function are ($4.50, 45,000) and ($5, 36,000).

(a) Determine the demand function $q = f(p)$.

(b) What price would result in a demand of 58,500 units?

(c) Determine the y intercept and interpret its meaning.

(d) Determine the x intercept and interpret its meaning.

5.45 Two points (p, q) on a linear supply function are ($10, 450,000) and ($15, 750,000).

(a) Determine the supply function $q = f(p)$.

(b) What price would result in suppliers offering 100,000 units for sale?

(c) Interpret the slope of the supply function.

(d) What is the x intercept? Interpret the meaning of this point.

5.46 Annual sales for a company have been increasing linearly at a rate of $4.5 million per year since 1972. Sales in 1975 were $260 million. Assume S equals annual sales in millions of dollars and t equals time in years (measured since 1972).

(a) Determine the function $S = f(t)$.

(b) What were annual sales in 1972?

(c) What are annual sales expected to equal in 1990?

Exercises 5.47 to 5.50 are related to Sec. 5.3.

5.47 A publisher has a fixed cost of $90,000 associated with the production of a college mathematics book. The contribution to profit and fixed cost from the sale of each book is $2.50.

(a) Determine the number of books which must be sold in order to break even.

(b) What is the expected profit if 30,000 books are sold?

5.48 A local college basketball team has added a national power to next year's schedule. The other team has agreed to play the game for a guaranteed fee of $10,000 plus 20 percent of the gate receipts. Assume ticket prices are $5.

(*a*) Determine the number of tickets which must be sold to recover the $10,000 guaranty.

(*b*) If college officials hope to net a profit of $25,000 from the game, how many tickets must be sold?

5.49 In Exercise 5.48, it is assured that 10,000 persons will attend.

(*a*) What ticket price would allow the college to break even?

(*b*) What ticket price would allow the college to earn the desired profit of $25,000?

5.50 *Equipment Selection* A firm has two equipment alternatives it can choose from in producing a new product. One automated piece of equipment costs $100,000 and produces items at a cost of $2.50 per unit. Another semiautomated piece of equipment costs $40,000 and produces items at a cost of $3 per unit.

(*a*) What volume of output makes the two pieces of equipment equally costly?

(*b*) If 100,000 units are going to be produced, which piece of equipment is the least costly? What is the minimum cost?

Exercises 5.51 to 5.54 are related to Sec. 5.4.

5.51 Determine the equilibrium price and quantity if

$$q_d = 50,000 - 75p \quad \text{and} \quad q_s = 10,000 + 25p$$

5.52 Using simultaneous equations, determine the linear function which contains the points (7.5, 4) and (6.0, 6).

5.53 Using simultaneous equations, determine the quadratic function which contains the points $(-1, 2)$, $(2, 8)$, and $(4, 32)$.

5.54 A company is combining peanuts, cashews, and almonds to form 1,000 pounds of a mixed-nut blend. Peanuts cost $0.60 per pound, cashews $1.10 per pound, and almonds $1.40 per pound. The number of pounds of cashews used in the blend should equal the number of pounds of almonds. If the blend is to cost $695, determine the number of pounds of each type of nut which should be used.

CHAPTER TEST

1 A company sells a product for $65 per unit. Raw material costs are $25 per unit, labor costs are $20 per unit, shipping costs are $5 per unit, and annual fixed costs are $75,000.

(*a*) Determine the profit function $P = f(x)$, where x equals the number of units sold.

(*b*) How many units must be sold in order to earn an annual profit of $150,000?

2 A piece of equipment had a book value of $60,000 when it was 2 years old and a book value of $37,500 when it was 5 years old. Assume that it is being depreciated by a straight-line method.

(*a*) What was the original book value?

(*b*) At what annual rate is the piece of equipment being depreciated?

(*c*) When will the book value equal 0?

3 A student organization is planning a ski week during semester break. It has arranged a package deal with a ski resort which provides for meals, equipment, lodging, and lift tickets at a cost of $180 per person plus a fixed cost of $2,000 for arranging special facilities and activities. Transportation costs are expected to equal $20 per person. Assume the student organization charges each student $225 for the complete package (transportation included).

(a) How many students will be required in order to break even?

(b) If the school subsidizes the trip by contributing $600, how many students will be required?

4 Determine the market equilibrium price and quantity if

$$q_d = 60,000 - 250p \qquad \text{and} \qquad q_s = 150p + 20,000$$

5 A company produces three products, each of which must be processed through three different departments. Table 5.5 summarizes the hours required per unit of each product in each department as well as the weekly capacities in each department. Formulate, *but do not solve*, the system of equations which, when solved, would indicate whether there are any combinations of the three products that would consume the weekly labor availability in all departments.

Table 5.5	Department 1	Department 2	Department 3
Product A	6	7	5
Product B	2	4	5
Product C	2	1	3
Hours available/week	80	60	100

CHAPTER OBJECTIVES After reading this chapter, you should be familiar with the nature and algebra of *linear inequalities*; you should be able to determine, graphically, the solution set for a system of linear inequalities; you should be familiar with the mathematical technique called *linear programming*; and you should be able to formulate linear programming problems and know how to solve such problems graphically when they involve two decision variables.

Although we have occasionally used inequalities in the previous chapters, this chapter discusses in a more formal manner the nature and algebra of *inequalities*. This is followed by a discussion of systems of *linear inequalities*. These are the last topics we need before presenting *linear programming*, a topic which integrates much of what we have been doing in the last three chapters. Linear programming is a powerful and widely applied mathematical technique.

In this chapter we will discuss the nature and structure of linear programming problems; we will see sample applications and graphical solution procedures for the two-variable situation. The last section of this chapter discusses special conditions which can arise in linear programming problems. The next chapter will discuss the *simplex method*, a solution procedure which is algebraically based and which is appropriate when graphical methods are not.

The Nature of Inequalities

Equations are used to represent a condition where two quantities are equal, e.g., number of work-hours used for production equals number of hours available. *Inequalities* express the condition that two quantities are not equal. There are different ways of expressing the condition of inequality. We have already used one method in the previous chapters. A statement such as $5 \neq 10$ indicates that the numbers 5 and 10 are *not* equal. We will be more interested in using the *inequality symbols*, $>$ or $<$ which, when placed between two numbers or expressions, "open" in the direction of the larger (in a real number sense) of the items being compared (see Sec. 0.1). The following examples illustrate the use of the inequality symbol. Note the comparisons among three items—*double inequalities*—and the way in which these are read.

$$3 < 5 \qquad 3 \text{ } is \text{ } less \text{ } than \text{ } 5$$
$$2 > -5 \qquad 2 \text{ } is \text{ } greater \text{ } than \text{ } -5$$
$$-10 < -2 \qquad -10 \text{ } is \text{ } less \text{ } than \text{ } -2$$
$$0 < 2 < 5 \qquad 2 \text{ } is \text{ } greater \text{ } than \text{ } 0 \text{ } and \text{ } less \text{ } than \text{ } 5$$
$$0 < x < 10 \qquad x \text{ } is \text{ } greater \text{ } than \text{ } 0 \text{ } and \text{ } less \text{ } than \text{ } 10$$

The direction of the inequality symbol is referred to as the *sense* of the inequality.

The inequalities illustrated are termed *strict inequalities* since the items being compared can never equal one another. We will be more concerned with situations in which items being compared may or may not be equal. To express this dual possibility, the inequality symbol is combined with half of an equals sign to form $\leq$ or $\geq$. The statement $x \leq 25$ implies that the variable x can assume values which are less than *or* equal to 25. The double inequality $0 \leq x \leq 25$ states that x may assume values which are greater than or equal to 0 and less than or equal to 25.

Very often a restriction is imposed which sets maximum or minimum values for some activity in a problem. In an investment problem, such as the portfolio example in the last chapter, the investor sets a goal of a minimum return on the investment. This goal might be stated as "the annual percentage return on the investment should be *at least* 7.5 percent," or, using inequality notation,

$$\text{Annual percentage return} \geq 7.5 \text{ percent}$$

Similarly, when a producer begins a production run with fixed quantities of raw materials, a restriction for the run is that

$$\begin{matrix} \text{Quantity of raw material} \\ \text{used in the production run} \end{matrix} \leq \begin{matrix} \text{quantity of raw} \\ \text{material available} \end{matrix}$$

The Algebra of Linear Inequalities

DEFINITION
A linear inequality involving n variables $x_1, x_2, x_3, \ldots, x_n$ has the general form

$$a_1x_1 + a_2x_2 + a_3x_3 + \cdots + a_nx_n \leq \text{ or } \geq b \qquad (6.1)$$

where $a_1, a_2, a_3, \ldots, a_n$ and b are real numbers and $a_1, a_2, a_3, \ldots, a_n$ cannot *all* equal zero.

The algebra of linear inequalities is very similar to the algebra of equations. Ultimately we will be concerned with defining solution sets for inequalities. For example, we may want to determine the value(s) of x which satisfy the inequality $20 - 4x \leq 36$. Given a problem like this, we need to know what algebraic operations can be used in obtaining the solution set. In most respects, the allowable operations are the same as with equations. *Equal quantities may be added to or subtracted from both sides of an inequality, and the inequality still holds.* Given the inequality $5 < 12$, 25 may be subtracted from both sides to yield $5 - 25 < 12 - 25$, or $-20 < -13$. The left side is still less than the right side by the same amount. If the original inequality has a solution set, the new inequality is an equivalent‡ inequality. Given the inequality $3x \leq x + 12$, adding 15 to both sides results in the equivalent inequality $3x + 15 \leq x + 27$.

Similarly, *both sides of an inequality may be multiplied or divided by the same positive number and the inequality still holds*. For example, multiplying both sides of the inequality $12 > -2$ by 5 results in the inequality $(5)(12) > 5(-2)$, or $60 > -10$, which has the same sense as the original inequality. Again, the solution set for the original inequality is equivalent to that for the new inequality. If both sides of the inequality $-2x \leq 4x - 18$ are divided by 2, the result is an equivalent inequality having the form $-x \leq 2x - 9$.

Both sides of an inequality may be multiplied or divided by a negative number. However, an important adjustment is necessary—*the sense of the inequality is reversed*. Multiplying both sides of the inequality $10 < 18$ by -2 results in the inequality $-20 > -36$. Similarly, dividing both sides of the same inequality by -2 results in $-5 > -9$.

Solution Sets for Linear Inequalities

To determine the solution set for a single inequality, solve for the variable of interest as you would in solving an equation. Just be sure that you remember the implications of multiplying or dividing by negative numbers.

---

‡ Do you remember what we mean by *equivalent?*

Example 6.1 To determine the solution set for the inequality $3x + 10 \leq 5x - 4$, 4 may be added to both sides to form

$$3x + 14 \leq 5x$$

Subtracting $3x$ from both sides results in

$$14 \leq 2x$$

Finally, dividing both sides by 2 yields the algebraic definition of the solution set

$$7 \leq x$$

That is, the original inequality is satisfied by any values of x which are greater than or equal to 7. (Check a few values—substitute values less than 7 and greater than 7 into the original inequality to see if the resulting statement is true.)

Example 6.2 **No Solution Set** To determine the solution set for the inequality $6x - 10 \geq 6x + 4$, the addition of 10 to both sides yields.

$$6x \geq 6x + 14$$

Subtracting $6x$ from both sides results in

$$0 \geq 14$$

which is a false statement. What is your conclusion? If you said the solution set is empty, you were correct.

Example 6.3 To determine the solution set for the inequality $4x + 6 \geq 4x - 3$, 6 is subtracted from both sides to yield

$$4x \geq 4x - 9$$

and subtracting $4x$ from both sides gives us

$$0 \geq -9$$

The variable x has disappeared, and we are left with an inequality which is true all the time. This indicates that the original inequality is true for *any and all (real) values of* x.

Example 6.4 **Two-Variable Inequality** Given the inequality $5x + 10y \leq 100$, we may want to define the values of x which satisfy the inequality. With linear equations of the form $ax + by = c$ we concluded in Chap. 3 that there are an infinite number of elements in the solution set. In order to specify any pair of values in the solution set, we needed to assume a value for one of the two variables and then solve for the remaining variable. Inequalities of the form $ax + by \leq c$ or $ax + by \geq c$ are satisfied by an infinite number of points—those that satisfy the *equality* part plus those satisfying the inequality part.

To determine the values of x satisfying the inequality $5x + 10y \leq 100$, solve for x, or

$$5x \leq 100 - 10y$$

and
$$x \leq 20 - 2y$$

The value of x depends on the value of y. For example, if $y = 6$, $x \leq 20 - 2(6)$, or $x \leq 8$.

___

EXERCISE
Determine the general expression for the values of y which satisfy the inequality.
(Ans: $y \leq 10 - x/2$)

___

Double Inequalities Occasionally we may want to determine the solution set for double inequalities. For example, what values of x satisfy the double inequality $-2x + 1 \leq x \leq 6 - x$? In order to determine the solution set for the double inequality, the solution sets for the two inequalities must be identified. The solution set for the double inequality consists of values common to the solution sets for the two inequalities. If

Example 6.5

$$S_1 = \{x \mid -2x + 1 \leq x\} \qquad \text{and} \qquad S_2 = \{x \mid x \leq 6 - x\}$$

the solution set S for the double inequality is

$$S = S_1 \cap S_2$$

The values of x satisfying the left inequality are determined as

$$-2x + 1 \leq x$$
$$1 \leq 3x$$
or
$$\tfrac{1}{3} \leq x$$

Thus $S_1 = \{x \mid x \geq \tfrac{1}{3}\}$.
Those values satisfying the right inequality are

$$x \leq 6 - x$$
$$2x \leq 6$$
or
$$x \leq 3$$

Thus $S_2 = \{x \mid x \leq 3\}$. Therefore, $S = S_1 \cap S_2 = \{x \mid \tfrac{1}{3} \leq x \leq 3\}$.

The Graphics of Linear Inequalities

When a linear inequality involves two variables, the solution set can be described graphically. The procedure for graphing is as follows:

1 Graph the line which represents the equality part of the inequality.

2 The solution set for the inequality will be represented by a *half-space* in two dimensions. That is, the solution set will be represented by the line found in step 1 *and* all points to one side of the line. Determine the side of the line satisfying the strict inequality by substituting

the coordinates of a point lying on one side of the line into the inequality [the most convenient point is the origin, $(0, 0)$, as long as it does not lie on the line]. If the chosen point satisfies the inequality, points on *that* side of the line are members of the solution set. If the coordinates do not satisfy the inequality, points on the other side of the line are members.

Example 6.6

To determine the graphical representation of the solution set for

$$-4x + 3y \leq -24$$

we first graph the equation $-4x + 3y = -24$. This is shown in Fig. 6.1*a*. The points on this line all satisfy the equality part of the inequality. The question is, Which side of the line satisfies the strict inequality? To answer this question, the coordinates of the origin are substituted into the inequality, or

$$-4(0) + 3(0) \overset{?}{\leq} -24$$

However,

$$0 \nleq -24$$

Since the origin $(0, 0)$ does not satisfy the inequality, points on the other side of the line satisfy the strict inequality. The half-space representing the solution set is shown as the shaded area in Fig. 6.1*b*.

Example 6.7

A firm manufactures two products. The products must be processed through one department. Product A requires 4 hours per unit, and product B requires 2 hours per unit. Total production time available for the coming week is 60 hours. A restriction in planning the production schedule, therefore, is that total hours used in producing the two products cannot exceed 60; or, if x_1 equals the number of units produced of product A and x_2 equals the number of units produced of product B, the restriction is represented by the inequality

$$4x_1 + 2x_2 \leq 60$$

FIGURE 6.1

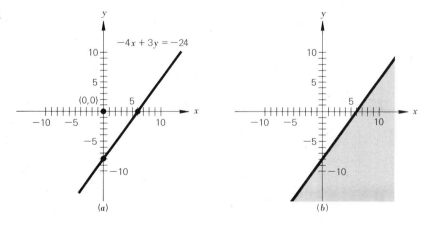

(a) (b)

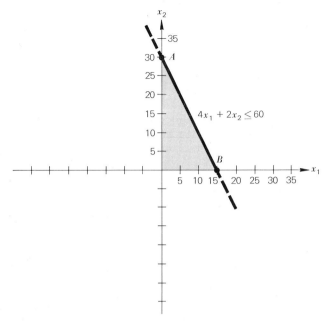

FIGURE 6.2

There are two other restrictions implied by the variable definitions. Since each variable represents a production quantity, neither variable can be negative. These restrictions are represented by the inequalities $x_1 \geq 0$ and $x_2 \geq 0$.

The solution set of the original inequality portrays the different combinations of the two products which can be manufactured with the 60 hours. Figure 6.2 illustrates the solution set graphically. Check to see whether the half-space has been identified correctly. The points satisfying the inequality $4x_1 + 2x_2 \leq 60$ would be the half-space including all points on and left of the line. However, the restriction that both variables not be negative confines us to the portion of the half-space in the first quadrant. Thus, the shaded area represents the combinations of products A and B which can be produced. A further distinction can be made in Fig. 6.2. All combinations of the two products represented by points on $\overline{AB}$ would use all 60 hours. Any points in the interior of the shaded area represent combinations of the two items which will require fewer than 60 hours. Is the origin a possible decision?

Systems of Linear Inequalities

In linear programming problems, we will be dealing with *systems* of linear inequalities. Our first interest will be in determining the solution set which satisfies all the inequalities. If S_j is the solution set for linear inequality j, the set of points S which satisfies n different linear inequalities can be represented by

$$S = S_1 \cap S_2 \cap S_3 \cap \cdot \cdot \cdot \cap S_n \quad \textbf{(6.2)}$$

Example 6.8 Assume that the products in the last example also need to be processed through another department in addition to the original department. Assume that product A requires 3 hours per unit and that product B requires 5 hours per unit. If the second department has 75 hours available each week, the inequality describing production in this department is

$$3x_1 + 5x_2 \leq 75$$

The solution set for this inequality is illustrated in Fig. 6.3. As with Fig. 6.2, the shaded area represents all combinations of products A and B which can be manufactured in the second department by using the 75 hours available.

    If our objective is to determine the combinations of the two products which can be processed through *both* departments, we are looking for the solution set for the system of linear inequalities

$$4x_1 + 2x_2 \leq 60 \qquad (6.3)$$
$$3x_1 + 5x_2 \leq 75 \qquad (6.4)$$
$$x_1 \geq 0 \qquad (6.5)$$
$$x_2 \geq 0 \qquad (6.6)$$

Figure 6.4 illustrates the composite of the two solution sets. Remember that the solution set for the system is the intersection of the solution sets for each inequality. And in Fig. 6.4 the solution set for the system is the shaded area $ABCD$ which is common to the two individual solution sets.

POINTS FOR THOUGHT AND DISCUSSION
Why are combinations of the two products within area AEB not possible? Why are combinations within BFC not possible? Is there any

FIGURE 6.3

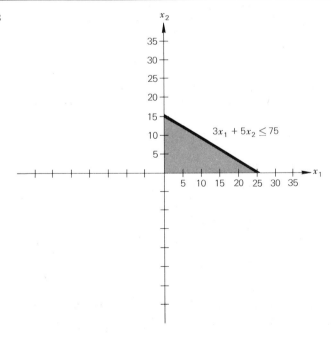

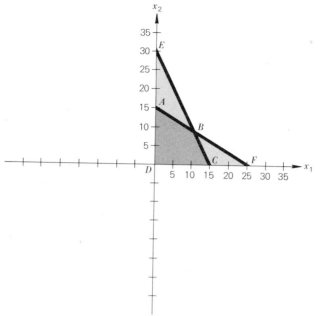

FIGURE 6.4

unique production characteristic associated with the combination of products represented by point B? How about the combinations along $\overline{AB}$? Those along $\overline{BC}$?

Graphically determine the solution set for the following system.

$$x_1 + x_2 \leq 10 \qquad (6.7)$$
$$x_1 \qquad \geq 3 \qquad (6.8)$$

Example 6.9

The shaded area in Fig. 6.5 illustrates the solution set for this system of inequalities. Verify that the correct half-spaces have been identified for each inequality.

Solution

Graphically determine the solution set for the following system.

$$2x_1 + 5x_2 \leq 20 \qquad (6.9)$$
$$2x_1 + 2x_2 \geq 24 \qquad (6.10)$$
$$2x_1 + x_2 = 10 \qquad (6.11)$$
$$x_1 \qquad \geq 0 \qquad (6.12)$$
$$x_2 \geq 0 \qquad (6.13)$$

Example 6.10

Figure 6.6 illustrates the system. Three points should be made here. First, the third member of this system is an equation having a line as its solution. Second, inequalities (6.12) and (6.13) have been accounted for by graphing in the first quadrant only. Third, there are no points

Solution

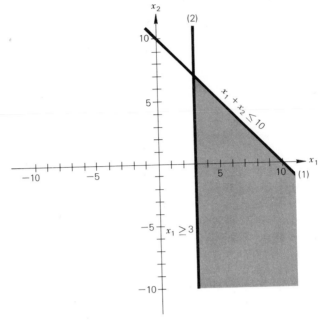

FIGURE 6.5

common to the five solution sets. Therefore the solution set contains no elements.

Follow-up Exercises

Algebraically solve for the values of x that satisfy the following inequalities.

6.1 $3x - 2 \leq 4x + 8$

6.2 $x + 6 \geq 10 - x$

6.3 $x \geq x + 5$

6.4 $2x \leq 2x - 10$

6.5 $-4x + 10 \geq -10 + x$

6.6 $3x + 6 \leq 3x - 5$

6.7 $15x + 6 \geq 10x - 24$

6.8 $-4x + 10 \leq x \leq 2x + 6$

6.9 $12 \geq x + 16 \geq -20$

6.10 $35 \leq 2x + 5 \leq 80$

6.11 $50 \leq 4x - 6 \leq 25$

6.12 $6x - 9 \leq 12x + 9 \leq 6x + 81$

6.13 Write the general expression for the values of x which are in the solution set of the inequality $2x + 8y \leq 80$. What are the values for x when $y = 5$? Determine the general expression for the values of y which are in the solution set. What are the values for y when $x = -40$?

6.14 For the inequality $-x + 2y \leq -20$, determine the general expression for the values of x which are members of the solution set. What values are permitted for x when $y = -10$? Determine the general expression for y. What values are permitted for y when $x = 20$?

In Exercises 6.15 to 6.20, graphically determine the half-space which satisfies the inequality.

6.15 $-4x + 2y \leq 20$

6.16 $-3x + 6y \geq -30$

6.17 $5x + 3y \leq 30$

6.18 $10x - 5y \geq 40$

6.19 $5x - 4y \leq -24$

6.20 $-2x - y \geq -14$

For the following systems, determine graphically the solution (if one exists) which satisfies the entire system.

6.21 $3x_1 + 2x_2 \leq 36$
$\qquad x_1 + 4x_2 \leq 16$

6.22 $2x_1 - 4x_2 \geq 20$
$\qquad x_1 + 3x_2 \leq 15$

6.23 $3x_1 + 4x_2 \leq 24$
$\qquad 4x_1 + 3x_2 \leq 24$

6.24 $x_1 + x_2 \leq 10$
$\qquad 3x_1 + x_2 \geq 12$

6.25 $4x_1 - 2x_2 \geq 4$
$\qquad x_1 \qquad\ \leq 5$
$\qquad\qquad x_2 \geq 2$

6.26 $x_1 + \ x_2 \leq 8$
$\qquad 2x_1 - 3x_2 \geq 6$
$\qquad\qquad x_1 \geq 0$
$\qquad\qquad x_2 \geq 0$

6.27 $x_1 + \ x_2 \leq 8$
$\qquad 3x_1 - \ x_2 \geq 9$
$\qquad x_1 + 2x_2 = 5$
$\qquad\qquad x_1 \geq 0$
$\qquad\qquad x_2 \geq 0$

6.28 $x_1 + 3x_2 \leq 12$
$\qquad -2x_1 - 6x_2 \leq -30$
$\qquad\qquad x_1 \geq 0$
$\qquad\qquad x_2 \geq 0$

6.29 A firm produces two products, each of which must be processed through three departments. The time requirements in each department are shown. Formulate the three inequalities associated with production during the coming week. Graphically determine the combinations of the two products which can be produced within the three departments.

Hours Required per Unit

	Department 1	Department 2	Department 3
Product A	2	3	1.5
Product B	4	2	3
Hours Available per Week	40	36	30

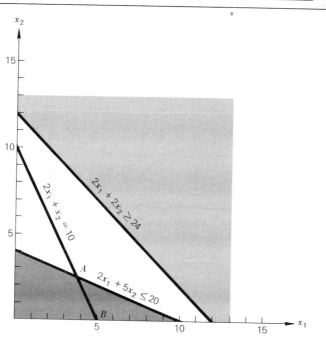

FIGURE 6.6

Introduction

Linear programming is a mathematical optimization technique. By "optimization" technique we are usually referring to a method which attempts to maximize or minimize some objective, e.g., maximize profits, minimize costs, etc. Linear programming is a subset of a larger area of mathematical optimization procedures called *mathematical programming*. Although the application of these mathematical programming methods very often requires the use of computers, none is directly concerned with computer "programming." They are both concerned with making an optimal set of decisions. Linear programming is a powerful and widely applied technique. There have been extensive applications of linear programming within the military and the oil industry. Although these sectors have been perhaps the heaviest users of linear programming, the services sector and public sector of the economy have applied the methods increasingly.

In any linear programming problem certain decisions need to be made. These decisions are represented by decision variables x_j used in the formulation of the linear programming model. The basic structure of a linear programming problem is either to maximize or to minimize an *objective function* while satisfying a set of *constraining conditions*, or *constraints*. The objective function is a mathematical representation of the overall goal stated in terms of the decision variables x_j. As mentioned before, the objective function may represent goals such as profit level, total revenue, total cost, pollution levels, percent return on investment, and so forth. The set of constraints, stated in terms of x_j, represents conditions which must be satisfied in determining levels for the decision variables. For example, in attempting to maximize profits from the production and sale of a group of products, sample constraints might reflect limited labor resources, limited raw materials, and limited demand for the products.

These problems are called *linear* programming problems because the objective function and constraints are all linear. A simple linear programming problem is stated below. The objective is to maximize z,

maximize $$z = 4x_1 + 2x_2$$

subject to $$x_1 + 2x_2 \leq 24$$
$$4x_1 + 3x_2 \geq 30$$

which is stated in terms of the two decision variables x_1 and x_2. In choosing values for x_1 and x_2, however, two constraints must be satisfied.

A Scenario

Since we have discussed product-mix examples in the last two chapters, let's expand upon this type of scenario. A firm manufactures two products, each of which must be processed through departments 1 and 2. Table 6.1 summarizes hourly requirements per unit for each product in

	Product *A*	Product *B*	Weekly Capacity	Table 6.1
Department 1	3 h per unit	2 h per unit	120 h	
Department 2	4 h per unit	6 h per unit	260 h	
Selling price	$25	$30		
Labor cost per unit	16	20		
Raw material cost per unit	4	4		

each department. Also presented are weekly capacities in each department, price per unit, labor cost per unit, and raw material cost per unit. The problem is to determine the number of units to produce of each product so as to maximize total contribution to fixed cost and profit.

If we let x_1 and x_2 equal the number of units produced and sold, respectively, of products *A* and *B*, then total profit contribution would be found by adding the contributions from both products. The contribution from each product would be computed by multiplying the profit margin per unit times the number of units produced and sold. Verify from Table 6.1 that the profit margins per unit are $5 and $6, respectively, for the two products. Letting z equal total contribution to fixed cost and profit, we have

$$z = 5x_1 + 6x_2$$

From the information given in the statement of the problem, the only restrictions in deciding the number of units to produce are the weekly capacities in the two departments. From our experiences in the last chapter you should be able to verify that these restrictions are represented by the inequalities

$$3x_1 + 2x_2 \leq 120 \quad \text{department 1}$$
$$4x_1 + 6x_2 \leq 260 \quad \text{department 2}$$

Although there is no formal statement of such a restriction, implicitly we know that x_1 and x_2 cannot be negative. Thus, we must account for these restrictions in formulating the linear programming model.

By combining these components, the linear programming model which represents the problem is as follows:

maximize

subject to

$$z = 5x_1 + 6x_2$$
$$3x_1 + 2x_2 \leq 120 \qquad (6.14)$$
$$4x_1 + 6x_2 \leq 260 \qquad (6.15)$$
$$x_1 \geq 0 \qquad (6.16)$$
$$x_2 \geq 0 \qquad (6.17)$$

Stop for a second and focus on the structure of this problem. If you recall Example 6.8, the set of constraints in this formulation determines for us the different combinations of the two products which can be produced given the capacity restrictions for departments 1 and 2. The only thing that has been added is the objective function. It provides some guidance as to what is important in selecting the quantities to produce. In this example we are concerned with profit. Linear programming solution methods will allow us to select from this set of possible production combinations the one (or ones) which will result in a maximum total contribution to fixed cost and profit.

Structural Constraints and Nonnegativity Constraints

The linear programming model is concerned with maximizing or minimizing a linear objective function subject to *structural constraints* and *nonnegativity constraints*, one for each decision variable. Structural constraints reflect such things as resource limitations and other restrictions explicitly identified in the statement of the problem. Constraints (6.14) and (6.15) in the previous formulation were structural ones. Nonnegativity constraints guarantee that each decision variable will not be negative. Constraints (6.16) and (6.17) in the previous problem were nonnegativity constraints. In almost all problems this restriction makes sense. Techniques are available to handle those cases where a variable is allowed to assume negative values.

6.3

SOME APPLICATIONS OF LINEAR PROGRAMMING

In the last section a simple product-mix problem was discussed. In this section, we will discuss two other areas of application.

Diet-Mix Models

We have discussed diet-mix problems in earlier chapters (see specifically Example 3.27 and Exercise 5.37). The classic diet-mix problem involves determining the items which should be included in a meal so as to (1) minimize the cost of the meal while (2) satisfying certain nutritional requirements. The nutritional requirements usually take the form of numerous daily vitamin requirements, restrictions encouraging variety in the meal (e.g., do not serve each person 10 pounds of boiled potatoes), and restrictions which consider taste and logical companion foods. The following example illustrates a simple diet-mix problem.

Example 6.11

A dietician is planning the menu for the evening meal at a university dining hall. Three main items will be served, each having different nutritional content. The dietician is interested in providing at least the minimum daily requirement of each of three vitamins in this one meal. Table 6.2 summarizes the *vitamin content per ounce of each type of food*, the cost per ounce of each food, and minimum daily levels for the three vitamins. Any combination of the three foods may be selected as long as the total serving size is at least 9 ounces.

The problem is to determine the number of ounces of each food to be included in the meal. The objective is to minimize the cost of each meal subject to satisfying minimum daily levels of the three vitamins as well as the restriction on minimum serving size.

To formulate the linear programming model for this problem, let x_j

	Vitamin 1	Vitamin 2	Vitamin 3	Cost per oz	Table
					6.2
Food 1	50 mg	20 mg	10 mg	$0.10	
Food 2	30 mg	10 mg	50 mg	0.15	
Food 3	20 mg	30 mg	20 mg	0.12	
Minimum daily vitamin requirement	290 mg	200 mg	210 mg		

equal the number of ounces of food j. The objective function should represent the total cost of the meal, or, to state it in dollars,

$$z = 0.10x_1 + 0.15x_2 + 0.12x_3 \qquad (6.18)$$

Since we are interested in providing *at least* the minimum daily levels of the three vitamins, there will be three "greater than or equal to" constraints. The constraint for each vitamin will have the form

Milligrams of vitamin intake $\geq$ minimum daily requirement

or   milligrams from food 1 + milligrams from food 2
  + milligrams from food 3 $\geq$ minimum daily requirement (milligrams)

The constraints are, respectively,

$$50x_1 + 30x_2 + 20x_3 \geq 290 \qquad (6.19)$$
$$20x_1 + 10x_2 + 30x_3 \geq 200 \qquad (6.20)$$
$$10x_1 + 50x_2 + 20x_3 \geq 210 \qquad (6.21)$$

The restriction that the serving size be at least 9 ounces is stated as

$$x_1 + x_2 + x_3 \geq 9 \qquad (6.22)$$

The complete formulation of the problem is as follows:

minimize $z = 0.10x_1 + 0.15x_2 + 0.12x_3$

subject to $50x_1 + 30x_2 + 20x_3 \geq 290$
          $20x_1 + 10x_2 + 30x_3 \geq 200$
          $10x_1 + 50x_2 + 20x_3 \geq 210$
          $x_1 + x_2 + x_3 \geq 9$
          $x_1, x_2, x_3 \geq 0 \qquad (6.23)$

Note the nonnegativity constraint (6.23). This ensures that negative quantities will not be served of any of the foods.

This is a very simplified problem involving the planning of one meal, the use of just three food types, and consideration of three vitamins. In actual practice models have been formulated which consider

Menu planning over longer periods of time (daily, weekly, etc.)

The interrelationships among all meals served during a given day

The interrelationships among meals served over the entire planning period

Many food items

Many nutritional requirements

These models are obviously very large in terms of the number of variables and number of constraints.

Transportation Models

Transportation models are possibly the most widely used linear programming models. Oil companies commit tremendous resources to the implementation of such models. The typical transportation problem involves the shipment of some *homogeneous* commodity from m sources of supply, or *origins*, to n points of demand, or *destinations*. By *homogeneous* we mean that there are no significant differences in the quality of the item provided by the different sources of supply. The product characteristics are essentially the same.

In the classic problem each origin can supply any of the destinations. And the demand at each destination may be supplied jointly from a combination of the origins or totally from one origin. Each origin usually has a specific capacity which represents the maximum number of units it can supply. Each destination has a specified demand which represents the number of units needed.

Given that each origin can supply units to each destination, some measure of the cost or effort of shipping a unit is specified for each origin-destination combination. This may take the form of a dollar cost, distance between the two points, or time required to move from one point to another. A typical problem is concerned with determining the number of units which should be supplied from each origin to each destination. The objective is to minimize the total transportation or delivery costs while ensuring that (1) the number of units shipped from any origin does not exceed the number of units available at that origin and (2) the demand at each destination is satisfied. Example 6.12 illustrates a simple transportation model.

**Example
6.12**

Highway Maintenance A medium-sized city has two locations in the city at which salt and sand stockpiles are maintained for use during winter icing and snow storms. During a storm, salt and sand are distributed from these two locations to four different city zones. Usually additional salt and sand are needed. However, it is usually impossible to get additional supplies during a storm since they are stockpiled at a central location some distance outside the city. City officials keep their fingers crossed that there will not be back-to-back storms.

The director of public works is interested in determining the minimum cost of allocating salt and sand supplies during a storm. Table 6.3 summarizes the cost of supplying 1 ton of salt or sand from each stockpile to each city zone. In addition, stockpile capacities and normal levels of demand for each zone are indicated (in tons).

In formulating the linear programming model for this problem, there are eight decisions to make—how many tons should be shipped from each stockpile to each zone. In some cases the best decision may be to ship no units from a particular stockpile to a given zone. Let's define our variables a little differently. Let x_{ij} equal the number of tons supplied from stockpile i to zone j. For example, x_{11} equals the number of tons

Zone				Maximum	Table
1	**2**	**3**	**4**	**Supply (Tons)**	6.3
Stockpile 1 $2.00	$3.00	$1.50	$2.50	900	
Stockpile 2 4.00	3.50	2.50	3.00	750	
Demand (Tons) 300	450	500	350		

supplied by stockpile 1 to zone 1. Similarly, x_{23} equals the number of tons supplied by stockpile 2 to zone 3. This *double-subscripted variable* conveys more information to the user than simply defining the variables in this problem as $x_1, x_2, \ldots, x_8$. Given this definition of the variables, the total cost of distributing salt and sand has the form

$$\text{Total cost} = 2x_{11} + 3x_{12} + 1.5x_{13} + 2.5x_{14} + 4x_{21}$$
$$+ 3.5x_{22} + 2.5x_{23} + 3x_{24} \quad (6.24)$$

This is the function we wish to minimize. Does its structure look right? Use your mental model to compute the total cost of shipping 200 tons from stockpile 1 to zone 3 and 100 tons from stockpile 2 to zone 1. Are we using the same function?

One class of constraints deals with the different stockpiles. For each stockpile a constraint should be formulated specifying that total shipments not exceed available supply. For stockpile 1, the sum of the shipments to each zone cannot exceed 900 tons, or

$$x_{11} + x_{12} + x_{13} + x_{14} \leq 900 \quad (6.25)$$

The same constraint for stockpile 2 is

$$x_{21} + x_{22} + x_{23} + x_{24} \leq 750 \quad (6.26)$$

The final class of constraints should guarantee that each zone receives its demanded quantity. For zone 1, the sum of the shipments from stockpiles 1 and 2 should equal 300 tons, or

$$x_{11} + x_{21} = 300 \quad (6.27)$$

The same constraints for the other three zones are, respectively,

$$x_{12} + x_{22} = 450 \quad (6.28)$$
$$x_{13} + x_{23} = 500 \quad (6.29)$$
$$x_{14} + x_{24} = 350 \quad (6.30)$$

The complete formulation of the linear programming model is as follows:

minimize $z = 2x_{11} + 3x_{12} + 1.5x_{13} + 2.5x_{14} + 4x_{21}$
$$+ 3.5x_{22} + 2.5x_{23} + 3x_{24}$$

subject to
$$x_{11} + x_{12} + x_{13} + x_{14} \leq 900$$
$$x_{21} + x_{22} + x_{23} + x_{24} \leq 750$$
$$x_{11} + x_{21} = 300$$
$$x_{12} + x_{22} = 450$$
$$x_{13} + x_{23} = 500$$
$$x_{14} + x_{24} = 350$$
$$x_{11}, x_{12}, x_{13}, x_{14}, x_{21}, x_{22}, x_{23}, x_{24} \geq 0$$

Follow-up Exercises

6.30 A firm manufactures two products. Each product must be processed through two departments. Product A requires 2 hours per unit in department 1 and 4 hours per unit in department 2. Product B requires 3 hours per unit in department 1 and 2 hours per unit in department 2. Departments 1 and 2 have, respectively, 60 and 80 hours available each week. Profit margins for the two products are, respectively, $3 and $4 per unit. If x_j equals the number of units produced of product j, formulate the linear programming model for determining the product-mix which maximizes total profit.

6.31 The dietician at a local penal institution is preparing the menu for tonight's *light* meal. Two food items will be served at the meal. The dietician is concerned about achieving minimum daily requirement of two vitamins. Table 6.4 summarizes vitamin content per ounce of each food, the minimum daily requirements of each, and cost per ounce of each food. If x_j equals the number of ounces of food j, formulate the linear programming model for determining the quantities of the two foods which will minimize the cost of the meal while ensuring that at least minimum levels of both vitamins will be satisfied.

Table 6.4	Food 1	Food 2	Minimum Daily Requirement
Vitamin 1	2 mg/oz	3 mg/oz	18 mg
Vitamin 2	4 mg/oz	2 mg/oz	22 mg
Cost per oz	$0.12	$0.15	

6.32 A chemical company manufactures liquid oxygen at two different locations in the South. It must supply three storage depots in the same region. Table 6.5 summarizes shipping cost per 1,000 gallons between any plant and any depot as well as monthly capacity at each plant and monthly demand at each depot. If x_{ij} equals the number of gallons (in thousands) shipped from plant i to depot j, formulate the linear programming model which allows for determining the minimum cost allocation schedule. Plant capacities are not to be violated, and depot demands are to be satisfied by the schedule.

| Table 6.5 | Depot | | | Supply |
	1	2	3	(1,000 gal)
Plant 1	50	40	35	100
Plant 2	30	45	40	140
Demand (1,000 gal)	80	75	65	

6.33 A firm manufactures three products which must be processed through some of or all four departments. Table 6.6 indicates the number of hours a unit of each product requires in the different departments and the number of pounds of raw material required. Also listed are labor and material costs per unit, selling price, and weekly capacities of both

	Product A	Product B	Product C	Weekly Availability	Table 6.6
Department 1	3.5	4	2	120 h	
Department 2		2	2	100 h	
Department 3	4	1		80 h	
Department 4	2	3	6	150 h	
Pounds of raw material per unit	5.5	4.0	3.5	250	
Selling price	$50	$60	$65		
Labor cost per unit	30	32	36		
Material cost per unit	11	8	7		

work-hours and raw materials. If the objective is to maximize total weekly profit, formulate the linear programming model for this exercise.

6.34 Referring to Exercise 6.33, write the constraints associated with each of the following conditions.

(a) Combined weekly production must be at least 40 units.

(b) The number of units of product A must be no more than twice the quantity of product C.

(c) Since products B and C are usually sold together, production levels of both should be the same.

6.35 A regional truck rental agency is planning for a heavy demand during the summer months. The agency has taken truck counts at different cities and has compared these with projected needs for each city (all trucks are the same size). Three metropolitan areas are expected to have more trucks than will be needed during the summer, while four cities are expected to have fewer trucks than will be demanded. To prepare for these months, trucks can be relocated from surplus areas to shortage areas by hiring drivers. Drivers are paid a flat fee which depends on the distance between the two cities. In addition, they receive per diem (daily) expenses. Table 6.7 summarizes costs of having a truck delivered between two cities. Also shown are the projected surpluses for each city which has an oversupply and projected shortages for each city needing additional trucks. (Note that total surplus exceeds total shortage.)

If the objective is to minimize the cost of reallocating the trucks, formulate the linear programming model which would allow for solving the problem. (*Hint:* Let x_{ij} equal the number of trucks delivered from surplus area i to shortage area j.)

	Shortage Area				Surplus of Trucks	Table 6.7
	1	2	3	4		
Surplus city 1	$100	$250	$300	$150	150	
Surplus city 2	400	75	100	200	125	
Surplus city 3	300	100	50	400	180	
Shortage of trucks	40	80	90	150		

When a linear programming model is stated in terms of two decision variables, it can be solved by graphical procedures. The graphical approach provides a nice visual frame of reference, and it is extremely helpful in understanding the kinds of things which can arise in solving linear programming problems. In this section we will develop the graphical solution approach.

Area of Feasible Solutions

In Sec. 6.2 we formulated a two-variable, product-mix problem. The formulation is rewritten as follows:

maximize $\qquad\qquad z = 5x_1 + 6x_2$ $\qquad\qquad$ (6.31)

subject to $\qquad\quad 3x_1 + 2x_2 \leq 120$ $\qquad\qquad$ (6.32)

$\qquad\qquad\qquad\;\; 4x_1 + 6x_2 \leq 260$ $\qquad\qquad$ (6.33)

$\qquad\qquad\qquad\qquad\;\; x_1, x_2 \geq 0$ $\qquad\qquad$ (6.34)

where x_1 and x_2 represent the number of units produced of products A and B. Since the problem involves two decision variables, we can determine the optimal solution graphically. *The first step in the graphical procedure is to identify the solution set for the system of constraints.* This solution set is often called the *area of feasible solutions*. It simply identifies all combinations of the decision variables which satisfy the constraints. These combinations are *candidates* for the optimal solution.

In Sec. 6.1 we showed how to determine the solution set for a system of linear inequalities. The solution set for inequalities (6.32) to (6.34) is indicated in Fig. 6.7. This is the area of feasible solutions for the linear programming problem.

NOTE
The coordinates of points A and C are identified as the intercept values. Because of inaccuracies in the graph it may be difficult to read the exact coordinates of some points such as point B. To determine the exact coordinates of such points, the *equations* of the lines intersecting at the point must be solved simultaneously. To determine the coordinates (20, 30), the equality portions of Eqs. (6.32) and (6.33) were solved simultaneously.

Each point within the area of feasible solutions in Fig. 6.7 represents a combination of the two products which can be produced. The problem now is to determine the combination(s) which maximize the objective function.

Incorporating the Objective Function

The linear programming solution procedure searches the area of feasible solutions for the optimal solution. Let's gradually develop a search

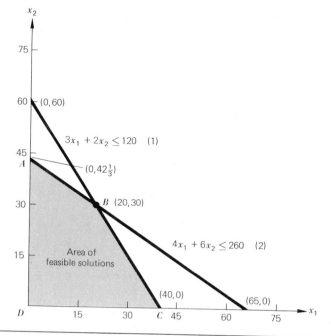

FIGURE 6.7

procedure by first examining some characteristics of objective functions. In the product-mix problem, let's identify combinations of the two products which would generate a desired profit level. For instance, if we wanted to determine the different combinations of the two products which would generate profits of $120, we would set the objective function equal to 120:

$$5x_1 + 6x_2 = 120$$

The solution set for this equation is indicated in Fig. 6.8. If we are interested in determining the combinations yielding a profit of $180, we would determine the solution set for the equation

$$5x_1 + 6x_2 = 180$$

This is also shown in Fig. 6.8. Similarly, the $240 profit line is indicated in Fig. 6.8. These three lines are often referred to as *isoprofit lines* because each point on the line represents the same profit.

Note that for these three profit lines we are interested in the portions which lie within the area of feasible solutions. For the $240 line there are some combinations of the two products which are not within the area of feasible solutions. If it were possible to produce these quantities, say 48 units of product A and no units of product B, a profit of $240 would be realized.

If we look at the three profit lines, profit levels increase as we move outward from the origin. Also, it seems as if the three profit lines are parallel to one another. This can be verified quickly by taking the profit function

$$z = 5x_1 + 6x_2 \qquad (6.35)$$

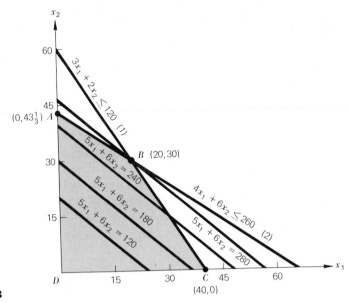

FIGURE 6.8

and rewriting it in the slope-intercept form. For our graph x_2 is equivalent to y (when the variables are defined as x and y). So if we solve Eq. (6.35) for x_2, we get

$$x_2 = \frac{-5}{6}x_1 + \frac{z}{6} \tag{6.36}$$

The slope for the objective function is $\frac{-5}{6}$, and it is not influenced by the value of z. It is determined solely by the coefficients of the two variables in the objective function. The x_2 (or y) intercept is defined by $z/6$, and it is apparent that as z changes in value, so does the x_2 intercept.

For this problem, each profit line has a slope of $\frac{-5}{6}$. If we are interested in maximizing profit, we want to move the profit line as far outward as possible while still touching a point within the area of feasible solutions. In sliding outward from the $240 line, the last point to be touched is B, with coordinates $(20, 30)$. This point lies on the $280 profit line. *Our conclusion: Profit is maximized at a value of $280 when 20 units and 30 units are manufactured, respectively, of products A and B.*

Example 6.13 **Minimization Problem** Determine the optimal solution to the linear programming problem

minimize
subject to

$$z = 3x_1 + 6x_2$$
$$4x_1 + x_2 \geq 20$$
$$x_1 + x_2 \leq 20$$
$$x_1 + x_2 \geq 10$$
$$x_1, x_2 \geq 0$$

Figure 6.9a indicates the area of feasible solutions. In an effort to determine the optimal solution, let's determine the shape of the objective function. To do this, let's assume an arbitrary value for z, say 60. The equation

$$3x_1 + 6x_2 = 60$$

is graphed in Fig. 6.9b. To determine the direction of movement of the objective function, we can choose a point on either side of the line. Selecting the origin, we find the value of the objective function at (0, 0) is

$$z = 3(0) + 6(0)$$
$$= 0$$

The value at the origin is less than 60, and our conclusion is that movement of the objective function toward the origin results in *lower* values of z. Since we want to minimize z, we will want to move the objective function, parallel to itself, as close to the origin as possible while still having it touch a point in the area of feasible solutions. The last point touched before the function moves entirely out of the area of feasible solutions is D, or (10, 0). The minimum value of z is computed as

$$z = 3(10) + 6(0)$$
$$= 30$$

Solution

Corner-Point Solutions

The search procedure can be simplified if we take advantage of the joint characteristics of the area of feasible solutions and the objective function. A *convex set* is a set of points such that if any two arbitrarily se-

FIGURE 6.9

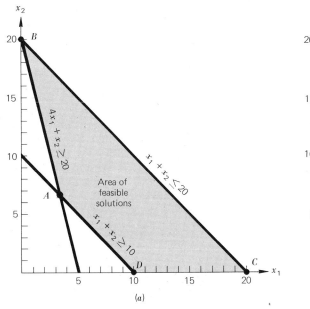

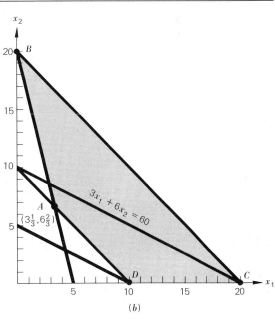

(a)   (b)

220

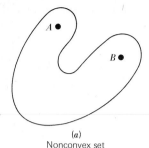

$A \bullet$

$B \bullet$

(a)
Nonconvex set

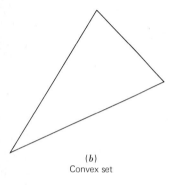

(b)
Convex set

FIGURE 6.10

lected points within the set are connected by a straight line, all elements on the line segment are also members of the set. Figure 6.10 illustrates the difference between a convex set and a nonconvex set. The set of points in Fig. 6.10b represents a convex set. If any two points within the set are connected by a line segment, each point on the line segment will also be a member of the set. In contrast to this, Fig. 6.10a illustrates a nonconvex set. For this set there are many pairs of points like A and B for which the connecting line segment contains points that are not members of the set.

This leads us to the following statements which are of fundamental importance in linear programming.

1 The solution set for a group of linear inequalities is a convex set. Therefore, the area of feasible solutions for a linear programming problem is a convex set.

2 Given a linear objective function in a linear programming problem, the optimal solution will always include a corner point on the area of feasible solutions. This is true regardless of the slope of the objective function and for either maximization or minimization problems.

The second statement simply implies that when a linear objective function is shifted through a convex area of feasible solutions, the last point touched before it moves entirely outside the area will include at least one corner point.

Therefore, the *corner-point approach* to solving linear programming problems is as follows:

1 Graphically sketch the area of feasible solutions.

2 Note the coordinates of each corner point on the area of feasible solutions.

3 Substitute the coordinates of the corner points into the objective function to determine the corresponding value of z.

4 An optimal solution occurs in a maximization problem at the corner point having the highest value of z and in a minimization problem at the corner point having the lowest value of z.

Example 6.14 In the product-mix example in this section, the objective function to be maximized was $z = 5x_1 + 6x_2$. Corner points on the area of feasible solutions were $(0, 0)$, $(0, 43\frac{1}{3})$, $(20, 30)$, and $(40, 0)$. Substituting these into the objective function, we arrive at the figures in Table 6.8. Note that an

Table 6.8

Corner Point	(x_1, x_2)	$z = 5x_1 + 6x_2$
A	$(0, 0)$	$5(0) + 6(0) = 0$
B	$(0, 43\frac{1}{3})$	$5(0) + 6(43\frac{1}{3}) = 260$
C	$(20, 30)$	$5(20) + 6(30) = 280*$
D	$(40, 0)$	$5(40) + 7(0) = 200$

optimal solution occurs at $x_1 = 20$ and $x_2 = 30$, resulting in a minimum value for z of 280.

For Example 6.13, Fig. 6.9 indicates four corner points on the area of feasible solutions. By using the corner-point method, the corner points and respective values of the objective function are summarized in Table 6.9. Given that the objective is to minimize z, the optimal solution occurs when $x_1 = 10$ and $x_2 = 0$ and $z = 30$.

Example 6.15

    Had the objective been to maximize z in this problem, the maximum value of 120 would have resulted when $x_1 = 0$ and $x_2 = 20$.

Corner Point	(x_1, x_2)	$z = 3x_1 + 6x_2$
A	$(3\frac{1}{3}, 6\frac{2}{3})$	$3(3\frac{1}{3}) + 6(6\frac{2}{3}) = 50$
B	$(0, 20)$	$3(0) + 6(20)\ \ = 120$
C	$(20, 0)$	$3(20) + 6(0)\ \ = 60$
D	$(10, 0)$	$3(10) + 6(0)\ \ = 30^*$

Table 6.9

Alternative Optimal Solutions

In the corner-point method it was suggested that an optimal solution will always occur at a corner point on the area of feasible solutions. There is the possibility of more than one optimal solution. Figure 6.11 illustrates a case where the objective function is to be maximized. If the objective function has the same slope as constraint (2), the last points touched before the function moves outside the area of feasible solutions are all points on $\overline{AB}$. In this situation there would exist an infinite number of points each of which will result in the same maximum value of z. For situations such as this, we say that there are *alternative optimal solutions* to the problem.

FIGURE 6.11

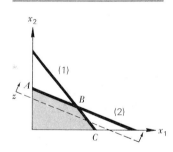

    Two conditions need to be met in order for alternative optimal solutions to exist: (1) the objective function must be parallel to a constraint which forms an *edge* or *boundary* on the area of feasible solutions; (2) the constraint must form a boundary on the area of feasible solutions in the direction of optimal movement of the objective function. This second condition would be violated in Fig. 6.11 if the problem were one of minimization, i.e., if we desired to shift the objective function in the other direction.

Solve the following linear programming problem by the corner-point method.

Example 6.16

maximize	$z = 20x_1 + 15x_2$	(6.37)
subject to	$3x_1 + 4x_2 \le 60$	(6.38)
	$4x_1 + 3x_2 \le 60$	(6.39)
	$x_1 \qquad\ \le 10$	(6.40)
	$\qquad x_2 \le 12$	(6.41)
	$x_1, x_2 \ge 0$	(6.42)

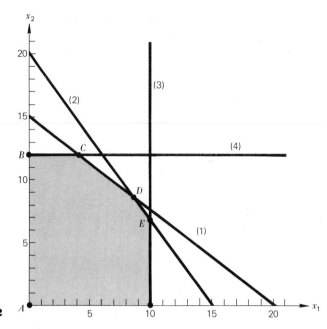

FIGURE 6.12

Solution   The area of feasible solutions is shown in Fig. 6.12. The corner points and their respective values for z are summarized in Table 6.10.

Table 6.10	Corner Point	(x_1, x_2)	$z = 20x_1 + 15x_2$
	A	$(0, 0)$	$20(0) + 15(0) = 0$
	B	$(0, 12)$	$20(0) + 15(12) = 180$
	C	$(4, 12)$	$20(4) + 15(12) = 260$
	D	$(\frac{60}{7}, \frac{60}{7})$	$20(\frac{60}{7}) + 15(\frac{60}{7}) = 300*$
	E	$(10, \frac{20}{3})$	$20(10) + 15(\frac{20}{3}) = 300*$
	F	$(10, 0)$	$20(10) + 15(0) = 200$

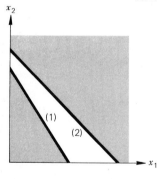

FIGURE 6.13

Note that there is a tie for the highest value of z between points D and E. If you compute the slope of the objective function, you will find that it is the same as for constraint (6.38). Thus, in Fig. 6.12 there are alternative optimal solutions along $\overline{DE}$.

No Feasible Solution

The system of constraints in a linear programming problem may not have any points which satisfy all the constraints. In such cases, there are no points in the solution set, and the linear programming problem is said to have *no feasible solution*. Figure 6.13 illustrates a problem having no feasible solution. Constraint 1 is a "less than or equal to" type while constraint 2 is a "greater than or equal to" type. A problem can certainly have both types of constraints. In this case the set of points satisfying one constraint includes none of the points satisfying the other.

Follow-up Exercises

6.36 Re-solve the product-mix problem with a new objective function $z = x_1 + 5x_2$.

6.37 Re-solve the product-mix problem with a new objective function $z = 5x_1 + x_2$.

Solve the following linear programming problems using the corner-point method.

6.38 Maximize $z = 6x_1 + 2x_2$
subject to $x_1 + x_2 \leq 10$
$2x_1 + x_2 \leq 16$
$x_1, x_2 \geq 0$

6.39 Minimize $z = 2x_1 + 4x_2$
subject to $3x_1 + 2x_2 \geq 24$
$4x_1 + 5x_2 \geq 60$
$x_1, x_2 \geq 0$

6.40 Maximize $z = 10x_1 + 15x_2$
subject to $x_1 + x_2 \geq 10$
$2x_1 + x_2 \leq 24$
$x_1 \leq 10$
$x_1 + x_2 \leq 15$
$x_1, x_2 \geq 0$

6.41 Minimize $z = 5x_1 + 3x_2$
subject to $2x_1 + x_2 \geq 10$
$x_1 + 3x_2 \geq 15$
$x_1 \leq 10$
$x_2 \leq 8$
$x_1, x_2 \geq 0$

6.42 Maximize $z = 2x_1 + 5x_2$
subject to $x_1 + x_2 \leq 8$
$x_1 \leq 6$
$x_1 \geq 4$
$x_2 \leq 5$
$x_2 \geq 2$
$x_1, x_2 \geq 0$

6.43 Solve Exercise 6.30 using the corner-point method. Fully interpret the results in terms of what product-mix is recommended. At these levels what percentage of capacity will be utilized in the two departments?

6.44 Solve Exercise 6.31 using the corner-point method. What does the minimum-cost meal consist of and what does it cost? What percentages of the minimum daily requirements will be realized for the two vitamins?

Exercises 6.45 to 6.48 have alternative optimal solutions. Solve each problem and identify the corner points which are optimal.

6.45 Maximize $z = 6x_1 + 4x_2$
subject to $x_1 + x_2 \leq 5$
$3x_1 + 2x_2 \leq 12$
$x_1, x_2 \geq 0$

6.46 Minimize $z = 12x_1 + 9x_2$
subject to $3x_1 + 6x_2 \geq 36$
$4x_1 + 3x_2 \geq 24$
$x_1 + x_2 \leq 15$
$x_1, x_2 \geq 0$

6.47 Minimize $z = 20x_1 + 5x_2$
subject to $x_1 + x_2 \geq 4$
$4x_1 + x_2 \geq 8$
$x_1 \geq 1$
$x_2 \leq 6$
$5x_1 + 4x_2 \leq 40$
$x_1, x_2 \geq 0$

6.48 Maximize $z = 5x_1 + 4x_2$
subject to $20x_1 + 10x_2 \leq 120$
$40x_1 + 32x_2 \leq 320$
$x_1 \leq 5$
$x_2 \leq 8$
$x_1, x_2 \geq 0$

Verify that the following problems have no feasible solution.

6.49 Minimize $z = 4x_1 + 2x_2$
subject to $4x_1 + 6x_2 \leq 36$
$x_1 + x_2 \geq 10$
$x_1, x_2 \geq 0$

6.50 Maximize $z = 15x_1 + 20x_2$
subject to $x_1 + x_2 \geq 12$
$6x_1 + 9x_2 \leq 54$
$15x_1 + 10x_2 \leq 90$
$x_1, x_2 \geq 0$

6.5   SUMMARY

In this chapter we extended the discussion of systems of linear equations to systems of linear inequalities. We followed by introducing linear programming. We have examined the structure of linear programming problems and some classic areas of application. We have also studied graphical solution procedures when problems involve two decision variables, and we illustrated some specialized conditions which can arise in solving linear programming problems.

Beyond two-variable problems graphical procedures are essentially useless. Chapter 7 discusses the *simplex method*, which is the most popular solution technique when graphical procedures are not practical. Chapter 7 is optional, depending upon your instructor's interests.

CHAPTER CHECKLIST

If you have read all sections of this chapter, you should

_____ **Understand the algebra of *linear inequalities***

_____ **Be able to determine, both algebraically and graphically, the solution set for a linear inequality**

_____ **Be able to graphically determine solution sets for systems of linear inequalities**

_____ **Understand the structure of *linear programming* problems and assumptions underlying the linear programming model**

_____ **Be familiar with three classic linear programming applications: *product-mix, diet-mix,* and *transportation models***

_____ **Understand the nature of *convex sets***

_____ **Be able to solve linear programming problems graphically when the problem involves two variables**

_____ **Understand the meaning of and reasons for *alternative optimal solutions* and *no feasible solution***

KEY TERMS AND CONCEPTS

inequality	structural constraints
sense of inequality	nonnegativity constraints
linear inequality	double-subscripted variable
solution set	area of feasible solutions

half-space

system of linear inequalities

linear programming

mathematical programming

objective function

isoprofit line

convex set

corner-point approach

alternative optimal solution

no feasible solution

ADDITIONAL EXERCISES

Exercises 6.51 to 6.61 are related to Sec. 6.1.

In Exercises 6.51 to 6.54, algebraically solve for the values of x which satisfy the given inequality.

6.51 $4x \leq 4x + 3$

6.52 $7x - 10 \geq 5x + 30$

6.53 $2x \leq 3x + 7 \leq 55$

6.54 $x \leq 13x - 5 \leq 5x + 8$

In Exercises 6.55 to 6.56, graphically determine the half-space which satisfies the inequality.

6.55 $3x - 5y \geq 10$

6.56 $4x + 6y \leq 2$

6.57 For the inequality $7x + 3y \leq 15$, determine the general expression for the values of x which are members of the solution set. What values of x are permitted if $y = -2$?

In Exercises 6.58 to 6.61, graphically determine the solution, if one exists, which satisfies the system of inequalities.

6.58 $\quad x_1 + 3x_2 \leq 7$
$\quad\quad 6x_1 - 9x_2 \leq 18$

6.59 $2x_1 - 2x_2 \leq 16$
$\quad\quad 4x_1 - 4x_2 \geq 32$

6.60 $2x_1 + 3x_2 \geq 8$
$\quad\quad x_1 - x_2 \leq 2$

6.61 $-x_1 - 5x_2 \geq -10$
$\quad\quad x_1 + 5x_2 \leq 10$

Exercises 6.62 to 6.64 are related to Sec. 6.3.

6.62 A producer of machinery wishes to maximize the profits from producing two products, product A and product B. The three major inputs for each product are steel, electricity, and work-hours. Table 6.11 summarizes the inputs per unit, available resources, and profit margin per unit. Formulate the linear programming model for this situation. Which constraint is the most restrictive?

	Product A	Product B	Monthly Total Available	
				Table 6.11
Energy	200 kWh	400 kWh	20,000 kWh	
Steel	100 lb	120 lb	10,000 lb	
Labor	5 h	8 h	400 h	
Profit per unit	$20	$50		

6.63 In Exercise 6.62, assume that energy costs $0.50 per kilowatthour, steel costs $4 per pound, and labor costs $8 per hour. An order for 10 units of product A must be filled using this month's production, and combined production for the two products cannot be less than 35 units. If the objective is to minimize total cost, formulate the linear programming model.

6.64 In a certain area there are two warehouses which supply food to four grocery stores. Table 6.12 summarizes the delivery cost per truckload from each warehouse to each store, the required number of truckloads per store per week, and the maximum number of truckloads available per week per warehouse. Formulate a linear programming model that would determine the number of deliveries from each warehouse to each store which would minimize total delivery cost.

Table 6.12	Store 1	Store 2	Store 3	Store 4	Maximum Number of Truckloads
Warehouse A	$25	$50	$25	$ 75	15
Warehouse B	$75	$25	$50	$100	25
Required number of truckloads	10	15	5	10	

Exercises 6.65 to 6.70 are related to Sec. 6.4.

Solve Exercises 6.65 to 6.68 using the corner-point method.

6.65 Maximize $z = 4x_1 + 3x_2$
subject to $x_1 = x_2$
$2x_1 + 5x_2 \le 20$
$x_1, x_2 \ge 0$

6.66 Minimize $z = 5x_1 + 2x_2$
subject to $x_1 + x_2 \ge 12$
$x_2 \ge 2$
$3x_1 + 2x_2 \le 30$
$x_1 \ge 0$

6.67 Re-solve Exercises 6.65, maximizing $z = 3x_1 + 4x_2$.

6.68 Minimize $z = 2x_1 + 8x_2$
subject to $7x_1 + 5x_2 \ge 35$
$x_1 + 4x_2 \ge 7$
$x_1, x_2 \ge 0$

6.69 Solve Exercise 6.62 using the corner-point method.

6.70 Solve Exercise 6.63 using the corner-point method.

CHAPTER TEST

1 Solve for the values of x which satisfy the given inequalities: (a) $5x - 7 \le 3x$, (b) $5x \le 9x + 7 \le 100 - x$.

2 Graphically determine the solution, if one exists, for this system of inequalities:

$$x_1 - x_2 \ge 5$$
$$x_1 + x_2 \le 15$$
$$x_1 \le 20$$
$$x_1, x_2 \ge 0$$

3 A company manufactures and sells five products. Costs per unit and selling price are given in Table 6.13. If the objective is to maximize total profit, formulate a linear programming model having the following con-

Products	A	B	C	D	E	Table
						6.13
Cost per unit	$50	$80	$300	$25	$10	
Selling price	$70	$90	$350	$50	$12	

straints: at least 20 units of product A and at least 10 units of product B must be produced; sufficient raw materials are not available for total production in excess of 75 units; the number of units produced of products C and E must be equal.

4 Solve using the corner-point method:

maximize

subject to

$$z = 2x_1 + x_2$$
$$x_1 + 2x_2 \leq 20$$
$$5x_1 + x_2 \leq 28$$
$$x_1, x_2 \geq 0$$

CHAPTER OBJECTIVES After reading this chapter, you should be familiar with the *simplex method*, which is an algebraically based procedure for solving linear programming problems, and you should understand the requirements for using the simplex method and know how to apply the technique for both maximization and minimization problems.

In this chapter we will examine a popular, algebraically based procedure for solving linear programming problems. First, we will survey the technique and discuss requirements for using it. Following this, the technique will be presented and illustrated for solving maximization problems which contain all "less than or equal to" constraints. The last section of the chapter will survey the procedure in solving minimization problems and problems containing other types of constraints.

NONGRAPHICAL SOLUTIONS   7.1

Overview of the Simplex Procedure

For all practical purposes, graphical solution procedures are applicable only for linear programming problems involving two variables. We can discuss the geometry of three-variable problems; however, most of us are not skilled at three-dimensional graphics. And beyond three variables, there is no geometric frame of reference. Since most realistic applications of linear programming involve far more than two variables, there is a need for a solution procedure other than the graphical method.

The most popular nongraphical procedure is called the *simplex method*. The simplex method is a sophisticated algebraic procedure for solving systems of simultaneous equations where an objective function is to be optimized. It is an *iterative* process, which identifies a feasible starting solution. The procedure then searches to see whether there exists a better solution. "Better" is measured by whether the value of the objective function can be improved. If a better solution is identified, the search resumes. The generation of each successive solution requires solving a system of linear equations. The search continues until no further improvement is possible in the objective function. An important characteristic of the simplex method is that *it guarantees that each successive solution will be feasible and that the value of the objective function will be at least as good as the value in the previous solution.*

Graphically, you may envision the procedure as searching different corner points on the area of feasible solutions. The solutions found at each iteration of the simplex method represent such corner points. Not all corner points are examined, however. The search chooses only a subset of these corner points, selecting a new one if and only if the objective function is at least as good as the current corner point. This idea is illustrated by Fig. 7.1. If we assume an objective of maximization, the simplex might move from an initial solution at corner point A to points B, C, and finally point D. Note the *isoprofit lines* z_1, z_2, z_3, and z_4. The isoprofit line moves outward, away from the origin, with each successive corner point. This illustrates a situation in which the value of z is increasing at each successive solution.

In a minimization problem successive solutions would have objective function values which are typically decreasing.

FIGURE 7.1

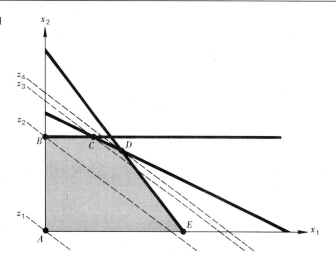

Requirements of the Simplex

There are three requirements in solving a linear programming problem by the simplex method:

1 All constraints must be stated as equations.

2 The right side of a constraint cannot be negative.

3 All variables are restricted to nonnegative values.

We stated earlier that the simplex method is a special routine for solving systems of simultaneous equations. Most linear programming problems contain constraints which are inequalities. Before we solve by the simplex, these inequalities must be restated as equations. The transformation from inequalities to equations varies depending on the nature of the inequality.

For each "less than or equal to" ($\leq$) constraint we add a variable to the left side of the constraint. This variable, called a *slack variable*, serves the function of balancing the two sides of the equation. For example, consider the constraint

$$x_1 + x_2 \leq 25 \tag{7.1}$$

This constraint restricts the values of x_1 and x_2 such that their sum is no greater than 25. The treatment of this constraint is to add a slack variable S, or

$$x_1 + x_2 + S = 25 \tag{7.2}$$

If the values of x_1 and x_2 are less than 25, the slack variable will "make up the difference" between the two sides of Eq. (7.2). To illustrate, if $x_1 = 5$ and $x_2 = 8$, the slack variable S must assume a value of 12 for the equation to be satisfied.

The slack variables become additional variables in the problem and must be treated like any other variables. This means that they are subject to requirement 3; that is, they cannot assume negative values.

Consider the two constraints

$$2x_1 + 3x_2 \leq 50 \qquad \text{department 1}$$
$$4x_1 + 2x_2 \leq 60 \qquad \text{department 2}$$

Example 7.1

where x_1 and x_2 equal, respectively, the number of units produced of two products. Assume that the two constraints represent limited labor availability in two departments; the coefficients on the variables represent the number of hours required to produce a unit of each product, and the right sides of the constraints equal the number of hours available in each department.

The treatment of these constraints is to add a slack variable to the left side of each. Or, the constraints are rewritten as

$$2x_1 + 3x_2 + S_1 = 50 \qquad \text{department 1}$$
$$4x_1 + 2x_2 + S_2 = 60 \qquad \text{department 2}$$

The slack variables S_1 and S_2 keep the two sides of their respective equations in balance. They also have a meaning which is easy to understand. They represent, in this problem, the number of unused hours in each department. For example, $x_1 = 5$ and $x_2 = 10$ suggests producing 5 units of product A and 10 units of product B. Substituting these values into the two constraints, we have

$$2(5) + 3(10) + S_1 = 50$$
$$4(5) + 2(10) + S_2 = 60$$

or

$$40 + S_1 = 50 \qquad \text{department 1}$$
$$40 + S_2 = 60 \qquad \text{department 2}$$

In other words, 40 hours would be used for production in each department. The slack variables would have to assume respective values of $S_1 = 10$ and $S_2 = 20$ to balance the equations. The interpretation of these values is that producing 5 units of product A and 10 units of product B will result in 10 hours being left over in department 1 and 20 hours being left over in department 2.

For each "greater than or equal to" ($\geq$) constraint we *subtract* a variable from the left side of the constraint. This variable, called a *surplus variable*, serves the same function as a slack variable: it keeps the two sides of the equation in balance. For the constraint

$$x_1 + x_2 \geq 10 \tag{7.3}$$

we subtract a surplus variable E, which gives the equivalent equation

$$x_1 + x_2 - E = 10 \tag{7.4}$$

If $x_1 = 20$ and $x_2 = 35$ in Eq. (7.4), the surplus variable E must equal 45 for the equation to be satisfied.

Example 7.2

Assume in Example 7.1 that combined production of the two products must be at least 25 units. The constraint representing this condition is

$$x_1 + x_2 \geq 25$$

Before we solve by the simplex method, the inequality must be transformed into the equivalent equation

$$x_1 + x_2 - E = 25$$

If $x_1 = 20$ and $x_2 = 35$, the surplus variable E must equal 30 for the equation to be satisfied. The interpretation of the surplus variable is that combined production exceeds the minimum quantity by 30 units.

The second requirement of the simplex method is that the right side of any constraint equation not be negative. If a constraint has a negative right side, the constraint can be multiplied by -1 to make the right side positive.

Example 7.3

For the following constraints, make the right side positive.

(a) $2x_1 - 5x_2 \leq -10$ (b) $x_1 + 6x_2 \geq -100$ (c) $5x_1 - 2x_2 = -28$

(a) Multiplying the constraint by -1 results in

$$-2x_1 + 5x_2 \geq 10$$

(b) Multiplying the constraint by -1 results in

$$-x_1 - 6x_2 \leq 100$$

(c) Multiplying the constraint by -1 results in

$$-5x_1 + 2x_2 = 28$$

Solution

The third requirement of the simplex method is that all variables be restricted to nonnegative values. There are specialized techniques for dealing with variables which *can* assume negative values; however, we will not examine these methods. The only point which should be mentioned is that slack and surplus variables are also restricted to being nonnegative.

Basic Feasible Solutions

Consider a problem having $m \leq$ constraints and n variables. Prior to solving by the simplex method, the m constraints would be changed into equations by adding m slack variables. This restatement results in a constraint set consisting of m equations and $m + n$ variables.

In Sec. 6.4, we examined this linear programming problem.

maximize

$$z = 5x_1 + 6x_2$$

subject to

$$3x_1 + 2x_2 \leq 120$$
$$4x_1 + 6x_2 \leq 260$$
$$x_1, x_2 \geq 0$$

Before we solve this problem by the simplex method, the constraint set must be transformed into the equivalent set

$$3x_1 + 2x_2 + S_1 = 120$$
$$4x_1 + 6x_2 + S_2 = 260$$
$$x_1, x_2, S_1, S_2 \geq 0$$

The constraint set involves two equations and four variables. Note that the slack variables are restricted to being nonnegative.

Of all the possible solutions to the constraint set, it can be proved that an optimal solution occurs when two of the four variables in this problem are set equal to zero and the system is solved for the other two variables. The question is, Which two variables should be set equal to 0? Let's enumerate the different possibilities. If S_1 and S_2 are set equal to 0, the constraint equations become

$$3x_1 + 2x_2 = 120$$
$$4x_1 + 6x_2 = 260$$

Solving for x_1 and x_2 results in $x_1 = 20$ and $x_2 = 30$.

If S_1 and x_1 are set equal to 0, the system becomes

$$2x_2 = 120$$
$$S_2 + 6x_2 = 260$$

Solving for x_2 and S_2 results in $x_2 = 60$ and $S_2 = -100$.

Table 7.1 Solution	Variables Set Equal to Zero	Values of Other Variables
1	S_1, S_2	$x_1 = 20, x_2 = 30$
*2	x_1, S_1	$x_2 = 60, S_2 = -100$
3	x_1, S_2	$x_2 = 43\frac{1}{3}, S_1 = 33\frac{1}{3}$
4	x_2, S_1	$x_1 = 40, S_2 = 100$
*5	x_2, S_2	$x_1 = 65, S_1 = -75$
6	x_1, x_2	$S_1 = 120, S_2 = 260$

Table 7.1 summarizes all the solution possibilities given that two of the four variables are assigned values of 0. Solutions 2 and 5 have an asterisk next to them. They have received special attention because they are not feasible solutions. They each contain a variable which has a negative value, violating the nonnegativity restriction. However, solutions 1, 3, 4, and 6 are feasible solutions to the linear programming problem.

Now, look at Fig. 7.2, which is the graphical representation of the two original constraints. Points in this figure are identified by the values for x_1 and x_2. If you examine the values of x_1 and x_2 for solutions 1, 3, 4, and 6 in Table 7.1, you will find that they correspond to the four corner points on the area of feasible solutions in Fig. 7.2. Specifically, solution 1 corresponds to corner point C, solution 3 corresponds to corner point B, solution 4 corresponds to corner point D, and solution 6 corresponds to corner point A. In fact, solutions 2 and 5, which are infeasible, correspond to points E and F in Fig. 7.2.

The important thing to note is that by setting all combinations of two

FIGURE 7.2

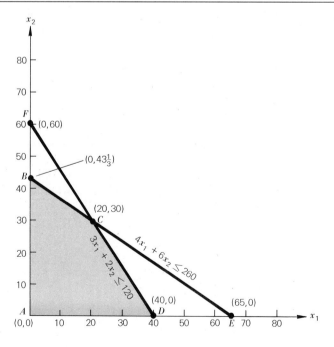

different variables equal to 0 and solving for the remaining variables, a set of potential solutions was identified for the linear programming problem. A subset of these solutions was automatically disqualified because it contained infeasible solutions (2 and 5). However, the remaining solutions corresponded to the corner points on the area of feasible solutions. Since we know that an optimal solution will occur at at least one of these corner points, further examination of these will reveal an optimal solution.

For a maximization problem having $m \leq$ constraints and n variables, the addition of m slack variables results in m constraint equations containing $m + n$ variables. *An optimal solution to this problem can be found by setting n of the variables equal to 0 and solving for the remaining m variables.* The simplex method uses this conclusion as the basis for its search. The question is, Which n variables should be set equal to 0.

As mentioned before, in the process of selecting different combinations of n variables to be set equal to 0, the simplex (1) *will never select a combination which would result in an infeasible solution* and (2) *will ensure that each new combination selected will result in a solution which has an objective function value at least as good as the current solution.*

The n variables set equal to 0 in any solution are called *nonbasic variables.* The other m variables whose values are found by solving the resulting system of equations are referred to as *basic variables.* The solutions represented by corner points on the feasible solution space are called *basic feasible solutions.*

Follow-up Exercises

7.1 Given linear programming problem:

maximize $z = 4x_1 + 2x_2 - 5x_3$

subject to

$$
\begin{aligned}
x_1 + x_2 + x_3 &\leq 100 \\
2x_1 \quad\;\; - x_3 &\leq 25 \\
x_2 \quad\quad &\leq 20 \\
x_3 &\leq 50 \\
x_1, x_2, x_3 &\geq 0
\end{aligned}
$$

transform the constraint set into an equivalent system of constraint equations. Do not attempt to *solve* the problem.

7.2 Given linear programming problem:

maximize $z = 10x_1 - 2x_2 + 5x_3 + 6x_4$

subject to

$$
\begin{aligned}
x_1 + x_2 + x_3 + x_4 &\leq 1{,}000 \\
x_1 \quad\;\; + x_3 \quad\quad &\leq 500 \\
5x_1 \quad\quad\;\; - 2x_4 &\leq 250 \\
x_2 \quad\quad\quad &\leq 50 \\
x_1 + 2x_2 \quad\; + x_4 &\leq 400 \\
x_1, x_2, x_3, x_4 &\geq 0
\end{aligned}
$$

transform the constraint set into an equivalent system of constraint equations. Do not attempt to solve the problem.

7.3 Given linear programming problem:

maximize $$z = 14x_1 + 10x_2$$

subject to
$$5x_1 + 4x_2 \leq 48$$
$$2x_1 + 5x_2 \leq 26$$
$$x_1, x_2 \geq 0$$

(a) Transform the $\leq$ constraints into equations.
(b) Enumerate all solutions for which two variables have been set equal to 0.
(c) From part b identify the basic feasible solutions.
(d) Graph the original constraint set and confirm that the basic feasible solutions are corner points on the area of feasible solutions.
(e) What is the optimal solution?

7.4 Given linear programming problem:

maximize $$z = 6x_1 + 4x_2$$

subject to
$$6x_1 + 10x_2 \leq 90$$
$$12x_1 + 8x_2 \leq 96$$
$$x_1, x_2 \geq 0$$

(a) Transform the $\leq$ constraints into equations.
(b) Enumerate all solutions for which two variables have been set equal to 0.
(c) From part b identify the basic feasible solutions.
(d) Graph the original constraint set and confirm that the basic feasible solutions are corner points on the area of feasible solutions.
(e) What is the optimal solution?

7.2 MAXIMIZATION PROBLEMS

This section will present the simplex method as it applies to solving maximization problems where all constraints are $\leq$ types.

The Algebra of the Simplex Method

Before presenting the simplex method formally, let's discuss the algebra upon which the method is based. The simplex arithmetic is based upon the Gauss-Jordan procedure discussed in Sec. 4.4. A rereading of this section is suggested if you are a little rusty with this method.

Let's return to the following maximization problem:

maximize $$z = 5x_1 + 6x_2 + 0S_1 + 0S_2$$

subject to
$$3x_1 + 2x_2 + S_1 \qquad = 120$$
$$4x_1 + 6x_2 \qquad + S_2 = 260$$
$$x_1, x_2, S_1, S_2 \geq 0$$

Note that the slack variables have been assigned objective function coefficients of 0. *Although there can be exceptions, slack and surplus variables are usually assigned coefficients of 0 in the objective function.* The reason is that these variables typically contribute nothing to the value of the objective function.

In the last section we concluded that at least one optimal solution to this problem can be found by setting two of the variables equal to 0 and solving for the values of the other two.

Let's illustrate how the Gauss-Jordan procedure can be used to identify these different solutions. If we represent the system of equations by showing only the variable coefficients and right-side constraints, we have

$$
\begin{array}{cccc}
x_1 & x_2 & S_1 & S_2 \\
3 & 2 & 1 & 0 \\
4 & 6 & 0 & 1
\end{array}
\quad
\begin{array}{c}
120 \\
260
\end{array}
\qquad
\begin{array}{c}
(7.5) \\
(7.6)
\end{array}
$$

Remember that the Gauss-Jordan procedure uses *row operations* to transform the original system of equations into an equivalent system. The equivalent system has the properties that only one variable remains in each equation and that the right side of the equation equals the value of that variable. In looking at the variable coefficients for this system of equations, a convenient starting point would be to set x_1 and x_2 equal to 0. The variable coefficients for S_1 and S_2 are already in the desired form. If x_1 and x_2 both equal 0, we can determine the corresponding values of S_1 and S_2 as $S_1 = 120$ and $S_2 = 260$. In this solution S_1 and S_2 are the basic variables, and x_1 and x_2 are the nonbasic variables.

Assume that we wish to set x_1 and S_1 equal to 0 and solve for x_2 and S_2. Compared with the original solution, we wish to replace S_1 with x_2 as a basic variable. And we would like the coefficients for x_2 and S_2 to have the form

$$
\begin{array}{cccc}
x_1 & x_2 & S_1 & S_2 \\
\blacksquare & 1 & \blacksquare & 0 \\
\blacksquare & 0 & \blacksquare & 1
\end{array}
\quad
\begin{array}{c}
\blacksquare \\
\blacksquare
\end{array}
\qquad
\begin{array}{c}
(7.7) \\
(7.8)
\end{array}
$$

Since the coefficients for S_2 are already in the desired form, we need only to change those for x_2 from $\binom{2}{6}$ to $\binom{1}{0}$. To create the 1, we multiply Eq. (7.5) by $\frac{1}{2}$, resulting in

$$
\begin{array}{cccc}
x_1 & x_2 & S_1 & S_2 \\
\frac{3}{2} & 1 & \frac{1}{2} & 0 \\
4 & 6 & 0 & 1
\end{array}
\quad
\begin{array}{c}
60 \\
260
\end{array}
\qquad
\begin{array}{c}
(7.5a) \\
(7.6)
\end{array}
$$

The 6 is changed to 0 by multiplying Eq. (7.5a) by -6 and adding this multiple to Eq. (7.6), or

$$
\begin{array}{cccc}
x_1 & x_2 & S_1 & S_2 \\
\frac{3}{2} & 1 & \frac{1}{2} & 0 \\
-5 & 0 & -3 & 1
\end{array}
\quad
\begin{array}{c}
60 \\
-100
\end{array}
\qquad
\begin{array}{c}
(7.5a) \\
(7.6a)
\end{array}
$$

By recalling that x_1 and S_1 were set equal to 0, the values of x_2 and S_2 can be read directly as $x_2 = 60$ and $S_2 = -100$. If you refer to Table 7.1, you will see that this solution is the same as solution 2.

If we want S_1 and S_2 to equal 0, x_1 will replace S_2 as a basic variable. And we would like the coefficients on x_1 and x_2 to have the form

$$
\begin{array}{cccc}
x_1 & x_2 & S_1 & S_2 \\
0 & 1 & \blacksquare & \blacksquare \\
1 & 0 & \blacksquare & \blacksquare
\end{array}
\quad
\begin{array}{c}
\blacksquare \\
\blacksquare
\end{array}
\qquad
\begin{array}{c}
(7.7) \\
(7.8)
\end{array}
$$

From the last solution the coefficients on x_2 are in the desired form, and we need to change those for x_1 from $\begin{pmatrix} \frac{3}{2} \\ -5 \end{pmatrix}$ to $\begin{pmatrix} 0 \\ 1 \end{pmatrix}$. The 1 is created by multiplying the Eq. (7.6a) by $-\frac{1}{5}$, resulting in

$$
\begin{array}{cccc|cc}
x_1 & x_2 & S_1 & S_2 & & \\
\frac{3}{2} & 1 & \frac{1}{2} & 0 & 60 & (7.5a) \\
1 & 0 & \frac{3}{5} & -\frac{1}{5} & 20 & (7.6b)
\end{array}
$$

The 0 is created by multiplying Eq. (7.6b) by $-\frac{3}{2}$ and adding this multiple to Eq. (7.5a), or

$$
\begin{array}{cccc|cc}
x_1 & x_2 & S_1 & S_2 & & \\
0 & 1 & -\frac{2}{5} & \frac{3}{10} & 30 & (7.5b) \\
1 & 0 & \frac{3}{5} & -\frac{1}{5} & 20 & (7.6b)
\end{array}
$$

With S_1 and S_2 set equal to 0, the values of x_1 and x_2 are read directly as $x_1 = 20$ and $x_2 = 30$, which corresponds to solution 1 in Table 7.1.

Adding the Objective Function

In solving by the simplex method, the objective function and constraints are combined to form a system of equations. The objective function is one of the equations, and z becomes an additional variable in the system. In rearranging the variables in the objective function so that they are on the left side of the equation, the problem is represented by the system of equations

$$
\begin{aligned}
z - 5x_1 - 6x_2 - 0S_1 - 0S_2 &= 0 & (0) \\
3x_1 + 2x_2 + S_1 &= 120 & (1) \\
4x_1 + 6x_2 \qquad\quad + S_2 &= 260 & (2)
\end{aligned}
$$

Note that the objective function is labeled as Eq. (0).

The objective is to solve this (3 × 5) system of equations so as to maximize the value of z. Since we are particularly concerned about the value of z and will want to know its value for any solution, z will always be a basic variable. The standard practice, however, is not to refer to z as a basic variable. The terms *basic variable* and *nonbasic variable* are usually reserved for the other variables in the problem.

The simplex operations are usually performed in a tabular format. The initial table, or *tableau*, for our problem is shown in Table 7.2. Note that there is one row for each equation and the table contains the coefficients of each variable in the equations. The b_i column contains the right-side constants of the equations; b_i is the right-side constant for equation i or row i.

In a maximization problem having all $\leq$ constraints, the starting so-

Table 7.2 Basic Variables	z	x_1	x_2	S_1	S_2	b_i	Row Number
	1	−5	−6	0	0	0	(0)
S_1	0	3	2	1	0	120	(1)
S_2	0	4	6	0	1	260	(2)

lution will have a set of basic variables consisting of the slack variables in the problem. By setting x_1 and x_2 equal to 0 in our problem, the initial solution is $S_1 = 120$, $S_2 = 260$, and $z = 0$. The basic variables and the rows in which their values are read are noted by the first column in the tableau.

Given any intermediate solution, the simplex compares the nonbasic variables with the set of basic variables. The purpose is to determine whether any nonbasic variable should replace a basic variable. A nonbasic variable will replace a basic variable only if (1) the objective function will be improved and (2) the new solution is feasible.

RULE 1: OPTIMALITY CHECK
In a maximization problem, the optimal solution has been found if all row (0) coefficients for the basic and nonbasic variables are greater than or equal to 0.

Since the row (0) coefficients for x_1 and x_2 are -5 and -6, respectively, the optimal solution has not been found. A negative row (0) coefficient for a nonbasic variable indicates that the objective function will increase in value if a positive quantity is assigned to the variable.

This last point can be seen more easily if we rewrite Eq. (0) so that z is written as a function of the nonbasic variables. The result is

$$z = 0 + 5x_1 + 6x_2 \tag{0a}$$

In this form, we can determine the effects of changes in the nonbasic variables. This equation indicates that the current value of z is 0, but assigning x_1 a value of 1 will result in z's increasing by 5. Similarly, assigning x_2 a value of 1 will result in z's increasing by 6. Thus, introducing positive quantities of either x_1 or x_2 would result in a better value for z.

RULE 2: NEW BASIC VARIABLE
In a maximization problem the nonbasic variable which will replace a basic variable is the one having the *most negative* row (0) coefficient. "Ties" may be broken arbitrarily.

In selecting a nonbasic variable to become a basic variable, the simplex method chooses the one which will result in the largest *marginal* (per unit) improvement in z. Since an improvement of 6 units is better than an improvement of 5 units, the simplex would choose x_2 to become a basic variable in the next solution. In the simplex tableau the column representing the new basic variable will be called the *key column*.

If z will increase by 6 units for *each* unit of x_2, we would like x_2 to become as large as possible. The simplex will allow x_2 to increase in value until one of the current basic variables is driven to 0. If Eqs. (1) and (2) are rewritten in terms of the nonbasic variables, we can observe the effects that changes in x_2 will have on the values of the current basic variables:

$$S_1 = 120 - 3x_1 - 2x_2 \qquad (1a)$$
$$S_2 = 260 - 4x_1 - 6x_2 \qquad (2a)$$

Looking at Eq. $(1a)$, S_1 equals 120 but will decrease in value by 2 units for each unit that x_2 increases. If x_2 is allowed to grow to a value of $120/2$, or 60 units, S_1 will be driven to a value of 0. Looking at Eq. $(2a)$, S_2 equals 260 but will decrease in value by 6 units for each unit that x_2 increases. S_2 will be driven to a value of 0 if x_2 is allowed to grow to a value of $260/6$, or $43\frac{1}{3}$ units. The question is, Which basic variable will be driven to a value of 0 first as x_2 is allowed to increase? The answer is S_2, when $x_2 = 43\frac{1}{3}$. If x_2 were allowed to grow to a value of 60, substitution into Eq. $(2a)$ would result in

$$S_2 = 260 - 6(60)$$
$$= -100$$

Since S_2 would be negative, this solution is not feasible. Our conclusion is that x_2 should replace S_2 as a basic variable in the next solution.

In using the tableau structure, the decision of which basic variable to replace is made by focusing upon the key column and the b_i column. The partial tableau in Table 7.3 illustrates a column which is supposed to represent the *key column* for an intermediate solution. The key column element a_{ik} represents the constant appearing in row i of the key (k) column. Similarly, b_i values represent the right side constants for row i.

Table 7.3	...	x_k	...	b_i	**Row Number**
	...	a_{0k}	...	b_0	**(0)**
	...	a_{1k}	...	b_1	**(1)**
	...	a_{mk}	...	b_m	**(m)**

RULE 3: DEPARTING BASIC VARIABLE
The basic variable to be replaced is found by determining the row i associated with

$$\min \frac{b_i}{a_{ik}} \qquad i = 1, \ldots, m$$

where $a_{ik} > 0$.

Rule 3 suggests that the ratio b_i/a_{ik} should be determined for rows (1) to (m) where $a_{ik} > 0$. The minimum ratio should be identified and the corresponding row i noted. The departing variable is the one whose value is currently read from this row. Table 7.4 illustrates this process for our example.

Key Column

Basic Variables	z	x_1	x_2	S_1	S_2	b_i	Row Number	b_i/a_{ik}
	1	-5	-6	0	0	0	(0)	
S_1	0	3	2	1	0	120	(1)	$120/2 = 60$
S_2	0	4	6	0	1	260	(2)	$260/6 = 43\frac{1}{3}$*

Table 7.4

In Table 7.4 attention is focused on the key column. The ratios b_i/a_{ik} are computed for rows (1) and (2). The minimum ratio is $43\frac{1}{3}$, associated with row (2). Since the value of S_2 is currently read from row (2), S_2 is the departing basic variable.

In the next solution we will want to read the value of the new basic variable x_2 from row (2). Thus, we need to apply the Gauss-Jordan procedures to change the column of coefficients under x_2 from $\begin{pmatrix} -6 \\ 2 \\ 6 \end{pmatrix}$ to $\begin{pmatrix} 0 \\ 0 \\ 1 \end{pmatrix}$. The 1 is created by multiplying row (2) by $\frac{1}{6}$. The two 0s are created by multiplying the *new* row (2) by $+6$ and -2 and adding these multiples, respectively, to rows (0) and (1). The next solution appears in Table 7.5. Note in Table 7.5 that a shorthand notation to the right of each row indicates how the elements of that row were computed. The notation R_j is used to represent row j.

Table 7.5

Basic Variables	z	x_1	x_2	S_1	S_2	b_i	Row Number	
	1	-1	0	0	1	260	(0)	$R_0' = R_0 + 6R_2'$
S_1	0	$\frac{10}{6}$	0	1	$-\frac{1}{3}$	$33\frac{1}{3}$	(1)	$R_1' = R_1 - 2R_2'$
x_2	0	$\frac{4}{6}$	1	0	$\frac{1}{6}$	$43\frac{1}{3}$	(2)	$R_2' = \frac{1}{6}R_2$

Note also in Table 7.5 that x_2 has replaced S_2 in the column of basic variables. Remembering that x_1 and S_2 are nonbasic variables, we know that their values are 0. The values of z, S_1, and x_2 can be read from the b_i column as $z = 260$, $S_1 = 33\frac{1}{3}$, and $x_2 = 43\frac{1}{3}$.

EXERCISE
Substitute the values for x_1 and x_2 back into the original formulation and verify (a) that the first constraint has slack equal to $33\frac{1}{3}$ units, (b) that the second constraint is satisfied as an equality ($S_2 = 0$), and (c) that the value of z equals 260.

With this new solution, the first thing to check is whether it is optimal. Applying Rule 1, we conclude that the solution is not optimal because of the -1 coefficient for x_1 in row (0). Since x_1 has the only nega-

Key Column (pointing to x_1)

Basic Variables	z	x_1	x_2	S_1	S_2	b_i	Row Number	b_i/a_{ik}
	1	-1	0	0	1	260	(0)	
S_1	0	$\frac{10}{6}$	0	1	$-\frac{1}{3}$	$33\frac{1}{3}$	(1)	$33\frac{1}{3} \div \frac{10}{6} = 20*$
x_2	0	$\frac{4}{6}$	1	0	$\frac{1}{6}$	$43\frac{1}{3}$	(2)	$43\frac{1}{3} \div \frac{4}{6} = 65$

Table 7.6

tive coefficient in row (0), it will become the new basic variable. To determine the departing basic variable, we focus on the elements in the x_1 column. As shown in Table 7.6, the minimum b_i/a_{ik} ratio is 20, and this minimum ratio is associated with row (1). Since the value of S_1 is currently read from row (1), S_1 is the departing variable.

In the next solution we will want to read the value of the new basic variable x_1 from row (1). As such, the column of coefficients under x_1 should be changed from $\begin{pmatrix} -1 \\ \frac{10}{6} \\ \frac{4}{6} \end{pmatrix}$ to $\begin{pmatrix} 0 \\ 1 \\ 0 \end{pmatrix}$.

The 1 is created by multiplying row (1) by $\frac{6}{10}$. The two 0s are created by multiplying the new row (1) by $+1$ and $-\frac{4}{6}$ and adding these multiples, respectively, to rows (0) and (2) (see equations to the right of Table 7.7). The new solution appears in Table 7.7.

Note in Table 7.7 that x_1 has replaced S_1 in the column of basic variables. With S_1 and S_2 equaling 0 in this solution, the values of z, x_1, and x_2 are read from the b_i column as $z = 280$, $x_1 = 20$, and $x_2 = 30$. With this new solution, our next step is to check for optimality. Applying Rule 1, we conclude that this solution is optimal because all row (0) coefficients are greater than or equal to 0. This answer agrees with the one we found when solving graphically in Sec. 6.4. The objective function is maximized at a value of 280 when $x_1 = 20$, $x_2 = 30$, $S_1 = 0$, and $S_2 = 0$.

Summary of Simplex Procedure

Let's generalize the simplex procedure *for maximization problems having all* $\leq$ *constraints.* First add slack variables to each constraint and place the variable coefficients and right-side constants in a simplex tableau. Then do the following:

1 Identify the initial solution by declaring each of the slack variables as basic variables in the solution. All other variables are nonbasic in the initial solution.

Table 7.7

Basic Variables	z	x_1	x_2	S_1	S_2	b_i	Row Number	
	1	0	0	$\frac{6}{10}$	$\frac{24}{30}$	280	(0)	$R_0'' = R_0' + R_1''$
x_1	0	1	0	$\frac{6}{10}$	$-\frac{6}{30}$	20	(1)	$R_1'' = \frac{6}{10}R_1'$
x_2	0	0	1	$-\frac{24}{60}$	$\frac{3}{10}$	30	(2)	$R_2'' = R_2' - \frac{4}{6}R_1''$

2 Determine whether the current solution is optimal by applying Rule 1. If it is optimal, stop! If it is not optimal, proceed to step 3.

3 Determine the nonbasic variable which should become a basic variable in the next solution by applying Rule 2.

4 Determine the basic variable which should be replaced in the next solution by applying Rule 3.

5 Apply the Gauss-Jordan operations to generate the new solution (or new tableau). Go to step 2.

Let's solve the following linear programming problem by using the simplex method.

Example 7.4

maximize $\qquad z = 2x_1 + 12x_2 + 8x_3$

subject to $\qquad\begin{aligned} 2x_1 + 2x_2 + x_3 &\leq 100 \\ x_1 - 2x_2 + 5x_3 &\leq 80 \\ 10x_1 + 5x_2 + 4x_3 &\leq 300 \\ x_1, x_2, x_3 &\geq 0 \end{aligned}$

Rewriting the problem with slack variables added in, we have the following.

maximize $\qquad z = 2x_1 + 12x_2 + 8x_3 + 0S_1 + 0S_2 + 0S_3$

subject to $\qquad\begin{aligned} 2x_1 + 2x_2 + x_3 + S_1 \qquad\qquad &= 100 \\ x_1 - 2x_2 + 5x_3 \qquad + S_2 \qquad &= 80 \\ 10x_1 + 5x_2 + 4x_3 \qquad\qquad + S_3 &= 300 \\ x_1, x_2, x_3, S_1, S_2, S_3 &\geq 0 \end{aligned}$

Restate the objective function by moving all variables to the left side of the equation. The initial simplex tableau is shown in Table 7.8.

1 In the initial solution x_1, x_2, and x_3 are nonbasic variables having values of 0. The basic variables are the slack variables with $S_1 = 100, S_2 = 80, S_3 = 300$, and $z = 0$.

2 Since all row (0) coefficients are *not* greater than or equal to 0, the initial solution is not optimal.

3 The most negative coefficient in row (0) is -12, and it is associated with x_2. Thus, x_2 will become a basic variable in the next solution.

Table 7.8

┌Key Column

Basic Variables	z	x_1	x_2	x_3	S_1	S_2	S_3	b_i	Row Number	b_i/a_{ik}
	1	−2	−12	−8	0	0	0	0	(0)	
S_1	0	2	2	1	1	0	0	100	(1)	100/2 = 50*
S_2	0	1	− 2	5	0	1	0	80	(2)	
S_3	0	10	5	4	0	0	1	300	(3)	300/5 = 60

4 In computing the b_i/a_{ik} ratios, the minimum ratio is **50**, and it corresponds to row **(1)**. Thus S_1 will become a nonbasic variable in the next solution. Note that no ratio was computed for row **(2)** because the a_{ik} value was negative.

5 The new solution is found by changing the coefficients under x_2

$$\text{from} \begin{pmatrix} -12 \\ 2 \\ -2 \\ 5 \end{pmatrix} \text{to} \begin{pmatrix} 0 \\ 1 \\ 0 \\ 0 \end{pmatrix}.$$

Table 7.9 indicates the next solution. The shorthand notation to the right of each row indicates how the elements of that row were computed. In this solution the basic variables and their values are $x_2 = 50$, $S_2 = 180$, $S_3 = 50$, and $z = 600$. Continuing the simplex procedure we next return to step 2.

2 Since the row **(0)** coefficient for x_3 is negative, this solution is not optimal.

3 The variable x_3 will become a basic variable in the next solution since it has the only negative coefficient in row **(0)**.

4 In computing the b_i/a_{ik} ratios, the minimum ratio is **30**, and it corresponds to row **(2)**. Thus, S_2 will become a nonbasic variable in the next solution.

5 The new solution is found by changing the coefficients under x_3

$$\text{from} \begin{pmatrix} -2 \\ \frac{1}{2} \\ 6 \\ \frac{3}{2} \end{pmatrix} \text{to} \begin{pmatrix} 0 \\ 0 \\ 1 \\ 0 \end{pmatrix}.$$

Table 7.10 indicates the next solution. The basic variables and their values in this solution are $x_2 = 35$, $x_3 = 30$, and $S_3 = 5$. The value of z is 660. We return to step 2.

2 Since all row **(0)** coefficients are greater than or equal to 0 in Table 7.10, this is the optimal solution.

The objective function is maximized at a value of 660 when $x_1 = 0$, $x_2 = 35$, $x_3 = 30$, $S_1 = 0$, $S_2 = 0$, and $S_3 = 5$.

Table 7.9

Key Column

Basic Variables	z	x_1	x_2	x_3	S_1	S_2	S_3	b_i	Row Number		b_i/a_{ik}
	1	10	0	−2	6	0	0	600	(0)	$R_0' = R_0 + 12R_1'$	
x_2	0	1	1	$\frac{1}{2}$	$\frac{1}{2}$	0	0	50	(1)	$R_1' = \frac{1}{2}R_1$	$50 \div \frac{1}{2} = 100$
S_2	0	3	0	6	1	1	0	180	(2)	$R_2' = R_2 + 2R_1'$	$180 \div 6 = 30^*$
S_3	0	5	0	$\frac{3}{2}$	$-\frac{5}{2}$	0	1	50	(3)	$R_3' = R_3 - 5R_1'$	$50 \div \frac{3}{2} = 33\frac{1}{3}$

Basic Variables	z	x_1	x_2	x_3	S_1	S_2	S_3	b_i	Row Number	
	1	11	0	0	$\frac{38}{6}$	$\frac{2}{6}$	0	660	(0)	$R''_0 = R'_0 + 2R''_2$
x_2	0	$\frac{3}{4}$	1	0	$\frac{5}{12}$	$-\frac{1}{12}$	0	35	(1)	$R''_1 = R'_1 - \frac{1}{2}R''_2$
x_3	0	$\frac{1}{2}$	0	1	$\frac{1}{6}$	$\frac{1}{6}$	0	30	(2)	$R''_2 = \frac{1}{6}R'_2$
S_3	0	$\frac{17}{4}$	0	0	$-\frac{11}{4}$	$-\frac{1}{4}$	1	5	(3)	$R''_3 = R'_3 - \frac{3}{2}R''_2$

Table 7.10

Follow-up Exercises

In Exercises 7.5 to 7.10, solve by the simplex method.

7.5 Maximize $\qquad z = 4x_1 + 2x_2$

subject to
$$\begin{aligned} x_1 + x_2 &\le 50 \\ 6x_1 &\le 240 \\ x_1, x_2 &\ge 0 \end{aligned}$$

7.6 Maximize $\qquad z = 4x_1 + 4x_2$

subject to
$$\begin{aligned} 4x_1 + 8x_2 &\le 24 \\ 24x_1 + 16x_2 &\le 96 \\ x_1, x_2 &\ge 0 \end{aligned}$$

7.7 Maximize $\qquad z = 10x_1 + 12x_2$

subject to
$$\begin{aligned} x_1 + x_2 &\le 150 \\ 3x_1 + 6x_2 &\le 300 \\ 4x_1 + 2x_2 &\le 160 \\ x_1, x_2 &\ge 0 \end{aligned}$$

7.8 Maximize $\qquad z = 6x_1 + 8x_2 + 10x_3$

subject to
$$\begin{aligned} x_1 + 2.5x_2 &\le 1{,}200 \\ 2x_1 + 3x_2 + 4x_3 &\le 2{,}600 \\ x_1, x_2, x_3 &\ge 0 \end{aligned}$$

7.9 Maximize $\qquad z = 10x_1 + 3x_2 + 4x_3$

subject to
$$\begin{aligned} 8x_1 + 2x_2 + 3x_3 &\le 400 \\ 4x_1 + 3x_2 &\le 200 \\ x_3 &\le 40 \\ x_1, x_2, x_3 &\ge 0 \end{aligned}$$

7.10 Maximize $\qquad z = 4x_1 - 2x_2 + x_3$

subject to
$$\begin{aligned} 6x_1 + 2x_2 + 2x_3 &\le 240 \\ 2x_1 - 2x_2 + 4x_3 &\le 40 \\ 2x_1 + 2x_2 - 2x_3 &\le 80 \\ x_1, x_2, x_3 &\ge 0 \end{aligned}$$

*7.11 Rule 3 discussed the identification of the departing basic variable in the simplex procedure. Why is consideration not given to the b_i/a_{ik} ratios which have $a_{ik} \le 0$?

*7.12 Rule 3 also indicated that the departing basic variable is associated with the row corresponding to the minimum ratio b_i/a_{ik}. Why is the departing variable identified by the *minimum* ratio?

This last section briefly summarizes the way in which other problem structures are handled by the simplex method.

Artificial Variables

The simplex method requires that additional variables, called *artificial variables*, be added to the left side of every $\geq$ constraint and every "equals" constraint. For $\geq$ constraints the artificial variable is added *in addition to subtracting a surplus variable*. The artificial variable has no real meaning in the problem. Its only function is to provide a convenient initial solution.

Example 7.5   Transform the following constraint set into the form required by the simplex method:

$$
\begin{aligned}
x_1 + x_2 &\leq 100 \\
2x_1 + 3x_2 &\geq 40 \\
x_1 - 2x_2 &= 25 \\
x_1, x_2 &\geq 0
\end{aligned}
$$

Solution   The transformed constraint set is

$$
\begin{aligned}
x_1 + x_2 + S_1 \qquad\qquad\qquad &= 100 \\
2x_1 + 3x_2 \qquad - E_1 + A_1 \qquad &= 40 \\
x_1 - 2x_2 \qquad\qquad\qquad + A_2 &= 25 \\
x_1, x_2, S_1, E_1, A_1, A_2 &\geq 0
\end{aligned}
$$

Artificial variables are usually assigned objective function coefficients which make them extremely undesirable in the problem. *For maximization problems artificial variables should be assigned objective function coefficients of $-M$, where M is assumed to be a very large number, much larger than any other coefficient in the objective function. For minimization problems artificial variables should be assigned objective function coefficients of $+M$.*

Example 7.6   If the original objective function in Example 7.5 had been

maximize $z = 5x_1 + 10x_2$

then it would be revised to have the form

maximize $z = 5x_1 + 10x_2 + 0S_1 + 0E_1 - MA_1 - MA_2$

In any linear programming problem the initial set of basic variables will consist of all the slack variables and artificial variables which appear in the problem.

Minimization Problems

The simplex procedure changes only slightly when minimization problems are solved. The only difference relates to the interpretation of row (0) coefficients. The following two rules are modifications of Rule 1 and Rule 2. These apply for minimization problems.

RULE 1A: OPTIMALITY CHECK
In a minimization problem, the optimal solution has been found if all row (0) coefficients for the basic and nonbasic variables are less than or equal to 0.

RULE 2A: NEW BASIC VARIABLE
In a minimization problem, the nonbasic variable which will replace a current basic variable is the one having the largest positive row (0) coefficient. Ties may be broken arbitrarily.

Solve the following linear programming problem using the simplex method.

Example 7.7

minimize $\qquad z = 5x_1 + 6x_2$

subject to
$$x_1 + x_2 \geq 10$$
$$2x_1 + 4x_2 \geq 24$$
$$x_1, x_2 \geq 0$$

Rewriting this problem with the constraints expressed as equations, we have

Solution

minimize $\quad z = 5x_1 + 6x_2 + 0E_1 + 0E_2 + MA_1 + MA_2$

subject to
$$x_1 + x_2 - E_1 \qquad + A_1 \qquad = 10$$
$$2x_1 + 4x_2 \qquad -E_2 \qquad + A_2 = 24$$
$$x_1, x_2, E_1, E_2, A_1, A_2 \geq 0$$

If all variables in the objective function are moved to the left side of the equation, the initial tableau for this problem appears in Table 7.11. Note that the artificial variables are the basic variables in this initial solution. However, in any problem containing artificial variables, the row (0) coefficients for the artificial variables do not equal 0. These coefficients must be changed to 0 if the value of z is to be read from row (0). In Table 7.11 we can accomplish this by multiplying rows (1) and (2) by $+M$ and adding these multiples to row (0). Table 7.12 shows the resulting tableau.

In this initial solution the nonbasic variables are x_1, x_2, E_1, and E_2.

Basic Variables	z	x_1	x_2	E_1	E_2	A_1	A_2	b_i	Row Number
	1	−5	−6	0	0	−M	−M	0	(0)
A_1	0	1	1	−1	0	1	0	10	(1)
A_2	0	2	4	0	−1	0	1	24	(2)

Table 7.11

Basic Variables	z	x_1	x_2 Key Column	E_1	E_2	A_1	A_2	b_i	Row Number		b_i/a_{ik}
	1	$-5+3M$	$-6+5M$	$-M$	$-M$	0	0	$34M$	(0)	$R'_0 = R_0 + MR_1 + MR_2$	
A_1	0	1	1	-1	0	1	0	10	(1)	R_1	$10/1 = 10$
A_2	0	2	4	0	-1	0	1	24	(2)	R_2	$24/4 = 6^*$

Table 7.12

The basic variables are the two artificial variables with $A_1 = 10$, $A_2 = 24$, and $z = 34M$.

Applying Rule 1a, we conclude that this solution is not optimal. The row (0) coefficients for x_1 and x_2 are both positive (remember that M is an extremely large number). In applying Rule 2a, x_2 is identified as the new basic variable. The minimum b_i/a_{ik} value is associated with row (2). Thus, A_2 will be the departing basic variable. Table 7.13 indicates the next solution.

In Table 7.13 the nonbasic variables are x_1, E_1, E_2, and A_2. For this solution $A_1 = 4$, $x_2 = 6$, and $z = 36 + 4M$.

Applying Rule 1a, we see that this solution is not optimal. The row (0) coefficients for x_1 and E_2 are both positive. In applying Rule 2a, x_1 is identified as the new basic variable. The b_i/a_{ik} ratios are $4 \div \frac{1}{2} = 8$ and $6 \div \frac{1}{2} = 12$ for rows (1) and (2). Since the minimum ratio is associated with row (1), A_1 is identified as the departing basic variable. Table 7.14 indicates the new solution.

The solution in Table 7.14 has $x_1 = 8$, $x_2 = 2$, and $z = 52$. Applying Rule 1a, we conclude that this solution is optimal. All row (0) coefficients are less than or equal to 0 for the basic and nonbasic variables.

Follow-up Exercises

7.13 Rewrite the following constraint set by adding in the appropriate slack, surplus, and artificial variables.

$$\begin{aligned} x_1 + x_2 + x_3 &\geq 25 \\ 6x_1 - 2x_2 &= 20 \\ x_1 + 4x_2 + 3x_3 &\leq 100 \\ x_1, x_2, x_3 &\geq 0 \end{aligned}$$

7.14 Rewrite the following constraint set by adding in the appropriate slack, surplus, and artificial variables.

$$\begin{aligned} x_1 - 2x_2 + 4x_3 &\leq 100 \\ x_1 + x_2 + x_3 &= 50 \\ 3x_1 - 2x_2 + 2x_3 &\geq 25 \\ x_1, x_2, x_3 &\geq 0 \end{aligned}$$

Table 7.13

Basic Variable	z	x_1	x_2 Key Column	E_1	E_2	A_1	A_2	b_i	Row Number	
	1	$-2+\dfrac{M}{2}$	0	$-M$	$-\dfrac{3}{2}+\dfrac{M}{4}$	0	$\dfrac{3}{2}-\dfrac{5M}{4}$	$36+4M$	(0)	$R''_0 = R'_0 + (6-5M)R'_2$
A_1	0	$\frac{1}{2}$	0	-1	$\frac{1}{4}$	1	$-\frac{1}{4}$	4	(1)	$R'_1 = R_1 - R'_2$
x_2	0	$\frac{1}{2}$	1	0	$-\frac{1}{4}$	0	$\frac{1}{4}$	6	(2)	$R'_2 = \frac{1}{4}R_2$

Basic Variable	z	x_1	x_2	E_1	E_2	A_1	A_2	b_i	Row Number
	1	0	0	-4	$-\frac{1}{2}$	$4-M$	$\frac{1}{2}-M$	52	(0)
x_1	0	1	0	-2	$\frac{1}{2}$	2	$-\frac{1}{2}$	8	(1)
x_2	0	0	1	1	$-\frac{1}{2}$	-1	$\frac{1}{2}$	2	(2)

$$R_0''' = R_0'' + \left(2 - \frac{M}{2}\right) R_1''$$

$$R_1'' = 2R_1'$$

$$R_2'' = R_2' - \tfrac{1}{2}R_1''$$

Table 7.14

7.15 (*a*) Solve the following linear programming problem using the simplex method.

Minimize $\qquad z = 3x_1 + 6x_2$

subject to $\qquad 4x_1 + x_2 \geq 20$

$\qquad\qquad\qquad x_1 + x_2 \leq 20$

$\qquad\qquad\qquad x_1 + x_2 \geq 10$

$\qquad\qquad\qquad x_1, x_2 \geq 0$

(*b*) Verify the solution in part *a* by solving graphically.

7.16 (*a*) Solve the following linear programming problem using the simplex method.

Minimize $\qquad z = 6x_1 + 10x_2$

subject to $\qquad x_1 \qquad\quad \leq 12$

$\qquad\qquad\qquad 2x_2 = 36$

$\qquad\qquad 3x_1 + 2x_2 \geq 54$

$\qquad\qquad\qquad x_1, x_2 \geq 0$

(*b*) Verify the solution in part *a* by solving graphically.

SUMMARY 7.4

This chapter has presented the simplex method of solution for linear programming problems. The treatment of the simplex falls far short of being complete. However, the chapter does present the fundamentals. In later courses you may look at the simplex in greater detail.

One point should be emphasized before we move on to new material. That is, the simplex method can be extremely tedious when it is performed with hand calculations. For problems of any meaningful size, the computer will be essential. Canned computer packages are readily available for solving linear programming problems by the simplex.

CHAPTER CHECKLIST

If you have read the entire chapter, you should

Understand the requirements for solving linear programming problems by the *simplex method* _____

Be able to convert inequality constraints into equivalent constraint equations _____

Be able to solve maximization problems having all $\leq$ constraints using the simplex method _____

Understand the treatment of *artificial variables* in $=$ and $\geq$ constraints _____

Be able to solve minimization problems using the simplex method _____

KEY TERMS AND CONCEPTS

slack variable

surplus variable

artificial variable

basic variable

nonbasic variable

basic feasible solution

Gauss-Jordan procedure

optimality check (maximization and minimization problems)

new basic variable (maximization and minimization problems)

key column

departing basic variable

simplex method

ADDITIONAL EXERCISES

Solve the following problems using the simplex method.

7.17 Maximize $\qquad z = 5x_1 + 9x_2$

subject to
$$4x_1 + 8x_2 \leq 600$$
$$12x_1 + 8x_2 \leq 960$$
$$x_1, x_2 \geq 0$$

7.18 Minimize $\qquad z = 100x_1 + 75x_2$

subject to
$$x_1 + x_2 \geq 200$$
$$x_2 \geq 100$$
$$x_1 \qquad \geq 80$$
$$x_1, x_2 \geq 0$$

7.19 Maximize $\qquad z = 4x_1 + 2x_2 + 6x_3$

subject to
$$x_1 + 2x_2 + x_3 \leq 100$$
$$3x_1 + 2x_2 + 3x_3 \leq 120$$
$$x_1, x_2, x_3 \geq 0$$

7.20 Minimize $\qquad z = 4x_1 + 4x_2$

subject to
$$2x_1 + 4x_2 \geq 160$$
$$2x_1 \qquad \geq 60$$
$$2x_2 \geq 40$$
$$x_1, x_2 \geq 0$$

7.21 Maximize $\qquad z = 6x_1 + 12x_2 + 5x_3 + 2x_4$

subject to
$$3x_1 + 4x_2 + 8x_3 + 6x_4 \leq 1,100$$
$$8x_1 + 2x_2 + 4x_3 + 2x_4 \leq 1,400$$
$$4x_1 + 6x_2 + 2x_3 + 4x_4 \leq 400$$
$$x_1, x_2, x_3, x_4 \geq 0$$

7.22 Maximize $\qquad z = 5x_1 + 8x_2 + x_3$

subject to
$$x_1 + x_2 + 3x_3 \leq 70$$
$$x_1 + 2x_2 + x_3 \leq 100$$
$$2x_1 + x_2 + x_3 \leq 80$$
$$x_1, x_2, x_3 \geq 0$$

7.23 Minimize $\qquad z = 8x_1 + 4x_2 + 7x_3$

subject to
$$4x_1 + 6x_2 + 2x_3 \geq 120$$
$$4x_1 + 2x_2 + 2x_3 \geq 80$$
$$2x_1 + 2x_2 + 4x_3 \geq 80$$
$$x_1, x_2, x_3 \geq 0$$

7.24 Maximize $\qquad z = 7x_1 + 2x_2 + 5x_3$

subject to
$$x_1 + 3x_2 + x_3 = 35$$
$$2x_1 + x_2 + x_3 \leq 50$$
$$x_1 + x_2 + 2x_3 \leq 40$$
$$x_1, x_2, x_3 \geq 0$$

CHAPTER TEST

1 Given the following linear programming problem:

maximize $\qquad z = 10x_1 + 8x_2 + 12x_3$

subject to
$$4x_1 - 2x_2 + x_3 \leq 25$$
$$x_1 + 3x_2 \geq -10$$
$$2x_1 + 3x_3 = -20$$
$$x_1, x_2, x_3 \geq 0$$

transform the constraint set into an equivalent system of constraint equations suitable for the simplex method.

2 Solve the following linear programming problem using the simplex method.

Maximize $\qquad z = 20x_1 + 24x_2$

subject to
$$3x_1 + 6x_2 \leq 60$$
$$4x_1 + 2x_2 \leq 32$$
$$x_1, x_2 \geq 0$$

3 You are given the linear programming problem

minimize $\qquad z = 5x_1 + 4x_2$

subject to
$$x_1 + x_2 \geq 10$$
$$2x_1 - x_2 = 15$$
$$x_1, x_2 \geq 0$$

(a) Set up the initial simplex tableau and revise it, if necessary, so that the row (0) coefficients equal 0 for all basic variables.
(b) Which basic variable will leave first?
(c) Which nonbasic variable will enter first?

CHAPTER OBJECTIVES   After reading this chapter, you should be familiar with the concept of a *matrix*; you should understand the fundamentals of the algebra of matrices; and you should be familiar with selected applications of matrix algebra.

This chapter discusses matrix algebra and its applications. The nature of matrices is presented, followed by a discussion of different types of matrices, the algebra of matrices, and some specialized matrix concepts. The last section in the chapter presents several applications of matrix algebra.

INTRODUCTION TO MATRICES   8.1

What Is a Matrix?

Whenever one is dealing with data, there should be concern for organizing them in such a way that they are meaningful and can be readily identified. Summarizing data in tables serves this function. Income tax tables are an example of this type of organization. A *matrix* is a common device for summarizing and displaying numbers or data.

DEFINITION
A *matrix* is a rectangular array of elements. The elements are usually, but not always, real-valued numbers.

Consider the test scores for five students on 3 examinations. These may be displayed in the matrix

$$\begin{array}{c} \\ \text{Student} \\ \end{array} \begin{array}{c} \\ 1 \\ 2 \\ 3 \\ 4 \\ 5 \end{array} \overset{\begin{array}{ccc} & \text{Test} & \\ 1 & 2 & 3 \end{array}}{\begin{pmatrix} 75 & 82 & 86 \\ 91 & 95 & 100 \\ 65 & 70 & 68 \\ 59 & 80 & 99 \\ 75 & 76 & 74 \end{pmatrix}}$$

The matrix is the array of test scores enclosed by the large parentheses. The array is rectangularly shaped, having five rows and three columns.

A matrix **A** containing elements a_{ij} has the general form

$$\mathbf{A} = \begin{pmatrix} a_{11} & a_{12} \cdots a_{1n} \\ a_{21} & a_{22} \cdots a_{2n} \\ \cdots \cdots \cdots \\ a_{m1} & a_{m2} \cdots a_{mn} \end{pmatrix}$$

This matrix is represented as having m rows and n columns. The subscripts on an element a_{ij} indicate that the element is located at the intersection of row i and column j of the matrix. For example, a_{21} is located at the intersection of row 2 and column 1. The element a_{35} would be located in row 3 and column 5 of the matrix.

EXERCISE
If the elements in the student test score matrix are denoted by a_{ij}, what are the elements a_{12}, a_{32}, a_{43}, and a_{16}? (Ans.: 82, 70, 99, no a_{16} element)

Matrix names are usually represented by capital letters and the elements of a matrix by lowercase, subscripted letters.

A matrix is characterized further by its *dimensions*. The dimensions are the number of rows and the number of columns contained within the matrix. If a matrix has m rows and n columns, it is said to have dimensions $m \times n$, which is read "m by n." The student test score matrix has dimensions 5×3, or it is a "5 by 3" matrix.

Purpose of Studying Matrix Algebra

Given that we know what a matrix is, it should be clear that matrices provide one way of storing and displaying numbers. If you have taken a computer programming course, you probably used matrices for storage of information. In the FORTRAN language you reserve storage space for data in the memory of the computer by use of the DIMENSION statement. The statement "DIMENSION $A(20, 30)$" reserves space for a matrix **A** which has dimensions of 20×30.

When numbers are stored within matrices, there is often a need to use them. Assuming that information is stored within a matrix in some logical pattern, the retrieval of individual items or groups of items is relatively easy. Frequently there is a need to manipulate the data. For instance, an instructor may want to determine a class average or student average using the student test score data in the previously defined matrix. Matrix algebra allows for manipulating data and for performing computations while keeping the data in a matrix form. This is convenient, especially in computerized applications.

There are other more theoretical areas of application of matrix algebra. We will not be concerned with these in this book.

SPECIAL TYPES OF MATRICES   8.2

Vectors

A *row vector* is a matrix having only one row. A row vector having n elements has dimensions $1 \times n$. The three test scores for student 1 might be represented by the (1×3) row vector

$$\mathbf{S} = (75 \quad 82 \quad 86)$$

The matrix **B** below is a (1×8) row vector.

$$\mathbf{B} = (3 \quad 4 \quad 7 \quad -6 \quad 2 \quad 0 \quad 1 \quad -2)$$

A *column vector* is a matrix having only one column. A column vector having m elements has dimensions $m \times 1$. The scores of the five students on the first examination might be represented by the (5×1) column vector

$$\mathbf{T} = \begin{pmatrix} 75 \\ 91 \\ 65 \\ 59 \\ 75 \end{pmatrix}$$

Square Matrices

A *square matrix* is a matrix having the same number of rows and columns. If the dimensions of a matrix are $m \times n$, a square matrix is such that $m = n$. The following matrices are square.

$$\mathbf{A} = (3) \qquad \mathbf{B} = \begin{pmatrix} 1 & 3 \\ -5 & 4 \end{pmatrix} \qquad \mathbf{C} = \begin{pmatrix} 2 & 0 & -3 \\ 1 & -4 & 5 \\ 0 & 2 & 6 \end{pmatrix}$$

Identity Matrix

If a matrix **A** is square, we might concern ourselves with a subset of elements a_{ij} which lie along the *primary diagonal* of the matrix. These elements are located in positions where $i = j$, for example, $a_{11}, a_{22}, a_{33}, a_{44}$, . . . , a_{nn}. The elements on the primary diagonal of matrix **B** are $b_{11} = 1$ and $b_{22} = 4$. The elements on the primary diagonal of matrix **C** are $c_{11} = 2$, $c_{22} = -4$, and $c_{33} = 6$.

An *identity matrix* **I**, sometimes called a *unit matrix*, is a square matrix for which the elements along the primary diagonal all equal 1 while all other elements equal 0. If e_{ij} denotes a generalized element within an identity matrix, then

$$e_{ij} = \begin{cases} 1 & \text{if } i = j \\ 0 & \text{if } i \neq j \end{cases}$$

The matrices

$$\mathbf{I} = \begin{pmatrix} 1 & 0 \\ 0 & 1 \end{pmatrix} \quad \text{and} \quad \mathbf{I} = \begin{pmatrix} 1 & 0 & 0 \\ 0 & 1 & 0 \\ 0 & 0 & 1 \end{pmatrix}$$

are (2×2) and (3×3) identity matrices.

Although we will see different applications of the identity matrix, one important property involves the multiplication of an identity matrix and another matrix. Multiplication of matrices is a legitimate algebraic operation under certain circumstances. Given a matrix **A** and an identity matrix **I**, if the multiplication of **A** and **I** is possible, $\mathbf{AI} = \mathbf{A}$. Similarly, if the multiplication of **I** and **A** is possible, then $\mathbf{IA} = \mathbf{A}$. When the identity matrix is multiplied with another matrix, the resulting product is the other matrix. Thus **I** is to matrix multiplication as the number 1 is to multiplication in the real number system; that is, $(a)(1) = (1)(a) = a$.

Transpose of a Matrix

There are times when a matrix needs to be rearranged. The rearrangement may be simply to see the array of numbers from a different perspective or to manipulate the data in a later stage. One rearrangement is to form the *transpose* of a matrix. *If the matrix **A** has elements a_{ij}, the transpose of **A**, denoted by $\mathbf{A}^t$, contains elements a_{ij}^t where $a_{ij}^t = a_{ji}$.* If the matrix **A** has dimensions $m \times n$, then $\mathbf{A}^t$ will have dimensions $n \times m$.

Example 8.1

To find the transpose of the matrix

$$\mathbf{A} = \begin{pmatrix} 3 & 2 \\ 4 & 0 \\ 1 & -2 \end{pmatrix}$$

we first determine the dimensions of $\mathbf{A}^t$. Since **A** is a (3×2) matrix, $\mathbf{A}^t$ will be a (2×3) matrix having the form

$$\mathbf{A}^t = \begin{pmatrix} a_{11}^t & a_{12}^t & a_{13}^t \\ a_{21}^t & a_{22}^t & a_{23}^t \end{pmatrix}$$

Using the previous definition, we get

$$a_{11}{}^t = a_{11} = 3 \qquad a_{21}{}^t = a_{12} = 2$$
$$a_{12}{}^t = a_{21} = 4 \qquad a_{22}{}^t = a_{22} = 0$$
$$a_{13}{}^t = a_{31} = 1 \qquad a_{23}{}^t = a_{32} = -2$$

or

$$\mathbf{A}^t = \begin{pmatrix} 3 & 4 & 1 \\ 2 & 0 & -2 \end{pmatrix}$$

Look back at **A** and $\mathbf{A}^t$ in Example 8.1. Do you notice any pattern? What you should observe is that the rows of **A** become the columns of $\mathbf{A}^t$ and the columns of **A** become the rows of $\mathbf{A}^t$. These relationships will be true for any matrix and its transpose, and they provide an easy method for determining the transpose.

Let's apply this logic in finding the transpose of

Example 8.2

$$\mathbf{B} = \begin{pmatrix} 3 & 0 & 6 \\ 5 & 1 & 3 \\ 2 & -1 & 4 \end{pmatrix}$$

To form the transpose of **B**, rows 1, 2, and 3 become columns 1, 2, and 3 of $\mathbf{B}^t$, or

$$\mathbf{B}^t = \begin{pmatrix} 3 & 5 & 2 \\ 0 & 1 & -1 \\ 6 & 3 & 4 \end{pmatrix}$$

(You might also have envisioned this in terms of columns 1, 2, and 3 of **B** becoming rows 1, 2, and 3 of $\mathbf{B}^t$.)

Follow-up Exercises

Find the transpose of each of the following matrices.

8.1 $(3 \quad -4 \quad 2)$

8.2 $\begin{pmatrix} 2 & 6 \\ -1 & 4 \end{pmatrix}$

8.3 $\begin{pmatrix} 6 \\ 8 \\ -7 \end{pmatrix}$

8.4 $\begin{pmatrix} 5 & 4 \\ -1 & 2 \\ 3 & 0 \end{pmatrix}$

8.5 $\begin{pmatrix} 1 & 0 & 0 \\ 0 & 1 & 0 \\ 0 & 0 & 1 \end{pmatrix}$

8.6 $\begin{pmatrix} 1 & 4 & 0 & -1 \\ 4 & 5 & 1 & 2 \\ -2 & 1 & 3 & -4 \end{pmatrix}$

8.7 $\begin{pmatrix} 3 & -4 & 0 \\ 6 & 2 & 6 \end{pmatrix}$

8.8 (10)

MATRIX OPERATIONS

8.3

In this section we will discuss some of the operations of matrix algebra.

Matrix Addition and Subtraction

Two matrices may be added or subtracted if and only if they have the same dimensions. If matrices **A** and **B** are added to form a new matrix **C**, then $\mathbf{C}$ will have the same dimensions as $\mathbf{A}$ and $\mathbf{B}$ and the elements of $\mathbf{C}$ are found by adding the corresponding elements of $\mathbf{A}$ and $\mathbf{B}$. That is,

$$c_{ij} = a_{ij} + b_{ij}$$

Example 8.3

Given

$$\mathbf{A} = \begin{pmatrix} 1 & 3 \\ 4 & -2 \end{pmatrix} \quad \text{and} \quad \mathbf{B} = \begin{pmatrix} -3 & 2 \\ 0 & 4 \end{pmatrix}$$

$$\mathbf{A} + \mathbf{B} = \begin{pmatrix} 1 & 3 \\ 4 & -2 \end{pmatrix} + \begin{pmatrix} -3 & 2 \\ 0 & 4 \end{pmatrix} = \begin{pmatrix} 1 + (-3) & 3 + 2 \\ 4 + 0 & -2 + 4 \end{pmatrix}$$

$$= \begin{pmatrix} -2 & 5 \\ 4 & 2 \end{pmatrix}$$

Example 8.4

Using the same matrices as in Example 8.3, we get

$$\mathbf{B} - \mathbf{A} = \begin{pmatrix} -3 - (1) & 2 - 3 \\ 0 - (4) & 4 - (-2) \end{pmatrix}$$

$$= \begin{pmatrix} -4 & -1 \\ -4 & 6 \end{pmatrix}$$

Example 8.5

A small community college is comparing its admission data for the last two years. The interest is in the distribution of in-state versus out-of-state students and male and female enrollments. Matrices $\mathbf{A}_1$ and $\mathbf{A}_2$ summarize the number of students admitted in the last two years.

$$\mathbf{A}_1 = \begin{matrix} & \text{Male} & \text{Female} \\ \text{In-state} & \\ \text{Out-of-state} \end{matrix} \begin{pmatrix} 360 & 290 \\ 85 & 60 \end{pmatrix} \quad \mathbf{A}_2 = \begin{matrix} & \text{Male} & \text{Female} \\ \text{In-state} & \\ \text{Out-of-state} \end{matrix} \begin{pmatrix} 400 & 310 \\ 80 & 90 \end{pmatrix}$$

Total admission for each category during the past two years can be determined by finding $\mathbf{A}_1 + \mathbf{A}_2$, or

$$\begin{pmatrix} 360 & 290 \\ 85 & 60 \end{pmatrix} + \begin{pmatrix} 400 & 310 \\ 80 & 90 \end{pmatrix} = \begin{pmatrix} 760 & 600 \\ 165 & 150 \end{pmatrix}$$

During the past two years, 760 in-state males, 600 in-state females, 165 out-of-state males, and 150 out-of-state females have been admitted.

$\mathbf{A}_2 - \mathbf{A}_1$ would reflect the changes in the number of students admitted in year 2 as compared with year 1:

$$\mathbf{A}_2 - \mathbf{A}_1 = \begin{pmatrix} 400 & 310 \\ 80 & 90 \end{pmatrix} - \begin{pmatrix} 360 & 290 \\ 85 & 60 \end{pmatrix} = \begin{pmatrix} 40 & 20 \\ -5 & 30 \end{pmatrix}$$

Compared with year 1, 40 more in-state males, 20 more in-state females, and 30 more out-of-state females were admitted. The only group showing a decline in admission was out-of-state males.

Scalar Multiplication

A *scalar* is a real number. *Scalar multiplication* of a matrix is the multiplication of a matrix by a scalar. The product is found by multiplying each element in the matrix by the scalar. For example, if k is a scalar and **A** the (3×2) matrix below, then

$$k\mathbf{A} = k \cdot \begin{pmatrix} 5 & 3 \\ -2 & 1 \\ 0 & 4 \end{pmatrix} = \begin{pmatrix} 5k & 3k \\ -2k & k \\ 0 & 4k \end{pmatrix}$$

If

$$\mathbf{T} = \begin{pmatrix} 4 & -2 \\ -3 & 1 \end{pmatrix}$$

then

$$-5\mathbf{T} = -5 \begin{pmatrix} 4 & -2 \\ -3 & 1 \end{pmatrix} = \begin{pmatrix} -20 & 10 \\ 15 & -5 \end{pmatrix}$$

Example 8.6

The community college in Example 8.5 is expecting a 20 percent increase in admissions for each category of students in the third year. The projected admission figures can be determined by multiplying $\mathbf{A}_2$ by 1.2 (120 percent), or

Example 8.7

$$\mathbf{A}_3 = 1.2 \begin{pmatrix} 400 & 310 \\ 80 & 90 \end{pmatrix} = \begin{pmatrix} 480 & 372 \\ 96 & 108 \end{pmatrix}$$

The Inner Product

The *inner product* results when a row vector is multiplied by a column vector. The resulting product is a scalar quantity. The inner product is a significant operation in matrix multiplication; so let's focus on this concept first. *The inner product is defined only if the row and column vectors contain the same number of elements.* Consider the multiplication of the following vectors:

$$(5 \quad -2) \begin{pmatrix} 4 \\ 6 \end{pmatrix}$$

The inner product is computed by multiplying corresponding elements in the two vectors and algebraically summing. That is, element 1 in the row vector is multiplied by the first element in the column vector, and the product is added to the product of element 2 in the row vector and element 2 in the column vector. For the vectors indicated, the inner product is computed as

$$(5 \quad -2) \begin{pmatrix} 4 \\ 6 \end{pmatrix} = (5)(4) + (-2)(6) = 8$$

By using summation notation, the inner product of a $(1 \times n)$ row vector **A** and an $(n \times 1)$ column vector **B** can be represented by

$$\mathbf{A} \cdot \mathbf{B} = \sum_{j=1}^{n} a_{1j} b_{j1} \qquad (8.1)$$

Example 8.8   The inner product of

$$\mathbf{M} = (5 \quad -2 \quad 0 \quad 1 \quad 3) \quad \text{and} \quad \mathbf{N} = \begin{pmatrix} -2 \\ -4 \\ 10 \\ 20 \\ 6 \end{pmatrix}$$

is computed as

$$\mathbf{MN} = (5 \quad -2 \quad 0 \quad 1 \quad 3) \begin{pmatrix} -2 \\ -4 \\ 10 \\ 20 \\ 6 \end{pmatrix}$$
$$= (5)(-2) + (-2)(-4) + (0)(10) + (1)(20) + (3)(6)$$
$$= -10 + 8 + 0 + 20 + 18$$
$$= 36$$

Matrix Multiplication

Assume that a matrix $\mathbf{A}$ having dimensions $m_A \times n_A$ is to be multiplied by a matrix $\mathbf{B}$ having dimensions $m_B \times n_B$:

$$\begin{array}{ccc} \mathbf{A} & \cdot & \mathbf{B} \\ (m_A \times n_A) & & (m_B \times n_B) \end{array}$$
$$\underbrace{\qquad\qquad}_{n_A = m_B} \overset{?}{}$$

The matrix product $\mathbf{AB}$ is defined if and only if the number of columns of $\mathbf{A}$ equals the number of rows of $\mathbf{B}$, or if $n_A = m_B$. If the multiplication can be performed (that is, $n_A = m_B$), the resulting product will be a matrix which has dimensions $m_A \times n_B$.

$$\begin{array}{ccccc} \mathbf{A} & \cdot & \mathbf{B} & = & \mathbf{C} \\ (m_A \times n_A) & & (m_B \times n_B) & & (m_A \times n_B) \end{array}$$
$$\underbrace{\qquad\qquad}_{n_A = m_B}$$

To determine elements of the product matrix, the following rule applies.

RULE
If AB = C, an element c_{ij} of the product matrix is
equal to the *inner product* of row *i* in matrix A and
column *j* of matrix B.

Find the matrix product **AB**, if possible, where

$$A = \begin{pmatrix} 2 & 4 \\ 3 & 1 \end{pmatrix} \qquad B = \begin{pmatrix} -4 \\ 2 \end{pmatrix}$$

Example 8.9

The first check is to determine whether the multiplication is possible. **A** is a (2×2) matrix and **B** is a (2×1) matrix.

Solution

$$\begin{array}{cccc} \mathbf{A} & \cdot & \mathbf{B} & \mathbf{C} \\ (2 \times 2) & & (2 \times 1) & = (2 \times 1) \end{array}$$

equal

The product is defined because the number of columns of **A** equals the number of rows of **B**. The resulting product matrix will have dimensions 2×1 and will have the general form

$$C = \begin{pmatrix} c_{11} \\ c_{21} \end{pmatrix}$$

To find c_{11}, the inner product is found by multiplying row 1 of **A** times column 1 of **B**, or

$$c_{11} = (2 \quad 4) \begin{pmatrix} -4 \\ 2 \end{pmatrix}$$
$$= (2)(-4) + (4)(2) = 0$$

Similarly, c_{21} is found by computing the inner product between row 2 of **A** and column 1 of **B**, or

$$c_{21} = (3 \quad 1) \begin{pmatrix} -4 \\ 2 \end{pmatrix}$$
$$= (3)(-4) + (1)(2) = -10$$

The product matrix is

$$C = \begin{pmatrix} 0 \\ -10 \end{pmatrix}$$

NOTE
As you first attempt matrix multiplication problems, you may find it
helpful to write out the general form of the product matrix. We did

this by first stating the general form of C as $\begin{pmatrix} c_{11} \\ c_{21} \end{pmatrix}$. With the elements identified in this manner, the subscripts of each element indicate how that element should be computed.

Example 8.10

Determine the matrix product **BA**, if possible, for the matrices in the last example.

Solution

The product **BA** involves multiplying a (2×1) matrix times a (2×2) matrix, or

$$
\begin{array}{ccc}
\mathbf{B} & \cdot & \mathbf{A} \\
(2 \times 1) & & (2 \times 2) \\
| & & | \\
1 & \neq & 2
\end{array}
$$

Since the number of columns of **B** does not equal the number of rows of **A**, the multiplication cannot be performed.

NOTE

This example illustrates that the commutative property which holds for the multiplication of real numbers *does not necessarily* hold for matrix multiplication. We *cannot* state that AB = BA for any two matrices A and B.

Example 8.11

Find, if possible, the product **PI** = **T** where

$$
\mathbf{P} = \begin{pmatrix} 1 & 0 & -1 \\ 2 & 6 & -2 \\ 0 & 10 & 1 \\ 3 & 4 & 5 \end{pmatrix} \quad \text{and} \quad \mathbf{I} = \begin{pmatrix} 1 & 0 & 0 \\ 0 & 1 & 0 \\ 0 & 0 & 1 \end{pmatrix}
$$

Solution

P is a (4×3) matrix, and **I** is a (3×3) identity matrix. Since the number of columns of **P** equals the number of rows of **I**, the multiplication can be performed and the product matrix **T** will have dimensions 4×3. Thus,

$$
\begin{array}{ccccc}
\mathbf{P} & \cdot & \mathbf{I} & = & \mathbf{T} \\
(4 \times 3) & & (3 \times 3) & & (4 \times 3)
\end{array}
$$

equal

T will have the general form

$$\mathbf{T} = \begin{pmatrix} t_{11} & t_{12} & t_{13} \\ t_{21} & t_{22} & t_{23} \\ t_{31} & t_{32} & t_{33} \\ t_{41} & t_{42} & t_{43} \end{pmatrix}$$

$$t_{11} = (1 \quad 0 \quad -1) \begin{pmatrix} 1 \\ 0 \\ 0 \end{pmatrix} = (1)(1) + (0)(0) + (-1)(0) = 1$$

$$t_{12} = (1 \quad 0 \quad -1) \begin{pmatrix} 0 \\ 1 \\ 0 \end{pmatrix} = (1)(0) + (0)(1) + (-1)(0) = 0$$

$$t_{13} = (1 \quad 0 \quad -1) \begin{pmatrix} 0 \\ 0 \\ 1 \end{pmatrix} = (1)(0) + (0)(0) + (-1)(1) = -1$$

$$t_{21} = (2 \quad 6 \quad -2) \begin{pmatrix} 1 \\ 0 \\ 0 \end{pmatrix} = (2)(1) + 6(0) + (-2)(0) = 2$$

$$t_{22} = (2 \quad 6 \quad -2) \begin{pmatrix} 0 \\ 1 \\ 0 \end{pmatrix} = (2)(0) + 6(1) + (-2)(0) = 6$$

$$t_{23} = (2 \quad 6 \quad -2) \begin{pmatrix} 0 \\ 0 \\ 1 \end{pmatrix} = (2)(0) + (6)(0) + (-2)(1) = -2$$

$$t_{31} = (0 \quad 10 \quad 1) \begin{pmatrix} 1 \\ 0 \\ 0 \end{pmatrix} = (0)(1) + (10)(0) + (1)(0) = 0$$

$$t_{32} = (0 \quad 10 \quad 1) \begin{pmatrix} 0 \\ 1 \\ 0 \end{pmatrix} = (0)(0) + (10)(1) + (1)(0) = 10$$

$$t_{33} = (0 \quad 10 \quad 1) \begin{pmatrix} 0 \\ 0 \\ 1 \end{pmatrix} = (0)(0) + (10)(0) + (1)(1) = 1$$

$$t_{41} = (3 \quad 4 \quad 5) \begin{pmatrix} 1 \\ 0 \\ 0 \end{pmatrix} = (3)(1) + (4)(0) + (5)(0) = 3$$

$$t_{42} = (3 \quad 4 \quad 5) \begin{pmatrix} 0 \\ 1 \\ 0 \end{pmatrix} = (3)(0) + (4)(1) + (5)(0) = 4$$

$$t_{43} = (3 \quad 4 \quad 5) \begin{pmatrix} 0 \\ 0 \\ 1 \end{pmatrix} = (3)(0) + (4)(0) + (5)(1) = 5$$

The product matrix **T** is

$$\mathbf{T} = \begin{pmatrix} 1 & 0 & -1 \\ 2 & 6 & -2 \\ 0 & 10 & 1 \\ 3 & 4 & 5 \end{pmatrix}$$

NOTE
This example illustrates the property mentioned earlier concerning identity matrices. That is, if an identity matrix is multiplied by another matrix, the product will be the other matrix. In this example PI = T. But P = T; thus PI = P.

Example 8.12

The instructor who gave the three tests to five students has decided to weight the first two tests at 30 percent each and the third at 40 percent. The instructor wishes to compute the final averages for the five students using matrix multiplication. The matrix of grades is

$$\mathbf{G} = \begin{pmatrix} 75 & 82 & 86 \\ 91 & 95 & 100 \\ 65 & 70 & 68 \\ 59 & 80 & 99 \\ 75 & 76 & 74 \end{pmatrix}$$

and the examination weights are placed in the row vector

$$\mathbf{W} = (0.30 \quad 0.30 \quad 0.40)$$

The instructor needs to multiply these matrices in such a way that the first examination score for *each* student is multiplied by 0.30, the second score by 0.30, and the last score by 0.40. Verify for yourself that the products **GW** and **WG** are not defined. If, however, **W** had been stated as a column vector, the matrix product **GW** would lead to the desired result.

We can transform **W** into a column vector by simply finding its transpose. The product $\mathbf{GW}^t$ is defined, it leads to a (5 × 1) product matrix, and most important it performs the desired computations.

$$\begin{array}{ccc} \mathbf{G} & \cdot & \mathbf{W}^t & = & \mathbf{A} \\ (5 \times 3) & & (3 \times 1) & & (5 \times 1) \end{array}$$

equal

The final averages are computed as

$$\begin{pmatrix} 75 & 82 & 86 \\ 91 & 95 & 100 \\ 65 & 70 & 68 \\ 59 & 80 & 99 \\ 75 & 76 & 74 \end{pmatrix} \begin{pmatrix} 0.30 \\ 0.30 \\ 0.40 \end{pmatrix} = \begin{pmatrix} 75(0.3) + 82(0.3) + 86(0.4) \\ 91(0.3) + 95(0.3) + 100(0.4) \\ 65(0.3) + 70(0.3) + 68(0.4) \\ 59(0.3) + 80(0.3) + 99(0.4) \\ 75(0.3) + 76(0.3) + 74(0.4) \end{pmatrix} = \begin{pmatrix} 81.5 \\ 95.8 \\ 67.7 \\ 81.3 \\ 74.9 \end{pmatrix}$$

The averages are 81.5, 95.8, 67.7, 81.3, and 74.9, respectively, for the five students.

Follow-up Exercises

Perform the following matrix operations.

8.9 $\begin{pmatrix} 3 & 1 \\ 4 & -2 \end{pmatrix} + \begin{pmatrix} 2 & 0 \\ 1 & -1 \end{pmatrix} - \begin{pmatrix} 5 & -4 \\ -3 & 2 \end{pmatrix}$ **8.10** $3\begin{pmatrix} 2 & -5 \\ 4 & 3 \end{pmatrix}$

8.11 $\begin{pmatrix} 3 & 1 & 5 \\ 2 & 0 & -6 \\ 1 & 5 & 3 \end{pmatrix} - \begin{pmatrix} 6 & -4 & 2 \\ 0 & 1 & 0 \\ -2 & 1 & -2 \end{pmatrix}$

8.12 $-2\begin{pmatrix} 1 & 0 & -1 \\ -1 & 0 & -2 \\ 1 & 3 & 4 \end{pmatrix}$ **8.13** $2\begin{pmatrix} -2 & 4 \\ 5 & 1 \end{pmatrix} - 3\begin{pmatrix} 2 & 1 \\ \frac{2}{3} & 4 \end{pmatrix}$

8.14 $-2\begin{pmatrix} \frac{1}{2} & -\frac{1}{3} \\ \frac{2}{3} & \frac{1}{4} \end{pmatrix} + 4\begin{pmatrix} \frac{3}{4} & \frac{2}{3} \\ \frac{5}{6} & -\frac{1}{2} \end{pmatrix}$

8.15 $k\begin{pmatrix} a_{11} & a_{12} \\ a_{21} & a_{22} \end{pmatrix}$ **8.16** $-c\begin{pmatrix} m & n \\ o & p \end{pmatrix}$

Compute the inner product for the following exercises.

8.17 $(3 \quad -6)\begin{pmatrix} 2 \\ 1 \end{pmatrix}$ **8.18** $(5 \quad 3)\begin{pmatrix} -2 \\ 7 \end{pmatrix}$

8.19 $(-2 \quad 0 \quad 3)\begin{pmatrix} 1 \\ -1 \\ 1 \end{pmatrix}$ **8.20** $(3 \quad -1 \quad 1 \quad 4)\begin{pmatrix} 0 \\ 5 \\ 2 \\ 4 \end{pmatrix}$

Perform the following matrix multiplications, if they are possible.

8.21 $\begin{pmatrix} 1 & 5 \\ 2 & -1 \end{pmatrix}\begin{pmatrix} 4 & 2 \\ -3 & 0 \end{pmatrix}$ **8.22** $\begin{pmatrix} 2 & 6 \\ -1 & 2 \\ 1 & 0 \end{pmatrix}\begin{pmatrix} 0 & 2 \\ -1 & 4 \end{pmatrix}$

8.23 $\begin{pmatrix} 1 & 0 & 0 \\ 0 & 1 & 0 \\ 0 & 0 & 1 \end{pmatrix}\begin{pmatrix} 2 & 6 & 4 \\ 1 & 0 & 1 \\ 0 & 0 & 2 \end{pmatrix}$ **8.24** $\begin{pmatrix} 1 & 0 \\ 0 & 1 \end{pmatrix}\begin{pmatrix} 2 & 4 \\ 5 & 1 \\ 0 & 3 \end{pmatrix}$

8.25 $(2 \quad 5)\begin{pmatrix} 1 & -2 & 1 \\ 3 & 4 & 5 \end{pmatrix}$

8.26 $\begin{pmatrix} 3 & 2 & 5 \\ 1 & -4 & 6 \end{pmatrix}\begin{pmatrix} 5 & 1 & 3 & 4 \\ 4 & 2 & 0 & 2 \\ 0 & 0 & 1 & -1 \end{pmatrix}$

8.27 $\begin{pmatrix} -2 \\ 1 \end{pmatrix}(2 \quad -4)$ **8.28** $\begin{pmatrix} a & b \\ c & d \end{pmatrix}\begin{pmatrix} 1 \\ 1 \end{pmatrix}$

8.29 $\begin{pmatrix} a & b \\ c & d \end{pmatrix}\begin{pmatrix} x_1 \\ x_2 \end{pmatrix}$

8.30 Does the commutative law of addition hold for matrices (for example, $\mathbf{A} + \mathbf{B} = \mathbf{B} + \mathbf{A}$)?

8.31 Does the associative law of addition hold for matrices [for example, $\mathbf{A} + (\mathbf{B} + \mathbf{C}) = (\mathbf{A} + \mathbf{B}) + \mathbf{C}$]?

8.32 The grades for four students on four examinations are summarized in the matrix

$$\mathbf{G} = \begin{array}{c} \\ \\ \\ \\ \\ \end{array}\overset{\text{Student}}{\underset{}{\begin{array}{cccc} 1 & 2 & 3 & 4 \\ \left(\begin{array}{cccc} 80 & 60 & 80 & 75 \\ 70 & 40 & 70 & 90 \\ 90 & 70 & 80 & 82 \\ 100 & 50 & 70 & 70 \end{array}\right) & & & \end{array}}} \begin{array}{c} 1 \\ 2 \\ 3 \\ 4 \end{array} \text{Examination}$$

The instructor has decided to weight the four tests according to the percentages indicated in the vector $\mathbf{W}$:

$$\mathbf{W} = (0.20 \quad 0.20 \quad 0.20 \quad 0.40)$$

Combine these matrices in a way which computes the average scores for each student.

8.4 MATRIX REPRESENTATION OF EQUATIONS

Matrices can be used to represent equations. This section discusses this type of representation.

Representation of an Equation

An equation may be represented by using the inner product. The expression

$$3x_1 + 5x_2 - 4x_3$$

can be represented by the inner product

$$(3 \quad 5 \quad -4) \begin{pmatrix} x_1 \\ x_2 \\ x_3 \end{pmatrix}$$

where the row vector contains the coefficients on the variables and the column vector contains the variables in the expression. Verify for yourself that the inner product does lead to the original expression.

Now, if we want to represent the *equation*

$$3x_1 + 5x_2 - 4x_3 = 25$$

this can be done by equating the inner product with a (1×1) matrix containing the right-side constant, or

$$(3 \quad 5 \quad -4) \begin{pmatrix} x_1 \\ x_2 \\ x_3 \end{pmatrix} = (25)$$

Remember that for two matrices to be equal, they must have the same dimensions. The inner product always results in a (1×1) matrix, which in this case contains one element—the expression $3x_1 + 5x_2 - 4x_3$.

In general, a linear equation of the form $a_1x_1 + a_2x_2 + a_3x_3 + \cdots + a_nx_n = b$ can be represented in a matrix form as

$$(a_1 \quad a_2 \quad a_3 \cdots a_n) \begin{pmatrix} x_1 \\ x_2 \\ x_3 \\ \cdot \\ \cdot \\ \cdot \\ x_n \end{pmatrix} = b \qquad (8.2)$$

Representation of Systems of Equations

While single equations may be represented by using the inner product, systems of equations can be represented by using matrix multiplication. The system

$$5x_1 + 3x_2 = 15$$
$$4x_1 - 2x_2 = 12$$

can be represented as

$$\begin{pmatrix} 5 & 3 \\ 4 & -2 \end{pmatrix} \begin{pmatrix} x_1 \\ x_2 \end{pmatrix} = \begin{pmatrix} 15 \\ 12 \end{pmatrix}$$

In general, an $(m \times n)$ system of equations having the form

$$a_{11}x_1 + a_{12}x_2 + \cdots + a_{1n}x_n = b_1$$
$$a_{21}x_2 + a_{22}x_2 + \cdots + a_{2n}x_n = b_2$$
$$\cdots \cdots \cdots \cdots \cdots \cdots \cdots$$
$$a_{m1}x_1 + a_{m2}x_2 + \cdots + a_{mn}x_n = b_m$$

can be represented by the matrix equation

$$\mathbf{AX = B}$$

where $\mathbf{A}$ is an $(m \times n)$ matrix containing the variable coefficients on the left side of the set of equations, $\mathbf{X}$ is an n-component column vector containing the n variables, and $\mathbf{B}$ is an m-component column vector containing the right-side constants for the m equations. This representation appears as

$$\begin{pmatrix} a_{11} & a_{12} \cdots a_{1n} \\ a_{21} & a_{22} \cdots a_{2n} \\ \cdots \cdots \cdots \cdots \\ a_{m1} & a_{m2} \cdots a_{mn} \end{pmatrix} \begin{pmatrix} x_1 \\ x_2 \\ \cdot \\ \cdot \\ \cdot \\ x_n \end{pmatrix} = \begin{pmatrix} b_1 \\ b_2 \\ \cdot \\ \cdot \\ \cdot \\ b_m \end{pmatrix} \qquad (8.3)$$

Example 8.13

The system of equations

$$x_1 - 2x_2 \qquad + 3x_4 + x_5 = 100$$
$$2x_1 \qquad - 3x_3 + x_4 \qquad = 60$$
$$4x_2 - x_3 + 2x_4 + x_5 = 125$$

can be represented in the matrix form $\mathbf{AX} = \dot{\mathbf{B}}$ as

$$\begin{pmatrix} 1 & -2 & 0 & 3 & 1 \\ 2 & 0 & -3 & 1 & 0 \\ 0 & 4 & -1 & 2 & 1 \end{pmatrix} \begin{pmatrix} x_1 \\ x_2 \\ x_3 \\ x_4 \\ x_5 \end{pmatrix} = \begin{pmatrix} 100 \\ 60 \\ 125 \end{pmatrix}$$

Verify that this representation is valid and that the 0s must be included in the **A** matrix when a variable does not appear in a particular equation.

Follow-up Exercises

Rewrite the following systems of equations in matrix form.

8.33 $\begin{aligned} 2x_1 - x_2 &= 10 \\ 3x_1 + 4x_2 &= 25 \end{aligned}$
8.34 $\begin{aligned} 4x_1 - 3x_2 &= 66 \\ x_1 + 5x_2 &= 22 \end{aligned}$

8.35 $\begin{aligned} x_1 + x_2 + x_3 &= 15 \\ x_1 - x_2 &= 4 \\ 2x_1 + x_3 &= 14 \end{aligned}$
8.36 $\begin{aligned} 2x_1 - x_2 + x_3 &= 24 \\ x_1 - x_3 &= 0 \\ 2x_2 - 3x_3 &= -6 \end{aligned}$

Restate the following matrix equations in algebraic form.

8.37 $\begin{pmatrix} 1 & 0 & 0 \\ 0 & 1 & 0 \\ 0 & 0 & 1 \end{pmatrix} \begin{pmatrix} x_1 \\ x_2 \\ x_3 \end{pmatrix} = \begin{pmatrix} 10 \\ 5 \\ -5 \end{pmatrix}$
8.38 $\begin{pmatrix} 1 & 0 & 2 \\ 0 & -1 & 1 \\ 2 & 1 & 0 \end{pmatrix} \begin{pmatrix} x_1 \\ x_2 \\ x_3 \end{pmatrix} = \begin{pmatrix} 40 \\ 30 \\ 65 \end{pmatrix}$

8.39 $\begin{pmatrix} 2 & -3 \\ 4 & 0 \end{pmatrix} \begin{pmatrix} x_1 \\ x_2 \end{pmatrix} = \begin{pmatrix} 10 \\ 18 \end{pmatrix}$
8.40 $\begin{pmatrix} 4 & -6 & 5 \\ 2 & 0 & 1 \end{pmatrix} \begin{pmatrix} x_1 \\ x_2 \\ x_3 \end{pmatrix} = \begin{pmatrix} 50 \\ -20 \end{pmatrix}$

8.41 $\begin{pmatrix} a & b & c \\ d & e & f \\ g & h & i \end{pmatrix} \begin{pmatrix} x_1 \\ x_2 \\ x_3 \end{pmatrix} = \begin{pmatrix} j \\ k \\ l \end{pmatrix}$
8.42 $(1 \quad -3 \quad +100) \begin{pmatrix} x^2 \\ x \\ 1 \end{pmatrix} = 725$

8.5   THE DETERMINANT

An important concept in matrix algebra is that of the *determinant. If a matrix is square, the elements of the matrix may be used to compute a real-valued number called the determinant.* The determinant of a matrix

$$\mathbf{A} = \begin{pmatrix} 2 & 5 \\ 3 & -2 \end{pmatrix}$$

can be denoted by either enclosing vertical lines around the matrix name or by placing vertical lines around the elements of the matrix. The determinant of **A** can be denoted by either

$$|\mathbf{A}| \qquad \text{or} \qquad \begin{vmatrix} 2 & 5 \\ 3 & -2 \end{vmatrix}$$

The determinant concept is of particular interest in solving simultaneous equations. There are different ways of finding the value of a determinant. First let's discuss specific techniques for handling (1×1), (2×2), and (3×3) matrices and follow with the more generalized *cofactor procedure.*

The Determinant of a (1 × 1) Matrix

The determinant of a (1×1) matrix is simply the value of the one element contained in the matrix. If $\mathbf{A} = (5)$, $|\mathbf{A}| = 5$. If $\mathbf{M} = (-10)$, $|\mathbf{M}| = -10$.

The Determinant of a (2 × 2) Matrix

Given a (2×2) matrix having the form

$$\mathbf{A} = \begin{pmatrix} a_{11} & a_{12} \\ a_{21} & a_{22} \end{pmatrix}$$

$$|\mathbf{A}| = a_{11}a_{22} - a_{21}a_{12} \qquad (8.4)$$

The computation involves a cross multiplication of elements on the two diagonals, as indicated:

$$|\mathbf{A}| = \begin{pmatrix} a_{11} \\ \qquad a_{22} \end{pmatrix} - \begin{pmatrix} \qquad a_{12} \\ a_{21} \end{pmatrix}$$

Example 8.14

If
$$\mathbf{A} = \begin{pmatrix} 1 & -2 \\ 3 & 4 \end{pmatrix}$$

then
$$|\mathbf{A}| = (1)(4) - (3)(-2)$$
$$= 4 + 6 = 10$$

Example 8.15

If
$$\mathbf{I} = \begin{pmatrix} 1 & 0 \\ 0 & 1 \end{pmatrix}$$

then
$$|\mathbf{I}| = (1)(1) - (0)(0)$$
$$= 1$$

The Determinant of a (3 × 3) Matrix

Given the (3×3) matrix

$$\mathbf{A} = \begin{pmatrix} a_{11} & a_{12} & a_{13} \\ a_{21} & a_{22} & a_{23} \\ a_{31} & a_{32} & a_{33} \end{pmatrix}$$

the determinant may be found by rewriting the first two columns of the matrix to the right of the original matrix.

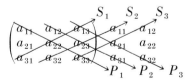

The determinant is computed by multiplying the elements on each *primary diagonal* (P_1, P_2, P_3) and adding these products. From this sum is subtracted the products of the elements lying on each *secondary diagonal* (S_1, S_2, S_3). Algebraically the determinant is computed as

$$|\mathbf{A}| = a_{11}a_{22}a_{33} + a_{12}a_{23}a_{31} + a_{13}a_{21}a_{32} - a_{31}a_{22}a_{13} \\ - a_{32}a_{23}a_{11} - a_{33}a_{21}a_{12} \tag{8.5}$$

Example 8.16

To find the determinant of the given matrix **A**

$$\mathbf{A} = \begin{pmatrix} 3 & 1 & 2 \\ -1 & 2 & 4 \\ 3 & -2 & 1 \end{pmatrix}$$

the first two columns rewrite to the right of the original (3×3) matrix:

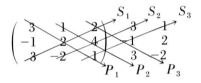

The determinant is computed as

$$\begin{aligned} |\mathbf{A}| &= (3)(2)(1) + (1)(4)(3) + (2)(-1)(-2) - (3)(2)(2) - (-2)(4)(3) \\ &\quad - (1)(-1)(1) \\ &= 6 + 12 + 4 - 12 + 24 + 1 \\ &= 47 - 12 = 35 \end{aligned}$$

The Method of Cofactors (Optional)

The methods that we have examined for (1×1), (2×2), and (3×3) matrices apply only for matrices of those dimensions. We cannot extend the (3×3) procedure to deal with (4×4), (5×5), or square matrices of a higher order. This section discusses a procedure which can be applied for all square matrices of size 2×2 or higher.

Our first concern will be with finding a *matrix of cofactors*. For any square matrix **A** there can be found a matrix of cofactors which we will denote as $\mathbf{A}_c$. The matrix of cofactors will have the same dimensions as **A** and will consist of elements a'_{ij} which are called *cofactors*. For each element a_{ij} contained in **A** there will be a corresponding cofactor a'_{ij}.

Determine the cofactor associated with element a_{ij} as follows:

1 Either mentally or with a pencil, cross off row i and column j in the original matrix. Focus upon the remaining elements in the matrix. The remaining elements are a *submatrix* of the original matrix.

2 Find the determinant of the remaining submatrix. This determinant is called the *minor* of the element a_{ij}.

3 The cofactor is found by multiplying the minor by either $+1$ or -1 depending on the position of the element a_{ij}. A formula for computing the cofactor is

$$a'_{ij} = (-1)^{i+j}(\text{the value of the minor})$$

(The essence of this formula is that if $i + j$ is an *even* number, the minor is multiplied by $+1$; if $i + j$ is *odd*, the minor is multiplied by -1.)

To find the matrix of cofactors for the (2×2) matrix

$$\mathbf{A} = \begin{pmatrix} 5 & -4 \\ 2 & -2 \end{pmatrix}$$

Example 8.17

let's begin with the cofactor corresponding to element a_{11}. Crossing off row 1 and column 1 leaves the (1×1) submatrix (-2). The determinant of this submatrix

$$\begin{pmatrix} 5 & -4 \\ 2 & -2 \end{pmatrix}$$

equals -2 and is therefore the minor. The cofactor is computed as

$$a'_{11} = (-1)^{1+1}(-2) = (-1)^2(-2)$$
$$= (1)(-2) = -2$$

For the remaining elements,

$$\begin{pmatrix} 5 & -4 \\ 2 & -2 \end{pmatrix} \qquad \begin{aligned} a'_{12} &= (-1)^{1+2}(2) \\ &= (-1)(2) &= -2 \end{aligned}$$

$$\begin{pmatrix} 5 & -4 \\ 2 & -2 \end{pmatrix} \qquad \begin{aligned} a'_{21} &= (-1)^{2+1}(-4) \\ &= (-1)(-4) &= 4 \end{aligned}$$

$$\begin{pmatrix} 5 & -4 \\ 2 & -2 \end{pmatrix} = \qquad \begin{aligned} a'_{22} &= (-1)^{2+2}(5) \\ &= (1)(5) &= 5 \end{aligned}$$

The matrix of cofactors $\mathbf{A}_c$ is

$$\mathbf{A}_c = \begin{pmatrix} -2 & -2 \\ 4 & 5 \end{pmatrix}$$

To find the matrix of cofactors for the (3×3) matrix in Example 8.16, let's begin with the element a_{11}. Crossing off row 1 and column 1, we are left with a (2×2) submatrix:

Example 8.18

$$\mathbf{A} = \begin{pmatrix} 3 & 1 & 2 \\ -1 & 2 & 4 \\ 3 & -2 & 1 \end{pmatrix}$$

The cofactor is computed as

$$a'_{11} = (-1)^{1+1} \begin{vmatrix} 2 & 4 \\ -2 & 1 \end{vmatrix} = (-1)^2[(2)(1) - (-2)(4)]$$
$$= 1(10) = 10$$

For element a_{12}, row 1 and column 2 are crossed off

$$\begin{pmatrix} 3 & 1 & 2 \\ -1 & 2 & 4 \\ 3 & -2 & 1 \end{pmatrix}$$

leaving the (2×2) submatrix

$$\begin{pmatrix} -1 & 4 \\ 3 & 1 \end{pmatrix}$$

The cofactor a'_{12} is computed as

$$a'_{12} = (-1)^{1+2} \begin{vmatrix} -1 & 4 \\ 3 & 1 \end{vmatrix} = (-1)^3(-1 - 12)$$
$$= -1(-13)$$
$$= 13$$

Now it is your turn! Verify that the matrix of cofactors is

$$\mathbf{A}_c = \begin{pmatrix} 10 & 13 & -4 \\ -5 & -3 & 9 \\ 0 & -14 & 7 \end{pmatrix}$$

This procedure seems tedious at first. It is, but you will get better at it. The level of tedium becomes greater with (4×4) matrices and those of higher dimensions. With a (4×4) matrix, crossing off a row and column leaves a (3×3) submatrix for which the determinant needs to be found. And this must be done 16 times—one for each element in the (4×4) matrix! This procedure can be programmed fairly easily on a computer, and unless your prof is an ogre, you will probably not have to compute the cofactor matrix manually for anything higher than a (10×10) matrix!

We began this section with the objective of determining a generalized approach for finding a determinant. The *method of cofactor expansion* allows you to compute the determinant of a matrix by (1) selecting *any* row or column of the matrix and (2) multiplying each element in the row or column by its corresponding cofactor and summing these products.

For the $(m \times m)$ matrix $\mathbf{A}$, the determinant can be found by expanding along any row i according to the equation

$$|\mathbf{A}| = a_{i1}a'_{i1} + a_{i2}a'_{i2} + \cdots + a_{im}a'_{im} \tag{8.6}$$

By using summation notation, Eq. (8.6) can be rewritten as

$$|\mathbf{A}| = \sum_{j=1}^{m} a_{ij}a'_{ij} \qquad i = 1, 2, 3, \ldots, m \tag{8.7}$$

Similarly, the determinant can be found by expanding in any column j according to the equation

$$|\mathbf{A}| = a_{1j}a'_{1j} + a_{2j}a'_{2j} + \cdots + a_{mj}a'_{mj} \tag{8.8}$$

or

$$|\mathbf{A}| = \sum_{i=1}^{m} a_{ij}a'_{ij} \qquad j = 1, 2, 3, \ldots, m \tag{8.9}$$

NOTE
If your objective is to find the determinant, it is not necessary to compute the entire matrix of cofactors! You need to determine only the cofactors for the row or column selected for expansion.

Repeating **A** and its matrix of cofactors **A**$_c$ from Example 8.17, we have

$$\mathbf{A} = \begin{pmatrix} 5 & -4 \\ 2 & -2 \end{pmatrix} \qquad \mathbf{A}_c = \begin{pmatrix} -2 & -2 \\ 4 & 5 \end{pmatrix}$$

Example 8.19

$|\mathbf{A}|$ can be found by expanding along row 1 as

$$\begin{aligned} |\mathbf{A}| &= (5)(-2) + (-4)(-2) \\ &= -2 \end{aligned}$$

or down column 2 as

$$\begin{aligned} |\mathbf{A}| &= (-4)(-2) + (-2)(5) \\ &= -2 \end{aligned}$$

By repeating **A** and **A**$_c$ from Example 8.18:

$$\mathbf{A} = \begin{pmatrix} 3 & 1 & 2 \\ -1 & 2 & 4 \\ 3 & -2 & 1 \end{pmatrix} \qquad \mathbf{A}_c = \begin{pmatrix} 10 & 13 & -4 \\ -5 & -3 & 9 \\ 0 & -14 & 7 \end{pmatrix}$$

Example 8.20

the determinant of **A** is computed by expanding down column 3 as

$$\begin{aligned} |\mathbf{A}| &= (2)(-4) + (4)(9) + (1)(7) \\ &= -8 + 36 + 7 = 35 \end{aligned}$$

EXERCISE
Verify that the value of the determinant is the same if you expand down the other two columns or across any of the rows.

The selection of a row or column for expanding by cofactors should not be arbitrary. Often you can take advantage of the content or form of a matrix. For example, let's find the determinant of the (4×4) matrix

Example 8.21

$$\mathbf{A} = \begin{pmatrix} 3 & 0 & 1 & 2 \\ 6 & -2 & -5 & 4 \\ -1 & 0 & 2 & 4 \\ 3 & 0 & -2 & 1 \end{pmatrix}$$

If we select column 2 for expansion, we will have to find only one cofactor—that corresponding to a_{22}. That is,

$$\begin{aligned} |\mathbf{A}| &= (0)a_{12}' + (-2)a_{22}' + (0)a_{32}' + (0)(a_{42}') \\ &= (-2)a_{22}' \end{aligned}$$

Crossing off row 2 and column 2, we are left with the (3×3) submatrix

$$\begin{pmatrix} 3 & 1 & 2 \\ -1 & 2 & 4 \\ 3 & -2 & 1 \end{pmatrix}$$

Compare this matrix with the one in Example 8.20. Since probably you have just about reached your limit, this problem has been "doctored." We have already computed the determinant of this matrix as 35. Thus,

$$a'_{22} = (-1)^{2+2}(35) = 35$$

and

$$|\mathbf{A}| = (-2)a'_{22}$$
$$= (-2)(35) = -70$$

Follow-up Exercises

Find the determinants of the following matrices.

8.43 $\mathbf{A} = (15)$ **8.44** $\mathbf{M} = (-18)$

8.45 $\mathbf{B} = \begin{pmatrix} 2 & 4 \\ 4 & 8 \end{pmatrix}$ **8.46** $\mathbf{C} = \begin{pmatrix} 1 & 3 \\ 4 & 12 \end{pmatrix}$

8.47 $\mathbf{A} = \begin{pmatrix} 1 & 3 & 0 \\ 4 & 0 & 2 \\ 1 & 2 & 3 \end{pmatrix}$ **8.48** $\mathbf{G} = \begin{pmatrix} 3 & -4 & 0 \\ 2 & 2 & 1 \\ -1 & 1 & -1 \end{pmatrix}$

Find the matrix of cofactors for each of the following matrices.

8.49 $\mathbf{A} = \begin{pmatrix} 3 & 5 \\ -2 & 6 \end{pmatrix}$ **8.50** $\mathbf{B} = \begin{pmatrix} 3 & -2 \\ -4 & 5 \end{pmatrix}$

8.51 $\mathbf{M} = \begin{pmatrix} 2 & 1 & 1 \\ 0 & 3 & 0 \\ 4 & -5 & 2 \end{pmatrix}$ **8.52** $\mathbf{A} = \begin{pmatrix} 4 & 2 & 4 \\ 0 & 1 & 0 \\ 2 & 1 & 2 \end{pmatrix}$

8.53 through 8.56 Find the determinants for the matrices in Exercises 8.49 to 8.52 by using the method of cofactor expansion.

8.57 Find the determinant of the matrix

$$\mathbf{A} = \begin{pmatrix} 5 & 2 & -3 & 1 \\ 0 & 0 & 3 & 0 \\ 1 & -1 & 2 & -2 \\ 2 & 4 & 1 & -1 \end{pmatrix}$$

8.58 Find the determinant of the matrix

$$\mathbf{A} = \begin{pmatrix} 0 & 0 & 3 \\ 0 & 3 & 0 \\ -3 & 0 & 0 \end{pmatrix}$$

8.6   ## THE INVERSE OF A MATRIX

For some matrices there can be identified another matrix called the *multiplicative-inverse matrix*. The relationship between a matrix $\mathbf{A}$ and its multiplicative inverse, denoted by $\mathbf{A}^{-1}$, is that the product of $\mathbf{A}$ and $\mathbf{A}^{-1}$, in either order, results in the identity matrix, or

$$\mathbf{A}\mathbf{A}^{-1} = \mathbf{A}^{-1}\mathbf{A} = \mathbf{I} \tag{8.10}$$

The multiplicative inverse is similar to the reciprocal in regular algebra. Multiplying a quantity b by its reciprocal $1/b$ results in a product of 1. In matrix algebra multiplying a matrix by its inverse results in the identity matrix.

Three important conditions exist concerning the inverse:

1 For a matrix A to have a multiplicative inverse, it must be square.

2 The multiplicative inverse of A will also be square, having the same dimensions as A.

3 Not every square matrix has a multiplicative inverse.

Henceforth in this section the term *inverse* will mean the multiplicative inverse.

We can verify that matrix **B** below is the inverse of matrix **A** by finding the products **AB** and **BA**.

Example 8.22

$$\mathbf{A} = \begin{pmatrix} 3 & 7 \\ 2 & 5 \end{pmatrix} \qquad \mathbf{B} = \begin{pmatrix} 5 & -7 \\ -2 & 3 \end{pmatrix}$$

$$\mathbf{AB} = \begin{pmatrix} 3 & 7 \\ 2 & 5 \end{pmatrix}\begin{pmatrix} 5 & -7 \\ -2 & 3 \end{pmatrix} = \begin{pmatrix} 1 & 0 \\ 0 & 1 \end{pmatrix}$$

$$\mathbf{BA} = \begin{pmatrix} 5 & -7 \\ -2 & 3 \end{pmatrix}\begin{pmatrix} 3 & 7 \\ 2 & 5 \end{pmatrix} = \begin{pmatrix} 1 & 0 \\ 0 & 1 \end{pmatrix}$$

Because both products result in a (2×2) identity matrix, we can state that matrix **B** is the inverse of **A**, or

$$\mathbf{B} = \mathbf{A}^{-1}$$

DEFINITION
If $\mathbf{A}^{-1}$ is the inverse of A, A is the inverse of $\mathbf{A}^{-1}$.

In the last example, we can make the statement that

$$\mathbf{A} = \mathbf{B}^{-1}$$

Verify that the matrix **A** meets the requirements to be the inverse of **B**.

Determining the Inverse

There are a couple of different ways to determine the inverse of a matrix. One method is based on the Gauss-Jordan procedure discussed in Sec. 4.4. Let's develop the general procedure by using an example. If you are fuzzy on the Gauss-Jordan procedure, a rereading of Sec. 4.4. is advised.

Example 8.23   Let's return to the matrix **A** in the last example. If there is another matrix **B** which is the inverse of **A**, it will have dimensions 2 × 2. Labeling the elements of **B** as below

$$\mathbf{B} = \begin{pmatrix} b_{11} & b_{12} \\ b_{21} & b_{22} \end{pmatrix}$$

we would expect the following matrix equation to be true:

$$\mathbf{AB} = \mathbf{I} \quad \text{or} \quad \begin{pmatrix} 3 & 7 \\ 2 & 5 \end{pmatrix} \begin{pmatrix} b_{11} & b_{12} \\ b_{21} & b_{22} \end{pmatrix} = \begin{pmatrix} 1 & 0 \\ 0 & 1 \end{pmatrix}$$

Multiplying on the left side of the equation gives

$$\begin{pmatrix} 3b_{11} + 7b_{21} & 3b_{12} + 7b_{22} \\ 2b_{11} + 5b_{21} & 2b_{12} + 5b_{22} \end{pmatrix} = \begin{pmatrix} 1 & 0 \\ 0 & 1 \end{pmatrix}$$

For two matrices to be equal, they must have the same dimensions and their respective elements must equal one another. To determine the elements of the inverse matrix **B**, we need to solve two pairs of equations. The pair used to solve for the values of b_{11} and b_{21} is

$$3b_{11} + 7b_{21} = 1$$
$$2b_{11} + 5b_{21} = 0$$

and the pair used to solve for the values of b_{12} and b_{22} is

$$3b_{12} + 7b_{22} = 0$$
$$2b_{12} + 5b_{22} = 1$$

If we were to solve these two systems individually by the Gauss-Jordan method, we would write them as

$$\begin{array}{cc|c} 3 & 7 & 1 \\ 2 & 5 & 0 \end{array} \quad \text{and} \quad \begin{array}{cc|c} 3 & 7 & 0 \\ 2 & 5 & 1 \end{array}$$

For each system we would perform row operations to transform the array of coefficients $\begin{pmatrix} 3 & 7 \\ 2 & 5 \end{pmatrix}$ into a (2 × 2) identity matrix. Since *both* systems have the same matrix of coefficients on the left side, we would perform the same row operations on both systems to solve them. We could streamline the process by augmenting the right-side coefficients for the first system with those for the second system of equations

$$\begin{pmatrix} 3 & 7 & 1 & 0 \\ 2 & 5 & 0 & 1 \end{pmatrix}$$

and perform the row operations one time only. Upon transforming the matrix of coefficients on the left side into a (2 × 2) identity matrix, the first column of values on the right side would contain the solution for the first system of equations and the second column the solution for the second system of equations. The transformed matrices would appear as

$$\begin{pmatrix} 1 & 0 & b_{11} & b_{12} \\ 0 & 1 & b_{21} & b_{22} \end{pmatrix}$$

and the (2×2) matrix to the right of the vertical line is the matrix **B**, or the inverse of **A**.

GAUSSIAN PROCEDURE
To determine the inverse of an $(m \times m)$ matrix A, do the following.

1 Augment the matrix A with an $(m \times m)$ identity matrix, as indicated:

$$(A|I)$$

2 Perform row operations on the entire augmented matrix so as to transform A into an $(m \times m)$ identity matrix. The resulting matrix will have the form

$$(I|A^{-1})$$

where A^{-1} can be read to the right of the vertical line.

If the matrix does not have an inverse, it will not be possible to transform A into an identity matrix.

Continuing the last example, we can find $\mathbf{A}^{-1}$ by the following steps:

Example 8.24

$$\begin{pmatrix} 3 & 7 & | & 1 & 0 \\ 2 & 5 & | & 0 & 1 \end{pmatrix}$$

$$\begin{pmatrix} 1 & \frac{7}{3} & | & \frac{1}{3} & 0 \\ 2 & 5 & | & 0 & 1 \end{pmatrix} \qquad \text{(multiplying row 1 by } \tfrac{1}{3})$$

$$\begin{pmatrix} 1 & \frac{7}{3} & | & \frac{1}{3} & 0 \\ 0 & \frac{1}{3} & | & -\frac{2}{3} & 1 \end{pmatrix} \qquad \begin{array}{l} \text{(multiplying row 1 by } -2 \\ \text{and adding to row 2)} \end{array}$$

$$\begin{pmatrix} 1 & \frac{7}{3} & | & \frac{1}{3} & 0 \\ 0 & 1 & | & -2 & 3 \end{pmatrix} \qquad \text{(multiplying row 2 by 3)}$$

$$\begin{pmatrix} 1 & 0 & | & 5 & -7 \\ 0 & 1 & | & -2 & 3 \end{pmatrix} \qquad \begin{array}{l} \text{(multiplying row 2 by } -\tfrac{7}{3} \\ \text{and adding to row 1)} \end{array}$$

The inverse of **A** is

$$\mathbf{A}^{-1} = \begin{pmatrix} 5 & -7 \\ -2 & 3 \end{pmatrix}$$

which we indicated in Example 8.22.

Find the inverse of the matrix

Example 8.25

$$\mathbf{B} = \begin{pmatrix} 1 & 2 & 0 \\ 1 & 0 & -1 \\ -1 & 3 & 2 \end{pmatrix}$$

Solution   Augmenting **B** with a (3×3) identity matrix, we have

$$\left(\begin{array}{ccc|ccc} 1 & 2 & 0 & 1 & 0 & 0 \\ 1 & 0 & -1 & 0 & 1 & 0 \\ -1 & 3 & 2 & 0 & 0 & 1 \end{array}\right)$$

$$\left(\begin{array}{ccc|ccc} 1 & 2 & 0 & 1 & 0 & 0 \\ 0 & -2 & -1 & -1 & 1 & 0 \\ -1 & 3 & 2 & 0 & 0 & 1 \end{array}\right) \quad \begin{array}{l} \text{(multiplying row 1 by } -1 \\ \text{and adding to row 2)} \end{array}$$

$$\left(\begin{array}{ccc|ccc} 1 & 2 & 0 & 1 & 0 & 0 \\ 0 & -2 & -1 & -1 & 1 & 0 \\ 0 & 5 & 2 & 1 & 0 & 1 \end{array}\right) \quad \text{(adding row 1 to row 3)}$$

$$\left(\begin{array}{ccc|ccc} 1 & 2 & 0 & 1 & 0 & 0 \\ 0 & 1 & \frac{1}{2} & \frac{1}{2} & -\frac{1}{2} & 0 \\ 0 & 5 & 2 & 1 & 0 & 1 \end{array}\right) \quad \text{(multiplying row 2 by } -\tfrac{1}{2})$$

$$\left(\begin{array}{ccc|ccc} 1 & 0 & -1 & 0 & 1 & 0 \\ 0 & 1 & \frac{1}{2} & \frac{1}{2} & -\frac{1}{2} & 0 \\ 0 & 5 & 2 & 1 & 0 & 1 \end{array}\right) \quad \begin{array}{l} \text{(multiplying row 2 by } -2 \\ \text{and adding to row 1)} \end{array}$$

$$\left(\begin{array}{ccc|ccc} 1 & 0 & -1 & 0 & 1 & 0 \\ 0 & 1 & \frac{1}{2} & \frac{1}{2} & -\frac{1}{2} & 0 \\ 0 & 0 & -\frac{1}{2} & -\frac{3}{2} & \frac{5}{2} & 1 \end{array}\right) \quad \begin{array}{l} \text{(multiplying row 2 by } -5 \\ \text{and adding to row 3)} \end{array}$$

$$\left(\begin{array}{ccc|ccc} 1 & 0 & -1 & 0 & 1 & 0 \\ 0 & 1 & \frac{1}{2} & \frac{1}{2} & -\frac{1}{2} & 0 \\ 0 & 0 & 1 & 3 & -5 & -2 \end{array}\right) \quad \text{(multiplying row 3 by } -2)$$

$$\left(\begin{array}{ccc|ccc} 1 & 0 & -1 & 0 & 1 & 0 \\ 0 & 1 & 0 & -1 & 2 & 1 \\ 0 & 0 & 1 & 3 & -5 & -2 \end{array}\right) \quad \begin{array}{l} \text{(multiplying row 3 by } -\tfrac{1}{2} \\ \text{and adding to row 2)} \end{array}$$

$$\left(\begin{array}{ccc|ccc} 1 & 0 & 0 & 3 & -4 & -2 \\ 0 & 1 & 0 & -1 & 2 & 1 \\ 0 & 0 & 1 & 3 & -5 & -2 \end{array}\right) \quad \text{(adding row 3 to row 1)}$$

Finding the Inverse Using Cofactors (Optional)

Another method for determining the inverse of a matrix utilizes the matrix of cofactors.

The cofactor procedure for finding the inverse of a square matrix A is as follows.

1 Determine the matrix of cofactors A_c for the matrix A.

2 Determine the adjoint matrix A_j which is the transpose of A_c:

$$\mathbf{A}_j = \mathbf{A}_c{}^t$$

3 The inverse of A is found by multiplying the adjoint matrix by the reciprocal of the determinant of A, or

$$\mathbf{A}^{-1} = \frac{1}{|\mathbf{A}|}\,\mathbf{A}_j$$

Let's determine the inverse of the (2 × 2) matrix in Example 8.24. For **Example 8.26**

$$\mathbf{A} = \begin{pmatrix} 3 & 7 \\ 2 & 5 \end{pmatrix}$$

the cofactor matrix $\mathbf{A}_c$ is

$$\mathbf{A}_c = \begin{pmatrix} 5 & -2 \\ -7 & 3 \end{pmatrix}$$

The adjoint matrix is the transpose of $\mathbf{A}_c$, or

$$\mathbf{A}_j = \begin{pmatrix} 5 & -7 \\ -2 & 3 \end{pmatrix}$$

The determinant of $\mathbf{A}$ is

$$|\mathbf{A}| = (3)(5) - (-2)(-7)$$
$$= 1$$

Therefore

$$\mathbf{A}^{-1} = \frac{1}{1} \begin{pmatrix} 5 & -7 \\ -2 & 3 \end{pmatrix}$$
$$= \begin{pmatrix} 5 & -7 \\ -2 & 3 \end{pmatrix}$$

Let's determine the inverse of the (3 × 3) matrix in Example 8.25. For **Example 8.27**

$$\mathbf{B} = \begin{pmatrix} 1 & 2 & 0 \\ 1 & 0 & -1 \\ -1 & 3 & 2 \end{pmatrix}$$

the matrix of cofactors $\mathbf{B}_c$ is

$$\mathbf{B}_c = \begin{pmatrix} 3 & -1 & 3 \\ -4 & 2 & -5 \\ -2 & 1 & -2 \end{pmatrix}$$

The adjoint matrix $\mathbf{B}_j$ is the transpose of $\mathbf{B}_c$, or

$$\mathbf{B}_j = \begin{pmatrix} 3 & -4 & -2 \\ -1 & 2 & 1 \\ 3 & -5 & -2 \end{pmatrix}$$

Verify that the determinant of $\mathbf{B}$ equals 1.
Therefore,

$$\mathbf{B}^{-1} = \frac{1}{1} \begin{pmatrix} 3 & -4 & -2 \\ -1 & 2 & 1 \\ 3 & -5 & -2 \end{pmatrix}$$
$$= \begin{pmatrix} 3 & -4 & -2 \\ -1 & 2 & 1 \\ 3 & -5 & -2 \end{pmatrix}$$

The Inverse and Systems of Equations

In Sec. 8.4 we discussed the matrix representation of systems of equations. The matrix inverse can be a useful concept in determining the solution set for a system of equations. Given a system of equations of the form $\mathbf{AX} = \mathbf{B}$ where $\mathbf{A}$ is a *square* matrix of coefficients, both sides of the matrix equation may be multiplied by $\mathbf{A}^{-1}$, yielding

$$\mathbf{A}^{-1}\mathbf{AX} = \mathbf{A}^{-1}\mathbf{B}$$

Because $\mathbf{A}^{-1}\mathbf{A} = \mathbf{I}$, we have

$$\mathbf{IX} = \mathbf{A}^{-1}\mathbf{B}$$
or
$$\mathbf{X} = \mathbf{A}^{-1}\mathbf{B} \qquad (8.11)$$

That is, the solution vector for the system of equations can be found by multiplying the inverse of the matrix of coefficients $\mathbf{A}$ by the vector of right-side constants $\mathbf{B}$. If $\mathbf{A}^{-1}$ does not exist, there is either no solution or an infinite number of solutions to the system of equations.

Example 8.28

Consider the system of equations

$$3x_1 + 7x_2 = 27$$
$$2x_1 + 5x_2 = 19$$

This system of equations may be written in matrix form as

$$\mathbf{AX} = \mathbf{B}$$
or
$$\begin{pmatrix} 3 & 7 \\ 2 & 5 \end{pmatrix} \begin{pmatrix} x_1 \\ x_2 \end{pmatrix} = \begin{pmatrix} 27 \\ 19 \end{pmatrix}$$

Our first step in solving this system of equations by the inverse method is to determine $\mathbf{A}^{-1}$. Conveniently, $\mathbf{A}$ is the same matrix for which we determined the inverse in Examples 8.24 and 8.26. Therefore, the solution vector $\mathbf{X}$ is calculated as

$$\mathbf{X} = \mathbf{A}^{-1}\mathbf{B}$$

$$= \begin{pmatrix} 5 & -7 \\ -2 & 3 \end{pmatrix} \begin{pmatrix} 27 \\ 19 \end{pmatrix} = \begin{pmatrix} (5)(27) + (-7)(19) \\ (-2)(27) + (3)(19) \end{pmatrix}$$

$$= \begin{pmatrix} 2 \\ 3 \end{pmatrix}$$

The solution to the system of equations is $x_1 = 2$ and $x_2 = 3$.

Example 8.29

Consider the system of equations

$$x_1 + 2x_2 \qquad = 5$$
$$x_1 \qquad - x_3 = -15$$
$$-x_1 + 3x_2 + 2x_3 = 40$$

The matrix of coefficients is

$$\mathbf{A} = \begin{pmatrix} 1 & 2 & 0 \\ 1 & 0 & -1 \\ -1 & 3 & 2 \end{pmatrix}$$

and again the example has been contrived (see Examples 8.25 and 8.27). The solution vector is calculated as

$$\mathbf{X} = \begin{pmatrix} 3 & -4 & -2 \\ -1 & 2 & 1 \\ 3 & -5 & -2 \end{pmatrix} \begin{pmatrix} 5 \\ -15 \\ 40 \end{pmatrix}$$

$$= \begin{pmatrix} 15 + 60 - 80 \\ -5 - 30 + 40 \\ 15 + 75 - 80 \end{pmatrix} = \begin{pmatrix} -5 \\ 5 \\ 10 \end{pmatrix}$$

or $x_1 = -5$, $x_2 = 5$, and $x_3 = 10$.

Follow-up Exercises

Determine the inverse, if it exists, for the following matrices, using the gaussian procedure.

8.59 $\begin{pmatrix} 1 & -1 \\ 2 & -3 \end{pmatrix}$
8.60 $\begin{pmatrix} 2 & 3 \\ 4 & 7 \end{pmatrix}$

8.61 $\begin{pmatrix} 4 & 2 \\ -2 & -1 \end{pmatrix}$
8.62 $\begin{pmatrix} 40 & 8 \\ 30 & 6 \end{pmatrix}$

8.63 $\begin{pmatrix} 1 & 0 \\ 0 & 1 \end{pmatrix}$
8.64 $\begin{pmatrix} -1 & 3 \\ 2 & -4 \end{pmatrix}$

8.65 $\begin{pmatrix} 0 & 3 & 1 \\ 1 & 1 & 0 \\ 2 & 3 & 3 \end{pmatrix}$
8.66 $\begin{pmatrix} 1 & 0 & -1 \\ -1 & 1 & -1 \\ -1 & 0 & 2 \end{pmatrix}$

Determine the inverse of the following matrices using the matrix of co-factors approach.

8.67 $\begin{pmatrix} 3 & 7 \\ 2 & 5 \end{pmatrix}$
8.68 $\begin{pmatrix} 3 & -15 \\ 5 & 25 \end{pmatrix}$

8.69 $\begin{pmatrix} 3 & 5 & 2 \\ 4 & 1 & 0 \\ -9 & -15 & -6 \end{pmatrix}$
8.70 $\begin{pmatrix} -5 & 6 & -7 \\ 10 & -11 & 13 \\ -1 & 1 & -1 \end{pmatrix}$

Using the results of Exercises 8.59 to 8.70, determine the solutions for the following systems of equations.

8.71 $\begin{aligned} x_1 - x_2 &= -1 \\ 2x_1 - 3x_2 &= -5 \end{aligned}$
8.72 $\begin{aligned} 2x_1 + 3x_2 &= 1 \\ 4x_1 + 7x_2 &= 3 \end{aligned}$

8.73 $\begin{aligned} -x_1 + 3x_2 &= 5 \\ 2x_1 - 4x_2 &= 0 \end{aligned}$
8.74 $\begin{aligned} 3x_2 + x_3 &= 1 \\ x_1 + x_2 &= 2 \\ 2x_1 + 3x_2 + 3x_3 &= 7 \end{aligned}$

8.75 $\begin{aligned} x_1 - x_3 &= -10 \\ -x_1 + x_2 - x_3 &= -40 \\ -x_1 + 2x_3 &= 40 \end{aligned}$
8.76 $\begin{aligned} 3x_1 + 7x_2 &= -3 \\ 2x_1 + 5x_2 &= -3 \end{aligned}$

8.77 $\begin{aligned} 3x_1 - 15x_2 &= 25 \\ 5x_1 + 25x_2 &= 40 \end{aligned}$
8.78 $\begin{aligned} 3x_1 + 5x_2 + 2x_3 &= 20 \\ 4x_1 + x_2 &= 40 \\ -9x_1 - 15x_2 - 6x_3 &= 30 \end{aligned}$

8.79 $\begin{aligned} -5x_1 + 6x_2 - 7x_3 &= 25 \\ 10x_1 - 11x_2 + 13x_3 &= -45 \\ -x_1 + x_2 - x_3 &= 4 \end{aligned}$

In this last section of the chapter we will see some selected areas of application of matrix algebra.

Educational Applications

Mathematical tools have been used more and more frequently to assist educational institutions in their operation. Example 8.30 illustrates a very simple application in admissions planning.

Example 8.30　　**College Admissions** The admissions office for a large university plans on admitting 7,500 students next year. The column vector $\mathbf{M}$ indicates the expected breakdown of the new students into the categories of in-state males (ISM), in-state females (ISF), out-of-state males (OSM), and out-of-state females (OSF):

$$\mathbf{M} = \begin{pmatrix} 3{,}000 \\ 2{,}750 \\ 1{,}000 \\ 750 \end{pmatrix} \begin{matrix} \text{ISM} \\ \text{ISF} \\ \text{OSM} \\ \text{OSF} \end{matrix}$$

Admissions personnel expect the students to choose their majors within the colleges of business (B), engineering (E), and arts and sciences (A&S) according to the percentages given in the matrix $\mathbf{P}$:

$$\begin{matrix} & \text{ISM} & \text{ISF} & \text{OSM} & \text{OSF} \\ \mathbf{P} = & \begin{pmatrix} 0.30 & 0.30 & 0.30 & 0.24 \\ 0.20 & 0.10 & 0.30 & 0.06 \\ 0.50 & 0.60 & 0.40 & 0.70 \end{pmatrix} & & & \end{matrix} \begin{matrix} \text{B} \\ \text{E} \\ \text{A\&S} \end{matrix}$$

The expected number of students entering each college can be computed by the multiplication $\mathbf{PM}$, or

$$\mathbf{D} = \mathbf{PM} = \begin{pmatrix} 2{,}205 \\ 1{,}220 \\ 4{,}075 \end{pmatrix}$$

You should verify the logic of the multiplication. Also verify that 2,205, 1,220, and 4,075 students are expected to enter the colleges of business, engineering, and arts and sciences, respectively.

This very simple application can be extended to generate projections of course demands which in turn allow for decisions about the allocation of faculty members. Similarly, the admissions projections allow for estimates for dormitory needs and decisions about auxiliary service needs (dining halls, infirmary, and so forth). If the school has gathered historical data, its different needs may be estimated by using a series of matrix multiplications. Figure 8.1 illustrates one possible sequence of projections.

Planning Models

Matrix algebra can provide a very useful way of planning for the future operations of a firm. One area of interest is production planning. Matrix

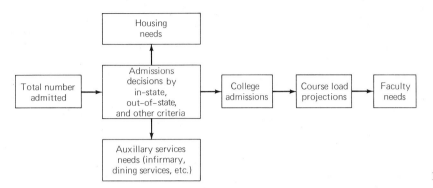

FIGURE 8.1

techniques have been used to calculate and display the parts requirements for a production schedule. The process begins by determining the number of units of finished products that are to be produced. Given that each final product is produced from component parts, a parts matrix may be formed which displays the quantity of each component part required in each final product. Matrix multiplications may be used to determine the quantities of each component part required for the entire production run as well as other information such as the costs of components.

Example 8.31 illustrates a parts requirements planning model for a car rental agency.

Parts Requirements Planning The national office of a car rental corporation is planning its maintenance program for the next year. Executives are interested in determining the company's needs for certain repair parts and expected costs for these categories of parts. The company rents full-size, midsized, and compact cars. The matrix **N** indicates the number of each size car available for renting in four regions of the country.

Example 8.31

$$
\mathbf{N} = \begin{pmatrix} \text{Full} \\ \text{Size} & \text{Midsized} & \text{Compact} \\ 16{,}000 & 40{,}000 & 50{,}000 \\ 15{,}000 & 30{,}000 & 20{,}000 \\ 10{,}000 & 10{,}000 & 15{,}000 \\ 12{,}000 & 40{,}000 & 30{,}000 \end{pmatrix} \begin{matrix} \text{East} \\ \text{Midwest} \\ \text{South} \\ \text{West} \end{matrix}
$$

Four repair parts of interest are points, spark plugs, batteries, and tires. Based upon studies of maintenance records in different parts of the country, analysts have determined the average number of repair parts needed per car during a year. These are summarized in the matrix **R**:

$$
\mathbf{R} = \begin{pmatrix} \text{Full} \\ \text{Size} & \text{Midsized} & \text{Compact} \\ 1.7 & 1.6 & 1.5 \\ 12.0 & 8.0 & 5.0 \\ 0.9 & 0.75 & 0.5 \\ 4.0 & 6.5 & 6.0 \end{pmatrix} \begin{matrix} \text{Points} \\ \text{Plugs} \\ \text{Batteries} \\ \text{Tires} \end{matrix}
$$

Executives want to determine what quantities of each repair part will be needed in each region. These can be calculated by performing the matrix multiplication $\mathbf{NR}^t$. These regional needs are shown in the matrix $\mathbf{P}$. Verify the elements of this matrix.

$$\mathbf{P} = \mathbf{NR}^t = \begin{pmatrix} \overset{\text{Points}}{166,200} & \overset{\text{Plugs}}{762,000} & \overset{\text{Batteries}}{69,400} & \overset{\text{Tires}}{624,000} \\ 103,500 & 520,000 & 46,000 & 375,000 \\ 55,500 & 275,000 & 24,000 & 195,000 \\ 129,400 & 614,000 & 55,800 & 488,000 \end{pmatrix} \begin{matrix} \text{East} \\ \text{Midwest} \\ \text{South} \\ \text{West} \end{matrix}$$

The column vector $\mathbf{C}$ contains the cost per unit for points, plugs, batteries, and tires:

$$\mathbf{C} = \begin{pmatrix} \$1.25 \\ \$0.80 \\ \$30.00 \\ \$35.00 \end{pmatrix}$$

Executives can compute regional costs for the four repair parts by performing the multiplication

$$\mathbf{T} = \mathbf{PC} = \begin{pmatrix} \$24,739,350 \\ \$15,050,375 \\ \$ 7,834,375 \\ \$19,406,950 \end{pmatrix} \begin{matrix} \text{East} \\ \text{Midwest} \\ \text{South} \\ \text{West} \end{matrix}$$

Expected annual costs of the four parts for the company are the sum of the four elements in $\mathbf{T}$, or \$67,031,050.

CHAPTER CHECKLIST

If you have read all sections of this chapter, you should

_____ **Understand what a *matrix* is and how it can be used**

_____ **Be familiar with the different kinds of matrices—*row vector, column vector, square matrix, identity matrix, transpose***

_____ **Understand the mechanics of *matrix addition* and *subtraction*, *scalar multiplication*, the *inner product*, and *matrix multiplication***

_____ **Understand the representation of equations using matrices**

_____ **Understand how to compute the value of a *determinant***

_____ **Understand *cofactors* and their use in computing determinants**

_____ **Understand the nature of the *multiplicative inverse* of a matrix and how it can be determined, using the gaussian procedure, the method of cofactors, or both**

_____ **Understand the use of the inverse matrix in solving systems of equations**

_____ **Be familiar with several applications of matrices and matrix algebra**

KEY TERMS AND CONCEPTS

matrix	inner product
dimensions	matrix multiplication
row vector	determinant
column vector	cofactor
square matrix	matrix of cofactors
identity matrix	minor
primary diagonal	method of cofactor expansion
secondary diagonal	multiplicative inverse matrix
transpose	gaussian procedure
matrix addition and subtraction	adjoint matrix
scalar multiplication	

ADDITIONAL EXERCISES

Exercises 8.80 to 8.83 are related to Sec. 8.2.

In Exercises 8.80 to 8.83, find the transpose of the given matrix.

8.80 $\begin{pmatrix} 1 & 3 & 5 & 7 \\ 2 & 4 & 6 & 8 \\ 9 & 11 & 13 & 15 \\ 10 & 12 & 14 & 16 \end{pmatrix}$
  8.81 $(3 \quad -8 \quad 9 \quad 0 \quad 14)$

8.82 $\begin{pmatrix} 8 \\ 5 \\ -23 \end{pmatrix}$
  8.83 $\begin{pmatrix} 0 & 1 & 0 & 1 \\ 2 & 3 & 4 & 5 \\ 1 & 0 & 0 & 1 \\ 6 & 7 & 8 & 9 \end{pmatrix}$

Exercises 8.84 to 8.96 are related to Sec. 8.3.

In Exercises 8.84 to 8.87, perform the indicated matrix operation.

8.84 $\begin{pmatrix} 6 & 9 & 0 \\ 3 & 5 & 7 \end{pmatrix} - \begin{pmatrix} 6 & 0 & 5 \\ 2 & 8 & 9 \end{pmatrix}$
  8.85 $3 \begin{pmatrix} 8 \\ 24 \\ 13 \end{pmatrix}$

8.86 $\begin{pmatrix} a & b \\ c & d \end{pmatrix} - \begin{pmatrix} x & -y \\ z & w \end{pmatrix} + \begin{pmatrix} h & i \\ j & -k \end{pmatrix}$

8.87 $5 \begin{pmatrix} 0.8 & 0.5 \\ 0.7 & 0.4 \\ 0.3 & 0.2 \end{pmatrix} + 6 \begin{pmatrix} 0.2 & 4 \\ 7 & 0 \\ 3.5 & 8 \end{pmatrix}$

In Exercises 8.88 and 8.89, compute the inner product.

8.88 $(5 \quad 6 \quad 7 \quad 8) \begin{pmatrix} 1 \\ -1 \\ 1 \\ -1 \end{pmatrix}$
  8.89 $(0 \quad 1 \quad 8) \begin{pmatrix} 7 \\ 14 \\ 21 \end{pmatrix}$

In Exercises 8.90 to 8.95, perform the matrix multiplication, if possible.

8.90 $\begin{pmatrix} 7 & 8 \\ 9 & 10 \end{pmatrix}\begin{pmatrix} 1 & 0 \\ 0 & 1 \end{pmatrix}$

8.91 $\begin{pmatrix} 1 & 0 \\ 0 & 1 \end{pmatrix}\begin{pmatrix} 7 & 8 \\ 9 & 10 \end{pmatrix}$

8.92 $(2 \quad 5 \quad 8 \quad 3)\begin{pmatrix} 1 & -1 \\ 4 & 2 \\ 6 & 0 \\ 7 & 5 \end{pmatrix}$

8.93 $\begin{pmatrix} 1 & -1 \\ 4 & 2 \\ 6 & 0 \\ 7 & 5 \end{pmatrix}(2 \quad 5 \quad 8 \quad 3)$

8.94 $\begin{pmatrix} x & y \\ z & o \end{pmatrix}\begin{pmatrix} 5 & -1 & 3 \\ 2 & -4 & 4 \end{pmatrix}$

8.95 $\begin{pmatrix} 0.5 & 1 & 0 \\ 0 & 0.5 & 1 \\ 1 & 0 & 0.5 \end{pmatrix}\begin{pmatrix} 8 & 10 \\ 4 & 9 \\ 6 & 7 \end{pmatrix}$

8.96 Under what conditions are the matrix products **AB** and **BA** both defined?

Exercises 8.97 to 8.100 are related to Sec. 8.4.

In Exercises 8.97 and 8.98, rewrite the system of equations in matrix form.

8.97 $\begin{aligned} 40x_1 + 35x_2 &= 100 \\ 5x_1 - 10x_2 &= 15 \end{aligned}$

8.98 $\begin{aligned} -9x_1 + 20x_2 - x_3 \quad\quad &= -20 \\ 17x_1 \quad\quad + x_3 - 7x_4 &= 15 \\ 52x_2 \quad\quad\quad &= 8 \end{aligned}$

In Exercises 8.99 and 8.100, restate the matrix equations in algebraic form.

8.99 $\begin{pmatrix} 8 & 7 & 6 \\ 5 & 4 & 3 \end{pmatrix}\begin{pmatrix} x_1 \\ x_2 \\ x_3 \end{pmatrix} = \begin{pmatrix} 5 \\ 7 \end{pmatrix}$

8.100 $\begin{pmatrix} 0 & 0 & 1 & 0 \\ 1 & 0 & 0 & 0 \\ 0 & 1 & 0 & 0 \\ 0 & 0 & 0 & 1 \end{pmatrix}\begin{pmatrix} x_1 \\ x_2 \\ x_3 \\ x_4 \end{pmatrix} = \begin{pmatrix} 3 \\ 2 \\ 1 \\ -1 \end{pmatrix}$

Exercises 8.101 to 8.110 are related to Sec. 8.5.

In Exercises 8.101 to 8.104, find the determinant for the given matrix.

8.101 $A = \begin{pmatrix} 7 & 6 \\ 2 & 5 \end{pmatrix}$

8.102 $B = \begin{pmatrix} 0 & 1 \\ 3 & 7 \\ 0 & 1 \end{pmatrix}$

8.103 $G = \begin{pmatrix} 1 & 0 & 5 \\ 0 & 1 & 3 \end{pmatrix}$

8.104 $T = \begin{pmatrix} 3 & 7 & 9 \\ 5 & 6 & -4 \\ -2 & 10 & 7 \end{pmatrix}$

In Exercises 8.105 and 8.106, find the matrix of cofactors.

8.105 $N = \begin{pmatrix} 1 & -1 & 1 \\ -1 & 1 & -1 \\ 1 & -1 & 1 \end{pmatrix}$

8.106 $H = \begin{pmatrix} 3 & 3 & 3 \\ 2 & 2 & 2 \\ 1 & 1 & 1 \end{pmatrix}$

For Exercises 8.107 and 8.108, use the method of cofactor expansion to find the determinant of each matrix given in Exercises 8.105 and 8.106.

8.109 Find the determinant of the matrix

$$\mathbf{C} = \begin{pmatrix} 3 & -1 & 2 & 0 \\ 4 & 6 & 0 & 1 \\ 7 & -1 & 0 & 5 \\ 0 & 1 & 0 & 1 \end{pmatrix}$$

8.110 Find the determinant of the matrix

$$\mathbf{D} = \begin{pmatrix} 1 & 0 & 0 & 0 \\ 0 & 1 & 0 & 0 \\ 0 & 0 & 1 & 0 \\ 0 & 0 & 0 & 1 \end{pmatrix}$$

Exercises 8.111 to 8.122 are related to Sec. 8.6.

In Exercises 8.111 to 8.114, find the inverse, if it exists, for the given matrix.

8.111 $\begin{pmatrix} 0 & 1 \\ 8 & 3 \end{pmatrix}$ **8.112** $\begin{pmatrix} 4 & 8 \\ 7 & 2 \end{pmatrix}$

8.113 $\begin{pmatrix} 1 & 8 & 7 \\ 2 & 3 & 5 \\ 7 & 4 & -1 \end{pmatrix}$ **8.114** $\begin{pmatrix} 4 & -4 & 3 \\ -3 & 2 & -2 \\ 1 & -1 & 0 \end{pmatrix}$

In Exercises 8.115 and 8.116, determine the inverse of the given matrix using the method of cofactors approach.

8.115 $\begin{pmatrix} 8 & 10 \\ 11 & 13 \end{pmatrix}$ **8.116** $\begin{pmatrix} 4 & 2 & 6 \\ 9 & 3 & 7 \\ -1 & 0 & 5 \end{pmatrix}$

In Exercises 8.117 to 8.122, use the results of Exercises 8.111 to 8.116 to determine the solution for each of the following systems of equations.

8.117 $x_2 = 4$
     $8x_1 + 3x_2 = 12$

8.118 $4x_1 + 8x_2 = 12$
     $7x_1 + 2x_2 = 9$

8.119 $x_1 + 8x_2 + 7x_3 = 0$
     $2x_1 + 3x_2 + 5x_3 = 4$
     $7x_1 + 4x_2 - x_3 = 2$

8.120 $2x_2 + x_3 = -2$
     $4x_1 - 4x_2 + 3x_3 = 7$
     $-3x_1 + 2x_2 - 2x_3 = -7$

8.121 $8x_1 + 10x_2 = 4$
     $11x_1 + 13x_2 = 4$

8.122 $x_1 - x_2 = 1$
     $4x_1 + 2x_2 + 6x_3 = 2$
     $9x_1 + 3x_2 + 7x_3 = 20$
     $-x_1 + 5x_3 = -10$

Exercises 8.123 to 8.126 are related to Sec. 8.7.

8.123 The admissions office for a large university plans on admitting 10,000 students next year. The vector **A** provides a breakdown of new students into the categories of in-state (IS) and out-of-state (OS). The matrix **C** indicates the percentages of students expected to choose majors in colleges A, B, C, and D within the university.

$$\text{IS} \quad \text{OS}$$
$$\mathbf{A} = (7{,}500 \quad 2{,}500)$$

$$\begin{array}{cccc} & \text{College} & & \\ A & B & C & D \end{array}$$
$$\mathbf{C} = \begin{pmatrix} 0.30 & 0.20 & 0.40 & 0.10 \\ 0.40 & 0.30 & 0.25 & 0.05 \end{pmatrix} \begin{array}{l} \text{IS} \\ \text{OS} \end{array}$$

Perform a matrix multiplication which will compute the number of new students expected to enter each college next year.

8.124 Refer to Exercise 8.123. The housing office estimates that students will select housing alternatives according to the percentages in **H**:

$$\begin{array}{cccc} & \text{Dorm} & \text{Fraternity or Sorority} & \text{Off-Campus} \end{array}$$
$$\mathbf{H} = \begin{pmatrix} 0.40 & 0.30 & 0.30 \\ 0.60 & 0.20 & 0.20 \end{pmatrix} \begin{array}{l} \text{IS} \\ \text{OS} \end{array}$$

Perform a matrix multiplication which will compute the number of new students expected to choose the different housing options.

8.125 A company manufactures three products, each of which requires certain amounts of raw materials and labor. The matrix **R** summarizes the requirements per unit of each product.

$$\begin{array}{cccc} & \text{Raw Material} & & \\ 1 & 2 & 3 & \text{Labor} \end{array}$$
$$\mathbf{R} = \begin{pmatrix} 2 & 4 & 5 & 5 \\ 3 & 2 & 3 & 8 \\ 1 & 3 & 5 & 4 \end{pmatrix} \begin{array}{l} \text{product } A \\ \text{product } B \\ \text{product } C \end{array}$$

Raw material requirements are stated in pounds per unit and labor requirements in hours per unit. The three raw materials cost $2, $3, and $1.50 per pound, respectively. Labor costs are $5 per hour. Assume 500, 1,000, and 400 units of products A, B, and C are to be produced.

(a) Perform a matrix multiplication which computes total quantities of the four resources required to produce products A, B, and C.

(b) Using your answer from part a, perform a matrix multiplication which calculates the combined total cost of production.

8.126 *Hospital Administration* A local hospital has gathered data regarding people admitted for in-patient services. The vector **P** indicates the percentages of all patients admitted to different hospital units. The vector **S** indicates the average length of patient stay (in days) for each hospital unit.

$$\mathbf{P} = \begin{pmatrix} 0.18 \\ 0.10 \\ 0.24 \\ 0.48 \end{pmatrix} \begin{array}{l} \text{obstetrical} \\ \text{cardiac} \\ \text{pediatric} \\ \text{other} \end{array} \qquad \mathbf{S} = (4 \quad 14 \quad 3 \quad 5)$$

The vector **C** summarizes current daily patient cost for the different hospital units:

$$\mathbf{C} = (\$280 \quad \$400 \quad \$240 \quad \$260)$$

If 200 new patients are admitted, perform a matrix multiplication to compute:

(a) The numbers of patients admitted to each hospital unit

(b) The total number of patient-days expected

(c) Total cost per day for the 200 patients

CHAPTER TEST

1 Find the transpose of $\mathbf{A}$ if

$$\mathbf{A} = \begin{pmatrix} 1 & -3 & 0 & 5 \\ 6 & -2 & 4 & 9 \end{pmatrix}$$

2 Find the inner product

$$(a \quad b \quad c \quad d) \begin{pmatrix} e \\ f \\ g \\ h \end{pmatrix}$$

3 Given the matrices

$$\mathbf{A} = \begin{pmatrix} 2 & -1 \\ 3 & 4 \end{pmatrix} \qquad \mathbf{B} = \begin{pmatrix} 2 & -5 \\ 1 & 0 \\ 7 & 4 \end{pmatrix} \qquad \mathbf{C} = \begin{pmatrix} -1 & 0 & 0 \\ 0 & -1 & 0 \\ 0 & 0 & -1 \end{pmatrix}$$

determine, if possible, (*a*) $\mathbf{AB}$, (*b*) $\mathbf{BA}$, (*c*) $\mathbf{BC}$.

4 Write the following system of equations as a matrix product:

$$\begin{aligned} x_1 \quad\quad\quad - x_4 &= 20 \\ x_2 + x_3 \quad\quad &= 15 \\ x_3 + x_4 &= 18 \\ x_4 &= 9 \end{aligned}$$

5 Find the determinant for the matrix

$$\mathbf{A} = \begin{pmatrix} 0 & 0 & -2 \\ 0 & 5 & 0 \\ -3 & 0 & 0 \end{pmatrix}$$

6 Find $\mathbf{A}^{-1}$ if

$$\mathbf{A} = \begin{pmatrix} 20 & -8 \\ -5 & 2 \end{pmatrix}$$

7 The solution to a system of equations having the form $\mathbf{AX} = \mathbf{B}$ can be found by the matrix multiplication

$$\mathbf{X} = \begin{pmatrix} 5 & -7 \\ -2 & 3 \end{pmatrix} \begin{pmatrix} 15 \\ 11 \end{pmatrix}$$

What was the original system of equations?

MATHEMATICS OF FINANCE

9

CHAPTER OBJECTIVES After reading this chapter, you should have an understanding of the notion of the time value of money; you should understand the concepts of *simple interest* and *compound interest*; you should be familiar with the mathematics of interest computations for two different cash flow structures: *single payments,* or deposits, and *annuities*; you should understand the meaning of an *effective annual interest rate* and its computation under certain circumstances; you should be familiar with mortgage computations.

This chapter is concerned with interest rates and their effects on the value of money. Interest rates have widespread influence over decisions made by businesses and by us in our personal lives. Corporations pay millions of dollars in interest each year for the use of money they have borrowed. We earn money on sums we have deposited in savings banks and credit unions. We also pay for the use of money which we have borrowed for school loans, mortgages, or credit card purchases.

The interest concept also has applications that are not related to money. Population growth, for example, may be characterized by an "interest rate," or rate of growth.

We will first examine the nature of interest and its computation. Then we will discuss several different investment situations and computations related to each. Finally, a special section will discuss computations related to mortgages.

Simple Interest

Interest is a fee which is paid for having the use of money. We pay interest on mortgages for having the use of the bank's money. We use the bank's money to pay a contractor or person from whom we are purchasing a home. Similarly, the bank pays us interest on money kept in savings accounts because it has temporary access to our money. The amount of money that is lent or invested is called the *principal*. Interest is usually paid in proportion to the principal and the period of time over which the money is used. The *interest rate* specifies the rate at which interest accumulates. The interest rate is typically stated as a *percentage of the principal* per period of time, for example, 8 percent per year or 1.5 percent per month.

Interest that is paid solely on the amount of the principal is called *simple interest*. Simple interest is usually associated with loans or investments which are short-term in nature. The computation of simple interest is based on the following formula:

Simple interest = principal × interest rate per time period

× number of time periods

or $$I = Pin \qquad (9.1)$$

where
I = simple interest (in dollars)
P = principal (in dollars)
i = interest rate per time period
n = number of time periods of loan

It is essential that the time periods for i and n be consistent with each other. That is, if i is expressed as a percentage per year, n should be expressed in number of years. Similarly, if i is expressed as a percentage per month, n must be stated in number of months.

Example 9.1   A credit union has issued a 3-year loan of $5,000. Simple interest is charged at a rate of 10 percent per year. The principal plus interest is to be repaid at the end of the third year. Compute the interest for the 3-year period. What amount will be repaid at the end of the third year?

Solution   Using the variable definitions from Eq. (9.1), we get P = $5,000, i = 0.10 per year, and n = 3 years. Therefore

$$I = (\$5,000)(0.10)(3)$$
$$= \$1,500$$

The amount to be repaid is the principal *plus* the accumulated interest, or

$$A = P + I$$
$$= \$5,000 + \$1,500$$
$$= \$6,500$$

A person "lends" $10,000 to a corporation by purchasing a bond from the corporation. Simple interest is computed quarterly at a rate of 2 percent per quarter, and a check for the interest is mailed each quarter to all bondholders. The bonds expire at the end of 5 years, and the final check includes the original principal plus interest earned during the last quarter. Compute the interest earned each quarter and the total interest which will be earned over the 5-year life of the bonds.

Example 9.2

In this problem $P = \$10,000$, $i = 0.02$ per quarter, and the period of the loan is 5 years. Since the time period for i is a quarter (or a year), we must consider 5 years as 20 quarters. And since we are interested in the amount of interest earned over one quarter, we must let $n = 1$. Therefore, quarterly interest equals

$$I = (\$10,000)(0.02)(1)$$
$$= \$200$$

To compute total interest over the 5-year period, we merely multiply the per-quarter interest of $200 by the number of quarters, 20, to obtain

$$\text{Total interest} = \$200 \times 20 = \$4,000$$

Compound Interest

A common procedure for computing interest is by *compounding interest*. Under this procedure the interest for each period is added to the principal for purposes of computing interest for the next period. The amount of interest computed using this procedure is called *compound interest*.

A simple example will illustrate this procedure. Assume that we have deposited $8,000 in a credit union which pays interest of 6 percent per year *compounded* quarterly. Assume that we want to determine the amount of money we will have on deposit at the end of 1 year if all interest is left in the savings account. At the end of the first quarter, interest is computed as

$$I_1 = (\$8,000)(0.06)(0.25)$$
$$= \$120$$

Note that n was defined as 0.25 *year*. With the interest left in the account, the principal on which interest is earned in the second quarter is the original principal plus $120 interest earned during the first quarter, or

$$P_2 = P_1 + I_1 = \$8,120$$

Interest earned during the second quarter is

$$I_2 = (\$8,120)(0.06)(0.25)$$
$$= \$121.80$$

Table 9.1 summarizes the computations for the four quarters. Note that for each quarter the accumulated principal plus interest is referred to as the *compound amount*.

Quarter	(P) Principal	(I) Interest	(S = P + I) Compound Amount	
1	$8,000.00	$120.00	$8,000 + $120	= $8,120
2	8,120.00	121.80	8,120 + 121.80	= 8,241.80
3	8,241.80	123.627	8,241.80 + 123.627	= 8,365.427
4	8,365.427	125.4814	8,365.427 + 125.4814 =	8,490.9084

Table 9.1

Two conclusions should soon become apparent. For a stated interest rate i:

1 Compound interest is greater than simple interest. This is because interest which has been earned subsequently earns interest itself.

2 The more frequently interest is compounded, the greater the interest earned. That is, a bank deposit having interest compounded monthly will earn more interest than an equal deposit having interest compounded quarterly.

In the last example, simple interest for the year would have been equal to

$$I = (\$8,000)(0.06)(1)$$
$$= \$480$$

The difference between the simple interest and the compound interest is $490.9084 − $480.00 = $10.9084. Compound interest exceeds simple interest in this example by approximately $11 over the 1-year period.

Follow-up Exercises

9.1 A company has issued a 5-year loan of $15,000 to a new vice president to finance a home improvement project. The terms of the loan are that it is to be paid back in full at the end of 5 years with simple interest computed at the rate of 6 percent per year. Determine the interest which must be paid on the loan for the 5-year period.

9.2 A student has received a $9,000 loan from a wealthy aunt in order to finance his 4-year college program. The terms are that the student repay his aunt in full at the end of 10 years with simple interest computed at a rate of 1 percent per year. Determine the interest which must be paid on the 10-year loan.

9.3 An elderly woman has purchased $60,000 worth of corporate bonds. The bonds expire in 10 years, and simple interest is computed semiannually at a rate of 5 percent per 6-month period. Interest checks are mailed to bondholders every 6 months. Determine the interest the woman can expect to earn every 6 months. How much interest can she expect over the 10-year period?

9.4 A major airline is planning to purchase new airplanes. It wants to borrow $50 million by issuing bonds. The bonds are for a 5-year period with simple interest computed quarterly at a rate of 1.75 percent per quarter. Interest is to be paid each quarter to bondholders. How much will the airline have to pay in quarterly interest? How much interest will they pay over the 5-year period?

9.5 There is $5,000 in a savings account which earns interest of 8 percent per year, compounded semiannually. Complete the following table with regard to semiannual compounding. What is total interest over the 2-year period?

Semiannual Period	(P) Principal	(I) Interest	(S = P + I) Compound Amount
1	$5,000	$200	$5,200.00
2			
3			
4			

9.6 The sum of $300,000 has been placed in an investment which earns interest at the rate of 12 percent per year, compounded quarterly. Complete the following table with regard to quarterly compounding. What is total interest for the year?

Quarter	(P) Principal	(I) Interest	(S = P + I) Compound Amount
1	$300,000	$9,000	$309,000
2			
3			
4			

9.7 Refer to Exercise 9.5.
(a) Determine the compound amount after 2 years if interest is compounded quarterly instead of semiannually.
(b) Under which compounding plan, semiannually or quarterly, is total interest higher? By how much?

9.8 Refer to Exercise 9.6.
(a) Determine the compound amount after 1 year if interest is compounded semiannually instead of quarterly.
(b) Under which compounding plan is total interest higher? By how much?

SINGLE-PAYMENT COMPUTATIONS 9.2

This section discusses the relationship between a sum of money at the present time and its value at some point in the future. The assumption in this and the remaining sections is that any interest is computed on a compounding basis.

Compound Amount

Assume that a sum of money is invested and that it earns interest which is compounded. One question related to such an investment is, What will the value of the investment be at some point in the future? The value of the investment is the original investment (principal) plus any earned interest. In our example illustrating calculations of compound interest in Sec. 9.1, we called this the *compound amount*. Given any principal invested at the beginning of a time period, the compound amount at the end of the period was calculated as

$$S = P + iP \tag{9.2}$$

Let's redefine our variables and then develop a generalized formula which can be used to calculate the compound amount. Let

P = principal (dollars)
i = interest rate per compounding period
n = number of compounding periods (number of periods in which the principal has earned interest)
S = compound amount

A *period*, for purposes of these definitions, may be any unit of time. If interest is compounded annually, a year is the appropriate period. If it is compounded monthly, a month is the appropriate period. It is again important to emphasize that the definition of a period must be the same for both i and n.

Suppose there has been an investment of P dollars which will earn interest at the rate of i percent per compounding period. From Eq. (9.2) we determined that the compound amount after one period is

$$S = P + iP$$

Factoring P from the terms on the right side of the equation, we can restate the compound amount as

$$S = P(1 + i) \tag{9.3}$$

If we are interested in determining the compound amount after two periods, it may be computed using the equation

$$\begin{pmatrix} \text{Compound amount} \\ \text{after two periods} \end{pmatrix} = \begin{pmatrix} \text{compound amount} \\ \text{after one period} \end{pmatrix}$$
$$+ \begin{pmatrix} \text{interest earned} \\ \text{during the second period} \end{pmatrix}$$

or
$$S = P(1 + i) + i[P(1 + i)]$$

Factoring P and $1 + i$ from both terms on the right side of the equation gives us

$$S = P(1 + i)(1 + i)$$
or
$$S = P(1 + i)^2 \tag{9.4}$$

Similarly, if we wish to determine the compound amount after three periods, it may be computed using the equation

$$\begin{pmatrix} \text{Compound amount} \\ \text{after three periods} \end{pmatrix} = \begin{pmatrix} \text{compound amount} \\ \text{after two periods} \end{pmatrix}$$
$$+ \begin{pmatrix} \text{interest earned} \\ \text{during the third period} \end{pmatrix}$$

or $$S = P(1 + i)^2 + i[P(1 + i)^2]$$

Factoring P and $(1 + i)^2$ from the terms on the right side of the equation, we have

$$S = P(1 + i)^2(1 + i)$$

or $$S = P(1 + i)^3 \qquad (9.5)$$

The compound-amount formulas developed so far are summarized below:

Compound amount after one period $= P(1 + i)$.
Compound amount after two periods $= P(1 + i)^2$.
Compound amount after three periods $= P(1 + i)^3$.

And the pattern continues so that the following definition is possible.

DEFINITION
If an amount of money P earns interest compounded at a rate of i percent per period, it will grow after n periods to the compound amount S computed by the formula

$$S = P(1 + i)^n \qquad (9.6)$$

Equation (9.6) is often referred to as the *compound-amount formula*. This relationship may be portrayed graphically as in Fig. 9.1.

Suppose that we have invested \$1,000 in a savings bank which declares interest at a rate of 5 percent per year compounded annually. If all interest is left in the account, what will the account balance be after 10 years?

Example 9.3

In all these examples we will assume that the investment is made at the very beginning of a compounding period. By using Eq. (9.6), the compound amount after 10 years (periods) is

Solution

$$S = \$1,000(1 + 0.05)^{10}$$

The question now becomes, How do we evaluate $(1 + 0.05)^{10}$? Among possible alternatives are:

1 Sit close to a pencil sharpener, load up on paper, and use a brute-force hand calculation approach.

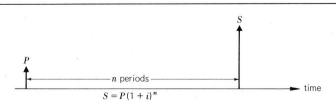

$$S = P(1 + i)^n$$

FIGURE 9.1

2 Use an electronic calculator.

3 Rewrite the equation by finding the logarithm of both sides and solving for the log of S.

The best alternative, however, has been saved for last. Since these kinds of computations are fairly common, especially for banking and financial institutions, sets of tables are available which provide values of $(1 + i)^n$ for given values of i and n. For your convenience Table 9.2 at the end of the chapter provides values of $(1 + i)^n$ values. The expression $(1 + i)^n$ is called the *compound-amount factor*.

For our problem we simply find the column associated with an interest rate per period of 5 percent and the row corresponding to 10 compounding periods. Figure 9.2 is an excerpt from these tables. The value of $(1 + 0.05)^{10}$ is 1.62889. Therefore

$$S = (\$1{,}000)(1.62889)$$
$$= \$1{,}628.89$$

n	i .05
1	1.05000
2	1.10250
3	1.15762
4	1.21550
5	1.27628
6	1.34009
7	1.40710
8	1.47745
9	1.55132
10	1.62889
11	1.71033
12	1.79585
13	1.88564
14	1.97993

FIGURE 9.2 The $1,000 investment will grow to $1,628.89, meaning that interest of $628.89 will be earned.

Example 9.4 A long-term investment of $250,000 has been made by a medium-sized company. The interest rate is 12 percent per year, and interest is compounded quarterly. If all interest is reinvested at the same *rate* of interest, what will the value of the investment be after 8 years?

NOTE
In almost all cases, the interest rate in a problem will be stated as an annual interest rate or as the interest rate per compounding period. When the former case occurs, the interest rate per compounding period is computed by the formula

$$i = \frac{\text{interest rate per year}}{\text{number of compounding periods per year}}$$

Solution In the compound-amount formula, Eq. (9.6), i is defined as the interest rate per compounding period and n as the number of compounding periods. In this problem compounding occurs every quarter of a year. The interest rate per quarter equals the annual interest rate divided by the number of compounding periods per year, or

$$i = \frac{0.12}{4} = 0.03$$

The number of compounding periods over the 8-year period is $8 \times 4 = 32$. Therefore

$$S = \$250{,}000(1 + 0.03)^{32}$$

From Table 9.2, $(1 + 0.03)^{32} = 2.57508$, and

$$S = \$250,000(2.57508)$$
$$= \$643,770$$

Over the 8-year period interest of $\$643,770 - \$250,000$, or $\$393,770$, is expected to be earned.

Present Value

The compound-amount formula

$$S = P(1 + i)^n$$

is an equation involving four variables—S, P, i, and n. And given the values of any three of these four, the equation can be solved for the remaining variable. To illustrate this point, suppose that a person can invest money in a savings account at the rate of 6 percent per year compounded quarterly. Assume that the person wishes to deposit a lump sum at the beginning of the year and have that sum grow to $\$20,000$ over the next 10 years. The question becomes, How much money should be deposited at the beginning of the year? Since we are given values for S, i, and n, we need to solve the equation for P. Doing this, we have

$$P = \frac{S}{(1 + i)^n} \qquad (9.7)$$

For the situation mentioned, $S = \$20,000$, $n = 40$ (10×4 compounding periods over the 10 years), and $i = 0.06/4 = 0.015$. The problem is illustrated in Fig. 9.3.

Refer to Table 9.2. We have $(1 + 0.015)^{40} = 1.81401$ and

$$P = \frac{\$20,000}{1.81401}$$
$$= \$11,025.297$$

In order to accumulate $\$20,000$ after 10 years, $\$11,025.30$ will have to be deposited.

Some kind soul, having used Eq. (9.7) without the benefit of an electronic calculator, concluded that multiplication by large decimal numbers is easier than division by such numbers. When it was recognized that Eq. (9.7) can be rewritten in the product form of Eq. (9.7a):

$$P = \left[\frac{1}{(1 + i)^n}\right] S \qquad (9.7a)$$

tables were constructed for values of $1/(1 + i)^n$, or $(1 + i)^{-n}$. The factor in brackets is called the *present-value factor*. Table 9.3 (at the end of the

$S = \$20,000$

FIGURE 9.3

$P = ?$

$i = 0.015$
$n = 40$

time

chapter) presents these values. The values in these tables are simply the reciprocal values for those in Table 9.2.

To solve the same problem using Table 9.3, the appropriate value is found for $i = 0.015$ and $n = 40$. Thus

$$P = (0.55126)(\$20,000)$$
$$= \$11,025.20$$

Note that this answer is not *exactly* the same as computed with Table 9.2—they are different by $0.10. This is due to rounding differences for the values in the two tables.

If you are wondering which table to use for these types of problems, you may use *either* one. In the following examples, Table 9.3 will be used.

Example 9.5

A young man has recently received an inheritance of $200,000. He wants to take a portion of his inheritance and invest it for his later years. His goal is to accumulate $300,000 in 15 years. How much of the inheritance should be invested if the money will earn 8 percent per year compounded semiannually? How much interest will be earned over the 15 years?

Solution

For this problem $S = \$300,000$, $n = 30$, and $i = 0.08/2 = 0.04$. Using Eq. (9.7a) and the appropriate value from Table 9.3, we get

$$P = (0.30831)(\$300,000)$$
$$= \$92,493$$

Over the 15-year period, interest of $300,000 − $92,493, or $207,507, will be earned.

In these applications P can be considered to be the *present value* of S. That is, P and S can be considered as *equivalent* if you consider the interest which can be earned on P during n compounding periods. In Example 9.5, $92,493 at the time of the inheritance is considered to be the present value of $300,000 at 15 years hence. It is considered the present value because if the $92,493 is invested at that point and if it earns 8 percent per year compounded semiannually, it will grow to a value of $300,000 in 15 years.

The present-value concept implies that a dollar in hand today is not equivalent to a dollar in hand at some point in the future. We can understand this in an *investment sense* from the preceding discussions. As consumers, we can also appreciate this idea by observing the effects of inflation on prices over time. Businesses often have to evaluate proposed projects which will generate cash flows in different periods. Today $20,000 of revenue is not equivalent to $20,000 in revenue 10 years from now. Thus, businesses very often use the present-value concept to translate all cash flows associated with a project into equivalent dollars at one common point in time.

Other Applications of the Compound-Amount Formula

The following examples illustrate other applications of the compound-amount formula. They illustrate problems in which the parameters i and n are unknown.

When a sum of money is invested, there may be a desire to know how long it will take for the principal to grow by a given percentage. Suppose we want to know how long it will take for an investment P to double itself, given that it receives compound interest of i percent per compounding period. If an investment doubles, the ratio of the compound amount S to the principal P is 2, or

Example 9.6

$$\frac{S}{P} = 2$$

Given the compound-amount formula

$$S = P(1 + i)^n$$

if both sides are divided by P, we get

$$\frac{S}{P} = (1 + i)^n$$

The ratio of S/P equals the compound-amount factor. An investment will double, then, when

$$(1 + i)^n = 2$$

Given the interest rate per compounding period for the investment, the number of compounding periods required would be found by selecting the appropriate column of Table 9.2 and determining the value of n for which $(1 + i)^n = 2$.

A lump sum of money is invested at a rate of 10 percent per year compounded quarterly. How long will it take the investment to double? To triple? To *increase by* 50 percent?

Example 9.7

For this investment the interest rate per compounding period is $0.10/4 = 0.025$. Referring to the column in Table 9.2 which corresponds to $i = 2.5$ percent, we read down, looking for a compound-amount factor equal to 2. There is no value of n for which $(1 + 0.025)^n$ equals exactly 2. However, for $n = 28$ the compound-amount factor equals 1.99649, and for $n = 29$ the compound-amount factor equals 2.04640. This suggests that after 28 quarters (or 7 years) the sum will almost have doubled in value. After 29 quarters ($7\frac{1}{4}$ years) the initial sum will have grown to slightly more than double its original value.

Solution

The sum will triple when $S/P = 3$ or when $(1 + .025)^n = 3$. Examining the same column in Table 9.2, we find that the investment will be slightly less than triple in value after 11 years [for $n = 44$, $(1 +$

$0.025)^{44} = 2.96380]$ and slightly more than triple after 11.25 years [for $n = 45$, $(1 + 0.025)^{45} = 3.03790]$.

For an investment to *increase by* 50 percent

$$S = P + 0.5P$$

or

$$S = 1.5P$$

and

$$\frac{S}{P} = 1.5$$

Refer again to Table 9.2. An investment will increase by slightly less than 50 percent after 4 years $[(1 + 0.025)^{16} = 1.48450]$ and by slightly more than 50 percent after $4\frac{1}{4}$ years $[(1 + 0.025)^{17} = 1.52161]$.

Example 9.8

College Enrollments The board of regents of a Southern state is planning the future college-level needs for the state. They have observed that the number of students attending state-operated schools—junior colleges, 4-year schools, and the state university—has been increasing at the rate of 7 percent per year. There are currently 80,000 students enrolled in the various schools. Assuming continued growth at the same rate, how long will it take for enrollments to reach 200,000 students?

Solution

Defining current enrollments as $P = 80,000$ and future enrollments as $S = 200,000$, we have

$$\frac{S}{P} = \frac{200,000}{80,000}$$

$$= 2.5$$

Therefore, from Table 9.2 with $i = 7$ percent,

at $n = 13$, $\qquad (1 + 0.07)^{13} = 2.40984$
and at $n = 14$, $\qquad (1 + 0.07)^{14} = 2.57853$

Enrollments will have increased beyond the 200,000 level after 14 years.

Example 9.9

A person wishes to invest $10,000 and wants the investment to grow to $20,000 over the next 10 years. At what annual interest rate would the $10,000 have to be invested for this growth to occur, assuming annual compounding?

Solution

In this problem, S, P, and n are specified, and the unknown is the interest rate i. Substituting the known parameters into the compound amount formula gives

$$20,000 = 10,000(1 + i)^{10}$$

or,

$$\frac{20,000}{10,000} = (1 + i)^{10}$$

$$2 = (1 + i)^{10}$$

To determine the interest rate, return to Table 9.2 and focus upon the row of values associated with $n = 10$. Read across the row until a value of 2 is identified in the table. There is no compound-amount factor which equals 2 exactly, however, when

$i = 7$ percent, $\qquad (1 + 0.07)^{10} = 1.96715$
and when $i = 8$ percent, $\quad (1 + 0.08)^{10} = 2.15892$

The original investment will grow to $20,000 over the 10 years if it is invested at an interest rate somewhere between 7 and 8 percent. A process called *interpolation* can be used to approximate the exact interest rate required. We will not devote time to this topic in this text.

Effective Interest Rates

Interest rates are typically stated as annual percentages. The stated annual rate is usually referred to as the *nominal rate*. We have seen that when interest is compounded semiannually, quarterly, and monthly, the interest earned during a year is greater than if compounded annually. When compounding is done more frequently than annually, an *effective annual interest rate* can be determined. This is the interest rate compounded annually which is equivalent to a nominal rate compounded more frequently than annually. The two rates would be considered equivalent if both result in the same compound amount.

Let r equal the effective annual interest rate, i the nominal annual interest rate, and m the number of compounding periods per year. The equivalence between the two rates suggests that if a principal P is invested for n years, the two compound amounts would be the same, or

$$P(1 + r)^n = P \left(1 + \frac{i}{m}\right)^{nm}$$

Dividing both sides of the equation by P results in

$$(1 + r)^n = \left(1 + \frac{i}{m}\right)^{nm}$$

Taking the nth root of both sides results in

$$1 + r = \left(1 + \frac{i}{m}\right)^{m}$$

and, by rearranging, the effective annual interest rate can be computed as

$$r = \left(1 + \frac{i}{m}\right)^{m} - 1 \qquad (9.8)$$

In Example 9.4 the investment was made with a nominal interest rate of 12 percent per year compounded quarterly. For this investment $i = 0.12$ and $m = 4$. The effective annual interest rate is

$$r = \left(1 + \frac{0.12}{4}\right)^{4} - 1$$

$$= (1 + 0.03)^4 - 1$$

From Table 9.2 we can determine that $(1 + 0.03)^4 = 1.12550$. Thus,

$$r = 1.12550 - 1$$
$$= 0.12550$$

The effective annual rate is 12.550 percent.

Follow-up Exercises

9.9 A sum of $500 is invested in a savings account which pays interest at a rate of 5 percent per year compounded annually. If the amount is kept on deposit for 8 years, what will the compound amount equal? How much interest will be earned during the 8 years?

9.10 A sum of $1,000 is invested in a savings account which pays interest at a rate of 5 percent per year compounded annually. If the amount is kept on deposit for 12 years, what will the compound amount equal? How much interest will be earned during the 12 years?

9.11 A company invests $750,000 in a mutual fund which is expected to yield interest at a rate of 10 percent per year compounded quarterly. If the interest rate projections are valid, to what amount should the $750,000 grow over the next 5 years? How much interest will be earned during this period?

9.12 A university endowment fund has invested $2 million in United States government certificates of deposit. Interest of 7 percent per year, compounded semiannually, will be earned for 10 years. To what amount will the investment grow during this period? How much interest will be earned?

9.13 The compound-amount factor $(1 + i)^n$ is the amount to which $1 would grow after n periods if it earns compound interest of i percent per period. Determine the compound amount and the interest earned if $1 is invested for 5 years at 12 percent per year (*a*) compounded semiannually, (*b*) compounded quarterly, and (*c*) compounded monthly.

9.14 Compute the compound amount and interest if $1 million is invested under the different conditions mentioned in Exercise 9.13.

9.15 The number of students at a local university is currently 36,000. Enrollments have been growing at a rate of 5 percent per year. If enrollments continue at the same rate, what is the student population expected to be 10 years from now?

9.16 A sales representative for the college division of a large publisher had sales of 25,000 books this past year. Her sales have been increasing at the rate of 8 percent per year. If her sales continue to grow at this rate, how many books should she expect to sell 5 years from now?

9.17 Consumer prices have been increasing at an average rate of 6 percent per year compounded quarterly. The base price on a particular model Chevrolet is $6,500. If prices on this model increase at the same rate as other consumer prices, what will the expected base price of this same model be 4 years from now?

9.18 If consumer prices are increasing at the rate of 9 percent per year compounded semiannually, an item which costs $2.25 today will cost what amount in 10 years?

9.19 If a savings account awards interest of 6 percent per year compounded quarterly, what amount must be deposited today in order to accumulate $10,000 after 7 years? How much interest will be earned during these 7 years?

9.20 If a credit union awards interest of 7 percent per year compounded semiannually, what amount must be deposited today in order to accumulate $25,000 after 10 years? How much interest will be earned during these 10 years?

9.21 What sum must be deposited today at 8 percent per year compounded quarterly if the goal is to have a compound amount of $100,000 five years from today? How much interest will be earned during this period?

9.22 What sum must be deposited today at 7 percent per year compounded annually if the goal is to have a compound amount of $50,000 at 30 years from today? How much interest will be earned during this period?

9.23 A sum of $10,000 earns interest at a rate of 8 percent per year compounded semiannually. How long will it take for the investment to grow to $24,000?

9.24 A sum of $1,500 earns interest at a rate of 5 percent per year compounded annually. How long will it take for the investment to grow to $5,000?

9.25 The nominal interest rate on an investment is 8 percent per year. Determine the effective annual interest rate if (*a*) interest is compounded semiannually, (*b*) interest is compounded quarterly.

9.26 The nominal interest rate on an investment is 10 percent per year. Determine the effective annual interest rate if (*a*) interest is compounded semiannually, (*b*) interest is compounded quarterly.

9.27 If $300,000 is to grow to $500,000 over a 10-year period, at what annual rate of interest must it be invested, given that interest is compounded semiannually?

9.28 If $2,500 is to grow to $4,000 over a 10-year period, at what annual rate of interest must it be invested, given that interest is compounded annually?

ANNUITIES AND THEIR FUTURE VALUE

9.3

An *annuity* is a series of periodic payments. Examples of annuities include regular deposits to a savings account, monthly car, mortgage, or insurance payments, and periodic payments to a person from a retirement fund. Although an annuity may vary in dollar amount, *we will assume that an annuity involves a series of equal payments. We will also assume that the payments are all made at the end of a compounding period.* One may certainly argue that the end of one period coincides with the beginning of the next period. The important point is that the payment does not qualify for interest in the previous period but will earn full interest during the next period. Figure 9.4 illustrates a series of payments R, each of which equals $1,000. These might represent year-end

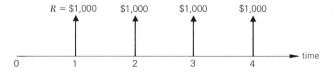

FIGURE 9.4

deposits in a savings account or quarterly tax payments by a self-employed person to the IRS.

The Sum of an Annuity

Just as we had an interest in determining the future value of a lump-sum investment in Sec. 9.2, there is often some benefit in determining the future value or sum of an annuity. Example 9.10 illustrates a problem of this type.

Example 9.10

A person plans to deposit $1,000 in a savings account at the end of this year and an equal sum at the end of each following year. If interest is expected to be earned at the rate of 6 percent per year compounded annually, to what sum will the investment grow at the time of the fourth deposit?

Solution

Figure 9.5 illustrates the annuity and the timing of the deposits. Let S_n equal the sum to which the deposits will have grown at the time of the nth deposit. We can determine the value of S_n by applying the compound-amount formula to *each* deposit, determining its value at the time of the nth deposit. These compound amounts may be summed for the four deposits to determine S_4. Figure 9.6 summarizes these calculations.

Note that the first deposit earns interest for 3 years while the fourth deposit earns no interest. Of the $4,374.71, the interest which has been earned on the first three deposits is $374.61.

The procedure used to determine S in Example 9.10 is manageable but impractical when the number of payments becomes large. Let's see if we can develop a simpler approach to determine S_n. Note in Example 9.10 that S_4 was determined by the sum

$$S_4 = 1{,}000 + 1{,}000(1 + 0.06) + 1{,}000(1 + 0.06)^2 + 1{,}000(1 + 0.06)^3 \qquad (9.9)$$

Let

R = amount of an annuity
i = interest rate per period
n = number of annuity payments (also the number of compounding periods)
S_n = sum (future value) of the annuity after n periods

FIGURE 9.5

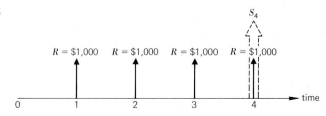

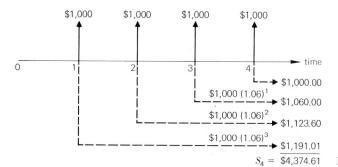

$S_4 = $4,374.61$ **FIGURE 9.6**

If we wish to determine the sum S_n that a series of deposits R (made at the end of each period) will grow to after n periods, first examine Eq. (9.9) for the four-period case. The comparable expression for the n-period case is

$$S_n = R + R(1 + i) + R(1 + i)^2 + \cdots + R(1 + i)^{n-1}$$

Factoring R from the terms on the right side gives

$$S_n = R[1 + (1 + i) + (1 + i)^2 + \cdots + (1 + i)^{n-1}] \qquad (9.10)$$

Multiplying both sides of the equation by $(1 + i)$ yields

$$(1 + i)S_n = (1 + i)R[1 + (1 + i) + (1 + i)^2 + \cdots + (1 + i)^{n-1}]$$

which simplifies to

$$S_n + iS_n = R[(1 + i) + (1 + i)^2 + (1 + i)^3 + \cdots + (1 + i)^n] \qquad (9.11)$$

Subtracting Eq. (9.10) from (9.11) results in

$$iS_n = R(1 + i)^n - R$$

or

$$iS_n = R[(1 + i)^n - 1]$$

Solving for S_n, we get

$$\boldsymbol{S_n = R\left[\frac{(1 + i)^n - 1}{i}\right]} \qquad \textbf{(9.12)}$$

The expression in brackets is called the *series compound-amount factor*. As with the compound-amount factor, tables have been constructed which contain values of this factor for different values of i and n. Table 9.4 (at the end of the chapter) contains values for this factor.

Re-solve Example 9.10 using Eq. (9.12).   **Example 9.11**

Since $i = 0.06$ and $n = 4$, the appropriate entry in Table 9.4 is 4.37461.   **Solution**
Substituting this value and $R = \$1,000$ into Eq. (9.12) yields

$$S_4 = \$1,000(4.37461)$$
$$= \$4374.61$$

which is the same answer as before.

NOTE

An assumption in this section is that interest is computed at the time of each payment. Annual payments earn interest compounded annually, quarterly payments earn interest compounded quarterly, and so forth. Differences between the timing of payments and interest computation (e.g., annual deposits to an account which earns interest compounded quarterly) can be handled by means other than those discussed in this chapter.

Example 9.12

A 12-year-old wants to begin saving for college. She plans to deposit $50 in a savings account at the end of each quarter for the next 6 years. Interest is earned at a rate of 6 percent per year compounded quarterly. What should her account balance be 6 years from now? How much interest will she earn?

Solution

In this problem $R = \$50$, $i = 0.06/4 = 0.015$, and $n = $ (6 years)(4 quarters per year) $= 24$ compounding periods. The appropriate entry in Table 9.4 is 28.63352. Substituting into Eq. (9.12), we have

$$S_{24} = \$50(28.63352)$$
$$= \$1,431.676$$

Over the 6-year period she will make 24 deposits of $50 for a total of $1,200. Interest for the period will be $1,431.676 - \$1,200.00 = \$231.676$.

Determining the Size of an Annuity

As with the compound-amount formula, Eq. (9.12) can be solved for any of the four parameters, given values for the other three. For example, we might have a goal of accumulating a particular sum of money by some future point in time. If the rate of interest which can be earned is known, the question becomes, What amount should be deposited each period in order to reach the goal?

To solve such a problem, Eq. (9.12) can be solved for R, or

$$R = \frac{S_n}{[(1 + i)^n - 1]/i}$$

This can be rewritten as

$$R = S_n \left[\frac{i}{(1 + i)^n - 1} \right] \qquad \textbf{(9.13)}$$

where the expression in brackets is the reciprocal of the series compound amount factor. This factor is often called the *sinking fund factor*. This is because the series of deposits used to accumulate some future sum of money is often called a *sinking fund*. Values for the sinking fund factor are found in Table 9.5 (at the end of the chapter).

A corporation wants to establish a sinking fund beginning at the end of this year. Annual deposits will be made at the end of this year and for the following 9 years. If deposits earn interest at the rate of 8 percent per year compounded annually, how much money must be deposited each year in order to have $12 million at the time of the tenth deposit? How much interest will be earned? **Example 9.13**

Figure 9.7 indicates the situation for this problem. In this problem S_{10} = $12 million, i = 0.08, and n = 10. The appropriate sinking fund factor in Table 9.5 is 0.06902. Substituting into Eq. (9.13) gives **Solution**

$$R = \$12,000,000(0.06902)$$
$$= \$828,240$$

Since 10 deposits of $828,240 will be made during this period, total deposits will equal $8,282,400. Because these deposits plus accumulated interest will equal $12 million, interest of $12,000,000 − $8,282,400 = $3,717,600 will be earned.

Assume in the last example that the corporation is going to make quarterly deposits and that interest is earned at the rate of 8 percent per year compounded quarterly. How much money should be deposited each quarter? How much less will the company have to deposit over the 10-year period as compared with annual deposits and annual compounding? **Example 9.14**

For this problem S_{40} = $12 million, i = 0.08/4 = 0.02, and n = 40. The appropriate sinking fund factor in Table 9.5 is 0.01655. Substituting into Eq. (9.13) yields **Solution**

$$R = \$12,000,000(0.01655)$$
$$= \$198,600$$

Since there will be 40 deposits of $198,600, total deposits over the 10-year period will equal $7,944,000. Compared with annual deposits and annual compounding in Example 9.13, total deposits required to accumulate the $12 million will be $8,282,400 − $7,944,000 = $338,400 less under the quarterly plan.

Follow-up Exercises

9.29 A person wishes to deposit $2,000 per year in a savings account which earns interest of 7 percent per year compounded annually. Assume the first deposit is made at the end of this current year and additional deposits at the end of each following year.

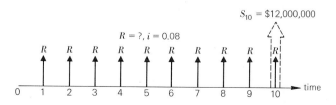

FIGURE 9.7

(*a*) To what sum will the investment grow at the time of the twenty-fifth deposit?

(*b*) How much interest will be earned?

9.30 A company wants to deposit $500,000 per year in an investment which earns interest of 8 percent per year compounded annually. Assume the first deposit is made at the end of the current year and additional deposits at the end of each following year.

(*a*) To what sum will the investment grow at the time of the twentieth deposit?

(*b*) How much interest will be earned?

9.31 A mother wishes to set up a savings account for her son's education. She plans on investing $200 when her son is 6 months old and every 6 months after. The account earns interest of 6 percent per year, compounded semiannually.

(*a*) To what amount will the account grow by the time of her son's eighteenth birthday?

(*b*) How much interest will be earned during this period?

9.32 A local university is planning to invest $25,000 every 3 months in an investment which earns interest at the rate of 10 percent per year compounded quarterly. The first investment will be at the end of this current quarter.

(*a*) To what sum will the investment grow at the end of 8 years?

(*b*) How much interest will be earned during this period?

9.33 A person wants to deposit $12,000 per year for 5 years. If interest is earned at the rate of 12 percent per year, compute the amount to which the deposits will grow by the end of the 5 years if:

(*a*) Deposits of $6,000 are made at the end of each 6-month period with interest compounded semiannually.

(*b*) Deposits of $3,000 are made at the end of every quarter with interest compounded quarterly.

(*c*) Deposits of $1,000 are made at the end of each month with interest compounded monthly.

9.34 A corporation wants to deposit $150,000 per year for 10 years. If interest is earned at the rate of 8 percent per year, compute the amount to which the deposits will grow if:

(*a*) Deposits of $150,000 are made at the end of each year with interest compounded annually.

(*b*) Deposits of $75,000 are made at the end of each 6-month period with interest compounded semiannually.

(*c*) Deposits of $37,500 are made at the end of each quarter with interest compounded quarterly.

9.35 How much money must be deposited at the end of each year if the objective is to accumulate $10,000 by the time of the eighth deposit? Assume interest is earned at the rate of 6 percent per year compounded annually. How much interest will be earned on the deposits?

9.36 How much money must be deposited at the end of each quarter if the objective is to accumulate $600,000 after 5 years? Assume interest is earned at the rate of 8 percent per year compounded quarterly. How much interest will be earned?

9.37 A family wants to begin saving for a trip to Europe. The trip is planned for 5 years from now, and the family wants to accumulate

$10,000 for the trip. If 10 deposits are made semiannually to an account which earns interest at the rate of 6 percent per year compounded semiannually, how much should each deposit equal? How much interest will be earned on their deposits?

9.38 A major city wants to establish a sinking fund to pay off debts of $20 million which come due in 7 years. The city can earn interest at the rate of 9 percent per year compounded semiannually. If the first deposit is made 6 months from now, what semiannual deposit will be required to accumulate the $20 million? How much interest will be earned on these deposits?

ANNUITIES AND THEIR PRESENT VALUE

Just as there are problems relating annuities and their equivalent future value, there are applications which relate an annuity to its present-value equivalent. For example, we may be interested in determining the size of a deposit which will generate a series of payments (an annuity) for college, retirement years, and so forth. Or, given that a loan has been made, we may be interested in determining the series of payments (annuity) necessary to repay the loan with interest. This section discusses problems of these types.

The Present Value of an Annuity

The *present value* of an annuity is an amount of money today which is equivalent to a series of equal payments in the future. Assume you have won a lottery and lottery officials give you the choice of having a lump-sum payment today or a series of payments at the end of each of the next 5 years. The two alternatives would be considered equivalent (in a monetary sense) if by investing the lump sum today you could generate (with accumulated interest) annual withdrawals equal to the five installments offered by the lottery officials. An assumption is that the final withdrawal would deplete the investment completely. Consider the following example.

Lottery A person recently won a state lottery. The terms of the lottery are that the winner will receive annual payments of $20,000 at the end of this year and each of the following 3 years. If the winner could invest money today at the rate of 6 percent per year compounded annually, what is the present value of the four payments?

Example 9.15

Figure 9.8 illustrates the situation. If A is defined as the present value of the annuity, we might determine the value of A by computing the present value of each $20,000 payment. Applying Eq. (9.7a) and using values from Table 9.3, we find the sum of the four present values is $69,301.60. We can conclude that a deposit today of $69,301.60 which earns interest at the rate of 6 percent per year compounded annually could generate a series of four withdrawals of $20,000 at the end of each of the next four years.

Solution

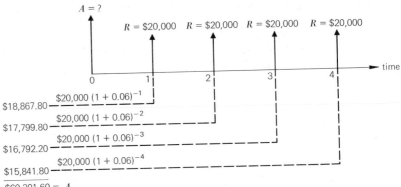

FIGURE 9.8

As with the future value of an annuity, the approach of summing the present values of each payment is possible but impractical. A more general and more efficient method of determining the present value of an annuity follows.

Let

R = amount of an annuity
i = interest rate per period
n = number of annuity payments (also, the number of compounding periods)
A = present value of the annuity

Equation (9.12), which determines the future value or sum of an annuity, is restated below.

$$S_n = R \frac{(1 + i)^n - 1}{i} \tag{9.12}$$

Looking at Fig. 9.9, we can think of S_n as being the equivalent future value of the annuity. If we know the value of S_n, the present value A of the annuity should simply be the present value of S_n, or

$$A = S_n(1 + i)^{-n}$$

Substituting the expression for S_n from Eq. (9.12) yields

$$A = R \frac{(1 + i)^n - 1}{i} (1 + i)^{-n}$$

or

$$A = R \left[\frac{(1 + i)^n - 1}{i(1 + i)^n} \right] \tag{9.14}$$

FIGURE 9.9

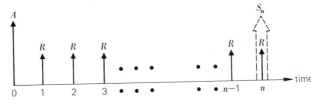

Equation (9.14) can be used to compute the present value A of an annuity consisting of n equal payments R, each made at the end of n periods. The expression in brackets is referred to as the *series present-worth factor*, and values for this factor are contained in Table 9.6 (at the end of the chapter).

Rework Example 9.15 using Equation (9.14).

Example 9.16

Since $i = 0.06$ and $n = 4$, the appropriate value from Table 9.6 is 3.46510. Substituting this value and $R = \$20,000$ into Eq. (9.14) yields

Solution

$$A = \$20,000(3.46510)$$
$$= \$69,302.00$$

The $0.40 difference between this answer and that found in Example 9.15 is due to rounding.

Parents of a teenage girl want to deposit a sum of money which will earn interest at the rate of 7 percent per year compounded semiannually. The deposit will be used to generate a series of eight semiannual payments of $2,500 beginning 6 months after the deposit. These payments will be used to help finance their daughter's college education. What amount must be deposited to achieve their goal? How much interest will be earned on this deposit?

Example 9.17

For this problem, $R = \$2,500$, $i = 0.07/2 = 0.035$, and $n = 8$. The appropriate value of the series present-worth factor is 6.87395. Substituting into Eq. (9.14) gives

Solution

$$A = (\$2,500)(6.87395)$$
$$= \$17,184.88$$

Since the $17,184.88 will generate eight payments totaling $20,000, interest of $20,000 − $17,184.88, or $2,815.12, will be earned.

Determining the Size of the Annuity

There are problems in which we may be given the present value of an annuity and need to determine the size of the corresponding annuity. For example, given a loan of $10,000 which is received today, what quarterly payments must be made to repay the loan in 5 years if interest is charged at the rate of 10 percent per year, compounded quarterly? The process of repaying a loan by installment payments is referred to as *amortizing* a loan.

For the loan example, the quarterly payments can be calculated by solving for R in Eq. (9.14). Solving for R, we get

$$R = \frac{A}{[(1 + i)^n - 1]/[i(1 + i)^n]}$$

or

$$R = A \left[\frac{i(1 + i)^n}{(1 + i)^n - 1} \right] \qquad (9.15)$$

The expression in brackets is sometimes called the *capital-recovery factor*. Table 9.7 (at the end of the chapter) contains values for this factor.

Example 9.18 Determine the quarterly payment necessary to repay the previously mentioned $10,000 loan. How much interest will be paid on the loan?

Solution For this problem $A = \$10,000$, $i = 0.10/4 = 0.025$, and $n = 20$. The corresponding factor in Table 9.7 is 0.06414. Substituting into Eq. (9.15) gives

$$R = \$10,000(0.06414)$$
$$= \$641.40$$

There will be 20 payments totaling $12,828; thus interest will equal $2,828 on the loan.

Example 9.19 **Retirement Planning** An employee has contributed with her employer to a retirement plan. At the date of her retirement, the total requirement benefits are $250,000. The retirement program provides for investment of this sum at an interest rate of 8 percent per year compounded semiannually. Semiannual disbursements will be made for 30 years to the employee or, in the event of her death, to her dependents. What semiannual payment should be generated? How much interest will be earned on the $250,000?

Solution For this problem $A = \$250,000$, $i = 0.08/2 = 0.04$, and $n = 60$. The appropriate value from Table 9.7 is 0.04420. Substituting into Eq. (9.15), we get

$$R = \$250,000(0.04420)$$
$$= \$11,050$$

Total payments over the 30 years will equal $663,000. Thus, interest of $663,000 − $250,000, or $413,000, will be earned over the 30 years.

Mortgages

Sooner or later, most of us succumb to the "American dream" of owning a home. Aside from the numerous pleasures of home ownership, there is *at least* one time during each month when we cringe from the effects of owning a home. That time is when we sign a check for the monthly mortgage payment. And whether we realize it or not, we spend an incredible amount of money to realize our dream.

Given a mortgage loan, many homeowners do not realize how the amount of their mortgage payment is calculated. It is calculated in the same way as were the loan payments in the last section. That is, they are calculated by using Eq. (9.15). Interest is typically compounded monthly, and the interest rate per compounding period can equal unusual fractions or decimal answers. If the annual interest rate is 8.5

percent, the value of i is $0.085/12 = \frac{17}{24}$ of a percent, or 0.0070833. Obviously Table 9.7 cannot be used for these interest rates.

Table 9.8 (at the end of the chapter) is an extension of Table 9.7 designed specifically for determining mortgage payments. Note that the interest rates are stated as annual percentages.

A person pays \$50,000 for a new house. A down payment of \$10,000 leaves a mortgage of \$40,000 with interest computed at 8.5 percent per year compounded monthly. Determine the monthly mortgage payment if the loan is to be repaid over (*a*) 20 years, (*b*) 25 years, and (*c*) 30 years. (*d*) Compute total interest under the three different loan periods.

Example 9.20

(*a*) From Table 9.8, the monthly payment per dollar of mortgage is 0.00867823 (corresponding to $n = 20 \times 12 = 240$ payments). Therefore

Solution

$$R = \$40,000(0.00867823)$$
$$= \$347.13$$

(*b*) For 25 years (or 300 monthly payments),

$$R = \$40,000(0.00805227)$$
$$= \$322.09$$

(*c*) For 30 years (or 360 monthly payments)

$$R = \$40,000(0.00768913)$$
$$= \$307.57$$

(*d*) Total payments are

for 20 years,   (240)(\$347.13) = \$83,311.20
for 25 years,   (300)(\$322.09) = \$96,627.00
for 30 years,   (360)(\$307.57) = \$110,725.20

Because these payments are all repaying a \$40,000 loan, interest on the loan is

for 20 years,   \$83,311.20 − \$40,000.00 = \$43,311.20
for 25 years,   \$96,627.00 − \$40,000.00 = \$56,627.00
for 30 years,   \$110,725.20 − \$40,000.00 = \$70,725.20

In the previous problem, determine the effects of a decrease in the interest rate to 8 percent (*a*) on monthly payments for the 25-year mortgage, (*b*) on total interest for the 25-year mortgage.

Example 9.21

(*a*) For $i = 8$ and 25 years,

Solution

$$R = 0.00771816(40,000)$$
$$= \$308.73$$

Therefore, monthly payments are less by an amount

$$\$322.09 - \$308.73 = \$13.36$$

(*b*) Total payments over the 25 years will equal

$$300(308.73) = \$92,619$$

The total interest is $52,619, which is $4,008.00 less than with the 8.5 percent mortgage.

Follow-up Exercises

9.39 Determine the present value of a series of 25 annual payments of $2,500 each which begins 1 year from today. Assume interest of 6 percent per year compounded annually.

9.40 Determine the present value of a series of 30 annual payments of $500 each which begins 1 year from today. Assume interest of 8 percent per year compounded annually.

9.41 Determine the present value of a series of 20 semiannual payments of $2,000 each which begins in 6 months. Assume interest of 9 percent per year compounded semiannually.

9.42 Determine the present value of a series of 36 quarterly payments of $5,000 each which begins in 3 months. Assume interest of 8 percent per year compounded quarterly.

9.43 A person wants to buy a life insurance policy which would yield a large enough sum of money to provide for 25 annual payments of $10,000 to surviving members of the family. The payments would begin 1 year from the time of death. It is assumed that interest could be earned on the sum received from the policy at a rate of 6 percent per year compounded annually.
(*a*) What amount of insurance should be taken out so as to ensure the desired annuity?
(*b*) How much interest will be earned on the policy benefits over the 25-year period?

9.44 Assume in Exercise 9.43 that semiannual payments of $5,000 are desired over the 25-year period, and interest is compounded semiannually.
(*a*) What amount of insurance should be taken out?
(*b*) How does this amount compare with that for Exercise 9.43?
(*c*) How much interest will be earned on the policy benefits?
(*d*) How does this compare with that for Exercise 9.43?

9.45 Given $100,000 today, determine the equivalent series of 10 annual payments which could be generated beginning in 1 year. Assume interest is 8 percent compounded annually.

9.46 Given $5 million today, determine the equivalent series of 24 annual payments which could be generated beginning in 1 year. Assume interest of 6 percent compounded annually.

9.47 Given $750,000 today, determine the equivalent series of 24 quarterly payments which could be generated beginning in 3 months. Assume interest of 10 percent per year compounded quarterly.

9.48 Given $10 million today, determine the equivalent series of 30 semiannual payments which could be generated beginning in 6 months. Assume interest of 5 percent per year compounded semiannually.

9.49 (*a*) Determine the monthly car payment necessary to repay a $5,000 automobile loan if interest is computed at 12 percent per year compounded monthly. Assume the period of the loan is 3 years.

(*b*) How much interest will be paid over the 3-year period?

9.50 (*a*) Determine the quarterly payment necessary to repay a $20,000 loan if interest is computed at the rate of 8 percent per year compounded quarterly. Assume the loan is to be repaid in 10 years.

(*b*) How much interest will be paid over the 10-year period?

For Exercises 9.51 to 9.54 compute the monthly mortgage payment, total payments, and total interest.

9.51 Mortgage loan of $30,000 at 9 percent per year for 25 years

9.52 Mortgage loan of $60,000 at 8 percent per year for 30 years

9.53 Mortgage loan of $50,000 at 8.75 percent per year for 20 years

9.54 Mortgage loan of $20,000 at 8.5 percent per year for 30 years

9.55 to 9.58 Rework Exercises 9.51 to 9.54, computing the difference between the amount of the monthly mortgage payment and the *total* interest paid if the interest rate increases by 1 percent.

9.59 A couple estimates that they can afford a mortgage payment of $325 per month. They can obtain a 25-year mortgage at an interest rate of 8 percent. What is the largest mortgage loan they can afford?

9.60 A couple estimates that they can afford a mortgage payment of $420 per month. They can obtain a 30-year mortgage at an interest rate of 8.5 percent. What is the largest mortgage loan they can afford?

SUMMARY   9.5

This chapter has discussed compound interest and its effect on the value of money. There are other cash flow situations which might have been discussed. However, time and space limitations do not permit their inclusion in the chapter.

It is important to review the different situations discussed in this chapter. We presented many different formulas, and the topic may seem more complicated than it really is. Figure 9.10 summarizes the three different cash flow situations discussed in the chapter. And there are really just three equations needed to solve any of the problems in the chapter. These equations also appear in Fig. 9.10.

In solving a problem, the first step is *recognition:* which of the three situations do you have? You should ask yourself whether you have a single-payment (deposit) situation or an annuity. If the problem involves a single-payment situation, Fig. 9.10*a* applies. If you are dealing with a series of equal payments (an annuity), you must determine whether the series of payments is being related to its future value or to its present value. If the former, Fig. 9.10*b* and its equation apply. If the series of payments is being related to its present value, Fig. 9.10*c* and its equation apply.

Once you have determined the appropriate situation, the next step is to define the parameters of *n* and *i* to be used in the equation. Once these have been specified, the appropriate table must be identified and the correct factor selected.

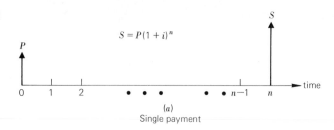

$$S = P(1 + i)^n$$

(a)
Single payment

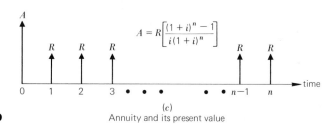

$$S_n = R\left[\frac{(1 + i)^n - 1}{i}\right]$$

(b)
Annuity and its future value

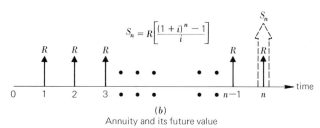

$$A = R\left[\frac{(1 + i)^n - 1}{i(1 + i)^n}\right]$$

(c)
Annuity and its present value

FIGURE 9.10

If you have trouble in dealing with six tables, remember that you can do all calculations using just three of them as long as you do not mind division.

CHAPTER CHECKLIST

If you have read the entire chapter, you should

_____ Understand the concept of *simple interest* and its computation

_____ Understand the difference between simple interest and *compound interest*

_____ Be able to determine the *compound amount* associated with any investment *P*

_____ Be able to determine the *present value* of a future sum of money

_____ Be able to determine either the interest rate or the period of time required for an investment to increase by a stated amount

_____ Understand the concept of *effective annual interest rates* and their computation

_____ Be able to perform computations relating to an *annuity* and its *future value*

Be able to perform computations relating to an *annuity* and its _____
present value

Be able to perform mortgage calculations _____

KEY TERMS AND CONCEPTS

simple interest	annuity
compound interest	sum of an annuity
principal	series compound-amount factor
interest rate	sinking fund
compound amount	sinking fund factor
interest rate per compounding period	present value of an annuity
present value	series present-worth factor
present-value factor	capital-recovery factor
effective annual interest rate	

IMPORTANT FORMULAS

$$I = Pin \tag{9.1}$$

$$S = P(1 + i)^n \tag{9.6}$$

$$P = \frac{1}{(1 + i)^n} S \tag{9.7a}$$

$$r = \left(1 + \frac{i}{m}\right)^m - 1 \tag{9.8}$$

$$S_n = R \frac{(1 + i)^n - 1}{i} \tag{9.12}$$

$$R = S_n \frac{i}{(1 + i)^n - 1} \tag{9.13}$$

$$A = R \frac{(1 + i)^n - 1}{i(1 + i)^n} \tag{9.14}$$

$$R = A \frac{i(1 + i)^n}{(1 + i)^n - 1} \tag{9.15}$$

ADDITIONAL EXERCISES

Exercises 9.61 to 9.70 are related to Sec. 9.2.

9.61 *Fire Protection* The number of fires reported each year in a major United States city has been increasing at a rate of 4 percent per year. The number of fires reported for the year 1977 was 12,000. If the number of fires continues to increase at the same rate, how many will be expected in 1985?

9.62 A sum of $2 million has been invested at an interest rate of 12 percent per year. If the investment is made for a period of 10 years, determine the compound amount if interest is compounded (*a*) semiannually; (*b*) quarterly; (*c*) bimonthly.

9.63 Prices for a particular commodity have been increasing at an annual rate of 6 percent compounded annually. The current price of the commodity is $25. What was the price of the same item 4 years ago?

9.64 A sum of money will be deposited today at 6 percent per year. The goal is to have this sum grow to $20,000 in 8 years. What sum must be deposited if interest is compounded (*a*) annually, (*b*) semiannually?

9.65 *Real Estate* Real estate prices within a state have been increasing at an average rate of 7 percent per year. How long will it take for current prices to increase by 50 percent if prices continue to increase at the same rate?

9.66 *Alcoholism* A state health agency has gathered data on the number of known alcoholics in the state. The number is currently 60,000. Data indicate that this number has been increasing at a rate of 1.5 percent per year and is expected to increase at the same rate in the future. How long will it take for the number of alcoholics in the state to reach a level of 80,000?

9.67 *Public Utilities* A major water utility estimates that the average daily consumption of water within a certain city is 30 million gallons. It has projected that the average daily consumption will equal 40 million gallons in 5 years. What annual rate of growth has the utility used in making its estimate of future consumption?

9.68 If compounding is done annually, at what interest rate must a sum be invested if it is to double in value over the next 9 years?

9.69 The nominal interest rate on an investment is 6 percent per year. Determine the effective annual interest rate if interest is compounded (*a*) semiannually, (*b*) quarterly.

9.70 The nominal interest rate on an investment is 4 percent per year. Determine the effective annual interest rate if interest is compounded (*a*) semiannually, (*b*) quarterly.

Exercises 9.71 to 9.76 are related to Sec. 9.3.

9.71 Quarterly deposits of $3,000 are to be made in an account which earns interest at the rate of 10 percent per year compounded quarterly. To what sum will the investment grow by the time of the twentieth deposit? How much interest will be earned during this period?

9.72 A person wishes to deposit $1,000 per year for 10 years. If interest is earned at the rate of 6 percent per year, compute the amount that the deposits will grow to by the end of 10 years if:

(*a*) Deposits of $1,000 are made at the end of each year with interest compounded annually.

(*b*) Deposits of $500 are made at the end of each 6-month period with interest compounded semiannually.

(*c*) Deposits of $250 are made at the end of every quarter with interest compounded quarterly.

9.73 How much money must be deposited at the end of each 6-month period if the objective is to accumulate $5,000 by the time of the eighth deposit? Assume that interest is earned at the rate of 7 percent per year compounded semiannually. How much interest will be earned on these deposits?

9.74 A small community wants to establish a sinking fund to pay off debts of $1 million associated with the construction of a sewage treatment plant. The community can earn interest at the rate of 8 percent per year compounded quarterly. The debt comes due in 6 years. If the first deposit is made 3 months from now, what quarterly deposit will be required to accumulate the $1 million? How much interest will be earned on these deposits?

*9.75 Interest can be earned on a savings account at the rate of 7 percent per year compounded annually. A person wishes to make deposits of $1,000 at the end of each year. How long will it take for the deposits and accumulated interest to grow to a sum which will exceed $10,000?

*9.76 Interest can be earned on a savings account at the rate of 8 percent per year compounded quarterly. If deposits of $10,000 are made at the end of each quarter, how long will it take for the deposits and accumulated interest to grow to a sum which exceeds $500,000?

Exercises 9.77 to 9.85 are related to Sec. 9.4.

9.77 Determine the present value of a series of 20 quarterly payments of $800 each which begins in 3 months. Assume interest is 10 percent per year compounded quarterly.

9.78 A person recently won a state lottery. The terms of the lottery are that the winner will receive annual payments of $10,000 at the end of this year and each of the following 19 years. If money can be invested today at the rate of 7 percent per year compounded annually, what is the present value of the 20 lottery payments?

9.79 Given $500,000 today, determine the equivalent series of 36 semiannual payments which could be generated beginning in 6 months. Assume interest can be earned at a rate of 8 percent per year compounded semiannually.

9.80 (*a*) Determine the monthly car payment necessary to repay a $4,000 automobile loan if interest is computed at 18 percent per year compounded monthly. Assume the period of the loan is 3 years. (*b*) How much interest will be paid over the 3-year period?

*9.81 A lump sum of $100,000 is invested at the rate of 6 percent per year compounded annually. How many annual withdrawals of $10,000 can be made (assume that the first withdrawal occurs in one year)?

*9.82 A family has inherited $50,000. If they choose to invest the $50,000 at 8 percent per year compounded quarterly, how many quarterly withdrawals of $5,000 can be made (assume that the first withdrawal is 3 months after the investment is made)?

9.83 Determine the monthly mortgage payment, total payments, and total interest on a 25-year mortgage loan of $40,000 if the interest rate is 8.75 percent per year.

9.84 Determine the monthly mortgage payment, total payments, and total interest on a 30-year mortgage loan of $50,000 if the interest rate is 9.5 percent per year.

9.85 A person estimates that she can afford a mortgage payment of $400 per month. If she can obtain a 25-year mortgage at an interest rate of 9 percent, what is the highest mortgage she can afford?

Table 9.2

Compound-Amount Factor $(1 + i)^n$

_i_

n	0.01 (1%)	0.015 (1½%)	0.02 (2%)	0.025 (2½%)	0.03 (3%)	0.035 (3½%)	0.04 (4%)	0.045 (4½%)	0.05 (5%)	0.06 (6%)	0.07 (7%)	0.08 (8%)
1	1.01000	1.01500	1.02000	1.02500	1.03000	1.03500	1.04000	1.04500	1.05000	1.06000	1.07000	1.08000
2	1.02010	1.03022	1.04040	1.05062	1.06090	1.07122	1.08160	1.09202	1.10250	1.12360	1.14490	1.16640
3	1.03030	1.04567	1.06120	1.07689	1.09272	1.10871	1.12486	1.14116	1.15762	1.19101	1.22504	1.25971
4	1.04060	1.06136	1.08243	1.10381	1.12550	1.14752	1.16985	1.19252	1.21550	1.26247	1.31079	1.36048
5	1.05101	1.07728	1.10408	1.13140	1.15927	1.18768	1.21665	1.24618	1.27628	1.33822	1.40255	1.46932
6	1.06152	1.09344	1.12616	1.15969	1.19405	1.22925	1.26531	1.30226	1.34009	1.41851	1.50073	1.58687
7	1.07213	1.10984	1.14868	1.18868	1.22987	1.27227	1.31593	1.36086	1.40710	1.50363	1.60578	1.71382
8	1.08285	1.12649	1.17165	1.21840	1.26677	1.31680	1.36856	1.42210	1.47745	1.59384	1.71818	1.85093
9	1.09368	1.14338	1.19509	1.24886	1.30477	1.36289	1.42331	1.48609	1.55132	1.68947	1.83845	1.99900
10	1.10462	1.16054	1.21899	1.28008	1.34391	1.41059	1.48024	1.55296	1.62889	1.79084	1.96715	2.15892
11	1.11566	1.17794	1.24337	1.31208	1.38423	1.45996	1.53945	1.62285	1.71033	1.89829	2.10485	2.33163
12	1.12682	1.19561	1.26824	1.34488	1.42576	1.51106	1.60103	1.69588	1.79585	2.01219	2.25219	2.51817
13	1.13809	1.21355	1.29360	1.37851	1.46853	1.56395	1.66507	1.77219	1.88564	2.13292	2.40984	2.71962
14	1.14947	1.23175	1.31947	1.41297	1.51259	1.61869	1.73167	1.85194	1.97993	2.26090	2.57853	2.93719
15	1.16096	1.25023	1.34586	1.44829	1.55796	1.67534	1.80094	1.93528	2.07892	2.39655	2.75903	3.17216
16	1.17257	1.26898	1.37278	1.48450	1.60470	1.73398	1.87298	2.02237	2.18287	2.54035	2.95216	3.42594
17	1.18430	1.28802	1.40024	1.52161	1.65284	1.79467	1.94790	2.11337	2.29201	2.69277	3.15881	3.70001
18	1.19614	1.30734	1.42824	1.55965	1.70243	1.85748	2.02581	2.20847	2.40661	2.85433	3.37993	3.99601
19	1.20810	1.32695	1.45681	1.59865	1.75350	1.92250	2.10684	2.30786	2.52695	3.02559	3.61652	4.31570
20	1.22019	1.34685	1.48594	1.63861	1.80611	1.98978	2.19112	2.41171	2.65329	3.20713	3.86968	4.66095
21	1.23239	1.36705	1.51566	1.67958	1.86029	2.05943	2.27876	2.52024	2.78596	3.39956	4.14056	5.03383
22	1.24471	1.38756	1.54597	1.72157	1.91610	2.13151	2.36991	2.63365	2.92526	3.60353	4.43040	5.43654
23	1.25716	1.40837	1.57689	1.76461	1.97358	2.20611	2.46471	2.75216	3.07152	3.81974	4.74052	5.87146
24	1.26973	1.42950	1.60843	1.80872	2.03279	2.28332	2.56330	2.87601	3.22509	4.04893	5.07236	6.34118
25	1.28243	1.45094	1.64060	1.85394	2.09377	2.36324	2.66583	3.00543	3.38635	4.29187	5.42743	6.84847
26	1.29525	1.47270	1.67341	1.90029	2.15659	2.44595	2.77246	3.14067	3.55567	4.54938	5.80735	7.39635
27	1.30820	1.49480	1.70688	1.94780	2.22128	2.53156	2.88336	3.28200	3.73345	4.82234	6.21386	7.98806
28	1.32129	1.51722	1.74102	1.99649	2.28792	2.62017	2.99870	3.42969	3.92012	5.11168	6.64883	8.62710
29	1.33450	1.53998	1.77584	2.04640	2.35656	2.71187	3.11865	3.58403	4.11613	5.41838	7.11425	9.31727
30	1.34784	1.56308	1.81136	2.09756	2.42726	2.80679	3.24339	3.74531	4.32194	5.74349	7.61225	10.06265
31	1.36132	1.58652	1.84758	2.15000	2.50008	2.90503	3.37313	3.91385	4.53803	6.08810	8.14511	10.86766
32	1.37494	1.61032	1.88454	2.20375	2.57508	3.00670	3.50805	4.08998	4.76494	6.45338	8.71527	11.73708
33	1.38869	1.63447	1.92223	2.25885	2.65233	3.11194	3.64838	4.27403	5.00318	6.84058	9.32533	12.67604
34	1.40257	1.65898	1.96067	2.31532	2.73190	3.22086	3.79431	4.46636	5.25334	7.25102	9.97811	13.69013
35	1.41660	1.68388	1.99988	2.37320	2.81386	3.33359	3.94608	4.66734	5.51601	7.68608	10.67658	14.78534
36	1.43076	1.70913	2.03988	2.43253	2.89827	3.45026	4.10393	4.87737	5.79181	8.14725	11.42394	15.96817
37	1.44507	1.73477	2.08068	2.49334	2.98522	3.57102	4.26808	5.09686	6.08140	8.63608	12.22361	17.24562
38	1.45952	1.76079	2.12229	2.55568	3.07478	3.69601	4.43881	5.32621	6.38547	9.15425	13.07927	18.62527
39	1.47412	1.78721	2.16474	2.61957	3.16702	3.82537	4.61636	5.56589	6.70475	9.70350	13.99482	20.11529
40	1.48886	1.81401	2.20803	2.68506	3.26203	3.95925	4.80102	5.81636	7.03998	10.28571	14.97445	21.72452
41	1.50375	1.84122	2.25220	2.75219	3.35989	4.09783	4.99306	6.07810	7.39198	10.90286	16.02266	23.46248
42	1.51878	1.86884	2.29724	2.82099	3.46069	4.24125	5.19278	6.35161	7.76158	11.55703	17.14425	25.33948
43	1.53397	1.89687	2.34318	2.89152	3.56451	4.38970	5.40049	6.63743	8.14966	12.25045	18.34435	27.36664
44	1.54931	1.92533	2.39005	2.96380	3.67145	4.54334	5.61651	6.93612	8.55715	12.98548	19.62845	29.55597
45	1.56481	1.95421	2.43785	3.03790	3.78159	4.70235	5.84117	7.24825	8.98500	13.76461	21.00245	31.92044
46	1.58045	1.98352	2.48661	3.11385	3.89504	4.86694	6.07482	7.57442	9.43425	14.59048	22.47262	34.47408
47	1.59626	2.01327	2.53634	3.19169	4.01189	5.03728	6.31781	7.91527	9.90597	15.46591	24.04570	37.23201
48	1.61222	2.04347	2.58707	3.27148	4.13225	5.21358	6.57052	8.27146	10.40126	16.39387	25.72890	40.21057
49	1.62834	2.07413	2.63881	3.35327	4.25621	5.39606	6.83334	8.64367	10.92133	17.37750	27.52993	43.42741
50	1.64463	2.10524	2.69158	3.43710	4.38390	5.58493	7.10668	9.03263	11.46740	18.42015	29.45702	46.90161
51	1.66107	2.13682	2.74541	3.52303	4.51542	5.78039	7.39095	9.43910	12.04077	19.52536	31.51901	50.65374
52	1.67768	2.16887	2.80032	3.61111	4.65060	5.98271	7.68658	9.86386	12.64280	20.69688	33.72534	54.70604
53	1.69446	2.20140	2.85633	3.70139	4.79041	6.19210	7.99405	10.30773	13.27494	21.93869	36.08612	59.08252
54	1.71141	2.23442	2.91346	3.79392	4.93412	6.40883	8.31381	10.77158	13.93869	23.25502	38.61215	63.80912
55	1.72852	2.26794	2.97173	3.88877	5.08214	6.63314	8.64636	11.25630	14.63563	24.65032	41.31500	68.91385
56	1.74580	2.30196	3.03116	3.98599	5.23461	6.86530	8.99222	11.76284	15.36741	26.12934	44.20705	74.42696
57	1.76326	2.33649	3.09178	4.08564	5.39165	7.10558	9.35191	12.29216	16.13578	27.69710	47.30154	80.38112
58	1.78090	2.37153	3.15362	4.18778	5.55340	7.35428	9.72598	12.84531	16.94257	29.35892	50.61265	86.81161
59	1.79870	2.40711	3.21669	4.29247	5.72000	7.61168	10.11502	13.42335	17.78970	31.12046	54.15553	93.75654
60	1.81669	2.44321	3.28103	4.39978	5.89160	7.87809	10.51962	14.02740	18.67918	32.98769	57.94642	101.25706

Table 9.3

$$\text{Present-Value Factor} \quad \frac{1}{(1+i)^n} = (1+i)^{-n}$$

n	0.01 (1%)	0.015 (1½%)	0.02 (2%)	0.025 (2½%)	0.03 (3%)	0.035 (3½%)	0.04 (4%)	0.045 (4½%)	0.05 (5%)	0.06 (6%)	0.07 (7%)	0.08 (8%)
1	0.99009	0.98522	0.98039	0.97560	0.97087	0.96618	0.96153	0.95693	0.95238	0.94339	0.93457	0.92592
2	0.98029	0.97066	0.96116	0.95181	0.94259	0.93351	0.92455	0.91572	0.90702	0.88999	0.87343	0.85733
3	0.97059	0.95631	0.94232	0.92859	0.91514	0.90194	0.88899	0.87629	0.86383	0.83961	0.81629	0.79383
4	0.96098	0.94218	0.92384	0.90595	0.88848	0.87144	0.85480	0.83856	0.82270	0.79209	0.76289	0.73502
5	0.95146	0.92826	0.90573	0.88385	0.86260	0.84197	0.82192	0.80245	0.78352	0.74725	0.71298	0.68058
6	0.94204	0.91454	0.88797	0.86229	0.83748	0.81350	0.79031	0.76789	0.74621	0.70496	0.66634	0.63016
7	0.93271	0.90102	0.87056	0.84126	0.81309	0.78599	0.75991	0.73482	0.71068	0.66505	0.62274	0.58349
8	0.92348	0.88771	0.85349	0.82074	0.78940	0.75941	0.73069	0.70318	0.67683	0.62741	0.58200	0.54026
9	0.91433	0.87459	0.83675	0.80072	0.76641	0.73373	0.70258	0.67290	0.64460	0.59189	0.54393	0.50024
10	0.90528	0.86166	0.82034	0.78120	0.74409	0.70891	0.67556	0.64392	0.61391	0.55839	0.50834	0.46319
11	0.89632	0.84893	0.80426	0.76214	0.72242	0.68494	0.64958	0.61619	0.58467	0.52678	0.47509	0.42888
12	0.88744	0.83638	0.78849	0.74355	0.70137	0.66178	0.62459	0.58966	0.55683	0.49696	0.44401	0.39711
13	0.87866	0.82402	0.77303	0.72542	0.68095	0.63940	0.60057	0.56427	0.53032	0.46883	0.41496	0.36769
14	0.86996	0.81184	0.75787	0.70772	0.66111	0.61778	0.57747	0.53997	0.50506	0.44230	0.38781	0.34046
15	0.86134	0.79985	0.74301	0.69046	0.64186	0.59689	0.55526	0.51672	0.48101	0.41726	0.36244	0.31524
16	0.85282	0.78803	0.72844	0.67362	0.62316	0.57670	0.53390	0.49464	0.45811	0.39364	0.33873	0.29189
17	0.84437	0.77638	0.71416	0.65719	0.60501	0.55720	0.51337	0.47317	0.43629	0.37136	0.31657	0.27026
18	0.83601	0.76491	0.70015	0.64116	0.58739	0.53836	0.49362	0.45280	0.41552	0.35034	0.29586	0.25024
19	0.82773	0.75360	0.68643	0.62552	0.57028	0.52015	0.47464	0.43330	0.39573	0.33051	0.27750	0.23171
20	0.81954	0.74247	0.67297	0.61027	0.55367	0.50256	0.45638	0.41464	0.37688	0.31180	0.25841	0.21454
21	0.81143	0.73149	0.65977	0.59538	0.53754	0.48557	0.43883	0.39678	0.35894	0.29415	0.24151	0.19865
22	0.80339	0.72068	0.64683	0.58086	0.52189	0.46915	0.42195	0.37970	0.34184	0.27750	0.22571	0.18394
23	0.79544	0.71000	0.63415	0.56669	0.50669	0.45328	0.40572	0.36335	0.32557	0.26179	0.21094	0.17031
24	0.78756	0.69954	0.62172	0.55287	0.49193	0.43795	0.39012	0.34770	0.31006	0.24697	0.19714	0.15769
25	0.77976	0.68921	0.60953	0.53939	0.47760	0.42314	0.37511	0.33273	0.29530	0.23299	0.18424	0.14601
26	0.77204	0.67902	0.59757	0.52623	0.46369	0.40883	0.36068	0.31840	0.28124	0.21981	0.17219	0.13520
27	0.76440	0.66898	0.58586	0.51339	0.45018	0.39501	0.34681	0.30469	0.26784	0.20736	0.16093	0.12518
28	0.75683	0.65909	0.57437	0.50087	0.43707	0.38165	0.33347	0.29157	0.25509	0.19563	0.15040	0.11591
29	0.74934	0.64935	0.56311	0.48866	0.42434	0.36874	0.32065	0.27901	0.24294	0.18455	0.14056	0.10732
30	0.74192	0.63976	0.55207	0.47674	0.41198	0.35627	0.30831	0.26700	0.23137	0.17411	0.13136	0.09937
31	0.73457	0.63030	0.54124	0.46511	0.39998	0.34423	0.29646	0.25550	0.22035	0.16425	0.12277	0.09201
32	0.72730	0.62099	0.53063	0.45377	0.38833	0.33258	0.28505	0.24449	0.20986	0.15495	0.11474	0.08520
33	0.72010	0.61181	0.52022	0.44270	0.37702	0.32134	0.27409	0.23397	0.19987	0.14618	0.10723	0.07888
34	0.71297	0.60277	0.51002	0.43190	0.36604	0.31047	0.26355	0.22389	0.19035	0.13791	0.10021	0.07304
35	0.70591	0.59386	0.50002	0.42137	0.35538	0.29997	0.25341	0.21425	0.18129	0.13010	0.09366	0.06763
36	0.69892	0.58508	0.49022	0.41109	0.34503	0.28983	0.24366	0.20502	0.17265	0.12274	0.08753	0.06262
37	0.69200	0.57644	0.48061	0.40106	0.33498	0.28003	0.23429	0.19619	0.16443	0.11579	0.08180	0.05798
38	0.68515	0.56792	0.47118	0.39128	0.32522	0.27056	0.22528	0.18775	0.15660	0.10923	0.07645	0.05369
39	0.67836	0.55953	0.46194	0.38174	0.31575	0.26141	0.21662	0.17966	0.14914	0.10305	0.07145	0.04971
40	0.67165	0.55125	0.45289	0.37243	0.30655	0.25257	0.20828	0.17192	0.14204	0.09722	0.06678	0.04603
41	0.66500	0.54311	0.44401	0.36334	0.29762	0.24403	0.20027	0.16452	0.13528	0.09171	0.06241	0.04262
42	0.65841	0.53508	0.43530	0.35448	0.28895	0.23577	0.19257	0.15744	0.12883	0.08652	0.05832	0.03946
43	0.65189	0.52718	0.42676	0.34583	0.28054	0.22780	0.18516	0.15066	0.12270	0.08162	0.05451	0.03654
44	0.64544	0.51939	0.41840	0.33740	0.27237	0.22010	0.17804	0.14417	0.11686	0.07700	0.05094	0.03383
45	0.63905	0.51171	0.41019	0.32917	0.26443	0.21265	0.17119	0.13796	0.11129	0.07265	0.04761	0.03132
46	0.63272	0.50415	0.40215	0.32114	0.25673	0.20546	0.16461	0.13202	0.10599	0.06853	0.04449	0.02900
47	0.62646	0.49670	0.39426	0.31331	0.24925	0.19851	0.15828	0.12633	0.10094	0.06465	0.04158	0.02685
48	0.62026	0.48936	0.38653	0.30567	0.24199	0.19180	0.15219	0.12089	0.09614	0.06099	0.03886	0.02486
49	0.61411	0.48212	0.37895	0.29822	0.23495	0.18532	0.14634	0.11569	0.09156	0.05754	0.03632	0.02302
50	0.60803	0.47500	0.37152	0.29094	0.22810	0.17905	0.14071	0.11071	0.08720	0.05428	0.03394	0.02132
51	0.60201	0.46798	0.36424	0.28384	0.22146	0.17299	0.13530	0.10594	0.08305	0.05121	0.03172	0.01974
52	0.59605	0.46106	0.35710	0.27692	0.21501	0.16714	0.13009	0.10138	0.07909	0.04831	0.02965	0.01827
53	0.59015	0.45425	0.35009	0.27016	0.20875	0.16149	0.12508	0.09701	0.07532	0.04558	0.02771	0.01692
54	0.58431	0.44754	0.34323	0.26357	0.20267	0.15603	0.12028	0.09283	0.07174	0.04300	0.02589	0.01567
55	0.57852	0.44092	0.33650	0.25715	0.19676	0.15075	0.11565	0.08883	0.06832	0.04056	0.02420	0.01451
56	0.57280	0.43441	0.32990	0.25087	0.19103	0.14566	0.11120	0.08501	0.06507	0.03827	0.02262	0.01343
57	0.56712	0.42799	0.32343	0.24475	0.18547	0.14073	0.10693	0.08135	0.06197	0.03610	0.02114	0.01244
58	0.56151	0.42166	0.31709	0.23878	0.18006	0.13597	0.10281	0.07784	0.05902	0.03406	0.01975	0.01151
59	0.55595	0.41543	0.31087	0.23296	0.17482	0.13137	0.09886	0.07449	0.05621	0.03213	0.01846	0.01066
60	0.55044	0.40929	0.30478	0.22728	0.16973	0.12693	0.09506	0.07128	0.05353	0.03031	0.01725	0.00987

Table 9.4

Series Compound-Amount Factor $\dfrac{(1+i)^n - 1}{i}$

n	0.01 (1%)	0.015 (1½%)	0.02 (2%)	0.025 (2½%)	0.03 (3%)	0.035 (3½%)	0.04 (4%)	0.045 (4½%)	0.05 (5%)	0.06 (6%)	0.07 (7%)	0.08 (8%)
1	1.00000	1.00000	1.00000	1.00000	1.00000	1.00000	1.00000	1.00000	1.00000	1.00000	1.00000	1.00000
2	2.01000	2.01500	2.02000	2.02500	2.03000	2.03500	2.04000	2.04500	2.05000	2.06000	2.07000	2.08000
3	3.03010	3.04522	3.06040	3.07562	3.09090	3.10622	3.12160	3.13702	3.15250	3.18360	3.21490	3.24640
4	4.06040	4.09090	4.12160	4.15251	4.18362	4.21494	4.24646	4.27819	4.31012	4.37461	4.43994	4.50611
5	5.10100	5.15226	5.20404	5.25632	5.30913	5.36246	5.41632	5.47070	5.52563	5.63709	5.75073	5.86660
6	6.15201	6.22955	6.30812	6.38773	6.46840	6.55015	6.63297	6.71689	6.80191	6.97531	7.15329	7.33592
7	7.21353	7.32299	7.43428	7.54743	7.66246	7.77940	7.89829	8.01915	8.14200	8.39383	8.65402	8.92280
8	8.28567	8.43283	8.58296	8.73611	8.89233	9.05168	9.21422	9.38001	9.54910	9.89746	10.25980	10.63662
9	9.36852	9.55933	9.75462	9.95451	10.15910	10.36849	10.58279	10.80211	11.02656	11.49132	11.97798	12.48755
10	10.46221	10.70272	10.94972	11.20338	11.46387	11.73139	12.00610	12.28820	12.57789	13.18079	13.81644	14.48656
11	11.56683	11.86326	12.16871	12.48346	12.80779	13.14199	13.48635	13.84117	14.20678	14.97164	15.78359	16.64548
12	12.68250	13.04121	13.41208	13.79555	14.19202	14.60196	15.02580	15.46403	15.91712	16.86994	17.88845	18.97712
13	13.80932	14.23682	14.68033	15.14044	15.61779	16.11303	16.62683	17.15991	17.71298	18.88213	20.14064	21.49529
14	14.94742	15.45038	15.97393	16.51895	17.08632	17.67698	18.29191	18.93210	19.59863	21.01506	22.55049	24.21492
15	16.09689	16.68213	17.29341	17.93192	18.59891	19.29568	20.02358	20.78405	21.57856	23.27596	25.12902	27.15211
16	17.25786	17.93236	18.63929	19.38022	20.15688	20.97102	21.82453	22.71933	23.65749	25.67252	27.88805	30.32428
17	18.43044	19.20135	20.01207	20.86473	21.76158	22.70501	23.69751	24.74170	25.84036	28.21287	30.84021	33.75022
18	19.61474	20.48937	21.41231	22.38634	23.41443	24.49969	25.64541	26.85508	28.13238	30.90565	33.99903	37.45024
19	20.81089	21.79671	22.84055	23.94600	25.11686	26.35718	27.67122	29.06356	30.53900	33.75999	37.37896	41.44626
20	22.01900	23.12366	24.29736	25.54465	26.87037	28.27968	29.77808	31.37142	33.06595	36.78559	40.99549	45.76196
21	23.23919	24.47052	25.78331	27.18327	28.67648	30.26947	31.96920	33.78313	35.71925	39.99272	44.86517	50.42292
22	24.47158	25.83757	27.29898	28.86285	30.53678	32.32890	34.24796	36.30337	38.50521	43.39229	49.00573	55.45675
23	25.71630	27.22514	28.84496	30.58442	32.45288	34.46041	36.61788	38.93703	41.43047	46.99582	53.43614	60.89329
24	26.97346	28.63352	30.42186	32.34903	34.42647	36.66652	39.08260	41.68919	44.50199	50.81557	58.17667	66.76475
25	28.24319	30.06302	32.03029	34.15776	36.45926	38.94985	41.64590	44.56521	47.72709	54.86451	63.24903	73.10594
26	29.52563	31.51396	33.67090	36.01170	38.55304	41.31310	44.31174	47.57064	51.11345	59.15638	68.67647	79.95441
27	30.82088	32.98667	35.34432	37.91200	40.70963	43.75906	47.08421	50.71132	54.66912	63.70576	74.48382	87.35076
28	32.12909	34.48147	37.05121	39.85980	42.93092	46.29062	49.96758	53.99333	58.40258	68.52811	80.69769	95.33882
29	33.45038	35.99870	38.79223	41.85629	45.21885	48.91079	52.96628	57.42303	62.32271	73.63979	87.34653	103.96593
30	34.78489	37.53868	40.56807	43.90270	47.57541	51.62267	56.08493	61.00706	66.43884	79.05818	94.46078	113.28321
31	36.13274	39.10176	42.37944	46.00027	50.00268	54.42947	59.32833	64.75238	70.76078	84.80168	102.07304	123.34586
32	37.49406	40.68828	44.22702	48.15027	52.50275	57.33450	62.70146	68.66624	75.29882	90.88977	110.21815	134.21353
33	38.86900	42.29861	46.11157	50.35403	55.07784	60.34121	66.20952	72.75622	80.06377	97.34316	118.93342	145.95062
34	40.25769	43.93309	48.03380	52.61288	57.73017	63.45315	69.85790	77.03025	85.06695	104.18375	128.25876	158.62667
35	41.66027	45.59208	49.99448	54.92820	60.46208	66.67401	73.65222	81.49661	90.32030	111.43478	138.23688	172.31680
36	43.07687	47.27596	51.99437	57.30141	63.27594	70.00760	77.59831	86.16396	95.83632	119.12086	148.91346	187.10214
37	44.50764	48.98501	54.03425	59.73394	66.17422	73.45786	81.70224	91.04134	101.62813	127.26811	160.33740	203.07032
38	45.95272	50.71988	56.11494	62.22729	69.15944	77.02889	85.97033	96.13820	107.70954	135.90420	172.56102	220.31594
39	47.41225	52.48068	58.23724	64.78297	72.23423	80.72490	90.40914	101.46442	114.09502	145.05845	185.64029	238.94122
40	48.88637	54.26789	60.40198	67.40255	75.40125	84.55027	95.02551	107.03032	120.79977	154.76196	199.63511	259.05651
41	50.37523	56.08191	62.61002	70.08761	78.66329	88.50953	99.82653	112.84668	127.83976	165.04768	214.60957	280.78104
42	51.87898	57.92314	64.86222	72.83980	82.02319	92.60737	104.81959	118.92478	135.23175	175.95054	230.63224	304.24352
43	53.39777	59.79198	67.15947	75.66080	85.48389	96.84862	110.01238	125.27640	142.99333	187.50757	247.77649	329.58300
44	54.93175	61.68886	69.50266	78.55232	89.04840	101.23833	115.41287	131.91384	151.14300	199.75803	266.12085	356.94964
45	56.48107	63.61420	71.89271	81.51613	92.71986	105.78167	121.02939	138.84996	159.70015	212.74351	285.74931	386.50561
46	58.04588	65.56841	74.33056	84.55493	96.50145	110.48403	126.87056	146.09821	168.68516	226.50812	306.75174	418.42606
47	59.62634	67.55194	76.81718	87.66788	100.39650	115.35097	132.94539	153.67263	178.11942	241.09861	329.22438	452.90015
48	61.22260	69.56521	79.35352	90.85957	104.40840	120.38825	139.26320	161.58790	188.02539	256.56452	353.27009	490.13216
49	62.83483	71.60869	81.94059	94.13107	108.54064	125.60184	145.83373	169.85935	198.42666	272.95840	378.99900	530.34273
50	64.46318	73.68282	84.57940	97.48434	112.79686	130.99791	152.66708	178.50302	209.34799	290.33590	406.52892	573.77015
51	66.10781	75.78807	87.27099	100.92145	117.18077	136.58283	159.77376	187.53566	220.81539	308.75605	435.98592	620.67176
52	67.76889	77.92489	90.01641	104.44449	121.69619	142.36323	167.16471	196.97476	232.85616	328.28142	467.50497	671.32551
53	69.44658	80.09376	92.81674	108.05560	126.34708	148.34594	174.85130	206.83863	245.49897	348.97830	501.23031	726.03155
54	71.14104	82.29517	95.67307	111.75699	131.13749	154.53805	182.84535	217.14637	258.77392	370.91700	537.31644	785.11407
55	72.85245	84.52959	98.58653	115.55091	136.07162	160.94688	191.15916	227.91795	272.71261	394.17202	575.92861	848.92320
56	74.58098	86.79754	101.55826	119.43969	141.15376	167.58003	199.80553	239.17426	287.34824	418.82234	617.24361	917.83705
57	76.32679	89.09550	104.58943	123.42568	146.38838	174.44533	208.79775	250.93710	302.71566	444.95168	661.45066	992.26402
58	78.09005	91.43599	107.68121	127.51132	151.78003	181.55091	218.14967	263.22927	318.85144	472.64879	708.75220	1072.64514
59	79.87096	93.80763	110.83484	131.69911	157.33343	188.90520	227.87565	276.07459	335.79401	502.00771	759.36485	1159.45675
60	81.66966	96.21465	114.05153	135.99159	163.05343	196.51688	237.99068	289.49795	353.58371	533.12818	813.52038	1253.21329

Table 9.5

Sinking Fund Factor $\dfrac{i}{(1+i)^n - 1}$

n	0.01 (1%)	0.015 (1½%)	0.02 (2%)	0.025 (2½%)	0.03 (3%)	0.035 (3½%)	0.04 (4%)	0.045 (4½%)	0.05 (5%)	0.06 (6%)	0.07 (7%)	0.08 (8%)
1	1.00000	1.00000	1.00000	1.00000	1.00000	1.00000	1.00000	1.00000	1.00000	1.00000	1.00000	1.00000
2	0.49751	0.49627	0.49504	0.49382	0.49261	0.49140	0.49019	0.48899	0.48780	0.48543	0.48309	0.48076
3	0.33002	0.32838	0.32675	0.32513	0.32353	0.32193	0.32034	0.31877	0.31720	0.31410	0.31105	0.30803
4	0.24628	0.24444	0.24262	0.24081	0.23902	0.23725	0.23549	0.23374	0.23201	0.22859	0.22522	0.22192
5	0.19603	0.19408	0.19215	0.19024	0.18835	0.18648	0.18462	0.18279	0.18097	0.17740	0.17389	0.17045
6	0.16254	0.16052	0.15852	0.15654	0.15459	0.15266	0.15076	0.14887	0.14701	0.14336	0.13979	0.13631
7	0.13862	0.13655	0.13451	0.13249	0.13050	0.12854	0.12660	0.12470	0.12281	0.11913	0.11555	0.11207
8	0.12069	0.11858	0.11650	0.11446	0.11245	0.11047	0.10852	0.10660	0.10472	0.10103	0.09746	0.09401
9	0.10674	0.10460	0.10251	0.10045	0.09843	0.09644	0.09449	0.09257	0.09069	0.08702	0.08348	0.08007
10	0.09558	0.09343	0.09132	0.08925	0.08723	0.08524	0.08329	0.08137	0.07950	0.07586	0.07237	0.06902
11	0.08645	0.08429	0.08217	0.08010	0.07807	0.07609	0.07414	0.07224	0.07038	0.06679	0.06335	0.06007
12	0.07884	0.07667	0.07455	0.07248	0.07046	0.06848	0.06655	0.06466	0.06282	0.05928	0.05590	0.05269
13	0.07241	0.07024	0.06811	0.06604	0.06402	0.06206	0.06014	0.05827	0.05645	0.05296	0.04965	0.04652
14	0.06690	0.06472	0.06260	0.06053	0.05852	0.05657	0.05466	0.05282	0.05102	0.04758	0.04434	0.04129
15	0.06212	0.05994	0.05782	0.05576	0.05376	0.05182	0.04994	0.04811	0.04634	0.04296	0.03979	0.03682
16	0.05794	0.05576	0.05365	0.05159	0.04961	0.04768	0.04582	0.04401	0.04226	0.03895	0.03585	0.03297
17	0.05425	0.05207	0.04996	0.04792	0.04595	0.04404	0.04219	0.04041	0.03869	0.03544	0.03242	0.02962
18	0.05098	0.04880	0.04670	0.04467	0.04270	0.04081	0.03899	0.03723	0.03554	0.03235	0.02941	0.02670
19	0.04805	0.04587	0.04378	0.04176	0.03981	0.03794	0.03613	0.03440	0.03274	0.02962	0.02675	0.02412
20	0.04541	0.04324	0.04115	0.03914	0.03721	0.03536	0.03358	0.03187	0.03024	0.02718	0.02439	0.02185
21	0.04303	0.04086	0.03878	0.03678	0.03487	0.03303	0.03128	0.02960	0.02799	0.02500	0.02228	0.01983
22	0.04086	0.03870	0.03663	0.03464	0.03274	0.03093	0.02919	0.02754	0.02597	0.02304	0.02040	0.01803
23	0.03888	0.03673	0.03466	0.03269	0.03081	0.02901	0.02729	0.02568	0.02413	0.02127	0.01871	0.01642
24	0.03707	0.03492	0.03287	0.03091	0.02904	0.02727	0.02558	0.02398	0.02247	0.01967	0.01718	0.01497
25	0.03540	0.03326	0.03122	0.02927	0.02742	0.02567	0.02401	0.02243	0.02095	0.01822	0.01581	0.01367
26	0.03386	0.03173	0.02969	0.02776	0.02593	0.02420	0.02256	0.02102	0.01956	0.01690	0.01456	0.01250
27	0.03244	0.03031	0.02829	0.02637	0.02456	0.02285	0.02123	0.01971	0.01829	0.01569	0.01342	0.01144
28	0.03112	0.02900	0.02698	0.02508	0.02329	0.02160	0.02001	0.01852	0.01712	0.01459	0.01239	0.01048
29	0.02989	0.02777	0.02577	0.02389	0.02211	0.02044	0.01887	0.01741	0.01604	0.01357	0.01144	0.00961
30	0.02875	0.02663	0.02464	0.02277	0.02101	0.01937	0.01783	0.01639	0.01505	0.01264	0.01058	0.00882
31	0.02767	0.02557	0.02359	0.02173	0.01999	0.01837	0.01685	0.01544	0.01413	0.01179	0.00979	0.00810
32	0.02667	0.02364	0.02261	0.02076	0.01904	0.01744	0.01594	0.01456	0.01328	0.01100	0.00907	0.00745
33	0.02572	0.02364	0.02168	0.01985	0.01815	0.01657	0.01510	0.01374	0.01249	0.01027	0.00840	0.00685
34	0.02483	0.02276	0.02081	0.01900	0.01732	0.01575	0.01431	0.01298	0.01175	0.00959	0.00779	0.00630
35	0.02400	0.02193	0.02000	0.01820	0.01653	0.01499	0.01357	0.01227	0.01107	0.00897	0.00723	0.00580
36	0.02321	0.02115	0.01923	0.01745	0.01580	0.01428	0.01288	0.01160	0.01043	0.00839	0.00671	0.00534
37	0.02246	0.02041	0.01850	0.01674	0.01511	0.01361	0.01223	0.01098	0.00983	0.00785	0.00623	0.00492
38	0.02176	0.01971	0.01782	0.01607	0.01445	0.01298	0.01163	0.01040	0.00928	0.00735	0.00579	0.00453
39	0.02109	0.01905	0.01717	0.01543	0.01384	0.01238	0.01106	0.00985	0.00876	0.00689	0.00538	0.00418
40	0.02045	0.01842	0.01655	0.01483	0.01326	0.01182	0.01052	0.00934	0.00827	0.00646	0.00500	0.00386
41	0.01985	0.01783	0.01597	0.01426	0.01271	0.01129	0.01001	0.00886	0.00782	0.00605	0.00465	0.00356
42	0.01927	0.01726	0.01541	0.01372	0.01219	0.01079	0.00954	0.00840	0.00739	0.00568	0.00433	0.00328
43	0.01872	0.01672	0.01488	0.01321	0.01169	0.01032	0.00908	0.00798	0.00699	0.00533	0.00403	0.00303
44	0.01820	0.01621	0.01438	0.01273	0.01122	0.00987	0.00866	0.00758	0.00661	0.00500	0.00375	0.00280
45	0.01770	0.01571	0.01390	0.01226	0.01078	0.00945	0.00826	0.00720	0.00626	0.00470	0.00349	0.00258
46	0.01722	0.01525	0.01345	0.01182	0.01036	0.00905	0.00788	0.00684	0.00592	0.00441	0.00325	0.00238
47	0.01677	0.01480	0.01301	0.01140	0.00996	0.00866	0.00752	0.00650	0.00561	0.00414	0.00303	0.00220
48	0.01633	0.01437	0.01260	0.01100	0.00957	0.00830	0.00718	0.00618	0.00531	0.00389	0.00283	0.00204
49	0.01591	0.01396	0.01220	0.01062	0.00921	0.00796	0.00686	0.00588	0.00503	0.00366	0.00263	0.00188
50	0.01551	0.01357	0.01182	0.01025	0.00886	0.00763	0.00655	0.00560	0.00477	0.00344	0.00245	0.00174
51	0.01512	0.01319	0.01145	0.00990	0.00853	0.00732	0.00625	0.00533	0.00452	0.00323	0.00229	0.00161
52	0.01475	0.01283	0.01110	0.00957	0.00821	0.00702	0.00598	0.00507	0.00429	0.00304	0.00213	0.00148
53	0.01439	0.01248	0.01077	0.00925	0.00791	0.00674	0.00571	0.00483	0.00407	0.00286	0.00199	0.00137
54	0.01405	0.01215	0.01045	0.00894	0.00762	0.00647	0.00546	0.00460	0.00386	0.00269	0.00186	0.00127
55	0.01372	0.01183	0.01014	0.00865	0.00734	0.00621	0.00523	0.00438	0.00366	0.00253	0.00173	0.00117
56	0.01340	0.01152	0.00984	0.00837	0.00708	0.00596	0.00500	0.00418	0.00348	0.00238	0.00162	0.00108
57	0.01310	0.01122	0.00956	0.00810	0.00683	0.00573	0.00478	0.00398	0.00330	0.00224	0.00151	0.00100
58	0.01280	0.01093	0.00928	0.00784	0.00658	0.00550	0.00458	0.00379	0.00313	0.00211	0.00141	0.00093
59	0.01252	0.01066	0.00902	0.00759	0.00635	0.00529	0.00438	0.00362	0.00297	0.00199	0.00131	0.00086
60	0.01224	0.01039	0.00876	0.00735	0.00613	0.00508	0.00420	0.00345	0.00282	0.00187	0.00122	0.00079

Table 9.6

Series Present-Worth Factor $\dfrac{(1+i)^n - 1}{i(1+i)^n}$

n	0.01 (1%)	0.015 (1½%)	0.02 (2%)	0.025 (2½%)	0.03 (3%)	0.035 (3½%)	0.04 (4%)	0.045 (4½%)	0.05 (5%)	0.06 (6%)	0.07 (7%)	0.08 (8%)
1	0.99009	0.98522	0.98039	0.97560	0.97087	0.96618	0.96153	0.95693	0.95238	0.94339	0.93457	0.92592
2	1.97039	1.95588	1.94156	1.92742	1.91346	1.89969	1.88609	1.87266	1.85941	1.83339	1.80801	1.78326
3	2.94098	2.91220	2.88388	2.85602	2.82861	2.80163	2.77509	2.74896	2.72324	2.67301	2.62431	2.57709
4	3.90196	3.85438	3.80772	3.76197	3.71709	3.67307	3.62989	3.58752	3.54595	3.46510	3.38721	3.31212
5	4.85343	4.78264	4.71345	4.64582	4.57970	4.51505	4.45182	4.38997	4.32947	4.21236	4.10019	3.99271
6	5.79547	5.69718	5.60143	5.50812	5.41719	5.32855	5.24213	5.15787	5.07569	4.91732	4.76653	4.62287
7	6.72819	6.59821	6.47199	6.34939	6.23028	6.11454	6.00205	5.89270	5.78637	5.58238	5.38928	5.20637
8	7.65167	7.48592	7.32548	7.17013	7.01969	6.87395	6.73274	6.59588	6.46321	6.20979	5.97129	5.74663
9	8.56601	8.36051	8.16223	7.97086	7.78610	7.60768	7.43533	7.26879	7.10782	6.80169	6.51523	6.24688
10	9.47130	9.22218	8.98258	8.75206	8.53020	8.31660	8.11089	7.91271	7.72173	7.36008	7.02358	6.71008
11	10.36762	10.07111	9.78684	9.51420	9.25262	9.00155	8.76047	8.52891	8.30641	7.88687	7.49867	7.13896
12	11.25507	10.90750	10.57534	10.25776	9.95400	9.66333	9.38507	9.11858	8.86325	8.38384	7.94268	7.53607
13	12.13374	11.73153	11.34837	10.98318	10.63495	10.30273	9.98564	9.68285	9.39357	8.85268	8.35765	7.90377
14	13.00370	12.54338	12.10624	11.69091	11.29607	10.92052	10.56312	10.22282	9.89864	9.29498	8.74546	8.24403
15	13.86505	13.34323	12.84926	12.38137	11.93793	11.51741	11.11838	10.73954	10.37965	9.71224	9.10791	8.55947
16	14.71787	14.13126	13.57771	13.05500	12.56110	12.09411	11.65229	11.23401	10.83776	10.10589	9.44664	8.85136
17	15.56225	14.90764	14.29187	13.71219	13.16611	12.65132	12.16566	11.70719	11.27406	10.47725	9.76322	9.12163
18	16.39826	15.67256	14.99203	14.35336	13.75351	13.18968	12.65929	12.15999	11.68958	10.82760	10.05908	9.37188
19	17.22600	16.42616	15.67846	14.97889	14.32379	13.70983	13.13393	12.59329	12.08532	11.15811	10.33559	9.60359
20	18.04555	17.16863	16.35143	15.58916	14.87747	14.21240	13.59032	13.00793	12.46221	11.46992	10.59401	9.81814
21	18.85698	17.90013	17.01120	16.18454	15.41502	14.69797	14.02915	13.40472	12.82115	11.76407	10.83552	10.01680
22	19.66037	18.62082	17.65804	16.76541	15.93691	15.16712	14.45111	13.78442	13.16300	12.04158	11.06124	10.20074
23	20.45582	19.33086	18.29220	17.33211	16.44360	15.62041	14.85684	14.14777	13.48857	12.30337	11.27218	10.37105
24	21.24338	20.03040	18.91393	17.88498	16.93554	16.05836	15.24696	14.49547	13.79864	12.55035	11.46933	10.52875
25	22.02315	20.71961	19.52345	18.42437	17.41314	16.48151	15.62207	14.82920	14.09394	12.78335	11.65358	10.67477
26	22.79520	21.39863	20.12103	18.95061	17.87684	16.89035	15.98276	15.14661	14.37518	13.00316	11.82577	10.80997
27	23.55960	22.06761	20.70689	19.46401	18.32703	17.28536	16.32938	15.45130	14.64303	13.21053	11.98670	10.93516
28	24.31644	22.72671	21.28127	19.96488	18.76410	17.66701	16.66306	15.74287	14.89812	13.40616	12.13711	11.05107
29	25.06578	23.37607	21.84438	20.45354	19.18845	18.03576	16.98371	16.02188	15.14107	13.59072	12.27767	11.15840
30	25.80770	24.01583	22.39645	20.93029	19.60044	18.39204	17.29203	16.28888	15.37245	13.76483	12.40904	11.25778
31	26.54228	24.64614	22.93770	21.39540	20.00042	18.73627	17.58849	16.54439	15.59281	13.92908	12.53181	11.34979
32	27.26958	25.26713	23.46833	21.84917	20.38876	19.06886	17.87355	16.78889	15.80267	14.08404	12.64655	11.43499
33	27.98969	25.87895	23.98856	22.29188	20.76579	19.39020	18.14764	17.02286	16.00254	14.23022	12.75379	11.51388
34	28.70266	26.48172	24.49859	22.72378	21.13183	19.70068	18.41119	17.24675	16.19290	14.36814	12.85400	11.58693
35	29.40858	27.07559	24.99862	23.14515	21.48722	20.00066	18.66461	17.46101	16.37419	14.49824	12.94767	11.65456
36	30.10750	27.66068	25.48884	23.55625	21.83225	20.29049	18.90828	17.66604	16.54685	14.62098	13.03520	11.71719
37	30.79950	28.23712	25.96945	23.95731	22.16723	20.57052	19.14257	17.86223	16.71128	14.73678	13.11701	11.77517
38	31.48466	28.80505	26.44064	24.34860	22.49246	20.84108	19.36786	18.04999	16.86789	14.84601	13.19347	11.82886
39	32.16303	29.36458	26.90258	24.73034	22.80821	21.10249	19.58448	18.22965	17.01704	14.94907	13.26492	11.87858
40	32.83468	29.91584	27.35547	25.10277	23.11477	21.35507	19.79277	18.40158	17.15908	15.04629	13.33170	11.92461
41	33.49968	30.45896	27.79948	25.46612	23.41240	21.59910	19.99305	18.56610	17.29436	15.13801	13.39412	11.96723
42	34.15810	30.99405	28.23479	25.82060	23.70135	21.83488	20.18562	18.72354	17.42320	15.22454	13.45244	12.00669
43	34.81000	31.52123	28.66156	26.16644	23.98190	22.06268	20.37079	18.87421	17.54591	15.30617	13.50696	12.04323
44	35.45545	32.04062	29.07996	26.50384	24.25427	22.28279	20.54884	19.01838	17.66277	15.38318	13.55790	12.07707
45	36.09450	32.55233	29.49015	26.83302	24.51871	22.49545	20.72003	19.15634	17.77406	15.45583	13.60552	12.10840
46	36.72723	33.05648	29.89231	27.15416	24.77544	22.70091	20.88465	19.28837	17.88006	15.52436	13.65002	12.13740
47	37.35369	33.55319	30.28658	27.46748	25.02470	22.89943	21.04293	19.41470	17.98101	15.58902	13.69160	12.16426
48	37.97395	34.04255	30.67311	27.77315	25.26670	23.09124	21.19513	19.53560	18.07715	15.65002	13.73047	12.18913
49	38.58807	34.52468	31.05207	28.07136	25.50165	23.27656	21.34147	19.65129	18.16872	15.70757	13.76679	12.21216
50	39.19611	34.99968	31.42360	28.36231	25.72976	23.45561	21.48218	19.76200	18.25592	15.76186	13.80074	12.23348
51	39.79813	35.46767	31.78784	28.64615	25.95912	23.62861	21.61748	19.86795	18.33897	15.81307	13.83247	12.25322
52	40.39419	35.92874	32.14494	28.92308	26.16624	23.79576	21.74758	19.96933	18.41807	15.86139	13.86212	12.27150
53	40.98435	36.38053	32.49505	29.19324	26.37499	23.95726	21.87267	20.06634	18.49340	15.90697	13.88983	12.28843
54	41.56866	36.83053	32.83828	29.45682	26.57766	24.11329	21.99295	20.15918	18.56514	15.94997	13.91573	12.30410
55	42.14719	37.27146	33.17478	29.71397	26.77442	24.26405	22.10861	20.24802	18.63347	15.99054	13.93993	12.31861
56	42.71999	37.70587	33.50469	29.96485	26.96546	24.40971	22.21981	20.33303	18.69854	16.02881	13.96255	12.33205
57	43.28712	38.13387	33.82813	30.20961	27.15093	24.55044	22.32674	20.41438	18.76051	16.06491	13.98370	12.34449
58	43.81863	38.55553	34.14523	30.44840	27.33100	24.68642	22.42956	20.49223	18.81954	16.09898	14.00345	12.35601
59	44.40458	38.97097	34.45610	30.68137	27.50583	24.81779	22.52842	20.56673	18.87575	16.13111	14.02192	12.36667
60	44.95503	39.38026	34.76088	30.90865	27.67556	24.94473	22.62348	20.63802	18.92928	16.16142	14.03918	12.37655

Table 9.7

Capital-Recovery Factor $\dfrac{i(1+i)^n}{(1+i)^n - 1}$

n	0.01 (1%)	0.015 (1½%)	0.02 (2%)	0.025 (2½%)	0.03 (3%)	0.035 (3½%)	0.04 (4%)	0.045 (4½%)	0.05 (5%)	0.06 (6%)	0.07 (7%)	0.08 (8%)
1	1.01000	1.01500	1.02000	1.02500	1.03000	1.03500	1.04000	1.04500	1.05000	1.06000	1.07000	1.08000
2	0.50751	0.51127	0.51504	0.51882	0.52261	0.52640	0.53019	0.53399	0.53780	0.54543	0.55309	0.56076
3	0.34002	0.34338	0.34675	0.35013	0.35353	0.35693	0.36034	0.36377	0.36720	0.37410	0.38105	0.38803
4	0.25628	0.25944	0.26262	0.26581	0.26902	0.27225	0.27549	0.27874	0.28201	0.28859	0.29522	0.30192
5	0.20603	0.20908	0.21215	0.21524	0.21835	0.22148	0.22462	0.22779	0.23097	0.23739	0.24389	0.25045
6	0.17254	0.17552	0.17852	0.18154	0.18459	0.18766	0.19076	0.19387	0.19701	0.20336	0.20979	0.21631
7	0.14862	0.15155	0.15451	0.15749	0.16050	0.16354	0.16660	0.16970	0.17281	0.17913	0.18555	0.19207
8	0.13069	0.13358	0.13650	0.13946	0.14245	0.14547	0.14852	0.15160	0.15472	0.16103	0.16746	0.17401
9	0.11674	0.11960	0.12251	0.12545	0.12843	0.13144	0.13449	0.13757	0.14069	0.14702	0.15348	0.16007
10	0.10558	0.10843	0.11132	0.11425	0.11723	0.12024	0.12329	0.12637	0.12950	0.13586	0.14237	0.14902
11	0.09645	0.09929	0.10217	0.10510	0.10808	0.11109	0.11414	0.11724	0.12038	0.12679	0.13335	0.14007
12	0.08884	0.09167	0.09455	0.09748	0.10046	0.10348	0.10655	0.10966	0.11282	0.11927	0.12590	0.13269
13	0.08241	0.08524	0.08811	0.09104	0.09403	0.09706	0.10014	0.10327	0.10645	0.11296	0.11965	0.12652
14	0.07690	0.07972	0.08260	0.08553	0.08853	0.09157	0.09466	0.09782	0.10102	0.10758	0.11434	0.12129
15	0.07212	0.07494	0.07782	0.08076	0.08377	0.08682	0.08994	0.09311	0.09634	0.10296	0.10979	0.11682
16	0.06794	0.07076	0.07365	0.07659	0.07961	0.08268	0.08582	0.08901	0.09226	0.09895	0.10585	0.11297
17	0.06425	0.06707	0.06996	0.07292	0.07595	0.07904	0.08219	0.08541	0.08869	0.09544	0.10242	0.10962
18	0.06098	0.06380	0.06670	0.06967	0.07271	0.07581	0.07899	0.08223	0.08554	0.09235	0.09941	0.10670
19	0.05805	0.06087	0.06378	0.06676	0.06981	0.07294	0.07613	0.07940	0.08274	0.08962	0.09675	0.10412
20	0.05541	0.05824	0.06115	0.06414	0.06722	0.07036	0.07358	0.07687	0.08024	0.08718	0.09439	0.10185
21	0.05303	0.05586	0.05878	0.06178	0.06487	0.06803	0.07128	0.07460	0.07799	0.08500	0.09228	0.09983
22	0.05086	0.05370	0.05663	0.05964	0.06275	0.06593	0.06919	0.07254	0.07597	0.08304	0.09040	0.09803
23	0.04888	0.05173	0.05466	0.05769	0.06081	0.06401	0.06730	0.07068	0.07413	0.08127	0.08871	0.09642
24	0.04707	0.04992	0.05287	0.05591	0.05905	0.06227	0.06558	0.06898	0.07247	0.07967	0.08718	0.09497
25	0.04540	0.04826	0.05122	0.05427	0.05743	0.06067	0.06401	0.06743	0.07095	0.07822	0.08581	0.09367
26	0.04386	0.04673	0.04969	0.05276	0.05594	0.05920	0.06256	0.06602	0.06956	0.07690	0.08456	0.09250
27	0.04244	0.04531	0.04829	0.05137	0.05456	0.05785	0.06123	0.06471	0.06829	0.07569	0.08342	0.09144
28	0.04112	0.04400	0.04698	0.05008	0.05329	0.05660	0.06001	0.06352	0.06712	0.07459	0.08239	0.09048
29	0.03989	0.04277	0.04577	0.04889	0.05211	0.05544	0.05887	0.06241	0.06604	0.07357	0.08144	0.08962
30	0.03874	0.04163	0.04464	0.04777	0.05102	0.05437	0.05783	0.06139	0.06505	0.07264	0.08058	0.08882
31	0.03767	0.04057	0.04357	0.04673	0.05000	0.05337	0.05686	0.06044	0.06413	0.07179	0.07979	0.08811
32	0.03667	0.03957	0.04261	0.04576	0.04905	0.05244	0.05594	0.05956	0.06328	0.07100	0.07907	0.08745
33	0.03573	0.03864	0.04168	0.04485	0.04816	0.05157	0.05510	0.05874	0.06249	0.07027	0.07840	0.08685
34	0.03483	0.03776	0.04081	0.04400	0.04732	0.05075	0.05431	0.05798	0.06175	0.06959	0.07779	0.08630
35	0.03400	0.03693	0.04000	0.04320	0.04654	0.04999	0.05357	0.05727	0.06107	0.06897	0.07723	0.08580
36	0.03321	0.03615	0.03923	0.04245	0.04580	0.04928	0.05288	0.05660	0.06043	0.06839	0.07671	0.08534
37	0.03246	0.03541	0.03850	0.04174	0.04511	0.04861	0.05223	0.05598	0.05983	0.06785	0.07623	0.08492
38	0.03176	0.03471	0.03782	0.04107	0.04446	0.04798	0.05163	0.05540	0.05928	0.06735	0.07579	0.08453
39	0.03109	0.03405	0.03717	0.04043	0.04384	0.04738	0.05106	0.05485	0.05876	0.06689	0.07538	0.08418
40	0.03045	0.03342	0.03655	0.03983	0.04326	0.04682	0.05052	0.05434	0.05828	0.06646	0.07500	0.08386
41	0.02985	0.03283	0.03597	0.03926	0.04271	0.04629	0.05001	0.05386	0.05782	0.06605	0.07465	0.08356
42	0.02927	0.03226	0.03541	0.03872	0.04219	0.04579	0.04954	0.05339	0.05739	0.06568	0.07433	0.08328
43	0.02872	0.03172	0.03488	0.03821	0.04169	0.04532	0.04908	0.05298	0.05699	0.06533	0.07403	0.08303
44	0.02820	0.03121	0.03438	0.03773	0.04122	0.04487	0.04866	0.05258	0.05661	0.06500	0.07375	0.08280
45	0.02770	0.03071	0.03390	0.03726	0.04078	0.04445	0.04826	0.05220	0.05626	0.06470	0.07349	0.08258
46	0.02722	0.03025	0.03345	0.03682	0.04036	0.04405	0.04788	0.05184	0.05592	0.06441	0.07325	0.08238
47	0.02677	0.02980	0.03301	0.03640	0.03996	0.04366	0.04752	0.05150	0.05561	0.06414	0.07303	0.08220
48	0.02633	0.02937	0.03260	0.03600	0.03958	0.04330	0.04718	0.05118	0.05531	0.06389	0.07283	0.08204
49	0.02591	0.02896	0.03220	0.03562	0.03921	0.04296	0.04686	0.05088	0.05503	0.06366	0.07263	0.08188
50	0.02551	0.02857	0.03182	0.03525	0.03887	0.04263	0.04655	0.05060	0.05477	0.06344	0.07245	0.08174
51	0.02512	0.02819	0.03145	0.03490	0.03853	0.04232	0.04625	0.05033	0.05452	0.06323	0.07229	0.08161
52	0.02475	0.02783	0.03110	0.03457	0.03821	0.04202	0.04598	0.05007	0.05429	0.06304	0.07213	0.08148
53	0.02439	0.02748	0.03077	0.03425	0.03791	0.04174	0.04571	0.04983	0.05407	0.06286	0.07199	0.08137
54	0.02405	0.02715	0.03045	0.03394	0.03762	0.04147	0.04546	0.04960	0.05386	0.06269	0.07186	0.08127
55	0.02372	0.02683	0.03014	0.03365	0.03734	0.04122	0.04523	0.04938	0.05366	0.06253	0.07173	0.08117
56	0.02340	0.02652	0.02984	0.03337	0.03708	0.04096	0.04500	0.04918	0.05348	0.06238	0.07162	0.08108
57	0.02310	0.02622	0.02956	0.03310	0.03683	0.04073	0.04478	0.04898	0.05330	0.06224	0.07151	0.08100
58	0.02280	0.02593	0.02928	0.03284	0.03658	0.04050	0.04458	0.04879	0.05313	0.06211	0.07141	0.08093
59	0.02252	0.02566	0.02902	0.03259	0.03635	0.04029	0.04438	0.04862	0.05297	0.06199	0.07131	0.08086
60	0.02224	0.02539	0.02876	0.03235	0.03613	0.04008	0.04420	0.04845	0.05282	0.06187	0.07122	0.08079

Table 9.8
Monthly Payment per Dollar of Mortgage Loan

Mortgage Period

Annual Interest Rate	15 Years (180 Payments)	20 Years (240 Payments)	25 Years (300 Payments)	30 Years (360 Payments)
7.50	0.00927012	0.00805593	0.00738991	0.00699214
7.75	0.00941275	0.00820948	0.00755328	0.00716412
8.00	0.00955652	0.00836440	0.00771816	0.00733764
8.25	0.00970140	0.00852065	0.00788450	0.00751266
8.50	0.00984739	0.00867823	0.00805227	0.00768913
8.75	0.00999448	0.00883710	0.00822143	0.00786700
9.00	0.01014266	0.00899725	0.00839196	0.00804622
9.25	0.01029192	0.00915866	0.00856381	0.00822675
9.50	0.01044224	0.00932131	0.00873696	0.00840854
9.75	0.01059362	0.00948516	0.00891137	0.00859154
10.00	0.01074605	0.00965021	0.00908700	0.00877571

CHAPTER TEST

1 A principal of $20,000 has been invested at an interest rate of 8 percent per year compounded semiannually. If the principal is invested for 8 years, determine the compound amount at the end of this period.

2 Real estate prices in one locality have been increasing at a rate of 8 percent per year compounded annually. A house which sells for $60,000 today would have sold for what price 3 years ago?

3 Quarterly deposits of $2,500 are to be made in an account which earns interest at the rate of 6 percent per year compounded quarterly.

(*a*) To what sum will the investment grow by the time of the fortieth deposit?

(*b*) How much interest will be earned during this period?

4 A sinking fund is to be established to repay debts totaling $20,000. The debts come due in 5 years. If interest can be earned at the rate of 10 percent per year compounded semiannually, what semiannual deposit will be required to accumulate the $20,000 (assume the first deposit is made in 6 months)? How much interest will be earned on these deposits?

5 Given $25,000 today, determine the equivalent series of 12 annual payments which could be generated beginning in 1 year. Assume interest of 7 percent per year compounded annually.

6 The nominal interest rate on an investment is 8 percent per year. Determine the effective annual rate if interest is compounded quarterly.

7 A mortgage loan of $40,000 is available at an annual interest rate of 9 percent. What is the difference between the monthly mortgage payments if the loan is for 20 years versus 30 years?

NONLINEAR FUNCTIONS

10

CHAPTER OBJECTIVES After reading this chapter, you should understand the fundamental differences between linear and nonlinear functions; you should be familiar with the algebraic and graphical characteristics of *quadratic functions, exponential functions*, and simple *logarithmic functions*; you should have the ability to sketch the graph of these and other nonlinear functions; and you will be acquainted with selected applications of quadratic and exponential functions.

Until this point, our attentions have been focused primarily on linear (versus nonlinear) mathematics. However, as useful and convenient as the linear mathematics has been, there are a variety of phenomena which are not linear and cannot be adequately approximated by using linear functions. In this chapter we will be introduced to some of the more common nonlinear functional forms. The purposes of this chapter are to acquaint you with the characteristics of these nonlinear forms, to create insight which will allow you to anticipate the behavior of these types of functions, and to illustrate a few areas of application in which nonlinear functions are appropriate.

WHEN LINEAR FUNCTIONS ARE INAPPROPRIATE

Table 10.1

x	y	Δx	Δy
0	0		
1	1	1	1
2	4	1	3
3	9	1	5

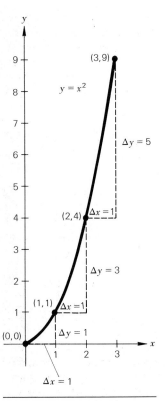

FIGURE 10.1

Any function which does not graph as a straight line in two dimensions or as a plane in three dimensions can be thought of as being nonlinear. For our purposes, *nonlinear functions* can be thought of as mathematical functions which graph as curved lines in two dimensions and as curved surfaces in three dimensions. Aside from this geometric point of view, we can think of the differences between linear and nonlinear functions in terms of "response." Given the general function

$$y = f(x) \tag{10.1}$$

if $f(x)$ is a linear function, the dependent variable y changes in direct proportion to the change in the independent variable x. For example, in the linear function

$$y = -6x + 10 \tag{10.2}$$

y *decreases* by 6 units for every unit that x increases. The slope of a linear function indicates the *constant* rate of change in the dependent variable given a unit increase in the independent variable.

For nonlinear functions, the response of the dependent variable is not in direct or exact proportion to changes in the independent variable. To illustrate, if

$$y = x^2 \tag{10.3}$$

the dependent variable y is computed by squaring the value of the independent variable x. Substituting a few values for x into Eq. (10.3), we can see from Table 10.1 that as x increases from 0 to 1, the change in x, Δx (read "delta x"), and the change in y, Δy (read "delta y"), are the same. But as x increases from 1 to 2, $\Delta x = 1$ and $\Delta y = 3$. Similarly, as x increases from 2 to 3, y increases by 5 units. The changes in y, Δy, are neither constant nor in *direct* proportion to the changes in x, Δx. Figure 10.1 illustrates these responses.

There are many situations in which the relationship between variables is nonlinear. A good example of this from economics is the *law of diminishing returns*.

An increase in some inputs relative to other fixed inputs will cause total output to increase; but after a point the extra output resulting from the same additions of extra inputs is likely to become less and less.†

Example 10.1

Law of Diminishing Returns An example of the law of diminishing returns might be the response of sales of a product to changes in the number of salespeople employed or to the amount of advertising expenditures. Suppose that a new company has defined a certain geographic area to be a pilot sales district for testing new products. One of their concerns is the number of salespeople to assign to the district.

---

† Paul A. Samuelson, *Economics: An Introductory Analysis*, 5th ed., McGraw-Hill Book Company, New York, 1961, p. 26.

Salespeople	Dollar Sales	Additional Sales	Table
0	0	0	10.2
1	$100,000	$100,000	
2	210,000	110,000	
3	330,000	120,000	
4	430,000	100,000	
5	500,000	70,000	
6	530,000	30,000	
7	540,000	10,000	

Company analysts suspect that sales (in dollars) will depend upon the number of salespeople assigned to the district. Company analysts have projected sales for different numbers of salespeople, as indicated in Table 10.2.

If we think of the number of salespersons as being the *input* and sales as the *output,* sales increase with each additional salesperson. However, if we examine the additional sales associated with each additional salesperson, the *additional sales* increase up to the third salesperson but begin to decrease thereafter. We can state that the point at which the fourth salesperson is added to the district is the point of *diminishing returns,* the point at which the extra or marginal output (sales) associated with additional inputs (salespeople) decreases compared with the marginal returns of previous inputs.

Economists have spent much time studying the laws and behavior of *supply* and *demand.* As discussed in Chap. 5, one theory states that a primary determinant of the quantity demanded of certain commodities is the price charged for the commodity. A general functional representation of this relationship is

$$q = f(p) \qquad (10.4)$$

where q = number of units demanded

$\quad p$ = price per unit

In some cases the relationship between price and quantity demanded is linear, or it can be reasonably approximated by a linear function. We discussed this case in Chap. 5. In other instances, the relationship is nonlinear and cannot be adequately approximated using a linear function. Figure 10.2 illustrates a demand function for the sale of lobster in the New England region. The smooth curve is an approximation to data points which were gathered in a consumer expenditure poll. The relationship between retail price and annual per capita consumption is obviously nonlinear.

The question you should be asking yourself is, When do you use a linear function and when do you use a nonlinear function to represent the relationship between variables? The answer to this question depends on whether the logical structure of how the variables are interrelated is clear and explicit. In the case where the structure is clear, the mathematical representation should take the exact form of the relation-

Example 10.2

FIGURE 10.2
Demand relationship for lobster

ship. A good example of this situation is the determination of the total revenue function associated with selling a product. If the firm sells each unit for the same price p, the total revenue R from selling q units is determined by multiplying the price times the quantity, or

$$R = pq$$

In many other cases, the way in which variables are interrelated is not exactly known. In these instances, it is first necessary to collect relevant data by using an appropriate sampling procedure. An example of this type of data gathering occurred in Example 10.2. Sample data points were found by surveying consumers about the quantities of lobster they expected to purchase given different retail prices. Once the data have been gathered, the objective is to identify the mathematical function which best "fits" the data. Different functional forms, linear and nonlinear, may be fit to the same set of data points and some determination reached as to which form most accurately approximates the relationship suggested by the data points. Figure 10.3 illustrates a set of data points which have been fit with three different functions, two linear and one nonlinear. There are different criteria which may be used to determine which function is "best." The methods can vary from simply "eyeballing" a curve to fit the data points to more rigorous statistical procedures such as regression analysis. Once the mathematical function (model) has been identified, the analysis of the model can begin.

10.2

QUADRATIC FUNCTIONS AND THEIR CHARACTERISTICS

One of the more common nonlinear functional forms is the quadratic function.

FIGURE 10.3

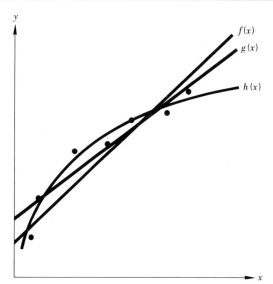

Mathematical Form

DEFINITION
A *quadratic function* involving the independent variable x and the dependent variable y has the general form

$$y = f(x) = ax^2 + bx + c \qquad (10.5)$$

where a, b, and c are constants and $a \neq 0$.

Can you reason why the coefficient of x^2 cannot equal 0? If $a = 0$ and b and c are nonzero, Eq. (10.5) becomes

$$y = bx + c$$

which is a linear function. As long as $a \neq 0$, b and c can assume any values.

Which of the following functions are quadratic functions?

Example 10.3

(*a*) $y = f(x) = 5x^2$ 　　　　(*b*) $u = f(v) = -10v^2 - 6$
(*c*) $y = f(x) = 7x - 2$ 　　　　(*d*) $g = f(h) = -6$
(*e*) $y = f(x) = x^2 + 10x$ 　　　　(*f*) $y = f(x) = 6x^2 - 40x + 15$
(*g*) $y = f(x) = 2x^3 + 4x^2 - 2x + 5$

Solution

(*a*) $y = 5x^2$ is a quadratic function. According to the general form of Eq. (10.5), $a = 5$, $b = 0$, and $c = 0$.
(*b*) $u = -10v^2 - 6$ is a quadratic function where, according to Eq. (10.5), $a = -10$, $b = 0$, and $c = -6$.
(*c*) $y = 7x - 2$ is *not* a quadratic function since there is no x^2 term, or $a = 0$.
(*d*) $g = -6$ is not a quadratic function for the same reason as presented in (*c*).
(*e*) $y = x^2 + 10x$ is a quadratic function where $a = 1$, $b = 10$, and $c = 0$.
(*f*) $y = 6x^2 - 40x + 15$ is a quadratic function where $a = 6$, $b = -40$, and $c = 15$.
(*g*) $y = 2x^3 + 4x^2 - 2x + 5$ is not a quadratic function because it does not have the form of Eq. (10.5). More explicitly, it is not a quadratic because it contains a third-degree term—$2x^3$.

Graphical Representation

All quadratic functions having the form of Eq. (10.5) graph as *parabolas*. Figure 10.4 illustrates two parabolas which have different orientations. A parabola which "opens" upward, such as that in Fig. 10.4*a*, is said to be *concave up*. A parabola which "opens" downward, such as that in Fig. 10.4*b*, is said to be *concave down*.† The point at which a parabola

† A more detailed discussion of the *concavity* of functions will be presented in Chap. 12.

Axis of symmetry

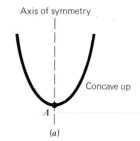

Concave up

A

(a)

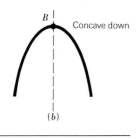

B

Concave down

(b)

FIGURE 10.4

either "bottoms out" when it is concave up or "peaks out" when it is concave down is called the *vertex* of the parabola. Points *A* and *B* are the respective *vertices* for the two parabolas in Fig. 10.4.

NOTE
It can be shown that the coordinates of the vertex of a parabola are

$$\left(\frac{-b}{2a}, \frac{4ac - b^2}{4a}\right)$$

where *a*, *b*, and *c* are the parameters of Eq. (10.5).

The dashed vertical line which passes through the vertex of each parabola is an imaginary line called the *axis of symmetry*. The parabola is divided into two halves which are symmetrical about the axis of symmetry. That is, if you fold one side of the parabola using the axis of symmetry as a hinge, you will find that the two halves are mirror images of each other. The axis of symmetry is described by the equation $x = b/(2a)$ where *a* and *b* are parameters in Eq. (10.5).

Example 10.4

Sketch the quadratic function $y = f(x) = x^2$.

Solution

To sketch any mathematical function which involves two variables, it is necessary to define the set of points which satisfy the function. We can describe this set as

$$S = \{(x, y)|y = x^2\}$$

Sample values for *x* and the corresponding values for *y* are shown in Fig. 10.5 along with the sketch of the parabola.

FIGURE 10.5

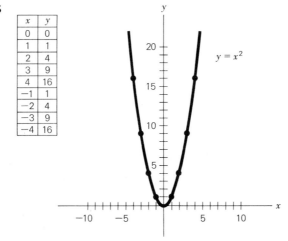

x	y
0	0
1	1
2	4
3	9
4	16
−1	1
−2	4
−3	9
−4	16

$y = x^2$

For this quadratic function, $a = 1$, $b = 0$, and $c = 0$. The x coordinate of the vertex is

$$x = \frac{-b}{2a} = -\frac{0}{2(1)} = 0$$

and the y coordinate is

$$y = \frac{4ac - b^2}{4a} = \frac{4(1)(0) - (0)^2}{4(1)} = 0$$

Given that $(0, 0)$ is the vertex, the y axis is the axis of symmetry. You can verify the symmetry about the y axis by noting that equal movements along the x axis to either side of the vertex result in the same values for y. For example, note that the value of y is the same when x equals $+1$ or -1, $+2$ or -2, $+3$ or -3, and $+4$ or -4.

Figure 10.5 is only a *sketch* of the function. The more data points identified and plotted, the more accurate the sketch will be for any function.

Special Insights to Sketching Quadratic Functions

Given the general quadratic form of Eq. (10.5), the concavity of the parabola can be determined by the sign of the coefficient on the x^2 term. If *a is positive*, the function will graph as a parabola which is *concave up*. If *a is negative*, the parabola is *concave down*.

What is the concavity of the parabola representing each quadratic function identified in Example 10.3?

Example 10.5

(*a*) The graph of $y = 5x^2$ is concave *up* since $a = +5$.
(*b*) The graph of $u = -10v^2 - 6$ is concave *down* since $a = -10$.
(*c*) The graph of $y = x^2 + 10x$ is concave *up* since $a = +1$.
(*d*) The graph of $y = 6x^2 - 40x + 15$ is concave *up* since $a = +6$.

Solution

Knowing the concavity and a few other key data points can allow for a quick and easy sketch of the parabola which represents a quadratic function. If we know the concavity, also knowing (1) the location of the vertex, (2) the y intercept, and (3) the x intercept(s) for the function can allow for a rough sketch of the function.

The *y intercept* for a function was defined in Chap. 3 as the point at which the function crosses the y axis. The y coordinate of the y intercept is the value of y when x equals 0, or $f(0)$.

What are the y intercepts for the quadratic functions in Example 10.5?

Example 10.6

(*a*) For $y = 5x^2$, $f(0) = 0$, or the y intercept occurs at $(0, 0)$.
(*b*) For $u = -10v^2 - 6$, $f(0) = -6$, or the u intercept occurs at $(0, -6)$.

Solution

(c) For $y = x^2$, $f(0) = 0$, or the y intercept occurs at $(0, 0)$.
(d) For $y = 6x^2 - 40x + 15$, $f(0) = 15$, or the y intercept occurs at $(0, 15)$.

The *x intercept* for a function was also defined in Chap. 3 as the point(s) at which the function crosses the x axis. Equivalently, the x intercept represents the value(s) of x when y equals 0. For quadratic functions, there may be one x intercept, two x intercepts, or *no x* intercept. These possibilities are shown in Fig. 10.6.

There are a number of ways of determining the x intercepts for a quadratic function if any exist. The x intercepts are found by determining the roots of the equation

$$ax^2 + bx + c = 0 \qquad (10.6)$$

Two methods of determining the roots to Eq. (10.6) were discussed in Sec. 0.6. These methods are illustrated in the following example.

Example 10.7

Determining Roots by Factoring Some quadratic functions can be factored (Sec. 0.3) into either two binomials or a binomial and a monomial. If a quadratic function can be factored, it is an easy matter to determine the roots of Eq. (10.6). For example, the values of x which satisfy the quadratic equation

$$6x^2 - 2x = 0 \qquad (10.7)$$

can be determined by first factoring $2x$ from the expression on the left-hand side of the equation, yielding

$$(2x)(3x - 1) = 0 \qquad (10.8)$$

By setting each factor equal to 0, the roots of the equation are identified as

$$2x = 0 \quad \text{or} \quad \boldsymbol{x = 0}$$

and $\qquad 3x - 1 = 0 \quad \text{or} \quad \boldsymbol{x = \frac{1}{3}}$

Similarly, the values of x satisfying the equation

$$x^2 + 6x + 9 = 0$$

FIGURE 10.6

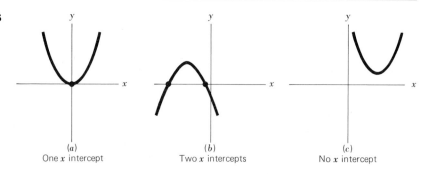

(a)
One x intercept

(b)
Two x intercepts

(c)
No x intercept

are found by factoring the left side of the equation, yielding

$$(x + 3)(x + 3) = 0$$

When the factors are set equal to 0, it is found that the only value which satisfies the equation is $x = -3$.

When a quadratic function cannot be factored, the approach illustrated in Example 10.7 fails to identify the roots of the quadratic equation. Applying the *quadratic formula* will *always* identify the roots of a quadratic equation *if any exist*.

ALGEBRA FLASHBACK

The *quadratic formula*, which is used to identify roots of equations of the form of Eq. (10.6), is

$$x = \frac{-b \pm \sqrt{b^2 - 4ac}}{2a}$$

Recall from Sec. 0.6 that (1) if $b^2 - 4ac > 0$, there will be two real roots; (2) if $b^2 - 4ac = 0$, there will be one real root; and (3) if $b^2 - 4ac < 0$, there will be no real roots

---

Given the quadratic function $y = f(x) = x^2 - x - 3.75$, the x intercepts occur when $x^2 - x - 3.75 = 0$. Referring to Eq. (10.6), we get $a = 1$, $b = -1$, $c = -3.75$. Substituting these values of a, b, and c into the quadratic formula, we compute the roots of the equation as

Example 10.8

$$x = \frac{-(-1) \pm \sqrt{(-1)^2 - 4(1)(-3.75)}}{2(1)}$$

$$= \frac{1 \pm \sqrt{1 + 15}}{2}$$

$$= \frac{1 \pm \sqrt{16}}{2}$$

$$= \frac{1 \pm 4}{2}$$

or, using the plus sign, we have

$$x = \tfrac{5}{2} = 2.5$$

Using the minus sign gives

$$x = -\tfrac{3}{2} = -1.5$$

Thus, there are two values of x which satisfy the quadratic equation, and the parabola representing the quadratic function would cross the x axis at two locations: $x = 2.5$ and $x = -1.5$. This case is similar to that of Fig. 10.6b.

Let's use the information developed thus far to illustrate how the sketch of a quadratic function can be made when its concavity, the location of the vertex, the y intercept, and the x intercept(s) are known.

Example 10.9

Sketch the quadratic function $y = f(x) = 3x^2 + 6x - 45$.

Solution

Since $a = 3$ is greater than 0, we can immediately state that the function will graph as a parabola which is concave up. The y intercept equals $f(0)$, or -45. The x intercepts can be identified by factoring as indicated:

$$3x^2 + 6x - 45 = 0$$

or

$$(3x - 9)(x + 5) = 0$$

Setting each factor equal to 0 yields

$$3x - 9 = 0$$
$$\boldsymbol{x = 3}$$

when

and

$$x + 5 = 0$$

when

$$\boldsymbol{x = -5}$$

Thus, the parabola crosses the x axis where $x = 3$ and $x = -5$. The coordinates of the vertex are

$$x = \frac{-b}{2a} = \frac{-6}{2(3)} = -1$$

and

$$y = \frac{4ac - b^2}{4a} = \frac{4(3)(-45) - (6)^2}{4(3)}$$

$$= \frac{-540 - 36}{12}$$

$$= \frac{-576}{12}$$

$$= -48$$

FIGURE 10.7

The parabola is sketched in Fig. 10.7.

NOTE
Because of the symmetry of parabolas, whenever a parabola has two x intercepts, the x coordinate of the vertex will always be midway between the x intercepts. Whenever the parabola has one x intercept, the vertex occurs at that point.

In this example, the x coordinate of the vertex will lie halfway between $x = -5$ and $x = 3$, or at $x = -1$, which is the same value as that determined by formula.

Determining the Equation of Quadratic Functions

In Exercise 5.46 we saw that the parameters a, b, and c of a quadratic function can be determined if the coordinates are known for three points which lie on the graph of the function. When the coordinates of the three points are substituted into Eq. (10.5), the result is a system of three equations stated in terms of a, b, and c. The values for these parameters can be found by solving the equations simultaneously. Example 10.10 illustrates this procedure by solving Exercise 5.46.

Determine the equation of the quadratic function which passes through the points $(1, 8)$, $(3, 20)$, and $(-2, 5)$.

Example 10.10

Substituting the coordinates of the three points into Eq. (10.5) yields

Solution

$$
\begin{array}{lll}
8 = a(1)^2 + b(1) + c & or & a + b + c = 8 \quad (10.9) \\
20 = a(3)^2 + b(3) + c & or & 9a + 3b + c = 20 \quad (10.10) \\
5 = a(-2)^2 + b(-2) + c & or & 4a - 2b + c = 5 \quad (10.11)
\end{array}
$$

Verify that the solution of the resulting system of equations is $a = 1$, $b = 2$, and $c = 5$. The function which passes through the three given points is

$$y = x^2 + 2x + 5$$

Polynomial Functions

Linear and quadratic functions are examples of the general set of functions called *polynomial functions*.

DEFINITION
A *polynomial function* involving the independent variable x and the dependent variable y has the general form

$$y = f(x)$$

where
$$f(x) = a_n x^n + a_{n-1} x^{n-1} + \cdots + a_1 x_1 + a_0 \qquad (10.12)$$

a_j **equals a real number for each** j, **and** n **is a positive integer.**

Polynomial functions can be characterized by the *degree* of the polynomial. The degree of a polynomial is the exponent of the highest powered term in the expression. Equation (10.12) would be considered an *nth-degree* polynomial function provided that $a_n \neq 0$. A linear function is a *first-degree* polynomial function, whereas a quadratic function is a *second-degree* function. A *third-degree* function such as

$$y = x^3 - 2x^2 + 5x + 10$$

is referred to as a *cubic function*.

The graphs of polynomial functions of degree three and higher can be considerably less predictable than linear and quadratic functions. The higher the degree of a function, the greater the chance that the graph of the function will have numerous peaks and valleys. Most of the applications in this book will involve functions which are of degree three or less. However, in studying differential calculus and the behavior of functions, we will see functions which are of degree greater than three. Consequently, you should sketch a few of the polynomial functions in Exercises 10.18 to 10.25. In Chap. 12 procedures will be presented which facilitate graphing polynomial functions.

Follow-up Exercises

In Exercises 10.1 to 10.8 determine which functions are quadratic and identify values for the parameters a, b, and c.

10.1 $f(x) = -3x^3 + 2x^2 + 10$ **10.2** $f(v) = v^2 - 6$
10.3 $f(s) = -s^2 + 6x - \frac{1}{2}$ **10.4** $f(x) = 4x - 10$
10.5 $f(n) = n^2/3$ **10.6** $f(t) = t^2/4 - t/7$
10.7 $f(x) = 40x^2 - 6x$ **10.8** $f(t) = (2t^{1/2})^2 + 3t - 10$

In Exercises 10.9 to 10.14, determine the concavity of the quadratic function, its y intercept, its x intercepts if there are any, and the coordinates of the vertex. Sketch the parabola.

10.9 $y = f(x) = -2x^2$ **10.10** $y = f(x) = -x^2 + 3x - 2$
10.11 $y = f(x) = 3x^2 - 4x + 2$ **10.12** $y = f(x) = x^2 - 3x - 18$
10.13 $y = f(x) = -x^2 - 10$ **10.14** $y = f(x) = 2x^2 - 5x - 3$

10.15 Sketch the following three quadratic functions, making note of the values of $|a|$ for each and the relative steepness of the three parabolas.

$$y = x^2 \qquad y = 0.01x^2 \qquad y = 100x^2$$

10.16 Determine the equation of the quadratic function which passes through the points $(0, -4)$, $(5, -29)$, and $(-2, -8)$.
10.17 Determine the equation of the quadratic function which passes through the points $(1, 6)$, $(-2, -3)$, and $(3, 22)$.

In Exercises 10.18 to 10.25, sketch the polynomial function and determine the degree of the function.

10.18 $y = f(x) = x^3$ **10.19** $y = f(x) = -x^3$
10.20 $y = f(x) = x^4$ **10.21** $y = f(x) = -x^4$
10.22 $y = f(x) = x^5$ **10.23** $y = f(x) = -x^5$
10.24 $y = f(x) = x^3 - 10$ **10.25** $y = f(x) = x^4 + 20$

10.3   QUADRATIC FUNCTIONS: APPLICATIONS

In this section some examples will be presented which will illustrate a few areas of application of quadratic functions.

Example 10.11 **Quadratic Revenue Functions** Often the demand for the product of a firm can be described as a function of the price which the firm charges for the product. Assume that a firm has determined that the quantity demanded of one of its products depends on the price charged. The function describing this relationship is

$$q = f(p)$$

or

$$q = 1,500 - 50p$$

where q equals the quantity demanded in thousands of units and p equals the price in dollars.

Total revenue R from selling q units is stated as the product of p and q, or

$$R = pq$$

Because q is stated as a function of p, total revenue can be stated as a function of price, or

$$\begin{aligned} R &= h(p) \\ &= p \cdot f(p) \\ &= p(1,500 - 50p) \\ &= 1,500p - 50p^2 \end{aligned}$$

You should recognize this as a quadratic function. The total revenue function is sketched in Fig. 10.8. Notice that the restricted domain (see Chap. 2) of the function consists of nonnegative values of p. Why does this make sense?

The total revenue expected from charging a particular price can be computed by substituting the value of p into the total revenue function. For example, the total revenue which corresponds to a price of $10 is

$$\begin{aligned} h(10) &= 1,500(10) - 50(10)^2 \\ &= 15,000 - 5,000 \\ &= \$10,000 \end{aligned}$$

POINTS FOR THOUGHT AND DISCUSSION
Given the x intercepts in Fig. 10.8, what value of p results in the maximum value of R? What is the expected maximum total revenue? What would happen if $p > 30$?

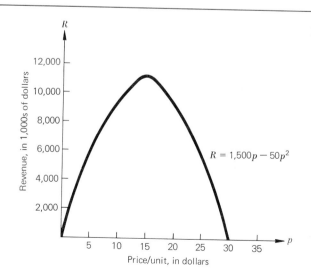

$$R = 1,500p - 50p^2$$

Revenue, in 1,000s of dollars

Price/unit, in dollars

FIGURE 10.8

Example 10.12 **Quadratic Supply Functions** Market surveys of suppliers of a particular product have resulted in the conclusion that the form of the supply function (see Chap. 5) is quadratic. Suppliers were asked what quantities they would be willing to supply at different market prices. Results of the survey indicated that at market prices of $25, $30, and $40 the quantities which suppliers would be willing to offer to the market were 112.5, 250.0, and 600.0 (thousand) units, respectively. Using the procedure discussed in Example 10.10, we can determine the equation of the quadratic supply function by substituting the three price-quantity combinations into the general equation

$$q_s = f(p)$$
$$q_s = ap^2 + bp + c$$

or

The resulting system of equations is

$$625a + 25b + c = 112.5$$
$$900a + 30b + c = 250$$
$$1,600a + 40b + c = 600$$

which, when solved, yields values of $a = 0.5$, $b = 0$, and $c = -200$. Thus the quadratic supply function, shown in Fig. 10.9, is represented by the equation

$$q_s = f(p) = 0.5p^2 - 200$$

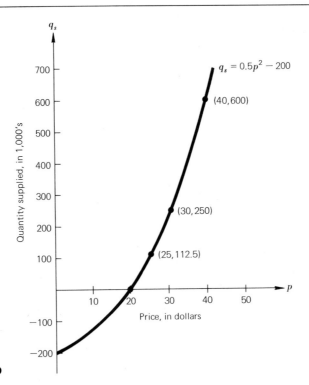

FIGURE 10.9

The quantity supplied at any market price can be determined by substituting the price into the supply function. For example, the quantity supplied at a price of $50 is

$$f(50) = 0.5(50)^2 - 200$$
$$= 0.5(2,500) - 200$$
$$= 1,250 - 200$$
$$= 1,050 \text{ (thousand) units}$$

POINTS FOR THOUGHT AND DISCUSSION
State the restricted domain of the supply function. Is it the same as indicated in Fig. 10.9? Interpret the meaning of the x intercept. Does this interpretation seem reasonable? Interpret the meaning of the y intercept. Does this interpretation make sense?

Quadratic Demand Functions Related to the previous example, a consumer survey was conducted to determine the demand function for the same product. Researchers asked consumers if they would purchase the product at various prices and from their responses constructed estimates of market demand at various market prices. After sample data points were plotted, it was concluded that the demand relationship was represented best by a quadratic function. Researchers concluded that the quadratic representation was valid for selling prices between $5 and $45.

Example 10.13

Three data points chosen for "fitting" the curve were (5, 2,025.0)(10, 1,600.0), and (20, 900.0). Substituting these data points into the general equation for a quadratic function and solving the resulting system simultaneously give the demand function

or

$$q_d = g(p)$$
$$q_d = p^2 - 100p + 2,500$$

where p equals the selling price in dollars and q_d equals demand stated in thousands of units. Figure 10.10 illustrates the demand function.

The quantity demanded at any price can be calculated by substituting the price into the demand function. For example, at a price of $30, the quantity demanded is

$$q(30) = (30)^2 - 100(30) + 2,500$$
$$= 900 - 3,000 + 2,500$$
$$= 400 \text{ (thousand) units}$$

Supply-Demand Equilibrium Market equilibrium between supply and demand can be estimated for the supply and demand functions in the last two examples by determining the market price which equates quantity supplied and quantity demanded. This condition is expressed by the equation

Example 10.14

or

$$q_s = q_d$$
$$0.5p^2 - 200 = p^2 - 100p + 2,500$$

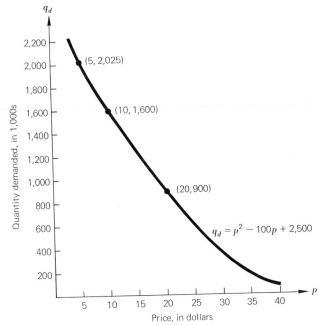

FIGURE 10.10

The equation can be rearranged so that

$$0.5p^2 - 100p + 2,700 = 0 \qquad (10.13)$$

Using the quadratic formula to determine the roots to Eq. (10.13), we get

$$p = \frac{-(-100) \pm \sqrt{(-100)^2 - 4(0.5)(2,700)}}{2(0.5)}$$

$$= \frac{100 \pm \sqrt{4,600}}{1}$$

$$= 100 \pm 67.82$$

The two values of p which satisfy Eq. (10.13) are $p = \$32.18$ and $p = \$167.82$. The second root is outside the relevant domain of the demand function and is therefore meaningless. However, $q_s = q_d$ when the selling price is \$32.18. Substitution of $p = 32.18$ into the supply and demand functions results in values of $q_s = 317.77$ and $q_d = 317.55$. (Rounding is the reason for the difference between these two values.) Thus market equilibrium occurs when the market price equals \$32.18 and the quantity supplied and demanded equals 317,770 units. Figure 10.11 illustrates the two functions.

POINT FOR THOUGHT AND DISCUSSION
Why were there two roots to Eq. (10.13)?

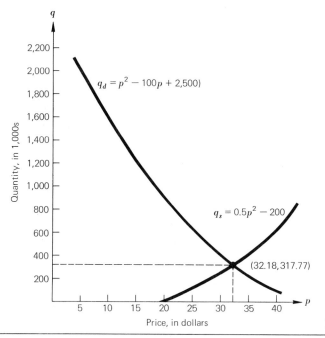

FIGURE 10.11

Emergency Response: Location Model

Emergency Response: Location Model Figure 10.12 illustrates the relative locations of three cities along a coastal highway. The three cities are popular resorts, and their populations swell during the summer months. The three cities believe their emergency rescue and health treatment capabilities are inadequate during the vacation season. They have decided to support jointly an emergency response facility which dispatches rescue trucks and trained paramedics. A key question concerns the location of the facility.

In choosing the location, it has been agreed that the distance from the facility to each city should be kept as short as possible to ensure quick response times. Another consideration is the size of the summer population of each city, since this is one measure of the potential need for emergency response services. The larger the summer population of a city, the greater the desire to locate the facility close to the city. Analysts have decided that the criterion for selecting the location is to minimize the sum of the products of the summer populations of each town and the square of the distance between the town and the facility. This can be stated more succinctly as

minimize $$S = \sum_{j=1}^{3} p_j d_j^2$$

where p_j equals the summer population for city j, stated in thousands, and d_j is the distance between city j and the rescue facility.

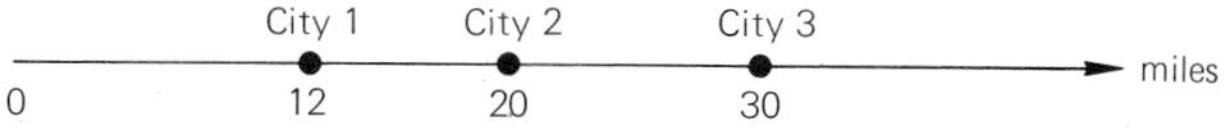

Example 10.15

FIGURE 10.12

If the summer populations are, respectively, 150,000, 100,000, and 200,000 for the three cities, compute the general expression for S. (*Hint:* Let x equal the location of the facility relative to the zero point of the scale in Fig. 10.12, and let x_j equal the location of city j. The distance between the facility and city j is calculated by the equation $d_j = x - x_j$.)

Solution With x defined as above, S can be stated as a function of x. The function is defined as

$$S = f(x)$$

$$= \sum_{j=1}^{3} p_j(x - x_j)^2$$

$$= 150(x - 12)^2 + 100(x - 20)^2 + 200(x - 30)^2$$
$$= 150x^2 - 3,600x + 21,600 + 100x^2 - 4,000x$$
$$\quad + 40,000 + 200x^2 - 12,000x + 180,000$$
$$= 450x^2 - 19,600x + 241,600$$

Note that this function is quadratic in form, and it will graph as a parabola which is concave up. S will be minimized at the vertex of the parabola, or where

$$x = \frac{-b}{2a} = \frac{-(-19,600)}{2(450)}$$

$$= \frac{19,600}{900}$$

$$= 21.77$$

According to Fig. 10.12, the emergency response facility will be located 21.77 miles to the right of the zero point, or 1.77 miles to the right of city 2.

We will reconsider this example in Chap. 13 and solve it by another method.

Follow-up Exercises

10.26 The demand function for a particular product is

$$q = f(p) = 200,000 - 1,000p$$

where q is stated in units and p is stated in dollars. Determine the quadratic total revenue function where R is a function of p, or $R = g(p)$. What is the concavity of the function? What is the y intercept? What does total revenue equal at a price of $10?

10.27 The demand function for a particular product is

$$q = f(p) = 4,500 - 2.5p$$

where q is stated in units and p is stated in dollars. Determine the quadratic total revenue function where R is a function of p, or $R = g(p)$. What is the concavity of the function? What is the y intercept? What does total revenue equal at a price of $20?

10.28 Total revenue in Exercise 10.26 can be stated in terms of either price p or demand q. Can you restate total revenue as a function of q rather than p? That is, determine the function $R = h(q)$. (*Hint:* Solve for p in the demand function and multiply this expression by q.)

10.29 In Exercise 10.27 restate the function for total revenue as a function of q. (See Exercise 10.28 for a hint.)

10.30 The supply function $q_s = f(p)$ for a product is quadratic. Three points which lie on the supply function are (40, 700), (50, 1,600) and (75, 4,725).

(*a*) Determine the equation for the function.

(*b*) Make any observations you can about the relevant domain of the function.

(*c*) Compute and interpret the x intercept.

(*d*) What quantity will be supplied at a price of $30?

10.31 The supply function $q_s = f(p)$ for a product is quadratic. Three points which lie on the function are (60, 2,200), (70, 4,800), and (100, 15,000).

(*a*) Determine the equation for the supply function.

(*b*) Make any observations you can about the relevant domain of the function.

(*c*) Compute and interpret the x intercept.

(*d*) What quantity will be supplied at a price of $80?

10.32 The demand function $q_d = f(p)$ for a product is quadratic. Three points which lie on the function are (10, 3,600), (20, 2,500), and (30, 1,600). Determine the equation for the demand function. What quantity will be demanded at a market price of $40?

10.33 The demand function $q_d = f(p)$ for a product is quadratic. Three points which lie on the function are (10, 6,400), (20, 3,600), and (30, 1,600). Determine the equation for the demand function. What quantity will be demanded at a market price of $40?

10.34 The supply and demand functions for a product are $q_s = p^2 - 900$ and $q_d = p^2 - 140p + 4,900$. Determine the market equilibrium price and quantity.

10.35 The supply and demand functions for a product are $q_s = 5p^2 - 4,500$ and $q_d = 4p^2 - 400p + 10,000$. Determine the market equilibrium price and quantity.

EXPONENTIAL FUNCTIONS

10.4

Another set of functional forms which have many important applications in business and economics is *exponential functions*. In this section we will study their characteristics.

ALGEBRA FLASHBACK

Some important properties of exponents are repeated here for your review. Assume a and b are positive numbers and x and y are real-valued. Then

    I. $b^x \cdot b^y = b^{x+y}$

        Example: $2^2 2^3 = 2^5 = 32$

    II. $\dfrac{b^x}{b^y} = b^{x-y} \qquad b \neq 0$

        Example: $\dfrac{3^6}{3^3} = (3)^{6-3} = 3^3 = 27$

III. $(b^x)^y = b^{xy}$

Example: $(10^3)^2 = (10)^{(3)(2)} = 10^6 = 1,000,000$

IV. $a^x b^x = (ab)^x$

Example: $3^4 2^4 = [(3)(2)]^4 = 6^4 = 1,296$

V. $b^{x/y} = \sqrt[y]{b^x}$

Example: $8^{2/3} = \sqrt[3]{8^2} = \sqrt[3]{64} = 4$

VI. $b^0 = 1 \qquad b \neq 0$

Example: $5,000^0 = 1$

VII. $b^{-x} = \dfrac{1}{b^x} \qquad b \neq 0$

Example: $(2)^{-3} = \dfrac{1}{2^3} = \dfrac{1}{8}$

If you are a little rusty on exponents, you are strongly advised to read Sec. 0.5.

Characteristics of Exponential Functions

An *exponential function* of the form $y = f(x)$ is one in which x appears as either an exponent or part of an exponent. Examples of exponential functions include

$$y = 10^x$$
$$y = (2)^{x^2-5}$$
and
$$y = 10(3)^{x/2}$$

There are different classes of exponential functions. One important class is that having the form

$$y = f(x) = ab^{mx} \qquad \qquad (10.14)$$

where a, b, and m are real-valued constants. One restriction is that $b > 0$ but $b \neq 1$.

POINT FOR THOUGHT AND DISCUSSION
What are the characteristics of Eq. (10.14) if $b = 1$?

Let's examine some exponential functions of the form $y = b^x$ [assuming $a = m = 1$ in Eq. (10.14)]. This will give us a feeling for the behavior of exponential functions in general.

Example 10.16 $y = b^x$ **where** $b > 1$ Sketch the following exponential functions where the *base* b is greater than 1.

$$y = f(x) = 2^x$$
$$y = g(x) = (2.5)^x$$
$$y = h(x) = 3^x$$

x		0	+1	+2	+3	−1	−2	−3	Table 10.3
$f(x) = 2^x$		1	2	4	8	0.5	0.25	0.125	
$g(x) = (2.5)^x$		1	2.5	6.25	15.625	0.4	0.160	0.064	
$h(x) = 3^x$		1	3	9	27	0.333	0.111	0.037	

Solution

These functions can be sketched by assuming values for the independent variable and by calculating the corresponding value of the dependent variable. Table 10.3 indicates sample values for the three functions.

ALGEBRA FLASHBACK
The exponent property $b^{-x} = 1/b^x$ must be used to evaluate the functions for negative values of x. See Sec. 0.2 for further discussion.

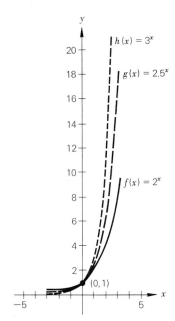

FIGURE 10.13

The three functions are sketched in Fig. 10.13. Notice that for these three functions

1 Each function is defined for all values of x (the domain is the set of real numbers).

2 The graph of each function lies entirely *above* the x axis (the range is the set of positive real numbers).

3 The graph of each function is *asymptotic* to the x axis. That is, the value of y approaches but never reaches a value of 0 as x approaches a value of negative infinity (denoted as $x \rightarrow -\infty$).

4 All three functions have the same y intercept, (0, 1).

5 y is an increasing function of x; that is, over the domain of the function any increase in x is accompanied by an increase in y. More precisely, this property suggests that for $x_1 < x_2, f(x_1) < f(x_2)$. Such functions are often said to be *monotonically increasing*.

$y = b^x$ where $0 < b < 1$ Sketch the following exponential functions where the base b is positive but less than 1:

Example 10.17

$$y = f(x) = (0.2)^x$$
$$y = g(x) = (0.6)^x$$
$$y = h(x) = (0.9)^x$$

Solution

Table 10.4 indicates sample values for x and for the three functions. The three functions are sketched in Fig. 10.14. Note that for these functions

x		0	+1	+2	+3	−1	−2	−3	Table 10.4
$f(x) = (0.2)^x$		1	0.2	0.04	0.008	5	25	125	
$g(x) = (0.6)^x$		1	0.6	0.36	0.216	1.666	2.777	4.629	
$h(x) = (0.9)^x$		1	0.9	0.81	0.729	1.111	1.234	1.372	

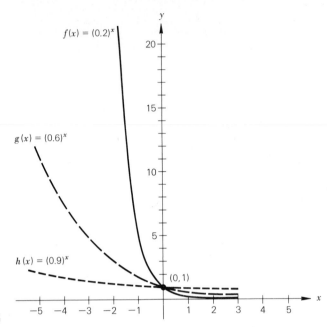

FIGURE 10.14

1 Each function is defined for all values of x (the domain is the set of real numbers).

2 The graph of each function is entirely above the x axis (the range is the set of positive real numbers).

3 The graph of each function is asymptotic to the x axis. That is, the value of y approaches but never reaches a value of 0 as x approaches positive infinity ($x \rightarrow +\infty$).

4 All three functions have the same y intercept, $(0, 1)$.

5 y is a decreasing function of x in that any increase in the value of x is accompanied by a decrease in the value of y. More precisely, this property suggests that for $x_1 < x_2$, $f(x_1) > f(x_2)$. Such functions are often said to be *monotonically decreasing*.

Base-e Exponential Functions

A special class of exponential functions is of the form

$$y = f(x) = ae^{mx} \qquad (10.15)$$

Note that the base of the exponential function is e, which is an irrational number equal to 2.71828. . . . The value of e is approximated by evaluating the expression $(1 + 1/n)^n$ as n approaches $+\infty$. Although we will not dwell on the origin of this constant, you will gain insights as we go along as to why such an unusual constant is used as the base for such a popular class of exponential functions. And, indeed, base-e exponential functions are more widely applied in business and economics than any other class of exponential functions.

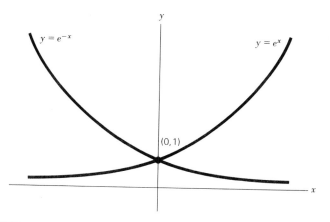

FIGURE 10.15

Two special exponential functions in this class are $y = e^x$ and $y = e^{-x}$. Figure 10.15 illustrates the graphs of these two functions.

NOTE
Calculating values for $(2.71828 \ldots)^x$ or $(2.71828 \ldots)^{-x}$ can be tedious. Since these calculations are needed regularly, values for e^x and e^{-x} are readily available. Many pocket calculators have e^x or e^{-x} functions. Values are also found in Table A.1 at the end of the book.

Modified Exponential Functions Certain applications of exponential functions involve functions of the form

$$y = f(x) = 1 - e^{-mx}$$

Graph the function $y = 1 - e^{-x}$ where $x \geq 0$.

Example 10.18

Table 10.5 contains some sample data points for this function. The function is shown in Fig. 10.16. Note how the graph of the function is asymptotic to the line $y = 1$. The value of y approaches but never quite reaches a value of 1. This is because e^{-x} can never equal 0. If e^{-x} is

Solution

FIGURE 10.16

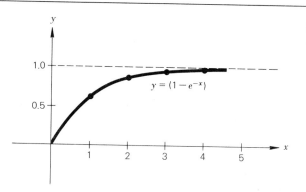

Table	x	0	1	2	3	4
10.5						
	e^{-x}	1	0.3678	0.1353	0.0498	0.0183
	$1 - e^{-x}$	0	0.6322	0.8647	0.9502	0.9817

rewritten as $1/e^x$, the resulting quotient will never equal 0, regardless of how large the denominator becomes. The quotient approaches a value of 0 as the value of x becomes more and more positive.

Follow-up Exercises

10.36 Which of the following functions can be considered to be exponential functions? For those which are not, indicate why they are not.
(a) $y = f(x) = e^{3x}$ 　　　　　(b) $y = g(x) = 5x^5$
(c) $u = v(t) = \sqrt{t}$ 　　　　　(d) $z = f(y) = \sqrt{2}y$
(e) $g = h(s) = 4^{(s^2 - 2s + 1)}$
10.37 Describe the appearance of the function $y = ab^{mx}$ if $b = 1$.
10.38 (a) Sketch the functions

$$y = f(x) = 2^x$$
$$y = g(x) = 2^{0.5x}$$
$$y = h(x) = 2^{2x}$$

(b) If these functions are compared with the general exponential function described by Eq. (10.14), the differences are in the value of m. What conclusion can be drawn about the behavior of exponential functions and the value of m?
10.39 (a) Sketch the functions

$$y = f(x) = 3^x$$
$$y = g(x) = 0.1(3^x)$$
$$y = h(x) = 2(3^x)$$

(b) If these functions are compared with Eq. (10.14), the differences are in the values of a. What conclusions can be drawn regarding the behavior of exponential functions and the value of a?
10.40 (a) Sketch the functions

$$y = f(x) = -(3)^x$$
$$y = g(x) = -0.1(3^x)$$
$$y = h(x) = -2(3^x)$$

(b) If these functions are compared with Eq. (10.14), the differences are in the values of a. What conclusions can be drawn regarding the behavior of exponential functions and the value of a?
10.41 Sketch the following exponential functions:
(a) $y = e^{x/2}$ 　　　　　(b) $y = e^{-x/2}$
†(c) $y = e^{x+2}$ 　　　　　†(d) $y = e^{2x-1}$
†(e) $y = e^{x^2}$ 　　　　　†(f) $y = e^{-x^2}$
10.42 Use the following table to determine data points and sketch the function $y = 1 - e^{-x/2}$ where $x \geq 0$.

† *Note:* These are exponential functions which have a different structure from Eq. (10.15).

x	0	1	2	3	4	5
$e^{-x/2}$	1					
$1 - e^{-x/2}$	0					

APPLICATIONS OF EXPONENTIAL FUNCTIONS

Exponential functions have particular application to *growth processes* and *decay processes*. Examples of growth processes include population growth, appreciation in the value of assets, inflation, growth in the rate at which particular resources are used (such as energy), and growth in the gross national product (GNP). Examples of decay processes include the declining value of certain assets such as machinery, the decline in the rate of incidence of certain diseases as medical research and technology improve, the decline in the purchasing power of a dollar, and the decline in the efficiency of a machine as it ages.

When a growth process is characterized by a constant percent increase in value, it is referred to as an *exponential growth process*. When a decay process is characterized by a constant percent decline in value, it is referred to as an *exponential decay process*. If the population of a country is growing constantly at a rate of 8 percent, it can be described by an *exponential growth function*. If the incidence of infant mortality is declining continually at a rate of 5 percent, it can be described by an exponential decay function.

Although exponential growth and decay functions are usually stated as a function of time, the independent variable may represent something other than time. Regardless of the nature of the independent variable, the effect is that *equal increases in the independent variable result in constant percent changes (increases or decreases) in the value of the dependent variable.*

Following are examples which illustrate some of the areas of application of exponential functions.

Compound Interest In Chap. 9 we determined that the equation

Example 10.19

$$S = P(1 + i)^n \qquad (10.16)$$

could be used to determine the amount S that an investment of P dollars would grow to if it receives interest of i percent per compounding period for n compounding periods.† If S is considered to be a function of n, Eq. (10.16) can be viewed as having the form of Eq. (10.14). That is,

$$S = f(n)$$

or

$$S = ab^{mn}$$

where $a = P$, $b = 1 + i$, and $m = 1$.

Assume that $P = \$1,000$, and $i = 0.06$ per year. Equation (10.16) becomes $S = f(n)$, or

$$S = (1,000)(1.06)^n$$

---

† Assuming reinvestment of any accrued interest.

To determine the value of S given any value of n, it is necessary to evaluate the exponential term $(1.06)^n$. If we want to know to what sum that $1,000 will grow after 25 years, we must evaluate $(1.06)^{25}$. As we discussed in Chap. 9, these kinds of calculations are so common that tables have been constructed to evaluate the expression $(1 + i)^n$. We called this expression the *compound-amount factor* in Chap. 9, and values for this factor are found in Table 9.2. From Table 9.2, $(1 + 0.06)^{25} = 4.29187$, and

$$S = 1,000(4.29187)$$
$$= \$4,291.87$$

Rearranging Eq. (10.16) and solving for P, we get

$$P = S(1 + i)^{-n} \qquad (10.17)$$

This equation is essentially the same as Eq. (9.7a). Given that money can be invested at a rate of interest of i percent per period, Eq. (10.17) allows one to determine how many dollars P should be invested today in order to accumulate S dollars after n compounding periods. In other terms, we can think of P as being the equivalent *present value* of having S dollars n periods from now.

In a given problem, if S and i are known, P can be defined as an exponential function stated in terms of n. If Eq. (10.17) is compared with the form of Eq. (10.14), $a = S,\ b = 1 + i$, and $m = -1$. As with the compound-amount factor $(1 + i)^n$, values of the *present-worth factor* $(1 + i)^{-n}$ are readily available for calculations involving Eq. (10.17). These are found in Table 9.3.

Example 10.20

Compound Interest: Continuous Compounding

When compounding of interest occurs more than once a year, we can restate Eq. (10.16) as

$$S = P \left(1 + \frac{i}{m}\right)^{mt} \qquad (10.18)$$

where i equals the annual interest rate, m equals the number of compounding periods per year, and t equals the number of years. Note that the product mt equals the number of compounding periods over t years.

Banks often use *continuous compounding* schemes on savings accounts as a way of promoting business. Continuous compounding means that compounding is occurring all the time. Another way of thinking of continuous compounding is that there are an infinite number of compounding periods each year. In Eq. (10.18), continuous compounding would suggest that we determine the value of S as m approaches $+\infty$. Since i/m can be written as $1/(m/i)$, Eq. (10.18) can be rewritten as

$$S = P \left(1 + \frac{1}{m/i}\right)^{mt}$$

And since $mt = (m/i)(it)$,

$$S = P \left[\left(1 + \frac{1}{m/i}\right)^{m/i}\right]^{it} \qquad (10.19)$$

When we discussed base-e exponential functions, we stated that

$$e = \left(1 + \frac{1}{n}\right)^n \qquad \text{as } n \longrightarrow +\infty \qquad (10.20)$$

Confirm that the expression in brackets has the same structure as Eq. (10.20) and that as m approaches $+\infty$.

$$\left[1 + \frac{1}{m/i}\right]^{m/i} \longrightarrow e = 2.718 \ldots$$

Therefore, for continuous compounding, Eq. (10.19) simplifies to

$$\boldsymbol{S = Pe^{it}} \qquad \qquad \textbf{(10.21)}$$

Refer to Example 10.19; \$1,000 invested for 25 years in an investment which earns 6 percent per year compounded continuously will grow to a sum

Example 10.21

$$S = \$1,000e^{0.06(25)}$$
$$= 1,000e^{1.5}$$

From Table A.1 at the end of the book, we have

$$e^{1.5} = 4.4817$$

and
$$S = \$1,000(4.4817)$$
$$= \$4,481.70$$

By comparing this value with that found in Example 10.19, continuous compounding results in additional interest of $4,481.70 - 4,291.87 = \$189.83$ over the 25-year period. From this example one *may* conclude that the additional interest resulting from continuous compounding is not as significant as was first thought.

Exponential Growth Process: Population. As mentioned at the beginning of this section, *exponential growth processes* are characterized by a constant percent increase in value over time. Such processes may be described by the general function

Example 10.22

$$V = f(t)$$

or
$$\boldsymbol{V = V_0 e^{kt}} \qquad \qquad \textbf{(10.22)}$$

where V equals the value of the function at time t, V_0 equals the value of the function at $t = 0$, k is the percent rate of growth, and t is time measured in the appropriate units (hours, days, weeks, years, etc.).

The population of a country was 100 million in 1970. It has been growing since that time exponentially at a constant rate of 4 percent per year. The function which describes the size of the population P (in millions) is

$$P = f(t)$$
$$= 100e^{0.04t}$$

where 100 (million) is the population at $t = 0$ (1970) and 0.04 is the rate of exponential growth.

The projected population for 1995 (assuming continued annual growth at the same rate) is found by evaluating $f(25)$, where $t = 25$ corresponds to 1995. The projected population for the country is

$$
\begin{aligned}
P &= f(25) \\
&= 100e^{0.04(25)} \\
&= 100e \\
&= 271.82 \text{ (millions)}
\end{aligned}
$$

Example 10.23

Exponential Growth Processes Continued A question of interest in growth functions is, How long will it take for the value of the function to increase by some multiple? In Example 10.22 there may be a question concerning how long it will take for the population to double. We looked at this question in an investment sense in Chap. 9. In Eq. (10.22), the value V_0 will double when

$$
\frac{V}{V_0} = 2
$$

Dividing both sides of Eq. (10.22) by V_0, we get

$$
\frac{V}{V_0} = e^{kt}
$$

Therefore the value will double when

$$
e^{kt} = 2
$$

To illustrate this, the population in Example 10.22 will double when $V = 200$, or

$$
200 = 100e^{0.04t}
$$

Dividing both sides by 100 yields

$$
2 = e^{0.04t}
$$

From Table A.1 we see that

$$
e^{0.70} \doteq 2\dagger
$$

A better approximation is

$$
e^{0.69314} \doteq 2
$$

In order to determine how long it takes the population of 100 million to double, we must find the value of t which makes

$$
e^{0.69314} \doteq e^{0.04t}
$$

These expressions will be equal when their exponents are equal, or when

$$
0.04t = 0.69314
$$

or

$$
t \doteq 17.33 \text{ years}\ddagger
$$

---

† The symbol $\doteq$ means "is approximately equal to."
‡ Solving for t can be easier if you understand logarithms. An alternative and equivalent approach would be to find the natural logarithms (next section) of both sides of the equation $2 = e^{0.04t}$ and equate these, solving for t.

POINTS FOR THOUGHT AND DISCUSSION
What relationship would exist between V and V_0 if the value tripled? Quadrupled? Determine how long it will take for this to occur in the last example.

Bill Collection A major financial institution offers a credit card which can be used internationally. The question arose among executives as to how long it takes to collect the accounts receivable for credit issued in any given month. Data gathered over a number of years have indicated that the collection percentage for credit issued in any month is an exponential function of the time since the credit was issued. Specifically, the function which approximates this relationship is

Example 10.24

$$P = f(t)$$
or
$$P = 0.95(1 - e^{-0.7t}) \qquad t \geq 0$$

where P equals the percentage of accounts receivable (in dollars) collected t *months* after the credit is granted. Sample data points for this function are shown in Table 10.6. The values for $e^{-0.7t}$ are found in Table A.1 at the end of the book. The function is sketched in Fig. 10.17. Note the figures in Table 10.6. For $t = 0$, $f(t) = 0$, which suggests that no accounts will have been collected at the time credit is issued. When $t = 1$, the function has a value of 0.4782. This indicates that after 1 month 47.82 percent of accounts receivable (in dollars) will have been collected. After 2 months, 71.56 percent will have been collected.

t	0	1	2	3	4	**Table 10.6**
$e^{-0.7t}$	1	0.4965	0.2466	0.1225	0.0608	
$1 - e^{-0.7t}$	0	0.5035	0.7534	0.8775	0.9392	
$0.95(1 - e^{-0.7t})$	0	0.4782	0.7156	0.8336	0.8922	

FIGURE 10.17

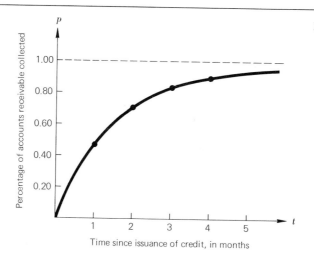

Percentage of accounts receivable collected

Time since issuance of credit, in months

POINTS FOR THOUGHT AND DISCUSSION
What value does P approach as t increases without limit? Why will the value of P never equal 1? Do you think that a restricted domain would apply in this type of application?

Follow-up Exercises

10.43 An investment of $100,000 is made which earns interest at the rate of 8 percent per year. If the principal is invested for a period of 5 years, compute the compound amount if interest is compounded (a) annually, (b) semiannually, (c) quarterly, (d) continuously.

10.44 An investment of $10,000 is made which earns interest at the rate of 12 percent per year. If the principal is invested for a period of 4 years, compute the compound amount if interest is compounded (a) semiannually, (b) quarterly, (c) monthly, (d) continuously.

10.45 A person desires to make an investment of P dollars which will earn interest at the rate of 7 percent per year. The goal is to have the principal P and accrued interest grow to $5,000 after 10 years.
(a) Using Eq. (10.17) as a guide, write the exponential function $P = f(n)$ which would allow for computing the amount P which needs to be invested.
(b) Using Table 9.3, determine the value of P.

10.46 *Population Growth.* The population P of a European country was 20 million on January 1, 1970. Since that time, it has been growing exponentially at a constant rate of 4.5 percent per year.
(a) Write the general exponential growth function $P = f(t)$ for the population of this country.
(b) If the rate and pattern of growth continue, what is the population expected to be in 1990? In 2010?

10.47 In Exercise 10.46, determine the year in which the population can be expected to double. In what year will the population have increased by 50 percent?

10.48 A bank advertises continuous compounding of interest on savings accounts at a rate of 5.5 percent per year. How long will it take a sum to double in value? Triple in value?

10.49 *Real Estate.* For the past 5 years, real estate prices in one California region have been increasing at an exponential rate of 6 percent per year. A home was purchased 5 years ago for $36,000.
(a) What is its value today?
(b) Assuming appreciation continues at the same rate, what will its value be 10 years from today?

10.50 *Solid Waste.* Within a major United States city, the annual tonnage of solid waste (garbage) has been increasing at an exponential rate of 7.5 percent per year. Assume the current daily tonnage is 4,000 tons and the rate and pattern of growth continue.
(a) What daily tonnage will be expected 10 years from now?
(b) Current capacity for handling solid waste is 6,000 tons per day. When will this capacity no longer be sufficient?

10.51 *Exponential Decay Functions.* An *exponential decay process* is one characterized by a constant percent decrease in value over time. Such processes may be described by the general function

$$V = f(t)$$
$$= V_0 e^{-kt} \qquad \textbf{(10.23)}$$

where V equals the value of the function at time t, V_0 equals the value of the function at $t = 0$, and k is the percentage rate of decay. Compare Eq. (10.23) with Eq. (10.22) and note the differences.

The resale value V (stated in dollars) of a certain piece of industrial equipment has been found to behave according to the function $V = 100,000e^{-0.1t}$ where t = years since original purchase.
(a) What is the original value of a piece of the equipment?
(b) What is the expected resale value after 5 years? After 10 years?
10.52 In Exercise 10.51, how long does it take for the resale value of the asset to reach 50 percent of its original value?
10.53 *Advertising Response.* A large record company sells tapes and albums by direct mail only. Advertising is done through network television. Much experience with this type of sales approach has allowed analysts to determine the expected response to an advertising program. Specifically, the response function for classical music albums and tapes is $R = f(t) = 1 - e^{-0.03t}$, where R is the percentage of customers in the target market actually purchasing the album or tape and t is the number of times an advertisement is run on national TV.
(a) What percentage of the target market is expected to buy a classical music offering if advertisements are run one time on TV? 10 times? 20 times?
(b) Sketch the response function $R = f(t)$.

LOGARITHMIC FUNCTIONS

This section discusses another class of functions which are directly related to exponential functions.

Logarithms

A *logarithm* is an exponent. More specifically, a logarithm is the *power* to which a *base* must be raised in order to yield a given number. Consider the equation

$$2^3 = 8$$

The exponent 3 can be considered as the logarithm, to the base 2, of the number 8. That is, 3 is the power to which 2 must be raised in order to generate the number 8. We can state this logarithmic property as

$$3 = \log_2 8$$

In general, the logarithm equation

$$x = \log_b y \qquad (10.24)$$

implies that a "base" b, when raised to the "power" x, will result in the number y. Or, the equivalent exponential equation is

$$b^x = y \qquad (10.25)$$

We will concern ourselves with situations where the base b is restricted to positive values other than 1.

Example 10.25 Following are statements of equivalent pairs of exponential and logarithmic equations.

Logarithmic Equation	Exponential Equation
$4 = \log_2 16$	$2^4 = 16$
$2 = \log_{10} 100$	$10^2 = 100$
$3 = \log_3 27$	$3^3 = 27$
$-1 = \log_{10} 0.1$	$10^{-1} = 0.1$

Exponential Equation	Logarithmic Equation
$10^4 = 10,000$	$4 = \log_{10} 10,000$
$4^3 = 64$	$3 = \log_4 64$
$5^2 = 25$	$2 = \log_5 25$
$10^{-2} = 0.01$	$-2 = \log_{10} 0.01$

The two most commonly used bases for logarithms are base 10 and base e. Most of us have probably had some experience with *base-10*, or *common logarithms*.† Logarithms which use $e = 2.718 \ldots$ as the base are called *natural logarithms*.‡ Logarithms of this form arise from the use of exponential functions which employ e as the base.

Common logarithms can be denoted by

$$x = \log_{10} y$$

However, because most logarithmic computations involve the base 10, a more common way of expressing such logarithms is

$$x = \log y$$

where the base, though not indicated, is implicitly 10. Base-e or natural logarithms can be denoted by

$$x = \log_e y$$

but are more commonly denoted by

$$x = \ln y$$

A logarithm having a base b other than 10 or e would be expressed as

$$x = \log_b y$$

Procedures for determining values of common logarithms will not be presented. The examples in this book will deal solely with natural logarithms. Values for $\ln y$ can be found in Table A.2 at the end of the book.

---

† These are sometimes referred to as *Briggsian* logarithms (after H. Briggs, who first used them).
‡ Natural logs are named after John Napier, the Scot, as *Napierian* logarithms.

Properties of Logarithms

Just as there are basic properties associated with exponents, there is a similar set of properties which holds for logarithms. Some of the more important properties are as follows.

I. $\log_b uv = \log_b u + \log_b v$
Example: $\log_{10}(100)(1,000) = \log_{10} 100 + \log_{10} 1,000 = 2 + 3 = 5$

II. $\log_b (u/v) = \log_b u - \log_b v$

Example: $\log_{10} \dfrac{10,000}{100} = \log_{10} 10,000 - \log_{10} 100 = 4 - 2 = 2$

III. $\log_b u^n = n \log_b u$
Example: $\log_{10} 100^2 = 2 \log_{10} 100 = 2(2) = 4$

IV. $\log_b b = 1$
Example: $\log_{10} 10 = 1$ $(10^1 = 10)$
Example: $\ln e = 1$ $(e^1 = e)$

V. $\log_b 1 = 0$
Example: $\log_{10} 1 = 0$ $(10^0 = 1)$
Example: $\ln 1 = 0$ $(e^0 = 1)$

Logarithmic Functions

DEFINITION
A *logarithmic function* has the form

$$y = f(x)$$
or
$$y = \log_b x \qquad (10.26)$$
where
$$b > 0 \text{ but } b \neq 1.$$

Graph the function $y = f(x) = \ln x$ where $x > 0$.

Example 10.26

The function $y = \ln x$ can be graphed by using two procedures. If values of $\ln x$ are available (from tables or an electronic calculator), the function can be graphed directly. Using Table A.2 at the end of the book, we summarize sample values of $\ln x$ in Table 10.7. The general shape of this function is indicated in Fig. 10.18.

Solution

An alternative procedure for graphing a logarithmic function is to rewrite the function in its equivalent exponential form. The equivalent exponential form of $y = \ln x$ is

$$e^y = x$$

x	0.1	0.5	1	10	100	200	300
$\ln x$	-2.3026	-0.6932	0	2.3026	4.6052	5.2983	5.703

Table 10.7

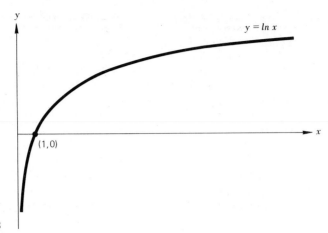

FIGURE 10.18

By *assuming values for y* and computing the corresponding values of x, a set of data points may be generated. What is needed is a means of evaluating the expression e^y. Using Table A.1 at the end of the book to evaluate e^y, we summarize sample data points in Table 10.8. If these points are graphed (remembering that x is the independent variable in the function of interest $y = \ln x$), they will lie on the curve in Fig. 10.18.

An examination of Fig. 10.18 indicates that the natural logarithm function $y = \ln x$ is monotonically increasing; also, $y > 0$ when $x > 1$, $y = 0$ when $x = 1$, and $y < 0$ when $0 < x < 1$.

Table 10.8

y	-1	-0.5	0	1	2	3	4
$x = e^y$	0.3679	0.6065	1.000	2.7183	7.3891	20.086	54.598

Follow-up Exercises

10.54 For each of the following exponential equations, write the equivalent logarithmic equation.

(a) $2^5 = 32$ (b) $4^2 = 16$

(c) $(0.5)^3 = 0.0625$ (d) $3^4 = 81$

(e) $(2)^{-3} = 0.125$ (f) $(0.5)^{-3} = 8$

(g) $(0.2)^{-2} = 25$ (h) $5^3 = 125$

(i) $6^2 = 36$ (j) $(0.1)^{-4} = 10{,}000$

10.55 For each of the following logarithmic equations, write the equivalent exponential equation.

(a) $\log_2 64 = 6$ (b) $\log_3 243 = 5$

(c) $\log_{0.5} 2 = -1$ (d) $\log_4 4 = 1$

(e) $\log_{10} 0.01 = -2$ (f) $\ln 1 = 0$

(g) $\ln e = 1$ (h) $\log_5 0.04 = -2$

(i) $\log_{16} 4 = 0.5$ (j) $\log_{16} 2 = 0.25$

10.56 Determine the following from Table A.2.

(a) $\ln 5$ (b) $\ln 25$

(c) $\ln 1$ (d) $\ln 300$

(e) $\ln 100$ (f) $\ln 250$

(g) $\ln 60$ (h) $\ln 45$

10.57 Sketch the following functions for $x > 0$.
(a) $y = \ln x^2$ (b) $y = \ln 0.1x$

CHAPTER CHECKLIST

If you have read *all* the sections of this chapter, you should

Understand the fundamental differences between linear functions _____
and nonlinear functions

Be familiar with the algebraic and graphical characteristics of *quad-* _____
ratic functions

Be able to sketch quadratic functions _____

Be familiar with the general form of *polynomial functions* _____

Be able to sketch polynomial functions _____

Be familiar with selected applications of quadratic functions _____

Be familiar with the algebraic and graphical characteristics of simple _____
exponential functions

Be able to sketch simple exponential functions _____

Be familiar with selected applications of exponential functions _____

Understand what a *logarithm* is _____

Be familiar with the characteristics of simple *logarithmic functions* _____

Be able to graph simple logarithmic functions _____

KEY TERMS AND CONCEPTS

nonlinear function

quadratic function

parabola

vertex

axis of symmetry

quadratic formula

polynomial function

exponential function

monotonically increasing
  (decreasing)

modified exponential functions

exponential growth function

exponential decay function

logarithm

common logarithm

natural logarithm

logarithmic function

IMPORTANT FORMULAS

$f(x) = ax^2 + bx + c$ (10.5)   (quadratic function)

$\left(-\dfrac{b}{2a}, \dfrac{4ac - b^2}{4a}\right)$ (vertex of parabola)

$$x = \frac{-b \pm \sqrt{b^2 - 4ac}}{2a} \qquad \text{(quadratic formula)}$$

$S = P(1 + i)^n$	(10.16)	(compound-amount formula)
$P = S(1 + i)^{-n}$	(10.17)	(present-value formula)
$S = Pe^{it}$	(10.21)	(compound amount, continuous compounding)
$V = V_0 e^{kt}$	(10.22)	(exponential growth process)

ADDITIONAL EXERCISES

Exercises 10.58 to 10.69 are related to Sec. 10.2.

In Exercises 10.58 to 10.63, determine which functions are quadratic and identify the parameters a, b, and c of each quadratic function.

10.58 $f(x) = 2x^5 + 5x^2 + 4$ **10.59** $f(x) = 3x^2 - 8x + 9$

10.60 $f(x) = \dfrac{x^4}{4} - 2x^3 + 1$ **10.61** $f(x) = \dfrac{5x^2}{4}$

10.62 $f(x) = (x - 5)^2$ **10.63** $f(x) = (x - 3)^3$

In Exercises 10.64 to 10.67, determine the concavity of the quadratic function, its y intercept, its x intercept(s), and the coordinates of the vertex. Sketch the parabola.

10.64 $y = f(x) = -\dfrac{x^2}{4} + x$ **10.65** $y = f(x) = \dfrac{x^2}{4} - x$

10.66 $y = f(x) = 5x^2 - 3x + 8$ **10.67** $y = f(x) = x^2 - 8x + 16$

10.68 (a) Determine the equation of the quadratic function which passes through the points $(1, -1)$, $(3, 3)$, and $(-1, 1)$.
(b) Find the coordinates of the vertex.
(c) Sketch the parabola.

10.69 Given the two quadratic functions

$$y = f(x) = (2x - 3)^2$$
and
$$y = g(x) = -x^2 + 3x + 1.5$$

(a) sketch the two functions on the same set of axes and (b) determine the coordinates of any points of intersection.

Exercises 10.70 to 10.74 are related to Sec. 10.3.

10.70 The total revenue R (in dollars) from selling q units of a product can be represented by the function

$$R = f(q) = -2q^2 + 10,000q$$

(a) What does total revenue equal if 50 units are sold?
(b) What values of q will make total revenue equal 0?
(c) What quantity will maximize total revenue?
(d) What is the maximum total revenue?

10.71 The demand function for a particular product is

$$q = f(p) = 120,000 - 3p$$

where q equals the quantity demanded and p equals the price in dollars.
(a) Determine the quadratic total revenue function $R = g(p)$.
(b) What is the concavity of the revenue function?
(c) What is the y intercept? What are the x intercepts?
(d) What price will result in maximum total revenue?
(e) What is the maximum revenue?

10.72 In Exercise 10.71 the total revenue function can be stated as a function of the quantity sold q. Determine the total revenue function $R = h(q)$. (*Hint:* Solve for p in the demand function and multiply the resulting expression by q.)

10.73 The supply and demand functions for a product are $q_s = p^2 - 2,500$ and $q_d = p^2 - 200p + 10,000$, where p is stated in dollars and q_s and q_d are both in thousands of units. Determine the market equilibrium price and quantity.

10.74 An amusement park charges a fixed daily admission fee. Management has varied the daily fee periodically to observe the effect on the average number of persons attending. They have determined the following function which expresses the average daily attendance q as a function of the fee p, stated in cents.

$$q = f(p) = 18,000 - 120p$$

(a) Determine the function which states average daily revenue R as a function of p.
(b) What is average daily revenue expected to equal if an admission fee of $0.50 is charged?
(c) What admission fee will result in a maximum value for R?
(d) What is the maximum value for R?

Exercises 10.75 to 10.78 are related to Sec. 10.4.

10.75 Which of the following functions can be considered to be exponential? For those which are not, indicate why.
(a) $f(x) = \sqrt[3]{x}$ (b) $h(t) = e^{5t}$
(c) $g(y) = \sqrt[y]{18}$ (d) $u(x) = 500(1 - e^{-x})$

10.76 Sketch the exponential functions
(a) $y = 1^x$ (b) $y = 3^x$

10.77 Sketch the exponential functions
(a) $y = 2^{x^2}$ (b) $y = (2)^{x/4}$

10.78 Sketch the exponential functions
(a) $y = -(2)^x$ (b) $y = -3(2)^x$

Exercises 10.79 to 10.86 are related to Sec. 10.5.

10.79 A sum of $50,000 is invested at a rate of 6 percent per year compounded continuously. Determine the compound amount S if the investment is for a period of 10 years. How much interest is earned during this period?

10.80 *Present Value: Continuous Compounding.* Assuming continuous compounding, the present value P of S dollars t years in the future can be expressed by the function

$$P = f(t) = Se^{-it} \tag{10.27}$$

(a) Assuming interest of 6 percent per year compounded continuously, what sum should be deposited today if $60,000 is desired 20 years from now?

(b) What deposit would be required if interest is compounded annually?

(c) How much more interest is earned over the 20-year period with continuous compounding?

10.81 The population of a particular species of fish has been estimated at 200 million. Scientists suspect that the population is growing exponentially at a rate of 4.5 percent per year. If the rate and pattern of growth continue, what is the fish population expected to equal in 20 years?

10.82 *Public Utilities.* The number of new telephones installed each day in a particular city is currently 300. Telephone company officials believe that the number of new telephones installed each day will continue to increase exponentially at a rate of 6 percent per year. If this pattern holds true, what is the daily rate of installation expected to be 5 years from today?

10.83 In Exercise 10.82, in what year will the number of new installations per day go over 450?

10.84 The population of a particular class of endangered species has been *decreasing* exponentially at a rate of 4 percent per year. If the current population of the species is 900,000, what is the population expected to equal in 10 years? (*Hint:* See Exercise 10.51.)

10.85 *Police Patrol Allocation.* A police department has determined that the average daily crime rate depends on the number of officers assigned to each shift. The function describing this relationship is

$$N = f(x)$$
$$= 200 - 5xe^{-0.02x}$$

where N equals the average daily crime rate and x equals the number of officers assigned to each shift. What is the average daily crime rate if 10 officers are assigned? If 40 officers are assigned?

10.86 *Product Reliability.* A manufacturer of batteries used in portable radios, toys, flashlights, etc., estimates that the percentage P of manufactured batteries having a useful life of at least t hours is described by the function

$$P = f(t) = e^{-0.1t}$$

What percentage of batteries is expected to last at least 10 hours? At least 20 hours?

Exercises 10.87 to 10.90 are related to Sec. 10.6.

10.87 For each exponential equation write the equivalent logarithmic equation.

(a) $3^5 = 243$ (b) $10^5 = 100,000$
(c) $6^3 = 216$ (d) $(2.5)^3 = 15.625$
(e) $7^3 = 243$ (f) $(0.2)^3 = 0.008$

10.88 For each of the following logarithmic equations, write the equivalent exponential equation.

(a) $\log_{1.5} 5.0625 = 4$ (b) $\log_5 125 = 3$
(c) $\log_5 0.008 = -3$ (d) $\log_{20} 8,000 = 3$

10.89 Determine the following from Table A.2.

(a) ln 75   (b) ln 1,000

(c) ln 5,000   (d) ln 900

10.90 *Welfare Management.* A welfare agency estimates that the average cost C of processing welfare applications is a function of the number of welfare analysts x. The average cost function is

$$C = 0.01x^2 - 20\ln x + 60$$

where C is stated in dollars. What is the average cost per application if there are 10 analysts?

CHAPTER TEST

1 For the quadratic function

$$f(x) = x^2 + 10x + 25$$

determine (a) the concavity, (b) the y intercept, (c) the x intercept(s), and (d) coordinates of the vertex of the parabola. (e) Sketch the function.

2 The demand function for a product is

$$q = f(p) = 400{,}000 - 30p$$

where q equals the quantity demanded and p equals the selling price in dollars. Determine the quadratic total revenue function $R = g(p)$.

3 Three points (p, q) on a quadratic supply function are (20, 400), (25, 850), and (30, 1,400). Set up (*only*) the system of equations which, when solved, would provide the parameters of the supply function $q_s = ap^2 + bp + c$.

4 Given $f(x) = 1{,}000e^{-x}$, determine $f(25)$.

5 An investment of \$10,000 receives interest of 7 percent per year compounded continuously. What is the compound amount S if the investment is for a period of 20 years? How much interest will be earned during this period?

6 Given

$$4^8 = 65{,}536$$

write the equivalent logarithmic equation.

CHAPTER OBJECTIVES After reading this chapter, you should understand the concept of the *limit* of a function; you should understand the differences between *continuous* and *discontinuous* functions; you should understand the meaning of and distinctions between the *average rate of change* and *instantaneous rate of change* of a function; you should be familiar with the *derivative*, its meaning, and its interpretations; and you should be able to apply the basic rules of *differentiation*.

INTRODUCTION 11.1

This is the first of five chapters which examine the *calculus* and its application to business, economics, and other areas of problem solving. Two major areas of study within the calculus are *differential calculus* and *integral calculus*. Differential calculus focuses on *rates of change* in analyzing a situation. Graphically, differential calculus solves the following problem: Given a function whose graph is a smooth curve and given a point in the domain of the function, what is the slope of the line tangent to the curve at this point? You will see later that this "slope" expresses the instantaneous rate of change of the function.

Integral calculus is oriented more toward summation of a special type. Graphically, the concepts of *area* in two dimensions or *volume* in three dimensions are important in integral calculus. In two dimensions, integral calculus solves the following problem: Given a function whose graph is a smooth curve and two points in the domain of the function, what is the area of the region bounded by the curve and the x axis between these two points?

This chapter and the next three which follow will discuss differential calculus and its applications. Chapter 15 will survey integral calculus and its applications. Chapter 16 will briefly illustrate the application of the integral calculus to probability theory. The goal in these chapters is to provide an appreciation for what the calculus is and where it can be applied. Though it would take several semesters of intensive study to understand most of the finer points of the calculus, your coverage will enable you to understand the tools for conducting analyses at elementary levels.

This chapter will concern itself with laying foundations for the remaining chapters. It will first examine two key concepts which are important in the theory of differential calculus. This discussion will be followed by an intuitive development of the concept of the *derivative*. The remainder of the chapter will provide the tools for finding derivatives as well as insights into interpreting the meaning of the derivative. Although proofs of the rules of differentiation are not presented in the main part of the chapter, selected proofs are presented in the appendix at the end of the chapter.

11.2   LIMITS AND CONTINUITY

Two concepts which are important in the theory of differential and integral calculus are the *limit of a function* and *continuity*. These concepts are discussed in this section. Since these concepts are frequently misunderstood, take care in reading these discussions.

Limits of Functions

In the calculus there is often a concern about the limiting value of a function as the independent variable approaches some specific value. This limiting value, when it exists, is called a *limit*. The notation

$$\lim_{x \to a} f(x) = L \tag{11.1}$$

is used to express the limiting value of a function. Equation (11.1) is read "the limit of $f(x)$, as x approaches the value a, equals L." The notion of a limit was alluded to in the last chapter when we mentioned asymptotes.

There are different procedures for determining the limit of a function. The temptation is simply to substitute the value $x = a$ into $f(x)$ and determine $f(a)$. This is actually a valid way of determining the limit for many but not all functions.

One approach that can be used is to substitute values of the independent variable into the function while observing the behavior of $f(x)$ as the value of x comes closer and closer to a. An important point in this procedure is that the value of the function is observed as the value of a is approached from both sides of a. The notation $\lim_{x \to a^-} f(x)$ represents the limit of $f(x)$ as x approaches a from the left (left-hand limit) or from below. The notation $\lim_{x \to a^+} f(x)$ represents the limit of $f(x)$ as x approaches a from the right (right-hand limit) or from above. *If the value of the function approaches the same number L as x approaches a from either direction, then the limit exists.* To state it more precisely,

---

If $\lim_{x \to a^-} f(x) = L$ and $\lim_{x \to a^+} f(x) = L$,

$$\lim_{x \to a} f(x) = L$$

If the limiting values of $f(x)$ are different when x approaches from each direction, then the function does not approach a limit as x approaches a. The following examples are illustrative.

Determine $\lim_{x \to 2} x^3$.

Example 11.1

In order to determine the limit, let's construct a table of assumed values for x and corresponding values for $f(x)$. Table 11.1 indicates these values. Note that the value of $x = 2$ has been approached from both the left and the right. And, from either direction, $f(x)$ is approaching the same value of 8. Since

Solution

$$\lim_{x \to 2^-} x^3 = \lim_{x \to 2^+} x^3 = 8 \qquad \lim_{x \to 2} x^3 = 8$$

x	1	1.5	1.9	1.95	1.99	1.995	1.999
$f(x) = x^3$	1	3.375	6.858	7.415	7.881	7.94	7.988

Table 11.1

Approaching $x = 2$ from the Left

x	3	2.5	2.1	2.05	2.01	2.005	2.001
$f(x) = x^3$	27	15.625	9.261	8.615	8.121	8.060	8.012

Approaching $x = 2$ from the Right

Note that this limit could have been determined by simply substituting $x = 2$ into $f(x)$.

Examination of the graph of the function in Fig. 11.1 confirms our result. The closer we get to a value of $x = 2$, the closer the value of $f(x)$ comes to 8.

Determine $\lim_{x \to 4} f(x)$

Example 11.2

where

$$f(x) = \begin{cases} 2x & \text{when } x \le 4 \\ 2x + 3 & \text{when } x > 4 \end{cases}$$

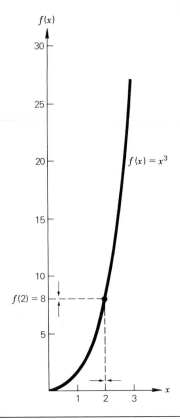

$$f(x)$$

$$f(x) = x^3$$

$$f(2) = 8$$

FIGURE 11.1

Solution This function is defined in two parts, depending on the value of x. Again, let's construct a table of values for $f(x)$ as x approaches 4 from both the left and right (Table 11.2). As x approaches a value of 4 from the left, $f(x)$ approaches a value of 8, or

$$\lim_{x \to 4^-} f(x) = 8$$

As x approaches 8 from the right, $f(x)$ approaches a value of 11, or

$$\lim_{x \to 4^+} f(x) = 11$$

Table 11.2

x	3	3.5	3.8	3.9	3.95	3.99
$f(x)$	6.0	7.0	7.6	7.8	7.9	7.98

Approaching $x = 4$ from the Left

x	5	4.5	4.3	4.1	4.05	4.01
$f(x)$	13.0	12.0	11.6	11.2	11.1	11.02

Approaching $x = 4$ from the Right

Since

$$\lim_{x \to 4^-} f(x) \ne \lim_{x \to 4^+} f(x)$$

the function does not approach a limiting value as $x \to 4$, and $\lim_{x \to 4} f(x)$ does not exist. Figure 11.2 shows the graph of this function. Recall from Chap. 2 that the solid circle (●) indicates that $x = 4$ is included in the domain for the lower line segment, and the open circle (○) indicates that $x = 4$ is not included in the domain for the upper line segment. The break in the function at $x = 4$ is the reason that the limit does not exist. An important point, with regard to this function, is that $f(x)$ does approach a limit for any values other than $x = 4$.

Determine

$$\lim_{x \to 3} \frac{x^2 - 9}{x - 3}$$

Example 11.3

Since the denominator equals 0 when $x = 3$, we can conclude that the function is undefined at this point. And, it would be tempting to conclude that no limit exists when $x = 3$. You will see in a minute, though, that this function does approach a limit as x approaches (gets closer to) 3, even though the function is not defined at $x = 3$.

Solution

Table 11.3 indicates values of $f(x)$ as x approaches 3 from both the left and the right. And, since

$$\lim_{x \to 3^-} f(x) = 6 \qquad \text{and} \qquad \lim_{x \to 3^+} f(x) = 6$$

$$\lim_{x \to 3} \frac{x^2 - 9}{x - 3} = 6$$

Even though the function is undefined when $x = 3$, the function approaches a value of 6 as the value of x comes closer to 3. Figure 11.3 indicates the graph of the function.

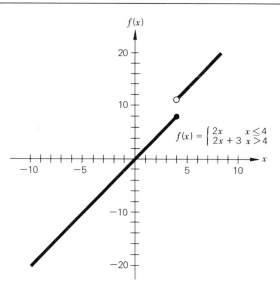

$$f(x) = \begin{cases} 2x & x \le 4 \\ 2x + 3 & x > 4 \end{cases}$$

FIGURE 11.2

Table 11.3	x	2	2.5	2.9	2.95	2.99
	$f(x)$	5.0	5.5	5.9	5.95	5.99

Approaching $x = 3$ from the Left

x	4	3.5	3.1	3.05	3.01
$f(x)$	7.0	6.5	6.1	6.05	6.01

Approaching $x = 3$ from the Right

An intuitive definition of a limit is now presented.

DEFINITION
The notation

$$\lim_{x \to a} f(x) = L$$

means that as x gets close to a, for $x \neq a$, $f(x)$ gets close to L.

A key point with the limit concept is that we are not interested in the value of $f(x)$ when $x = a$. We are interested in the behavior of the values of $f(x)$ as x comes closer and closer to a value of a.

Follow-up Exercises

For the following exercises, determine the limit (if it exists) by constructing a table of values for $f(x)$.

11.1 $\lim_{x \to 5} 2x^2$

11.2 $\lim_{x \to -2} (4x - 5)$

FIGURE 11.3

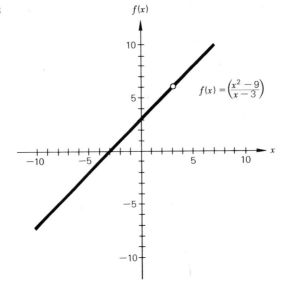

$$f(x) = \left(\frac{x^2 - 9}{x - 3}\right)$$

11.3 $\lim\limits_{x \to 5} f(x)$ where $f(x) = \begin{cases} x & \text{for } x < 5 \\ 10 - x & \text{for } x \geq 5 \end{cases}$

11.4 $\lim\limits_{x \to 3} f(x)$ where $f(x) = \begin{cases} x^2 & \text{for } x < 3 \\ 12 - x & \text{for } x \geq 3 \end{cases}$

11.5 $\lim\limits_{x \to 1} g(x)$ where $g(x) = \begin{cases} 5 - 2x & \text{for } x < 1 \\ 2x & \text{for } x \geq 1 \end{cases}$

11.6 $\lim\limits_{x \to 4} h(x)$ where $h(x) = \begin{cases} x^2 & \text{for } x < 4 \\ 0.5x^2 & \text{for } x \geq 4 \end{cases}$

11.7 $\lim\limits_{x \to 7} \dfrac{x^2 - 49}{x - 7}$

11.8 $\lim\limits_{x \to -2} \dfrac{x^2 - 4}{x + 2}$

11.9 $\lim\limits_{x \to -1} \dfrac{3x^2 - 9x - 12}{3x + 3}$

11.10 $\lim\limits_{x \to 1/2} \dfrac{2x^2 + x - 1}{2x - 1}$

11.11 $\lim\limits_{x \to \infty} (\tfrac{1}{2})^x$

11.12 $\lim\limits_{x \to \infty} e^{-x}$

11.13 $\lim\limits_{x \to 0} \dfrac{1}{x}$

11.14 $\lim\limits_{x \to 2} \dfrac{1}{x - 2}$

Some Properties of Limits

This section discusses some properties of limits which are useful in terms of actually determining the limiting value of a function. We will soon see that the process of determining limits need not always involve evaluation of $f(x)$ at a series of points on either side of $x = a$.

Properties of Limits

1 If $f(x) = c$, where c is real,

$$\lim_{x \to a} (c) = c$$

2 If $f(x) = x^n$, where n is a positive integer, then

$$\lim_{x \to a} x^n = a^n$$

3 If $f(x)$ has a limit as $x \to a$ and c is real, then .

$$\lim_{x \to a} c \cdot f(x) = c \cdot \lim_{x \to a} f(x)$$

4 If $f(x)$ and $g(x)$ have limits defined as $x \to a$,

$$\lim_{x \to a} [f(x) \pm g(x)] = \lim_{x \to a} f(x) \pm \lim_{x \to a} g(x)$$

5 If $f(x)$ and $g(x)$ have limits defined as $x \to a$,

$$\lim_{x \to a} [f(x) \cdot g(x)] = \lim_{x \to a} f(x) \cdot \lim_{x \to a} g(x)$$

6 If $f(x)$ and $g(x)$ have limits defined as $x \to a$,

$$\lim_{x \to a} \frac{f(x)}{g(x)} = \frac{\lim\limits_{x \to a} f(x)}{\lim\limits_{x \to a} g(x)} \qquad \text{provided } \lim_{x \to a} g(x) \neq 0$$

Example 11.4

$$\lim_{x \to -5} 10 = 10 \qquad \text{(Property 1)}$$

Example 11.5

$$\lim_{x \to -1} x^4 = (-1)^4 = 1 \qquad \text{(Property 2)}$$

Example 11.6

$$\lim_{x \to 5} (x^2 - x + 10) = \lim_{x \to 5} x^2 - \lim_{x \to 5} x + \lim_{x \to 5} 10$$
$$= 5^2 - 5 + 10$$
$$= 30$$

(Properties 1, 2, and 3)

Example 11.7

$$\lim_{x \to -2} 5x^3 = 5 \cdot \lim_{x \to -2} x^3$$
$$= (5)(-2)^3$$
$$= (5)(-8) = -40 \quad \text{(Properties 3 and 4)}$$

Example 11.8

$$\lim_{x \to 0} [(x^5 - 1)(x^3 + 4)] = \lim_{x \to 0} (x^5 - 1) \cdot \lim_{x \to 0} (x^3 + 4)$$
$$= (\lim_{x \to 0} x^5 - \lim_{x \to 0} 1)(\lim_{x \to 0} x^3 + \lim_{x \to 0} 4)$$
$$= (0 - 1)(0 + 4)$$
$$= (-1)(4)$$
$$= -4$$

(Properties 1, 2, 4, and 5)

Example 11.9

$$\lim_{x \to 2} \frac{x^3 - 1}{x^2} = \frac{\lim_{x \to 2} (x^3 - 1)}{\lim_{x \to 2} x^2}$$
$$= \frac{\lim_{x \to 2} x^3 - \lim_{x \to 2} 1}{\lim_{x \to 2} x^2}$$
$$= \frac{2^3 - 1}{2^2} = \frac{8 - 1}{4}$$
$$= \tfrac{7}{4}$$

(Properties 1, 2, 4, and 6)

These properties make the process of evaluating limits considerably easier for certain classes of functions. Limits of these types of functions may be evaluated by *substitution* to determine $f(a)$. For these classes of functions

$$\lim_{x \to a} f(x) = f(a) \qquad (11.2)$$

Polynomial functions are a commonly used class of functions for which Eq. (11.2) is valid. This follows from Properties 1 through 4.

$$\lim_{x \to -2} (3x^2 - 4x + 10) = f(-2)$$
$$= 3(-2)^2 - 4(-2) + 10$$
$$= 12 + 8 + 10$$
$$= 30$$

Example 11.10

In Example 11.3 we determined that

$$\lim_{x \to 3} \frac{x^2 - 9}{x - 3} = 6$$

Even though the function is not defined at $x = 3$, the value of the function approaches 6 as x approaches 3. This function is an example of a group of "quotient" functions which can be simplified by factoring. The function in Example 11.3 can be simplified as follows:

$$f(x) = \frac{x^2 - 9}{x - 3}$$
$$= \frac{(x + 3)(x - 3)}{x - 3}$$
$$= x + 3 \qquad \text{for all } x \neq 3$$

It should be pointed out that $f(x) = [(x + 3)(x - 3)]/(x - 3)$ and $g(x) = x + 3$ are *not* the same function, but they *are* the same everywhere $f(x)$ is defined. As illustrated in Fig. 11.4, $g(x)$ is a line, and $f(x)$ is a line with a "hole" at $x = 3$. However, since we do not care what happens at

FIGURE 11.4

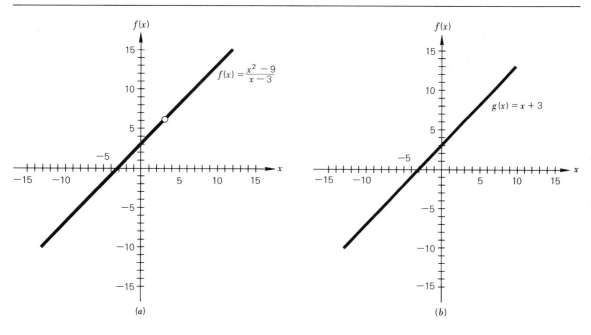

(a)

(b)

$x = 3$, we can study the behavior of $f(x)$ by studying the behavior of $g(x)$.

This simplification has reduced the function to a form for which the substitution approach is valid. That is,

$$\lim_{x \to 3} \frac{x^2 - 9}{x - 3} = \lim_{x \to 3} (x + 3)$$
$$= 3 + 3$$
$$= 6$$

Example 11.11

$$\lim_{x \to -1} \frac{4x^2 + x - 3}{x + 1} = \lim_{x \to -1} \frac{(4x - 3)(x + 1)}{x + 1}$$
$$= \lim_{x \to -1} (4x - 3)$$
$$= 4(-1) - 3$$
$$= -7$$

One special case that we will consider is that of limits at an endpoint on the domain of a function. Consider the function $f(x) = \sqrt{x}$. The domain for this function is $x \geq 0$. If we are interested in $\lim_{x \to 0} \sqrt{x}$, we cannot determine both the left-hand and the right-hand limits. We can determine $\lim_{x \to 0^+} \sqrt{x}$, but not $\lim_{x \to 0^-} \sqrt{x}$. *Our concern always will be in determining limits from within the domain of a function.* In this instance, the limit must be determined based on the right-hand limit. Since $\lim_{x \to 0^+} \sqrt{x} = 0$, $\lim_{x \to 0} \sqrt{x} = 0$.

Limits and Asymptotes

Chapter 10 alluded to the notion of *asymptotes*, which are characteristics of the graphs of certain functions. The following definitions will help to formalize these concepts.

DEFINITION
The line $x = a$ is a *vertical asymptote* of the graph of $f(x)$ if and only if

$$\lim_{x \to a^-} f(x) = \infty \qquad (\text{or } -\infty)$$

or

$$\lim_{x \to a^+} f(x) = \infty \qquad (\text{or } -\infty)$$

FIGURE 11.5

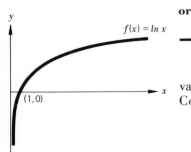

$f(x) = \ln x$

$(1, 0)$

This definition suggests that as x approaches a particular value, the value of the function approaches either positive or negative infinity. Consider the function $f(x) = \ln x$, shown in Fig. 11.5. For this function

$$\lim_{x \to 0^+} \ln x = -\infty$$

and we can state that the graph of $f(x)$ has a vertical asymptote at $x = 0$.

DEFINITION
The line $y = a$ is a *horizontal asymptote* of the graph of $f(x)$ if and only if

$$\lim_{x \to \infty} f(x) = a$$

or

$$\lim_{x \to -\infty} f(x) = a$$

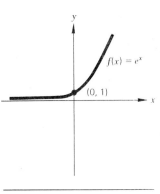

This definition suggests that as x approaches a value of positive infinity or negative infinity, the value of $f(x)$ approaches but never quite reaches a value of a. Consider the function $f(x) = e^x$ shown in Fig. 11.6. For this function

$$\lim_{x \to -\infty} e^x = 0$$

and we can state that $f(x)$ has a horizontal asymptote at $y = 0$.

FIGURE 11.6

Continuity

In an informal sense, a function is described as *continuous* if it can be sketched without lifting your pen or pencil from the paper. Most of the functions that we will examine in the calculus will be continuous functions. Figure 11.7 indicates the sketches of four different functions. Those depicted in Fig. 11.7a and 11.7b are continuous since they can be drawn without lifting your pencil. Those in Fig. 11.7c and 11.7d are not continuous because of the "breaks" in the functions. A function which is not continuous is termed *discontinuous*. A more formal definition of the property of continuity follows:

DEFINITION
A function $f(x)$ is said to be *continuous* at $x = a$ if (1) the function is defined at $x = a$ and (2)

$$\lim_{x \to a} f(x) = f(a) \qquad (11.3)$$

In Example 11.1 we determined that

$$\lim_{x \to 2} x^3 = 8$$

Example 11.12

Because $\lim_{x \to 2} x^3 = f(2) = 8$, Eq. (11.3) is satisfied and we can state that the function $f(x) = x^3$ is continuous when $x = 2$.

In Example 11.3 we determined that

$$\lim_{x \to 3} \frac{x^2 - 9}{x - 3} = 6$$

Example 11.13

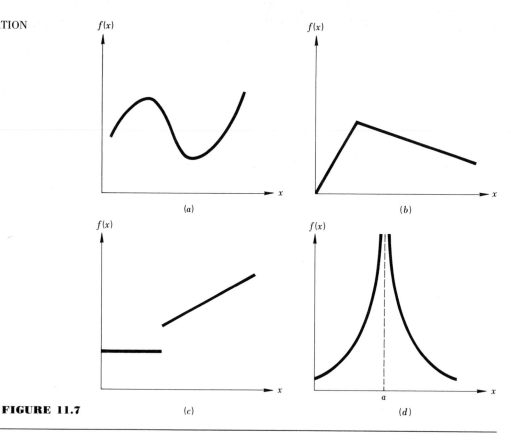

FIGURE 11.7

Because $x = 3$ is not in the domain of the function, $f(3)$ is not defined and we can state that the function $(x^2 - 9)/(x - 3)$ is *discontinuous* at $x = 3$.

DEFINITION
A function is continuous over an interval $a \le x \le b$ if it is continuous at every point within the interval.

Example 11.14   The function $f(x) = x^2 - 2x + 5$ is continuous when x is real-valued because

$$\lim_{x \to a} (x^2 - 2x + 5) = f(a)$$
$$= a^2 - 2a + 5 \qquad \text{for all real } a$$

Example 11.15   Determine whether there are any discontinuities for the function

$$f(x) = \frac{1}{x^3 - x}$$

This function is not defined when

$$x^3 - x = 0$$
or
$$x(x^2 - 1) = 0$$
or
$$x(x + 1)(x - 1) = 0$$

The product on the left side of the equation equals 0 when $x = 0$, $x = -1$, or $x = +1$. Thus, the function is discontinuous at these three points. Figure 11.8 presents a sketch of the graph of the function. Note that this function has vertical asymptotes described by the equations $x = 1$, $x = -1$, and $x = 0$.

Follow-up Exercises

For the following exercises, find the indicated limit.

11.15 $\lim\limits_{x \to 0} (4x^3 - x)$

11.16 $\lim\limits_{x \to -1} (3x^2 - 2x + 1)$

11.17 $\lim\limits_{x \to -3} \left(\dfrac{x^2}{4} - \dfrac{x}{2} + 10 \right)$

11.18 $\lim\limits_{x \to 2} \dfrac{x - 2}{x + 6}$

11.19 $\lim\limits_{x \to 4} \dfrac{x^2 - 5}{1 - x}$

11.20 $\lim\limits_{x \to -2} (x - 4)(x^2 + 3x)$

11.21 $\lim\limits_{x \to 0} (3 - x^2)(5x + 6)$

11.22 $\lim\limits_{x \to 3} (-12)$

11.23 $\lim\limits_{x \to 0} 250$

11.24 $\lim\limits_{x \to 6} \dfrac{x^2 - 36}{x - 6}$

11.25 $\lim\limits_{x \to -2} \dfrac{x^2 - 4}{x + 2}$

11.26 $\lim\limits_{x \to -2} \dfrac{3x^2 + x - 10}{x + 2}$

11.27 $\lim\limits_{x \to 2} \dfrac{3x^2 + x - 14}{x - 2}$

11.28 $\lim\limits_{x \to a} (x^3 - 2x)$

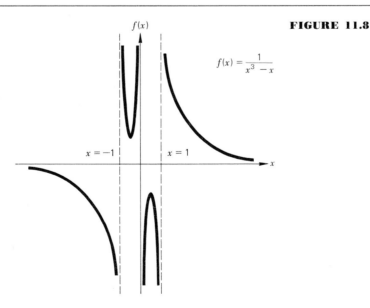

$$f(x) = \frac{1}{x^3 - x}$$

$x = -1$ $x = 1$

FIGURE 11.8

11.29 $\lim\limits_{x \to -b} (x^2 - 2x + 1)$

11.30 $\lim\limits_{x \to \infty} (1/x)$

11.31 $\lim\limits_{x \to -\infty} \dfrac{2x + 1}{2x}$

11.32 $\lim\limits_{x \to \infty} \dfrac{x}{2x + 1}$

In the following exercises, determine whether there are any discontinuities and, if so, where they occur.

11.33 $f(x) = 3x^2 - 2x + 10$

11.34 $f(x) = 1/x$

11.35 $f(x) = (2x + 6)(x - 5)$

11.36 $f(x) = x^7$

11.37 $f(x) = \dfrac{x}{x - 3}$

11.38 $f(x) = \dfrac{3}{6 - x}$

11.39 $f(x) = |x|$

11.40 $g(x) = |-x|$

11.41 $h(x) = \dfrac{5}{-2x^2 + 9x - 9}$

11.42 $v(x) = \dfrac{2x - 1}{x^2 - 2x + 1}$

11.43 $g(x) = \dfrac{4 - x}{3x^3 - 27x}$

11.44 $h(x) = \dfrac{5}{2x^3 - 2x}$

11.3   AVERAGE RATE OF CHANGE

Average Rate of Change and Slope

As discussed in Chap. 3, the slope of a straight line can be determined by applying the two-point formula:

$$m = \frac{\Delta y}{\Delta x} = \frac{y_2 - y_1}{x_2 - x_1} \qquad (11.4)$$

Figure 11.9 illustrates the graph of a linear function. With linear functions the slope is constant over the domain of the function. The slope provides an *exact measure* of the rate of change in the value of y with respect to a change in the value of x. If the function in Fig. 11.9 repre-

FIGURE 11.9

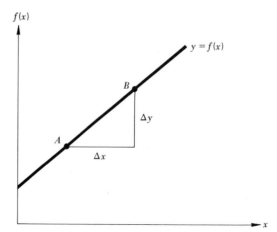

sents a linear cost function and x equals the number of units produced, the slope indicates the rate at which total cost increases with respect to changes in the level of output.

With nonlinear functions the rate of change in the value of y with respect to a change in x is not constant. However, one way of describing nonlinear functions is by the *average rate of change* over some interval.

Assume that a person takes an automobile trip and that the distance traveled d can be described as a function of time t by the nonlinear function

$$d = f(t) = 8t^2 + 8t$$

Example 11.16

where d is measured in miles, t is measured in hours, and $0 \le t \le 5$. During this 5-hour journey the speed of the car may change continuously (e.g., because of traffic lights, rest stops, etc.).

After 1 hour, the total distance traveled is

$$f(1) = 8(1)^2 + 8(1)$$
$$= 16 \text{ (miles)}$$

The average rate of change in the distance traveled with respect to a change in time during a time interval (better known as *average velocity*) is computed as

$$\frac{\text{Distance traveled}}{\text{Time traveled}}$$

For the first hour of this trip, the average velocity equals

$$\frac{\Delta d}{\Delta t} = \frac{f(1) - f(0)}{1 - 0} = \frac{16 - 0}{1} = 16 \text{ (miles per hour)}$$

The distance traveled at the end of 2 hours is

$$f(2) = 8(2^2) + 8(2)$$
$$= 32 + 16$$
$$= 48 \text{ miles}$$

The distance traveled *during* the second hour is

$$\Delta d = f(2) - f(1)$$
$$= 48 - 16$$
$$= 32 \text{ miles}$$

The average velocity *for the second hour* equals

$$\frac{\Delta d}{\Delta t} = \frac{32}{1} = 32 \text{ (miles per hour)}$$

And, the average velocity is different compared with that for the first hour.

The average velocity *during the first 2 hours* is the total distance traveled during that period divided by the time traveled, or

$$\frac{\Delta d}{\Delta t} = \frac{f(2) - f(0)}{2 - 0} = \frac{48 - 0}{2} = 24 \text{ (miles per hour)}$$

POINT FOR THOUGHT AND DISCUSSION
Consider the function

$$d = f(t) = 55t$$

which expresses the distance traveled d (in miles) as a function of time
t (in hours). Compare this function with the function in Example
11.16. What is the difference with regard to average velocity?

Consider the two points A and B in Fig. 11.10. The straight line connecting these two points on $f(x)$ is referred to as a *secant line*. At point A the independent variable has a value of x, and the corresponding value of the dependent variable can be determined by evaluating $f(x)$. At point B the independent variable has changed in value to $x + \Delta x$, and the corresponding value of the dependent variable can be determined by evaluating $f(x + \Delta x)$. In moving from point A to point B, the change in the value of x is $(x + \Delta x) - x$, or Δx. The associated change in the value of y is $\Delta y = f(x + \Delta x) - f(x)$. The ratio of these changes is

$$\frac{\Delta y}{\Delta x} = \frac{f(x + \Delta x) - f(x)}{\Delta x} \qquad (11.5)$$

Equation (11.5) is sometimes referred to as the *difference quotient*. Given any two points on a function having coordinates $(x, f(x))$ and

FIGURE 11.10

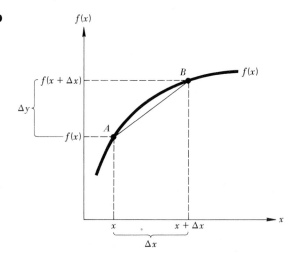

$((x + \Delta x), f(x + \Delta x))$, the difference quotient provides a general expression which

1 represents the *average rate of change* in the value of y with respect to the change in x while moving from one point to the other

2 computes the slope of the secant line connecting the two points

---

(a) Find the general expression for the difference quotient of the function $y = f(x) = x^2$.

(b) Find the slope of the line connecting $(-2, 4)$ and $(3, 9)$ using the two-point formula.

(c) Find the slope in part b using the expression for the difference quotient found in part a.

Example 11.17

(a) Given two points on the function $f(x) = x^2$ which have coordinates $(x, f(x))$ and $(x + \Delta x, f(x + \Delta x))$, we have

Solution

$$\frac{f(x + \Delta x) - f(x)}{\Delta x} = \frac{(x + \Delta x)^2 - x^2}{\Delta x}$$

$$= \frac{[x^2 + x(\Delta x) + x(\Delta x) + (\Delta x)^2] - x^2}{\Delta x}$$

$$= \frac{[x^2 + 2x(\Delta x) + (\Delta x)^2] - x^2}{\Delta x}$$

$$= \frac{2x(\Delta x) + (\Delta x)^2}{\Delta x}$$

Factoring Δx from each term in the numerator and canceling with Δx in the denominator, we get

$$\frac{f(x + \Delta x) - f(x)}{\Delta x} = \frac{\Delta x(2x + \Delta x)}{\Delta x}$$

$$= 2x + \Delta x \qquad (11.6)$$

NOTE

The evaluation of $f(x + \Delta x)$ and $f(x)$ for a specific function causes the greatest difficulty for students. If, for this function, you were asked to find $f(3)$, you would substitute the value of 3 into the function wherever the independent variable appears, or $f(3) = 3^2 = 9$. When asked to find $f(x + \Delta x)$ in this example, we substituted $x + \Delta x$ into the function where the independent variable appeared and evaluated $(x + \Delta x)^2$. Similarly, when finding $f(x)$, we substituted the value x where the independent variable appeared and evaluated x^2. *Whenever you are asked to determine the difference quotient, $f(x)$ will always be the specific function with which you are working.*

(b) Using the two-point slope formula, we get

$$\frac{\Delta y}{\Delta x} = \frac{9 - 4}{3 - (-2)} = \frac{5}{5} = 1$$

The slope of the secant line connecting $(-2, 4)$ and $(3, 9)$ on $f(x)$ equals 1.

(c) Letting $(x, f(x))$ and $(x + \Delta x, f(x + \Delta x))$ correspond to the points $(-2, 4)$ and $(3, 9)$ on the function, assume that x corresponds to the coordinate -2 and $x + \Delta x$ corresponds to the coordinate of 3. Thus,

$$(x, f(x)) \quad ((x + \Delta x), f(x + \Delta x))$$

$$(-2, 4) \quad (3, 9)$$

So $\quad x = -2$
and $\quad x + \Delta x = 3$
Therefore $\quad (-2) + \Delta x = 3$
or $\quad \Delta x = 5$

This value for Δx simply means that the distance separating these two points along the x axis is 5 units.

If we substitute the values of $x = -2$ and $\Delta x = 5$ into Eq. (11.6), the difference quotient for these two points equals $2(-2) + 5 = 1$. This is exactly the same result as we got in part b.

EXERCISE
In the last example, let $x = 3$ and $(x + \Delta x) = -2$. Evaluate the difference quotient and see if you arrive at the same result as in the example. Conclusions?

Follow-up Exercises

11.45 For the function $y = f(x) = 3x^2$, determine the average rate of change in the value of y in moving from $x = -1$ to $x = 3$.
11.46 For the function $y = f(x) = -x^2/2$, determine the average rate of change in the value of y in moving from $x = 2$ to $x = 5$.
11.47 For the function $y = f(x) = 2x^2 - 4x + 1$ determine the average rate of change in the value of y in moving from $x = 1$ to $x = 3$.
11.48 For the function $y = f(x) = -2x^3$ determine the average rate of change in the value of y in moving from $x = -2$ to $x = 0$.
11.49 The following table indicates annual sales (in dollars) for a company during a selected period. At what average rate did annual sales increase between 1974 and 1977? Between 1974 and 1975? Between 1975 and 1976? Between 1975 and 1977?

Year	1974	1975	1976	1977
Annual Sales (millions)	$20.0	$22.5	$24.8	$28.2

11.50 Annual attendance at professional baseball games has been decreasing in recent years. Figures for the years 1972 to 1977 are shown in the table. Determine the average rate of change in annual attendance between 1972 and 1974, 1974 and 1977, and 1972 and 1977.

Year	1972	1973	1974	1975	1976	1977
Annual Attendance (millions)	25.6	24.8	24.5	24.0	23.1	22.5

11.51 *Forest Management.* Figure 11.11 indicates data points which have been gathered regarding the annual demand for timber from commercial forest land. Demand is measured in billions of cubic feet. Demand is increasing but not at a constant rate. Determine the average rate of change in demand between 1970 and 1975, 1970 and 1973, and 1973 and 1975.

11.52 A person takes an automobile trip. The distance traveled d (in miles) is described as a function of time t (in hours):

$$d = f(t) = 5t^2 + 10t \qquad \text{where } 0 \le t \le 5$$

(*a*) What is the average speed during the first hour? Fifth hour?

(*b*) What is the average speed for the 5-hour trip?

For Exercises 11.53 to 11.60, (*a*) determine the general expression for the difference quotient, and (*b*) use the difference quotient to compute the slope of the secant line connecting points at $x = 1$ and $x = 3$.

11.53 $y = f(x) = x^2 - 4x + 5$ **11.54** $y = f(x) = -x^2 + 9$

11.55 $y = f(x) = 10x + 6$ **11.56** $y = f(x) = 5$

*__11.57__ $y = f(x) = x^3$ *__11.58__ $y = f(x) = -2x^3$

*__11.59__ $y = f(x) = 1/x$ *__11.60__ $y = f(x) = -3/x$

THE DERIVATIVE   11.4

In this section the concept of the *derivative* will be developed. This concept is fundamental to all that follows, so study this material carefully.

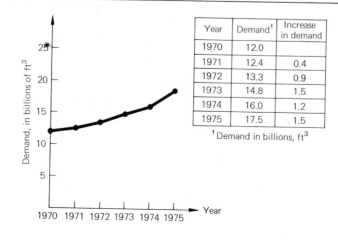

Year	Demand[†]	Increase in demand
1970	12.0	
1971	12.4	0.4
1972	13.3	0.9
1973	14.8	1.5
1974	16.0	1.2
1975	17.5	.1.5

[†] Demand in billions, ft^3

FIGURE 11.11
Annual demand for commercial forestland

Instantaneous Rate of Change

A distinction needs to be made between the concepts of *average rate of change* and *instantaneous rate of change*. Example 11.16 discussed a situation in which the distance traveled d was described as a function of time t by the function

$$d = f(t) = 8t^2 + 8t \qquad \text{where } 0 \le t \le 5$$

Suppose that we are interested in determining how fast the car is moving at the *instant* that $t = 1$. We might determine this instantaneous velocity by examining the average velocity during time intervals near $t = 1$.

For instance, the average velocity during the second hour (between $t = 1$ and $t = 2$) can be determined as

$$\frac{\Delta d}{\Delta t} = \frac{f(2) - f(1)}{2 - 1}$$

$$= \frac{[8(2^2) + 8(2)] - [8(1^2) + 8(1)]}{1}$$

$$= \frac{48 - 16}{1}$$

$$= 32 \text{ (miles per hour)}$$

The average velocity between $t = 1$ and $t = 1.5$ can be determined as

$$\frac{\Delta d}{\Delta t} = \frac{f(1.5) - f(1)}{1.5 - 1}$$

$$= \frac{[8(1.5)^2 + 8(1.5)] - [8(1^2) + 8(1)]}{0.5}$$

$$= \frac{30 - 16}{0.5}$$

$$= 28 \text{ (miles per hour)}$$

The average velocity between $t = 1$ and $t = 1.1$ can be determined as

$$\frac{\Delta d}{\Delta t} = \frac{f(1.1) - f(1)}{1.1 - 1}$$

$$= \frac{[8(1.1)^2 + 8(1.1)] - [8(1^2) + 8(1)]}{0.1}$$

$$= \frac{18.48 - 16}{0.1}$$

$$= 24.8 \text{ (miles per hour)}$$

The average velocity between $t = 1$ and $t = 1.01$ can be determined as

$$\frac{\Delta d}{\Delta t} = \frac{f(1.01) - f(1)}{1.01 - 1}$$

$$= \frac{[8(1.01)^2 + 8(1.01)] - [8(1^2) + 8(1)]}{0.01}$$

$$= \frac{16.2408 - 16}{0.01}$$

$$= 24.08 \text{ (miles per hour)}$$

These computations have been determining the average velocity over shorter and shorter time intervals measured *from* $t = 1$. As the time interval becomes shorter (or as the second value of t is chosen closer and closer to 1), the average velocity $\Delta d/\Delta t$ is approaching a limiting value. This limiting value can be considered as the *instantaneous* velocity at $t = 1$. To determine this limiting value, we could compute

$$\lim_{t \to 1} \frac{f(t) - f(1)}{t - 1} = \lim_{t \to 1} \frac{8t^2 + 8t - 16}{t - 1}$$
$$= \lim_{t \to 1} \frac{8(t^2 + t - 2)}{t - 1}$$
$$= \lim_{t \to 1} \frac{8(t + 2)(t - 1)}{t - 1}$$
$$= \lim_{t \to 1} 8(t + 2)$$
$$= 8(1 + 2)$$
$$= 24$$

Thus, the *instantaneous* velocity of the automobile when $t = 1$ is 24 miles per hour. Note that the average velocity is measured over a time interval and the instantaneous velocity is measured at a point in time. The instantaneous velocity is a "snapshot" of what is happening at a particular instant.

The instantaneous rate of change of a smooth, continuous function can be represented geometrically by the slope of the tangent line drawn at the point of interest.

Let's first determine the meaning of *tangent line*. Consider Fig. 11.12. The tangent line at A is the *limiting position* of the secant line AB as point B comes closer and closer to A. Note how the position of the secant line rotates in a clockwise manner as B is drawn closer to A (AB, AB', AB'', and AB'''). The limiting position of AB is the line segment MN.

FIGURE 11.12

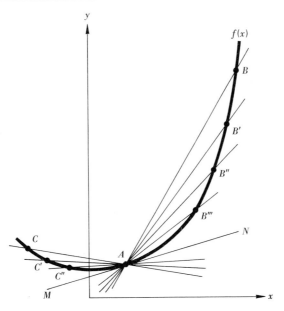

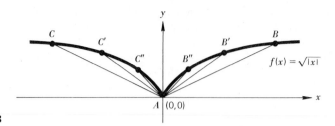

FIGURE 11.13

This same limiting position results whether A is approached with secant lines from the left or right of A. The sequence of secant lines AC, AC', and AC'' have the same limiting position MN as C is drawn closer to A. *Since MN is the limiting position whether the approach is from the left or right, MN is the tangent line at point A.*

Not all continuous functions have unique tangent lines at each point on the function. For example, the function $y = f(x) = \sqrt{|x|}$, shown in Fig. 11.13, does not have a tangent at $(0, 0)$. The secant lines drawn from $(0, 0)$ to points on the left or right do not converge to the same limiting position.

DEFINITION
The slope of a curve at $x = a$ is the slope of the tangent line at $x = a$.

Later we will have a particular interest in determining the instantaneous rate of change in functions. Since the instantaneous rate of change is represented by the slope of the tangent line at the point of interest, we will need a way of determining these tangent slopes. Suppose in Fig. 11.14 that we are interested in finding the slope of the tangent line at A. There are several different methods we might use to determine this slope. If we were good at mechanical drawing, we might construct a tangent line at point A using graph paper, read from the line coordinates of any two points, and substitute these coordinates into the two-point formula.

An alternative approach would be to identify another point B on the curve. If we connect A and B with a straight line, the slope of the line segment AB can be computed and used as an "approximation" to the slope of MN. Obviously, the slope of AB is not a good approximation. However, let's continue, still referring to Fig. 11.14. At point B the value of the independent variable is $x + \Delta x$; the distance between A and B along the x axis is Δx. If the two-point formula is applied, the slope of AB is computed by using the difference quotient:

$$\frac{\Delta y}{\Delta x} = \frac{f(x + \Delta x) - f(x)}{\Delta x} \tag{11.5}$$

Now, let's observe what happens to our approximation if a second point is chosen closer to point A. If point C is chosen as the second point, the slope of the line segment AC is still a poor approximation, but it is better than that of AB. And, if you look at the slopes of AD and AE, you should conclude that as the second point is chosen closer and closer to A, the approximation becomes better. In fact, as the value of Δx gets close to 0, the slope of the tiny line segment connecting A with the second point becomes an excellent approximation. The exact tangent slope can be determined by finding the limit of the different quotient as $\Delta x \rightarrow 0$, or the *derivative* as defined by Eq. (11.7).

$$\frac{dy}{dx} = \lim_{\Delta x \to 0} \frac{f(x + \Delta x) - f(x)}{\Delta x} \quad \textbf{(11.7)}$$

The following points should be made regarding Eq. (11.7).

1 Equation (11.7) is the general expression for the *derivative* of the function $y = f(x)$.

2 The derivative is an expression which represents the *instantaneous rate of change* in the dependent variable given a change in the independent variable. The notation dy/dx is used to represent the *instantaneous* rate of change in y with respect to a change in x. This notation is distinguished from $\Delta y/\Delta x$ which represents the average rate of change.

3 The derivative is a general expression for the tangent slope of the graph of a function at any point x in the domain of the function.

4 If the limit in Eq. (11.7) does not exist, the derivative does not exist.

FIGURE 11.14

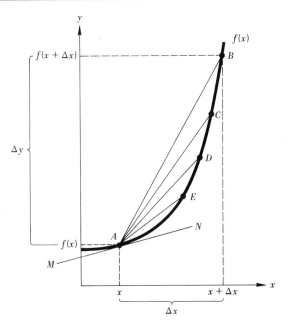

The Limit Approach to Finding the Derivative

In order to determine the derivative of a function $y = f(x)$:

1 Determine the difference quotient for $f(x)$ using Eq. (11.5).

2 Find the limit of the difference quotient as $\Delta x \to 0$.

NOTE

If
$$\lim_{\Delta x \to 0} \frac{f(x + \Delta x) - f(x)}{\Delta x}$$

does not exist for a function, the function does not have a derivative.

The following examples illustrate the *limit approach* for determining the derivative.

Example 11.18

Determine the derivative of the function $y = f(x) = -5x + 9$.

Solution

The function $f(x)$ is linear with a constant slope of -5. With the slope always -5, we should find that the derivative is -5. Forming the difference quotient, we get

$$\frac{\Delta y}{\Delta x} = \frac{f(x + \Delta x) - f(x)}{\Delta x}$$

$$= \frac{[-5(x + \Delta x) + 9] - (-5x + 9)}{\Delta x}$$

$$= \frac{-5x - 5\Delta x + 9 + 5x - 9}{\Delta x}$$

$$= \frac{-5\Delta x}{\Delta x}$$

or
$$\frac{\Delta y}{\Delta x} = -5$$

Now, determining the limit of the difference quotient as $\Delta x \to 0$, we have

$$\frac{dy}{dx} = \lim_{\Delta x \to 0} (-5)$$
$$= -5$$

Thus, the derivative is exactly what we anticipated.

Example 11.19

Determine the derivative of the function $y = f(x) = x^2$.

Solution

In Example 11.17 we found that the difference quotient for $y = f(x) = x^2$ was

$$\frac{\Delta y}{\Delta x} = 2x + \Delta x$$

The derivative is found as

$$\frac{dy}{dx} = \lim_{\Delta x \to 0} (2x + \Delta x)$$

or $\qquad \frac{dy}{dx} = 2x$

NOTE
To determine the instantaneous rate of change (or equivalently, the tangent slope) at any point on the graph of a function $f(x)$ simply substitute the value of the independent variable into the expression for dy/dx. The tangent slope at $x = c$ can be denoted by $\left.\dfrac{dy}{dx}\right|_{x=c}$, which is read "the derivative of y with respect to x at $x = c$."

For the function $y = f(x) = x^2$ in Example 11.19,

Example 11.20

(a) Determine the instantaneous rate of change in $f(x)$ at $x = -3$.
(b) Determine the instantaneous rate of change in $f(x)$ at $x = 0$.
(c) Determine the instantaneous rate of change in $f(x)$ at $x = +3$.

(a) $\left.\dfrac{dy}{dx}\right|_{x=-3} = 2(-3) = -6$

Solution

(b) $\left.\dfrac{dy}{dx}\right|_{x=0} = 2(0) = 0$

(c) $\left.\dfrac{dy}{dx}\right|_{x=3} = 2(3) = +6$

POINTS FOR THOUGHT AND DISCUSSION
From Chap. 10 we know that the function $y = x^2$ is quadratic. Sketch the function and confirm that the tangent slope values which we found in Example 11.20 a, b, and c seem reasonable. The derivative expression $dy/dx = 2x$ suggests that as x becomes more negative, the tangent slope becomes more negative and as x becomes more positive, the tangent slope becomes more positive. Does this seem correct in light of your sketch?

For the function $y = f(x) = -2x^2 + 3x - 10$

Example 11.21

(a) Determine the derivative expression.
(b) Determine the instantaneous rate of change in $f(x)$ at $x = 5$.
(c) Determine where on the function the tangent slope equals 0.

Solution   (a) The difference quotient for $f(x)$ is

$$\frac{\Delta y}{\Delta x} = \frac{f(x + \Delta x) - f(x)}{\Delta x}$$

$$= \frac{[-2(x + \Delta x)^2 + 3(x + \Delta x) - 10] - (-2x^2 + 3x - 10)}{\Delta x}$$

$$= \frac{[-2(x^2 + 2x\,\Delta x + \Delta x^2) + 3x + 3\Delta x - 10] + 2x^2 - 3x + 10}{\Delta x}$$

$$= \frac{-2x^2 - 4x\,\Delta x - 2\Delta x^2 + 3x + 3\Delta x - 10 + 2x^2 - 3x + 10}{\Delta x}$$

Simplifying the numerator gives

$$\frac{\Delta y}{\Delta x} = \frac{-4x(\Delta x) - 2(\Delta x)^2 + 3\Delta x}{\Delta x}$$

Factoring Δx from the numerator and simplifying yield

$$\frac{\Delta y}{\Delta x} = \frac{\Delta x(-4x - 2\Delta x + 3)}{\Delta x} = -4x - 2\Delta x + 3$$

The derivative of the function is

$$\frac{dy}{dx} = \lim_{\Delta x \to 0} (-4x - 2\Delta x + 3)$$

or

$$\frac{dy}{dx} = -4x + 3$$

(b) $\left. \dfrac{dy}{dx} \right|_{x=5} = -4(5) + 3$

$$= -17$$

(c) The tangent slope will equal 0 whenever $dy/dx = 0$, or for this function when $-4x + 3 = 0$. Solving for x, we have

$$-4x = -3$$

or

$$x = \tfrac{3}{4}$$

The only point where the tangent slope equals 0 occurs where $x = \tfrac{3}{4}$.

EXERCISE:
Verify that $x = \tfrac{3}{4}$ is the x coordinate of the vertex of the parabola representing this function using the appropriate formula in Chap. 10.

If a function is not continuous at a point, it cannot have a derivative at that point. However, some functions are continuous and yet not differentiable at all points within the domain.

Example 11.22   Consider $f(x) = |2x|$ shown in Fig. 11.15. Suppose we wish to find the derivative of $f(x)$ at $x = 0$. Evaluating Eq. (11.7) at $x = 0$ gives us

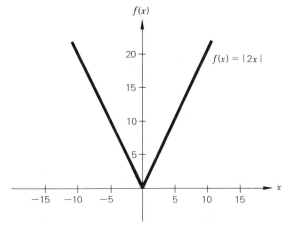

$f(x)$

$f(x) = |2x|$

FIGURE 11.15

$$\frac{dy}{dx} = \lim_{\Delta x \to 0} \frac{f(0 + \Delta x) - f(0)}{\Delta x}$$

$$= \lim_{\Delta x \to 0} \frac{|2(0 + \Delta x)| - |2(0)|}{\Delta x}$$

$$= \lim_{\Delta x \to 0} \frac{|2\Delta x|}{\Delta x}$$

Evaluating both the left- and right-hand limits, we have

$$\lim_{\Delta x \to 0^-} \frac{|2\Delta x|}{\Delta x} = -2 \quad and \quad \lim_{\Delta x \to 0^+} \frac{|2\Delta x|}{\Delta x} = 2$$

Since these two limits are not the same,

$$\lim_{\Delta x \to 0} \frac{|2\Delta x|}{\Delta x}$$

does not exist. Therefore, the function $f(x) = |2x|$ is not differentiable *at the point* $x = 0$.

Instantaneous Rate of Change Revisited

In the last section we found that the derivative dy/dx can be interpreted as a measure of the instantaneous rate of change in y with respect to a change in x. The derivative, representing the rate of change at a given instant, can be used to approximate changes which would occur in y given a change in the value of x. The following example illustrates the use of dy/dx in approximating these changes.

Example 11.23

In Example 11.20 we evaluated the derivative of the function $y = f(x) = x^2$ at different values of x. We determined that the tangent slope at $x = 3$ is $+6$. Using the instantaneous rate of change interpretation, we can state that "at the instant" when $x = 3$, y is increasing at a rate of 6 units for each unit that x increases. And this provides an approxi-

Table 11.4	x	Δx	$f(x)$	Actual Change $f(x) - f(3)$	Projected Change $6(\Delta x)$	Actual Change − Projected Change
	3.1	0.1	9.61	0.61	$6(0.1) = \;\;0.6$	0.01
	3.5	0.5	12.25	3.25	$6(0.5) = \;\;3.0$	0.25
	4.0	1.0	16.00	7.00	$6(1.0) = \;\;6.0$	1.00
	5.0	2.0	25.00	16.00	$6(2.0) = 12.0$	4.00
	6.0	3.0	36.00	27.00	$6(3.0) = 18.0$	9.00

mation of what will happen if x increases from the value of 3. The derivative suggests that for each unit that x increases beyond 3, y will increase by approximately 6 units. To test this approximation, we can compare the values of $f(x)$ when x increases by 1 unit from a value of 3 to 4.

In moving from $x = 3$ to $x = 4$,

$$\begin{aligned} \Delta y &= f(4) - f(3) \\ &= 4^2 - 3^2 \\ &= 16 - 9 \\ &= 7 \end{aligned}$$

The difference between the "actual" change in y and the approximated or "projected" change based on the derivative is $7 - 6 = 1$ unit. Therefore the derivative provides an *approximation* of the actual change. Table 11.4 presents similar comparisons for values of x closer to 3 and for values of x greater than 4. A close examination of this table reveals that *the smaller the change in x, or Δx, the better the approximation provided by dy/dx*. This is illustrated in Fig. 11.16. The vertical separation between the curve representing $y = x^2$ and the tangent line at $x = 3$ is small close to $x = 3$ but increases as one moves farther from $x = 3$.

Follow-up Exercises

In Exercises 11.61 to 11.70, (*a*) determine the derivative of $f(x)$ using the limit approach, and (*b*) determine the tangent slope at $x = -1$ and $x = 2$.

FIGURE 11.16

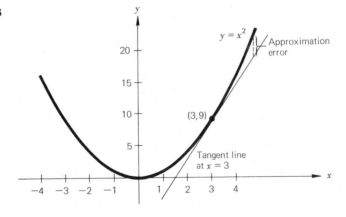

11.61 $f(x) = 3x - 5$

11.62 $f(x) = 20$

11.63 $f(x) = -x^2$

11.64 $f(x) = 4x^2$

11.65 $f(x) = 5x^2 - 5$

11.66 $f(x) = -x^2 + 6x$

*__11.67__ $f(x) = 1/x$

*__11.68__ $f(x) = x^3$

*__11.69__ $f(x) = -2x^3$

*__11.70__ $f(x) = x^4$

In Exercises 11.71 to 11.76, the function $f(x)$ and its derivative dy/dx are given. Determine the tangent slope when $x = 0$ and $x = -1$ and determine any values of x where the tangent slope equals 0.

11.71 $f(x) = 6x^2 - 3x + 10$

   $dy/dx = 12x - 3$

11.72 $f(x) = 4x^2 - 2x + 9$

   $dy/dx = 8x - 2$

11.73 $f(x) = 25x - 9$

   $dy/dx = 25$

11.74 $f(x) = -30$

   $dy/dx = 0$

11.75 $f(x) = x^3 - 3x^2$

   $dy/dx = 3x^2 - 6x$

11.76 $f(x) = x^5$

   $dy/dx = 5x^4$

11.77 For the function in Exercise 11.71 determine the instantaneous rate of change in $f(x)$ when $x = 1$. Use this to estimate the value of $f(x)$ at $x = 1.5$, $x = 2$, and $x = 3$. Compute $f(1.5)$, $f(2)$, and $f(3)$, and determine how accurately dy/dx predicts these values.

11.78 For the function in Exercise 11.72 determine the instantaneous rate of change in $f(x)$ when $x = 2$. Use this to estimate the value of $f(x)$ at $x = 2.5$, $x = 3$, and $x = 4$. Compute $f(2.5)$, $f(3)$, and $f(4)$, and determine how accurate the projections are when dy/dx is used.

DIFFERENTIATION   11.5

The process of finding a derivative is called *differentiation*. Fortunately, for us, the process does not have to be as agonizing as it may have seemed when we used the limit approach. A set of rules of differentiation exists for finding the derivatives of many common functional forms. Although there are many functions for which the derivative does not exist, *our concern will be with continuous functions which are differentiable*.

Rules of Differentiation

The rules of differentiation presented in this section have been developed by using the limit approach. The mathematics involved in proving these rules can be fairly complicated. For our purposes it will suffice to present the rules without proof. The appendix at the end of the chapter presents proofs of selected differentiation rules for anyone interested.

The rules of differentiation apply to functions which have specific structural characteristics. A rule will state that if a function has specific characteristics, then the derivative of the function will have a resulting form. As you study these rules, remember that each of these functions can be graphed and that the derivative is a general expression for the tangent slope. An alternative to the dy/dx notation is to let $f'(x)$ (read "f prime of x") represent the derivative of the function $y = f(x)$.

RULE 1: CONSTANT FUNCTION
If $f(x) = c$, where c is any constant,
$f'(x) = 0$.

Example 11.24

Consider the function $f(x) = 5$. This function has the form indicated in Rule 1. Thus, $f'(x) = 0$. If you consider what the function looks like graphically, this result seems reasonable. The function $f(x) = 5$ graphs as a horizontal line crossing the y axis at 5. The tangent slope at all points along such a function equals 0.

RULE 2: POWER RULE
If $f(x) = x^n$, where n is a real number,
$f'(x) = nx^{n-1}$.

Example 11.25

Consider the function $f(x) = x$. This function is the same as $f(x) = x^1$. Applying Rule 2, we know $n = 1$ and

$$f'(x) = 1 \cdot x^{1-1}$$
$$= x^0$$
$$= 1$$

This implies that for the function $f(x) = x$, the tangent slope equals 1 at all points. You should recognize that $f(x) = x$ is a linear function with slope of 1.

Example 11.26

Consider the function $f(x) = x^5$. Applying Rule 2, we have $n = 5$ and

$$f'(x) = 5x^{5-1}$$
$$= 5x^4$$

Example 11.27

Consider the function $f(x) = 1/x^3$.

ALGEBRA FLASHBACK

$$\frac{1}{x^n} = x^{-n}$$

Rewriting $f(x)$ as $f(x) = x^{-3}$, we have $n = -3$ and

$$f'(x) = -3x^{-3-1}$$
$$= -3x^{-4}$$
$$= \frac{-3}{x^4}$$

Consider the function $f(x) = \sqrt[3]{x^2}$.

Example 11.28

ALGEBRA FLASHBACK

$$\sqrt[n]{x^m} = x^{m/n}$$

Rewriting $f(x)$ as $f(x) = x^{2/3}$ gives us $n = \frac{2}{3}$ and

$$f'(x) = \tfrac{2}{3}x^{2/3 - 1}$$

$$= \frac{2x^{-1/3}}{3}$$

Rewriting with a positive exponent yields

$$f'(x) = \frac{2}{3x^{1/3}}$$

which can be written, using a radical, as

$$f'(x) = \frac{2}{3\sqrt[3]{x}}$$

RULE 3: CONSTANT TIMES A FUNCTION
If $f(x) = c \cdot g(x)$, where c is a constant and $g(x)$ is a differentiable function, $f'(x) = c \cdot g'(x)$.

Consider the function $f(x) = 10x^2$. Applying Rule 3 gives us $g(x) = x^2$ and $c = 10$, and

Example 11.29

$$f'(x) = 10(2x)$$
$$= 20x$$

Consider the function $f(x) = -3/x$. This function can be rewritten as

Example 11.30

$$f(x) = -3\left(\frac{1}{x}\right) = -3x^{-1}$$

Applying Rules 2 and 3 gives

$$f'(x) = (-3)(-1)(x^{-1-1})$$
$$= 3x^{-2}$$

$$= \frac{3}{x^2}$$

RULE 4: SUM OR DIFFERENCE OF FUNCTIONS
If $f(x) = u(x) \pm v(x)$, where $u(x)$ and $v(x)$ are differentiable, $f'(x) = u'(x) \pm v'(x)$.

This rule implies that the derivative of a function formed by the sum (difference) of two or more component functions is the sum (difference) of the derivatives of the component functions.

Example 11.31

Consider the function $f(x) = x^2 - 5x + 10$. Applying Rules 1 through 4, we have

$$f'(x) = 2x - 5 + 0$$
$$= 2x - 5$$

RULE 5: PRODUCT RULE

If $f(x) = u(x) \cdot v(x)$, where $u(x)$ and $v(x)$ are differentiable, then

$$f'(x) = u'(x) \cdot v(x) + v'(x) \cdot u(x)$$

Example 11.32

Consider the function $f(x) = (x^2 - 5)(x - x^3)$. Applying Rule 5, we have $u(x) = x^2 - 5$ and $v(x) = x - x^3$. Therefore

$$f'(x) = (2x)(x - x^3) + (1 - 3x^2)(x^2 - 5)$$
$$= 2x^2 - 2x^4 + x^2 - 5 - 3x^4 + 15x^2$$
$$= -5x^4 + 18x^2 - 5$$

Example 11.33

In the last example the function could have been rewritten in the equivalent form

$$f(x) = (x^2 - 5)(x - x^3)$$
$$= x^3 - x^5 - 5x + 5x^3$$
$$= -x^5 + 6x^3 - 5x$$

Finding the derivative of this form of the function does not require the use of Rule 5. The derivative is

$$f'(x) = -5x^4 + 18x^2 - 5$$

which is the same result as obtained before.

NOTE

As with the last two examples, many functions can be algebraically manipulated into an equivalent form. This can be useful for two reasons. First, rewriting a function in an equivalent form can allow the use of derivative rules which are more efficient or easier to remember. Second, finding the derivative of both the original function and an equivalent form of the function provides a check on your answer.

RULE 6: QUOTIENT RULE
If $f(x) = u(x)/v(x)$, where $u(x)$ and $v(x)$ are differentiable and $v(x) \neq 0$, then

$$f'(x) = \frac{v(x) \cdot u'(x) - u(x) \cdot v'(x)}{[v(x)]^2}$$

Verbally, this rule states that the derivative is found by multiplying the denominator by the derivative of the numerator, then subtracting the product of the numerator and the derivative of the denominator, and finally dividing the result by the square of the denominator.

In Example 11.27 we used the power rule to determine that the derivative of $f(x) = 1/x^3$ is $f'(x) = 3/x^4$. Since $f(x)$ has the form of a quotient, we can, as an alternative approach, apply Rule 6 as follows:

Example 11.34

$$f'(x) = \frac{x^3(0) - (1)(3x^2)}{(x^3)^2}$$

$$= \frac{-3x^2}{x^6}$$

$$= \frac{-3}{x^4}$$

Consider the function $f(x) = (3x^2 - 5)/(1 - x^3)$. Applying Rule 6 gives us

Example 11.35

$$f'(x) = \frac{(1 - x^3)(6x) - (3x^2 - 5)(-3x^2)}{(1 - x^3)^2}$$

$$= \frac{6x - 6x^4 + 9x^4 - 15x^2}{(1 - x^3)^2}$$

$$= \frac{3x^4 - 15x^2 + 6x}{(1 - x^3)^2}$$

RULE 7: POWER OF A FUNCTION†
If $f(x) = [u(x)]^n$, where $u(x)$ is a differentiable function,

$$f'(x) = n \cdot [u(x)]^{n-1} \cdot u'(x)$$

This rule looks very similar to the power rule (Rule 2). In fact, the power rule is the special case of this rule where $u(x)$ equals x. When $u(x) = x$, $u'(x) = 1$ and applying Rule 7 results in

$$f'(x) = n(x)^{n-1}(1)$$
$$= nx^{n-1}$$

† We will revisit this rule later with discussion in chain-rule terminology.

Example 11.36
Consider the function $f(x) = \sqrt{7x^4 - 5x - 9}$. Rewriting the function gives $f(x) = (7x^4 - 5x - 9)^{1/2}$. In this form, $f(x)$ has the structure to which Rule 7 applies, where $u(x) = 7x^4 - 5x - 9$. Applying Rule 7 yields

$$f'(x) = \tfrac{1}{2}(7x^4 - 5x - 9)^{(1/2)-1}(28x^3 - 5)$$
$$= (14x^3 - \tfrac{5}{2})(7x^4 - 5x - 9)^{-1/2}$$

which can be rewritten as

$$f'(x) = \frac{14x^3 - \tfrac{5}{2}}{(7x^4 - 5x - 9)^{1/2}}$$

or

$$f'(x) = \frac{14x^3 - \tfrac{5}{2}}{\sqrt{7x^4 - 5x - 9}}$$

Example 11.37
Consider the function

$$f(x) = \left(\frac{3x}{1 - x^2}\right)^5$$

This function has the form stated in Rule 7 where $u(x)$ equals the quotient function $3x/(1 - x^2)$. Applying Rule 7 gives

$$f'(x) = 5\left(\frac{3x}{1 - x^2}\right)^4 \frac{(1 - x^2)(3) - (3x)(-2x)}{(1 - x^2)^2}$$
$$= 5\left(\frac{3x}{1 - x^2}\right)^4 \frac{3 - 3x^2 + 6x^2}{(1 - x^2)^2}$$
$$= 5\left(\frac{3x}{1 - x^2}\right)^4 \frac{3 + 3x^2}{(1 - x^2)^2}$$

RULE 8
If $f(x) = e^{u(x)}$, where $u(x)$ is differentiable, then

$$f'(x) = u'(x)e^{u(x)}$$

Example 11.38
Referring to Rule 8 the exponent $u(x) = x$, consider the function $f(x) = e^x$. Therefore

$$f'(x) = (1)e^x$$
$$= e^x$$

NOTE
The derivative of $f(x) = e^x$ is a special case of the group of functions having the form $f(x) = e^{u(x)}$. In this case $u(x) = x$. The result is that the function and its derivative are exactly the same, or

$$f(x) = f'(x) = e^x$$

Consider the function $f(x) = e^{-x^2+2x}$. Applying Rule 8, we have

$$f'(x) = (-2x + 2)e^{-x^2+2x}$$

**Example
11.39**

RULE 9
If $f(x) = \ln [u(x)]$, where $u(x)$ is differentiable, then

$$f'(x) = u'(x)/u(x)$$

Consider the function $f(x) = \ln x$. Referring to Rule 9, we let $u(x) = x$.
Therefore

$$f'(x) = \frac{1}{x}$$

**Example
11.40**

Consider the function $f(x) = \ln (5x^2 - 2x + 1)$. Referring to Rule 9, we
have $u(x) = 5x^2 - 2x + 1$ and

$$f'(x) = \frac{10x - 2}{5x^2 - 2x + 1}$$

**Example
11.41**

Instantaneous Rate of Change—Again

In Example 11.16 the function

$$d = f(t) = 8t^2 + 8t$$

described the distance (in miles) an automobile traveled as a function of
time (in hours). The instantaneous velocity of the car at any point in time
is found by evaluating the derivative at that value of t. To determine the
instantaneous velocity at $t = 3$, the derivative

$$f'(t) = 16t + 8$$

must be evaluated at $t = 3$, or

$$f'(3) = 16(3) + 8$$
$$= 56 \text{ (miles per hour)}$$

An object is dropped from a cliff which is 1,296 feet above the ground.
The distance that the object falls is described as a function of time. The
function is

$$d = f(t) = 16t^2$$

**Example
11.42**

where d equals the distance in feet and t equals time measured in seconds from the time the object is dropped.

(a) How far will the object drop after 2 seconds?
(b) What is the instantaneous velocity of the object at $t = 2$?
(c) What is the velocity of the object at the instant it hits the ground?

Solution   (a) The object will drop

$$f(2) = 16(2^2)$$
$$= 64 \text{ feet}$$

(b) Since $f'(t) = 32t$, the object will have a velocity equal to

$$f'(2) = 32(2)$$
$$= 64 \text{ feet per second}$$

at $t = 2$.

(c) In order to determine the velocity of the object when it hits the ground, we must know *when* it will hit the ground. The object will hit the ground after traveling 1,296 feet, or when

$$16t^2 = 1,296$$

If we solve for t,

$$t^2 = \frac{1,296}{16} = 81$$

and $t = \pm 9$. Since a negative root is meaningless, we can conclude that the object will hit the ground after 9 seconds. The velocity at this instant in time will be

$$f'(9) = 32(9)$$
$$= 288 \text{ feet per second}$$

Follow-up Exercises

In Exercises 11.79 to 11.114 find $f'(x)$.

11.79 $f(x) = -25$

11.80 $f(x) = \frac{3}{5}$

11.81 $f(x) = 15 - 3x/2$

11.82 $f(x) = 4x - 5$

11.83 $f(x) = -4x^2$

11.84 $f(x) = 3x^2/5$

11.85 $f(x) = \sqrt[3]{x^5}$

11.86 $f(x) = 1/\sqrt{2x}$

11.87 $f(x) = \dfrac{8}{x^5}$

11.88 $f(x) = \dfrac{3}{x^2} - 2x$

11.89 $f(x) = (x^2 - 1)(3x + 10)$

11.90 $f(x) = (x - x^3)(2x^{3/2} + x^5)$

11.91 $f(x) = (x^3 - 2x^2 + 9)(6 - 3x)$

11.92 $f(x) = (x^5 - 3x^4)(6x + 3x^2)$

11.93 $f(x) = 2x/(5 - 2x^2)$

11.94 $f(x) = (x^2 - 4)/(3x^2 - 6x + 1)$

11.95 $f(x) = 7x^2/(2x^7 - 14x)$

11.96 $f(x) = 1/(x^5 - 1)$

11.97 $f(x) = (2x - 5)^3$

11.98 $f(x) = (-x^2 + 3x - 1)^4$

11.99 $f(x) = \sqrt{x^5 - 5}$

11.100 $f(x) = \sqrt[3]{(x - 1)^2}$

11.101 $f(x) = 1/(x^2 - 9)^3$

11.102 $f(x) = (\sqrt{x} - 2x)^4$

11.103 $f(x) = e^{x^3}$

11.104 $f(x) = e^{-x^2/2}$

11.105 $f(x) = 10xe^x$

11.106 $f(x) = (e^{2x} - 1)^3$

11.107 $f(x) = \ln(4x^2 - 2x + 9)$

11.108 $f(x) = 4x^2 \ln x$

11.109 $f(x) = ax^2 + bx + c$

11.110 $f(x) = mx + b$

11.111 $f(x) = \ln 1$

11.112 $f(x) = e$

11.113 $f(x) = e^{ax+b}$

11.114 $f(x) = \ln cx$

In Exercises 11.115 to 11.120, (a) find $f'(1)$ and (b) determine the values of x at which the tangent slope of the graph of $f(x)$ equals 0.

11.115 $f(x) = 4x - 5$

11.116 $f(x) = 4x^2 + 2x - 5$

11.117 $f(x) = x^3/3 - 4x + 9$

11.118 $f(x) = x^4/4 - x^2/2$

11.119 $f(x) = ax^2 + bx + c$

11.120 $f(x) = 1/x$

11.121 The function $y = f(t) = t^3$, where $0 \le t \le 30$, describes the height y (in hundreds of feet) of a rocket t seconds after it has been launched.

(a) What is the average velocity during the time interval $1 \le t \le 4$?

(b) What is the instantaneous velocity at $t = 5$? At $t = 20$?

11.122 A ball is tossed from ground level with an initial velocity of 64 feet per second. The function which describes the height s of the ball is

$$s = f(t) = 64t - 16t^2$$

where s is measured in feet and t is time measured in seconds since the ball was thrown.

(a) What is the velocity of the ball at $t = 1$ second?

(b) When will the ball return to the ground?

(c) What is the velocity of the ball when it hits the ground?

11.123 A ball is dropped from the roof of a building which is 256 feet high. The distance that the ball falls is described by the function

$$s = f(t) = 16t^2$$

where s equals the distance in feet and t equals time measured in seconds from when the ball was dropped.

(a) What is the average velocity during the time interval $1 \le t \le 2$?

(b) What is the instantaneous velocity at $t = 1$?

(c) What is the velocity of the ball at the instant it hits the ground?

11.124 *Epidemic Control.* An epidemic is spreading through a large Western state. Health officials estimate that the number of persons who will be afflicted by the disease is a function of time since the disease was first detected. Specifically, the function is

$$n = f(t) = 300t^3 - 20t^2$$

where n equals the number of persons and $0 \le t \le 60$, measured in days.

(a) How many persons are expected to have caught the disease after 20 days?

(b) What is the average rate at which the disease is expected to spread between $t = 10$ and $t = 20$?

(c) At what rate is the disease spreading at $t = 30$?

*11.125 *Fund Raising.* Total contributions C to a national charity are estimated to be a function of the length of the charity's annual fund raising campaign. The function is

$$C = f(t) = 1,000,000(1 - e^{-0.04t})$$

where C is measured in dollars and t is measured in days.

(a) What are total contributions expected to equal if the campaign lasts 20 days?

(b) At what rate are contributions being received at $t = 20$?

11.126 *Population Growth.* The size of the population P of a country is described by the function

$$P = f(t) = 50e^{0.05t}$$

where P is measured in millions and t is measured in years ($t = 0$ corresponds to 1970).

(a) What was the population in 1975?

(b) At what average rate did the population increase between 1970 and 1975?

(c) At what instantaneous rate is the population expected to be growing in 1990?

11.6   HIGHER-ORDER DERIVATIVES

Given a function $f(x)$, there are other derivative expressions which can be identified. This section discusses these *higher-order derivatives* and their interpretation.

The Second Derivative

The derivative $f'(x)$ of the function $f(x)$ is often referred to as the *first derivative* of the function. The adjective *first* is used to distinguish this derivative from other derivatives associated with a function. The *order* of the first derivative is 1.

The *second derivative* of a function is the derivative of the first derivative. Denoted by either d^2y/dx^2 or $f''(x)$, the second derivative is found by applying the same rules of differentiation as were used in finding the first derivative. Table 11.5 illustrates the computation of first and second derivatives for several functions.

Just as the first derivative is a measure of the instantaneous rate of change in the value of y with respect to a change in x, the *second derivative* is a measure of the instantaneous rate of change in the value of the first derivative with respect to a change in x. Described differently, the second derivative is a *measure of the instantaneous rate of change in the tangent slope with respect to a change in x.*

Consider the function $f(x) = -x^2$. The first and second derivatives of this function are

$$f'(x) = -2x \qquad f''(x) = -2$$

Table 11.5	$f(x)$	$f'(x)$	$f''(x)$
	x^5	$5x^4$	$20x^3$
	$x^2 - 3x + 10$	$2x - 3$	2
	$mx + b$	m	0
	e^{x^2}	$2xe^{x^2}$	$2e^{x^2} + 4x^2e^{x^2}$
	$x^3 - 2x^2 + 5x$	$3x^2 - 4x + 5$	$6x - 4$
	$x^{3/2}$	$\frac{3}{2}x^{1/2}$	$\frac{3}{4}x^{-1/2}$

Figure 11.17 illustrates the graphs of $f(x)$, $f'(x)$, and $f''(x)$. These graphs have been sketched directly above one another so that some important observations can be made more easily. The function $f(x)$ is a parabola which is concave down with the vertex at $(0, 0)$. Looking at the sketch of $f(x)$, we see the tangent slope is positive to the left of the vertex but becomes *less positive* as x approaches 0. To the right of the vertex the tangent slope is negative and becomes *more negative* (decreases) as x increases. The graph of $f'(x)$ indicates the value of the slope at any point on $f(x)$. Note that values of $f'(x)$ are positive, but becoming less positive, as x approaches 0 from the left. And, $f'(x)$ becomes more and more negative as the value of x becomes more positive. Thus, the graph of $f'(x)$ is consistent with our observations of the sketch of $f(x)$.

The second derivative is a measure of the instantaneous rate of change in the first derivative or in the slope of the graph of a function. Since $f''(x) = -2$, this suggests that the rate of change in the first derivative is constant over the entire function. Specifically $f''(x) = -2$ suggests that everywhere on the function the slope is *decreasing* at an instantaneous rate of 2 units for each unit that x increases. If you look at $f'(x)$ and its graph, $f'(x)$ is a linear function with slope of -2.

Some earlier examples in this chapter discussed functions having the form $d = f(t)$ where d represents the distance traveled after time t. We concluded that the instantaneous velocity at any time t was represented by the first derivative $f'(t)$. The second derivative of this type of function $f''(t)$ provides a measure of the instantaneous rate of change *in the velocity* with respect to a change in time. Measured in units of distance per unit of time squared (for example; ft/sec.^{2} and miles/hr.^{2}), this second derivative represents the instantaneous *acceleration* of an object. If

$$d = f(t) = t^3 - 2t^2 + 3t$$

the expression representing the *instantaneous* velocity is

$$f'(t) = 3t^2 - 4t + 3$$

and the expression representing the *instantaneous* acceleration is

$$f''(t) = 6t - 4$$

Third and Higher-Order Derivatives

Further derivatives can be determined for functions. These derivatives become less easy to understand from an intuitive standpoint. However, they will be useful to us later, and they have particular value at higher levels of mathematical analysis.

DEFINITION
The nth-order derivative of $f(x)$ denoted by $f^{(n)}(x)$ is found by differentiating the derivative of order $n - 1$. That is,

$$f^{(n)}(x) = \frac{d}{dx} [f^{(n-1)}(x)]$$

FIGURE 11.17

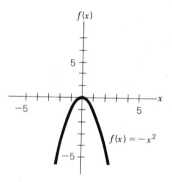

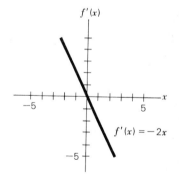

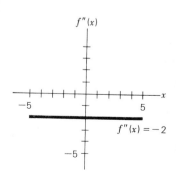

Example 11.43

Find all derivatives of

$$f(x) = x^6 - 2x^5 + x^4 - 3x^3 + x^2 - x + 1$$

Solution

$$f'(x) = 6x^5 - 10x^4 + 4x^3 - 9x^2 + 2x - 1$$
$$f''(x) = 30x^4 - 40x^3 + 12x^2 - 18x + 2$$
$$f'''(x) = 120x^3 - 120x^2 + 24x - 18$$
$$f^{(4)}(x) = 360x^2 - 240x + 24$$
$$f^{(5)}(x) = 720x - 240$$
$$f^{(6)}(x) = 720$$
$$f^{(7)}(x) = 0$$

All additional higher-order derivatives will also equal 0.

NOTE
For polynomial functions of *degree n*, the first derivative is a polynomial function of degree $n - 1$. Each successive derivative is a polynomial function of degree one less than the previous derivative (until the degree of a derivative equals 0).

Follow-up Exercises

In Exercises 11.127 to 11.136, (a) find $f''(x)$ and (b) evaluate $f'(1)$ and $f''(1)$.

11.127 $f(x) = 12$

11.128 $f(x) = 10 - 5x$

11.129 $f(x) = -3x^2$

11.130 $f(x) = -x^2 + 2x - 5$

11.131 $f(x) = x^3$

11.132 $f(x) = 4x^3 - 2x^2$

11.133 $f(x) = x^5 - 1$

11.134 $f(x) = x^4 - 2x^3 + 5x^2$

11.135 $f(x) = e^x$

11.136 $f(x) = \ln cx$

11.137 The distance traveled by a falling object is described by the function

$$s = 16t^2$$

where s is measured in feet and t is measured in seconds.
(a) What is the velocity at $t = 5$?
(b) What is the acceleration at $t = 5$?

11.138 A ball thrown from the roof of a building which is 300 feet high will be at a height of h feet after t seconds as described by the function

$$h = f(t) = -16t^2 + 50t + 300$$

(a) What is the height of the ball after 3 seconds?
(b) What is the velocity of the ball after 4 seconds? (A negative sign implies movement *toward* the ground.)
(c) What is the acceleration of the ball at $t = 0$? $t = 1$?

In Exercises 11.139 to 11.144, find all higher-order derivatives.

11.139 $f(x) = -4x^3$

11.140 $f(x) = x^5 - 2x^3 + 10x$

11.141 $f(x) = x^6$

11.142 $f(x) = -x^4$

11.143 $f(x) = ax^2 + bx + c$

11.144 $f(x) = ax^3 + bx^2 + cx + d$

DIFFERENTIATION OF SPECIAL
FUNCTIONAL FORMS (OPTIONAL)

This section discusses techniques for differentiating some functional forms not covered by Rules 1 through 9.

Chain Rule

Rule 7 (power of a function) was presented expeditiously and without the attention it should have been given. As stated in Sec. 11.5, Rule 7 is a special case of the more general *chain rule*.

RULE 10: CHAIN RULE
If $y = f(u)$ is a differentiable function and
$u = g(x)$ is a differentiable function, then

$$\frac{dy}{dx} = \frac{dy}{du} \cdot \frac{du}{dx}$$

Recall that in Chap. 2 we examined composite functions—functions whose values depend upon other functions. The chain rule applies to composite functions. For example, assume that

$$y = f(u) = 20 - 3u$$

and
$$u = g(x) = 5x - 4$$

The chain rule is concerned with determining the instantaneous change in y with respect to a change in x, or dy/dx. If x increases by 1 unit, u increases by 5 units. And an increase in u of 5 units results in a *decrease* in y of $(3)(5) = 15$ units. This information also is determined by applying the chain rule, or

$$\frac{dy}{dx} = \frac{dy}{du} \cdot \frac{du}{dx}$$
$$= (-3)(5)$$
$$= -15$$

Given $y = f(u) = u^2 - 2u + 1$ and $u = g(x) = x^2 - 1$,

$$\frac{dy}{dx} = \frac{dy}{du} \cdot \frac{du}{dx}$$
$$= (2u - 2)(2x)$$

Example 11.44

We can rewrite dy/dx strictly in terms of x by substituting $u = x^2 - 1$. This results in

$$\frac{dy}{dx} = [2(x^2 - 1) - 2](2x)$$
$$= (2x^2 - 4)(2x)$$
$$= 4x^3 - 8x$$

**Example
11.45** Given $y = f(u) = u^3 - 5u$ where $u = g(x) = x^4 + 3x$,

$$\frac{dy}{dx} = \frac{dy}{du} \cdot \frac{du}{dx}$$
$$= (3u^2 - 5)(4x^3 + 3)$$

Rewriting this as a function of x gives

$$\frac{dy}{dx} = [3(x^4 + 3x)^2 - 5](4x^3 + 3)$$
$$= [3(x^8 + 6x^5 + 9x^2) - 5](4x^3 + 3)$$
$$= (3x^8 + 18x^5 + 27x^2 - 5)(4x^3 + 3)$$
$$= 12x^{11} + 72x^8 + 108x^5 - 20x^3 + 9x^8 + 54x^5$$
$$+ 81x^2 - 15$$
$$= 12x^{11} + 81x^8 + 162x^5 - 20x^3 + 81x^2 - 15$$

EXERCISE:
Rewriting y as a function of x, $y = (x^4 + 3x)^3 - 5(x^4 + 3x)$. Expand y into one large polynomial function and see if $f'(x)$ is the same as obtained in the example.

Other Derivatives

The derivative dx/dy is a measure of the instantaneous rate of change in x with respect to a change in y. With many functions we may have a real interest in knowing the value of dx/dy. In some cases a function of the form $y = f(x)$ can be solved explicitly for x, creating a function of the form $x = g(y)$. In other cases it may be impossible to solve explicitly for x. The following derivative property is useful in determining dx/dy.

RULE 11
Given a differentiable function of the form
$y = f(x)$,

$$\frac{dx}{dy} = \frac{1}{dy/dx} \qquad \text{provided } \frac{dy}{dx} \neq 0 \qquad (11.8)$$

**Example
11.46** Given $y = f(x) = 5x - 20$, we can solve for x in terms of the variable y:

$$x = g(y)$$
$$= 4 + \frac{y}{5}$$

Differentiating $g(y)$ with respect to y yields

$$\frac{dx}{dy} = \frac{1}{5}$$

Checking our answer with the property stated by Eq. (11.8), let's differentiate $f(x)$ with respect to x:

$$\frac{dy}{dx} = 5$$

According to Eq. (11.8),

$$\frac{dx}{dy} = \frac{1}{dy/dx} = \frac{1}{5}$$

which agrees with our original answer.

Find dx/dy associated with the function $y = f(x) = x^3 - 3x^2 + 5$.

Example 11.47

Applying our derivative rules, we have

Solution

$$\frac{dy}{dx} = 3x^2 - 6x$$

According to Eq. (11.8),

$$\frac{dx}{dy} = \frac{1}{3x^2 - 6x} \qquad x \neq 0 \text{ or } 2$$

Follow-up Exercises

In Exercises 11.145 to 11.154, apply the chain rule to determine dy/dx.

11.145 $y = f(u) = 4u - 5$ and $u = g(x) = x^2$
11.146 $y = f(u) = -5u + 10$ and $u = g(x) = x - 1$
11.147 $y = f(u) = c$ and $u = g(x) = x^2 + 5$
11.148 $y = f(u) = u^2 - 5u + 1$ and $u = g(x) = x$
11.149 $y = f(u) = u^2/3$ and $u = g(x) = x^3 + 4$
11.150 $y = f(u) = u^{1/2}$ and $u = g(x) = 1/x + 1$
11.151 $y = f(u) = 2u^2 + 7u - 4$ and $u = g(x) = -x^2$
11.152 $y = f(u) = 1/u$ and $u = g(x) = x^2 - 1$
11.153 $y = f(u) = u^4 - 4u^3 + 6u$ and $u = g(x) = x + 3$
11.154 $y = f(u) = \sqrt{u}$ and $u = g(x) = 10$

In Exercises 11.155 to 11.158, determine dx/dy and state the values of x for which dx/dy is not defined.

11.155 $f(x) = x^3 - 3x^2 + 5x - 1$ **11.156** $f(x) = 15 - \frac{3}{2}x$
11.157 $f(x) = 6x^2 - 5x + 1$ **11.158** $f(x) = x^4 - 2x^3$

In Exercises 11.159 to 11.162, find dy/dx.

11.159 $x = g(y) = my + b$ **11.160** $x = g(y) = -\frac{2}{3}y + 1$
11.161 $x = g(y) = -3y^2 + 2y - 5$
11.162 $x = g(y) = -5y^3$

SUMMARY   11.8

This chapter has introduced the theory and concepts of differential calculus. It provides important foundations which are critical to all that follows. Two important concepts—the limit of a function and continuous versus discontinuous functions—were presented first. Both these concepts are important in developing the notion of the derivative. A second step in the development of the derivative was the discussion of the average rate of change of a function. An understanding of this concept is necessary before the derivative is presented since the derivative is a measure of the instantaneous rate of change of a function.

The remainder of the chapter concentrated on the differentiation of functions. The limit approach was presented to illustrate the theoretical determination of the derivative. Following this, a set of basic rules of differentiation was presented and illustrated. These rules were applied in finding first derivatives and higher-order derivatives.

A thorough understanding of this material is essential before you move on to the following chapters. Review the Chapter Checklist to determine where you stand.

CHAPTER CHECKLIST

If you have read *all* sections of this chapter, you should

_____ **Understand the notion of the *limit* of a function**

_____ **Understand how to determine limits, if they exist**

_____ **Understand certain properties of limits**

_____ **Understand the relationships between *asymptotes* and limits**

_____ **Understand the notion and characteristics of *continuous functions***

_____ **Understand the distinction between *average rate of change* and *instantaneous rate of change***

_____ **Understand the *difference quotient* and its meaning**

_____ **Understand the meaning of a *tangent line***

_____ **Understand the meaning and interpretations of the *derivative***

_____ **Be able to determine the derivative of simple polynomial functions using the *limit approach***

_____ **Know the rules of differentiation and how to apply them**

_____ **Understand the meaning of the second derivative**

KEY TERMS AND CONCEPTS

limit	average rate of change
left- and right-hand limits	secant line
asymptote (horizontal and vertical)	difference quotient
continuous versus discontinuous functions	instantaneous rate of change
	tangent line

**tangent slope of a curve
  at a point**

derivative

**limit approach for
  determining the derivative**

differentiation

second derivative

higher-order derivatives

chain rule

IMPORTANT FORMULAS

$$\frac{\Delta y}{\Delta x} = \frac{f(x + \Delta x) - f(x)}{\Delta x}$$

difference quotient (11.5)

$$\frac{dy}{dx} = \lim_{\Delta x \to 0} \frac{f(x + \Delta x) - f(x)}{\Delta x}$$

derivative (11.7)

Rules of Differentiation

1 If $f(x) = c$, $f'(x) = 0$ (constant function)

2 If $f(x) = x^n$, $f'(x) = nx^{n-1}$ (power rule)

3 If $f(x) = c \cdot g(x)$, $f'(x) = c \cdot g'(x)$ (constant times a function)

4 If $f(x) = u(x) \pm v(x)$, $f'(x) = u'(x) \pm v'(x)$ (sum or difference)

5 If $f(x) = u(x)v(x)$, $f'(x) = u'(x)v(x) + v'(x)u(x)$ (product rule)

6 If $f(x) = u(x)/v(x)$, $f'(x) = \dfrac{v(x)u'(x) - u(x)v'(x)}{[v(x)]^2}$ (quotient rule)

7 If $f(x) = [u(x)]^n$, $f'(x) = n[u(x)]^{n-1}u'(x)$ (power of a function)

8 If $f(x) = e^{u(x)}$, $f'(x) = u'(x)e^{u(x)}$

9 If $f(x) = \ln[u(x)]$, $f'(x) = \dfrac{u'(x)}{u(x)}$

10 $\dfrac{dy}{dx} = \dfrac{dy}{du}\dfrac{du}{dx}$ (chain rule)

11 $\dfrac{dx}{dy} = \dfrac{1}{dy/dx}$ $\dfrac{dy}{dx} \neq 0$ (inverse-function rule)

ADDITIONAL EXERCISES

Exercises 11.163 to 11.178 are related to Sec. 11.2.

In Exercises 11.163 to 11.170, determine the limit if it exists.

11.163 $\displaystyle\lim_{x \to -3} (3x - 2)$

11.164 $\displaystyle\lim_{x \to -2} \frac{x^2 - 3x - 10}{x + 2}$

11.165 $\displaystyle\lim_{x \to 2} \frac{|x^2 - 6x + 1|}{x - 1}$

11.166 $\displaystyle\lim_{x \to -1} (x^5 + x^4 + x^3 + x^2 + x + 1)$

*11.167 $\displaystyle\lim_{x \to \infty} \frac{1}{x}$

*11.168 $\displaystyle\lim_{x \to -\infty} \frac{-x^2 + 1}{x + 1}$

*11.169 $\displaystyle\lim_{x \to \infty} \frac{5x^3 + 2x^2 + 1}{x^2 - x + 7}$

*11.170 $\displaystyle\lim_{x \to -\infty} \frac{x + 1}{x}$

In Exercises 11.171 to 11.178, determine whether there are any discontinuities and, if so, where they occur.

11.171 $f(x) = e^x$

11.172 $v(x) = \dfrac{x^2 - 9}{16 - x^4}$

*11.173 $f(x) = \begin{cases} 2/x^2 & \text{if } x \neq 6 \\ 10 & \text{if } x = 6 \end{cases}$

*11.174 $f(x) = \begin{cases} x^2 - 5 & \text{if } x > 5 \\ -x^2 & \text{if } x < 5 \end{cases}$

11.175 $f(x) = \ln x,\ x > 0$

11.176 $f(x) = ax^2 + bx + c$

*11.177 $f(x) = \dfrac{ax + b}{ax^2 + bx + c}$

11.178 $f(x) = \dfrac{a}{x^2 - b}$

Exercises 11.179 to 11.188 are related to Sec. 11.3.

11.179 For the function $y = h(x) = x^3 - 2x^2 - 4$, determine the average rate of change in $f(x)$ between $x = 2$ and $x = 4$.

11.180 Enrollments at a university have increased annually, as indicated in the following table.

Year	1972	1973	1974	1975	1976
Student Enrollment	18,000	18,650	19,200	19,100	19,050

At what average rate did student enrollments change between 1972 and 1976? Between 1974 and 1976?

In Exercises 11.181 to 11.188, (a) determine the general expression for the difference quotient and (b) use the difference quotient to compute the slope of the secant line connecting points at $x = 1$ and $x = 2$.

11.181 $y = f(x) = -10$

11.182 $y = f(x) = 2x - 5$

11.183 $y = f(x) = 2x^2 - x + 3$

11.184 $y = f(x) = x^2/4$

*11.185 $y = f(x) = x^3 - 1$

*11.186 $y = f(x) = 10/x$

*11.187 $y = f(x) = ax + b$

*11.188 $y = f(x) = ax^2 + bx + c$

Exercises 11.189 to 11.194 are related to Sec. 11.4.

In Exercises 11.189 to 11.194, (a) determine dy/dx using the limit approach, (b) determine the tangent slope at $x = 2$, and (c) determine any values of x where the tangent slope equals 0.

11.189 $f(x) = 9$

*11.190 $f(x) = x^3/3$

*11.191 $f(x) = -1/x$

11.192 $f(x) = 12 - 4x$

*11.193 $f(x) = ax + b$

*11.194 $f(x) = ax^2 + bx + c$

Exercises 11.195 to 11.222 are related to Sec. 11.5.

In Exercises 11.195 to 11.214, find $f'(x)$.

11.195 $f(x) = \ln (5x/3)$

11.196 $f(x) = e^{x^2} - e^x - x$

11.197 $f(x) = 5x^3/3 + 2x^2$

11.198 $f(x) = (x^3 - 1)^4$

11.199 $f(x) = \sqrt{x^7}$

11.200 $f(x) = 1/\sqrt[3]{x}$

11.201 $f(x) = x^2/\sqrt{x}$

11.202 $f(x) = \sqrt{x^3 - 2x^2 + 10}$

11.203 $f(x) = (x - 7)(x^3 - 3x^2 + 2x)$

11.204 $f(x) = 8x^2/(7 - x^3)$

11.205 $f(x) = (9 - x^2)(x + 3)^4$ **11.206** $f(x) = 7/\sqrt[3]{x - 1}$

11.207 $f(x) = e^{5x-10}$ **11.208** $f(x) = 5x^2 e^{x^2}$

11.209 $f(x) = (e^x + 12)^3$ **11.210** $f(x) = \dfrac{3x^2 - 4x + 5}{1 - x}$

11.211 $f(x) = \ln(ax^2 + bx + c)$ **11.212** $f(x) = \ln(10)$

11.213 $f(x) = (\ln x)(x^5 + 8x)$

11.214 $f(x) = \ln[(x + 1)/(x - 1)]$

In Exercises 11.215 to 11.222, (a) find $f'(2)$ and (b) determine values of x where the tangent slope of the graph of $f(x)$ equals 0.

11.215 $f(x) = x^2 - 10x + 20$ **11.216** $f(x) = 50 - 20x$

11.217 $f(x) = (8x + 3)^3$ **11.218** $f(x) = (x - 7)/(3x + 3)$

11.219 $f(x) = \sqrt{(x + 10)^3}$

11.220 $f(x) = 6x^3 - 5x^2 + 10x - 6$

11.221 $f(x) = e^{4x^2-10}$ **11.222** $f(x) = \ln(4x^2 - 2x)$

Exercises 11.223 to 11.232 are related to Sec. 11.6.

In Exercises 11.223 to 11.228, (a) find $f''(x)$ and (b) evaluate $f'(1)$ and $f''(1)$.

11.223 $f(x) = 1/x$ **11.224** $f(x) = x^3 + 3$

11.225 $f(x) = e^x + e^{-x}$

11.226 $f(x) = 5x^4 + 4x^3 + 3x^2 + 2x$

11.227 $f(x) = x - 5$ **11.228** $f(x) = e^{x/2}$

In Exercises 11.229 to 11.232, find all higher-order derivatives.

11.229 $f(x) = 2x^6 - 4x^5 + 2x^2 - 3$

11.230 $f(x) = x^3 - 2x^2 + 5x + 8$

11.231 $f(x) = -5x^4 + 3x^3 - 2x^2$

11.232 $f(x) = (x^2 + 7)(x - 9)$

Exercises 11.233 to 11.244 are related to Sec. 11.7.

In Exercises 11.233 to 11.238, apply the chain rule to find dy/dx.

11.233 $y = f(u) = u^3 - 4$ and $u = g(x) = x^3$

11.234 $y = f(u) = u^{1/3}$ and $u = g(x) = x^2 + 2$

11.235 $y = f(u) = \sqrt{u^2 + 3u}$ and $u = g(x) = \dfrac{1}{x}$

11.236 $y = f(u) = e^{5u-1}$ and $u = g(x) = 5 - \dfrac{1}{x^2}$

11.237 $y = f(u) = (2u + 3)^2$ and $u = g(x) = 2x + 3$

11.238 $y = f(u) = \dfrac{5u + 1}{2 - u}$ and $u = g(x) = x^2$

In Exercises 11.239 to 11.244, determine dx/dy if it exists.

11.239 $x = g(y) = y^2 - 5y + 8$ **11.240** $x = g(y) = \dfrac{1}{y - 3}$

11.241 $x = g(y) = \sqrt{2y^2 - 3y + 2}$

11.242 $y = f(x) = e^x$

11.243 $y = f(x) = 2x^3 + 4x^2 - \dfrac{3x}{2} + 1$

11.244 $y = f(x) = x^2 e^x$

CHAPTER TEST

1 Determine

(a) $\displaystyle \lim_{x \to 3} \frac{x^2 - x - 6}{x - 3}$

(b) $\displaystyle \lim_{x \to \infty} \frac{4}{(2x - 1)/x}$

2 Determine whether there are any discontinuities on $f(x)$ and, if so, where they occur if

$$f(x) = \frac{x^2 - 25}{4x^2 - 2x + 5}$$

3 Determine dy/dx using the limit approach if

$$f(x) = -3x^2 + x + 10$$

4 Find $f'(x)$ if

(a) $f(x) = 4/\sqrt[5]{x^2}$
(b) $f(x) = x^8 - 7x^4 - x^2 + 9$
(c) $f(x) = (12 - x^2)/(x^3 + 5)$
(d) $f(x) = (e^{x^2} - x^5)^4$
(e) $f(x) = (4x^2 - 5)(\ln x^3)$

5 Given $f(x) = 5x^2 - 5x - 35$, determine the locations of any points on the graph of $f(x)$ where the tangent slope equals $+5$.

6 Find all higher-order derivatives of $f(x)$ if

$$f(x) = \frac{x^3}{3} - \frac{4x^2}{2} + 5x - 1$$

7 Find dy/dx if

$$y = f(u) = u^4 - 2u \quad \text{and} \quad u = g(x) = x^2 - 15$$

8 Find dx/dy if $f(x) = 10x - 15$.

APPENDIX
PROOFS OF SELECTED RULES
OF DIFFERENTIATION

The first proof is a "partial" proof in that it proves Rule 2 when n is a positive integer. The proof of this rule for all other values of n is beyond the scope of this text.

Rule 2 Modified

If $f(x) = x^n$, where n is a positive integer, then $f'(x) = nx^{n-1}$.

Proof

$$f(x) = x^n$$
$$f(x + \Delta x) = (x + \Delta x)^n$$
$$f(x + \Delta x) - f(x) = (x + \Delta x)^n - x^n$$

By the *binomial theorem*, for n = a positive integer,

$$(x + \Delta x)^n = x^n + nx^{n-1}(\Delta x) + \frac{n(n-1)}{2}x^{n-2}(\Delta x)^2 + \cdots + (\Delta x)^n$$

Substituting into $f(x + \Delta x) - f(x)$ yields

$$f(x + \Delta x) - f(x) = x^n + nx^{n-1}(\Delta x) + \frac{n(n-1)}{2}x^{n-2}(\Delta x)^2$$
$$+ \cdots + (\Delta x)^n - x^n$$

Dividing by Δx and taking the limit as $\Delta x \to 0$, we get

$$\lim_{\Delta x \to 0} \frac{f(x + \Delta x) - f(x)}{\Delta x} = \lim_{\Delta x \to 0} \left[x^n + nx^{n-1}\Delta x + \frac{n(n-1)}{2}x^{n-2}(\Delta x)^2 \right.$$
$$\left. + \cdots + (\Delta x)^n - x^n \right] / \Delta x$$
$$= \lim_{\Delta x \to 0} \left[nx^{n-1} + \frac{n(n-1)}{2}x^{n-2}(\Delta x) \right.$$
$$\left. + \cdots + (\Delta x)^{n-1} \right]$$

or $$f'(x) = nx^{n-1}$$

Rule 3

If $f(x) = c \cdot g(x)$, where c is a constant and $g(x)$ is a differentiable function, then $f'(x) = c \cdot g'(x)$.

Proof

$$f(x) = c \cdot g(x)$$
$$f(x + \Delta x) = c \cdot g(x + \Delta x)$$
$$f(x + \Delta x) - f(x) = c \cdot g(x + \Delta x) - c \cdot g(x)$$
$$= c[g(x + \Delta x) - g(x)]$$
$$\frac{f(x + \Delta x) - f(x)}{\Delta x} = \frac{c[g(x + \Delta x) - g(x)]}{\Delta x}$$
$$= c\frac{g(x + \Delta x) - g(x)}{\Delta x}$$
$$\lim_{\Delta x \to 0} \frac{f(x + \Delta x) - f(x)}{\Delta x} = \lim_{\Delta x \to 0} c\frac{g(x + \Delta x) - g(x)}{\Delta x}$$
$$= c \cdot \lim_{\Delta x \to 0} \frac{g(x + \Delta x) - g(x)}{\Delta x}$$

or $$f'(x) = c \cdot g'(x)$$

Rule 4

If $f(x) = u(x) \pm v(x)$, where $u(x)$ and $v(x)$ are differentiable, then $f'(x) = u'(x) \pm v'(x)$.

The proof presented is for the "sum" of $u(x)$ and $v(x)$.

Proof

$$f(x) = u(x) + v(x)$$
$$f(x + \Delta x) = u(x + \Delta x) + v(x + \Delta x)$$
$$f(x + \Delta x) - f(x) = [u(x + \Delta x) + v(x + \Delta x)] - [u(x) + v(x)]$$
$$\frac{f(x + \Delta x) - f(x)}{\Delta x} = \frac{[u(x + \Delta x) + v(x + \Delta x)] - [u(x) + v(x)]}{\Delta x}$$
$$= \left[\frac{u(x + \Delta x) - u(x)}{\Delta x} + \frac{v(x + \Delta x) - v(x)}{\Delta x}\right]$$

$$\lim_{\Delta x \to 0} \frac{f(x + \Delta x) - f(x)}{\Delta x}$$
$$= \lim_{\Delta x \to 0} \left[\frac{u(x + \Delta x) - u(x)}{\Delta x} + \frac{v(x + \Delta x) - v(x)}{\Delta x}\right]$$
$$= \lim_{\Delta x \to 0} \frac{u(x + \Delta x) - u(x)}{\Delta x} + \lim_{\Delta x \to 0} \frac{v(x + \Delta x) - v(x)}{\Delta x}$$

or
$$f'(x) = u'(x) + v'(x)$$

Rule 5

If $f(x) = u(x) \cdot v(x)$, where $u(x)$ and $v(x)$ are differentiable, then

$$f'(x) = u'(x) \cdot v(x) + v'(x) \cdot u(x)$$

Proof

$$f(x) = u(x) \cdot v(x)$$
$$f(x + \Delta x) = u(x + \Delta x) \cdot v(x + \Delta x)$$
$$f(x + \Delta x) - f(x) = u(x + \Delta x) \cdot v(x + \Delta x) - u(x) \cdot v(x)$$

Adding *and* subtracting the quantity $u(x + \Delta x) \cdot v(x)$ to the right side give

$$f(x + \Delta x) - f(x) = u(x + \Delta x) \cdot v(x + \Delta x) - u(x + \Delta x) \cdot v(x)$$
$$+ u(x + \Delta x) \cdot v(x) - u(x)v(x)$$
$$= u(x + \Delta x)[v(x + \Delta x) - v(x)]$$
$$+ v(x)[u(x + \Delta x) - u(x)]$$

$$\frac{f(x + \Delta x) - f(x)}{\Delta x}$$
$$= \frac{u(x + \Delta x)[v(x + \Delta x) - v(x)] + v(x)[u(x + \Delta x) - u(x)]}{\Delta x}$$
$$= u(x + \Delta x)\frac{v(x + \Delta x) - v(x)}{\Delta x} + v(x)\frac{u(x + \Delta x) - u(x)}{\Delta x}$$

$$\lim_{\Delta x \to 0} \frac{f(x + \Delta x) - f(x)}{\Delta x} = \lim_{\Delta x \to 0} u(x + \Delta x)\frac{v(x + \Delta x) - v(x)}{\Delta x}$$
$$+ \lim_{\Delta x \to 0} v(x)\frac{u(x + \Delta x) - u(x)}{\Delta x}$$

$$= \lim_{\Delta x \to 0} u(x + \Delta x) \cdot \lim_{\Delta x \to 0} \frac{v(x + \Delta x) - v(x)}{\Delta x}$$

$$+ \lim_{\Delta x \to 0} v(x) \cdot \lim_{\Delta x \to 0} \frac{u(x + \Delta x) - u(x)}{\Delta x}$$

or
$$f'(x) = u(x) \cdot v'(x) + v(x) \cdot u'(x)$$
$$= v'(x) \cdot u(x) + u'(x) \cdot v(x)$$

Rule 6

If $f(x) = u(x)/v(x)$, where $u(x)$ and $v(x)$ are differentiable and $v(x) \neq 0$, then

$$f'(x) = \frac{v(x) \cdot u'(x) - u(x) \cdot v'(x)}{[v(x)]^2}$$

Proof

$$f(x) = \frac{u(x)}{v(x)}$$

$$f(x + \Delta x) = \frac{u(x + \Delta x)}{v(x + \Delta x)}$$

$$f(x + \Delta x) - f(x) = \frac{u(x + \Delta x)}{v(x + \Delta x)} - \frac{u(x)}{v(x)}$$

which can be rewritten as

$$f(x + \Delta x) - f(x) = \frac{u(x + \Delta x) \cdot v(x) - u(x) \cdot v(x + \Delta x)}{v(x + \Delta x) \cdot v(x)}$$

Adding *and* subtracting the quantity $[u(x)v(x)]/[v(x + \Delta x)v(x)]$ yield

$$f(x + \Delta x) - f(x) = \frac{u(x + \Delta x) \cdot v(x) - u(x) \cdot v(x + \Delta x)}{v(x + \Delta x) \cdot v(x)}$$

$$+ \frac{u(x) \cdot v(x)}{v(x + \Delta x) \cdot v(x)} - \frac{u(x) \cdot v(x)}{v(x + \Delta x) \cdot v(x)}$$

Rearranging gives

$$f(x + \Delta x) - f(x)$$

$$= \frac{u(x + \Delta x) \cdot v(x) - u(x) \cdot v(x) - v(x + \Delta x) \cdot u(x) + u(x) \cdot v(x)}{v(x + \Delta x) \cdot v(x)}$$

$$= \frac{v(x)[u(x + \Delta x) - u(x)] - u(x)[v(x + \Delta x) - v(x)]}{v(x + \Delta x) \cdot v(x)}$$

$$\frac{f(x + \Delta x) - f(x)}{\Delta x}$$

$$= \frac{v(x)[u(x + \Delta x) - u(x)] - u(x)[v(x + \Delta x) - v(x)]}{v(x + \Delta x) \cdot v(x)} \bigg/ \Delta x$$

$$= \frac{v(x) \dfrac{u(x + \Delta x) - u(x)}{\Delta x} - u(x) \dfrac{v(x + \Delta x) - v(x)}{\Delta x}}{v(x + \Delta x) \cdot v(x)}$$

$$\lim_{\Delta x \to 0} \frac{f(x + \Delta x) - f(x)}{\Delta x}$$

$$= \lim_{\Delta x \to 0} \frac{v(x) \dfrac{u(x + \Delta x) - u(x)}{\Delta x} - u(x) \dfrac{v(x + \Delta x) - v(x)}{\Delta x}}{v(x + \Delta x) \cdot v(x)}$$

$$= \frac{\lim\limits_{\Delta x \to 0} v(x) \cdot \lim\limits_{\Delta x \to 0} \dfrac{u(x + \Delta x) - u(x)}{\Delta x} - \lim\limits_{\Delta x \to 0} u(x) \cdot \lim\limits_{\Delta x \to 0} \dfrac{v(x + \Delta x) - v(x)}{\Delta x}}{\lim\limits_{\Delta x \to 0} v(x + \Delta x) \cdot \lim\limits_{\Delta x \to 0} v(x)}$$

or $$f'(x) = \frac{v(x) \cdot u'(x) - u(x) \cdot v'(x)}{v(x) \cdot v(x)}$$

$$= \frac{v(x) \cdot u'(x) - u(x) \cdot v'(x)}{[v(x)]^2}$$

CLASSICAL OPTIMIZATION: METHODOLOGY

12

CHAPTER OBJECTIVES After reading this chapter, you should have a better understanding of the meaning of the first and second derivatives; you should have a better understanding of the concept of concavity; you should be able to examine a function and determine the conditions for optimizing (maximizing or minimizing) the value of the function; your ability to understand the general behavior of a function should be improved; and you should be able to sketch the general shape of functions with greater ease.

In this chapter the tools developed in Chap. 11 will be extended. We will further our understanding of the first and second derivatives. We will see how these derivatives can be useful in describing the behavior of mathematical functions. A major objective of the chapter is to develop a method for determining where a function achieves maximum or minimum values. *Classical optimization* refers to calculus-based procedures used to locate maximum and minimum values on a function. Finally, we will examine an approach which can facilitate the sketching of functions.

12.1 DERIVATIVES: ADDITIONAL INTERPRETATIONS

In this section we will continue to expand our understanding of derivatives.

The First Derivative

As mentioned in the last chapter, the first derivative represents the instantaneous rate of change in $f(x)$ with respect to a change in x.

DEFINITION
The function $f(x)$ is said to be an *increasing function* on an interval I if for any x_1 and x_2 within the interval, $x_1 < x_2$ implies that $f(x_1) < f(x_2)$.

If the first derivative is positive throughout an interval on $f(x)$, then the tangent slope is positive and $f(x)$ *is an increasing function on the interval*. That is, at any point within the interval, a slight increase in the value of x will be accompanied by an increase in the value of $f(x)$. The curves in Fig. 12.1a and Fig. 12.1b are the graphs of increasing functions of x because the tangent slope at any point is positive.

FIGURE 12.1

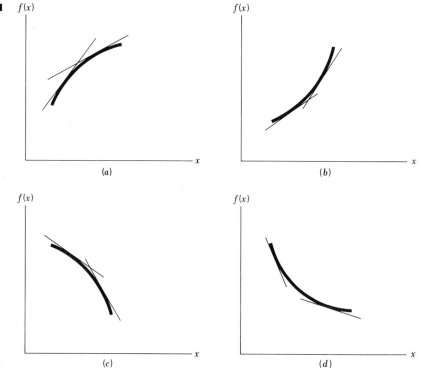

(a)

(b)

(c)

(d)

DEFINITION
The function $f(x)$ is said to be a *decreasing function*
on an interval *I* if for any x_1 and x_2 within the interval,
$x_1 < x_2$ implies that $f(x_1) > f(x_2)$.

If the first derivative is negative throughout an interval on $f(x)$, then
the tangent slope is negative and $f(x)$ *is a decreasing function on the interval*. That is, at any point within the interval a slight increase in the
value of x will be accompanied by a decrease in the value of $f(x)$. The
curves in Fig. 12.1c and *d* are the graphs of decreasing functions of x.

NOTE
If a function is increasing (decreasing) on
an interval, the function is increasing (decreasing) at every point within the interval.

Given $f(x) = 5x^2 - 20x + 3$, determine the intervals over which $f(x)$ **Example**
can be described as (*a*) an increasing function, (*b*) a decreasing function, **12.1**
and (*c*) neither increasing or decreasing.

To determine whether $f(x)$ is increasing or decreasing, we should first **Solution**
find $f'(x)$:

$$f'(x) = 10x - 20$$

$f(x)$ will be an increasing function when $f'(x) > 0$, or when

$$10x - 20 > 0$$
or $$10x > 20$$
or $$x > 2$$

$f(x)$ will be a decreasing function when $f'(x) < 0$, or when

$$10x - 20 < 0$$
or $$10x < 20$$
or $$x < 2$$

$f(x)$ will be neither increasing or decreasing when $f'(x) = 0$, or when

$$10x - 20 = 0$$
or $$10x = 20$$
or $$x = 2$$

Summarizing, $f(x)$ is a decreasing function when $x < 2$, neither increasing or decreasing at $x = 2$, and an increasing function when $x > 2$.
Sketch the graph of $f(x)$ to see if these conclusions seem reasonable.

The Second Derivative

The second derivative is the derivative of the first derivative. Although we will almost always use $f''(x)$ to represent the second derivative, we might express it using the notation

$$\frac{d(dy/dx)}{dx} \quad \text{or} \quad \frac{d}{dx}\left(\frac{dy}{dx}\right) \quad \text{or} \quad \frac{d^2y}{dx^2}$$

This notation can be read as "the derivative of dy/dx with respect to x." It is a measure of the instantaneous rate of change in dy/dx with respect to a change in x. In other words, it tells you the rate at which the slope of the tangent line is changing with respect to a change in x—whether the slope of the tangent is increasing or decreasing at a particular instant.

If $f''(x)$ is negative on an interval of $f(x)$, the first derivative is decreasing, or graphically the tangent slope is decreasing in value on the interval. If $f''(x)$ is positive on an interval of $f(x)$, the first derivative is increasing, or graphically the tangent slope is increasing on the interval.

Examine Fig. 12.2. Either mentally construct tangent lines or lay a straightedge on the curve to represent the tangent line at various points. Along the curve from A to B the slope is slightly negative and becomes more and more negative as we get closer to B. In fact, the tangent slope goes from a value of 0 at A to its most negative value at point B. Thus the slope is decreasing in value over the interval between A and B, and we would expect $f''(x)$ to be negative on this interval (that is, $f''(x) < 0$).

Having reached its most negative value at point B, the slope continues to be negative on the interval between B and C; but the slope becomes less and less negative, eventually equaling 0 at C. If the slope assumes values which are becoming *less negative* (for example, -5, -4, -3, -2, -1, 0), the slope is increasing in value. As such, we would expect $f''(x)$ to be positive on this interval (that is, $f''(x) > 0$).

FIGURE 12.2 $f(x)$

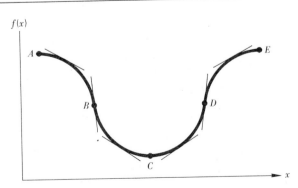

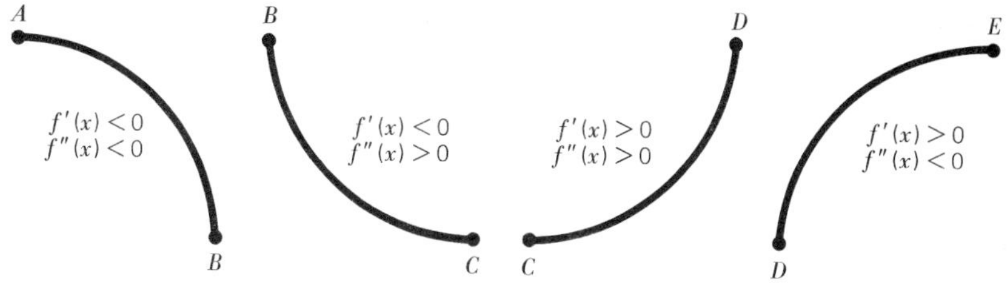

$f'(x) < 0$
$f''(x) < 0$

$f'(x) < 0$
$f''(x) > 0$

$f'(x) > 0$
$f''(x) > 0$

$f'(x) > 0$
$f''(x) < 0$

FIGURE 12.3

Between C and D the slope becomes more and more positive assuming its largest positive value at D. Since the slope is increasing in value on this interval, we would expect $f''(x)$ to be positive.

Between D and E the slope continues to be positive, but it is becoming less and less positive, eventually equaling 0 at E. If the slope is assuming values which are positive but becoming smaller (for example, 5, 4, 3, 2, 1, 0), it is decreasing in value and we would expect $f''(x)$ to be negative on the interval.

Figure 12.3 summarizes the first- and second-derivative conditions for the four regions of the function. These relationships can be difficult to understand. Take your time studying these figures and retrace the logic if necessary.

Concavity and Inflection Points

In Chap. 10 the notion of concavity was briefly introduced. A more formal definition of concavity follows.

DEFINITION
The graph of a function $f(x)$ is *concave up (down)* on an interval if $f'(x)$ increases (decreases) on the entire interval.

This definition suggests that the graph of a function is concave up on an interval if the tangent slope *increases* over the entire interval. For any point within such an interval *the curve will lie above its tangent line*. Similarly, the graph of a function is concave down on an interval if the tangent slope *decreases* over the entire interval. For any point within such an interval *the curve will lie below its tangent line*.

In Fig. 12.4 the graph of $f(x)$ is *concave down* between A and B, and it is *concave up* between B and C. Note that between A and B the curve lies below its tangent lines and between B and C the curve lies above its tangent lines. Point B is where the concavity changes from concave down to concave up. A point at which the concavity changes is called an *inflection point*. Thus, point B is an inflection point.

There are relationships between the second derivative and the concavity of the graph of a function which are going to be of considerable value later in this chapter. These relationships are as follows:

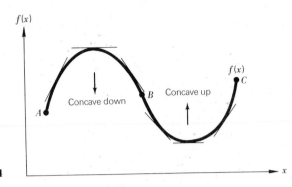

$f(x)$

Concave down

B Concave up

$f(x)$
C

A

x

FIGURE 12.4

1 If $f''(x) < 0$ on an interval $a \le x \le b$, the graph of $f(x)$ is *concave down* over that interval. For any point $x = c$ in such an interval, $f(x)$ is said to be concave down at $[c, f(c)]$.

2 If $f''(x) > 0$ on any interval $a \le x \le b$, $f(x)$ is *concave up* over that interval. For any point $x = c$ in such an interval, $f(x)$ is said to be concave up at $[c, f(c)]$

3 If $f''(x) = 0$ at any point $x = c$ in the domain of $f(x)$, no conclusion can be drawn about the concavity at $[c, f(c)]$.

Be very careful not to reverse the logic of these relationships! Because of relationship 3 we *cannot* make statements about the sign of the second derivative knowing the concavity of the graph of a function. For example, we cannot state that if the graph of a function is concave down at $x = a$, then $f''(a) < 0$.

Example 12.2   We should be quite familiar with quadratic functions by now. Given the quadratic function $f(x) = ax^2 + bx + c$, determine the concavity of its graph.

Solution   Given $f(x)$,

$$f'(x) = 2ax + b \qquad \text{and} \qquad f''(x) = 2a$$

If $a > 0$, then $f''(x) = 2a > 0$. Thus from relationship 2, the graph of $f(x)$ is concave up whenever $a > 0$. If $a < 0$, then $f''(x) = 2a < 0$. Thus from relationship 1, the graph of $f(x)$ is concave down whenever $a < 0$. This is entirely consistent with our discussions in Chap. 10 which concluded that if $a > 0$, $f(x)$ graphs as a parabola which is concave up. And, if $a < 0$, $f(x)$ graphs as a parabola which is concave down.

Example 12.3   For $f(x) = x^3 - 2x^2 + x - 1$ determine the concavity at $x = -2$ and $x = 3$.

Solution $f'(x) = 3x^2 - 4x + 1$
          and $f''(x) = 6x - 4$

Evaluating $f''(x)$ at $x = -2$ gives

$$f''(-2) = 6(-2) - 4 = -16$$

Since $f''(-2) < 0$, the graph of the function is concave down at $x = -2$.
Evaluating $f''(x)$ at $x = 3$, we get

$$f''(3) = 6(3) - 4 = 14$$

Since $f''(3) > 0$, the graph of the function is concave up at $x = 3$.

Determine the concavity of $f(x) = x^4$ at $x = 0$.

Example 12.4

Solution

$$f'(x) = 4x^3$$
$$f''(x) = 12x^2$$
$$f''(0) = 12(0)^2 = 0$$

Because $f''(0) = 0$, according to relationship 3 we can make no statement about the concavity at $x = 0$. However, substituting a sufficient number of values for x into $f(x)$ and plotting these pairs of values, we can conclude that $f(x)$ has the graphical shape shown in Fig. 12.5. And from this sketch it is obvious that the graph is concave up at $x = 0$.

At times we may have a need to locate points of inflection on the graph of a function. *A necessary condition (something which must be true) for the existence of an inflection point at $x = a$ is that $f''(a) = 0$.* That is, by finding all values of x for which $f''(x) = 0$, you will identify the *candidate locations* for inflection points.† For many functions, all values satisfying this condition will, in fact, be inflection points. For some functions, such as $f(x) = x^4$ in the last example, the condition $f''(a) = 0$ does not guarantee that an inflection point exists at $x = a$.

Therefore a practical test to identify inflection points is the following:

1 Find all points a where $f''(a) = 0$.

2 If $f''(x)$ changes sign when passing through $x = a$, there is an inflection point at $x = a$.

The essence of this test is to choose points slightly to the left and right of $x = a$ and determine if the concavity is different on each side. If $f''(x)$ is positive to the left and negative to the right, or vice versa, an inflection point exists at $x = a$.

FIGURE 12.5

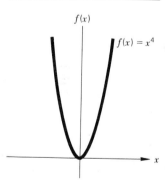

Use the test for inflection points to verify that an inflection point does *not* exist at $x = 0$ for $f(x) = x^4$.

Example 12.5

---

† Other candidates for inflection points occur where $f''(x)$ is discontinuous. However, we will not encounter such candidates in this book.

Solution Given that $f''(x) = 12x^2$, $f''(x) = 0$ when $12x^2 = 0$, or when $x = 0$. Thus, $x = 0$ is the only candidate for being an inflection point. If $f''(x)$ is evaluated at $x = -0.1$ and $x = +0.1$, then

$$f''(-0.1) = 12(-0.1)^2$$
$$= 0.12 > 0$$

and

$$f''(+0.1) = 12(+0.1)^2$$
$$= 0.12 > 0$$

Since the second derivative has the same sign to the left and right of $x = 0$, there is no inflection point at $x = 0$.

Example 12.6 Determine the location(s) of all inflection points on the graph of

$$f(x) = \frac{x^4}{12} - \frac{x^3}{2} + x^2 + 10$$

Solution Given $f(x)$,

$$f'(x) = \frac{4x^3}{12} - \frac{3x^2}{2} + 2x$$

$$= \frac{x^3}{3} - \frac{3x^2}{2} + 2x$$

$$f''(x) = \frac{3x^2}{3} - \frac{6x}{2} + 2$$

$$= x^2 - 3x + 2$$

If $f''(x)$ is set equal to 0,

$$x^2 - 3x + 2 = 0$$

or

$$(x - 2)(x - 1) = 0$$

Therefore, $f''(x) = 0$ when $x = 2$ and $x = 1$. If $f''(x)$ is evaluated to the left and right of $x = 1$,

$$f''(1.1) = -0.09 < 0$$
$$f''(0.9) = 0.11 > 0$$

Since the sign of $f''(x)$ changes, an inflection point exists at $x = 1$. If $f''(x)$ is evaluated to the left and right of $x = 2$,

$$f''(2.1) = 0.11 > 0$$
$$f''(1.9) = -0.09 < 0$$

Thus, an inflection point also exists at $x = 2$.

Follow-up Exercises

For each of the following functions (*a*) determine whether $f(x)$ is increasing or decreasing at $x = 1$. Determine the values of x for which $f(x)$ is (*b*) an increasing function, (*c*) a decreasing function, and (*d*) neither increasing nor decreasing.

12.1 $f(x) = 10 - 2x$

12.2 $f(x) = 3x + 7$

12.3 $f(x) = x^2 - 2x + 1$

12.4 $f(x) = 6x^2 - 7x + 12$

12.5 $f(x) = x^3 + 10$ **12.6** $f(x) = -2x^3$
12.7 $f(x) = x^4 - 15$ **12.8** $f(x) = -3x^4$
12.9 $f(x) = x^5/5$ **12.10** $f(x) = -10x^5 + 40$

For each of the following functions, use $f''(x)$ to determine the concavity conditions at $x = -2$ and $x = +3$.

12.11 $f(x) = 4x^2 + 2x + 5$ **12.12** $f(x) = 3x^2 - 7x + 9$
12.13 $f(x) = -x^3$ **12.14** $f(x) = x^3/4$
12.15 $f(x) = x^3 - 7x^2 + 4x - 10$
12.16 $f(x) = -x^3 + 3x^2 - x + 9$
12.17 $f(x) = x^4 - 4x^3 - x$
12.18 $f(x) = x^5 + x^3/3 - 4x + 12$
12.19 $f(x) = e^x$ **12.20** $f(x) = e^{x^2}$
12.21 $f(x) = (x - 5)^4$ **12.22** $f(x) = (8 - x)^3$

For each of the following functions identify the locations of any inflection points.

12.23 $f(x) = x^5$ **12.24** $f(x) = -x^4/2$
12.25 $f(x) = 4x^3 - 2x^2 + 15$ **12.26** $f(x) = x^4/12 + x^3 + 4x^2$
12.27 $f(x) = x^5/20 - x^3/6$ **12.28** $f(x) = (x - 4)^3$
12.29 $f(x) = (6 - x)^4$ **12.30** $f(x) = e^x$
12.31 $f(x) = e^{-x^2}$ **12.32** $f(x) = -x^3 + 5x^2$

IDENTIFICATION OF MAXIMA AND MINIMA   12.2

In applications of mathematics, a nonlinear function can represent some decision criterion. For example, a function may represent profit, revenue, cost, or pollution levels, stated as a function of a variable which is at least partially under the control of the decision maker. For instance, profit may be stated as a function of the number of dollars spent on advertising. With that assumption the decision maker can determine, within certain limits, how much to spend on advertising. The goal is to decide how much to spend so as to maximize profit. If the graph of the profit function has the general shape shown in Fig. 12.6, the decision maker would want to locate the greatest value of $f(x)$, which in this case occurs at $[x^*, f(x^*)]$.

In this section we will examine functions with the purpose of identifying maximum and minimum values.

Relative Maxima and Minima

DEFINITION
If $f(x)$ is defined on an interval which contains $x = a$, $f(x)$ is said to reach a *relative* or *local maximum* at $x = a$ if $f(a) \geq f(x)$ for all x within the interval.

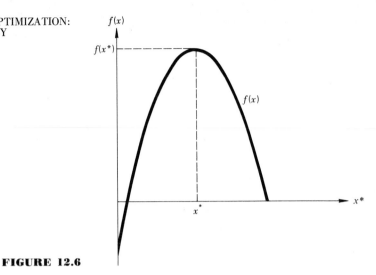

DEFINITION
If $f(x)$ is defined on an interval which contains $x = a$, $f(x)$ is said to reach a *relative* or *local minimum* at $x = a$ if $f(a) \leq f(x)$ for all x within the interval.

Both definitions focus upon the value of $f(x)$ within an interval. A relative maximum refers to a point where the value of $f(x)$ is greater than the value of $f(x)$ for points which are nearby. A relative minimum refers to a point where the value of $f(x)$ is lower than the value of $f(x)$ for points which are nearby. If we use these definitions and examine Fig. 12.7, $f(x)$ has *relative maxima* at points a and c, or when $x = x_a$ and $x = x_c$. Similarly, $f(x)$ has *relative minima* at points b and d, or when $x = x_b$ and $x = x_d$.

FIGURE 12.7

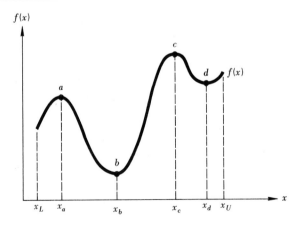

DEFINITION
A function $f(x)$ is said to reach an *absolute* or *global*
maximum at $x = a$ if $f(a) > f(x)$ for any other x in the
domain of $f(x)$.

DEFINITION
A function $f(x)$ is said to reach an *absolute* or *global*
minimum at $x = a$ if $f(a) > f(x)$ for any other x in the
domain of $f(x)$.

If we refer again to Fig. 12.7, $f(x)$ reaches a global maximum at point
c, or when $x = x_c$. It reaches a global minimum at point b, or when
$x = x_b$. It should be noted that a point on the graph of a function can be
both a relative maximum (minimum) and a global maximum (minimum).
We will see later in the chapter, however, that the global maximum or
minimum for a function does not have to occur at a relative maximum or
minimum.

Stationary Points

We will have a particular interest in relative maxima and minima. It will
be important to know how to identify and distinguish between them.

DEFINITION
Given the differentiable function $f(x)$, necessary conditions for the
existence of a relative maximum or minimum at $x = a$ are that

$$1.\ f'(a) = 0 \qquad or \qquad 2.\ f'(a)\ \text{is undefined}$$

FIGURE 12.8

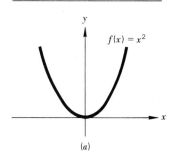

(a)

Points which satisfy either of the conditions in this definition are *candidates* for relative maxima or minima. Such points are often referred to
as *critical points*. Figure 12.8 illustrates the graphs of two functions
which have relative minima at $x = 0$. For $f(x) = x^2$, $f'(0) = 0$ (or the
tangent slope equals 0 at $x = 0$). For $f(x) = |x|$, $f'(0)$ is not defined (or
there is no unique tangent line at $x = 0$).

In this book we will focus our attention upon functions which have
relative maxima and minima satisfying condition 1 in the definition. We
will not examine functions which have relative maxima or minima characterized by condition 2.

Points which satisfy condition 1 are often referred to as *stationary
points*. These are points on the graph of a function where the tangent
slope equals 0. The locations of these points are found by setting $f'(x)$
equal to 0 and solving for the values of x (if any exist) which satisfy the
equation.

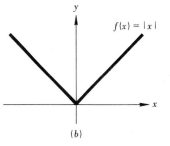

(b)

Example 12.7
Determine the location(s) of any stationary points on the graph of

$$f(x) = \frac{x^3}{3} - \frac{x^2}{2} - 6x + 100$$

Solution
First, the general expression for the tangent slope is

$$f'(x) = \frac{3x^2}{3} - \frac{2x}{2} - 6$$
$$= x^2 - x - 6$$

If $f'(x)$ is set equal to 0, then

$$x^2 - x - 6 = 0$$

when
$$(x - 3)(x + 2) = 0$$

When the two factors are set equal to 0, it can be determined that there are two stationary points (or points of zero slope) which occur when $x = 3$ and $x = -2$.

The only statements we can make about the behavior of $f(x)$ at these points is that the tangent slope equals 0. And, nowhere else on the graph of $f(x)$ is the slope equal to 0. Further testing is necessary to determine whether there is a relative maximum or minimum at $x = 3$ and $x = -2$.

Aside from relative maxima and minima, there is one other situation where the tangent slope can equal 0. *Stationary inflection points* are points on a function where the slope equals 0 ("stationary") and the concavity of the function changes ("inflection point"), thus, the term *stationary inflection point*.

Figure 12.9 illustrates the different possibilities for stationary points. Figure 12.9*a* and *b* illustrates relative maximum and minimum points, whereas Fig. 12.9*c* and *d* illustrates two different types of stationary inflection points. In Fig. 12.9*c* the graph of the function has a tangent slope of 0 at point *a*, and it is also changing from being concave down to concave up. In Fig. 12.9*d* the graph has a tangent slope of 0 and is changing from being concave up to concave down.

In summary, any stationary point will be a relative maximum, a relative minimum, or a stationary inflection point.

POINT FOR THOUGHT AND DISCUSSION
For polynomial functions $f(x)$ of degree n, the largest possible number of stationary points is $n - 1$. Thus, a function $f(x)$ of degree 5 can have *as many as* four stationary points. Why is this so?

POINT FOR THOUGHT AND DISCUSSION
What comment can be made regarding stationary points on constant functions [for example, $f(x) = 10$]?

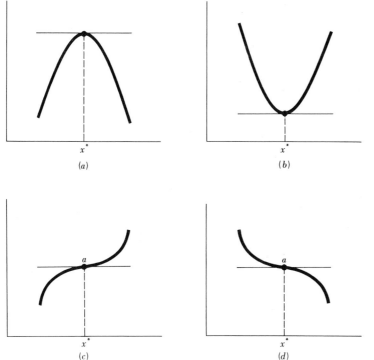

(a)

(b)

(c)

(d)

FIGURE 12.9

The First-Derivative Test

In an effort to locate relative maximum or minimum points, the first step is to locate all stationary points on the graph of the function. Given that a stationary point may be either a relative maximum or minimum or a stationary inflection point, some test must be devised to distinguish among these. There are a number of tests available. One test which is easy to understand intuitively is the *first-derivative test.*

After the locations of stationary points are identified, the first-derivative test suggests looking at the tangent slope conditions to the left and right of the stationary point. Figure 12.10 illustrates the four stationary point possibilities and their tangent slope conditions to either side of x^*. For a relative maximum, the tangent slope is positive to the left (x_l) and negative to the right (x_r). For a relative minimum, the tangent slope is negative to the left and positive to the right. For stationary inflection points, the tangent slope has the *same sign* to the left or the right of the stationary point.

Another way of describing this test is the following.

1 For a relative maximum, the value of the function is increasing to the left and decreasing to the right.

2 For a relative minimum, the value of the function is decreasing to the left and increasing to the right.

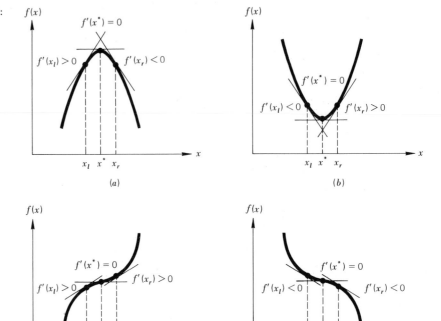

FIGURE 12.10

3 For stationary inflection points, the value of the function is either increasing to both the left *and* right or decreasing to both the left and right.

FIRST-DERIVATIVE TEST

1 Find all stationary points x^*.

2 For any stationary point x^* determine the value of $f'(x)$ to the left and right of x^*.

i. **If $f'(x) > 0$ to the left and $f'(x) < 0$ to the right, there is a relative maximum for $f(x)$ at x^*.**

ii. **If $f'(x) < 0$ to the left and $f'(x) > 0$ to the right, there is a relative minimum for $f(x)$ at x^*.**

iii. **If $f'(x)$ has the same sign to both the left and right, a stationary inflection point exists at x^*.**

Example 12.8 Determine the location(s) of any stationary points on the graph of $f(x) = 2x^2 - 12x - 10$, and determine the nature of any stationary points.

The first derivative is

$$f'(x) = 4x - 12$$

When the first derivative is set equal to 0,

$$4x - 12 = 0$$
or
$$4x = 12$$
and
$$\boldsymbol{x = 3}$$

Since $f(3) = 2(3^2) - 12(3) - 10 = -28$, there is a stationary point located at $(3, -28)$.

To test the stationary point, let's select $x_l = 2.9$ and $x_r = 3.1$.

$$f'(2.9) = 4(2.9) - 12$$
$$= 11.6 - 12$$
$$= -0.4$$
$$f'(3.1) = 4(3.1) - 12$$
$$= 12.4 - 12$$
$$= +0.4$$

Because the first derivative is negative to the left of $x = 3$ and positive to the right, the point $(3, -28)$ is a relative minimum on $f(x)$. Note that $f(x)$ is a quadratic function which graphs as a parabola that is concave up.

In Example 12.7 we determined that the graph of the function **Example 12.9**

$$f(x) = \frac{x^3}{3} - \frac{x^2}{2} - 6x + 100$$

has stationary points when $x = 3$ and $x = -2$. Determine the nature of these stationary points.

Given $f(x)$,

$$f'(x) = x^2 - x - 6$$

In testing the stationary point at $x = 3$, let's select $x_l = 2.9$ and $x_r = 3.1$.

$$f'(2.9) = (2.9)^2 - 2.9 - 6$$
$$= -0.49$$
$$f'(3.1) = (3.1)^2 - 3.1 - 6$$
$$= 0.51$$

Since $f'(x)$ is negative to the left of $x = 3$ and positive to the right, a relative minimum occurs for $f(x)$ when $x = 3$.

In testing the stationary point at $x = -2$, let's select $x_l = -2.1$ and $x_r = -1.9$.

$$f'(-2.1) = (-2.1)^2 - (-2.1) - 6$$
$$= 0.51$$
$$f'(-1.9) = (-1.9)^2 - (-1.9) - 6$$
$$= -0.49$$

Since $f'(x)$ is positive to the left of $x = -2$ and negative to the right, a relative maximum occurs for $f(x)$ when $x = -2$.

The Second-Derivative Test

The most expedient test of stationary points is the *second-derivative test*. Intuitively, the second-derivative test attempts to determine the concavity of the function at a stationary point x^*. We concluded in Sec. 12.1 that if $f''(x) < 0$ at a point on the graph of $f(x)$, the curve is *concave down* at that point. If $f''(x) > 0$ at a point on the graph of $f(x)$, the curve is *concave up* at that point. Thus, the second-derivative test suggests finding the value of $f''(x^*)$. Of greater interest, though, is the *sign* of $f''(x^*)$. If $f''(x^*) > 0$, we know that not only is the slope equal to 0 at x^* but also the function is concave up at x^*. If we refer to the four stationary point possibilities in Fig. 12.9, only one is concave up at x^*, that being the relative minimum in Fig. 12.9*b*.

If $f''(x^*) < 0$, the slope is 0 and the function is concave down at x^*. Again referring to Fig. 12.9, we find that the only stationary point accompanied by concave-down conditions is the relative maximum in Fig. 12.9*a*.

As stated in Sec. 12.1, if $f''(x^*) = 0$, no conclusions can be drawn regarding the concavity at x^*. Another test such as the first-derivative test is required to determine the nature of these stationary points.

SECOND-DERIVATIVE TEST

1 Find all stationary points x^*.
2 For any stationary point x^* determine the value of $f''(x^*)$.

  i. If $f''(x^*) > 0$, the function is concave up at x^* and there is a *relative minimum* for $f(x)$ at x^*.

  ii. If $f''(x^*) < 0$, the function is concave down at x^* and there is a *relative maximum* for $f(x)$ at x^*.

  iii. If $f''(x^*) = 0$, no conclusions can be drawn about the stationary point. Another test such as the first-derivative test is necessary.

Example 12.10
Examine the following function for any stationary points and determine their nature.
$$f(x) = -\tfrac{3}{2}x^2 + 6x - 20$$

Solution
We should recognize this as a quadratic function which graphs as a parabola that is concave down. There should be one stationary point which is a relative maximum.

The first derivative is
$$f'(x) = -3x + 6$$

If $f'(x)$ is set equal to 0,
$$-3x + 6 = 0$$
$$-3x = -6$$
$$\boldsymbol{x = 2}$$

The only stationary point occurs at $x = 2$.

If we continue with the second-derivative test,

$$f''(x) = -3$$

and

$$f''(2) = -3 < 0$$

Since the second derivative is negative at $x = 2$, we can conclude that the graph of $f(x)$ is concave down at this point, and the stationary point is a relative maximum.

The value of $f(x)$ at the relative maximum is

$$f(2) = -\tfrac{3}{2}(2^2) + 6(2) - 20$$
$$= -6 + 12 - 20$$
$$= -14$$

which is the local maximum value for $f(x)$. Figure 12.11 presents a sketch of the function.

Examine the following function for any stationary points and determine their nature if

$$f(x) = \frac{x^4}{4} - \frac{9x^2}{2}$$

Example 12.11

If $f'(x)$ is identified and set equal to 0,

Solution

$$f'(x) = \frac{4x^3}{4} - \frac{18x}{2}$$
$$= x^3 - 9x$$
$$x^3 - 9x = 0$$

when

$$x(x^2 - 9) = 0$$

or when

$$x(x + 3)(x - 3) = 0$$

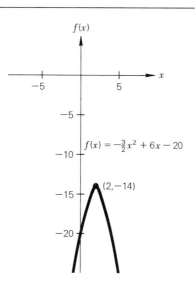

FIGURE 12.11

$f(x) = -\tfrac{3}{2}x^2 + 6x - 20$

$(2, -14)$

If the three factors are set equal to 0, stationary points are found at

$$x = 0, \qquad x = -3, \qquad \text{and} \qquad x = 3$$

The second derivative is

$$f''(x) = 3x^2 - 9$$

To test the stationary point at $x = 0$,

$$f''(0) = 3(0^2) - 9$$
$$= -9 < 0$$

Therefore a *relative maximum* occurs when $x = 0$.
The value of $f(x)$ at $x = 0$ is

$$f(0) = \frac{0^4}{4} - \frac{9(0^2)}{2} = 0$$

To test the stationary point at $x = -3$,

$$f''(-3) = 3(-3)^2 - 9$$
$$= 27 - 9 = 18 > 0$$

Therefore a *relative minimum* occurs when $x = -3$.
The value of $f(x)$ at $x = -3$ is

$$f(-3) = \frac{(-3)^4}{4} - \frac{9(-3)^2}{2}$$

$$= \frac{81}{4} - \frac{81}{2} = \frac{-81}{4}$$

To test the stationary point at $x = 3$,

$$f''(3) = 3(3^2) - 9$$
$$= 27 - 9 = 18 > 0$$

Therefore, a *relative minimum* occurs at $x = 3$. At $x = 3$, $f(3) = (3^4)/4 - 9(3^2)/2 = \frac{-81}{4}$, which is another relative minimum value on $f(x)$. Figure 12.12 contains a sketch of the function.

Example 12.12

Examine the following function for any stationary points and determine their nature.

$$f(x) = -10{,}000e^{-0.03x} - 120x + 10{,}000$$

Solution

If we find $f'(x)$ and set it equal to 0,

$$f'(x) = -10{,}000(-0.03)e^{-0.03x} - 120$$
$$= 300e^{-0.03x} - 120$$

$$300e^{-0.03x} - 120 = 0$$
when
$$300e^{-0.03x} = 120$$
or when
$$e^{-0.03x} = \frac{120}{300} = 0.4$$

If we refer to Table A.1 at the end of the book, we find

$$e^{-0.92} \doteq 0.4$$

Therefore,
$$e^{-0.03x} \doteq 0.4$$
when
$$-0.03x = -0.92$$
or when
$$x = \mathbf{30.67}$$

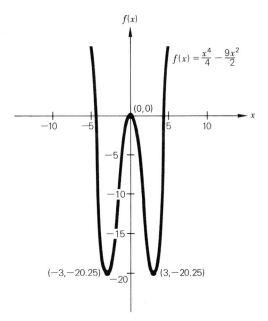

$$f(x) = \frac{x^4}{4} - \frac{9x^2}{2}$$

(0,0)

(−3,−20.25)

(3,−20.25)

FIGURE 12.12

The only stationary point occurs when $x \doteq 30.67$.

Continuing with the second-derivative test, we have

$$f''(x) = -0.03(300)e^{-0.03x}$$
$$= -9e^{-0.03x}$$
$$f''(30.67) = -9e^{-0.03(30.67)}$$
$$= -9e^{-0.92}$$
$$= -9(0.4)$$
$$= -3.6 < 0$$

Therefore, a *relative maximum* occurs at $x = 30.67$. At $x = 30.67$,

$$f(30.67) = -10,000e^{-0.03(30.67)} - 120(30.67) + 10,000$$
$$= -10,000(0.4) - 3,680.4 + 10,000$$
$$= 2,319.6$$

which is a relative maximum value for $f(x)$. Figure 12.13 contains a sketch of the function.

When the Second-Derivative Test Fails

As indicated in the description of the second-derivative test, if $f''(x^*) = 0$, the second derivative does not allow for any conclusion about what is happening to $f(x)$ at x^*. Consider the following example.

Examine the following function for any stationary points and determine their nature.

**Example
12.13**

$$f(x) = -x^5$$

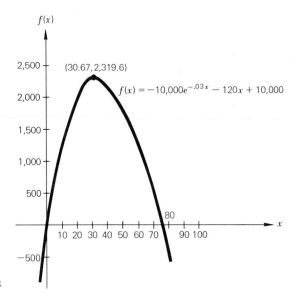

$f(x)$

(30.67, 2,319.6)

$f(x) = -10,000e^{-.03x} - 120x + 10,000$

FIGURE 12.13

Solution   If $f'(x)$ is identified and set equal to 0,

$$f'(x) = -5x^4$$
$$-5x^4 = 0$$

FIGURE 12.14

when $$x = 0$$

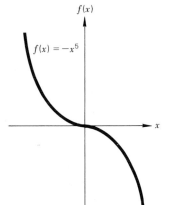

$f(x)$

$f(x) = -x^5$

Continuing with the second-derivative test, we get

$$f''(x) = -20x^3$$

Testing at $x = 0$ yields

$$f''(0) = -20(0)^3$$
$$= 0$$

Thus, there is no conclusion about x^*.

Let's use the first-derivative test to determine the nature of the stationary point. If $x_l = -0.1$ and $x_r = 0.1$, then

$$f'(-0.1) = -5(-0.1)^4$$
$$= -0.0005$$
$$f'(0.1) = -5(0.1)^4$$
$$= -0.0005$$

Since $f'(-0.1)$ and $f'(0.1)$ are both negative, a stationary inflection point occurs at $x = 0$. Figure 12.14 presents a sketch of the function.

Higher-Order Derivative Test (Optional)

There are several ways to reach a conclusion about the nature of a stationary point when the second-derivative test fails. One method which is efficient but not easy to understand intuitively is the *higher-order derivative test*. This test will always be conclusive.

HIGHER-ORDER DERIVATIVE TEST

1 Given a stationary point x^* on $f(x)$, find the lowest-order derivative for which the value of the derivative is nonzero *at* x^*. Denote this derivative as $f^{(n)}(x)$ where n is the order of the derivative.

2 If the order n of this derivative is *even*, $f(x^*)$ is a *relative maximum* if $f^{(n)}(x^*) < 0$ and a *relative minimum* if $f^{(n)}(x^*) > 0$

3 If the order n of this derivative is *odd*, the stationary point is a *stationary inflection point*.

Identify any stationary points and determine their nature if

$$f(x) = (x - 2)^4$$

If we find $f'(x)$ and set it equal to 0,

$$f'(x) = 4(x - 2)^3(1)$$
$$= 4(x - 2)^3$$
$$4(x - 2)^3 = 0$$

when
$$x = 2$$

The second derivative is

$$f''(x) = 4(3)(x - 2)^2$$
$$= 12(x - 2)^2$$

and
$$f''(2) = 12(2 - 2)^2$$
$$= 0$$

Thus, there is no conclusion based upon the second derivative. If we proceed using the higher-order derivative test, the third derivative is

$$f'''(x) = 24(x - 2)$$

and
$$f'''(2) = 24(2 - 2) = 0$$

Since $f'''(2) = 0$, there is no conclusion based on the third derivative.
The fourth derivative is

$$f^{(4)}(x) = 24$$

and
$$f^{(4)}(2) = 24$$

This is the first derivative not equaling 0 at $x = 2$. Since the order of the derivative ($n = 4$) is even, a relative maximum or minimum exists at $x = 2$. To determine which is the case, we look at the sign of $f^{(4)}(2)$. Since $f^{(4)}(2) > 0$, we can conclude that there is a relative minimum at $x = 2$, and $f(2) = 0$ is a relative minimum value of $f(x)$. Figure 12.15 contains a sketch of the function.

Example 12.14

Solution

FIGURE 12.15

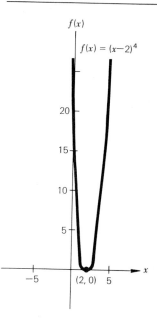

NOTE
The second-derivative test is actually a special case of the higher-order derivative test—the case where the lowest-order derivative not equaling 0 is the second derivative ($n = 2$).

Follow-up Exercises

For each of the following functions determine the location of all stationary points and determine their nature. (*Note:* not all functions have stationary points. This may be the case for some of the functions in this problem set.) Also, compute $f(x^*)$ for each stationary point x^*.

12.33 $f(x) = -3x^2 + 24x + 10$

12.34 $f(x) = 4x^2 - 4x + 9$

12.35 $f(x) = 4x^3$

12.36 $f(x) = -x^3/3$

12.37 $f(x) = \dfrac{x^3}{3} - \dfrac{x^2}{2} - 6x$

12.38 $f(x) = \dfrac{x^3}{6} - x^2$

12.39 $f(x) = \dfrac{x^4}{4} - 8x^2 + 10$

12.40 $f(x) = 2x^2 - \dfrac{x^4}{4}$

12.41 $f(x) = \dfrac{x^5}{5} - \dfrac{3x^4}{4} - \dfrac{4x^3}{3}$

12.42 $f(x) = \dfrac{2x^5}{5} + \dfrac{x^4}{4} - 5x^3$

12.43 $f(x) = (2x - 5)^3$

12.44 $f(x) = -(4x - 2)^4$

12.45 $f(x) = e^{x^2}$

12.46 $f(x) = e^{-x^2}$

12.47 $f(x) = x^6$

12.48 $f(x) = -3x^4 + 10$

12.49 $f(x) = -5{,}000e^{-0.02x} - 50x + 5{,}000$

12.50 $f(x) = 2{,}000e^{-0.05x} + 200x - 3{,}000$

*12.51 *Original Equation Test.* It was mentioned in the last section that other techniques exist for determining the nature of stationary points. One test involves comparing the value of $f(x^*)$ with the values of $f(x)$ just to the left and right of x^*. Refer to Fig. 12.9, and determine a set of rules which would allow one to distinguish among the four stationary point possibilities.

*12.52 Compare the relative efficiencies associated with performing the original equation test and the first-derivative test of stationary points.

*12.53 Compare the relative efficiencies associated with performing the first-derivative, second-derivative, and higher-order derivative tests of stationary points.

12.3 RESTRICTED-DOMAIN CONSIDERATIONS

The last section concentrated on procedures for identifying relative maxima and minima. This section will examine procedures for identifying global maxima and minima when the domain of a function is restricted.

When the Domain Is Restricted

Very often in applied problems the set of possible values for the independent variable(s) is restricted. For example, if profit P is stated as a function of the number of units produced x, it is likely that x will be restricted to values such that $0 \le x \le x_C$. In this case x is restricted to nonnegative values (there is no production of negative quantities) which are less than or equal to some upper limit x_C. The value of x_C may reflect production capacity, as defined by limited labor or raw materials or by the physical capacity of the plant itself.

In searching for the global maximum or global minimum of a function, consideration must be given not only to the relative maxima and minima of the function but also to the *endpoints* for the domain of the function. For example, look at the function graphed in Fig. 12.16. Note that the domain of the function is restricted to values between 0 and x_u. If there is interest in identifying the global maximum for $f(x)$, it can be seen that it occurs at x_u, the upper limit on the domain. The global minimum occurs at x_2, which is also a relative minimum on the function.

PROCEDURE FOR IDENTIFYING GLOBAL MAXIMUM AND MINIMUM POINTS

Given the continuous function $f(x)$ defined over the interval $x_l \le x \le x_u$:

1 Locate all stationary points x^* which lie within the domain of the function. Compute the value of the function $f(x^*)$ at each of these points.

2 Compute the value of $f(x)$ at the lower limit of the domain x_l and at the upper limit of the domain x_u.

3 Compare the values of $f(x^*)$ with $f(x_l)$ and $f(x_u)$. The global maximum is the largest of these values. The global minimum is the smallest of these values.

Determine the locations and values of the global maximum and global minimum for the function

Example 12.15

$$f(x) = \frac{x^3}{3} - \frac{7x^2}{2} + 6x + 5$$

where $2 \le x \le 10$.

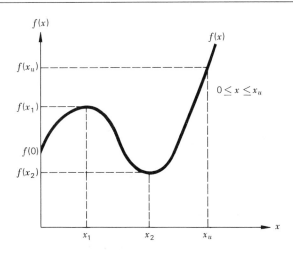

FIGURE 12.16

Solution   *Step 1* Finding the first derivative, we have

$$f'(x) = \frac{3x^2}{3} - \frac{14x}{2} + 6$$

$$= x^2 - 7x + 6$$

If $f'(x)$ is set equal to 0,

$$x^2 - 7x + 6 = 0$$

or

$$(x - 6)(x - 1) = 0$$

Thus, $x = 6$ and $x = 1$

The stationary point at $x = 1$ is not within the domain of the function. Thus, there is no need to consider this point in searching for the global maximum or minimum.

The second derivative is

$$f''(x) = 2x - 7$$

To test $x = 6$, $$f''(6) = 2(6) - 7$$

$$= 5 > 0$$

Since $f''(6) > 0$, there is a relative minimum at $x = 6$. The value of $f(x)$ at $x = 6$ is

$$f(6) = \frac{6^3}{3} - \frac{7(6^2)}{2} + 6(6) + 5$$

$$= 72 - 126 + 36 + 5$$

$$= -13$$

Step 2 The values of $f(x)$ at the endpoints of the domain are

$$f(2) = \frac{2^3}{3} - \frac{7(2^2)}{2} + 6(2) + 5$$

$$= \tfrac{8}{3} - 14 + 12 + 5$$

$$= 5\tfrac{2}{3}$$

and

$$f(10) = \frac{(10)^3}{3} - \frac{7(10)^2}{2} + 6(10) + 5$$

$$= \frac{1,000}{3} - \frac{700}{2} + 65$$

$$= 48\tfrac{1}{3}$$

Step 3 Comparing $f(2)$, $f(6)$, and $f(10)$, we find the global minimum of -13 occurs when $x = 6$ and the global maximum of $48\tfrac{1}{3}$ occurs when $x = 10$. Figure 12.17 presents a sketch of the function.

Follow-up Exercises

In the following exercises, determine the locations and values of the global maximum and global minimum for $f(x)$.

12.54 $f(x) = x^3 + 10; \ 1 \le x \le 5$

12.55 $f(x) = -4x^2 + 6x - 10; \ 0 \le x \le 10$

12.56 $f(x) = x^3/3 - x^2/2 - 6x; \ 0 \le x \le 5$

12.57 $f(x) = x^4/4 - 4x^2 + 16; \ 5 \le x \le 10$

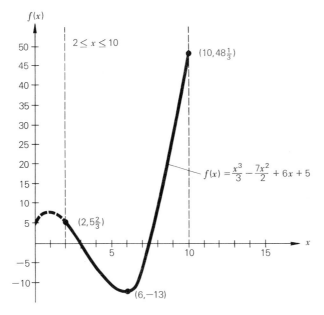

$$f(x) = \frac{x^3}{3} - \frac{7x^2}{2} + 6x + 5$$

FIGURE 12.17

12.58 $f(x) = x^4/4 - 7x^3/3 + 5x^2; \ 0 \le x \le 4$
12.59 $f(x) = x^5/5 - 5x^4/4 - 14x^3/3 - 10; \ 0 \le x \le 6$
12.60 $f(x) = x^4/4 - 8x^2 + 25; \ 0 \le x$
12.61 $f(x) = x^6/6 - x^5 + 2.5x^4; \ -5 \le x \le 5$
12.62 $f(x) = 10,000e^{-0.03x} - 120x + 10,000; \ 20 \le x \le 60$
12.63 $f(x) = 1,000e^{-0.02x} + 10x - 1,250; \ 10 \le x \le 30$

CURVE SKETCHING 12.4

Sketching functions can be simpler when the information we have acquired in this chapter is given. One can get a feeling for the general shape of a function without determining and plotting a large number of data points. This section discusses some of the key determinants of the shape of the graph of a function.

Key Data Points

In determining the general shape of the graph of a function, the following points are the most significant:

Stationary points

Intercepts

Inflection points

To illustrate this, consider the function

$$f(x) = \frac{x^3}{3} - 4x^2 + 12x + 5$$

The easiest data point to locate on the graph of a function is the y intercept. This is evaluated as $f(0)$, or for this function

$$f(0) = 5$$

Thus one data point is (0, 5).

Depending on the function, the x intercepts may or may not be easy to identify. For this function they would be somewhat difficult. So rather than spend a lot of time searching for them, let's see what kind of sketch we can arrive at without them.

The first derivative is

$$f'(x) = x^2 - 8x + 12$$

Setting $f'(x)$ equal to 0 gives

$$x^2 - 8x + 12 = 0$$
or
$$(x - 2)(x - 6) = 0$$

Stationary points occur at $x = 2$ and $x = 6$.

Now, use the second-derivative test:

$$f''(x) = 2x - 8$$

To test $x = 2$,

$$f''(2) = 2(2) - 8$$
$$= -4 < 0$$

Thus, a relative maximum occurs at $x = 2$.

The value of $f(x)$ at $x = 2$ is

$$f(2) = \frac{2^3}{3} - 4(2^2) + 12(2) + 5$$

$$= \tfrac{8}{3} - 16 + 24 + 5$$
$$= 15\tfrac{2}{3}$$

At $(2, 15\tfrac{2}{3})$ there is a relative maximum on the graph of $f(x)$. To test $x = 6$,

$$f''(6) = 2(6) - 8$$
$$= 4 > 0$$

Thus, a relative minimum occurs at $x = 6$.

The value of $f(x)$ at $x = 6$ is

$$f(6) = \frac{6^3}{3} - 4(6^2) + 12(6) + 5$$

$$= 72 - 144 + 72 + 5$$
$$= 5$$

At (6, 5) there is a relative minimum on the graph of $f(x)$.

Inflection point candidates are found when $f''(x)$ is set equal to 0, or when

$$2x - 8 = 0$$
$$x = 4$$

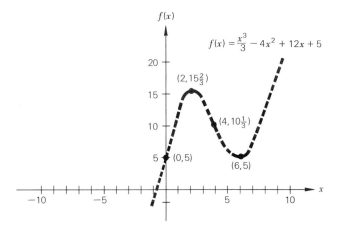

$$f(x) = \frac{x^3}{3} - 4x^2 + 12x + 5$$

FIGURE 12.18

Checking the sign of $f''(x)$ to the left and right of $x = 4$, we find

$$f''(3.9) = -0.2 < 0$$
$$f''(4.1) = +0.2 > 0$$

Since $f''(x)$ changes sign when passing through $x = 4$, we can conclude that there is an inflection point when $x = 4$, or at $(4, 10\frac{1}{3})$.

Figure 12.18 presents a graphical summary of the information we have gathered. The dotted-line segments represent a continuation of this sketch of the function based on the four data points.

You may have some question as to how we would know that the function behaves in the manner indicated by the dotted-line segments. For instance, how do we know that the graph of the function does not continue as indicated in Fig. 12.19? The curve in Fig. 12.19a indicates additional relative maximum and minimum points, respectively, at A and D. These would have to be stationary points; however, the only stationary points on the graph occur at $x = 2$ and $x = 6$. There is another way to eliminate this sketch as a possibility. In order to have a relative minimum at point A, an inflection point would have to occur between points A and B. In order to have a relative maximum at point D, an inflection point would have to occur between C and D. We have already concluded that the only change of concavity on $f(x)$ occurs when $x = 4$.

Although the curve in Fig. 12.19b does not have any additional stationary points, the behavior of this function would require inflection points to the left of the relative maximum and to the right of the relative minimum. This is because the curve becomes concave up to the left of the relative maximum and concave down to the right of the relative minimum.

Ultimate Direction

Another useful observation in sketching a function is to determine the *ultimate direction* or behavior of the function as $x \to +\infty$ and as $x \to -\infty$. For polynomial functions, the ultimate behavior of $f(x)$ is linked to the behavior of the highest-powered term in the function. The theory is that as x becomes more and more positive or negative, eventually a

FIGURE 12.19

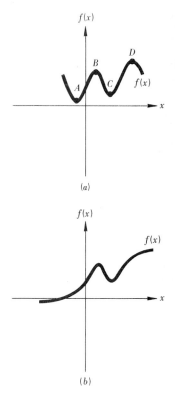

point will be reached where the highest-powered term will contribute more to the value of $f(x)$ than all other terms in the function.

For the function that we first examined, the highest-powered term is $x^3/3$. Thus to determine the behavior of $f(x)$ as x becomes more and more positive, determine the behavior of $x^3/3$ as x becomes more and more positive.

As $x \to +\infty$, $\qquad\qquad \dfrac{x^3}{3} \to +\infty$

Therefore, as $x \to +\infty$, $\qquad f(x) = \dfrac{x^3}{3} - 4x^2 + 12x + 5 \to +\infty$

Similarly,

as $x \to -\infty$, $\qquad\qquad \dfrac{x^3}{3} \to -\infty$

Therefore, as $x \to -\infty$ $\qquad f(x) = \dfrac{x^3}{3} - 4x^2 + 12x + 5 \to -\infty$

These observations support the shape of the curve in Fig. 12.18.

**Example
12.16**

Sketch the function

$$f(x) = \frac{x^4}{4} - \frac{8x^3}{3} + 8x^2$$

Solution

The y intercept for the graph of $f(x)$ is 0. Thus, one point on the function is $(0, 0)$.

The first derivative is

$$f'(x) = x^3 - 8x^2 + 16x$$

If $f'(x)$ is set equal to 0,

$$x^3 - 8x^2 + 16x = 0$$
$$x(x^2 - 8x + 16) = 0$$
or $\qquad\qquad x(x - 4)(x - 4) = 0$

If the factors are set equal to 0, stationary points are found at $x = 0$ and $x = 4$.

Testing $x = 0$, we find

$$f''(x) = 3x^2 - 16x + 16$$
$$f''(0) = 3(0)^2 - 16(0) + 16$$
$$= 16 > 0$$

Therefore, a relative minimum occurs at $x = 0$. Testing $x = 4$ yields

$$f''(4) = 3(4^2) - 16(4) + 16$$
$$= 48 - 64 + 16$$
$$= 0$$

No conclusion can be drawn about $x = 4$ based upon the second derivative. Continuing with the higher-order derivative test, we get

$$f'''(x) = 6x - 16$$
$$f'''(4) = 6(4) - 16$$
$$= 8 > 0$$

Since the order of the derivative is odd, a stationary inflection point occurs when $x = 4$. The value of $f(x)$ at this point is

$$f(4) = \frac{4^4}{4} - \frac{8(4^3)}{3} + 8(4^2)$$
$$= 64 - 170\tfrac{2}{3} + 128$$
$$= 21\tfrac{1}{3}$$

Candidates for inflection points are found by setting $f''(x)$ equal to 0, or

$$3x^2 - 16x + 16 = 0$$
or
$$(3x - 4)(x - 4) = 0$$
when
$$x = \tfrac{4}{3} \quad \text{and} \quad x = 4$$

We have already concluded that a stationary inflection point occurs at $x = 4$. Confirm for yourself that $(\tfrac{4}{3}, 8.69)$ is also an inflection point.

The ultimate behavior of $f(x)$ is linked to the behavior of the term $x^4/4$. As $x \to +\infty$, $x^4/4 \to +\infty$ and $f(x) \to +\infty$. As $x \to -\infty$, $x^4/4 \to +\infty$, and $f(x) \to +\infty$.

Using the information we have gathered, we can sketch the approximate shape of $f(x)$. This sketch is shown in Fig. 12.20.

NOTE

A useful tidbit of information in confirming the existence of inflection points is that for continuous functions *there must be at least one inflection point between any two adjacent stationary points*. This information could have been useful in confirming that an inflection point does exist at $x = \tfrac{4}{3}$ in the last example. With stationary points at $x = 0$ and $x = 4$, there *must be* an inflection point between them. The only candidate inflection point in this range was at $x = \tfrac{4}{3}$.

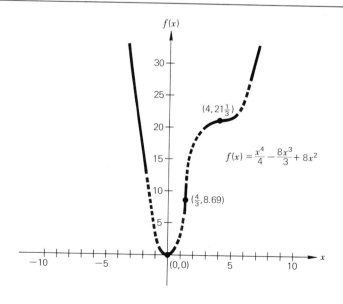

FIGURE 12.20

Follow-up Exercises

Sketch the graphs of the following functions.

12.64 $f(x) = x^3 - 7x^2 + 4x - 10$

12.65 $f(x) = -x^3 + 3x^2 - x + 9$

12.66 $f(x) = \dfrac{x^3}{6} - x^2$ **12.67** $f(x) = \dfrac{x^4}{4} - 8x^2 + 10$

12.68 $f(x) = \dfrac{2x^5}{5} - \dfrac{6x^4}{4} + \dfrac{8x^3}{3}$ **12.69** $f(x) = \dfrac{x^5}{5} + \dfrac{x^4}{8} - 2.5x^3$

12.70 $f(x) = -(5x - 15)^3$

12.5   SUMMARY

In this chapter we have continued to develop our understanding of the first and second derivatives and the information they convey about mathematical functions. A major objective in the chapter was to develop a methodology for determining maximum and minimum values on functions. We also have seen how, with a few key data points, one can determine an approximate sketch of a function without having to plot large numbers of data points. If there is a requirement for very precise sketches, the procedures discussed in the last section probably will not be adequate.

This chapter, as with Chap. 11, has been a "tools" chapter. With the tools that we have now acquired we will proceed to applications. Chapter 13 is a chapter devoted entirely to a wide variety of applications of the differential calculus we have studied.

CHAPTER CHECKLIST

If you have read *all* the sections of this chapter, you should

_____ Understand the relationship between the first derivative and *increasing (decreasing) functions*

_____ Understand what is meant by *concavity* and the relationships which exist between the second derivative and concavity

_____ Know the meaning of *inflection points* and be able to identify their locations

_____ Understand the meaning of the conditions for the existence of *relative maximum (minimum)* points

_____ Understand the meaning of and conditions for the existence of *global maximum (minimum)* points

_____ Know how to identify *stationary points* and determine their nature

_____ Know how to identify global maximum and minimum points

_____ Be able to sketch the graph of a function by identifying a few key points

KEY TERMS AND CONCEPTS

increasing function

decreasing function

stationary

relative (local) maximum

relative (local) minimum

global maximum (minimum)

critical point

stationary point

stationary inflection point

first-derivative test

second-derivative test

higher-order derivative test

ultimate direction

ADDITIONAL EXERCISES

Exercises 12.71 to 12.92 are related to Sec. 12.1.

In Exercises 12.71 to 12.76, determine the intervals over which $f(x)$ is (a) an increasing function, (b) a decreasing function, and (c) stationary.

12.71 $f(x) = mx + b$

12.72 $f(x) = -20$

12.73 $f(x) = x^2 - 5x + 6$

12.74 $f(x) = x^6$

***12.75** $f(x) = ax^4$

***12.76** $f(x) = ax^2 + bx + c$

In Exercises 12.77 to 12.84, determine whether $f''(x)$ reveals the concavity conditions at $x = -1$ and $x = 0$.

12.77 $f(x) = x^2 + 3x - 2$

12.78 $f(x) = e^{x+1}$

12.79 $f(x) = \dfrac{x^4}{12} + \dfrac{3x^3}{2} + x^2 + 2x + 1$

12.80 $f(x) = (x + 2)^4$

12.81 $f(x) = x^4/6 + x^3/2$

12.82 $f(x) = 2x^5 + 20x^2 - 10$

12.83 $f(x) = \ln(x + 2)$

12.84 $f(x) = 5/(3 - x^2)$

In Exercises 12.85 to 12.92, identify the locations of any inflection points.

12.85 $f(x) = x^3/6 - x^2 + 9$

12.86 $f(x) = e^{x^2-1}$

12.87 $f(x) = x^6$

12.88 $f(x) = x^4/6 + 5x^3 + 12x^2 - 4$

12.89 $f(x) = 2x^6 - x^5$

12.90 $f(x) = (x - \tfrac{1}{2})^5$

12.91 $f(x) = 1 + 2e^{x/2}$

12.92 $f(x) = \dfrac{x^4}{12} + \dfrac{x^3}{6} - 3x^2 + 120$

Exercises 12.93 to 12.104 are related to Sec. 12.2.

In Exercises 12.93 to 12.104, determine the location of all stationary points and determine their nature. Compute $f(x^*)$ for each stationary point x^*.

12.93 $f(x) = 2x^2 - 5x + 3$

12.94 $f(x) = -x^2/2 + 6x - 7$

12.95 $f(x) = 2x^4$

12.96 $f(x) = x^4 - 9x^2/2$

12.97 $f(x) = x^3 - 2x^2 + 4$

12.98 $f(x) = -2x^3 + \dfrac{3x^2}{2} + 3x + 1$

12.99 $f(x) = x^5 - x^4 - x^3/3$ **12.100** $f(x) = (-x + 2)^5$

12.101 $f(x) = e^{2x-1}$ **12.102** $f(x) = e^{-x^2+3}$

12.103 $f(x) = -500e^{-0.09x} + 30x - 2{,}000$

12.104 $f(x) = x(\ln x)$

Exercises 12.105 to 12.120 are related to Sec. 12.3.

In Exercises 12.105 to 12.110, determine the locations and values of the global maximum and global minimum for $f(x)$.

12.105 $f(x) = 2x^2 - 5x + 15;\ -1 \le x \le +1$

12.106 $f(x) = 2x^3/3 + 3x^2 + 4x - 1;\ -3 \le x \le 0$

12.107 $f(x) = 2x^5/5 - 27x^2;\ -2 \le x \le 1$

12.108 $f(x) = -x^6 + x^4 + 2x^3/3;\ -1 \le x \le 2$

12.109 $f(x) = x^4 + 5x^3 + 5.5x^2 + 6;\ -2 \le x \le 0$

12.110 $f(x) = -1{,}500e^{-0.05x} - 100x + 4{,}500;\ -10 \le x \le 10$

Exercises 12.111 to 12.114 are related to Sec. 12.4.

In Exercises 12.111 to 12.114, sketch the graph of $f(x)$.

12.111 $f(x) = -2x^3 + 7x^2 - 4x - 9$

12.112 $f(x) = \dfrac{x^4}{4} + x^3 + x^2 + 5$

12.113 $f(x) = (x + 3)^3$

12.114 $f(x) = \dfrac{2x^5}{5} + \dfrac{x^4}{4} - x^3 + 1$

CHAPTER TEST

1 Given $f(x) = -3x^2 + 24x - 15$, for what values of x is $f(x)$ an increasing function?

2 Sketch a portion of a function which has the characteristics that $f'(x) > 0$ and $f''(x) > 0$.

3 Given $f(x) = x^3/3 - 2x^2 - 21x + 1$, determine the location of all stationary points and determine their nature.

4 Given $f(x) = x^4/12 - x^2$, identify the locations of any inflection points.

5 The function $f(x) = -x^3/3 - x^2/2 + 2x$ has stationary points at $x = 1$ and $x = -2$. If the domain of $f(x)$ is $-1 \le x \le 2$, determine the locations and values of the global maximum and global minimum.

6 Sketch the function $f(x) = (x - 4)^3$.

CLASSICAL OPTIMIZATION: APPLICATIONS

13

CHAPTER OBJECTIVES After reading this chapter, you should have some sense of the breadth of possible applications of classical optimization techniques.

Chapter 12 provided the tools of classical optimization. That is, it gave us a method for examining functions in order to locate maximum and minimum points. This chapter, as with Chap. 5, is devoted entirely to applications. Specifically, this chapter presents applications of classical optimization problems.

REVENUE, COST, AND PROFIT APPLICATIONS

13.1

Revenue Applications

The following applications focus on revenue maximization. Recall from Chap. 5 that the money which flows *into* an organization from either selling products or providing services is referred to as *revenue*. And, the most fundamental way of computing total revenue from selling a product (or service) is

$$\text{Total revenue} = (\text{price})(\text{quantity sold})$$

An assumption in this relationship is that the selling price is the same for all units sold.

Example 13.1

The demand for the product of a firm varies with the price that the firm charges for the product. And the firm has determined that annual total revenue R (stated in \$1,000s) is a function of the price p (stated in dollars). Specifically,

$$R = f(p) = -50p^2 + 500p$$

(a) Determine the price which should be charged in order to maximize total revenue.
(b) What is the maximum value of annual total revenue?

Solution

(a) The revenue function is quadratic, and it graphs as a parabola which is concave down. Thus the maximum value of R will occur at the vertex. The first derivative of the revenue function is

$$f'(p) = -100p + 500$$

If we set $f'(p)$ equal to 0,

$$-100p + 500 = 0$$
$$-100p = -500$$

or
$$p = 5$$

There is one stationary point on the graph of $f(p)$, and it occurs when $p = 5$. Although we know that a relative maximum occurs when $p = 5$, let's formally verify this using the second-derivative test:

$$f''(p) = -100 \quad \text{and} \quad f''(5) = -100 < 0$$

Therefore, a relative maximum occurs on $f(p)$ at $p = 5$.
(b) The maximum value of R is found by substituting $p = 5$ into $f(p)$, or

$$f(5) = -50(5^2) + 500(5)$$
$$= -1,250 + 2,500$$
$$= 1,250$$

Thus, annual total revenue is expected to be maximized at \$1,250 (in 1,000s) or \$1.25 million when the firm charges \$5 per unit. Figure 13.1 presents a sketch of the revenue function.

NOTE
This has been mentioned earlier in the text when we have dealt with applications; however, it is worth repeating. It is quite common for students to work through a word problem, find the solution, but have no ability to interpret the results within the framework of the application. If you become caught up in the mechanics of finding a solution and temporarily lose your frame of reference regarding the original problem, reread the problem, making special note of how the variables are defined. Also review the specific questions asked in the

problem. This should assist in reminding you of what the objectives
are and the direction in which you should be heading.

Public Transportation Management The transit authority for a major metropolitan area has experimented with the fare structure for the city's public bus system. It has abandoned the zone fare structure in which the fare varies depending on the number of zones through which a passenger passes. The new system is a fixed-fare system in which a passenger may travel between any two points in the city for the same fare.

**Example
13.2**

The transit authority has surveyed citizens to determine the number of persons who would use the bus system if the fixed fare were equal to different amounts. From the survey results, systems analysts have determined an approximate demand function which expresses the daily ridership as a function of the fare charged. Specifically, the demand function is

$$q = 10{,}000 - 125p$$

where q equals the number of riders per day and p equals the fare in cents.

(a) Determine the fare which should be charged in order to maximize daily bus fare revenue.

(b) What is the expected maximum revenue?

(c) How many riders per day are expected under this fare?

(a) The first step is to determine a function which states daily revenue as a function of the fare p. The reason for selecting p as the independent variable is that the question was to determine the fare which would result in maximum total revenue. Also, the fare is a *decision variable*—a variable whose value can be decided by the transit authority management.

Solution

FIGURE 13.1

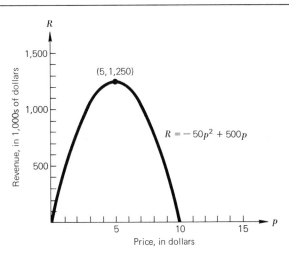

$R = -50p^2 + 500p$

The general expression for total revenue is, as stated before,

$$R = pq$$

But in this form, R is stated as a function of two variables—p and q. *At this time* we cannot deal with the optimization of functions involving more than one independent variable. The demand function, however, establishes a relationship between the variables p and q which allows us to transform the revenue function into one where R is stated as a function of one independent variable p. The right side of the demand function is an expression, stated in terms of p, which is equivalent to q. If we substitute this expression for q in the revenue function, we get

$$\begin{aligned} R &= f(p) \\ &= p(10{,}000 - 125p) \\ &= 10{,}000p - 125p^2 \end{aligned}$$

The first derivative is

$$f'(p) = 10{,}000 - 250p$$

If the derivative is set equal to 0,

$$\begin{aligned} 10{,}000 - 250p &= 0 \\ 10{,}000 &= 250p \\ \mathbf{40} &= \boldsymbol{p} \end{aligned}$$

The second derivative must be identified next to determine the nature of the stationary point:

$$\begin{aligned} f''(p) &= -250 \\ f''(40) &= -250 < 0 \end{aligned}$$

Thus, a relative maximum occurs for $f(p)$ when $p = 40$. The interpretation of this result is that daily revenue will be maximized when a fixed fare of \$0.40 is charged.

(b)
$$\begin{aligned} f(40) &= 10{,}000(40) - 125(40)^2 \\ &= 400{,}000 - 200{,}000 \\ &= 200{,}000 \end{aligned}$$

Since the fare is stated in cents, the maximum expected daily revenue is 200,000 cents, or \$2,000.

(c) The number of riders expected each day with this fare is found by substituting the fare into the demand function, or

$$\begin{aligned} q &= 10{,}000 - 125(40) \\ &= 10{,}000 - 5{,}000 \\ &= 5{,}000 \text{ riders per day} \end{aligned}$$

Figure 13.2 presents a sketch of the daily revenue function.

Cost Applications

As mentioned earlier, costs represent cash *outflows* for an organization. Most organizations seek ways to minimize these outflows, or costs. This section presents applications which deal with the minimization of some measure of cost.

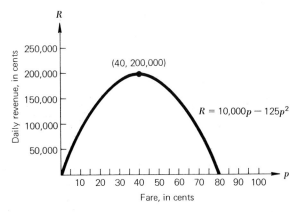

FIGURE 13.2

Inventory Management A common problem in organizations is determining how much of a needed item should be kept on hand. For retailers, the problem may relate to how many units of each product should be kept in stock. For producers, the problem may involve how much of each raw material should be kept available. This problem is identified with an area called *inventory control*, or *inventory management*. Concerning the question of how much "inventory" to keep on hand, there may be costs associated with having too little or too much inventory on hand.

Example 13.3

A retailer of motorized bicycles has examined cost data and has determined a cost function which expresses the annual cost of purchasing, owning, and maintaining inventory as a function of the size (number of units) of each order it places for the bicycles. The cost function is

$$C = f(q) = \frac{4,860}{q} + 15q + 750,000$$

where C equals annual inventory cost, stated in dollars, and q equals the number of cycles ordered each time the retailer replenishes the supply.

(*a*) Determine the order size which minimizes annual inventory cost.
(*b*) What is minimum annual inventory cost expected to equal?

(*a*) The first derivative is

Solution

$$f'(q) = -4,860q^{-2} + 15$$

If $f'(q)$ is set equal to 0,

$$-4,860q^{-2} + 15 = 0$$

when

$$\frac{-4,860}{q^2} = -15$$

Multiplying both sides by q^2 and dividing both sides by -15 yield

$$\frac{4,860}{15} = q^2$$

$$324 = q^2$$

and

$$\mathbf{18 = q}$$

The nature of the stationary point is checked by finding $f''(q)$:

$$f''(q) = 9{,}720q^{-3}$$

$$= \frac{9{,}720}{q^3}$$

and

$$f''(18) = \frac{9{,}720}{(18)^3}$$

$$= 1.667 > 0$$

Thus, a relative minimum occurs for $f(q)$ when $q = 18$. Annual inventory costs will be minimized when 18 cycles are ordered each time the retailer replenishes the supply.

(b) Minimum annual inventory costs are calculated by determining $f(18)$, or

$$f(18) = \frac{4{,}860}{18} + 15(18) + 750{,}000$$

$$= 270 + 270 + 750{,}000$$

$$= \$750{,}540$$

Figure 13.3 presents a sketch of the cost function.

Example 13.4

Minimizing Average Cost per Unit The total cost of producing q units of a certain product is described by the function

$$C = 100{,}000 + 1{,}500q + 0.2q^2$$

where C is the total cost stated in dollars. Determine how many units q should be produced in order to minimize the *average cost per unit*.

Solution

Average cost per unit is calculated by dividing the total cost by the number of units produced. For example, if the total cost of producing 10 units of a product equals \$275, the average cost per unit is \$275/10 = \$27.50. Thus, the function representing average cost per unit in this example is

$$\overline{C} = f(q) = \frac{C}{q} = \frac{100{,}000}{q} + 1{,}500 + 0.2q$$

FIGURE 13.3

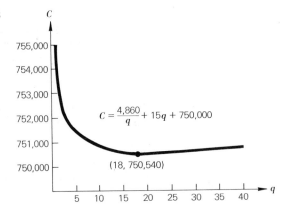

The first derivative is

$$f'(q) = -100,000q^{-2} + 0.2$$

If $f'(q)$ is set equal to 0,

$$0.2 = \frac{100,000}{q^2}$$

or

$$q^2 = \frac{100,000}{0.2}$$

$$= 500,000$$

Finding the square root of both sides, we have

$q = 707.11$ (units)

The nature of the stationary point is tested with the second-derivative test.

$$f''(q) = 200,000q^{-3}$$

$$= \frac{200,000}{q^3}$$

$$f''(707.11) = \frac{200,000}{(707.11)^3}$$

$$= 0.00056 > 0$$

Thus, a relative minimum occurs for $f(q)$ when $q = 707.11$. Figure 13.4 presents a sketch of $f(q)$.

EXERCISE
For Example 13.4
a. Determine the minimum average cost per unit; and
b. What is the total cost of production at this level of output?
(Answer: a) \$1,782.84; b) \$1,260,663.90)

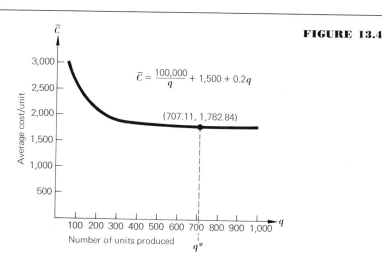

FIGURE 13.4

$$\bar{C} = \frac{100,000}{q} + 1,500 + 0.2q$$

(707.11, 1,782.84)

Average cost/unit

Number of units produced

q^*

Profit Applications

This section contains two examples which deal with profit maximization.

Example 13.5

Sales Force Allocation Example 10.1 discussed the *law of diminishing returns* as an illustration of a nonlinear function. A major cosmetic and beauty supply firm, which specializes in a door-to-door sales approach, has found that the response of sales to the allocation of additional sales representatives behaves according to the law of diminishing returns. For one regional sales district, the company has determined that annual profit P, stated in hundreds of dollars, is a function of the number of sales representatives x assigned to the district. Specifically, the function relating these two variables is

$$P = f(x) = -12.5x^2 + 1,375x - 1,500$$

(*a*) What number of representatives will result in maximum profit for the district?

(*b*) What is the expected maximum profit?

Solution

(*a*) The derivative of the profit function is

$$f'(x) = -25x + 1,375$$

If $f'(x)$ is set equal to 0,

$$-25x = -1375$$

or $$x = 55$$

Checking the nature of the stationary point, we find

$$f''(x) = -25 \quad \text{and} \quad f''(55) = -25 < 0$$

Thus, a relative maximum occurs for $f(x)$ when $x = 55$.

(*b*) The expected maximum profit is

$$f(55) = -12.5(55)^2 + 1,375(55) - 1,500$$
$$= -37,812.5 + 75,625 - 1,500$$
$$= 36,312.5$$

We can conclude that annual profit will be maximized at a value of $36,312.5 (100s), or $3,631,250 if 55 representatives are assigned to the district. Figure 13.5 presents a sketch of the profit function.

POINTS FOR THOUGHT AND DISCUSSION
What do the x intercepts represent in Fig. 13.5? Interpret the meaning of the y intercept. Discuss the law of diminishing returns as it pertains to the shape of this profit function.

Example 13.6

Solar Energy A manufacturer has developed a new design for solar collection panels. Marketing studies have indicated that annual

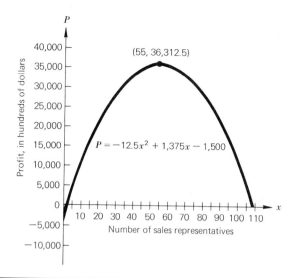

$P = -12.5x^2 + 1,375x - 1,500$

(55, 36,312.5)

Number of sales representatives

FIGURE 13.5

demand for the panels will depend on the price charged. The demand function for the panels has been estimated as

$$q = 100,000 - 200p \qquad (13.1)$$

where q equals the number of units demanded each year and p equals the price in dollars. Engineering studies indicate that the total cost of producing q panels is represented well by the function

$$C = 150,000 + 100q + 0.003q^2 \qquad (13.2)$$

Formulate the profit function $P = f(q)$ which states the annual profit P as a function of the number of units q which are produced and sold.

We have been asked to develop a function which states profit P as a function of q, the number of units produced and sold. As opposed to Example 13.5, *we must construct* the profit function. Equation (13.2) is a total cost function stated in terms of q; so, that component of the profit function is already available. However, we need to formulate a total revenue function stated in terms of q.

Solution

Again it is necessary to remember the basic structure for computing total revenue;

$$R = pq \qquad (13.3)$$

Because we want R to be stated in terms of q, we need to replace p in Eq. (13.3) by an equivalent expression which can be derived from the demand function. Solving for p in Eq. (13.1), we find

$$200p = 100,000 - q$$
or
$$p = 500 - 0.005q \qquad (13.4)$$

We can substitute the right side of this equation into Eq. (13.3) to yield the revenue function

$$R = (500 - 0.005q)q$$
$$= 500q - 0.005q^2$$

Now that both the revenue and cost functions have been stated in terms of q, the profit function can be defined as

$$P = f(q)$$
$$= R - C$$
$$= 500q - 0.005q^2 - (150,000 + 100q + 0.003q^2)$$
$$= 500q - 0.005q^2 - 150,000 - 100q - 0.003q^2$$

or $\qquad P = -0.008q^2 + 400q - 150,000$

EXERCISE
In Example 13.6 determine a) how many units q should be produced to maximize annual profit; b) what price should be charged for each panel to generate a demand equal to the answer in part (a); and c) the maximum annual profit.
(Answer: a) $q = 25,000$ units; b) $p = \$375$; c) $\$4,850,000$.)

Example 13.7 **Restricted Domain** Assume in the last example that the manufacturer's annual production capacity is 20,000 units. Re-solve Example 13.6 with this added restriction.

Solution With the added restriction, the domain of the function is defined as $0 \le q \le 20,000$. From Chap. 12, it should be recalled that we must com-

---

FIGURE 13.6

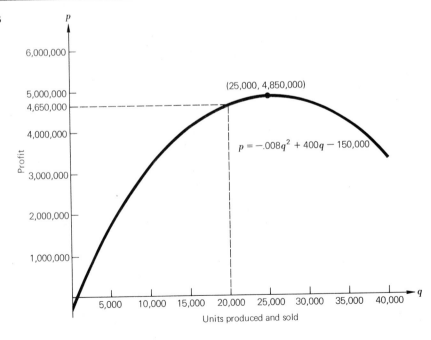

pare the values of $f(q)$ at the endpoints of the domain with the values of $f(q^*)$ for any q^* value where $0 \leq q^* \leq 20{,}000$.

The only stationary point on the profit function occurred at $q^* = 25{,}000$, which is outside the domain. Thus, profit will be maximized at one of the endpoints. Evaluating $f(q)$ at the endpoints, we find

$$f(0) = -150{,}000$$
$$f(20{,}000) = -0.008(20{,}000)^2 + 400(20{,}000) - 150{,}000$$
$$= -3{,}200{,}000 + 8{,}000{,}000 - 150{,}000$$
$$= 4{,}650{,}000$$

Profit is maximized at a value of $\$4{,}650{,}000$ when $q = 20{,}000$, or when the manufacturer operates at capacity.

The price which should be charged is

$$p = 500 - 0.005(20{,}000)$$
$$= 500 - 100$$
$$= \$400$$

Figure 13.6 presents a sketch of the profit function.

Follow-up Exercises

13.1 A firm has determined that total revenue is a function of the price charged for its product. Specifically the total revenue function is

$$R = f(p) = -25p^2 + 875p$$

where p equals the price in dollars.
(a) Determine the price p which results in maximum total revenue.
(b) What is the maximum value of R?

13.2 The demand function for a firm's product is

$$q = 50{,}000 - 25p$$

where q equals the number of units demanded and p equals the price in dollars.
(a) Determine the price which should be charged to maximize total revenue.
(b) What is the maximum value of total revenue?
(c) How many units are expected to be demanded?

13.3 *Beach Management.* A community which is located in a resort area is trying to decide on the parking fee to charge at the town-owned beach. There are other beaches in the area, and there is competition for bathers among the different beaches. The town has determined the following function which expresses the average number of cars per day q as a function of the parking fee p stated in cents.

$$q = 4{,}000 - 16p$$

(a) Determine the fee which should be charged to maximize daily beach revenues.
(b) What is the maximum daily beach revenue expected to equal?
(c) How many cars are expected on any average day?

13.4 *Import Tax Management.* The United States government is studying the import tax structure for color television sets imported from other countries into the United States. The government is trying is determine the amount of the tax to charge on each TV set. The government realizes that the demand for imported TV sets will be affected by the tax. It estimates that the demand for imported sets D, measured in hundreds of TV sets, will be related to the import tax x, measured in cents, according to the function

$$D = 50,000 - 25x$$

(a) Determine the import tax which will result in maximum tax revenues from importing TV sets.
(b) What is the maximum revenue?
(c) What will the demand for imported color TV sets equal with this tax?

13.5 A manufacturer has determined a cost function which expresses the annual cost of purchasing, owning, and maintaining its raw material inventory as a function of the size of each order. The cost function is

$$C = \frac{9,000}{q} + 10q + 900,000$$

where q equals the size of each order (in tons) and C equals the annual inventory cost.
(a) Determine the order size q which minimizes annual inventory cost.
(b) What are minimum inventory costs expected to equal?

13.6 In Exercise 13.5, assume that the maximum amount of the raw material which can be accepted in any one shipment is 25 tons.
(a) Given this restriction, determine the order size q which minimizes annual inventory cost.
(b) What are the minimum annual inventory costs?
(c) How do these results compare with those in Exercise 13.5?

13.7 A major distributor of tennis balls is thriving because tennis has taken over as one of the country's most popular participant sports. One of the distributor's major problems is keeping up with the demand for tennis balls. Balls are purchased periodically from a sporting goods manufacturer. The annual cost of purchasing, owning, and maintaining the inventory of tennis balls is described by the function

$$C = \frac{120,000}{q} + 0.12q + 2,000,000$$

where q equals the order size (in dozens of tennis balls) and C equals the annual inventory cost.
(a) Determine the order size q which minimizes annual inventory cost.
(b) What are the minimum inventory costs expected to equal?

13.8 The distributor in Exercise 13.7 has storage facilities to accept up to 1,500 dozens of balls in any one shipment.
(a) Determine the order size q which minimizes annual inventory costs.
(b) What are the minimum inventory costs?
(c) How do these results compare with those in Exercise 13.7?

13.9 The total cost of producing q units of a certain product is described by the function

$$C = 200,000 + 5,000q + 0.1q^2$$

where C is the total cost stated in dollars.

(a) Determine how many units q should be produced in order to minimize the *average cost per unit*.

(b) What is the minimum average cost per unit?

(c) What is the total cost of production at this level of output?

13.10 Re-solve Exercise 13.9 if the maximum production capacity is 1,250 units.

13.11 *Public Utilities.* A cable TV antenna company has determined that its profitability depends upon the monthly fee it charges its customers. Specifically, the relationship which describes annual profit P (stated in dollars) as a function of the monthly rental fee r (stated in dollars) is

$$P = -50,000r^2 + 785,000r - 250,000$$

(a) Determine the monthly rental fee r which will lead to maximum profit.

(b) What is the expected maximum profit?

13.12 In Exercise 13.11 assume that the local public utility commission has restricted the CATV company to a monthly fee not to exceed $6.75.

(a) What fee leads to a maximum profit for the company?

(b) What is the effect of the utility commission's ruling on the profitability of the firm?

13.13 A company estimates that the demand for its product fluctuates with the price it charges. The demand function is

$$q = 250,000 - 500p$$

where q equals the number of units demanded and p equals the price in dollars. The total cost of producing q units of the product is estimated by the function

$$C = 200,000 + 200q + 0.001q^2$$

(a) Determine how many units q should be produced in order to maximize annual profit.

(b) What price should be charged?

(c) What is the annual profit expected to equal?

13.14 If annual capacity is 60,000 units in Exercise 13.13, how many units q will result in maximum profit?

13.15 An equivalent way of solving Example 13.2 is to state total revenue as a function of q, the number of riders per day. Formulate the function $R = g(q)$ for Example 13.2, and determine the number of riders q which will result in maximum total revenue. Verify that the maximum value of R and the price which should be charged are the same as obtained in Example 13.2.

MARGINAL APPROACH TO PROFIT MAXIMIZATION

13.2

An alternative approach to finding the profit maximization point involves *marginal analysis.* Popular among economists, marginal analysis examines *incremental effects* on profitability. Given that a firm is producing a certain number of units each year, marginal analysis would be concerned with the effect on profit if *1* additional unit is produced and sold.

To utilize the marginal approach to profit maximization, the following conditions must hold:

1 It must be possible to identify the total revenue function *and* the total cost function.

2 The revenue and cost functions must be stated in terms of the level of output or number of units produced and sold.

Marginal Revenue

One of the two important concepts in marginal analysis is marginal revenue. *Marginal revenue* is the additional revenue derived from selling 1 additional unit of a product. If each unit of a product sells at the same price, the marginal revenue is always equal to the price. For example, the linear revenue function

$$R = 10q$$

represents a pricing situation where each unit sells for $10. The marginal revenue from selling 1 additional unit is $10 at any level of output q.

In Example 13.6 a demand function for solar panels was stated as

$$q = 100,000 - 200p$$

From this demand function we formulated the nonlinear total revenue function

$$R = 500q - 0.005q^2 \qquad (13.5)$$

Marginal revenue for this example is not constant. We can illustrate this by computing total revenue for different levels of output. Table 13.1 illustrates these calculations for selected values of q.

The third column represents the marginal revenue associated with moving from one level of output to another. Note that although the differences are slight, the marginal revenue values are changing at each different level of output.

Given a total revenue function $R(q)$, the derivative $R'(q)$ represents the instantaneous rate of change in total revenue given a change in the number of units sold. $R'(q)$ also represents a general expression for the

Table 13.1	Level of Output q	Total Revenue R	Marginal Revenue ΔR
	100	$49,950.00	—
	101	$50,448.995	$498.995
	102	$50,947.98	$498.985
	103	$51,446.955	$498.975

slope of the total revenue function. For purposes of marginal analysis, the derivative is used to represent the marginal revenue, or

$$MR = R'(q) \qquad (13.6)$$

The derivative, as discussed in Chap. 11, provides an approximation to actual changes in the value of a function. As such, $R'(q)$ can be used to approximate the marginal revenue from selling the next unit. If we find $R'(q)$ for the revenue function in Eq. (13.5),

$$R'(q) = 500 - 0.010q$$

To approximate the marginal revenue from selling the 101st unit, we evaluate $R'(q)$ at $q = 100$, or

$$\begin{aligned} R'(100) &= 500 - 0.010(100) \\ &= 500 - 1 \\ &= 499 \end{aligned}$$

And this is a very close approximation to the actual value of $498.995 shown in Table 13.1.

Marginal Cost

The other important concept in marginal analysis is marginal cost. *Marginal cost* is the additional cost incurred as a result of producing and selling 1 additional unit of a product. Linear cost functions assume that the variable cost per unit is constant; for such functions the marginal cost is the same at any level of output. An example of this is the cost function

$$C = 150,000 + 3.5q$$

where variable cost per unit is $3.50.

A nonlinear cost function results in variable marginal costs. This can be illustrated by the cost function

$$C = 150,000 + 100q + 0.003q^2 \qquad (13.7)$$

which was stated in Example 13.6. We can illustrate that the marginal costs do fluctuate at different levels of output by computing total costs for selected values of q. Table 13.2 illustrates these calculations.

Level of Output q	Total Cost C	Marginal Cost ΔC	Table 13.2
100	$160,030.00	—	
101	$160,130.603	$100.603	
102	$160,231.212	$100.609	
103	$160,331.827	$100.615	

Given a total cost function $C(q)$, the derivative $C'(q)$ represents the instantaneous rate of change in total cost given a change in the number of units produced. $C'(q)$ also represents a general expression for the slope of the total cost function. For purposes of marginal analysis, the derivative is used to represent the marginal cost, or

$$MC = C'(q) \qquad (13.8)$$

As with $R'(q)$, $C'(q)$ can be used to approximate the marginal cost associated with producing the next unit. The derivative of the cost function in Eq. (13.7) is

$$C'(q) = 100 + 0.006q$$

To approximate the marginal cost from producing the 101st unit, we evaluate $C'(q)$ at $q = 100$, or

$$C'(100) = 100 + 0.006(100)$$
$$= \$100.60$$

Comparing this approximation with the actual value in Table 13.2, we see that the two values are very close.

Marginal Profit Analysis

As indicated earlier, the marginal profit analysis is concerned with the effect on profit if 1 additional unit of a product is produced and sold. As long as the additional revenue brought in by the next unit exceeds the cost of producing and selling that unit, there is a net profit from producing and selling that unit and total profit increases. A quick rule of thumb concerning the production of an additional unit is (assuming profit is of greatest importance)

If $MR > MC$, produce the next unit.

If the additional revenue from selling the next unit is exceeded by the cost of producing and selling the additional unit, there is a net loss from that next unit and total profit decreases. Thus,

If $MR < MC$, do not produce the next unit.

For many production situations, the marginal revenue exceeds the marginal cost at lower levels of output (if $MR < MC$, why produce?). Although economies of scale can complicate the analysis slightly, as long as $MR > MC$, it is worthwhile from a profit standpoint to continue producing. Eventually a level of output is reached at which $MR = MC$.

Beyond this point $MR < MC$, and total profit begins to decrease. Thus, from a theoretical standpoint, if the point can be identified where for the last unit produced and sold $MR = MC$, total profit will be maximized. A condition for maximizing total profit is to identify the point where

$$MR = MC \qquad (13.9)$$

or, stated in terms of derivatives, the point where

$$R'(q) = C'(q) \qquad (13.10)$$

This equation is a natural result of differentiating the profit equation

$$P(q) = R(q) - C(q)$$

and setting the derivative equal to 0:

$$P'(q) = R'(q) - C'(q)$$
and $$P'(q) = 0$$
when $$R'(q) - C'(q) = 0$$
or $$R'(q) = C'(q)$$

A sufficient condition for a relative maximum at q^* for a profit function $P(q)$ is that $P''(q^*) < 0$, and since

$$P(q) = R(q) - C(q)$$

a sufficient condition for a relative maximum on $P(q)$ is that

$$R''(q^*) < C''(q^*) \qquad (13.11)$$

Re-solve Example 13.6 using the marginal approach.

**Example
13.8**

Solution

In Example 13.6,

$$R = 500q - 0.005q^2$$
and $$C = 150{,}000 + 100q + 0.003q^2$$

The revenue and cost functions are distinct, and both are stated in terms of the level of output q. We have already determined that

$$R'(q) = 500 - 0.01q$$
and $$C'(q) = 100 + 0.006q$$
$$R'(q) = C'(q)$$

when

$$500 - 0.01q = 100 + 0.006q$$
$$-0.016q = -400$$
or $$q = 25{,}000$$

Since $\quad\quad R''(q) = -0.01 \quad$ and $\quad C''(q) = 0.007$

$$R''(q^*) < C''(q^*)$$

or $\quad\quad\quad\quad -0.01 < 0.006$

and there is a relative maximum on the profit function when $q = 25,000$. Figure 13.7 presents the graphs of $R(q)$ and $C(q)$.

Take a moment to examine Fig. 13.7. The following observations are worth noting:

Points C and D represent points where the revenue and cost functions intersect. These represent break-even points.

Between points C and D the revenue function is above the cost function, indicating that a profit will be earned within this interval. For levels of output to the right of D, the cost function lies above the revenue function, indicating that a negative profit (loss) will be incurred.

The *vertical* distance between the two functions represents the profit or loss, depending on the level of output.

In the interval $0 \leq q \leq 25,000$, the tangent slope of the revenue function is positive and greater than the slope of the cost function. Stated in terms of MR and MC, $MR > MC$ in this interval.

Also in the interval $0 \leq q \leq 25,000$ (for points to the right of C), the vertical distance separating the two curves becomes greater, indicating that profit is increasing on the interval.

At $q = 25,000$ the tangent slopes at points A and B are the same, indicating that $MR = MC$. Also at $q = 25,000$ the vertical distance separating the two curves is greater than at any other point in the profit region; thus, this is the point of profit maximization.

FIGURE 13.7

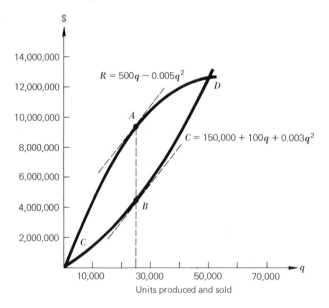

For $q > 25,000$ the tangent slope of the revenue function is positive but less than that for the cost function. Thus, $MR < MC$ and for each additional unit profit decreases, actually resulting in a loss beyond point D.

In Example 13.5 we were asked to determine the number of sales representatives x which would result in maximum profit P for a cosmetic and beauty supply firm. The profit function was stated as

$$P = f(x) = -12.5x^2 + 1,375x - 1,500$$

Using the marginal approach, determine the number of representatives which will result in maximum profit for the firm.

Example 13.9

We cannot use the marginal approach in this example because we cannot identify the total revenue and total cost functions which were combined to form the profit function!

Solution

Figure 13.8 illustrates a sketch of a linear revenue function and a non-linear cost function. To the left of q^*, the slope of the revenue function exceeds the slope of the cost function, indicating that $MR > MC$. At q^* the slopes of the two functions are the same. And the vertical distance separating the two functions is greater at q^* than for any other value of q in the profit region between points A and B. Points A and B are break-even points.

Example 13.10

Follow-up Exercises

13.16 The total cost and total revenue functions for a product are

$$C(q) = 300 + 20q + 0.1q^2$$
$$R(q) = 60q$$

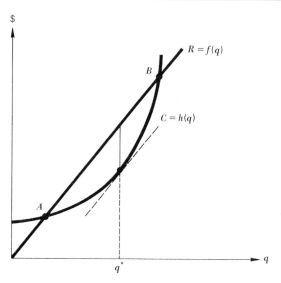

$R = f(q)$

B

$C = h(q)$

A

q^*

q

FIGURE 13.8

(a) Using the marginal approach, determine the profit-maximizing level of output.

(b) What is the maximum profit?

13.17 The total cost and total revenue functions for a product are

$$C(q) = 100 + 5q + 0.2q^2$$
$$R(q) = 150q$$

(a) Using the marginal approach, determine the profit-maximizing level of output.

(b) What is the maximum profit?

13.18 The profit function for a firm is

$$P(q) = -4q^2 + 20,000q - 1,000$$

(a) Using the marginal approach, determine the profit-maximizing level of output.

(b) What is the maximum profit?

13.19 The total cost and total revenue functions for a product are

$$C(q) = 1,000,000 + 200q + 0.001q^2$$
$$R(q) = 1000q - 0.004q^2$$

(a) Using the marginal approach, determine the profit-maximizing level of output.

(b) What is the maximum profit?

13.20 The total cost and total revenue functions for a product are

$$C(q) = 50,000 + 20q + 0.0001q^2$$
$$R(q) = 60q - 0.004q^2$$

(a) Using the marginal approach, determine the profit-maximizing level of output.

(b) What is the maximum profit?

13.21 Re-solve Exercise 13.13 using the marginal approach.

13.3   ADDITIONAL APPLICATIONS

The following examples are additional applications of classical optimization procedures.

Example 13.11

Real Estate A large multinational conglomerate is interested in purchasing some prime boardwalk real estate at a major ocean resort. The conglomerate is interested in acquiring a rectangular lot which is directly next to the boardwalk. The only restriction is that the lot have an area of 100,000 square feet. Figure 13.9 presents a sketch of the layout with x equaling the boardwalk frontage for the lot and y equaling the depth of the lot (both measured in feet).

The seller of the property is pricing the lots at $500 per foot of frontage along the boardwalk and $200 per foot of depth away from the boardwalk. The conglomerate is interested in determining the dimensions of the lot which will minimize the total purchase cost.

Solution The objective in this problem is to minimize the purchase cost. Refer to

Fig. 13.9. Total purchase cost for a lot having dimensions of x feet by y feet is

$$C = 500x + 200y \qquad (13.12)$$

where C is cost in dollars.

The problem is to determine the values of x and y which minimize C. However, C is stated as a function of two variables, and we are unable, as yet, to handle functions which have two independent variables.

Because the conglomerate has specified that the area of the lot must equal 100,000 square feet, a relationship which exists between x and y is

$$xy = 100,000 \qquad (13.13)$$

Given this relationship, we can solve for either variable in terms of the other. For instance,

$$y = \frac{100,000}{x} \qquad (13.14)$$

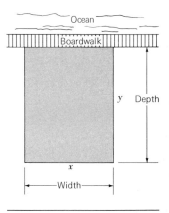

We can substitute the right side of this equation into the cost function wherever the variable y appears, or

FIGURE 13.9

$$C = f(x)$$
$$= 500x + 200 \left(\frac{100,000}{x}\right)$$
$$= 500x + \frac{20,000,000}{x} \qquad (13.15)$$

Equation (13.15) is a restatement of Eq. (13.12), only in terms of one independent variable. We can now determine the value of x which minimizes the purchase cost C.

The first derivative is

$$C'(x) = 500 - 20,000,000x^{-2}$$

If $C'(x)$ is set equal to 0,

$$500 = \frac{20,000,000}{x^2}$$
$$x^2 = \frac{20,000,000}{500}$$
$$= 40,000$$

or

$$x = \pm 200$$

If we recall the definition of x, the stationary point at $x = -200$ is meaningless. To test $x = 200$,

$$C''(x) = 40,000,000x^{-3}$$
$$= \frac{40,000,000}{x^3}$$
$$C''(200) = \frac{40,000,000}{(200)^3}$$
$$= \frac{40,000,000}{8,000,000}$$
$$= 5 > 0$$

Thus, a relative minimum occurs for $C(x)$ at $x = 200$.

Total costs will be minimized when the width of the lot equals 200 feet. The depth of the lot can be found by substituting $x = 200$ into Eq. (13.14), or

$$y = \frac{100,000}{200}$$
$$= 500$$

If the lot is 200 feet by 500 feet, total cost will be minimized at a value of

$$C = \$500(200) + \$200(500)$$
$$= \$200,000$$

Example 13.12 **Emergency Response: Location Model** Example 10.15 discussed a problem in which three resort cities had agreed jointly to build and support an emergency response facility which would house rescue trucks and trained paramedics. The key question dealt with the location of the facility. The criterion selected was to choose the location so as to minimize S, the sum of the products of the summer populations of each town and the square of the distance between the town and the facility. Figure 13.10 shows the relative locations of the three cities.

The criterion function to be minimized was determined to be

$$S = f(x) = 450x^2 - 19,600x + 241,600$$

where x is the location of the facility relative to the zero point in Fig. 13.10. (You may want to reread Example 10.15.) Given the criterion function, the first derivative is

$$f'(x) = 900x - 19,600$$

If $f'(x)$ is set equal to 0,

$$900x = 19,600$$
and $$x = \mathbf{21.77}$$

Checking the nature of the stationary point, we find

$$f''(x) = 900$$
$$f''(21.77) = 900 > 0$$

Thus, a relative minimum occurs for $f(x)$ when $x = 21.77$. The criterion S is minimized at $x = 21.77$, and the facility should be located as shown in Fig. 13.11.

Example 13.13 **Bill Collection** Example 10.24 discussed the collection of accounts receivable for credit issued to people who use a major credit card. The financial institution determined that the percentage of ac-

FIGURE 13.10

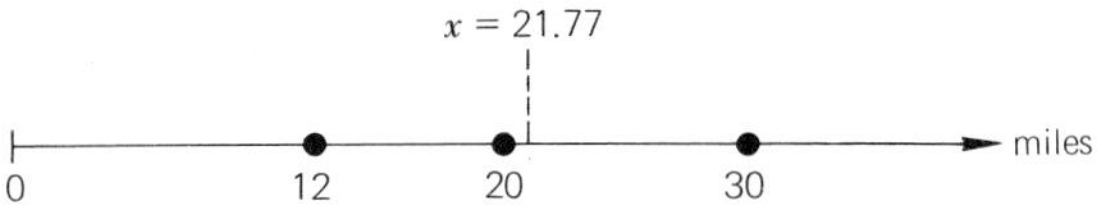

$$x = 21.77$$

FIGURE 13.11

counts receivable P (in dollars) collected t months after the credit was issued is

$$P = 0.95(1 - e^{-0.7t})$$

The average credit issued in any one month is $100 million. The financial institution estimates that *for new credit* issued in any month, collection efforts cost $1 million per month. That is, if credit is issued today, it costs $1 million for every month the institution attempts to collect these accounts receivable. Determine the number of months that collection efforts should be continued if the objective is to maximize the *net collections N* (dollars collected minus collection costs).

Solution

Given that $100 million of credit is issued, the amount of receivables collected (in millions of dollars) equals

$$(100)(0.95)(1 - e^{-0.7t})$$

Therefore, net collections N are described by the function

$$
\begin{aligned}
N &= f(t) \\
&= (100)(0.95)(1 - e^{-0.7t}) - (1)t \\
&= 95(1 - e^{-0.7t}) - t \\
&= 95 - 95e^{-0.7t} - t
\end{aligned}
$$

The first derivative is

$$f'(t) = 66.5e^{-0.7t} - 1$$

If $f'(t)$ is set equal to 0,

$$
\begin{aligned}
66.5e^{-0.7t} &= 1 \\
e^{-0.7t} &= 0.01503
\end{aligned}
$$

From Table A.1 at the end of the book,

$$e^{-4.2} = 0.01503$$

Thus, $e^{-0.7t} = 0.01503$ when

$$-0.7t = -4.2$$

or

$$t = 6$$

The only stationary point on $f(t)$ occurs when $t = 6$. Maximum net collections are

$$
\begin{aligned}
f(6) &= 95 - 95e^{-0.7(6)} - 6 \\
&= 95 - 95(0.0150) - 6 \\
&= 95 - 1.425 - 6 \\
&= 87.575
\end{aligned}
$$

or $87.575 million.

For each $100 million of credit issued, net collections will be maximized at a value of $87.575 million if collection efforts continue for 6 months.

EXERCISE
a) Verify that the stationary point at $t = 6$ is a relative maximum; and b) What is the total amount collected over the six-month period?
(Answer: b) $93.575 million)

Example 13.14

Equipment Replacement A decision faced by many organizations is determining the optimal point in time to replace a major piece of equipment. Major pieces of equipment are often characterized by two cost components—capital cost and operating cost. *Capital cost* is purchase cost less any salvage value. If a machine costs $10,000 and is later sold for $2,000, the capital cost is $8,000. *Operating cost* includes costs of owning and maintaining a piece of equipment. Gasoline, oil, insurance, and repair costs associated with owning and operating a vehicle would be considered operating costs.

Some organizations focus on the *average* capital cost and *average* operating cost when they determine when to replace a piece of equipment. These costs tend to trade off against one another. That is, as one cost increases, the other decreases. Average capital cost for a piece of equipment tends to decrease over time. For a new automobile which decreases in value from $6,000 to $5,000 in the first year, the average capital cost for that year is $1,000. If the automobile decreases in value to $2,000 after 5 years, the average capital cost is $4,000/5, or $800 per year. Average operating cost tends to increase over time as equipment becomes less efficient. The average annual operating cost of a car tends to increase as the car ages.

A taxi company in a major city wants to determine how long it should keep its cabs. Each cab comes fully equipped at a cost of $8,000. The company estimates average capital cost and average operating cost to be a function of x, the number of miles the car is driven. The salvage value of the car, in dollars, is expressed by the function

$$S(x) = 6,000 - 0.06x$$

This means that the car decreases $2,000 in value as soon as the cab is driven, and it decreases in value at the rate of $0.06 per mile.

The average operating cost, stated in dollars per mile, is estimated by the function

$$O(x) = 0.0000003x + 0.15$$

Determine the number of miles the car should be driven prior to replacement if the objective is to minimize the *sum* of average capital cost and average operating cost.

Average capital cost per mile equals the purchase cost less the salvage **Solution**
value, all divided by the number of miles driven, or

$$C(x) = \frac{8,000 - (6,000 - 0.06x)}{x}$$

$$= \frac{2,000 + 0.06}{x}$$

$$= \frac{2,000}{x} + 0.06$$

The sum of average capital cost and average operating cost is

$$f(x) = O(x) + C(x)$$

$$= 0.0000003x + 0.15 + \frac{2,000}{x} + 0.06$$

$$= 0.0000003x + 0.21 + \frac{2,000}{x}$$

$$f'(x) = 0.0000003 - 2,000x^{-2}$$

If $f'(x)$ is set equal to 0, then

$$0.0000003 = \frac{2,000}{x^2}$$

$$x^2 = \frac{2,000}{0.0000003}$$

$$= 6,666,666,666.67$$

or
$$x = \mathbf{81,649.6}$$

Checking this stationary point, we have

$$f''(x) = 4,000x^{-3}$$

$$= \frac{4,000}{x^3}$$

$$f''(81,649.6) = \frac{4,000}{81,649.6} > 0$$

Therefore, a relative minimum occurs for $f(x)$ when $x = 81,649.6$,

$$f(81,649.6) = 0.0000003(81,649.6) + 0.21 + \frac{2,000}{81,649.6}$$

$$= 0.02450 + 0.21 + 0.02450$$
$$= 0.259$$

Average capital and operating costs are minimized at a value of $0.259
per mile when a taxi is driven 81,649.6 miles. Total capital and
operating costs will equal

$$(\$0.259)(81,649.6) = \$21,147.25$$

Figure 13.12 illustrates the two component cost functions and the
sum of the two functions. Notice that the average operating cost per
mile $O(x)$ increases with increasing values of x and that average capital
cost per mile $C(x)$ decreases with increasing values of x.

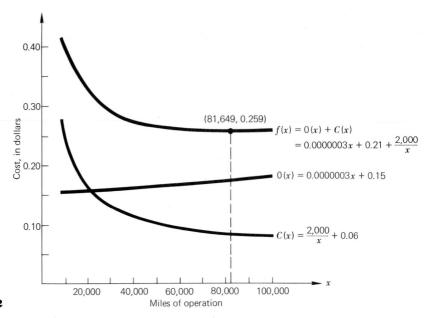

FIGURE 13.12

**Example
13.15**

Welfare Management A newly created state welfare agency is attempting to determine the number of analysts to hire to process welfare applications. Efficiency experts estimate that the average cost C of processing an application is a function of the number of analysts x. Specifically, the cost function is

$$C = f(x) = 0.001x^2 - 5 \ln x + 60$$

Determine the number of analysts who should be hired in order to minimize the average cost per application.

Solution The derivative of $f(x)$ is

$$f'(x) = 0.002x - 5\frac{1}{x}$$

$$= 0.002x - \frac{5}{x}$$

If $f'(x)$ is set equal to 0,

$$0.002x = \frac{5}{x}$$

$$0.002x^2 = 5$$

$$x^2 = \frac{5}{0.002}$$

$$x^2 = 2,500$$

$$\mathbf{x = 50}$$

To check the nature of the stationary point,

$$f''(x) = 0.002 + 5x^{-2}$$

$$= 0.002 + \frac{5}{x^2}$$

$$f''(50) = 0.002 + \frac{5}{(50)^2}$$

$$= 0.002 + \frac{5}{2,500}$$

$$= 0.002 + 0.002$$

$$= 0.004 > 0$$

Therefore, a relative minimum occurs for $f(x)$ when $x = 50$. The value of $f(x)$ at the stationary point is

$$f(50) = 0.001(50)^2 - 5 \ln 50 + 60$$

$$= 0.001(2,500) - 5(3.912) + 60$$

$$= 2.5 - 19.56 + 60$$

$$= \$42.94$$

Average processing cost per application is minimized at a value of $42.94 when 50 analysts are employed. Figure 13.13 presents a sketch of the average cost function.

Police Patrol Allocation A police department has determined that the average daily crime rate in the city depends upon the number of officers assigned to each shift. Specifically, the function describing this relationship is

$$N = f(x)$$
$$= 200 - 5xe^{-0.02x}$$

where N equals the average daily crime rate and x equals the number of officers assigned to each shift. Police analysts indicate the function is

Example 13.16

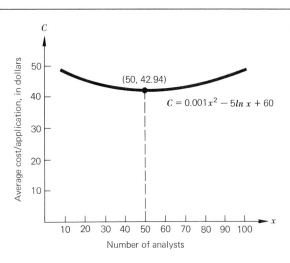

FIGURE 13.13

valid for $0 \leq x \leq 60$. Determine the number of officers which will result in a minimum average daily crime rate.

Solution   The derivative of $f(x)$ is

$$f'(x) = -5e^{-0.02x} - 5x(-0.02)e^{-0.02x}$$
$$= -5e^{-0.02x} + 0.1xe^{-0.02x}$$

If $f'(x)$ is set equal to 0,

$$-5e^{-0.02x} + 0.1xe^{-0.02x} = 0$$

Factoring $e^{-0.02x}$ on the left side, we have

$$e^{-0.02x}(-5 + 0.1x) = 0$$

Since $e^{-0.02x}$ will never equal 0, the only stationary point occurs when

$$-5 + 0.1x = 0$$
$$\text{or} \qquad 0.1x = 5$$
$$\boldsymbol{x = 50}$$

To check the nature of the stationary point,

$$f''(x) = (-0.5)(-0.02)e^{-0.02x} + 0.1e^{-0.02x} + 0.1x(-0.02)e^{-0.02x}$$
$$= 0.1e^{-0.02x} + 0.1e^{-0.02x} - 0.002xe^{-0.02x}$$
$$= e^{-0.02x}(0.2 - 0.002x)$$
$$f''(50) = (0.3679)[0.2 - 0.002(50)]$$
$$= (0.3679)(0.2 - 0.1)$$
$$= 0.03679 > 0$$

Therefore, a relative minimum occurs for $f(x)$ when $x = 50$.

Because x^* lies within the domain of the function, we must compare $f(x^*)$ with $f(0)$ and $f(60)$.

$$f(50) = 200 - 5(50)e^{-0.02(50)}$$
$$= 200 - 250e^{-1.0}$$
$$= 200 - 250(0.3679)$$
$$= 200 - 91.975$$
$$= \boldsymbol{108.025}$$
$$f(0) = 200 - 5(0)e^{-0.02(0)}$$
$$= 200 - 0$$
$$= \boldsymbol{200}$$
$$f(60) = 200 - 5(60)e^{-0.02(60)}$$
$$= 200 - 300e^{-1.2}$$
$$= 200 - 300(0.3012)$$
$$= 200 - 90.36$$
$$= \boldsymbol{109.64}$$

Since $f(50)$ is less than $f(0)$ and $f(60)$, the global minimum occurs at $x = 50$. The average daily crime rate is expected to be minimized at a value of 108.025 crimes if 50 officers are assigned to each shift.

Follow-up Exercises

13.22 An owner of a ranch wishes to build a rectangular riding corral having an area of 10,000 square yards. If the corral appears as in Fig.

13.14, determine the dimensions x and y which will require the minimum length of fencing. (*Hint:* Set up a function for the total length of fencing required, stated in terms of x and y. Then, remembering that $xy = 10,000$, restate the length function in terms of either x or y.)

13.23 A small beach club has been given 200 yards of flotation barrier to enclose a swimming area. The desire is to create the largest rectangular swim area given the 200 yards of flotation barrier. Figure 13.15 illustrates the proposed layout. Note that the flotation barrier is required only on three sides of the swimming area. Determine the dimensions x and y which result in the largest swim area. What is the maximum area? (*Hint:* Remember that $x + 2y = 200$.)

13.24 An automobile dealer wishes to create a parking area for storing new cars. The parking area is to have a total area of 240,000 square feet and will have dimensions as indicated in Fig. 13.16. Because of security concerns, the section of fence across the front of the lot will be more heavy-duty and taller than the fence used along the sides and rear of the lot. The cost of fence for the front is $10 per foot, and that used for the other three sides costs $5 per foot. Determine the dimensions x and y which result in a minimum total cost of fence. What is the minimum cost? (*Hint:* $xy = 240,000$.)

13.25 Figure 13.17 illustrates an area which is to be fenced. In addition to enclosing the area, a piece of fence should divide the total area in half. If 1,200 feet of fence are available, determine the dimensions x and y which result in the maximum enclosed area. What is the maximum area? (*Hint:* $2x + 3y = 1,200$.)

13.26 Figure 13.18 illustrates the relative locations of three cities. A major department store wishes to build a new store to service the three cities. The location of the store x should be such that the sum of the squares of the distance between the store and each city is minimized. This criterion can be stated as

minimize $$S = \sum_{j=1}^{3} (x_j - x)^2$$

where x_j is the location of the city j and x is the location of the department store. Determine the location x which minimizes S.

13.27 A national charity is planning a fund raising campaign in a major United States city having a population of 1 million. The percentage of the population who will make a donation is estimated by the function

$$R = 1 - e^{-0.02x}$$

where R equals the percentage of the population and x equals the number of days the campaign is conducted.

Past experience indicates that the average contribution in this city is $1.50 per donor. Costs of the campaign are estimated at $10,000 per day.

(*a*) How many days should the campaign be conducted if the objective

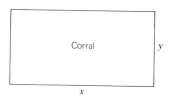

FIGURE 13.14

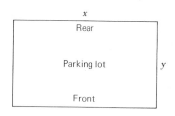

FIGURE 13.15

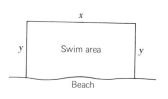

FIGURE 13.16

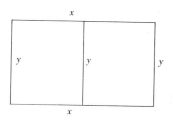

FIGURE 13.17

FIGURE 13.18

is to maximize net proceeds (total contributions minus total costs) from the campaign?

(b) What are maximum net proceeds expected to equal? What percentage of the population is expected to donate?

13.28 A national record distribution company sells records and tapes by mail only. Advertising is done on local TV stations. A promotion program is being planned for a major metropolitan area for a new country western album. The target audience—those who might be interested in this type of album—is estimated at 500,000. Past experience indicates that for this city and this type of album the percentage of the target market R actually purchasing an album or tape is a function of the length of the advertising campaign t. Specifically, this *sales response function* is

$$R = 1 - e^{-0.025t}$$

The profit margin on each album is $2. Advertising costs include a fixed cost of $10,000 and a variable cost of $1,500 per day.

(a) Determine how long the campaign should be conducted if the goal is to maximize *net profit* (gross profit minus advertising costs).

(b) What is the expected maximum net profit?

(c) What percentage of the target market is expected to purchase the album?

13.29 Assume in Example 13.13 that the average amount of credit issued each month is $50 million instead of $100 million. Re-solve the problem.

13.30 A police department purchases new patrol cars for $9,000. The department estimates average capital cost and average operating cost to be a function of x, the number of miles the car is driven. The salvage value of a patrol car (in dollars) is expressed by the function

$$S(x) = 7,500 - 0.055x$$

Average operating cost, stated in dollars per mile, is estimated by the function

$$O(x) = 0.0000004x + 0.16$$

(a) Determine how many miles the car should be driven prior to replacement if the objective is to minimize the sum of average capital cost and average operating cost per mile.

(b) What is the minimum cost per mile?

(c) What is the salvage value expected to equal?

13.31 A major airline purchases a particular type of plane at a cost of $750,000. The company estimates that average capital cost and average operating cost are a function of x, the number of hours of flight time. The salvage value of a plane (in dollars) is expressed by the function

$$S(x) = 700,000 - 500x$$

Average operating cost, stated in dollars per hour of flight time, is estimated by the function

$$O(x) = 200 + 0.05x$$

(*a*) Determine how many hours a plane should be flown before replacement if the objective is to minimize the sum of average capital and average operating cost per hour?

(*b*) What is the minimum cost per hour?

(*c*) What is the salvage value expected to equal?

13.32 A new state welfare agency wants to determine how many analysts to hire for processing of welfare applications. It is estimated that the average cost C of processing an application is a function of the number of analysts x. Specifically, the cost function is

$$C = 0.005x^2 - 16 \ln x + 70$$

(*a*) If the objective is to minimize the average cost per application, determine the number of analysts who should be hired.

(*b*) What is the minimum average cost of processing an application expected to equal?

13.33 A firm has estimated that the average production cost per unit $\overline{C}$ fluctuates with the number of units produced x. The average cost function is

$$\overline{C} = 0.002x^2 - 1,000 \ln x + 7,500$$

where $\overline{C}$ is stated in dollars per unit and x is stated in hundreds of units.

(*a*) Determine the number of units which should be produced in order to minimize the average production cost per unit.

(*b*) What is the minimum average cost expected to equal?

(*c*) What are total production costs expected to equal?

13.34 A police department has determined that the daily crime rate depends upon the number of officers assigned to each shift. Specifically, the function describing this relationship is

$$N = 500 - 7.5xe^{-0.03x}$$

where N equals the daily crime rate and x equals the number of officers assigned to each shift.

(*a*) Determine the number of officers which will result in a minimum daily crime rate.

(*b*) What is the minimum rate expected to equal?

13.35 A firm's annual profit is stated as a function of the number of salespeople employed. The profit function is

$$P = 10xe^{-0.004x}$$

where P equals profit stated in thousands of dollars and x equals the number of salespeople.

(*a*) Determine the number of salespeople which will maximize annual profit.

(*b*) What is the maximum profit expected to equal?

SUMMARY 13.4

This chapter has presented a variety of applications of classical optimization problems. Additional applications will be included in the end-of-chapter exercises. This chapter also ends our discussion of single-variable differential calculus, that is, the differential calculus of functions involving one independent variable. Chapter 14 surveys the differential calculus of functions involving two independent variables.

ADDITIONAL EXERCISES

13.36 A vendor at a local stadium has determined that the amount of money spent by spectators on concessions depends on the number of concession stands operating. The function is

$$R = f(x) = -20x^2 + 400x$$

where R equals concession sales per game (in \$100s) and x equals the number of stands operating. Determine (a) the number of stands which will result in the maximum sales per game and (b) the maximum value for R.

13.37 The demand function for a firm's product is

$$q = 100,000 - 12.5p$$

where q equals the number of units demanded and p equals the price in dollars.
(a) Determine the revenue function $R = f(p)$.
(b) What price will result in the maximum value of total revenue?
(c) How many units will be demanded at this price?

13.38 Two points (p, q) on a linear demand function are (20, 4,000) and (30, 2,000). Assume p equals the price in dollars and q the quantity demanded.
(a) Determine the demand function $q = f(p)$.
(b) Determine the total revenue function $R = g(p)$.
(c) Sketch the revenue function.

*13.39 A local travel agent is organizing a charter flight to a well-known resort. The agent has quoted a price of \$300 per person if 100 or fewer sign up for the flight. For every person over the 100, the price for *all* will decrease by \$2.50. For instance, if 101 people sign up, each will pay \$297.50. Let x equal the number of persons above 100.
(a) Determine the function which states price per person p as a function of x, or $p = f(x)$.
(b) In part a, is there any restriction on the domain?
(c) Formulate the function $R = h(x)$, which states total ticket revenue R as a function of x.
(d) What value of x results in the maximum value of R?
(e) What is the maximum value of R?
(f) What price per ticket results in the maximum R?

*13.40 *Wage Incentive Plan.* A producer of a perishable product offers a wage incentive to the drivers of its trucks. A standard delivery route takes an average of 20 hours. Drivers are paid at the rate of \$10 per hour up to a *maximum* of 20 hours (if the trip requires 30 hours, the drivers receive payment for only 20 hours). There is an incentive for drivers to make the trip in less than 20 hours. For each hour under 20, the hourly wage increases by \$1. Assume x equals the number of hours required to complete the trip.
(a) Determine the function $w = f(x)$ where w equals the hourly wage in dollars.

(b) What trip time x will maximize the driver's salary for the trip?
(c) What is the hourly wage associated with this trip time?
(d) What is the maximum salary?
(e) How does this salary compare with that received for a 20-hour trip?

13.41 The total cost of producing q units of a certain product is described by the function

$$C = 12,500,000 + 100q + 0.02q^2$$

(a) Determine how many units q should be produced in order to minimize the *average cost per unit*.
(b) What is the minimum average cost per unit?
(c) What is the total cost of production at this level of output?

13.42 A law of economics states that the average cost per unit is minimized when the marginal cost equals the average cost. Show that this is true for the cost function in Exercise 13.41.

13.43 A firm sells each unit of a product for $250. The cost function which describes the total cost C as a function of the number of units produced and sold x is

$$C(x) = 50x + 0.1x^2 + 150$$

(a) Formulate the profit function $P = f(x)$.
(b) How many units should be produced and sold in order to maximize total profit?
(c) What is total revenue at this level of output?
(d) What is total cost at this level of output?

13.44 Re-solve Exercise 13.43 using the marginal approach.

13.45 A person wishes to enclose the largest possible rectangular area using 40,000 feet of fence. Determine the dimensions of the largest rectangular area. What is the maximum area?

13.46 *Poster Problem.* Figure 13.19 is a sketch of a poster which is being designed for a political campaign. The printed area should contain 600 square inches. A margin of 2 inches should appear on each side of the printed matter and a 3-inch margin on the top and bottom.
(a) Determine the dimensions of the printed area which minimize the *area* of the poster.
(b) What are the optimal dimensions of the poster?
(c) What is the minimum poster area?

13.47 A person wants to purchase a rectangular piece of property in order to construct a warehouse. The warehouse should have an area of 10,000 square feet. Zoning ordinances specify that there should be at least 30 feet between the building and the side boundaries of the lot and at least 40 feet between the building and the front and rear boundaries of the lot. Figure 13.20 is a sketch of the proposed lot.
(a) Determine the dimensions of the warehouse which will minimize the area of the lot.
(b) What are the optimal dimensions of the lot?
(c) What is the minimum lot area?

13.48 Determine two numbers x and y whose sum is 50 and whose product is as large as possible. What is the maximum product of the two numbers?

13.49 Determine two positive numbers whose product equals 40 and whose sum is as small as possible. What is the minimum sum?

FIGURE 13.19

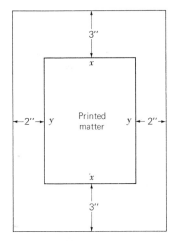

FIGURE 13.20

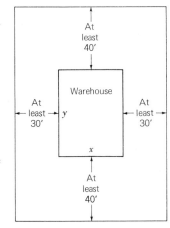

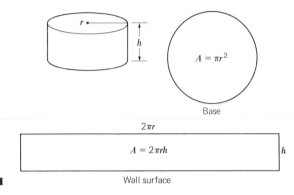

FIGURE 13.21

---

*__13.50__ *Solid Waste Management.* A local city is planning to construct a solid waste treatment facility. One of the major components of the plant is a solid waste agitation pool. This pool is to be circular in shape and is supposed to have a volume capacity of 1 million cubic feet. Municipal engineers have estimated construction costs as a function of the surface area of the base and wall of the pool. Construction costs are estimated at $10 per square foot for the base of the pool and $20 per square foot of wall surface. Figure 13.21 presents a sketch of the pool. Note that r equals the radius of the pool in feet and h equals the depth of the pool in feet. Determine the dimensions r and h which provide a capacity of 1 million cubic feet at a minimum cost of construction. (*Hint:* The area A of a circle having radius r is $A = \pi r^2$, the surface area A of a circular cylinder having radius r and height h is $A = 2\pi rh$ and the volume V is $V = \pi r^2 h$.)

*__13.51__ *Pipeline Construction.* A major oil company is planning to construct a pipeline to deliver crude oil from a major well site to a point where the crude will be loaded on tankers and shipped to refineries. Figure 13.22 illustrates the relative locations of the well site A and the destination point C. Points A and C are on opposite sides of a river which is 25 miles wide. Point C is also 100 miles south of A along the river. The oil company is proposing a pipeline which will run south along the east side of the river, and at some point x will cross the river to point C. Construction costs are $100,000 per mile along the bank of the river and $125,000 per mile for the section crossing the river. Determine the crossing point x which will result in the minimum construction costs for the pipeline.

FIGURE 13.22

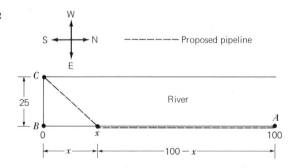

CHAPTER TEST

1 The demand function for a product is

$$q = f(p) = 50{,}000 - 7.5p$$

where q equals the quantity demanded and p equals the price in dollars. Formulate the total revenue function $R = g(p)$.

2 The total revenue function for a product is

$$R = f(x) = -3x^2 + 200x$$

where R is measured in hundreds of dollars and x equals the number of units sold (in 100s). The total cost of producing x (hundred) units is described by the function

$$C = g(x) = 2x^2 - 150x + 5{,}000$$

where C is measured in hundreds of dollars.
(a) Formulate the profit function $P = h(x)$.
(b) How many units should be produced and sold in order to maximize total profit?
(c) What is the maximum profit?

3 An importer wants to fence in a storage area near the local shipping docks. The area will be used for temporary storage of shipping containers. The area is to be rectangular with an area of 100,000 square feet. The fence will cost \$10 per running foot.
(a) Determine the dimensions of the area which will result in fencing costs being minimized.
(b) What is the minimum cost?

4 A retailer has determined that the annual cost C of purchasing, owning, and maintaining one of its products behaves according to the function

$$C = f(q) = \frac{20{,}000}{q} + 0.5q + 50{,}000$$

where q is the size (in units) of each order purchased from suppliers.
(a) What order quantity q results in minimum annual cost?
(b) What is the minimum annual cost?

5 A national charity is planning a fund raising campaign in a major city. The population of the city is 1.5 million. The percentage of the population who will make a donation is described by the function

$$R = 1 - e^{-0.06x}$$

where R equals the percentage of the population and x equals the number of days the campaign is conducted. Past experience indicates that the average contribution per donor is \$1. Costs of the campaign are estimated at \$5,000 per day. Formulate the function $N = f(x)$ which expresses net proceeds N (total contributions minus total costs) as a function of x. (*Note:* This is a formulation problem.)

CHAPTER OBJECTIVES After reading this chapter, you should have a general familiarity with the calculus of functions which contain two independent variables; you should be familiar with the graphical representation of these functions; you should understand the meaning of the derivatives of these functions and how to find these derivatives; you should know how to locate and verify the existence of relative maxima and minima for these functions; and you should be familiar with some applications of classical optimization of functions which contain two independent variables.

Chapters 11, 12, and 13 have provided a methodology for examining functions which involve one independent variable. In applied problems, stating that a decision criterion or objective depends on only one variable may oversimplify a situation. When functions involve more than one independent variable, they are referred to as *multivariate functions*, or *functions of several variables*. Methods of differential calculus are available for examining such functions and for determining optimal values (maxima and minima). As we examine some of these procedures in this chapter, you will see that they are very similar to those we used for functions of one independent variable.

This chapter will concentrate on *bivariate functions* (functions involving two independent variables). The graphics of these functions will be illustrated first. Then there will follow a discussion of the derivatives of these functions and their interpretation. Next procedures for determining optimal values of these functions will be developed. The last section discusses applications of bivariate functions.

14.1 GRAPHICAL REPRESENTATION OF BIVARIATE FUNCTIONS

Graphical Representation

A function involving a dependent variable z and two independent variables x and y may be represented by using the notation

$$z = f(x, y) \tag{14.1}$$

We established a long time ago that the number of variables in a function determines the number of dimensions required to graph the function. Whereas two dimensions are required to graph single-variable functions, three dimensions are required to graph bivariate functions.

We established earlier in the book that linear functions involving one independent variable graph as *straight lines* in two dimensions. Linear functions involving two independent variables graph as *planes* in three dimensions. Generally speaking, nonlinear functions involving one independent variable graph as *curves* in two dimensions. And, nonlinear functions containing two independent variables graph as *surfaces* in three dimensions. Being associated with nonlinear functions, these surfaces are curved as opposed to the flat surfaces associated with linear functions. Examples of nonlinear surfaces include the undulating surface of a golf green, a mogul-laden ski slope, and a billowing sail on a sailboat. An important point is that these functions are represented by *surfaces*, not solids.

Sketching Bivariate Functions

Although graphing in three dimensions is difficult, we will now discuss a procedure that can be used in some instances to sketch the general shape of the graph of a bivariate function. An understanding of the graphics of these functions will assist us with the material which follows.

Consider the bivariate function

$$z = f(x, y) = 25 - x^2 - y^2 \tag{14.2}$$

where $0 \le x \le 5$ and $0 \le y \le 5$. In order to sketch this function, let's fix the value of one of the independent variables and graph the resulting function. For example, if we let $y = 0$, the function $f(x, y)$ becomes

$$z = 25 - x^2 - 0^2$$
or
$$z = 25 - x^2 \tag{14.3}$$

By fixing the value of one of the variables, the function is restated in terms of one independent variable. That is, once the value of one inde-

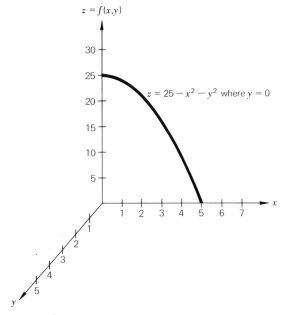

FIGURE 14.1

x	0	1	2	3	4	5
$z = 25 - x^2$	25	24	21	16	9	0

Table 14.1

pendent variable is specified, the value of the dependent variable varies with the value of the remaining independent variable. Given Eq. (14.3), Table 14.1 indicates selected values for x and resulting values of z.

Figure 14.1 is a partial sketch of the function with the value of y fixed at 0. If we let $y = 0$, the sketch of Eq. (14.3) must be in the xz plane. A close examination of Eq. (14.3) reveals that the relationship between z and x is quadratic. And the sketch in Fig. 14.1 is part of a parabola which is concave down.

If we let $x = 0$ in the original function, $f(x, y)$ becomes

$$z = 25 - 0^2 - y^2$$

or
$$z = 25 - y^2 \qquad (14.4)$$

Table 14.2 indicates selected values of y and the resulting values of z.

Figure 14.2 is a partial sketch of $f(x, y)$. With $x = 0$, the sketch of Eq. (14.4) is in the yz plane. Equation (14.4) indicates a quadratic relationship between y and z. And, if you were to look at Fig. 14.2 in a direction parallel to the x axis, you would see that this equation graphs as a portion of a parabola which is concave down. Figure 14.3 indicates what you would see if sighting along the x axis.

y	0	1	2	3	4	5
$z = 25 - y^2$	25	24	21	16	9	0

Table 14.2

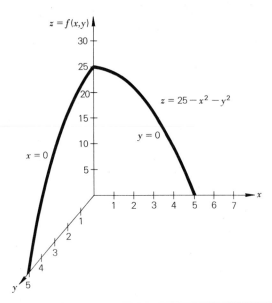

FIGURE 14.2

DEFINITION
Given $z = f(x, y)$, a *trace* is the graphical representation of $f(x, y)$ when one variable is held constant.

Refer to Fig. 14.2. The two portions of $f(x, y)$ which are illustrated
are *traces*. One is a trace where $y = 0$, and the other is a trace where
$x = 0$. Each trace represents a *rib* on the surface which represents the
function.

Figure 14.4 presents a sketch of the function which includes four additional traces. By letting $y = 1$, the function becomes

$$f(x, y) = 25 - x^2 - 1^2$$
$$= 24 - x^2$$

FIGURE 14.3

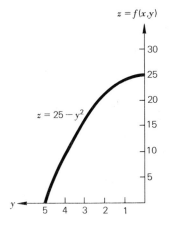

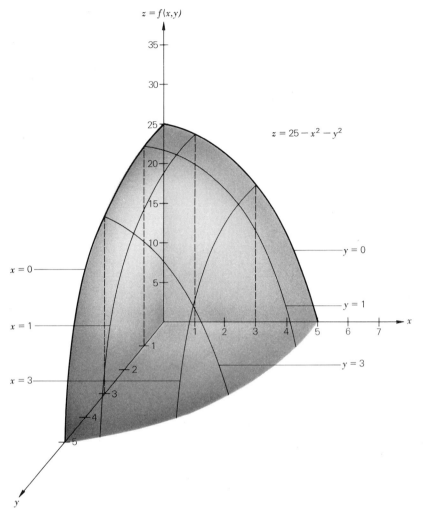

FIGURE 14.4

The trace representing this function is parallel to the xz plane and 1 unit out along the positive y axis. Similarly, letting $y = 3$, we have

$$f(x, y) = 25 - x^2 - 3^2$$
$$= 16 - x^2$$

The trace representing this function graphs parallel to the xz plane and 3 units out along the y axis.

Traces have also been sketched by letting $x = 1$ and $x = 3$. These six traces in combination begin to resemble a skeletal structure of the surface. And if we were to graph more traces associated with other assumed values for x and y, we would get a more accurate representation of the surface representing $f(x, y)$.

Therefore, a procedure which can sometimes provide a rough sketch of a function of the form $z = f(x, y)$ is to assume selected values for x and y and graph the traces which represent the resulting function.

NOTE
An important observation should be made regarding the graphics of a function $f(x, y)$. Whenever x is held constant, the resulting trace graphs in a plane which is parallel to the yz plane. Whenever y is held constant, the resulting trace graphs in a plane which is parallel to the xz plane.

Follow-up Exercises

Sketch the following functions.

14.1 $f(x, y) = 16 - x^2 - y^2$,   where $0 \leq x \leq 4$ and $0 \leq y \leq 4$
14.2 $f(x, y) = 9 - x^2 - y^2$,   where $0 \leq x \leq 3$ and $0 \leq y \leq 3$
14.3 $f(x, y) = 4 - x^2 - y^2$,   where $0 \leq x \leq 2$ and $0 \leq y \leq 2$
14.4 $f(x, y) = 25 - x^2/4 - y^2/4$, where $0 \leq x \leq 10$ and $0 \leq y \leq 10$
14.5 $f(x, y) = x^2 + y^2$,   where $0 \leq x \leq 5$ and $0 \leq y \leq 5$

14.2   PARTIAL DERIVATIVES

Although more involved, the calculus of bivariate functions is very similar to that of single-variable functions. In this section we will discuss derivatives of bivariate functions and their interpretation.

Derivatives of Bivariate Functions

With single-variable functions, the derivative represents the instantaneous rate of change in the dependent variable with respect to a change in the independent variable. For bivariate functions, derivatives can also be identified. We will focus on *partial derivatives* which represent the instantaneous rate of change in the dependent variable, but with respect to changes in the two independent variables, separately. Given a function $z = f(x, y)$, a partial derivative can be found with respect to each independent variable. The partial derivative taken with respect to x is denoted by

$$\frac{\partial z}{\partial x} \quad \text{or} \quad f_x$$

The partial derivative taken with respect to y is denoted by

$$\frac{\partial z}{\partial y} \quad \text{or} \quad f_y$$

Although both forms are used to denote the partial derivative, we will use the subscripted notation f_x or f_y in this chapter.

Partial derivatives are found by using the same differentiation rules we used in the last three chapters. The only exception is that *when a partial derivative is found with respect to one independent variable, the other independent variable is assumed to be held constant.* For instance, in finding the partial derivative with respect to x, y is assumed to be constant. And a very important point is that *the variable which is assumed constant must be treated like a constant in applying the rules of differentiation.*

Find the partial derivatives with respect to x and y for the function

$$f(x, y) = 5x^2 + 6y^3$$

Example 14.1

First, to find the partial derivative with respect to x, the variable y must be assumed held constant. Differentiating term by term, we find that the derivative of $5x^2$ with respect to x is $10x$. In differentiating the second term, remember that y is assumed to be constant. Thus, this term has the general form of

$$6(\text{constant})^3$$

Solution

And the product of 6 times the cube of a constant is simply a constant. Since a constant does not change in value as other variables change in value—or, remember from Chap. 11 that the derivative of a constant equals 0—the derivative of the second term equals 0. And,

$$f_x = 10x$$

In finding the partial derivative with respect to y, the variable x is assumed held constant. In differentiating term by term, $5x^2$ is viewed as being a constant since x is assumed constant and the derivative equals 0. The derivative of $6y^3$ with respect to y is $18y^2$. Thus,

$$f_y = 18y^2$$

Find f_x and f_y for the function

$$f(x, y) = 4xy$$

Example 14.2

To find f_x, y is assumed to be constant. The term $4xy$ is in the form of a product. To differentiate such product terms, you can use two approaches. The first approach is simply to apply the product rule. In viewing $4xy$ as the product of $4x$ and y, the product rule yields

$$f_x = (4)(y) + (0)(4x)$$
or
$$f_x = 4y$$

Solution

An *alternative approach* is to remember which variable is assumed constant. When y is held constant, we can rearrange $4xy$ to have the form

$$(4y)x$$

By grouping the 4 and y, this term has the general form of a constant $4y$ times x. And the derivative of a constant times x is the constant, or

$$f_x = 4y$$

To find f_y, x is assumed constant. Applying the product rule, we find

$$f_y = (0)(y) + (1)(4x)$$
or
$$f_y = 4x$$

Or, by using the alternative approach, the factor $4x$ is constant with x held constant, and $f(x, y)$ can be viewed as having the form

$$f(x, y) = \text{constant} \cdot y$$

The derivative with respect to y is the constant, or

$$f_y = 4x$$

**Example
14.3**

Find f_x and f_y if

$$f(x, y) = 3x^2 - 10xy^3 + 5y^2 - 100$$

Solution

To find f_x, the biggest problem is the second term in the function. So let's focus on the derivative of $-10xy^3$. With y held constant, this term can be rearranged (mentally or explicitly) to have the form

$$(-10y^3)x$$

With $-10y^3$ being constant, the derivative equals $-10y^3$. Thus,

$$\boldsymbol{f_x = 6x - 10y^3}$$

For f_y the second term can be viewed as having the form

$$(-10x)y^3 \qquad \text{or} \qquad (\text{constant})(y^3)$$

The derivative with respect to y is

$$(\text{constant})(3y^2) \qquad \text{or} \qquad (-10x)(3y^2) = -30xy^2$$

Again, the product rule will generate the same result. Therefore,

$$\boldsymbol{f_y = -30xy^2 + 10y}$$

**Example
14.4**

Find f_x and f_y if

$$f(x, y) = e^{x^2+y^2}$$

Solution

Using our differentiation rules for exponential functions, we have

$$f_x = 2xe^{x^2+y^2}$$
$$f_y = 2ye^{x^2+y^2}$$

**Example
14.5**

Find f_x and f_y if

$$f(x, y) = (3x - 2y^2)^3$$

Solution

Remembering the power of a function rule, we have

$$f_x = 3(3x - 2y^2)^2(3)$$
$$= 9(3x - 2y^2)^2$$
$$f_y = 3(3x - 2y^2)^2(-4y)$$
$$= -12y(3x - 2y^2)^2$$

Interpreting Partial Derivatives

One interpretation of partial derivatives is the instantaneous rate-of-change interpretation. As with single-variable functions, partial derivatives can be used to approximate changes in the value of the dependent variable, given a change in *one* of the independent variables. For example, f_x can be used to approximate the change in $f(x, y)$, given a change in x with y assumed constant. The partial derivative f_y can be used to approximate the change in $f(x, y)$, given a change in y with x assumed constant. The following example illustrates this interpretation.

Advertising Expenditures A national manufacturer esti-mates that the number of units it sells each year is a function of its expenditures on radio and TV advertising. The function specifying this relationship is

Example 14.6

$$z = 50{,}000x + 40{,}000y - 10x^2 - 20y^2 - 10xy$$

where z equals the number of units sold annually, x equals the amount spent for TV advertising, and y equals the amount spent for radio adver-tising (both in $1,000s).

Assume that the firm is currently spending $40,000 on TV advertising ($x = 40$) and $20,000 on radio advertising ($y = 20$). With these expendi-tures,

$$\begin{aligned}
f(40, 20) &= 50{,}000(40) + 40{,}000(20) - 10(40)^2 - 20(20)^2 - 10(40)(20) \\
&= 2{,}000{,}000 + 800{,}000 - 16{,}000 - 8{,}000 - 8{,}000 \\
&= 2{,}768{,}000
\end{aligned}$$

or it is projected that 2,768,000 units will be sold.

Suppose we are interested in determining the effect on annual sales if $1,000 more is spent on TV advertising. The partial derivative f_x should provide us with an approximation of this effect:

$$f_x = 50{,}000 - 20x - 10y$$

Because we are interested in the instantaneous rate of change, given that expenditures are currently $40,000 and $20,000, we evaluate f_x at $x = 40$ and $y = 20$:

$$\begin{aligned}
f_x(40, 20) &= 50{,}000 - 20(40) - 10(20) \\
&= 50{,}000 - 800 - 200 \\
&= 49{,}000
\end{aligned}$$

Evaluating the partial derivative, we can state that an increase in TV expenditures of $1,000 should result in additional sales of approximately 49,000 units.

To determine how accurate this approximation is, let's evaluate $f(41, 20)$:

$$\begin{aligned}
f(41, 20) &= 50{,}000(41) + 40{,}000(20) - 10(41)^2 - 20(20)^2 - 10(41)(20) \\
&= 2{,}050{,}000 + 800{,}000 - 16{,}810 - 8{,}000 - 8{,}200 \\
&= 2{,}816{,}990
\end{aligned}$$

The actual increase in sales is projected as

$$f(41, 20) - f(40, 20) = 2,816,990 - 2,768,000$$
$$= 48,990 \text{ units}$$

The difference between the actual increase and the increase estimated by using f_x is 10 units.

Now suppose that we are interested in determining the effect if an additional \$1,000 is spent on radio, rather than TV, advertising. The partial derivative taken with respect to y will approximate this change:

$$f_y = 40,000 - 40y - 10x$$

Evaluating f_y at $x = 40$ and $y = 20$, we get

$$f_y(40, 20) = 40,000 - 40(20) - 10(40)$$
$$= 40,000 - 800 - 400$$
$$= 38,800$$

Thus an increase of \$1,000 in radio advertising expenditures will lead to an approximate increase of 38,800 units.

Actual sales are estimated at

$$f(40, 21) = 50,000(40) + 40,000(21) - 10(40)^2 - 20(21)^2 - 10(40)(21)$$
$$= 2,000,000 + 840,000 - 16,000 - 8,820 - 8,400$$
$$= 2,806,780 \text{ units}$$

The actual increase in sales is

$$f(40, 21) - f(40, 20) = 2,806,780 - 2,768,000$$
$$= 38,780 \text{ units}$$

Again, the approximate change estimated by using f_y is in error by only 20 units.

From a comparative standpoint, if \$1,000 is to be allocated to either TV or radio, it appears that the greater return will come from TV.

The other interpretation of derivatives deals with the tangent slope. As with single-variable functions, the partial derivatives f_x and f_y have a tangent slope interpretation. These interpretations are:

1 f_x represents a general expression for the tangent slope of the family of traces which are parallel to the xz plane.

2 f_y represents a general expression for the tangent slope of the family of traces which are parallel to the yz plane.

The partial derivative f_x estimates the change in z given a change in x, assuming y is held constant. If you remember Sec. 14.1, traces which were graphed while a constant value for y is assumed, graphed parallel to the xz plane. Thus f_x concerns the slope of these traces.

Similarly, f_y assumes that x is held constant. When x was held constant in Sec. 14.1, the result was a family of traces which were parallel to the yz plane. And, f_y represents the slope of these traces.

Second Derivatives

As with single-variable functions, we can determine second derivatives for bivariate functions. These will be of considerable importance to us in the next section when we seek to optimize the value of a function.

For functions of the form $f(x, y)$, there are *four* different second derivatives. These are divided into two types: *pure second partial derivatives* and *mixed or cross partial derivatives*. The two pure partial derivatives are denoted by f_{xx} and f_{yy}. The pure partial derivative with respect to x, f_{xx}, is found by first finding f_x and then differentiating f_x with respect to x. Similarly, f_{yy} is found by determining the expression for f_y and then differentiating f_y with respect to y.

The two cross partial derivatives are denoted by f_{xy} and f_{yx}. The cross partial derivative f_{xy} is found by determining f_x and then differentiating f_x with respect to y. Similarly, f_{yx} is found by determining f_y and then differentiating f_y with respect to x.

Determine all first and second derivatives for the function

$$f(x, y) = 8x^3 - 4x^2y + 10y^3$$

Example 14.7

We start with the first derivatives:

Solution

$$f_x = 24x^2 - 8xy$$
$$f_y = -4x^2 + 30y^2$$

The pure partial derivative f_{xx} is found by differentiating f_x with respect to x, or

$$f_{xx} = 48x - 8y$$

f_{yy} is found by differentiating f_y with respect to y, or

$$f_{yy} = 60y$$

The cross partial derivative f_{xy} is found by differentiating f_x with respect to y, or

$$f_{xy} = -8x$$

f_{yx} is found by differentiating f_y with respect to x, or

$$f_{yx} = -8x$$

NOTE
For all functions which we will examine, the cross partial derivatives will be the same; that is, $f_{xy} = f_{yx}$. Notice that this is true for the last example. This property provides a possible check on errors which may have been made in finding f_x, f_y, f_{xy}, and f_{yx}.

We will not dwell on the interpretation of these second derivatives. However, a few points should be made. The pure partial derivatives f_{xx} and f_{yy} convey information about the concavity of a function (just as the second derivative does for single-variable functions). Specifically, f_{xx} *offers information about the concavity of traces which are parallel to the xz plane. Similarly, f_{yy} provides information about the concavity of traces which are parallel to the yz plane.*

The interpretation of the cross partial derivatives f_{xy} and f_{yx} is less intuitive than with the pure partial derivatives. However, they will be significant in the next section.

Follow-up Exercises

In Exercises 14.6 to 14.15, determine f_x and f_y.

14.6 $f(x, y) = 10x^3y^2$ **14.7** $f(x, y) = -5x^2 + 4y^2 - 2xy$

14.8 $f(x, y) = 3x^2 + 5y^2 - 4xy$

14.9 $f(x, y) = 5x^4 - 3x^3y + 2xy^2 - y^3$

14.10 $f(x, y) = \ln x(\ln y)$ **14.11** $f(x, y) = (x^2 - 2y^2)^4$

14.12 $f(x, y) = (2x^3 - 4y^2)^3$ **14.13** $f(x, y) = e^{x+y}$

14.14 $f(x, y) = e^{3x^2+y}$ **14.15** $f(x, y) = x^2/y^3$

In Exercises 14.16 to 14.23, determine all second partial derivatives.

14.16 $f(x, y) = x^2 + 3y^2 - 10$ **14.17** $f(x, y) = 5x^3y^2$

14.18 $f(x, y) = -x^2 - 2y^2 + 2xy$ **14.19** $f(x, y) = x^3/y^2$

14.20 $f(x, y) = x^3 + y^2 - 4x^2y^3$ **14.21** $f(x, y) = \ln 3xy$

14.22 $f(x, y) = e^{x^2+y^2}$ **14.23** $f(x, y) = 160x^3y^2 - xy^2$

14.24 Given $f(x, y) = 100x^2 + 200y^2 - 10xy$:
(a) Determine $f(40, 50)$.
(b) Using partial derivatives, estimate the change expected in $f(x, y)$ if x increases by 1 unit.
(c) Compare the actual change with the estimated change.
(d) Repeat parts b and c assuming a possible increase in y of 1 unit.

14.25 Given $f(x, y) = 20x^3 - 30y^3 + 10x^2y$:
(a) Determine $f(10, 10)$.
(b) Using partial derivatives, estimate the change expected in $f(x, y)$ if x increases by 1 unit.
(c) Compare the actual change with the estimated change.
(d) Repeat parts b and c assuming a possible increase in y of 1 unit.

14.26 A firm estimates that the number of units it sells each year is a function of the advertising expenditures for TV and radio. The function expressing this relationship is

$$z = 2{,}000x + 5{,}000y - 20x^2 - 10y^2 - 50xy$$

where z equals the number of units sold, x equals the amount spent on TV advertising, and y equals the amount spent on radio advertising (the latter two variables expressed in $1,000s). The firm is presently allocating $50,000 to TV and $30,000 to radio.
(a) What are annual sales expected to equal?
(b) Using partial derivatives, estimate the effect on annual sales if an additional $1,000 is allocated to TV.
(c) Using partial derivatives, estimate the effect on annual sales if an additional $1,000 is allocated to radio.
(d) Where does it seem that the $1,000 is better spent?

The process of finding optimum values on bivariate functions is very similar to that used for single-variable functions. This section discusses the process.

Stationary Points

As with single-variable functions, we will have a particular interest in identifying relative maximum and minimum points on the surface representing a function $f(x, y)$. Relative maximum and minimum points have the same meaning in three dimensions as in two dimensions.

DEFINITION
A function $z = f(x, y)$ is said to have a *relative maximum* at $x = a$ and $y = b$ if for all points (x, y) sufficiently "close" to (a, b)

$$f(a, b) \geq f(x, y)$$

A relative maximum usually appears as the top or peak of a mound on the surface representing $f(x, y)$.

DEFINITION
A function $z = f(x, y)$ is said to have a *relative minimum* at $x = a$ and $y = b$ if for all points (x, y) sufficiently "close" to (a, b)

$$f(a, b) \leq f(x, y)$$

A relative minimum usually appears as the bottom of a valley on the surface representing $f(x, y)$.

Figure 14.5 illustrates both a relative maximum point and a relative minimum point. If you examine the slope conditions at a relative maximum or at a relative minimum, you should conclude that a line drawn tangent at the point in any direction has a slope equal to 0. Given that the first partial derivatives f_x and f_y represent general expressions for the tangent slope of traces which are parallel, respectively, to the xz and yz planes, we can state the following definition.

DEFINITION
A *necessary condition* for the existence of a relative maximum or a relative minimum of a function $f(x, y)$ is that both first partial derivatives equal 0, or

$$f_x = 0 \quad and \quad f_y = 0 \tag{14.5}$$

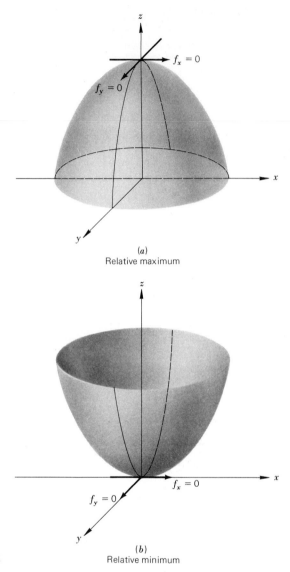

(a)
Relative maximum

(b)
Relative minimum

FIGURE 14.5

An important part of this definition is that *both* f_x and f_y equal 0. As illustrated in Fig. 14.6, there can be an infinite number of points on a surface where f_x equals 0. In Fig. 14.6 a tangent drawn parallel to the xz plane anywhere along the trace AB will have a slope of 0 ($f_x = 0$). However, the only point where *both* f_x and f_y equal zero is at A. At the other points along AB, a tangent drawn parallel to the yz plane has a negative slope ($f_y < 0$).

Similarly, Fig. 14.7 illustrates a trace AC along which $f_y = 0$ but $f_x < 0$ except at point A.

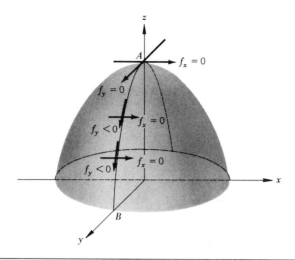

FIGURE 14.6

DEFINITION
Any points on the graph of $f(x, y)$ where $f_x = 0$ *and*
$f_y = 0$ will be referred to as *stationary points*.

Locate any stationary points on the graph of the function

$$f(x, y) = 4x^2 - 12x + y^2 + 2y - 10$$

First, find the expressions for f_x and f_y;

$$f_x = 8x - 12$$
$$f_y = 2y + 2$$

**Example
14.8**

Solution

FIGURE 14.7

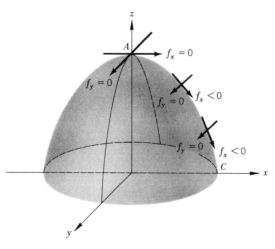

To determine the values of x and y at which f_x and f_y both equal 0,

$$f_x = 0 \qquad \text{when } 8x - 12 = 0$$
$$x = \tfrac{3}{2}$$

or

$$f_y = 0 \qquad \text{when } 2y + 2 = 0$$
$$y = -1$$

or

Thus, the only stationary point on the graph of $f(x, y)$ occurs when $x = \tfrac{3}{2}$ and $y = -1$.

NOTE
As with single-variable functions, stationary points in three dimensions are specified by the associated values of the *independent variables*.

Example 14.9

Determine any stationary points on the graph of the function

$$f(x, y) = -2x^2 - y^2 + 8x + 10y - 5xy$$

Solution

Finding the first-derivative expressions, we have

$$f_x = -4x + 8 - 5y$$
$$f_y = -2y + 10 - 5x$$

We wish to determine the values of x to y which make f_x and $f_y = 0$,

or

$$-4x + 8 - 5y = 0 \tag{14.6}$$
$$-2y + 10 - 5x = 0 \tag{14.7}$$

In order to determine these values, Eqs. (14.6) and (14.7) must be solved simultaneously. Rewriting these equations, we have

$$4x + 5y = 8 \tag{14.8}$$
$$5x + 2y = 10 \tag{14.9}$$

Multiplying both sides of Eq. (14.8) by -2 and both sides of Eq. (14.9) by 5 and adding the resulting equations, we get

$$\begin{array}{rcl} -8x - 10y &=& -16 \\ 25x + 10y &=& 50 \\ \hline 17x &=& 34 \\ x &=& 2 \end{array}$$

If $x = 2$ is substituted into Eq. (14.9), we find

$$5(2) + 2y = 10$$
$$2y = 0$$

and

$$y = 0$$

Thus, a stationary point (x^*, y^*, z) occurs when $x = 2$ and $y = 0$.

Example 14.10

Determine any stationary points on the graph of the function

$$f(x, y) = 2x^2 + 4xy - x^2y - 4x$$

Finding the first-derivative expressions and setting them equal to 0 yield   **Solution**

$$f_x = 4x + 4y - 2xy - 4 = 0 \qquad (14.10)$$
$$f_y = 4x - x^2 = 0 \qquad (14.11)$$

These two equations must be solved simultaneously. However, the equations are not linear. If we focus on Eq. (14.11), f_y will equal 0 when

$$4x - x^2 = 0$$
$$x(4 - x) = 0$$

or $\qquad \boldsymbol{x = 0} \qquad$ and $\qquad \boldsymbol{x = 4}$

To determine the values of y which correspond to these values of x and which make f_x equal 0, let's substitute these values, one at a time, into Eq. (14.10).
For $x = 0$, $\qquad 4(0) + 4y - 2(0)y - 4 = 0$
$$4y = 4$$
$$\boldsymbol{y = 1}$$

Thus, one stationary point occurs on the graph of $f(x, y)$ when $x = 0$ and $y = 1$.
For $x = 4$, $\qquad 4(4) + 4y - 2(4)y - 4 = 0$
$$16 + 4y - 8y - 4 = 0$$
$$-4y = -12$$
$$\boldsymbol{y = 3}$$

Another stationary point occurs when $x = 4$ and $y = 3$.

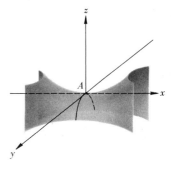

FIGURE 14.8
Saddle point

Distinguishing among Stationary Points

Once a stationary point has been identified, it is necessary to determine its nature. Aside from relative maximum and minimum points, there is one other situation in which f_x and f_y both equal 0. Figure 14.8 illustrates this situation which is referred to as a *saddle point*. A saddle point is a portion of a surface which has the shape of a saddle. At point A—"where you sit on the horse"—the values of f_x and f_y both equal 0. However, the function does not reach either a relative maximum or a relative minimum at A. If you slice through the surface at point A with the plane having the equation $x = 0$, the resulting edge or trace indicates a relative maximum at A. However, in slicing through the surface with the plane having the equation $y = 0$, the resulting trace indicates a relative minimum at A. Figure 14.9 illustrates these observations.

FIGURE 14.9

The conditions which allow you to distinguish among relative maximum, relative minimum, or saddle points follow. The test of a stationary point is a second-derivative test (as used in single-variable problems) which, from an intuitive standpoint, investigates the concavity conditions at the stationary point.

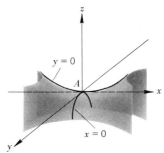

TEST OF STATIONARY POINT
Given that a stationary point is located at (x^*, y^*, z), determine the value of $D(x^*, y^*)$ where

$$D(x^*, y^*) = f_{xx}(x^*, y^*)f_{yy}(x^*, y^*) - [f_{xy}(x^*, y^*)]^2 \qquad (14.12)$$

1 If $D(x^*, y^*) > 0$, the stationary point is a *relative maximum* if *both* $f_{xx}(x^*, y^*)$ and $f_{yy}(x^*, y^*)$ are negative, and the stationary point is a *relative minimum* if *both* $f_{xx}(x^*, y^*)$ and $f_{yy}(x^*, y^*)$ are positive.

2 If $D(x^*, y^*) < 0$, the stationary point is a *saddle point*.

3 If $D(x^*, y^*) = 0$, other techniques (beyond the scope of this text) are required to determine the nature of the stationary point.

Example 14.11 In Example 14.8 we determined that a stationary point occurs on the graph of the function

$$f(x, y) = 4x^2 - 12x + y^2 + 2y - 10$$

when $x = \frac{3}{2}$ and $y = -1$. Determine the nature of the stationary point.

Solution In Example 14.8 we determined that

$$f_x = 8x - 12$$
$$f_y = 2y + 2$$

The four second derivatives are

$$f_{xx} = 8 \qquad f_{xy} = 0$$
$$f_{yy} = 2 \qquad f_{yx} = 0$$

Evaluating $D(x^*, y^*)$, we have

$$D(\tfrac{3}{2}, -1) = (8)(2) - 0^2$$
$$= 16 > 0$$

Since $D(x^*, y^*) > 0$ and $f_{xx}(\tfrac{3}{2}, -1) = 8$ and $f_{yy}(\tfrac{3}{2}, -1) = 2$, all of which are greater than 0, we can conclude that a relative minimum occurs when $x = \frac{3}{2}$ and $y = -1$. The value of the function at this relative minimum is

$$f(\tfrac{3}{2}, -1) = 4(\tfrac{3}{2})^2 - 12(\tfrac{3}{2}) + (-1)^2 + 2(-1) - 10$$
$$= 9 - 18 + 1 - 2 - 10$$
$$= -20$$

Example 14.12 Given the function

$$f(x, y) = -2x^2 + 24x - y^2 + 30y$$

determine the location and nature of any stationary points.

Solution Finding the first derivatives and setting them equal to 0, we have

$$f_x = -4x + 24 = 0 \qquad \text{or} \qquad \mathbf{x = 6}$$
$$f_y = -2y + 30 = 0 \qquad \text{or} \qquad \mathbf{y = 15}$$

The second derivatives are

$$f_{xx} = -4 \qquad f_{xy} = 0$$
$$f_{yy} = -2 \qquad f_{yx} = 0$$

Evaluating $D(x^*, y^*)$, we get

$$D(6, 15) = (-4)(-2) - 0^2$$
$$= 8 > 0$$

Since $D(6, 15)$ is positive and both f_{xx} and f_{yy} are negative, a relative maximum occurs at $x = 6$ and $y = 15$. The value of $f(x, y)$ at the relative maximum is

$$f(6, 15) = -2(6^2) + 24(6) - (15)^2 + 30(15)$$
$$= -72 + 144 - 225 + 450$$
$$= 297$$

In Example 14.10 we determined that stationary points occur on the graph of the function

$$f(x, y) = 2x^2 + 4xy - x^2y - 4x$$

when $x = 0$ and $y = 1$ and when $x = 4$ and $y = 3$. Determine the nature of the two stationary points.

Example 14.13

From Example 14.10

$$f_x = 4x + 4y - 2xy - 4$$
$$f_y = 4x - x^2$$

Solution

The second derivatives are

$$f_{xx} = 4 - 2y \qquad f_{xy} = 4 - 2x$$
$$f_{yy} = 0 \qquad f_{yx} = 4 - 2x$$

Evaluating $D(x^*, y^*)$ at $x = 0$ and $y = 1$, we get

$$D(0, 1) = [4 - 2(1)](0) - [4 - 2(0)]^2$$
$$= (2)(0) - 4^2$$
$$= -16 < 0$$

Since $D(x^*, y^*) < 0$, a saddle point occurs on $f(x, y)$ when $x = 0$ and $y = 1$.

For the other stationary point

$$D(4, 3) = [4 - 2(3)](0) - [4 - 2(4)]^2$$
$$= (-2)(0) - (-4)^2$$
$$= -16 < 0$$

Another saddle point occurs on $f(x, y)$ when $x = 4$ and $y = 3$.

Given the function

$$f(x, y) = -x^2 - y^3 + 12y^2$$

determine the location and nature of all stationary points.

Example 14.14

Finding the first derivatives and setting them equal to 0 give us

Solution

$$f_x = -2x = 0 \qquad \text{or} \qquad \boldsymbol{x = 0}$$
$$f_y = -3y^2 + 24y = 0$$
$$3y(-y + 8) = 0 \qquad \text{when} \qquad \boldsymbol{y = 0} \qquad \text{and} \qquad \boldsymbol{y = 8}$$

There are two stationary points—one when $x = 0$ and $y = 0$ and another when $x = 0$ and $y = 8$.

The second derivatives are

$$f_{xx} = -2 \qquad\qquad f_{xy} = 0$$
$$f_{yy} = -6y + 24 \qquad f_{yx} = 0$$

Evaluating $D(x^*, y^*)$ at the first stationary point, we get

$$D(0, 0) = (-2)[-6(0) + 24] - 0^2$$
$$= (-2)(24) - 0$$
$$= -48 < 0$$

Therefore, a saddle point occurs when $x = 0$ and $y = 0$. For the other stationary point,

$$D(0, 8) = (-2)[-6(8) + 24] - 0^2$$
$$= (-2)(-24)$$
$$= 48 > 0$$

The values of the two pure partial derivatives at the stationary point are $f_{xx}(0, 8) = -2$ and $f_{yy}(0, 8) = -6(8) + 24 = -24$. Since both are negative, we conclude that a relative maximum occurs on the graph of $f(x, y)$ at $x = 0$ and $y = 8$.

Follow-up Exercises

In the following exercises, determine the location of all stationary points, their nature, and the value of $f(x^*, y^*)$.

14.27 $f(x, y) = x^2 - x + 2y^2 - 2y$

14.28 $f(x, y) = 2x^2 - 20x + y^2 - 30y + 10$

14.29 $f(x, y) = -3x^2 + 36x - 2y^2 + 40y$

14.30 $f(x, y) = \dfrac{x^2}{2} + 5x - \dfrac{y^2}{4} - 3y - 5$

14.31 $f(x, y) = -2x^2 + 8x + 3y^2 - 6y$

14.32 $f(x, y) = \dfrac{x^2}{4} - 2x - \dfrac{y^2}{3} + 6y$

14.33 $f(x, y) = x^2 - 3xy + 5x + 2y^2 - 6y$

14.34 $f(x, y) = 2x^2 + 5xy - 19x - 4y^2 + 19y$

14.35 $f(x, y) = 10x^2 - 10xy - 30x + 8y^2 + 37y$

14.36 $f(x, y) = -4x^2 + 6xy + 22x - 6y^2 + 6y$

14.37 $f(x, y) = -x^3 + 24x^2 - 4y^2 + 100$

14.38 $f(x, y) = 10x^2 + 2y^3 - 30y^2$

14.39 $f(x, y) = x^2 + 4xy - xy^2$

14.4   APPLICATIONS OF BIVARIATE OPTIMIZATION

This section presents some applications of the optimization of bivariate functions.

Example 14.15   **Advertising Expenditures** Example 14.6 involved a manufacturer who estimated annual sales (in units) to be a function of the expenditures made for radio and TV advertising. The function specifying this relationship was stated as

$$z = 50,000x + 40,000y - 10x^2 - 20y^2 - 10xy$$

where z equals the number of units sold each year, x equals the amount spent for TV advertising, and y equals the amount spent for radio advertising (x and y both in \$1,000s). Determine how much money should be spent on TV and radio in order to maximize the number of units sold.

Solution

The first partial derivatives are

$$f_x = 50,000 - 20x - 10y$$
$$f_y = 40,000 - 40y - 10x$$

Rearranging the derivative expressions and setting them equal to 0, we have

$$20x + 10y = 50,000$$
$$10x + 40y = 40,000$$

If both sides of the second equation are multiplied by -2 and the result is added to the first equation, then

$$
\begin{aligned}
20x + 10y &= 50,000 \\
-20x - 80y &= -80,000 \\
\hline
-70y &= 30,000 \\
y &= \mathbf{428.57}
\end{aligned}
$$

Substituting y into one of the original equations yields

$$
\begin{aligned}
20x + 10(428.57) &= 50,000 \\
20x &= 50,000 - 4,285.7 \\
20x &= 45,714.3 \\
x &= \mathbf{2,285.72}
\end{aligned}
$$

Thus a stationary point occurs on the graph of $f(x, y)$ when $x = 2,285.72$ and $y = 428.57$.

The second derivatives are

$$f_{xx} = -20 \qquad f_{xy} = -10$$
$$f_{yy} = -40 \qquad f_{yx} = -10$$

Testing the stationary point, we find

$$
\begin{aligned}
D(2,285.72, 428.57) &= (-20)(-40) - (-10)^2 \\
&= 800 - 100 \\
&= 700 > 0
\end{aligned}
$$

Since $D > 0$ and both f_{xx} and f_{yy} are negative, we can conclude that annual sales are maximized when 2,285.72 (\$1,000s) is spent for TV advertising and 428.57 (\$1,000s) is spent for radio advertising.

Expected annual sales are estimated as

$$
\begin{aligned}
f(2,285.72, 428.57) &= 50,000(2,285.72) + 40,000(428.57) \\
&\quad - 10(2,285.72)^2 - 20(428.57)^2 \\
&\quad - 10(2,285.72)(428.57) \\
&= 65,714,296.00 \text{ units}
\end{aligned}
$$

Example 14.16 **Pricing Model** A manufacturer sells two related products, the demand for which is characterized by the following two demand functions:

$$q_1 = 150 - 2p_1 - p_2 \tag{14.13}$$
$$q_2 = 200 - p_1 - 3p_2 \tag{14.14}$$

where p_j equals the price (in dollars) of product j and q_j equals the demand (in thousands of units) for product j. Examination of these demand functions indicates that the two products are related. The demand for one product depends not only on the price charged for the product itself but also on the price charged for the other product.

The firm wants to determine the price it should charge for each product in order to maximize total revenue from the sale of the two products.

Solution This problem is exactly like the single-product problems discussed in Chap. 13. The only difference is that there are two products and two pricing decisions to be made.

Total revenue from selling the two products is determined by the equation

$$R = p_1 q_1 + p_2 q_2 \tag{14.15}$$

This equation, however, is stated in terms of four variables. But, as with the single-product problems, we can substitute the right side of Eqs. (14.13) and (14.14) into Eq. (14.15) to yield

$$
\begin{aligned}
R &= f(p_1, p_2) \\
&= p_1(150 - 2p_1 - p_2) + p_2(200 - p_1 - 3p_2) \\
&= 150p_1 - 2p_1^2 - p_1 p_2 + 200p_2 - p_1 p_2 - 3p_2^2 \\
&= 150p_1 - 2p_1^2 - 2p_1 p_2 + 200p_2 - 3p_2^2
\end{aligned}
$$

We can now proceed to examine the revenue surface for relative maximum points.

The first partial derivatives are

$$f_{p_1} = 150 - 4p_1 - 2p_2$$
$$f_{p_2} = -2p_1 + 200 - 6p_2$$

Rearranging these derivative expressions and setting them equal to 0, we have

$$4p_1 + 2p_2 = 150 \tag{14.16}$$
$$2p_1 + 6p_2 = 200 \tag{14.17}$$

If Eq. (14.16) is multiplied by -2 and added to Eq. (14.16), we get

$$
\begin{aligned}
4p_1 + 2p_2 &= 150 \\
-4p_1 - 12p_2 &= -400 \\
\hline
-10p_2 &= -250 \\
p_2 &= \mathbf{25}
\end{aligned}
$$

Substituting $p_2 = 25$ into Eq. (14.16) yields

$$
\begin{aligned}
4p_1 + 2(25) &= 150 \\
4p_1 &= 100 \\
\boldsymbol{p_1} &= \mathbf{25}
\end{aligned}
$$

Thus, a stationary point occurs on the graph of the revenue function when $p_1 = 25$ and $p_2 = 25$.

The second derivatives are

$$f_{p_1 p_1} = -4 \qquad f_{p_1 p_2} = -2$$
$$f_{p_2 p_2} = -6 \qquad f_{p_2 p_1} = -2$$

And,

$$D(25, 25) = (-4)(-6) - (-2)^2$$
$$= 24 - 4$$
$$= 20 > 0$$

Since $D(x^*, y^*) > 0$ and $f_{p_1 p_1}$ and $f_{p_2 p_2}$ are both negative, a relative maximum exists on $f(p_1, p_2)$ when $p_1 = 25$ and $p_2 = 25$. In order to maximize total revenue, each product should sell for \$25. Expected demand at these prices can be determined by substituting p_1 and p_2 into the demand equations, or

$$q_1 = 150 - 2(25) - (25) = 75 \text{ (thousand units)}$$
$$q_2 = 200 - (25) - 3(25) = 100 \text{ (thousand units)}$$

Maximum total revenue can be determined by substituting p_1 and p_2 into the total revenue function. Or, since we know the price and expected demand for each product, we can use Eq. (14.15):

$$R = (25)(75) + (25)(100)$$
$$= 1,875 + 2,500$$
$$= 4,375(\$1,000\text{s}) \text{ or } \$4,375,000$$

Warehouse Location   A large food chain is planning to locate a warehouse in a region of upstate New York. This warehouse will supply three major cities, the relative locations of which are indicated in Fig. 14.10. The firm wants to select a preliminary site by using the following criterion: determine the location (x, y) which minimizes the *sum of the squares* of the distances from each city to the warehouse.

Example 14.17

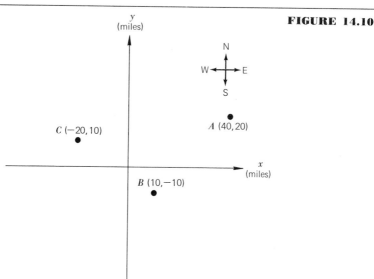

FIGURE 14.10

Solution   The unknowns in this problem are x and y, the coordinates of the warehouse location. We need to determine an expression for the square of the distance separating the warehouse and each of the cities. The Pythagorean theorem provides this for us. Given two points (x_1, y_1) and (x_2, y_2), the square of the distance d separating these two points is found by using the equation

$$d^2 = (x_2 - x_1)^2 + (y_2 - y_1)^2 \qquad \text{(14.18)}$$

To illustrate, the square of the distance separating the warehouse with location (x, y) and city A located at $(40, 20)$ is

$$d^2 = (x - 40)^2 + (y - 20)^2$$

Finding similar expressions for the square of the distance separating cities B and C and the warehouse and summing for the three cities, we get

$$s = f(x, y)$$
$$= [(x - 40)^2 + (y - 20)^2] + [(x - 10)^2 + (y + 10)^2]$$
$$+ [(x + 20)^2 + (y - 10)^2]$$

The right side of this function may be expanded or left in this form for purposes of taking derivatives. Let's leave it as it is. The first partial derivatives are

$$f_x = 2(x - 40)(1) + 2(x - 10)(1) + 2(x + 20)(1)$$
$$= 2x - 80 + 2x - 20 + 2x + 40$$
$$= 6x - 60$$
$$f_y = 2(y - 20)(1) + 2(y + 10)(1) + 2(y - 10)(1)$$
$$= 2y - 40 + 2y + 20 + 2y - 20$$
$$= 6y - 40$$

If the two partial derivatives are set equal to 0, we find that a stationary point occurs on the graph of $f(x, y)$ when $x = 10$ and $y = 6\frac{2}{3}$. The second partial derivatives are

$$f_{xx} = 6 \qquad f_{xy} = 0$$
$$f_{yy} = 6 \qquad f_{yx} = 0$$
$$D(10, 6\tfrac{2}{3}) = (6)(6) - 0^2 = 36 > 0$$

Since $D > 0$ and f_{xx} and f_{yy} are both greater than 0, we can conclude that a relative minimum occurs on $f(x, y)$ when $x = 10$ and $y = 6\frac{2}{3}$, or when the warehouse is located as indicated in Fig. 14.11.

Example 14.18   **Least-Squares Model**   Organizations gather data regularly on a multitude of variables which are related to their operation. One major area of analysis deals with determining whether there are any patterns to the data—are there any apparent relationships among the variables of interest? For example, the demand functions to which we have con-

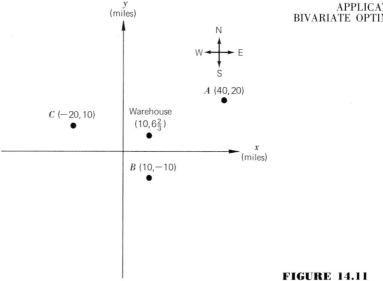

FIGURE 14.11

tinually referred, have most likely been determined by gathering data on the demand for a product at different prices. And, analysis of this data translates into a formal statement of the demand function.

Consider the four data points (x_1, y_1), (x_2, y_2), (x_3, y_3), and (x_4, y_4) in Fig. 14.12, which have been gathered for the variables x and y. Suppose there is evidence suggesting that x and y are related and that the nature of the relationship is linear. And, suppose that we would like to fit a straight line to these points, the equation of which would be used as an approximation of the actual relationship existing between x and y. The

FIGURE 14.12

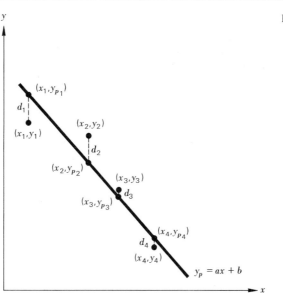

question becomes, What line best fits the data points? There are an infinite number of straight lines which we can attempt to fit to these data points, each having the general form

$$y_p = ax + b \tag{14.19}$$

The difference between each line would be differences in the slope a and/or the y intercept b. Note that y has a subscript of p in Eq. (14.19). This is because the line fit to the data points can be used to *predict* values of y, given a known value of x.

In Fig. 14.12, the predicted values of y, given the x coordinates of the four data points, are indicated on the line. The vertical distance separating the actual data point and the corresponding point on the line is a measure of the error introduced by using the line to predict the location of the data point. The error, indicated by the d_j values in Fig. 14.12, is called the *deviation* between the actual value of y and the predicted value of y for the jth data point, or

$$d_j = y_j - y_{p_j}$$

Given that we wish to find the "best" line to fit to the data points, the next question is, How do you define *best*? One of the most popular methods of finding the line of best fit is the least-squares model. The least-squares model defines *best* as the line which minimizes the sum of the squared deviations for all the data points. In Fig. 14.12 we would seek the line which minimizes

$$S = d_1^2 + d_2^2 + d_3^2 + d_4^2$$
$$= \sum_{j=1}^{4} d_j^2$$
$$= \sum_{j=1}^{4} (y_j - y_{p_j})^2 \tag{14.20}$$

For any line $y_{p_j} = ax_j + b$ chosen to fit the data points, Eq. (14.20) can be rewritten as

$$S = f(a, b)$$
$$= \sum_{j=1}^{4} [y_j - (ax_j + b)]^2 \tag{14.21}$$

For any straight line having slope a and y intercept b, the sum of the squared deviations S can be determined. The least-squares model seeks the values of a and b which result in a minimum value for S.

Consider the simple case where a firm has collected three price-demand data points. Table 14.3 indicates the price-quantity combinations. Figure 14.13 is a graph of their locations. Suppose that we wish to determine the line of best fit to these data points using the least-squares model. The least-squares function is generated by using Eq. (14.21).

Table 14.3			
y (Demand in thousands of units)	50	30	20
x (Price in dollars)	5	10	15

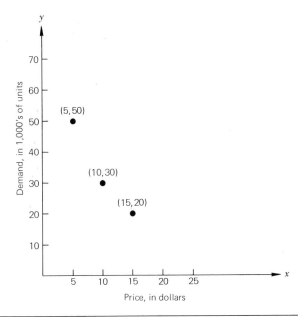

FIGURE 14.13

$$S = f(a, b)$$
$$= \sum_{j=1}^{3} [y_j - (ax_j + b)]^2$$
$$= [50 - (5a + b)]^2 + [30 - (10a + b)]^2 + [20 - (15a + b)]^2$$

To determine the values of a and b which minimize S, we find the partial derivatives with respect to a and b.

$$
\begin{aligned}
f_a &= 2[50 - (5a + b)](-5) + 2[30 - (10a + b)](-10) \\
&\quad + 2[20 - (15a + b)](-15) \\
&= -500 + 50a + 10b - 600 + 200a + 20b - 600 + 450a + 30b \\
&= 700a + 60b - 1{,}700 \\
f_b &= 2[50 - (5a + b)](-1) + 2[30 - (10a + b)](-1) \\
&\quad + 2[20 - (15a + b)](-1) \\
&= -100 + 10a + 2b - 60 + 20a + 2b - 40 + 30a + 2b \\
&= 60a + 6b - 200
\end{aligned}
$$

If these two derivatives are set equal to 0, these two equations result:

$$700a + 60b = 1{,}700 \qquad (14.22)$$
$$60a + 6b = 200 \qquad (14.23)$$

Multiplying the second equation by -10 and adding it to the first equation yield

$$
\begin{aligned}
700a + 60b &= 1{,}700 \\
-600a - 60b &= -2{,}000 \\
\hline
100a &= -300 \\
\boldsymbol{a} &= \boldsymbol{-3}
\end{aligned}
$$

Substituting $a = 3$ into Eq. (14.23) yields

$$
\begin{aligned}
60(-3) + 6b &= 200 \\
6b &= 380 \\
\boldsymbol{b} &= \boldsymbol{63\tfrac{1}{3}}
\end{aligned}
$$

To verify that the stationary point results in a minimum value for S,

$$f_{aa} = 700 \qquad f_{ab} = 60$$
$$f_{bb} = 6 \qquad f_{ba} = 60$$
$$D(-3, 63\tfrac{1}{3}) = (700)(6) - (60)^2$$
$$= 4,200 - 3,600$$
$$= 600 > 0$$

Since $D > 0$ and both f_{aa} and f_{bb} are positive, we can conclude that the sum of the squares of the deviations S is minimized when $a = -3$ and $b = 63\tfrac{1}{3}$, or when the data points are fit with a straight line having a slope of -3 and y intercept of $63\tfrac{1}{3}$. The equation of this line is

$$y_p = -3x + 63\tfrac{1}{3}$$

Follow-up Exercises

14.40 A manufacturer estimates that annual sales (in units) are a function of the expenditures made for TV and radio advertising. The function specifying the relationship is

$$z = 20,000x + 30,000y - 5x^2 - 10y^2 - 10xy$$

where z equals the number of units sold each year, x equals the amount spent for TV advertising, and y equals the amount spent for radio advertising (both x and y in \$1,000s).
(a) Determine how much should be spent for radio and TV advertising in order to maximize the number of units sold.
(b) What is the maximum number of units expected to equal?
14.41 A company sells two products. Total revenue from the two products is estimated to be a function of the numbers of units sold of the two products. Specifically, the function is

$$R = 10,000x + 5,000y - 10x^2 - 10y^2 - 10xy$$

where R equals total revenue and x and y equal the numbers of units sold of the two products.
(a) How many units of each product should be produced in order to maximize total revenue?
(b) What is the maximum revenue?
14.42 A firm sells two products. The demand functions for the two products are

$$q_1 = 300 - 2p_1 - p_2$$
$$q_2 = 300 - 2p_1 - 3p_2$$

where p_j equals the price of product j and q_j equals the demand (in thousands of units) for product j.
(a) Determine the price which should be charged for each product in order to maximize total revenue from the two products.
(b) How many units will be demanded of each product at these prices?
(c) What is maximum total revenue expected to equal?
14.43 A company is planning to locate a warehouse which will supply three major department stores. The relative locations of the three department stores on a set of coordinate axes are (40, 10), (0, 30), and $(-10, -20)$ where the coordinates are stated in miles. Figure 14.14 indi-

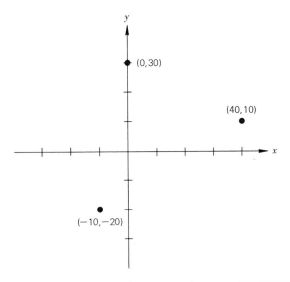

FIGURE 14.14

cates the relative locations of the department stores. Determine the warehouse location (x, y) which minimizes the sum of the squares of the distances from each city to the warehouse.

14.44 *Airport Location.* A new airport is being planned to service four metropolitan areas. The relative locations of the metropolitan areas on a set of coordinate axes are $(20, 5)$, $(0, 30)$, $(10, -10)$, and $(-5, -5)$, where the coordinates are stated in miles. Figure 14.15 indicates the relative locations of the four cities. Determine the airport location (x, y) which minimizes the sum of the squares of the distances from the airport to each metropolitan area.

14.45 In Example 14.17, assume that the number of tons of grocery products expected to be delivered weekly to the three cities equals 200, 400, and 300, respectively, for cities A, B, and C. Also assume that the firm wishes to determine the location (x, y) which minimizes the sum of

FIGURE 14.15

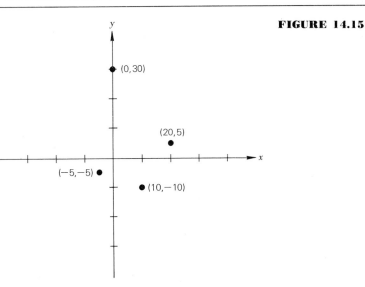

the products of the weekly demand at each city *times* the square of the distance separating the city and the warehouse. This objective can be stated as

minimize
$$\sum_{j=1}^{3} v_j d_j^2$$

where v_j equals the weekly volume for city j and d_j equals the distance from city j to the warehouse. Determine the location of the warehouse.
14.46 Given the price-demand data points in Table 14.4, determine the equation of the line of best fit to these data points using the least-squares model.

Table 14.4

y (Demand in thousands of units)	100	80	60
x (Price in dollars)	10	20	30

CHAPTER CHECKLIST

If you have read *all* the sections of this chapter, you should

_____ Have some familiarity with the graphics of *bivariate functions*, including an understanding of the meaning of a *trace*

_____ Know how to find *first* and *second partial derivatives*

_____ Be able to interpret the meaning of first partial derivatives and understand the information conveyed by pure second partial derivatives

_____ Understand the meaning of stationary points for bivariate functions, know how to locate them, and be able to determine their nature

_____ Be familiar with some applications of bivariate optimization

KEY TERMS AND CONCEPTS

multivariate functions	saddle point
bivariate functions	pure second partial derivatives
trace	mixed or cross partial derivatives
partial derivative	stationary point

IMPORTANT FORMULAS

$$D(x^*, y^*) = f_{xx}(x^*, y^*)f_{yy}(x^*, y^*) - [f_{xy}(x^*, y^*)]^2 \qquad (14.12)$$

ADDITIONAL EXERCISES

Exercises 14.47 to 14.62 are related to Sec. 14.2.

In Exercises 14.47 to 14.56, determine f_x and f_y.

14.47 $f(x, y) = 4x^4y^4$
14.48 $f(x, y) = -(xy)^3 + xy + 5y^2 + 3$

14.49 $f(x, y) = 3x^2y + xy^2 - 2y + 2$

14.50 $f(x, y) = -2x^4y + x^3y^2 - 3x^2y^3 + x + 2$

14.51 $f(x, y) = \dfrac{x^4}{2} + 5x^3y^3 + 2x^2y + 4xy$

14.52 $f(x, y) = (2x + y^4)^2$

14.53 $f(x, y) = \left(\dfrac{x^4}{4} - \dfrac{2y^5}{5}\right)^3$ **14.54** $f(x, y) = (y^2 - 4)(\ln x)$

14.55 $f(x, y) = e^x(1 + e^y)$ **14.56** $f(x, y) = e^{x^2y}$

In Exercises 14.57 to 14.62, determine all second partial derivatives.

14.57 $f(x, y) = x^5y^4/10$ **14.58** $f(x, y) = 3x + 4x^3y + y^2$

14.59 $f(x, y) = 2x^2/(y^2 + 2)$ **14.60** $f(x, y) = e^{2x^2+y}$

14.61 $f(x, y) = x^2(\ln y)$ **14.62** $f(x, y) = (x + y)^3$

Exercises 14.63 to 14.69 are related to Sec. 14.3.

In Exercises 14.63 to 14.69, determine the location of all stationary points, their nature, and the value of $f(x^*, y^*)$.

14.63 $f(x, y) = x^2 + y^2 - xy + 3x$

14.64 $f(x, y) = -x^2 + 3x + \dfrac{y^3}{3} + 2y^2$

14.65 $f(x, y) = 3x^2 - 2xy + 10y + y^2 + 2x$

14.66 $f(x, y) = \dfrac{2x^3}{3} + 2x^2y - 8y + 11$

14.67 $f(x, y) = x^3 + \dfrac{5x^2}{2} + 8xy - 2y^2 + 15$

14.68 $f(x, y) = 5x^2 + 2xy + 3y^2 - 30y - 10x + 8$

14.69 $f(x, y) = -4x^2 + 3y^2 + 2xy + 5x + 2y$

Exercises 14.70 to 14.72 are related to Sec. 14.4.

14.70 A firm sells two products. The annual total revenue R behaves as a function of the number of units sold. Specifically,

$$R = 400x - 4x^2 + 1,960y - 8y^2$$

where x and y equal, respectively, the number of units sold of each product. The cost of producing the two products is

$$C = 100 + 2x^2 + 4y^2 + 2xy$$

(a) Determine the number of units which should be produced and sold in order to maximize annual profit.

(b) What does total revenue equal?

(c) What do total costs equal?

(d) What is the maximum profit?

14.71 Given the four data points (1, 2.5), (−2, 17.5), (4, −12.5), and (−1, 12.5), determine the equation of the line of best fit using the least-squares model.

*****14.72** A rectangular container is being designed which is to have a volume of 8,000 cubic inches. The objective is to minimize the amount of material used in constructing the container. Thus, the surface area is to be minimized. If x, y, and z represent the dimensions of the container (in inches), determine the dimensions which minimize the surface area. (*Hint:* $V = xyz$.)

CHAPTER TEST

1 Give two interpretations of f_x.

2 What is a *trace*?

3 Determine f_x and f_y if

$$f(x, y) = 5x^3 - 4y^2 + 5x^2y$$

4 Determine all second partial derivatives for the function

$$f(x, y) = 4x^5 + 6x^3 - 3x^2y^2$$

5 Given the function

$$f(x, y) = 3x^2 - 4xy + 3y^2 + 8x - 17y + 5$$

(*a*) Locate any stationary points and determine their nature.

(*b*) What is $f(x^*, y^*)$?

6 A researcher at a college of agriculture estimated that annual profit at a local farm can be described by the function

$$P = 1,200x + 1,600y - 2x^2 - 4y^2 - 4xy$$

where P equals annual profit in dollars, x equals the number of acres planted with soybeans, and y equals the number of acres planted with corn. Determine the number of acres of each crop which should be planted if the objective is to maximize annual profit. What is the expected maximum profit?

CHAPTER OBJECTIVES After reading this chapter, you should
have a general familiarity with integral calculus; you should have a
sense of the relationships that exist between differential calculus and
integral calculus; you should understand how to apply a set of basic
rules of *integration*; you should understand the concept of the *definite integral* and how it can be used to calculate areas; and you should
have an acquaintance with some areas of application of integral calculus.

In this chapter we will survey a second major area of study within the
calculus—*integral calculus*. As was mentioned at the beginning of
Chap. 11, differential calculus is useful in considering rates of change
and tangent slopes. An important concern of integral calculus is the
determination of areas which occur between curves and other defined
boundaries. Also, if the derivative of an unknown function is known,
integral calculus may provide a way of determining the original function.

As we begin this new area of study, it will be of value to know where
we are headed. First, integral calculus comprises a major area of study
within the calculus. We will devote only one chapter to this material.
The purpose is to survey the area in such a way that you have a feeling
for the concerns of integral calculus, how integral calculus relates to differential calculus, and where it can be applied.

In this chapter the nature of integral calculus will be introduced first by relating it to derivatives. As there were rules for finding derivatives in differential calculus, there are rules for finding *integrals* in integral calculus. These rules will be presented in Sec. 15.2. The next section will discuss the use of integral calculus in determining areas. This section will be followed by one which presents sample applications of integral calculus. The final section in the chapter will discuss specialized techniques for finding integrals when the set of rules presented earlier is not adequate.

15.1   ANTIDERIVATIVES

The Antiderivative Concept

Given a function $f(x)$, we are acquainted with how to find the derivative $f'(x)$. There may be occasions in which we are given the derivative $f'(x)$ and wish to determine the original function $f(x)$. Since the process of finding the original function is the reverse of differentiation, $f(x)$ is said to be an *antiderivative* of $f'(x)$.

Consider the derivative

$$f'(x) = 4 \tag{15.1}$$

By using a trial-and-error approach, it is not very difficult to conclude that the function

$$f(x) = 4x \tag{15.2}$$

has a derivative of the form of Eq. (15.1). Another function having the same derivative is

$$f(x) = 4x + 1$$

In fact, any function having the form

$$f(x) = 4x + C \tag{15.3}$$

where C equals a constant, will have the same derivative. Thus, given the derivative in Eq. (15.1), our conclusion is that the original function was one of the *family* of functions characterized by Eq. (15.3). This family of functions is a set of linear functions whose members all have a slope of $+4$ but different y intercepts C. Figure 15.1 illustrates selected members of this family of functions.

We can also state that the function

$$f(x) = 4x + C$$

is the *antiderivative* of

$$f'(x) = 4$$

Example 15.1

Find the antiderivative of $f'(x) = 0$.

Solution

We know that the derivative of any constant function is 0. Therefore the antiderivative is $f(x) = C$.

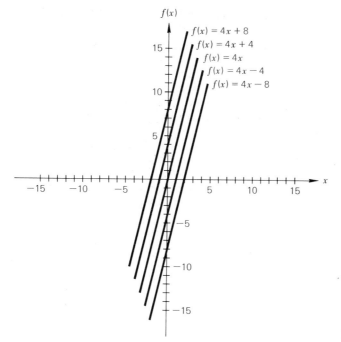

$f(x) = 4x + 8$
$f(x) = 4x + 4$
$f(x) = 4x$
$f(x) = 4x - 4$
$f(x) = 4x - 8$

FIGURE 15.1

Find the antiderivative of $f'(x) = 2x - 5$.

Example 15.2

Using a trial-and-error approach and working with each term separately, you should conclude that the antiderivative is

Solution

$$f(x) = x^2 - 5x + C$$

NOTE
An easy check on your antiderivative $f(x)$ is to differentiate it to determine $f'(x)$.

With additional information it may be possible to determine the precise function from which $f'(x)$ was derived. Assume for the original example that we are told that one point on the original function is (2,6). Since the coordinates of this point must satisfy the equation of the original function, we can solve for the y intercept C by substituting $x = 2$ and $f(x) = 6$ into Eq. (15.3), or

$$6 = 4(2) + C$$
$$-2 = C$$

Therefore, the specific member of the family of functions characterized by Eq. (15.3) is

$$f(x) = 4x - 2$$

Example 15.3 Assume in Example 15.1 that one point on the function $f(x)$ is $(-2, 5)$. Determine the specific function from which $f'(x)$ was derived.

Solution The antiderivative describing the family of possible functions was

$$f(x) = C$$

Substituting $x = -2$ and $f(x) = 5$ into this equation gives

$$5 = C$$

Thus, the specific function is $f(x) = 5$.

Example 15.4 Assume in Example 15.2 that one point on the function $f(x)$ is $(2, 20)$. Determine the specific function from which $f'(x)$ was derived.

Solution The antiderivative describing the family of possible functions was

$$f(x) = x^2 - 5x + C$$

Substituting $x = 2$ and $f(x) = 20$ into this equation, we have

$$20 = 2^2 - 5(2) + C$$
$$20 = -6 + C$$
$$26 = C$$

Thus the original function is

$$f(x) = x^2 - 5x + 26$$

Revenue and Cost Functions

In Chap. 13 we discussed the "marginal approach" for determining the profit-maximizing level of output. We stated that an expression for marginal revenue (MR) is the derivative of the total revenue function where the independent variable is the level of output. Similarly, we said that an expression for marginal cost (MC) is the derivative of the total cost function. If we have an expression for either marginal revenue or marginal cost, the respective antiderivatives will be the total revenue and total cost functions.

Example 15.5 **Marginal Revenue** The marginal revenue function for a company's product is

$$MR = 50,000 - x$$

where x equals the number of units produced and sold. If total revenue equals 0 when no units are sold, determine the total revenue function for the product.

Solution Because the marginal revenue function is the derivative of the total revenue function, the total revenue function is the antiderivative of MR. Using a trial-and-error approach gives

$$R(x) = 50,000x - \frac{x^2}{2} + C \qquad (15.4)$$

Since we are told that $R(0) = 0$, substitution of $x = 0$ into Eq. (15.4) yields

$$0 = 50,000(0) - \frac{0^2}{2} + C$$

or $0 = C$

Thus, the total revenue function for the company's product is

$$R(x) = 50,000x - \frac{x^2}{2}$$

Marginal Cost The function describing the marginal cost of producing a product is

$$MC = x + 100$$

where x equals the number of units produced. It is also known that total cost equals \$40,000 when $x = 100$. Determine the total cost function.

Example 15.6

To determine the total cost function, we must first find the antiderivative of the marginal cost function, or

Solution

$$C(x) = \frac{x^2}{2} + 100x + C \qquad (15.5)$$

Given that $C(100) = 40,000$, we can solve for the value of C, which happens to represent the fixed cost.

$$40,000 = \frac{(100)^2}{2} + 100(100) + C$$

$$40,000 = 5,000 + 10,000 + C$$

or $25,000 = C$

The specific function representing the total cost of producing the product is

$$C(x) = \frac{x^2}{2} + 100x + 25,000$$

Follow-up Exercises

In Exercises 15.1 to 15.8, determine the antiderivative of the given function.

15.1 $f'(x) = 2.5$ **15.2** $f'(x) = -5$
15.3 $f'(x) = -3x$ **15.4** $f'(x) = x/2$
15.5 $f'(x) = x^2$ **15.6** $f'(x) = x^3/3$
15.7 $f'(x) = x^2/2 + 5x - 2$
15.8 $f'(x) = x^3 + 2x^2 - 4x + 10$

In Exercises 15.9 to 15.14, determine $f(x)$ given $f'(x)$ and a point which satisfies $f(x)$.

15.9 $f'(x) = 7.5$; (1, 10)   **15.10** $f'(x) = 3x$; (2, 1)
15.11 $f'(x) = -x/2$; (4, 6)   **15.12** $f'(x) = x^2$; (3, 0)

15.13 $f'(x) = -x^2 + 2x$; (3, 12)   **15.14** $f'(x) = x^3 - 5x$; (2, 56)

15.15 The marginal revenue function for a company's product is

$$MR = 40,000 - 2x$$

where x equals the number of units sold. If total revenue equals 0 when no units are sold, determine the total revenue function for the product.

15.16 The function describing the marginal cost (in dollars) of producing a product is

$$MC = 2x + 300$$

where x equals the number of units produced. It is known that total cost equals $27,500 when 50 units are produced. Determine the total cost function.

15.17 The function describing the *marginal profit* from producing and selling a product is

$$MP = -2x + 500$$

where x equals the number of units and MP is the marginal profit measured in dollars. When 100 units are produced and sold, *total profit* equals $35,000. Determine the total profit function.

15.2   RULES OF INTEGRATION

Fortunately, we need not resort to a trial-and-error approach whenever we wish to identify an antiderivative. As with differentiation, a set of rules has been developed for finding antiderivatives. If a function has a particular form, a rule may be available which allows one to determine its antiderivative very easily. This is exactly how our rules of differentiation were applied.

Integration

The process of finding antiderivatives is more frequently called *integration*. And the family of functions obtained through this process is called the *indefinite integral*. The notation

$$\int f(x)\, dx \qquad (15.6)$$

is often used to indicate the indefinite integral of the function $f(x)$. The symbol $\int$ is the *integral sign*, $f(x)$ is the *integrand*, or the function for which we want to find the indefinite integral, and dx, as we will deal with it, indicates the variable with respect to which the integration process is performed. Two verbal descriptions of Eq. (15.6) are "integrate the function $f(x)$ with respect to the variable x" and "find the indefinite integral of $f(x)$ with respect to x."

NOTE
Keep in mind that finding an indefinite integral is the same as finding an antiderivative.

In Example 15.2 we found that the antiderivative of $2x - 5$ is $x^2 - 5x + C$. We can denote this, using integral notation, as

$$\int (2x - 5)\, dx = x^2 - 5x + C$$

A more formal definition of the indefinite integral follows.

DEFINITION
Given that $f(x)$ is a continuous function,

$$\int f(x)\, dx = F(x) + C \qquad (15.7)$$

if $F'(x) = f(x)$.

In this definition C is termed the *constant of integration*.

Rules of Integration

Following are a set of rules for finding the indefinite integral of some functional forms common in business and economics applications.

RULE 1: CONSTANT FUNCTIONS

$$\int k\, dx = kx + C \qquad \text{where } k \text{ is real}$$

Example 15.7 illustrates this rule.

(a) $\displaystyle\int (-2)\, dx = -2x + C$

(b) $\displaystyle\int \tfrac{3}{2}\, dx = \tfrac{3}{2}x + C$

(c) $\displaystyle\int \sqrt{2}\, dx = \sqrt{2}x + C$

(d) $\displaystyle\int 0\, dx = (0)x + C = C$

Example 15.7

RULE 2: POWER RULE

$$\int x^n\, dx = \frac{x^{n+1}}{n + 1} + C, \qquad n \neq -1$$

This rule is analogous to the power rule of differentiation. Note that this rule is not valid when $n = -1$. We will treat this exception shortly. Verbally, the rule states that when the integrand is x raised to some real-valued exponent, increase the exponent of x by 1, divide by the new exponent, and add the constant of integration. Example 15.8 provides several illustrations of this rule.

Example 15.8

(a) $\int x \, dx = \dfrac{x^2}{2} + C$

(b) $\int x^2 \, dx = \dfrac{x^3}{3} + C$

(c) $\int \sqrt{x} \, dx = \int x^{1/2} \, dx = \dfrac{x^{3/2}}{\frac{3}{2}} + C$

$\qquad\qquad\qquad\quad = \frac{2}{3}x^{3/2} + C$

(d) $\int \dfrac{1}{x^3} \, dx = \int x^{-3} \, dx = \dfrac{x^{-2}}{-2} + C$

$\qquad\qquad\quad = \dfrac{-1}{2x^2} + C$

NOTE
Do not forget the built-in checking mechanism. It takes only a few seconds and may save you from careless errors. Find the derivative of the indefinite integrals found above and see if they equal the respective integrands. Some algebraic manipulation may be needed to verify these results.

RULE 3

$\int kf(x) \, dx = k \int f(x) \, dx$ $\qquad$ where k is a real-valued constant

Verbally, this rule states that the indefinite integral of a constant k times a function $f(x)$ is found by multiplying the constant by the indefinite integral of $f(x)$. Another way of viewing this rule is to say that whenever a *constant* can be factored from the integrand, the constant may also be factored out of the integral. Example 15.9 provides some illustrations of this rule.

Example 15.9

(a) $\int 5x \, dx = 5 \int x \, dx$

$\qquad\qquad = 5 \left(\dfrac{x^2}{2} + C_1 \right)$

$$= \frac{5x^2}{2} + 5C_1$$

$$= \frac{5x^2}{2} + C$$

If $f(x) = \dfrac{5x^2}{2} + C$, $f'(x) = \frac{5}{2}(2x) = 5x$ ✔ **Check**

NOTE
With indefinite integrals we always include the constant of integration. In using Rule 3, the algebra suggests that any constant k factored out of the integral will be multiplied by the constant of integration (e.g., the $5C_1$ term in this example). This multiplication is unnecessary. We simply need a constant of integration to indicate the "indefinite nature" of the integral. Thus, the convention is to add C and not a multiple of C. In the last step the $5C_1$ term is rewritten as just C, since C can represent any constant as well as $5C_1$.

(b) $\displaystyle\int \frac{x^2}{2}\, dx = \int \tfrac{1}{2}x^2\, dx$

$$= \tfrac{1}{2} \int x^2\, dx$$

$$= \frac{1}{2} \frac{x^3}{3} + C$$

$$= \frac{x^3}{6} + C$$

If $f(x) = \dfrac{x^3}{6} + C$, $f'(x) = \dfrac{3x^2}{6} = \dfrac{x^2}{2}$ ✔ **Check**

(c) $\displaystyle\int \frac{3}{\sqrt{x}}\, dx = \int 3x^{-1/2}\, dx$

$$= 3 \int x^{-1/2}\, dx$$

$$= 3\frac{x^{1/2}}{\frac{1}{2}} + C$$

$$= 6x^{1/2} + C$$

If $f(x) = 6x^{1/2} + C$, $f'(x) = 6(\tfrac{1}{2})x^{-1/2}$ **Check**

$$= \frac{3}{x^{1/2}}$$

$$= \frac{3}{\sqrt{x}}$$ ✔

RULE 4

$$\int [f(x) \pm g(x)]\, dx = \int f(x)\, dx \pm \int g(x)\, dx$$

The integral of the sum (difference) of two functions is the sum (difference) of their respective integrals.

Example 15.10

(a) $\displaystyle \int (3x - 6)\, dx = \int 3x\, dx - \int 6\, dx$

$$= \frac{3x^2}{2} + C_1 - (6x + C_2)$$

$$= \frac{3x^2}{2} - 6x + C$$

Note again that even though the two integrals technically result in separate constants of integration, these constants may be considered together as one.

Check

If $f(x) = \dfrac{3x^2}{2} - 6x + C$, $f'(x) = 3x - 6$ ✔

(b) $\displaystyle \int (4x^2 - 7x + 6)\, dx = \int 4x^2\, dx - \int 7x\, dx + \int 6\, dx$

$$= \frac{4x^3}{3} - \frac{7x^2}{2} + 6x + C$$

Check

If $f(x) = \dfrac{4x^3}{3} - \dfrac{7x^2}{2} + 6x + C$, $f'(x) = \dfrac{12x^2}{3} - \dfrac{14x}{2} + 6$

$$= 4x^2 - 7x + 6 \text{ ✔}$$

RULE 5: POWER-RULE EXCEPTION

$$\int x^{-1}\, dx = \ln x + C$$

This is the exception associated with Rule 2 (the power rule) where $n = -1$ for x^n. Remember our differentiation rules? If $f(x) = \ln x$, $f'(x) = 1/x = x^{-1}$.

RULE 6

$$\int e^x\, dx = e^x + C$$

RULE 7

$$\int [f(x)]^n f'(x)\, dx = \frac{[f(x)]^{n+1}}{n+1} + C$$

where $n \neq -1$

This rule is similar to the power rule (Rule 2). In fact, the power rule is the special case of this rule where $f(x) = x$. If the integrand consists of the product of a function $f(x)$ raised to a power n and the derivative of $f(x)$, the indefinite integral is found by increasing the exponent of $f(x)$ by 1 and dividing by the new exponent.

Evaluate $\int (5x - 3)^3(5)\, dx$.

Example 15.11

As soon as you identify an integrand which contains a function raised to a power, you should immediately think of Rule 7. The first step is to define the function $f(x)$. In this case, the function which is raised to the third power is

$$f(x) = 5x - 3$$

Once $f(x)$ has been defined, $f'(x)$ should be determined. In this case

$$f'(x) = 5$$

If the integrand has the form $[f(x)]^n f'(x)$, then Rule 7 applies. The integrand in this example *does* have the required form, and

$$\int (5x - 3)^3(5)\, dx = \frac{(5x - 3)^4}{4} + C$$

Solution

If $f(x) = \dfrac{(5x - 3)^4}{4}$, $f'(x) = \frac{4}{4}(5x - 3)^3(5)$

$$= (5x - 3)^3(5) \checkmark$$

Check

Evaluate $\int \sqrt{2x^2 - 6}(4)\, dx$.

Example 15.12

The integrand can be rewritten as

$$\int (2x^2 - 6)^{1/2}(4)\, dx$$

Referring to Rule 7, we have

$$f(x) = 2x^2 - 6 \quad \text{and} \quad f'(x) = 4x$$

For Rule 7 to apply, $(2x^2 - 6)^{1/2}$ should be multiplied by $f'(x)$, or $4x$, in the integrand. Since the other factor in the integrand is 4 and not $4x$, we cannot evaluate the integral.

Solution

Example 15.13 Evaluate $\int (x^2 - 2x)^5(x - 1) \, dx$.

Solution For this integral

$$f(x) = x^2 - 2x \quad \text{and} \quad f'(x) = 2x - 2$$

Again it seems that the integrand is not in the proper form. To apply Rule 7, the second factor in the integrand should be $2x - 2$, and not $x - 1$. However, recalling Rule 3 and using some algebraic manipulations, we get

$$\int (x^2 - 2x)^5(x - 1) \, dx = \frac{2}{2} \int (x^2 - 2x)^5(x - 1) \, dx$$

$$= \tfrac{1}{2} \int (x^2 - 2x)^5(2)(x - 1) \, dx$$

$$= \tfrac{1}{2} \int (x^2 - 2x)^5(2x - 2) \, dx \qquad (15.8)$$

What we have done is manipulate the integrand into the proper form. Rule 3 indicated that *constants* can be removed to outside the integral sign. Similarly, we can move a constant which is a factor from outside the integral sign to inside. We multiplied the integrand by 2 and offset this multiplication by multiplying the integral by $\tfrac{1}{2}$. Effectively, we have simply multiplied the original integral by $\tfrac{2}{2}$, or 1. Thus, we have changed the appearance of the original integral but not its value.

Evaluating the integral in Eq. (15.8) gives

$$\int (x^2 - 2x)^5(x - 1) \, dx = \tfrac{1}{2} \int (x^2 - 2x)^5(2x - 2) \, dx$$

$$= \tfrac{1}{2} \frac{(x^2 - 2x)^6}{6} + C$$

$$= \frac{(x^2 - 2x)^6}{12} + C$$

Check If $f(x) = \dfrac{(x^2 - 2x)^6}{12}$, $f'(x) = \tfrac{6}{12}(x^2 - 2x)^5(2x - 2)$

$$= \frac{6(x^2 - 2x)^5(2)(x - 1)}{12}$$

$$= (x^2 - 2x)^5(x - 1) \; \checkmark$$

Example 15.14 Evaluate $\int (x^4 - 2x^2)^4(4x^2 - 4) \, dx$.

Solution For this integral

$$f(x) = x^4 - 2x^2 \quad \text{and} \quad f'(x) = 4x^3 - 4x$$

The integrand is not quite in the form of Rule 7. And, there is great temptation to perform the following operations.

$$\int (x^4 - 2x^2)^4(4x^2 - 4)\, dx = \frac{x}{x} \int (x^4 - 2x^2)^4(4x^2 - 4)\, dx$$

$$= \frac{1}{x} \int (x^4 - 2x^2)^4(4x^3 - 4x)\, dx$$

However, we have not discussed any property which allows us to factor *variables* through an integral sign. Constants yes; variables no! Therefore, given our current rules, we cannot evaluate the integral.

RULE 8

$$\int f'(x)e^{f(x)}\, dx = e^{f(x)} + C$$

This rule, as with the previous rule, requires that the integrand be in a very specific form. Rule 6 is actually the special case of this rule when $f(x) = x$.

Evaluate $\int 2xe^{x^2}\, dx$.

Example 15.15

Solution

As soon as you identify an integrand which contains e raised to a power that is a function of x, you should immediately think of Rule 8. As with Rule 7, the next step is to see if the integrand has the form required to apply Rule 8. For this integrand

$$f(x) = x^2 \qquad \text{and} \qquad f'(x) = 2x$$

Refer to Rule 8: the integrand has the appropriate form, and

$$\int 2xe^{x^2}\, dx = e^{x^2} + C$$

If $f(x) = e^{x^2}, f'(x) = e^{x^2}(2x)$ ✔

Evaluate $\int x^2 e^{3x^3}\, dx$.

Example 15.16

Solution

Referring to Rule 8, for this integrand we have

$$f(x) = 3x^3 \qquad \text{and} \qquad f'(x) = 9x^2$$

The integrand is currently not in a form which is suitable for using Rule 8. However,

$$\int x^2 e^{3x^3}\, dx = \frac{9}{9} \int x^2 e^{3x^3}\, dx$$

$$= \tfrac{1}{9} \int 9x^2 e^{3x^3}\, dx$$

$$= \tfrac{1}{9}e^{3x^3} + C$$

If $f(x) = \tfrac{1}{9}e^{3x^3} + C, f'(x) = \tfrac{1}{9}e^{3x^3}(9x^2) = x^2 e^{3x^3}$ ✔

RULE 9

$$\int \frac{f'(x)}{f(x)} \, dx = \ln f(x) + C$$

Example 15.17 Evaluate $\int \frac{6x}{3x^2 - 10} \, dx$.

Solution Referring to Rule 9, we have

$$f(x) = 3x^2 - 10 \quad \text{and} \quad f'(x) = 6x$$

Since the integrand has the form required by Rule 9,

$$\int \frac{6x \, dx}{3x^2 - 10} = \ln (3x^2 - 10) + C$$

Check If $f(x) = \ln (3x^2 - 10) + C$, $f'(x) = \dfrac{6x}{3x^2 - 10}$ ✔

Example 15.18 Evaluate $\int \frac{x - 1}{4x^2 - 8x + 10} \, dx$.

Solution Referring to Rule 9, we have

$$f(x) = 4x^2 - 8x + 10 \quad \text{and} \quad f'(x) = 8x - 8$$

At first glance, the form of the integrand does not seem to comply with that required by Rule 9. However, an algebraic manipulation allows us to rewrite the integrand in the required form, or

$$\int \frac{x - 1}{4x^2 - 8x + 10} \, dx = \frac{8}{8} \int \frac{x - 1}{4x^2 - 8x + 10} \, dx$$

$$= \frac{1}{8} \int \frac{8x - 8}{4x^2 - 8x + 10} \, dx$$

$$= \tfrac{1}{8} \ln (4x^2 - 8x + 10) + C$$

Check If $f(x) = \tfrac{1}{8} \ln (4x^2 - 8x + 10) + C$,

$$f'(x) = \frac{1}{8} \left[\frac{8x - 8}{4x^2 - 8x + 10} \right] = \frac{x - 1}{4x^2 - 8x + 10}$$ ✔

Follow-up Exercises

For Exercises 15.18 to 15.47, find the indefinite integral.

15.18 $\int 100 \, dx$ **15.19** $\int -50 \, dx$

15.20 $\int 3x \, dx$ **15.21** $\int \frac{x}{4} \, dx$

15.22 $\int (2x - 5)\, dx$

15.23 $\int (10 - 6x)\, dx$

15.24 $\int (mx + b)\, dx$, m and b constants

15.25 $\int x^4\, dx$

15.26 $\int \sqrt{x^3}\, dx$

15.27 $\int 5/\sqrt[3]{x^2}\, dx$

15.28 $\int \dfrac{dx}{x^5}$

15.29 $\int dx$

15.30 $\int (x^4 - 3x^3 - 3x^2)\, dx$

15.31 $\int (ax^2 + bx + c)\, dx$, a, b, and c constants

15.32 $\int (x - 10)^5\, dx$

15.33 $\int (x^2 - 5)^3(2x)\, dx$

15.34 $\int \sqrt{x + 25}\, dx$

15.35 $\int 4x/\sqrt{2x^2 - 5}\, dx$

15.36 $\int (x^3 + 16)^4(6x^2)\, dx$

15.37 $\int (4x^4 - 16x)^{3/2}(x^3 - 1)\, dx$

15.38 $\int (x^2 - 2x)^7(x - 1)\, dx$

15.39 $\int (x^2/6 - 20)^5(x)\, dx$

15.40 $\int 3x^2 e^{x^3}\, dx$

15.41 $\int e^{5x}\, dx$

15.42 $\int e^{mx}\, dx$, m constant

15.43 $\int (x - 1)e^{2x^2 - 4x}\, dx$

15.44 $\int \dfrac{2x}{x^2 + 5}\, dx$

15.45 $\int \dfrac{x^2 - 1}{x^3 - 3x}\, dx$

15.46 $\int \dfrac{10}{5x - 6}\, dx$

15.47 $\int \dfrac{dx}{mx + b}$, m and b constants

FIGURE 15.2

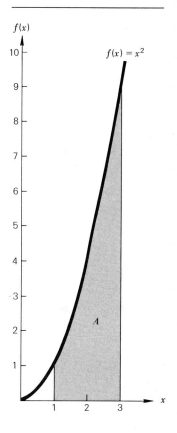

DEFINITE INTEGRALS 15.3

In this section we will introduce the definite integral and discuss its application in determining areas.

The Definite Integral

In this section we will see that the *definite integral* can be interpreted as an area and equivalently as a limit. Consider the function $f(x) = x^2$ which is shown in Fig. 15.2. Assume that we wish to determine the shaded area A under the curve between $x = 1$ and $x = 3$. One approach is to *approximate* the area by computing the areas of a set of rectangles which are contained within the shaded area. In Fig. 15.3 two rectangles

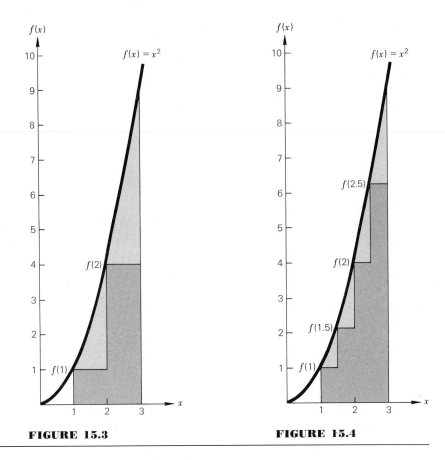

FIGURE 15.3   **FIGURE 15.4**

have been drawn within the area of interest. The width of each rectangle equals 1, and the heights are respectively $f(1)$ and $f(2)$. Using the area of these two rectangles to approximate the area of interest, we have

$$A^* = f(1) \cdot (1) + f(2) \cdot (1)$$

where A^* is the approximate area. Note that this approximation *underestimates* the actual area. The error introduced is represented by the lighter shaded areas.

In Fig. 15.4 four rectangles have been drawn within the area of interest. The width of each rectangle equals $\frac{1}{2}$, and the total area of the four rectangles is computed by using the equation

$$A^* = f(1) \cdot (0.5) + f(1.5) \cdot (0.5) + f(2) \cdot (0.5) + f(2.5) \cdot (0.5)$$

Compared with Fig. 15.3, the use of four rectangles rather than two results in a better approximation of the actual area. The lighter shaded area is smaller in Fig. 15.4.

In Fig. 15.5 eight rectangles have been drawn, each having a width equal to 0.25. The area of these rectangles is computed by using the equation

$$A^* = f(1) \cdot (0.25) + f(1.25) \cdot (0.25) + \cdots + f(2.75) \cdot (0.25)$$

Observe that this approximation is better than the others. In fact, if we continue to subdivide the interval between $x = 1$ and $x = 3$, making the base of each rectangle smaller and smaller, the approximation will come closer and closer to the actual area.

Let's now look at this process in a more general sense. Consider the function in Fig. 15.6. Suppose we are interested in determining the area beneath the curve but above the x axis between $x = a$ and $x = b$. Further suppose that the interval has been subdivided into n rectangles. Assume that the width of rectangle i is Δx_i and the height is $f(x_i)$. It is not necessary to assume that the width of each rectangle is the same. We can approximate the area of interest by summing the areas of the n rectangles, or

$$A^* = f(x_1)\Delta x_1 + f(x_2)\Delta x_2 + \cdots + f(x_n)\Delta x_n$$
$$= \sum_{i=1}^{n} f(x_i)\Delta x_i$$

As we observed for the function $f(x) = x^2$, the approximation becomes more and more accurate as the width of the rectangles becomes smaller and smaller, or concurrently with the number of rectangles becoming larger and larger. We can formalize this observation by stating that

$$\lim_{n \to \infty} \sum_{i=1}^{n} f(x_i)\Delta x_i = A \qquad (15.9)$$

That is, the actual area under the curve A is the limiting value of the sum of the areas of the n rectangles as the number of rectangles approaches infinity.

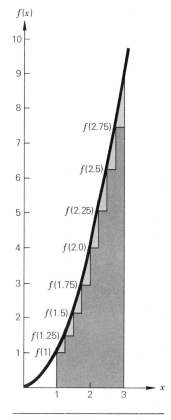

FIGURE 15.5

FIGURE 15.6

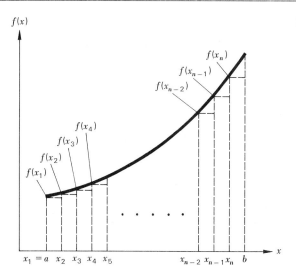

Just as the summation sign Σ applies when the sum of discrete elements is desired, the definite integral implies summation for continuous functions. And it can be shown that the area in Fig. 15.6 can be defined as the *definite integral* of $f(x)$ between $x = a$ and $x = b$, or

$$\int_a^b f(x)\,dx = \lim_{n \to \infty} \sum_{i=1}^n f(x_i)\Delta x_i = A \qquad (15.10)$$

The left side of Eq. (15.10) presents the notation of the *definite integral*. The values a and b which appear, respectively, below and above the integral sign are called the *limits of integration*. The *lower limit of integration* is a, and the *upper limit of integration* is b. The notation $\int_a^b f(x)\,dx$ can be verbalized as "the definite integral of $f(x)$ between a lower limit $x = a$ and an upper limit $x = b$," or more simply "the integral of $f(x)$ between a and b."

Evaluating Definite Integrals

The evaluation of definite integrals is facilitated by the following important theorem.

FUNDAMENTAL THEOREM OF INTEGRAL CALCULUS
If a function $f(x)$ is continuous over an interval and $F(x)$ is any anti-derivative of $f(x)$, then for any points $x = a$ and $x = b$ on the interval, where $a \le b$,

$$\int_a^b f(x)\,dx = F(b) - F(a) \qquad (15.11)$$

According to the fundamental theorem of integral calculus, the definite integral can be evaluated by (1) determining the indefinite integral $F(x) + C$ and (2) computing $F(b) - F(a)$, sometimes denoted by $F(x) \Big]_a^b$. As you will see in the following example, there is no need to include the constant of integration in evaluating definite integrals.

Example 15.19   Evaluate $\displaystyle\int_0^3 x^2\,dx$.

Solution   First, the indefinite integral is defined as

$$F(x) = \frac{x^3}{3} + C$$

Now $\qquad \int_0^3 x^2\,dx = \left(\dfrac{x^3}{3} + C\right)\Big]_0^3 = \left(\dfrac{3^3}{3} + C\right) - \left(\dfrac{0^3}{3} + C\right)$

$$= 9 + C - C$$
$$= 9$$

When evaluating definite integrals, we always subtract the value of the indefinite integral at the lower limit of integration from the value at the upper limit of integration. The constant of integration will always drop out in this computation, as it did in this example. Thus, there is no need to include the constant in evaluating definite integrals.

Evaluate $\displaystyle\int_1^4 (2x^2 - 4x + 5)\,dx.$

Example 15.20

Solution

$$F(x) = \frac{2x^3}{3} - \frac{4x^2}{2} + 5x$$

$$= \frac{2x^3}{3} - 2x^2 + 5x$$

Therefore, $\qquad \displaystyle\int_1^4 (2x^2 - 4x + 5)\,dx = \dfrac{2x^3}{3} - 2x^2 + 5x\,\Big]_1^4$

$$= \left[\frac{2(4)^3}{3} - 2(4)^2 + 5(4)\right]$$

$$- \left[\frac{2(1)^3}{3} - 2(1)^2 + 5(1)\right]$$

$$= \left(\tfrac{128}{3} - 32 + 20\right) - \left(\tfrac{2}{3} - 2 + 5\right)$$

$$= 30\tfrac{2}{3} - 3\tfrac{2}{3}$$

$$= 27$$

Evaluate $\displaystyle\int_{-2}^1 e^x\,dx.$

Example 15.21

Solution

$$F(x) = e^x$$

Therefore, $\qquad \displaystyle\int_{-2}^1 e^x\,dx = e^x\,\Big]_{-2}^1$

$$= e^1 - e^{-2}$$

or from Table A.1, $\qquad = 2.7183 - 0.1353$

$$= 2.5830$$

Definite Integrals and Areas

One of the practical effects of this discussion is that definite integrals can be used to compute areas. Because the methods of determining areas may vary slightly, let's discuss a couple of different cases.

CASE 1: ($f(x) > 0$)
When the value of a function is positive over the interval from $x = a$ to
$x = b$ ($b > a$)—that is, $f(x)$ lies above the x axis—the area which is
bounded by the function, the x axis, $x = a$, and $x = b$ is determined by

$$\int_a^b f(x)\, dx.$$

Figure 15.7 illustrates the situation.

Example
15.22

Determine the area which is beneath $f(x) = x^2$ and above the x axis
between $x = 1$ and $x = 3$.

Solution

This is the area which was illustrated earlier in Fig. 15.2. Therefore,

$$A = \int_1^3 x^2\, dx$$

We find

$$F(x) = \frac{x^3}{3}$$

Therefore,

$$\int_1^3 x^2\, dx = \frac{x^3}{3}\Bigg]_1^3$$

$$= \frac{3^3}{3} - \frac{1^3}{3}$$

$$= 9 - \tfrac{1}{3} = 8\tfrac{2}{3}$$

The area equals $8\tfrac{2}{3}$ *square* units.

Example
15.23

Determine the area indicated in Fig. 15.8.

Solution

Let's anticipate the answer by using familiar formulas for computing the
area of a rectangle and a triangle. As shown in Fig. 15.9, the area of
interest can be thought of as being composed of a rectangle and a triangle. Therefore,

FIGURE 15.7

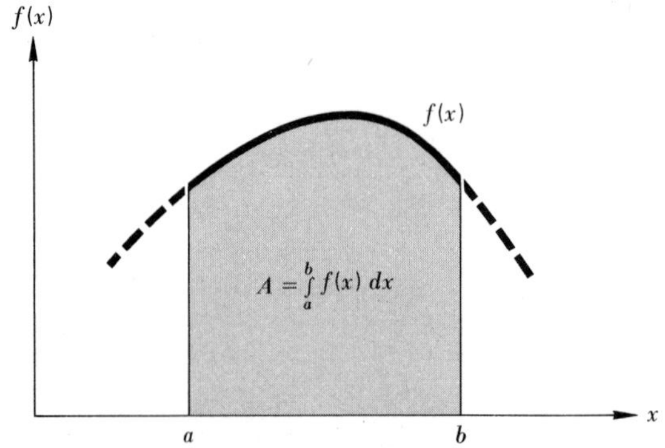

$$A = A_1 + A_2$$
$$= \tfrac{1}{2}bh + lw$$
$$= \tfrac{1}{2}(15)(7.5) + (15)(12.5)$$
$$= 56.25 + 187.5$$
$$= 243.75 \text{ square units}$$

Now, using the definite integral, we have

$$A = \int_5^{20} \left(\frac{x}{2} + 10 \right) dx$$

We find

$$F(x) = \frac{x^2}{4} + 10x$$

Therefore,

$$A = \left. \frac{x^2}{4} + 10x \right]_5^{20}$$

$$= \left[\frac{(20)^2}{4} + 10(20) \right] - \left[\frac{5^2}{4} + 10(5) \right]$$

$$= (100 + 200) - (6.25 + 50)$$

$$= 243.75 \text{ square units}$$

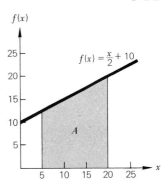

$f(x) = \frac{x}{2} + 10$

FIGURE 15.8

CASE 2: ($f(x) < 0$)
When the value of a function is negative over the interval from $x = a$ to $x = b$ $(b > a)$—that is, $f(x)$ lies below the x axis—the area which is bounded by the function, the x axis, $x = a$, and $x = b$ is determined by $\int_a^b f(x)\,dx$. *However, the definite integral evaluates the area as nega-tive when it lies below the x axis. Hence, the area will be* $- \int_a^b f(x)\,dx$.

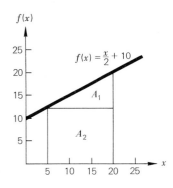

$f(x) = \frac{x}{2} + 10$

FIGURE 15.9

Determine the area indicated in Fig. 15.10.

$$A = \int_{2.5}^{3.5} -\frac{x^3}{2}\,dx$$

First,

$$F(x) = -\frac{x^4}{8}$$

Therefore,

$$A = \int_{2.5}^{3.5} -\frac{x^3}{2}\,dx = \left. -\frac{x^4}{8} \right]_{2.5}^{3.5}$$

$$= \left[-\frac{(3.5)^4}{8} \right] - \left[\frac{-(2.5)^4}{8} \right]$$

$$= -18.7578 - (-4.8828)$$

$$= -13.875 \text{ square units}$$

Hence, the actual enclosed area is 13.875 square units.

Example 15.24

Solution

FIGURE 15.10

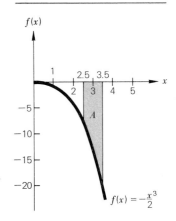

$f(x) = -\frac{x^3}{2}$

CASE 3: $(f(x) < 0 \text{ and } f(x) > 0)$

When the value of a function is positive over part of the interval from $x = a$ to $x = b$ and is negative over the remainder of the interval—part of the area between $f(x)$ and the x axis is above the x axis and part is below the x axis—then $\int_a^b f(x)\, dx$ calculates the *net area*. That is, areas above the x axis are evaluated as positive, and those below are evaluated as negative. The two are combined algebraically to yield the net value.

Example 15.25 Evaluate $\int_0^{15} (x - 5)\, dx$ to determine the *net* area, shown in Fig. 15.11.

Solution Again, we can predict the answer using the formula for the area of a triangle. Remembering that the area below the x axis will be evaluated as negative when we integrate, we have

$$A = -\tfrac{1}{2}(5)(5) + \tfrac{1}{2}(10)(10)$$
$$= -12.5 + 50$$
$$= 37.5 \text{ square units}$$

Evaluating the definite integral, we first find $F(x) = x^2/2 - 5x$. Therefore,

$$A = \frac{x^2}{2} - 5x \Bigg]_0^{15}$$
$$= \left[\frac{(15)^2}{2} - 5(15) \right] - \left[\frac{0^2}{2} - 5(0) \right]$$
$$= (112.5 - 75) - 0$$
$$= 37.5 \text{ square units}$$

FIGURE 15.11

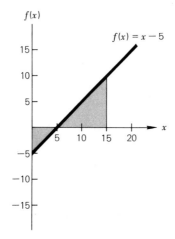

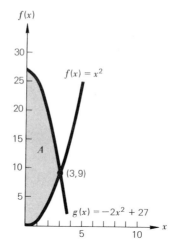

FIGURE 15.12

Finding Areas between Curves

The following examples illustrate procedures for determining areas between curves.

Determine the shaded area between $f(x)$ and $g(x)$ indicated in Fig. 15.12.

Example 15.26

In order to determine the area A, it is necessary to examine the composition of the area. The area cannot be determined by integrating only one of the functions. One way of determining A is shown in Fig. 15.13. If $g(x)$ is integrated between $x = 0$ and $x = 3$, the resulting area includes A, but it also includes an additional area which is not part of A. Having overestimated A, we need to subtract the *surplus*. The surplus area

Solution

FIGURE 15.13

$$\int_0^3 g(x)\,dx \quad - \quad \int_0^3 f(x)\,dx \quad = \quad A$$

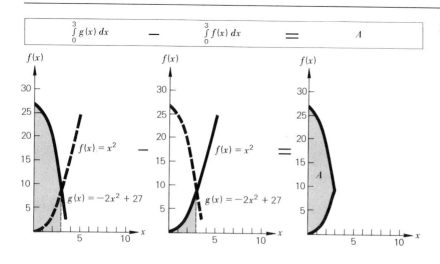

happens to be the area under $f(x)$ between $x = 0$ and $x = 3$. Thus, A can be determined as

$$A = \int_0^3 g(x)\,dx - \int_0^3 f(x)\,dx$$

or

$$A = \int_0^3 (-2x^2 + 27)\,dx - \int_0^3 x^2\,dx$$

$$= \left(\frac{-2x^3}{3} + 27x\right)\Big]_0^3 - \frac{x^3}{3}\Big]_0^3$$

$$= \left[\frac{-2(3)^3}{3} + 27(3)\right] - \left[\frac{-2(0)^3}{3} + 27(0)\right] - \left(\frac{3^3}{3} - \frac{0^3}{3}\right)$$

$$= (-18 + 81) - 0 - 9$$

$$= 54 \text{ square units}$$

NOTE
A property of definite integrals which can facilitate computations such as those in this example is

$$\int_a^b f(x)\,dx \pm \int_a^b g(x)\,dx = \int_a^b [f(x) \pm g(x)]\,dx$$

That is, if two or more definite integrals *having the same limits of integration* are to be added or subtracted, the integrands may be algebraically combined before they are integrated.

Using the information contained in the note, we could have solved the previous example as follows:

$$A = \int_0^3 (-2x^2 + 27)\,dx - \int_0^3 x^2\,dx$$

$$= \int_0^3 (-3x^2 + 27)\,dx$$

$$= -x^3 + 27x\Big]_0^3$$

$$= [-(3)^3 + 27(3)] - [-(0)^3 + 27(0)]$$

$$= -27 + 81 - 0$$

$$= 54$$

Example 15.27   Referring to Fig. 15.14, determine the combination of integrals which would compute the size of (*a*) area A_1, (*b*) area A_2, (*c*) area A_3.

Solution   This example presents no actual numbers. It really is an exercise in the logic of formulating combinations of definite integrals to define areas.

(*a*) The upper boundary on A_1 is determined by $f(x)$. If $f(x)$ is integrated between $x = 0$ and $x = a$, the result is an area including A_1 plus a

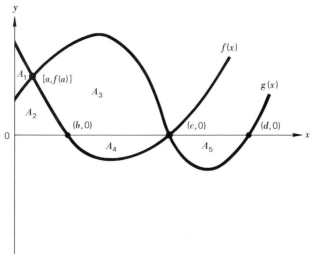

FIGURE 15.14

surplus area. The surplus area can be determined by integrating $g(x)$ between $x = 0$ and $x = a$. Thus,

$$A_1 = \int_0^a f(x) \, dx - \int_0^a g(x) \, dx$$

This is illustrated graphically in Fig. 15.15*a*.

(*b*) The upper boundary on A_2 is determined by $g(x)$ up until $x = a$ and by $f(x)$ when $a \le x \le b$. If $g(x)$ is integrated between $x = 0$ and $x = a$, the resulting area is a portion of A_2. The remaining portion of A_2 can be determined by integrating $f(x)$ between $x = a$ and $x = b$. Thus,

$$A_2 = \int_0^a g(x) \, dx + \int_a^b f(x) \, dx$$

This is illustrated graphically in Fig. 15.15*b*.

(*c*) The upper boundary on A_3 is determined entirely by $g(x)$. If we integrate $g(x)$ between $x = a$ and $x = c$, the resulting area includes A_3 plus a surplus area. The surplus area can be determined by integrating $f(x)$ between $x = a$ and $x = b$. Thus,

$$A_3 = \int_a^c g(x) \, dx - \int_a^b f(x) \, dx$$

This is illustrated graphically in Fig. 15.15*c*.

Verify for yourself in Fig. 15.14 that

$$A_4 = - \int_b^c f(x) \, dx \qquad \text{and} \qquad A_5 = - \int_c^d g(x) \, dx$$

The minus sign preceding the integrals compensates for the fact that the integrals will compute A_4 and A_5 as negative.

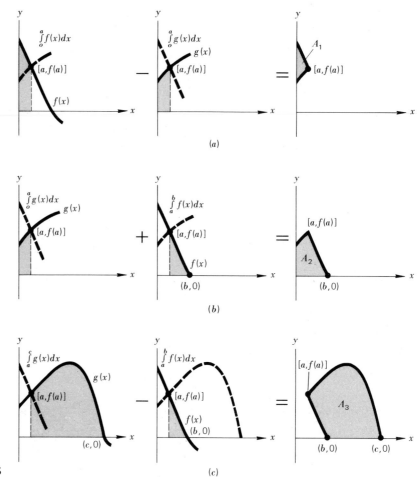

FIGURE 15.15

NOTE
A suggestion in using definite integrals to compute areas is always to
draw a sketch of the functions involved. Having a picture of the areas
of interest makes it easier to identify pertinent boundaries and to
understand the logic required to define the areas.

Follow-up Exercises

In Exercises 15.48 to 15.63, evaluate the definite integral.

15.48 $\displaystyle\int_0^2 (2x + 5)\, dx$ **15.49** $\displaystyle\int_1^2 3x^2\, dx$

15.50 $\displaystyle\int_2^4 (mx + b)\, dx$, m and b constants

15.51 $\displaystyle\int_5^{10} 10\,dx$ **15.52** $\displaystyle\int_0^2 4x^3\,dx$

15.53 $\displaystyle\int_0^1 (x-5)^2\,dx$ **15.54** $\displaystyle\int_4^9 \sqrt{x}\,dx$

15.55 $\displaystyle\int_{-1}^1 (x^2 - 2x + 5)\,dx$ **15.56** $\displaystyle\int_2^5 3x^5\,dx$

15.57 $\displaystyle\int_2^3 -6x^2\,dx$ **15.58** $\displaystyle\int_2^4 2e^x\,dx$

15.59 $\displaystyle\int_0^3 e^x\,dx$ **15.60** $\displaystyle\int_0^1 2xe^{x^2}\,dx$

15.61 $\displaystyle\int_1^2 dx/x$ **15.62** $\displaystyle\int_3^4 \frac{2x}{x^2 - 4}\,dx$

15.63 $\displaystyle\int_0^2 (ax^2 + bx + c)\,dx$, a, b, and c constants

In Exercises 15.64 to 15.71, (a) sketch $f(x)$ and (b) determine the size of the area between $f(x)$ and the x axis over the indicated interval.

15.64 $f(x) = -2x + 10$, between $x = 1$ and $x = 4$
15.65 $f(x) = x^2$, between $x = 5$ and $x = 10$
15.66 $f(x) = 4x^3$, between $x = 1$ and $x = 2$
15.67 $f(x) = 25 - 3x^2$, between $x = 0$ and $x = 2$
15.68 $f(x) = e^x$, between $x = 2$ and $x = 4$
15.69 $f(x) = -\frac{1}{2}x^3$, between $x = 2$ and $x = 10$
15.70 $f(x) = 20x - x^2$, between $x = 0$ and $x = 10$
15.71 $f(x) = x^2 - 10x$, between $x = 1$ and $x = 4$

15.72 Referring to Fig. 15.16, determine the combinations of definite integrals which would compute the area of (a) A_1, (b) A_2, (c) A_3, (d) A_4, (e) A_5.
15.73 Referring to Fig. 15.17, determine the combinations of definite integrals which would compute the area of (a) A_1, (b) A_2, (c) A_3.

FIGURE 15.16

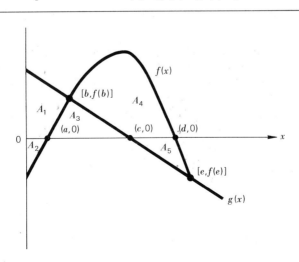

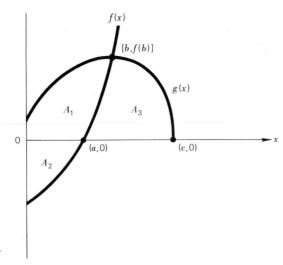

FIGURE 15.17

15.74 Given $f(x) = x^2/2$ and $g(x) = 24 - x^2$, (*a*) sketch the two functions. (*b*) For $x \geq 0$, determine the area bounded by the two functions and the *y* axis.

15.75 Given $f(x) = 2x + 2$ and $g(x) = 14 - x$, (*a*) sketch the two functions. (*b*) For $x \geq 0$, determine the area bounded by the two functions and the *y* axis.

15.76 Given $f(x) = x^2 - 20x$ and $g(x) = -x^2 + 20x$, (*a*) sketch the two functions. (*b*) Determine the area bounded by the two functions between $x = 0$ and $x = 20$.

15.4   APPLICATIONS OF INTEGRAL CALCULUS

The following examples illustrate sample areas of application of integral calculus.

Example 15.28

Revenue Earlier in the chapter we discussed how the total revenue function can sometimes be determined by integrating the marginal revenue function. As a simple extension of this concept, assume that the price of a product is constant at a value of $10 per unit, or the marginal revenue function is

$$MR = f(x)$$
$$= 10$$

where *x* equals the number of units sold. Total revenue from selling any quantity can be determined by integrating the marginal revenue function between 0 and the quantity sold. For example, the total revenue from selling 1,500 units can be computed as

$$\int_0^{1,500} 10\,dx = 10x \Big]_0^{1,500}$$
$$= 10(1,500)$$
$$= \$15,000$$

This is a rather elaborate procedure for calculating total revenue since we simply could have multiplied price by quantity sold to determine the same result. However, it does illustrate how the area beneath the marginal revenue function (Fig. 15.18) can be interpreted as total revenue or incremental revenue. The additional revenue associated with increasing sales from 1,500 to 1,800 units can be computed as

$$\int_{1,500}^{1,800} 10 \, dx = 10x \Big]_{1,500}^{1,800}$$
$$= \$18,000 - \$15,000$$
$$= \$3,000$$

Maintenance Expenditures An automobile manufacturer estimates that the annual rate of expenditure $r(t)$ for maintenance on one of its models is represented by the function

Example 15.29

$$r(t) = 100 + 10t^2$$

where t is the age of the automobile stated in years and $r(t)$ is measured in dollars per year. This function suggests that when the car is 1 year old, maintenance expenses are being incurred at a rate of

$$r(1) = 100 + 10(1)^2$$
$$= \$110 \text{ per year}$$

When the car is 3 years old, maintenance costs are being incurred at a rate of

$$r(3) = 100 + 10(3)^2$$
$$= \$190 \text{ per year}$$

As would be anticipated, the older the automobile, the more maintenance is required. Figure 15.19 illustrates the sketch of the rate of expenditure function.

The area under this curve between any two values of t is a measure of

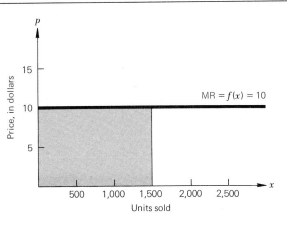

FIGURE 15.18

the expected maintenance cost during that time interval. The expected maintenance expenditures during the automobile's first 5 years are computed as

$$\int_0^5 (100 + 10t^2)\, dt = 100t + \frac{10t^3}{3}\Bigg]_0^5$$

$$= 100(5) + \frac{10(5)^3}{3}$$

$$= 500 + 416.67$$

$$= \$916.67$$

Of these expenditures, those expected to be incurred during the fifth year are estimated as

$$\int_4^5 (100 + 10t^2)\, dt = 100t + \frac{10t^3}{3}\Bigg]_4^5$$

$$= 916.67 - \left[100(4) + \frac{10(4)^3}{3}\right]$$

$$= 916.67 - (400 + 213.33)$$

$$= \$303.34$$

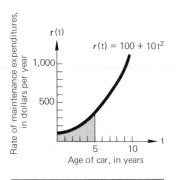

r(t)

r(t) = 100 + 10t²

1,000

500

5   10

Age of car, in years

Rate of maintenance expenditures, in dollars per year

FIGURE 15.9

Example 15.30

Fund Raising A state civic organization is conducting its annual fund raising campaign for its summer camp program for the disadvantaged. Campaign expenditures will be incurred at a rate of $10,000 per day. From past experience it is known that contributions will be high during the early stages of the campaign and will tend to fall off as the campaign continues. The function describing the rate at which contributions are received is

$$c(t) = -100t^2 + 20,000$$

where t represents the day of the campaign, and $c(t)$ is measured in dollars per day.

The organization wishes to maximize the net proceeds from the campaign.

(a) Determine how long the campaign should be conducted in order to maximize net proceeds.
(b) What are total campaign expenditures expected to equal?
(c) What are total contributions expected to equal?
(d) What are the net proceeds (total contributions less total expenditures) expected to equal?

Solution

(a) The function which describes the rate at which expenditures $e(t)$ are incurred is

$$e(t) = 10,000$$

Figure 15.20 illustrates the two functions. As long as the rate at which contributions are made exceeds the rate of expenditures for the campaign, net proceeds are positive. Refer to Fig. 15.20. Net proceeds will be positive up until the time when the graphs of the

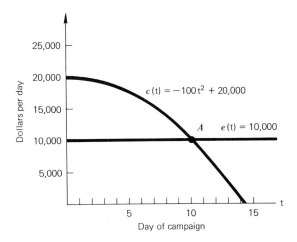

FIGURE 15.20

two functions intersect. Beyond this point, the rate of expenditure exceeds the rate of contribution. That is, contributions would be coming in at a rate of less than $10,000 per day.

The two functions intersect when

$$c(t) = e(t)$$

or when
$$-100t^2 + 20,000 = 10,000$$
$$-100t^2 = -10,000$$
$$t^2 = 100$$
$$\mathbf{t = 10 \ days}$$

(b) Total campaign expenditures are represented by the area under $e(t)$ between $t = 0$ and $t = 10$. This could be found by integrating $e(t)$ between these limits or more simply by multiplying:

$$E = (\$10,000 \text{ per day})(10 \text{ days})$$
$$= \$100,000$$

(c) Total contributions during the 10 days are represented by the area under $c(t)$ between $t = 0$ and $t = 10$, or

$$C = \int_0^{10} (-100t^2 + 20,000) \, dt$$

$$= -100 \frac{t^3}{3} + 20,000t \bigg]_0^{10}$$

$$= \frac{-100(10)^3}{3} + 20,000(10)$$

$$= -33,333.33 + 200,000$$
$$= \$166,666.67$$

(d) Net proceeds are expected to equal

$$C - E = \$166,666.67 - \$100,000$$
$$= \$66,666.67$$

Example 15.31

Nuclear Power An electric company has proposed building a nuclear power plant on the outskirts of a major metropolitan area. As might be expected, public opinion is divided and discussions have been heated. One lobbyist group opposing the construction of the plant has presented some disputed data regarding the consequences of a catastrophic accident at the proposed plant. The lobbyist group estimates that the rate at which deaths would occur within the metropolitan area because of radioactive fallout is described by the function

$$r(t) = 200,000e^{-0.1t}$$

where $r(t)$ represents the rate of deaths in persons per hour and t represents time elapsed since the accident, measured in hours. *Note: Although the dispute in this example is quite real, the data are all contrived!*

The population of the metropolitan area is 1.5 million persons.

(a) Determine the expected number of deaths 1 hour after a major accident.

(b) How long would it take for all people in the metropolitan area to succumb to the effects of the radioactivity?

Solution

(a) Figure 15.21 illustrates a sketch of the function $r(t)$. The area beneath this function between any two points t_1 and t_2 is a measure of the expected number of deaths during that time interval. Thus, the number of deaths expected during the first hour would be computed as

$$\int_0^1 200,000e^{-0.1t}\, dt = \int_0^1 -2,000,000(-0.1)e^{-0.1t}\, dt$$

$$= -2,000,000 \int_0^1 (-0.1)e^{-0.1t}\, dt$$

$$= -2,000,000e^{-0.1t}\Big]_0^1$$

$$= -2,000,000e^{-0.1} + 2,000,000e^0$$
$$= -2,000,000(e^{-0.1} - e^0)$$
$$= -2,000,000(0.9048 - 1)$$
$$= -2,000,000(-0.0952)$$
$$= 190,400 \text{ people}$$

(b) As morbid as it is, the entire population would succumb when

$$\int_0^{t_1} 200,000e^{-0.1t}\, dt = 1,500,000$$

or when

$$-2,000,000e^{-0.1t}\Big]_0^{t_1} = 1,500,000$$

Solving for t_1, we get

$$-2,000,000e^{-0.1t_1} + 2,000,000 = 1,500,000$$
$$-2,000,000e^{-0.1t_1} = -500,000$$
$$e^{-0.1t_1} = 0.25$$

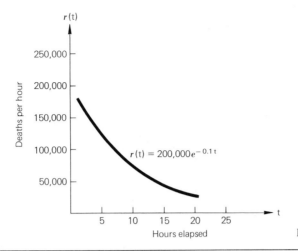

FIGURE 15.21

Since $e^{-1.39} \doteq 0.25$, the value of t_1 is found when

$$-0.1t_1 = -1.39$$

or
$$t_1 = \textbf{13.9 hours}$$

Consumer's Surplus One way of measuring the value or utility that a product holds for a consumer is the price that he or she is willing to pay for it. Economists contend that consumers actually receive bonus or surplus value from the products they purchase according to the way in which the marketplace operates.

Example 15.32

Figure 15.22 portrays the demand function for a product. Equilibrium occurs when a price of $10 is charged and demand equals 100 units. If money is used to represent the value of this product to consumers, our accounting practices would suggest that the total revenue ($10 \cdot 100$ units = $1,000) is a measure of the *economic value* of this product. The area of rectangle $ABCE$ represents this measure of value.

However, if you consider the nature of the demand function, there

FIGURE 15.22

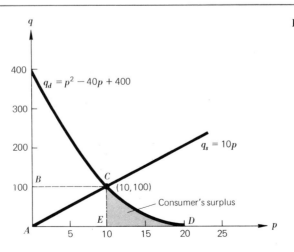

would have been a demand for the product at prices higher than $10. That is, there would have been consumers willing to pay almost $20 for the product. And, additional consumers would have been drawn into the market at prices between $10 and $20. If we assume that the price these people would be willing to pay is a measure of the utility the product holds for them, they actually receive a bonus when the market price is $10. Refer to Fig. 15.22. Economists would claim that a measure of the actual utility of the product is the area $ABCDE$. And when the market is in equilibrium, the extra utility received by consumers, referred to as the *consumer's surplus*, is represented by the shaded area CDE. This area can be found as

$$\int_{10}^{20} (p^2 - 40p + 400) \, dp = \frac{p^3}{3} - 20p^2 + 400p \Big]_{10}^{20}$$

$$= \left[\frac{(20)^3}{3} - 20(20)^2 + 400(20) \right]$$

$$- \left[\frac{(10)^3}{3} - 20(10)^2 + 400(10) \right]$$

$$= 2{,}666.67 - 2{,}333.33$$

$$= \$333.34$$

Our accounting methods would value the utility of the product at $1,000. Economists would contend that the actual utility is $1,333.34, or that the consumer's surplus equals $333.34.

Follow-up Exercises

15.77 The marginal revenue function for a firm's product is

$$MR = -0.02x + 20$$

where x equals the number of units sold.
(a) Determine the total revenue from selling 100 units of the product.
(b) What is the added revenue associated with an increase in sales from 100 to 150 units?

15.78 A manufacturer of jet engines estimates that the rate at which maintenance costs are incurred on its engines is a function of the number of hours of operation of the engine. For one engine used on commercial aircraft, the function is

$$r(x) = 50 + .025x^2$$

where x equals the number of hours of operation and $r(x)$ equals the rate at which repair costs are incurred in dollars per hour of operation.
(a) Determine the rate at which costs are being incurred after 100 hours of operation.
(b) What are total maintenance costs expected to equal during the first 100 hours of operation?

15.79 A company specializing in a mail-order sales approach is beginning a promotional campaign. Advertising expenditures will cost the firm $5,950 per day. Marketing specialists estimate that the rate at which profit (exclusive of advertising costs) will be generated from the

promotion campaign decreases over the length of the campaign. Specifically, the rate $r(t)$ for this campaign is estimated by the function

$$r(t) = -50t^2 + 10,000$$

where t represents the day of the campaign and $r(t)$ is measured in
dollars per day. In order to maximize *net* profit, the firm should conduct
the campaign as long as $r(t)$ exceeds the daily advertising cost.

(a) Graph the function $r(t)$ and the function $c(t) = 5,950$ which describes the rate at which advertising expenses are incurred.

(b) How long should the campaign be conducted?

(c) What are total advertising expenditures expected to equal during
the campaign?

(d) What *net* profit will be expected?

15.80 Rework Example 15.30, assuming that campaign expenditures
will be incurred at a rate of $5,000 per day and that

$$c(t) = -10t^2 + 9,000$$

15.81 Rework Example 15.31, assuming that $r(t) = 200,000e^{-0.05t}$.

15.82 Rework Example 15.31, assuming that the population equals
800,000 and $r(t) = 100,000e^{-0.1t}$.

15.83 You are given the demand function

$$q_d = p^2 - 30p + 200$$

and the supply function

$$q_s = 15p$$

where p is stated in dollars, q_d and q_s are stated in units, and $0 \leq p \leq 9$.

(a) Sketch the two functions.

(b) Determine the equilibrium price and quantity.

(c) Determine the value of the consumer's surplus if the market is in
equilibrium.

15.84 *Energy Conservation.* A small business is considering buying an
energy-saving device which will reduce its consumption of fuel. The device will cost $49,250. Engineering estimates suggest that savings from
using the device will occur at a rate of $s(t)$ dollars per year where

$$s(t) = 50,000e^{-t}$$

and t equals time measured in years. Determine how long it will take for
the firm to recover the cost of the device (that is, when the accumulated
fuel savings equal the purchase cost).

15.85 *Blood Bank Management.* A hospital blood bank conducts an
annual blood drive to replenish its inventory of blood. The hospital estimates that blood will be donated at a rate of $d(t)$ pints per day where

$$d(t) = 500e^{-0.4t}$$

and t equals the length of the blood drive in days. If the goal for the
blood drive is 1,000 pints, when will the hospital reach its goal?

15.86 *Forest Management.* The demand for commercial forestland
timber has been increasing rapidly over the past three to four decades.
The function describing the rate of demand for timber is

$$d(t) = 12 + 0.005t^2$$

where $d(t)$ is stated in billions of cubic feet per year and t equals time in years ($t = 0$ corresponds to January 1, 1965).

(a) Determine the rate of demand at the beginning of 1965.

(b) Determine the rate of demand at the beginning of 1980.

(c) Determine the *total* demand for timber during the period 1965 through 1980. (*Hint:* Integrate $d(t)$ between $t = 0$ and $t = 16$.)

15.87 *Solid Waste Management.* The rate $w(t)$ at which solid waste is being generated in a major United States city is described by the function

$$w(t) = 2e^{0.075t}$$

where $w(t)$ is stated in billions of tons per year and t equals time measured in years ($t = 0$ corresponds to January 1, 1976).

(a) Determine the rate at which solid waste is expected to be generated at the beginning of 1986.

(b) What total tonnage is expected to be generated during the 10-year period from 1976 through 1985?

15.88 *Epidemic Control.* A health research center specializes in the study of epidemics. They estimate that for one particular type of epidemic which occurred in one region of the country the rate at which new people were afflicted was described by the function

$$r(t) = 100e^{0.4t} - 100$$

where $r(t)$ is the rate of new afflictions, measured in people per day, and t equals time since the beginning of the epidemic, measured in days. How many persons were afflicted during the first 10 days? During the first 25 days?

15.89 *Learning Curves.* People in the manufacturing industries have observed in many instances that employees assigned to a new job or task become more efficient with experience. That is, as the employee repeats the task, he or she becomes more familiar with the operations, motions, and equipment required to perform the job. Some companies have enough experience with job training that they can project how quickly an employee will learn a job. Very often a *learning curve* can be constructed which estimates the rate at which a job is performed as a function of the number of times the job has been performed by an employee.

The *learning curve* for a particular job has been defined as

$$h(x) = \frac{10}{x} + 5 \qquad x > 0$$

where $h(x)$ equals the production rate measured in hours per unit and x equals the unit produced.

(a) Determine the production rate $h(x)$ at the time of the fifth unit ($x = 5$).

(b) Integrating the learning curve over a specified interval provides an estimate of the total number of production hours required over the corresponding range of output. Determine the total number of hours expected for producing the first 10 units by integrating $h(x)$ between $x = 1$ and $x = 10$.

(c) Sketch $h(x)$.

(d) Is there any limit suggested as to how efficient an employee can become at this job?

15.90 *Producer's Surplus*. Example 15.32 discussed the notion of consumer's surplus, which represents what economists believe to be a measure of the added utility consumers enjoy when the market is in equilibrium. Economists also suggest that producers receive a bonus or added utility when the market is in equilibrium. Figure 15.23 repeats the supply and demand functions presented in Example 15.32.

If you focus on the supply function q_s, it indicates that certain suppliers would be willing to supply units at prices less than the equilibrium price of $10. When the market price is $10, these suppliers earn more than they otherwise would have. If each supplier sells at the price he or she is willing to, the total revenue received would be represented by area *ACD*. Since total revenue at equilibrium is represented by *ABCD*, the shaded area represents a measure of the added value to suppliers. This added value is referred to as *producer's surplus*.

(*a*) Determine the producer's surplus in Example 15.32.
(*b*) Determine the producer's surplus for the functions described in Exercise 15.83.

WHEN OUR RULES OF INTEGRATION FAIL (OPTIONAL)

The nine integration rules which we discussed earlier in the chapter apply only to a subset of the functions which might be integrated. This subset includes the more common functions used in business and economics applications. A natural question is, What happens when our rules do not work? This section discusses a technique called *integration by parts*. We will also discuss the use of special tables of integration formulas.

Integration by Parts

Recall the product rule of differentiation from Chap. 11. This rule stated that if

$$f(x) = u(x)v(x)$$

then

$$f'(x) = v(x)u'(x) + u(x)v'(x)$$

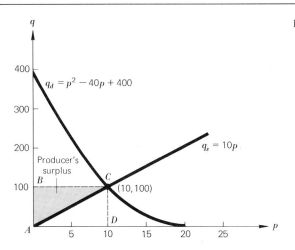

FIGURE 15.23

We can write this rule in a slightly different form as

$$\frac{d}{dx}[u(x)v(x)] = v(x)u'(x) + u(x)v'(x)$$

If we integrate both sides of this equation, the result is

$$u(x)v(x) = \int v(x)u'(x)\,dx + \int u(x)v'(x)\,dx$$

And, rewriting this equation, we get

$$\int u(x)v'(x)\,dx = u(x)v(x) - \int v(x)u'(x)\,dx \qquad (15.12)$$

This equation expresses a relationship which can be used to determine integrals where the integrand has the form $u(x)v'(x)$. Equation (15.12) is the *integration-by-parts formula*.

The integration-by-parts procedure is a trial-and-error method which may or may not be successful for a given integrand. If the integrand is in the form of a product and the other integration rules do not apply:

1 Define two functions $u(x)$ and $v(x)$ and determine whether the integrand has the form $u(x)v'(x)$.

2 If two functions are found such that $u(x)v'(x)$ equals the integrand, attempt to find the integral by evaluating the right side of Eq. (15.12). The key is whether you can evaluate $\int v(x)\,u'(x)\,dx$.

The following examples illustrate the approach.

Example 15.33

Determine $\int xe^x\,dx$.

Solution

The first temptation is to try to use Rule 8, which applies for integrals of the form $\int f'(x)e^{f(x)}\,dx$. With the exponent $f(x)$ defined as x, $f'(x) = 1$ and the integrand is not in an appropriate form to apply Rule 8.

Since the integrand is in the form of a product, let's try to define two functions $u(x)$ and $v(x)$ such that the integrand has the form $u(x)v'(x)$.

NOTE
A hint is to examine the factors of the integrand to determine if one of them has the form of the derivative of another function.

Let's define $v'(x)$ as equaling x and $u(x)$ as equaling e^x:

$$\int \overbrace{x}^{v'(x)}\ \overbrace{e^x}^{u(x)}\ dx$$

With these definitions we can determine $v(x)$ by integrating $v'(x)$ and $u'(x)$ by differentiating $u(x)$, or

$$v'(x) = x \text{ suggests that } v(x) = \frac{x^2}{2}$$

and

$$u(x) = e^x \text{ suggests that } u'(x) = e^x$$

With $u(x)$, $v(x)$, and their derivatives defined, we substitute into Eq. (15.12):

$$\int x e^x \, dx = e^x \frac{x^2}{2} - \int \frac{x^2}{2} e^x \, dx$$

An examination of $\int(x^2/2)e^x \, dx$ would suggest that this integral may be as difficult to evaluate as the original integral.

So, let's backtrack and start again. Let's redefine $v'(x)$ and $u(x)$ such that $v'(x) = e^x$ and $u(x) = x$:

$$\int \overbrace{x}^{u(x)} \overbrace{e^x}^{v'(x)} \, dx$$

Given these definitions,

$$u(x) = x \text{ suggests that } u'(x) = 1$$
$$v'(x) = e^x \text{ suggests that } v(x) = e^x$$

Substituting into Eq. (15.12) yields

$$\int x e^x \, dx = x e^x - \int e^x(1) \, dx$$

$$= x e^x - \int e^x \, dx$$

$$= x e^x - e^x + C$$

Differentiating this answer as a check, we find

$$\frac{d}{dx} [x e^x - e^x + C] = (1)e^x + e^x x - e^x$$

$$= x e^x \ \checkmark$$

Determine $\int x^2 \ln x \, dx$.

Example 15.34

If we let $u(x) = \ln x$ and $v'(x) = x^2$, then

Solution

$$u'(x) = \frac{1}{x} \quad \text{and} \quad v(x) = \int x^2 \, dx = \frac{x^3}{3}$$

Substituting into Eq. (15.12) gives

$$\int x^2 \ln x \, dx = (\ln x)\left(\frac{x^3}{3}\right) - \int \frac{x^3}{3} \frac{1}{x} \, dx$$

$$= \frac{x^3}{3} \ln x - \int \frac{x^2}{3} \, dx$$

$$= \frac{x^3}{3} \ln x - \frac{x^3}{9} + C$$

Checking this answer by differentiating, we get

$$\frac{d}{dx}\left[\frac{x^3}{3}\ln x - \frac{x^3}{9} + C\right] = \frac{3x^2}{3}\ln x + \frac{1}{x}\frac{x^3}{3} - \frac{3x^2}{9}$$

$$= x^2 \ln x + \frac{x^2}{3} - \frac{x^2}{3}$$

$$= x^2 \ln x \quad \checkmark$$

Example 15.35

Determine $\int \ln x \, dx$.

Solution

Although the integrand is not in the form of a product, we can imagine it to have the form

$$\int \ln x(1) \, dx$$

Letting $u(x) = \ln x$ and $v'(x) = 1$, we have

$$u'(x) = \frac{1}{x}$$

and

$$v(x) = \int 1 dx$$

$$= x$$

Substituting into Eq. (15.12) yields

$$\int \ln x \, dx = (\ln x)(x) - \int x \frac{1}{x} dx$$

$$= x \ln x - \int dx$$

$$= x \ln x - x + C$$

This answer can be checked by differentiating, or

$$\frac{d}{dx}[x \ln x - x + C] = (1) \ln x + \frac{1}{x}x - 1$$

$$= \ln x + 1 - 1$$

$$= \ln x \quad \checkmark$$

Integration by parts is often time-consuming, given the trial-and-error approach required. You are again reminded to first examine the integrand carefully to determine whether our other rules apply before you try this procedure.

Tables of Integrals

For cases where our rules and procedures are inadequate for determining indefinite integrals, special tables of integrals are available which may contain literally hundreds of integration formulas. Each formula applies to an integrand which has a particular functional form. To use the tables, you match the form of your integrand with the corresponding general form in the table. Once the appropriate formula has been identified, the indefinite integral follows directly from the formula.

Follow-up Exercises

In the following exercises, determine the indefinite integral (if possible) using integration by parts.

15.91 $\int xe^{-x}\, dx$

15.92 $\int 5xe^{x}\, dx$

15.93 $\int x \sqrt[3]{x+1}\, dx$

15.94 $\int x \sqrt{x+1}\, dx$

15.95 $\int x^3(3x^2)\, dx$

15.96 $\int xe^{-2x}\, dx$

15.97 $\int (x+4) \ln x\, dx$

15.98 $\int x^2 \ln 5x\, dx$

15.99 $\int x(x+2)^4\, dx$

15.100 $\int x(x-4)^5\, dx$

15.101 $\int \dfrac{x\, dx}{\sqrt{x-3}}$

15.102 $\int \dfrac{x}{(x-3)^2}\, dx$

15.103 $\int [\ln x/x^2]\, dx$

15.104 $\int (2x+5)(x+1)^{1/2}\, dx$

SUMMARY   15.6

The purpose of this chapter has been to survey integral calculus and to provide a sense of the concerns of integral calculus and where it can be applied. We have seen some of the interrelationships which exist between differential and integral calculus. The antiderivative concept is the most obvious link between these two areas of study within the calculus.

We have also seen that the process of integration can be performed by using a set of basic rules of integration. These rules are applied in a manner similar to that used in finding derivatives.

Our discussions also focused on the definite integral and its application. We were most interested in the use of definite integrals in computing the size of areas which exist between curves and other defined boundaries. These areas later had meaning in a series of applications discussed in Sec. 15.4. The final section discussed other techniques of integration which may be employed when the set of basic rules is not appropriate.

The application of integral calculus to probability theory will be illustrated in Sec. 16.5.

CHAPTER CHECKLIST

If you have read *all* the sections of this chapter, you should

Understand the *antiderivative* concept   _____

_____ Know how to find *indefinite integrals* using the basic rules of inte-ration

_____ Understand the computational aspects of the *definite integral*

_____ Have some sense of why definite integrals compute areas between a curve and the x axis

_____ Be able to determine areas bounded by the graphs of continuous functions and by other defined areas

_____ Be familiar with selected applications of integral calculus

_____ Understand *integration by parts*

_____ Be aware that alternative procedures exist for finding indefinite integrals when the procedures presented in this chapter are inadequate

KEY TERMS AND CONCEPTS

antiderivative

integration

indefinite integral

integral sign

integrand

constant of integration

definite integral

fundamental theorem of integral calculus

limits of integration (lower and upper)

integration by parts

IMPORTANT FORMULAS

$$\int k\,dx = kx + c \qquad k \text{ real} \tag{Rule 1}$$

$$\int x^n\,dx = \frac{x^{n+1}}{n+1} + C \qquad n \neq -1 \tag{Rule 2}$$

$$\int kf(x)\,dx = k\int f(x)\,dx \qquad k \text{ real} \tag{Rule 3}$$

$$\int [f(x) \pm g(x)]\,dx = \int f(x)\,dx \pm \int g(x)\,dx \tag{Rule 4}$$

$$\int x^{-1}\,dx = \ln x + C \tag{Rule 5}$$

$$\int e^x\,dx = e^x + C \tag{Rule 6}$$

$$\int [f(x)]^n f'(x)\,dx = \frac{[f(x)]^{n+1}}{n+1} + C \qquad n \neq -1 \tag{Rule 7}$$

$$\int f'(x)e^{f(x)}\,dx = e^{f(x)} + C \tag{Rule 8}$$

$$\int \frac{f'(x)}{f(x)}\,dx = \ln f(x) + C \tag{Rule 9}$$

$$\int_a^b f(x)\,dx = F(b) - F(a) \tag{15.11}$$

$$\int u(x)v'(x)\,dx = u(x)v(x) - \int v(x)u'(x)\,dx \tag{15.12}$$

ADDITIONAL EXERCISES

Exercises 15.105 to 15.113 are related to Sec. 15.1.

In Exercises 15.105 to 15.110, determine the antiderivative of the given function.

15.105 $f'(x) = 3$ **15.106** $f'(x) = 2x$
15.107 $f'(x) = x/2 + 2$ **15.108** $f'(x) = -4x^2$
15.109 $f'(x) = 5x^2 + x + 7$ **15.110** $f'(x) = 2x^3 - x^2 + 11$

In Exercises 15.111 to 15.113, determine $f(x)$ given $f'(x)$ and a point which satisfies $f(x)$.

15.111 $f'(x) = 8;\ (2,\ 20)$
15.112 $f'(x) = x^2 + 3x - 6;\ (1,\ 0)$

15.113 $f'(x) = \dfrac{-4x^3}{3} + x^2 + 2x + 1;\ (-1,\ \tfrac{1}{3})$

Exercises 15.114 to 15.139 are related to Sec. 15.2.

In Exercises 15.114 to 15.139, find the indefinite integral.

15.114 $\displaystyle\int 33\,dx$ **15.115** $\displaystyle\int -12\,dx$

15.116 $\displaystyle\int 9x\,dx$ **15.117** $\displaystyle\int (-x + 1)\,dx$

15.118 $\displaystyle\int (-5x + 3)\,dx$ **15.119** $\displaystyle\int (x/2 + 7)\,dx$

15.120 $\displaystyle\int (2x^3 - 4x^2)\,dx$ **15.121** $\displaystyle\int (x^4/5 + 3x^3 - 5)\,dx$

15.122 $\displaystyle\int (x - 1/x^3)\,dx$ **15.123** $\displaystyle\int (x + 3)^4\,dx$

15.124 $\displaystyle\int (2x^4 + 4x^3 - x^2 + 6x - 7)\,dx$

15.125 $\displaystyle\int (ax^4 + bx^3 + cx^2 + dx + e)\,dx$

15.126 $\displaystyle\int \sqrt{x^5}\,dx$ **15.127** $\displaystyle\int \sqrt[4]{1/x}\,dx$

15.128 $\displaystyle\int (4x^2 + 5)^{1/2}(8x)\,dx$ **15.129** $\displaystyle\int (x^2 + 3e^x + 2)\,dx$

15.130 $\displaystyle\int (\sqrt{x} + \sqrt[5]{x})\,dx$ **15.131** $\displaystyle\int (x^2 + 1)(2x)\,dx$

15.132 $\displaystyle\int (3x^2 - 2)^3(x)\,dx$

15.133 $\int (2x^3 - x^2)^2(3x^2 - x)\, dx$

15.134 $\int \dfrac{-x}{3 - x^2/2}\, dx$

15.135 $\int \dfrac{2 - x}{x^3}\, dx$

15.136 $\int \dfrac{7}{x - 3}\, dx$

15.137 $\int (e^{8x} + 2)\, dx$

15.138 $\int \dfrac{2x}{\sqrt{x^2 + 3}}\, dx$

15.139 $\int \dfrac{x}{(x^2 + 4)^3}\, dx$

Exercises 15.140 to 15.155 relate to Sec. 15.3.

In Exercises 15.140 to 15.151, evaluate the definite integral.

15.140 $\displaystyle\int_0^1 (x^2 - 3e^x - 2)\, dx$

15.141 $\displaystyle\int_1^3 (4x^2 + 5)\, dx$

15.142 $\displaystyle\int_{-2}^2 (6x + 7)\, dx$

15.143 $\displaystyle\int_{-1}^0 3x^2\, dx$

15.144 $\displaystyle\int_0^1 (-2x^5 + 3x^4)\, dx$

15.145 $\displaystyle\int_{-1}^1 (x - 3)/x^3\, dx$

15.146 $\displaystyle\int_1^2 (x^2/2 - 2x)\, dx$

15.147 $\displaystyle\int_{-3}^0 3x^2 e^{x^3}\, dx$

15.148 $\displaystyle\int_{-3}^3 (-5xe^{x^2+2}\, dx$

15.149 $\displaystyle\int_2^3 \dfrac{6x}{3x^2 - 7}\, dx$

15.150 $\displaystyle\int_0^1 x^{1/2}(1 + x)\, dx$

15.151 $\displaystyle\int_{-4}^0 e^{-1-6x}\, dx$

In Exercises 15.152 to 15.154, (a) sketch $f(x)$ and (b) determine the size of the area between $f(x)$ and the x axis over the indicated interval.

15.152 $f(x) = 3x + 2$ between $x = 0$ and $x = 3$
15.153 $f(x) = 4 - x^2$ between $x = 1$ and $x = 2$
15.154 $f(x) = 1/x$ between $x = 1$ and $x = 4$
15.155 Given $f(x) = x^3$ and $g(x) = x$, (a) sketch the two functions. (b) For $0 \le x \le 1$ determine the area of the region between the two curves.

Exercises 15.156 to 15.159 are related to Sec. 15.4.

15.156 Maintenance expenses for a piece of industrial equipment are estimated to be incurred at a rate described by the function

$$r(t) = 100 + 50t^2$$

where $r(t)$ is measured in dollars per year and t equals the age of the machine in years.
(a) Determine the rate at which costs are being incurred when the machine is 3 years old.
(b) What are total maintenance expenses expected to equal during the first 5 years of operation?
15.157 *Oil Consumption.* In 1976 the amount of oil used in a particular region of the United States was 5 billion barrels. The demand for oil

was growing at an exponential rate of 10 percent per year. The function describing annual rate of consumption $c(t)$ at time t is

$$c(t) = 5e^{0.1t}$$

where t is measured in years, $t = 0$ corresponds to January 1, 1976, and $c(t)$ is measured in billions of barrels per year. If the demand for oil continues to grow at this rate, how much oil is expected to be consumed in the 20-year period January 1, 1976, to January 1, 1996?

*15.158 *Velocity and Acceleration.* Given the function $s(t)$ which describes the position of a moving object as a function of time t, the velocity function is $v(t) = s'(t)$, and the acceleration function is $a(t) = v'(t) = s''(t)$.

An object in free fall experiences a constant downward acceleration of 32 feet per square second. The acceleration function for a particular object is $a(t) = -32$. The initial velocity of the object thrown from ground level is 80 feet per second.

(a) Determine the function $v(t)$ which describes the velocity of the object at time t.

(b) Determine the velocity at $t = 2$.

(c) Determine the function $s(t)$ which describes the height of the object at time t.

(d) What is the height at $t = 1$?

15.159 The demand for a product has been decreasing exponentially. The annual rate of demand $d(t)$ is

$$d(t) = 250,000e^{-0.15t}$$

where $t = 0$ corresponds to January 1, 1977. The demand continues to decrease at the same rate.

(a) Determine the annual rate of demand at $t = 4$.

(b) How many total units are expected to be demanded over the time interval 1977 through 1986 ($t = 0$ to $t = 10$)?

Exercises 15.160 to 15.163 are related to Sec. 15.5.

In Exercises 15.160 to 15.163, determine the indefinite integral using integration by parts.

15.160 $\int x^3 e^{x^2}\, dx$ **15.161** $\int \ln x(x + 4)\, dx$

15.162 $\int (-x)(2x + 3)^{1/2}\, dx$ **15.163** $\int e^{-x}(x + 5)\, dx$

CHAPTER TEST

1 Given $f'(x) = 4x^3 - 2x - 10$ and the point $(5, 100)$ which satisfies $f(x)$, determine $f(x)$.

2 Find the following indefinite integrals.

(a) $\int \dfrac{dx}{\sqrt[3]{x^5}}$

(b) $\int (x^4 - 10)^7(x^3)\, dx$

(c) $\int e^{-10x} \, dx$

3 Evaluate $\int_0^4 (x^2 - 3x + 1) \, dx$.

4 Given $f(x) = x^2$ and $g(x) = 8 + 2x$, (a) sketch the two functions. (b) For $x \geq 0$ determine the area bounded by the two functions and the y axis.

5 An automobile manufacturer estimates that the annual rate of expenditure $r(t)$ for maintenance on one of its models is represented by the function

$$r(t) = 120 + 8t^2$$

where t is the age of the automobile stated in years and $r(t)$ is measured in dollars per year.

(a) At what annual rate are maintenance costs being incurred when the car is 4 years old?

(b) What are total maintenance costs expected to equal during the first 3 years?

16

CHAPTER OBJECTIVES After reading this chapter, you should be familiar with the concept of a probability; you should understand the basic rules of probability for selected statistical environments; you should be familiar with probability distributions and their characteristics; and you should have an understanding of the use of expected monetary value as a basis for decision making under conditions of uncertainty. In addition, you should be familiar with the characteristics and usage of two of the more commonly used probability distributions—the binomial distribution and the normal distribution.

Much in life is characterized by uncertainty. Most decisions are made in an environment characterized by uncertainty. A decision concerning the number of units of a product to produce is usually based on an *estimate* of the number of units expected to be purchased. If the number to be purchased were known in advance, the decision would be to produce this quantity, incurring neither shortages nor overages. However, in many applications exact information is rarely obtainable.

Probability concepts can be very useful in dealing with the uncertainty which characterizes most decision-making environments. Probability theory takes advantage of the fact that, for many uncertain phenomena, there are "long run" patterns. For instance, on the single flip of a fair coin it is uncertain whether a head or a tail will occur. However, over many flips of the same coin—over the long run—approximately half of the outcomes should be heads and approximately half tails.

The purpose of this chapter is to introduce the fundamentals of probability theory. The first section discusses some special counting methods which are useful in probability theory. The next section introduces fundamental concepts of probability and the computation of probabilities. This is followed by a discussion of the use of probability in determining expected values. The last two sections discuss two of the more frequently used probability distributions—the binomial and the normal distributions. The last section also includes a brief discussion of integral calculus and its role in probability theory.

16.1   PERMUTATIONS AND COMBINATIONS

Before we introduce probability theory, the special counting methods of permutations and combinations will be discussed.

Permutations

A *permutation* is an ordered arrangement of a set of objects. Consider the three numerals 1, 2, and 3. One permutation of these numerals is 123. Another permutation is 132. In fact, all the different permutations of these three numerals are

$$123 \quad 132 \quad 213 \quad 231 \quad 312 \quad 321$$

DEFINITION
The number of permutations of *n* different objects taken *n* at a time is denoted by $_nP_n$ where

$$_nP_n = n(n-1)(n-2) \cdots 2 \cdot 1 \qquad (16.1)$$

Equation (16.1) can be rewritten by using *factorial* notation as

$$_nP_n = n! \qquad (16.2)$$

The notation $n!$ (read "n factorial") is a shorthand way of representing the product on the right side of Eq. (16.1). For example,

$$5! = 5 \cdot 4 \cdot 3 \cdot 2 \cdot 1$$

And, $\qquad 10! = 10 \cdot 9 \cdot 8 \cdot 7 \cdot 6 \cdot 5 \cdot 4 \cdot 3 \cdot 2 \cdot 1$

By definition, $\qquad\qquad\qquad 0! = 1.$

The number of different permutations of the three numerals 1, 2, and 3 taken three at a time is $_3P_3 = 3! = 3 \cdot 2 \cdot 1 = 6$. Note that this equals the number of different permutations enumerated previously.

Example 16.1   Six football teams compete in a particular conference. Assuming no ties, how many different end-of-season rankings are possible in the conference?

The number of different rankings is

$$_6P_6 = 6! = 6 \cdot 5 \cdot 4 \cdot 3 \cdot 2 \cdot 1$$
$$= 720$$

DEFINITION
The number of permutations of n different objects taken r at a time is denoted by

$$_nP_r = n(n - 1)(n - 2) \cdots (n - r + 1) \qquad (16.3)$$

The logic underlying Eq. (16.3) is that in selecting the first of the r objects, there are n choices. Once the first object is selected, there are $n - 1$ choices for the second object, or $(n)(n - 1)$ possible choices for the first two objects. Following selection of the second object there are $n - 2$ choices for the third object, or $(n)(n - 1)(n - 2)$ possible choices for the first three objects. Once $r - 1$ objects have been selected, the number of different choices for the rth object equals $n - (r - 1)$, or $n - r + 1$.

An alternative statement of Eq. (16.3) is

$$_nP_r = \frac{n!}{(n - r)!} \qquad (16.4)$$

This is obtained by multiplying the right side of Eq. (16.3) by $(n - r)!/(n - r)!$

A person wishes to place an "across the board" bet which selects the first three horses to finish a race in their correct order of finish. If eight horses are in the race, how many different possibilities exist for the first three horses (assuming no ties)?

Example 16.2

The number of possibilities is

Solution

$$_8P_3 = 8 \cdot 7 \cdot 6 = 336$$

or, according to Eq. (16.4),

$$_8P_3 = \frac{8!}{(8 - 3)!} = \frac{8 \cdot 7 \cdot 6 \cdot 5 \cdot 4 \cdot 3 \cdot 2 \cdot 1}{5 \cdot 4 \cdot 3 \cdot 2 \cdot 1}$$
$$= 8 \cdot 7 \cdot 6 = 336$$

Combinations

With permutations we were concerned with the number of different ways in which a set of objects can be arranged. In many situations there is an interest in the number of ways in which a set of objects can be selected without any particular concern for the order or arrangement of the objects. For example, one may be interested in determining the number of different possible committees of three people which can be formed from six candidate members. In this instance, the committee consisting of (A, B, C) is the same committee as (B, A, C), where $A, B,$

and C represent three of the candidates. Order of selection is not significant in determining the number of different committees.

A *combination* is a set of objects with no consideration given to the order or arrangement of the objects. A combination of r objects selected from a set of n objects is really a *subset* of the set of n items.

DEFINITION
The number of different combinations of r objects which can be selected from n different objects is denoted by $_nC_r$ where

$$_nC_r = \frac{n!}{r!(n-r)!}$$ (16.5)

To return to the committee example, the number of different combinations of six persons taken three at a time equals

$$_6C_3 = \frac{6!}{3!(6-3)!}$$

$$= \frac{6!}{3!3!}$$

$$= \frac{6 \cdot 5 \cdot 4 \cdot 3 \cdot 2 \cdot 1}{3 \cdot 2 \cdot 1 \cdot 3 \cdot 2 \cdot 1}$$

$$= 20$$

Example 16.3   Super Bowl organizers are selecting game officials. From 12 who are eligible, 5 officials will be selected. How many different teams of 5 officials can be selected from the 12?

Solution   The number of different teams of officials is

$$_{12}C_5 = \frac{12!}{5!(12-5)!}$$

$$= \frac{12!}{5!7!}$$

$$= \frac{12 \cdot 11 \cdot 10 \cdot 9 \cdot 8}{5 \cdot 4 \cdot 3 \cdot 2 \cdot 1}$$

$$= 792$$

Follow-up Exercises

In Exercises 16.1 to 16.6, evaluate each symbol.

16.1 $_5P_5$ **16.2** $_7P_2$

16.3 $_{10}P_5$ **16.4** $_3C_3$

16.5 $_{10}C_3$ **16.6** $_5C_4$

16.7 Eight people are to be seated at the head table at a banquet. How many different seating arrangements are possible?

16.8 A political candidate wishes to visit six different cities. In how many different orders can she visit these cities?

16.9 The same political candidate in Exercise 16.8 has time and funds to visit only four of the cities. How many different combinations of four cities can she visit?

16.10 A credit card company issues credit cards which have a three-letter prefix as part of the card number. A sample card number is ABC105. If each letter in the prefix is to be different, how many different prefixes are possible?

16.11 In Exercise 16.10, assume that the three-letter prefix is followed by three numerals, each different. How many different three-digit sequences are possible?

16.12 A small school has received financial assistance applications from 20 people. Only 5 will be granted financial assistance. How many different combinations of applicants are there who might receive financial aid?

BASIC PROBABILITY CONCEPTS   16.2

This section will introduce the notion of probability and some basic probability concepts.

Probabilities and Odds

The notion of probability is associated with *random processes*, or *random experiments*. A random experiment is a process which results in one of a number of possible *outcomes*, or *events*. The occurrence or absence of these outcomes or events is determined by chance. A classic illustration of a random experiment is the flipping of a fair coin. If we assume the coin does not come to rest on its edge, the two possible outcomes for the experiment are the occurrence of a head or the occurrence of a tail. And, the occurrence or nonoccurrence of either of these outcomes is determined by chance.

Other classic random experiments include rolling a die, drawing a card from a well-shuffled deck, and selecting a ball from an urn which contains a number of balls. There are many random processes around us which are less obvious. Many manufacturing processes produce defective products in a random manner. The time of arrival of telephone calls at a telephone exchange, cars at toll booths, and customers at supermarkets have been described as random processes. The process by which the sex of a child is determined is also random.

Although we can guess about the outcome of a random experiment, we cannot know for certain what outcome will occur. We can guess head or tail for the flip of a coin, but we cannot know for sure. With many random processes, however, there is long-run regularity. As mentioned earlier, the long-run expectation in flipping a coin is that approximately half of the outcomes will be heads and half tails. In the roll of a die, the long-run expectation is that each side of the die will occur approximately one-sixth of the time. These values reflect the expectation of the *relative frequency* of an event. The relative frequency of an event is the proportion of the time that the event occurs. It is computed by dividing the number of times m the event occurs by the number of times n the experiment is conducted. *The probability of an event can be thought of as the relative frequency m/n of the event over the long run.*†

Since the probability of an event is a proportion, we can state the following rule.

RULE 1
The probability of an event A, denoted by $P(A)$, is a number between 0 and 1, inclusive, or

$$0 \leq P(A) \leq 1 \tag{16.6}$$

Two special cases of Eq. (16.6) follow. If $P(A) = 0$, it is certain that event A will not occur. For example, if a coin is two-headed, $P(\text{tail}) = 0$ in a single flip of the coin. If $P(A) = 1$, it is certain that event A will occur. With the same coin, $P(\text{head}) = 1$. If $0 < P(A) < 1$, there is uncertainty about the occurrence of event A. For example, if $P(A) = .4$, we can state that there is a 40 percent chance that event A will occur.

**Example
16.4**
Table 16.1 indicates some characteristics of the first-year class at a junior college. Assume that a student will be selected at random from the freshman class and that each person has an equal chance of being selected. Using the relative frequency concept of probability, we can estimate the likelihood that the selected student will have certain characteristics. For example, the probability that the selected student will be a male is

$$P(M) = \frac{\text{number of males}}{\text{total number of first-year students}}$$
$$= \frac{750}{1,500} = 0.50$$

The probability that the selected student will be a preengineering student is

$$P(E) = \frac{150}{1,500} = 0.10$$

---

† For those who have read Chap. 11, the probability of an event can be defined in terms of the limit of the relative frequency m/n as the number of trials n approaches infinity.

**Table
16.1**

Sex ＼ Major	(B) Business	(L) Liberal Arts	(E) Preengineering	Total
Male (M)	350	300	100	750
Female (F)	250	450	50	750
Total	600	750	150	1,500

Major Sex	(B) Business	(L) Liberal Arts	(E) Preengineering	Total	Table 16.2
Male (M)	.233	.200	.067	.500	
Female (F)	.167	.300	.033	.500	
Total	.400	.500	.100	1.000	

The probability that the selected student will be a female majoring in business is

$$P(F \text{ and } B) = \frac{250}{1,500} = 0.166$$

Table 16.2 summarizes the probabilities of various events in selecting a student.

Notice that the sum of the probabilities for the events M and F equals 1. Similarly, the sum of the probabilities for the events B, L, and E equals 1.

POINT FOR THOUGHT AND DISCUSSION
Why do the probabilities for the two different sets of events $\{M, F\}$ and $\{B, L, E\}$ each total 1?

Probabilities may be classified in several ways. One classification is the distinction between *objective* and *subjective probabilities*. Objective probabilities are based upon definite historical experience or general knowledge. For example, probabilities assigned to the events associated with flipping a fair coin or rolling a die are based upon much historical and generally known experience. Other objective probabilities are assigned because of actual experimentation. For instance, if one has been told that a die is "loaded," one method of determining the probability of any side occurring is to roll the die many times while keeping a record of the relative frequency for each side.

Subjective probabilities are assigned in the absence of wide historical experience. They are based upon personal experiences and intuition. They are really expressions of personal judgment. A subjective probability would be the probability that you would assign to your receiving a grade of A in this course. Such an estimate would reflect your personal assessment of such factors as your aptitude in this type of course, your perception of the degree of difficulty of this course, and your assessment of the instructor and the way in which he or she will conduct the course and evaluate performance.

When *odds* are given in association with some event, they reflect someone's assessment of the likelihood of occurrence (or nonoccurrence) of the event. If an oddsmaker states odds of 3 to 1 that team A will win a football game, the oddsmaker is stating a belief that if the game were played four times, team A would win three of the four times. Or, these odds assign a probability of $\frac{3}{1 + 3} = \frac{3}{4}$ or 0.75 that team A will win. The odds of 3 to 1 favoring team A are equivalent to stating odds of 1 to 3 that the opponent team will win. Odds of 1 to 3 are equivalent to assigning a probability of $\dfrac{1}{1+3} = \frac{1}{4} = 0.25$.

Some Rules of Probability

RULE 2
If $P(A)$ represents the probability that an event A will occur, the probability that A will not occur, denoted by $P(\overline{A})$, is

$$P(\overline{A}) = 1 - P(A) \qquad (16.7)$$

If the probability that a business will earn a profit during its first year of operation is .85, the probability that it will not earn a profit during the first year is $1 - .85 = .15$.

Events are considered to be *mutually exclusive* if the occurrence of one event precludes the occurrence of any other events. In flipping a coin, the two possible outcomes are *heads* and *tails*. Since the occurrence of a head precludes any possibility of a tail, and vice versa, the events "heads" and "tails" are mutually exclusive events.

Example 16.5 Consider the events "king" and "spade" in drawing a card from a deck of cards. These events are not mutually exclusive because the selection of a king does not eliminate any possibility of a spade. The king could be the king of spades.

The events "heart", "spade", "club", and "diamond" are considered to be mutually exclusive. The occurrence of any one of these events eliminates any possibility of the other three events.

RULE 3
If events A and B are mutually exclusive, the probability of either A or B occurring is

$$P(A \cup B) = P(A) + P(B) \qquad (16.8)$$

Note the use of the union operator from set theory in this rule.

Example 16.6 **Public Works** The department of public works for a community is gearing up for winter. The department is planning its sand and salt needs for maintaining roads during and after snowstorms. An analysis of past winters has resulted in the following probability estimates regarding the expected number of major snowstorms. What is the probability of three or more major snowstorms during the coming year?

Number of Major Storms n	$P(n)$	Table 16.3
0	.10	
1	.25	
2	.30	
3	.20	
more than 3	.15	

Solution

The events in Table 16.3 which correspond to "3 or more" major snowstorms are $n = 3$ and $n =$ more than 3. These two events are mutually exclusive. Therefore, the probability of three or more major snowstorms is

$$P(3 \text{ or more}) = P(3) + P(\text{more than 3})$$
$$= .20 + .15$$
$$= 0.35$$

RULE 4
Given n mutually exclusive events $E_1, E_2, \ldots, E_n$, the probability of occurrence of one of the n events is

$$P(E_1 \cup E_2 \cup \cdots \cup E_n) = P(E_1) + P(E_2) + \cdots + P(E_n) \tag{16.9}$$

Example 16.7

In Example 16.6, what is the probability of having fewer than three major snowstorms?

Solution

The events corresponding to "fewer than three" storms are 0, 1, or 2 storms. Therefore

$$P(\text{less than 3}) = P(0 \cup 1 \cup 2)$$
$$= P(0) + P(1) + P(2)$$
$$= .10 + .25 + .30$$
$$= 0.65$$

NOTE
This problem could have been solved by using our answer from Example 16.5 and applying Rule 2. That is,

$$P(\text{less than 3}) = 1 - P(3 \text{ or more})$$

When a set of events is not mutually exclusive, Rule 3 must be modified to reflect the possibility that two events may occur at the same time.

RULE 5
The probability of occurrence of event A, event B, or both A and B is

$$P(A \cup B) = P(A) + P(B) - P(A \cap B) \qquad (16.10)$$

Note that the intersection operator is used to denote the joint or simultaneous occurrence of events A and B.

Rule 3 is the special case of Rule 5 where $P(A \cap B) = 0$. This is because A and B are assumed to be mutually exclusive in Rule 3, meaning that the events can never occur together.

Example 16.8
In Example 16.5 we concluded that for the experiment consisting of selecting one card at random from a deck of 52 cards, the events "king" and "spade" were not mutually exclusive. The probability of selecting a king, a spade, or both a king and a spade is determined by applying Rule 5, or

$$\begin{aligned}
P(\text{king} \cup \text{spade}) &= P(\text{king}) + P(\text{spade}) - P(\text{king} \cap \text{spade}) \\
&= P(\text{king}) + P(\text{spade}) - P(\text{king of spades}) \\
&= \tfrac{4}{52} + \tfrac{13}{52} - \tfrac{1}{52} \\
&= \tfrac{16}{52} = \tfrac{4}{13}
\end{aligned}$$

Note that $P(A \cap B)$ must be subtracted to offset the double counting of the event $A \cap B$. When $P(\text{king})$ is computed, the king of spades is included; and when $P(\text{spade})$ is computed, the king of spades is included. Thus, double counting has occurred, and $P(\text{king of spades})$ must be subtracted once.

A set of events is said to be *collectively exhaustive* if their union accounts for all possible outcomes of an experiment. The events "head" and "tail," associated with the flip of a coin, are collectively exhaustive since their union accounts for all possible outcomes. The events H_1H_2, H_1T_2, and T_1T_2 describe outcomes associated with flipping a coin twice. This set of events is not collectively exhaustive since the union of the events does not include the outcome T_1H_2.

For the same experiment, the set of events H_1H_2, H_1T_2, T_1T_2, and T_1H_2 is *both* mutually exclusive and collectively exhaustive.

Statistical Independence

Events may be classified as *independent* or *dependent*. If two events are independent, the occurrence or nonoccurrence of one event in no way affects the occurrence of the other event. Another way of stating this is that the occurrence or nonoccurrence of one event in no way affects the *probability* of occurrence of the other event.

Successive flips of a fair coin are an example of independent events. The occurrence of a head or tail on any one toss of the coin has no effect on the probability of a head or tail on the next or succeeding tosses of the coin.

Drawing cards from a deck or balls from an urn *with replacement* is an experiment characterized by independent events. *With replacement* means that the item selected is put back in the deck or the urn before the next item is selected. In the case of a deck of cards, the probability of drawing a heart on each draw is $\frac{13}{52}$ as long as the previously drawn card is replaced in the deck.

The simple probability of an event is often called a *marginal probability*. The marginal probability of a head is .5 when a fair coin is tossed. Very often there is an interest in computing the probability of two or more events occurring at the same time or in succession. For example, we may be interested in the probability of rolling a pair of dice and having a 5 occur on one die and a 2 on the other; or, we may be interested in the likelihood that five heads would occur in five successive tosses of a coin. The probability of the joint occurrence of two or more events is called a *joint probability*.

RULE 6
The joint probability that two independent events A and B will occur together or in succession equals the product of the marginal probabilities of A and B, or

$$P(A \cap B) = P(A) \cdot P(B) \qquad (16.11)$$

The probability that a machine will produce a defective part equals .05. The production process is characterized by statistical independence. That is, the probability of any item being defective is .05, regardless of the quality of previous units. What is the probability that two consecutive parts will be defective?

Example 16.9

If the event D represents the occurrence of a defective item, then

Solution

$$
\begin{aligned}
P(D_1 \cap D_2) &= P(D_1)P(D_2) \\
&= (.05)(.05) \\
&= .0025
\end{aligned}
$$

RULE 7
The joint probability that n independent events E_1, $E_2, \ldots, E_n$ will occur together or in succession is

$$P(E_1 \cap E_2 \cap \cdots \cap E_n) = P(E_1)P(E_2) \cdots P(E_n) \qquad (16.12)$$

A fair coin is tossed 3 consecutive times. Determine all possible outcomes for the experiment and the probabilities of these outcomes.

Example 16.10

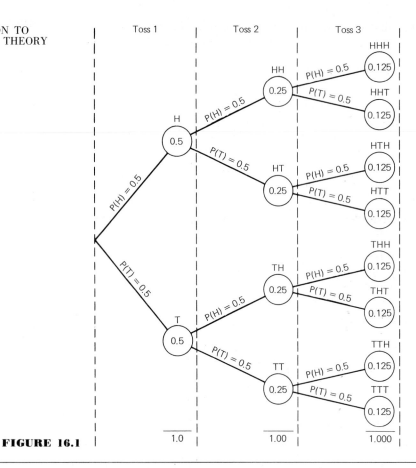

FIGURE 16.1

A device which is useful in problems such as this is a *probability tree*. A probability tree provides a logical method for determining and displaying all possible outcomes in an experiment. Figure 16.1 illustrates the probability tree for this experiment. For toss 1, the circles indicate the marginal probabilities of the two simple events which can occur. Given one of these outcomes for the first toss, there are two possible outcomes on the second toss. The circles indicate the joint probabilities of the various joint events which can occur for an experiment involving two tosses of a coin. Since the outcomes for toss 1 and toss 2 are independent events, these probabilities are computed by using Rule 6. For example,

$$P(H \cap T) = P(H)P(T)$$
$$= (.5)(.5) = .125$$

For three tosses there are eight possible joint outcomes. The circles indicate the joint probabilities of the different joint events, and they have been computed by applying Rule 7. For example,

$$P(T \cap H \cap T) = P(T)P(H)P(T)$$
$$= (.5)(.5)(.5) = .125$$

Note in Fig. 16.1 that for each toss the sum of the joint probabilities equals 1. This is so because the set of outcomes identified is collectively exhaustive.

In addition to marginal and joint probabilities, another type of probability is a *conditional probability*. The notation $P(A|B)$ represents the conditional probability of event A given that event B has occurred. The probability of a head on the third toss of a coin, given that the first two tosses both resulted in a head, is a conditional probability.

By definition, however, independent events have the property that the occurrence or nonoccurrence of one event has no influence on the probability of another event.

RULE 8
Given two independent events A and B, the conditional probability of event A given that event B has occurred is the marginal probability of A, or

$$P(A|B) = P(A) \tag{16.13}$$

The conditional probability of a 6 on the next roll of a die given that no 6s have occurred in the last 20 rolls equals $\frac{1}{6}$.

Statistical Dependence

Two events are *dependent* if the probability of occurrence of one event is affected by the occurrence or nonoccurrence of the other event. Examples of experiments consisting of dependent events include drawing cards from a deck or balls from an urn *without replacement*. If a card is selected which is not a heart and the card is kept out of the deck, the probability of selecting a heart on the next draw is not the same as it was for the first draw. Given the following events related to weather conditions:

Event A = it will snow
Event B = the temperature will be below freezing

the probability of event A is affected by event B.

A nationwide survey of 10,000 middle-aged men resulted in the data shown in Table 16.4. It is believed that the results from this survey of

Example 16.11

Table 16.4

	No Exercise (NE)	Some Exercise (SE)	Regular Exercise (RE)	Total
Heart Disease (HD)	700	300	100	1,100
No Heart Disease ($\overline{HD}$)	1,300	6,600	1,000	8,900
Total	2,000	6,900	1,100	10,000

10,000 men are representative of these particular attributes for the average middle-aged man in this country. Based upon these results, we can estimate probabilities related to heart disease and exercise habits. For example, the probability that a middle-aged man gets no exercise is

$$P(NE) = \frac{2,000}{10,000} = 0.20$$

The probability that a middle-aged man has heart disease is

$$P(HD) = \frac{1,100}{10,000} = 0.11$$

The joint probability that a middle-aged man exercises regularly and has heart disease is

$$P(HD \cap RE) = \frac{100}{10,000} = 0.01$$

Assume that we are interested in the conditional probability that a man will suffer from heart disease *given* that he does not exercise. The *given* information focuses our attentions upon the first column in Table 16.4, those who do not exercise. Of the 2,000 surveyed who do not exercise, 700 suffer heart disease. Therefore

$$P(HD|NE) = \frac{700}{2,000} = .35$$

The conditional probability that a man exercises regularly given that he suffers heart disease is

$$P(RE|HD) = \frac{100}{1,100} = .09$$

Conditional probabilities under conditions of statistical dependence can be computed by using the following rule.

RULE 9
Under conditions of statistical dependence, the conditional probability of event A given the occurrence of event B is

$$P(A|B) = \frac{P(A \cap B)}{P(B)} \qquad (16.14)$$

The conditional probability is found by dividing the joint probability of events A and B by the marginal probability of B.

Indirectly, we were using Eq. (16.14) when computing the conditional probabilities in Example 16.11. Applying Eq. (16.14) in that example, we get

$$P(HD|NE) = \frac{P(HD \cap NE)}{P(NE)}$$

$$= \frac{.07}{.2} = .35$$

and
$$P(RE|HD) = \frac{P(RE \cap HD)}{P(HD)}$$
$$= \frac{.01}{.11} = .09$$

A person selects a card at random from a deck of 52 cards. The person tells us that the selected card is red. What is the probability that the card is the king of hearts *given* that it is red?

Example 16.12

Applying Eq. (16.14) gives us

Solution

$$P(\text{king of hearts} \mid \text{red}) = \frac{P(\text{king of hearts} \cap \text{red})}{P(\text{red})}$$
$$= \frac{\frac{1}{52}}{\frac{26}{52}}$$
$$= \frac{1}{26}$$

If both sides of Eq. (16.14) are multiplied by $P(B)$, the resulting equation provides an expression for the joint probability $P(A \cap B)$, or

$$P(A \cap B) = P(B)P(A|B) \qquad (16.15)$$

What is the joint probability of selecting two aces in a row from a deck without replacement of the first card?

Example 16.13

$$P(A_1 \cap A_2) = P(A_1)P(A_2|A_1)$$
$$= \frac{4}{52} \cdot \frac{3}{51}$$
$$= \frac{12}{2,652}$$

Solution

A production run of 20 units resulted in five defective parts. If three parts are selected at random from the run, what is the probability that the first two are not defective and the third is defective (assume no replacement and equal likelihood of selection)?

Example 16.14

Let's determine the probability that the first two items will not be defective. If N denotes a nondefective item and D a defective item, then

Solution

$$P(N_1 \cap N_2) = P(N_1)P(N_2|N_1)$$
$$= \frac{15}{20} \cdot \frac{14}{19}$$
$$= \frac{210}{380} = \frac{21}{38}$$

Now considering the third item selected, we have

$$P(N_1 \cap N_2 \cap D_3) = P(N_1 \cap N_2)P(D_3|N_1 \cap N_2)$$
$$= \frac{21}{38} \cdot \frac{5}{18}$$
$$= \frac{105}{684} = \frac{35}{228}$$

Table 16.5	Highest Degree / Sex	College Degree (C)	High School Diploma (H)	No Degree (N)	Total
	Male (M)	30	35	15	80
	Female (F)	70	45	5	120
	Total	100	80	20	200

Follow-up Exercises

16.13 Table 16.5 indicates some characteristics of a pool of 200 applicants for an administrative position. Applicants are classified by sex and by *highest* educational degree received. If one applicant is selected at random (each having an equal chance of being selected), what is the probability that the applicant selected will (*a*) be a female, (*b*) have a high school diploma as the highest degree, (*c*) be a female with no degrees, (*d*) be a male with a college degree?

16.14 Table 16.6 indicates some characteristics of 10,000 borrowers from a major financial institution. Borrowers are classified according to the type of loan (personal or business) and level of risk. If one borrower's account is to be selected at random (each having an equal chance of selection) for purposes of review, what is the probability that the account selected will (*a*) be in the excellent risk category, (*b*) be a business loan, (*c*) be a personal loan in the poor risk category, (*d*) be a business loan with a good risk?

16.15 Odds that a political candidate will win the next election have been stated as 5 to 2. What is the probability that the candidate will win according to the stated odds? What are the odds that another candidate will win?

16.16 Three teams are participating in a tournament. Experts estimate that team *A* has a probability of .40 of winning the tournament. What is the probability that one of the other two teams will win the tournament?

16.17 A student estimates the probability of receiving an A in a course at .20 and the probability of receiving a B at .25. What is the probability that the student (*a*) will not receive an A, (*b*) will not receive a B, (*c*) will receive neither an A nor a B?

16.18 The number of units sold by a firm fluctuates daily. The owner of the firm estimates the probabilities for the different sales volumes (see Table 16.7). For any given day, what is the probability that (*a*) 10 or 11 units will be demanded, (*b*) more than 10 units will be demanded, (*c*) no more than 11 units will be demanded?

Table 16.6	Credit Risk / Type of Loan	Excellent Risk (E)	Good Risk (G)	Poor Risk (P)	Total
	Personal (P)	1,500	6,000	500	8,000
	Business (B)	500	1,300	200	2,000
	Total	2,000	7,300	700	10,000

Number of Units Sold (n)	P(n)	Table
		16.7
Fewer than 10	.10	
10	.25	
11	.30	
12	.20	
More than 12	.15	

16.19 The number of fire alarms pulled each hour fluctuates in a particular city. Analysts have estimated the probability of different numbers of alarms per hour as shown in Table 16.8. In any given hour, what is the probability that (a) more than five alarms will be pulled, (b) between five and seven alarms (inclusive) will be pulled, (c) no more than five alarms will be pulled?

16.20 A card is to be drawn at random from a well-shuffled deck. What is the probability that the card will be (a) an ace or king, (b) a face card (jack, queen, or king), (c) a 4 or a heart, (d) a face card or a club?

16.21 The probability that a machine will produce a defective part equals .08. If the process is characterized by statistical independence, what is the probability that (a) two items in succession will not be defective, (b) the first two items are defective and the third not defective, (c) five consecutive items will not be defective?

16.22 *Auditing.* An income tax return can be audited by the federal IRS and/or by the state of residence. The probability that an individual tax return will be audited by the IRS is .03. The probability that it will be audited by the state is .02. Assume that audit decisions are made independent of one another at the federal and state levels.
(a) What is the probability of being audited by both agencies?
(b) What is the probability of a state audit but not a federal audit?

16.23 A coin is weighted such that $P(H) = .4$ and $P(T) = .6$. Construct a probability tree denoting all possible outcomes if the coin is tossed 3 times. What is the probability of two heads in three tosses?

16.24 Three cards are selected at random from a deck of 52. If the drawn cards are not replaced in the deck, what is the probability of selecting an ace followed by a king, followed by a queen?

16.25 Table 16.9 indicates the results of a survey of voter behavior in a recent election. If a voter is selected at random from this group of 20,000, what are the following probabilities?
(a) The voter was a registered Republican but did not vote Republican.
(b) The voter voted for the Republican candidate.
(c) The voter was a registered Democrat given that he or she voted for the Democratic candidate.

Number of Alarms Pulled (n)	P(n)	Table
		16.8
Fewer than 5	.40	
5	.25	
6	.15	
7	.10	
More than 7	.10	

Voter Registration / Voter Preference	Democratic Candidate (DC)	Republican Candidate (RC)	Other Candidate (OC)	Total
Democrat (D)	7,500	1,000	500	9,000
Republican (R)	3,500	4,200	300	8,000
Other (O)	1,000	800	1,200	3,000
Total	12,000	6,000	2,000	20,000

Table
16.9

(d) The voter voted for the Republican candidate given that he or she was not a registered Democrat or Republican.

(e) The voter was a registered Democrat and did not vote for the Democratic or Republican candidate.

16.3   MATHEMATICAL EXPECTATION

This section discusses random variables, probability distributions, and mathematical expectation.

Random Variables

A *random variable* is a numerical value which fluctuates in no predictable manner. Very often the results or outcomes of an experiment are described by random variables. For instance, events in an experiment may be the number of heads which occur in three tosses of a coin. In an experiment concerned with crime prevention techniques, the outcomes may reflect the number of crimes per day. An experiment comparing lawn fertilizers may describe outcomes in terms of growth per week or perhaps density or thickness of grass. In each of these experiments, a value of the random variable corresponds to each possible outcome in the experiment.

If a random variable can assume only a finite number of distinct values, it is called a *discrete random variable*. The outcomes of an experiment which measures the number of items of a product demanded each day can be represented by a discrete random variable. The outcomes of an experiment which measures the number of cars passing through a toll booth each hour can be represented by a discrete random variable.

A random variable which can assume any value within some interval of numbers is called a *continuous random variable*. In an experiment which selects people at random and records some attribute such as height or weight, the outcomes can be represented by a continuous random variable. The outcomes of an experiment which measures the length of time that a transistor will operate before burning out can be described by a continuous random variable.

Probability Distributions

A *probability distribution* is a complete listing of all possible outcomes of an experiment along with the probabilities of each outcome. When

Number of Heads (x)	$P(x)$	Table
0	$\frac{1}{8}$	16.10
1	$\frac{3}{8}$	
2	$\frac{3}{8}$	
3	$\frac{1}{8}$	
	1	

the outcomes are described by a discrete random variable, the probability distribution lists all possible values of the random variable and the probabilities of each value. Since all possible outcomes are included, the sum of their probabilities should total 1.

Table 16.10 is a discrete probability distribution associated with tossing a fair coin 3 times. The discrete random variable x represents the number of heads occurring in three tosses.

With continuous probability distributions, the number of possible values for the random variable is infinite. And, the probability that the random variable will assume one specific value is very close to 0. To illustrate this, think of the random variable x which equals the annual rainfall in an area. The number of possible amounts of rain is infinite. For example, one possible value for x is 24.000056 inches. With an infinite number of possible values for x, the likelihood of any one value is extremely small. Thus, with continuous probability distributions, statements are not made regarding the probability that the random variable will assume a specific value. Rather, statements are usually made regarding the probability that the random variable will assume a value within a defined interval. In the rainfall example, we may want to know the probability that annual rainfall will be between 24 and 25 inches.

Mean and Standard Deviation

The *arithmetic mean*, or more simply the *mean*, of a random variable is one measure of the central tendency of the value of the random variable. The mean is a single value which is most frequently referred to as the *average* of the random variable. We have all heard and used the term *average* to best describe the value of some attribute in our daily lives. Average temperature, Environmental Protection Agency estimates of average gasoline mileage on a new car, and average age of a set of persons are examples.

The mean of a discrete probability distribution is found by multiplying each value of the random variable by its probability of occurring and algebraically summing these products for each value.

DEFINITION
If a discrete random variable x can assume n values $x_1, x_2, \ldots, x_n$ having respective probabilities of occurrence $p_1, p_2, \ldots, p_n$, the mean value μ (mu) of the random variable is

$$\mu = x_1 p_1 + x_2 p_2 + \cdots + x_n p_n \qquad (16.16)$$

Table 16.11	Quantity Demanded (x)	P(x)
	25	.10
	26	.20
	27	.25
	28	.30
	29	.10
	30	.05
		1.00

Example 16.15 Analysis has revealed that demand for a product varies randomly day to day. Table 16.11 presents a discrete probability distribution based on the study of historical data. The mean value for this random variable is

$$\mu = 25(.10) + 26(.20) + (27)(.25) + (28)(.30) + (29)(.10) + (30)(.05)$$
$$= 27.25$$

Note that the quantity demanded on any given day cannot equal the mean. However, *on the average*, daily demand will equal 27.25 units.

Whereas the mean of a random variable provides information about central tendency, the *standard deviation* yields information about the degree of variability in the value of a random variable. Consider the two probability distributions in Table 16.12. Both these distributions have the same mean $\mu = 50$. However, the possible variation in the values of the two random variables is quite different.

DEFINITION
Given a discrete random variable x which can assume n values x_1, $x_2, \ldots, x_n$ having respective probabilities of occurrence p_1, $p_2, \ldots, p_n$, the standard deviation σ (sigma) of the random variable is

$$\sigma = \sqrt{(x_1 - \mu)^2 p_1 + (x_2 - \mu)^2 p_2 + \cdots + (x_n - \mu)^2 p_n} \quad (16.17)$$

or, using summation notation, we have

$$\sigma = \sqrt{\sum_{j=1}^{n} (x_j - \mu)^2 p_j} \quad (16.18)$$

Example 16.16 Let's compute the standard deviations for the two distributions in Table 16.12. For the first distribution,

$$\sigma = \sqrt{(49 - 50)^2(.05) + (50 - 50)^2(.90) + (51 - 50)^2(.05)}$$
$$= \sqrt{.05 + 0 + .05}$$
$$= \sqrt{.10}$$
$$= 0.3162$$

x	$P(x)$	x	$P(x)$	Table
				16.12
49	.05	0	.05	
50	.90	50	.90	
51	.05	100	.05	

For the second distribution,

$$\sigma = \sqrt{(0 - 50)^2(.05) + (50 - 50)^2(.90) + (100 - 50)^2(.05)}$$
$$= \sqrt{125 + 0 + 125}$$
$$= \sqrt{250}$$
$$= 15.81$$

From this example we can conclude that the greater the variability in the value of a random variable, the greater the value of the standard deviation. Later we will see that the standard deviation has some very useful interpretations.

Expected Monetary Value

Consider a game in which a fair die is rolled. The participant in the game pays \$3 to play and receives a payoff of x dollars where x equals the number which comes up on the die. The question is whether it is worthwhile monetarily to participate in the game. *Expected monetary value*, or average dollar payoff, may be used to help make a decision about participating in the game. Table 16.13 presents a probability distribution showing the possible outcomes on a roll of the die, the corresponding dollar payoffs, and their probabilities of occurrence. Note that payoffs, being dependent upon the roll of the die, become the random variable. The mean of this distribution is

$$\mu = \$1(\tfrac{1}{6}) + \$2(\tfrac{1}{6}) + \$3(\tfrac{1}{6}) + \$4(\tfrac{1}{6}) + \$5(\tfrac{1}{6}) + \$6(\tfrac{1}{6})$$
$$= \frac{\$21}{6} = \$3.50$$

Thus, the *expected payoff* associated with this game is \$3.50. This represents the average dollar payoff over many plays of the game and when compared with the \$3 cost of playing the game, the *expected profit* per game is 50 cents.

Outcome of Roll	Payoff x	$P(x)$	Table 16.13
1	\$1	$\tfrac{1}{6}$	
2	\$2	$\tfrac{1}{6}$	
3	\$3	$\tfrac{1}{6}$	
4	\$4	$\tfrac{1}{6}$	
5	\$5	$\tfrac{1}{6}$	
6	\$6	$\tfrac{1}{6}$	
		$\overline{1}$	

Table 16.14	Daily Demand (x)	Number of Days Observed	P(x)
	21	20	.10
	22	60	.30
	23	100	.50
	24	20	.10
		200	1.00

Example 16.17

Expected monetary value can be the basis for deciding which decision alternative is best in a given situation. Consider a situation in which a retailer sells a single product. She purchases the product from a supplier at a cost of $5 per unit. She sells each unit at a price of $8. The item is perishable; if it is not sold on the first day, it has no value. That is, it cannot be sold, and there is no salvage value. The retailer must absorb the cost of the item as a $5 loss.

She has gathered historical data which confirm that daily demand for the product assumes four possible values. Table 16.14 summarizes this demand information in terms of a discrete probability distribution.

The retailer is trying to decide how many units to stock on a given day. She has decided that rather than try to second-guess the market each day, she would prefer to determine one quantity which will be stocked each day. Her goal is to select the quantity which maximizes expected daily profit.

Table 16.15 presents a *conditional profit table* which summarizes the daily profit which would result *given* any quantity demanded and corresponding stock decision. Note that the possible stock decisions correspond to the different discrete demand possibilities.

The conditional profit values are determined by computing the total profit from units sold and subtracting from this any loss which would have to be absorbed because of overstocking. For example, the decision to stock 21 units always results in a conditional profit of $63. The $63 results from selling all 21 units stocked with a profit per unit of $8 − $5 = $3. If demand equals 22 units or more, the 21 units stocked will always be sold. However, at these levels of demand, she has understocked.

Let's consider the decision to stock 22 units. If 21 units are demanded, 21 units will be sold, earning a profit of $63. However, since the retailer overstocked by 1 unit, the cost of the leftover unit must be absorbed, reducing the conditional profit to $63 − $5 = $58. If 22 units are stocked and 22 units are demanded, conditional profits of $66 result.

Table 16.15 Conditional Profit Table		Possible Stock Decision			
	Possible Demand	21	22	23	24
	21	63	58	53	48
	22	63	66	61	56
	23	63	66	69	64
	24	63	66	69	72

And if more than 22 units are demanded, the 22 units stocked will be sold, resulting in conditional profits of $66.

The conditional profits for the stock decisions of 23 and 24 units are computed in a similar manner. For example, the $53 conditional profit from stocking 23 units and having demand for 21 units results from 21 units being sold at a profit of $63, but this is reduced by $2 \cdot \$5 = \$10$ because of the overstocking of 2 units.

The expected daily profit for each stock decision can be determined by weighting each conditional profit by its likelihood of occurrence (which is the probability of the corresponding level of demand). Table 16.16 illustrates the computation for each stock decision.

Table 16.16

Stock 21

Conditional Profit	Probability of Occurrence	Expected Daily Profit
$63	× .10	= $ 6.30
63	× .30	= 18.90
63	× .50	= 31.50
63	× .10	= 6.30
		$63.00

Stock 22

Conditional Profit	Probability of Occurrence	Expected Daily Profit
$58	× .10	= $ 5.80
66	× .30	= 19.80
66	× .50	= 33.00
66	× .10	= 6.60
		$65.20

Stock 23

Conditional Profit	Probability of Occurrence	Expected Daily Profit
$53	× .10	= $ 5.30
61	× .30	= 18.30
69	× .50	= 34.50
69	× .10	= 6.90
		$65.00

Stock 24

Conditional Profit	Probability of Occurrence	Expected Daily Profit
$48	× .10	= $ 4.80
56	× .30	= 16.80
64	× .50	= 32.00
72	× .10	= 7.20
		$60.80

Table	Number Demanded per Day	
16.17	(x)	P(x)
	10	.08
	20	.22
	30	.36
	40	.18
	50	.16
		1.00

Based on expected daily profit, the best stock decision is to stock 22 items each day, resulting in an expected (average) daily profit of $65.20.

POINT FOR THOUGHT AND DISCUSSION
Why would the retailer not consider stocking fewer than 21 units or more than 24 units?

Follow-up Exercises

16.26 Construct the discrete probability distribution which corresponds to the experiment of tossing a *fair* coin 4 times. Let the random variable x equal the number of heads occurring in four tosses.

16.27 Construct the discrete probability distribution which corresponds to the experiment of rolling a *pair* of dice. Assume equal likelihood of occurrence of each side of a die, and let the random variable x equal the sum of the dots which come up on the pair.

16.28 Table 16.17 presents a discrete probability distribution associated with the daily demand for a product.
(a) Determine the mean daily demand.
(b) What is the standard deviation of daily demand?

16.29 A manufactured part consists of five electrical components. Each of the components has a limited lifetime. The company has tested the part to determine the reliability of the components. Table 16.18 presents a probability distribution where the random variable x indicates the number of components which fail during the first 100 hours of operation.

Table	Number of Components Failing	
16.18	(x)	P(x)
	0	.05
	1	.35
	2	.20
	3	.15
	4	.15
	5	.10
		1.00

x	P(x)	x	P(x)	Table
300	1	0	.15	16.19
		100	.05	
		200	.20	
		300	.20	
		400	.20	
		500	.05	
		600	.15	
			1.00	

(a) What is the mean number of components which fail during the first 100 hours of operation?

(b) What is the standard deviation of the random variable x?

(c) If the part will continue to operate if no more than one component fails, what percentage of the manufactured parts will continue to operate during the first 100 hours?

16.30 Compute the respective means and standard deviations for the two distributions in Table 16.19.

16.31 A game involves tossing a coin for which $P(H) = .4$. If a head occurs, the participant receives a payoff of $5. If a tail occurs, the participant receives no payoff. If it costs $3 to participate in the game, what is the expected profit associated with playing the game? Would you play?

16.32 A single card will be selected from a well-shuffled deck of 52 cards. A payoff will be made based upon the rank of the card. A 2 will result in payment of $2, a 10 in a payment of $10, and so forth. Jack, queen, king, and ace will result in payments of $15, $20, $25, and $30, respectively. What is the expected payoff associated with a single draw?

16.33 A perishable product is purchased by a retailer for $12 and sold at a price of $20. Daily demand varies at random according to the distribution in Table 16.20. If an item is stocked but not sold, the retailer must absorb the $12 cost as a loss. The retailer wishes to determine the level to stock each day so as to maximize expected daily profit.

(a) Set up the conditional profit table.

(b) What stock decision results in the maximum expected daily profit?

(c) What is the maximum expected daily profit?

16.34 *Salvage Value.* Rework Exercise 16.33 with the assumption that units unsold after the first day have a salvage value of $6.

16.35 Rework Example 16.17 if there is a salvage value of $2 for any units not sold on the first day.

16.36 *Expected Profit with Perfect Information.* Assume in Example 16.17 that there is a way of predicting exactly how many units will be demanded on a given day (an order-ahead system might achieve this). When demand is known ahead of time, the prudent stock decision is to stock the quantity demanded. This prevents overstocking and understocking. In Example 16.17, for instance, 21 units would be stocked whenever 21 units are demanded, 22 units stocked whenever 22 are demanded, and so forth. Using the appropriate conditional profits in Table 16.15, compute the expected profit (*expected profit with perfect informa-*

Table 16.20

Daily Demand

(x)	P(x)
10	.20
11	.40
12	.30
13	.10
	1.00

tion) for this situation. How does it compare with the maximum expected profit (without perfect information) of $65.20 from stocking 22 units?

16.4

THE BINOMIAL PROBABILITY DISTRIBUTION

This section discusses one of the more commonly used discrete probability distributions—the *binomial probability distribution*. First is a discussion of the characteristics of random processes which can be represented by the binomial distribution. This will be followed by a discussion of the binomial distribution and its applications.

Bernoulli Process

Many random processes are characterized by trials in which there are just two mutually exclusive outcomes. Manufactured parts may be sampled to determine whether they are of an acceptable quality or defective; the toss of a coin results in either a head or tail; patients arriving at an emergency room might be classified as male or female; survey questionnaires mailed to potential respondents may be classified as returned or not returned; and questions on a multiple-choice or true-false test may be judged as answered correctly or incorrectly. It is common to refer to the two possible outcomes as "successful" or "unsuccessful." The occurrence of a head in the toss of a coin may be declared a successful outcome. This assignment of labels, though, is completely arbitrary. The occurrence of a tail might just as easily, and appropriately, be termed a success (it depends on the side for which you are rooting).

Random processes such as tossing a fair coin are examples of *Bernoulli processes*. Bernoulli processes are characterized by the following:

1 There are n trials, each of which has two mutually exclusive outcomes that can be classified as either success or failure.

2 The probability of a success p remains fixed for each trial.

3 The random variable x is the total number of successes in n trials.

Example 16.18

A single die is rolled 25 times. A successful outcome is the occurrence of a 6. This is an example of a Bernoulli process. If a fair die is assumed, the probability of a success for each trial is $\frac{1}{6}$, or $p = \frac{1}{6}$. If the probability of success equals $\frac{1}{6}$, the probability of a failure q is $q = 1 - p$ or $q = 1 - \frac{1}{6} = \frac{5}{6}$. Each roll of the die is statistically independent of the others. The random variable x is the number of times a 6 occurs in the 25 rolls.

Example 16.19

One hundred parts will be selected from a manufacturing process which is judged to produce defective parts at random with a probability of 5 percent. The process resulting in defective parts is characterized by statistical independence. The probability of a defective part, the production of such being deemed a successful outcome, is $p = .05$. The probability of a failure is $q = 1 - .05 = .95$. The random variable x is the number of defective items identified in the 100 trials.

The Binomial Distribution

Consider a student who is taking a true-false quiz consisting of five questions. Assume that the probability of answering any one of the questions correctly is .8. Suppose we are interested in the probability that the student will answer exactly four questions correctly. This situation is a Bernoulli process where the probability of success on any trial is $p = .8$, the probability of a failure is $q = .2$, the number of trials is $n = 5$, and the random variable x equals the number of questions answered correctly.

One way of answering four questions correctly is to answer the first four correctly and the last incorrectly; or, stated in terms of success (S) or failure (F), the sequence of outcomes is $SSSSF$. The probability of this joint event is a joint probability for independent events computed by applying Rule 7 from Sec. 16.2, or

$$P(S \cap S \cap S \cap S \cap F) = (.8)(.8)(.8)(.8)(.2)$$
$$= .08192$$

Another way of getting four correct answers is the sequence $FSSSS$ and

$$P(F \cap S \cap S \cap S \cap S) = (.2)(.8)(.8)(.8)(.8)$$
$$= .08192$$

which is the same probability as computed for the joint event $SSSSF$. There are, in fact, five different ways in which four questions can be answered correctly. They are $SSSSF$, $SSSFS$, $SSFSS$, $SFSSS$, and $FSSSS$. Note that in applying Rule 7 to compute the probability of each of these sequences, the probability of success, $p = .8$, will be a factor 4 times and the probability of a failure will be a factor once. The only difference is the order of multiplication which has no effect on the product. Thus, the probability of answering four questions correctly is

$$p(x = 4) = \begin{pmatrix} \text{number of different ways} \\ \text{in which four questions can} \\ \text{be answered correctly} \end{pmatrix} \begin{pmatrix} \text{probability of answering} \\ \text{four questions correctly} \\ \text{in any one order} \end{pmatrix}$$
$$= 5(.08192)$$
$$= .4096$$

An alternative to enumerating the different ways in which four successes can occur in five trials is to recognize that this is a combinations question. The number of ways in which x successes can occur in n trials is found by applying Eq. (16.5), or

$$_nC_x = \frac{n!}{x!(n - x)!}$$

The number of ways in which four successes can occur in five trials is

$$_5C_4 = \frac{5!}{4!(5 - 4)!} = \frac{5!}{4!1!}$$
$$= 5$$

The *binomial probability distribution* is used to represent experiments which are Bernoulli processes. Given that the probability of success in any trial equals p and the probability of a failure equals q, the binomial distribution computes the probability of x successes in n trials as

$$P(x,n) = {_nC_x}\overbrace{(p \cdot p \cdot p \cdots p)}^{x \text{ times}}\overbrace{(q \cdot q \cdot q \cdots q)}^{n-x \text{ times}}$$

or $\qquad P(x,n) = {_nC_x}p^x q^{n-x}$ $\qquad\qquad\qquad$ (16.19)

If we continue with the quiz example, the possible outcomes for the quiz are zero, one, two, three, four, or five questions correct (successes). Let's compute the probabilities for the other outcomes.

$$P(0, 5) = {_5C_0}(.8)^0(.2)^5$$

$$= \frac{5!}{0!(5-0)!}(.00032)$$

$$= (1)(.00032)$$

$$= .00032$$

$$P(1, 5) = {_5C_1}(.8)^1(.2)^4$$

$$= \frac{5!}{1!(5-1)!}(.00128)$$

$$= 5(.000128)$$

$$= .0064$$

$$P(2, 5) = {_5C_2}(.8)^2(.2)^3$$

$$= \frac{5!}{2!(5-2)!}(.00512)$$

$$= 10(.00512)$$

$$= .0512$$

$$P(3, 5) = {_5C_3}(.8)^3(.2)^2$$

$$= \frac{5!}{3!(5-3)!}(.02048)$$

$$= 10(.02048)$$

$$= .2048$$

$$P(5, 5) = {_5C_5}(.8)^5(.2)^0$$

$$= \frac{5!}{0!(5-0)!}(.32768)$$

$$= .32768$$

Table 16.21 presents the binomial distribution for this experiment. Figure 16.2 presents a graphical representation of the distribution called a *histogram*. Each bar corresponds to an event, and the height of the bar equals the probability of the event.

**Example
16.20** **Internal Revenue** The IRS has determined that 40 percent of all personal income tax returns contain at least one error. If a sample of six

Number of Successes (x)	P(x)	Table 16.21
0	.00032	
1	.00640	
2	.05120	
3	.20480	
4	.40960	
5	.32768	
	1.00000	

returns is selected at random from last year's returns, construct the binomial distribution where the random variable x equals the number of returns found to contain errors.

Solution

This experiment can be considered to be a Bernoulli process where a return found to contain an error is considered a success and one found not to contain an error is considered a failure. For this experiment $p = .40$, $q = .60$, and $n = 6$.

The probability that none of the six returns will contain an error is

$$P(0, 6) = {}_6C_0(.4)^0(.6)^6$$

$$= \frac{6!}{0!(6 - 0)!} (.046656)$$

$$= (1)(.046656)$$

$$= .046656$$

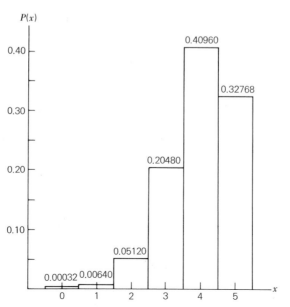

FIGURE 16.2

Table 16.22	Number of Successes (x)	P(x)
	0	.046656
	1	.186624
	2	.311040
	3	.276480
	4	.138240
	5	.036864
	6	.004096
		1.000000

The probability that exactly one return will contain an error is

$$P(1, 6) = {}_6C_1(.4)^1(.6)^5$$
$$= \frac{6!}{1!(6-1)!}(.031104)$$
$$= (6)(.031104)$$
$$= .186624$$

The probability that exactly two returns will contain an error is

$$P(2, 6) = {}_6C_2(.4)^2(.6)^4$$
$$= \frac{6!}{2!(6-2)!}(.020736)$$
$$= (15)(.020736)$$
$$= .31104$$

The probability that exactly three returns will contain an error is

$$P(3, 6) = {}_6C_3(.4)^3(.6)^3$$
$$= \frac{6!}{3!(6-3)!}(.013824)$$
$$= (20)(.013824)$$
$$= .27648$$

By continuing this process, the result is the probability distribution shown in Table 16.22.

The probability that no more than three returns will contain an error equals $P(0) + P(1) + P(2) + P(3)$, or .8208. The probability that more than four returns will contain errors equals $P(5) + P(6) = .04096$.

Mean and Standard Deviation of the Binomial Distribution

It can be shown that for a binomial probability distribution the mean value of the distribution is

$$\mu = np \tag{16.20}$$

This formula is what we should probably expect. If the binomial distribution relates to the number of heads occurring in 500 flips of a fair coin, the mean is

$$\mu = 500(.5)$$
$$= 250$$

which suggests that on the average we would expect to get 250 heads in 500 flips of a fair coin.

In Example 16.20, the probability that an income tax return contained an error was .4. In the selection of six returns, the mean is **Example 16.21**

$$\mu = 6(.4)$$
$$= 2.4$$

or on the average a selection of six returns at random would result in 2.4 being identified as containing errors.

It can be shown that the standard deviation of a binomial probability distribution can be computed by using the formula

$$\sigma = \sqrt{npq} \qquad (16.21)$$

For Example 16.20, the standard deviation is

$$\sigma = \sqrt{6(.4)(.6)}$$
$$= \sqrt{1.44}$$
$$= 1.2$$

Follow-up Exercises

16.37 Determine which of the following random variables are not variables in a Bernoulli process.
(a) x = the number of heads in the toss of a coin 20 times
(b) x = the heights of 10 students selected at random
(c) x = the number of 6s which appear in five rolls of a *pair* of dice
(d) x = scores earned by 100 different students on a standardized test
(e) x = the closing price of a stock for 10 randomly selected days
(f) x = the number of arrivals per hour at an emergency room observed for 20 randomly selected hours of operation
(g) x = the number of false alarms in a sample of 10 fire alarms where the probability that any alarm is a false alarm equals .18
16.38 A fair coin is to be flipped 4 times. What is the probability that exactly two heads will occur? No heads?
16.39 A fair die will be rolled 4 times. What is the probability that exactly three 1s will occur? No 1s?
16.40 *Drunken Driving.* A state has determined that of all traffic accidents in which a fatality occurs, 80 percent involve situations in which at least one driver has been drinking. If a sample of five fatal accidents is selected at random, construct the binomial distribution where the random variable x equals the number of accidents in which at least one driver was drinking.
16.41 It has been determined that 95 percent of all American households have at least one television set. If five residences are selected at random, construct the binomial distribution where the random variable x equals the number of residences having at least one television.

16.42 A firm which conducts consumer surveys by mail has found that 40 percent of those families receiving a questionnaire will return it. In a survey of 20 families, what is the probability that exactly 10 families will return the questionnaire? Exactly 8 families?

16.43 A student takes a true-false examination which consists of 10 questions. The student knows nothing about the subject and chooses answers at random. Assuming independence between questions and a probability of .5 of answering any question correctly, what is the probability that the student will pass the test (assume that passing means getting seven or more correct)?

16.44 *Immunization.* A particular influenza vaccine has been found to be 96 percent effective in providing immunity. In a random sample of five vaccinated people who have been exposed to this strain of influenza, what is the probability that none of the five will come down with the disease?

16.45 An urn contains five red balls, two green balls, and three blue balls. If 10 balls are selected at random with replacement between each draw, what is the probability that no green balls will be selected? What is the probability that four red balls will be selected?

16.46 A manufacturing process produces defective parts randomly at a rate of 20 percent. In a sample of 10 parts, what is the probability that fewer than 3 will be defective?

16.47 In Exercise 16.46, what is the mean number of defective parts expected? What is the interpretation of this value? What is the standard deviation for this distribution?

16.48 In a local hospital 45 percent of all babies born are males. On a particular day five babies are born. What is the probability that three or more of the babies are males? What is the mean of this distribution for $n = 5$? What is the standard deviation?

16.5   CONTINUOUS PROBABILITY DISTRIBUTIONS

As mentioned in Sec. 16.3, continuous probability distributions are characterized by random variables which can assume any value within some interval of numbers. This section discusses one of the most familiar and most widely applied continuous probability distributions—the *normal probability distribution.* Also, this section will illustrate a relationship between integral calculus and probability.

FIGURE 16.3

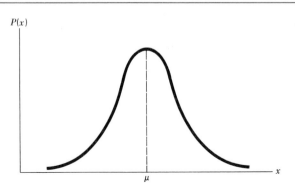

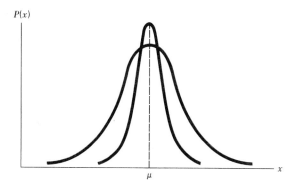

$P(x)$

μ

x

FIGURE 16.4

The Normal Probability Distribution

The normal probability distribution is one of the most important distributions in modern-day probability theory. The normal probability distribution is represented by the classic bell-shaped curve, or *normal curve*, shown in Fig. 16.3. The bell-shaped curve in Fig. 16.3 is typical of a family of bell-shaped curves which represent normal probability distributions, each different with regard to its mean and standard deviation. Figure 16.4 illustrates the graphs of two normal distributions having the same mean but different standard deviations. Figure 16.5 illustrates the graphs of two normal distributions which have different means but the same standard deviation.

The normal curve is symmetrical about an imaginary vertical line which passes through the mean μ. This means the height of the curve is the same if one moves equal distances to the left and right of the mean. The "tails" of the curve come closer and closer to the horizontal axis without ever reaching it, no matter how far one moves to the left or the right. If μ equals the mean and σ the standard deviation of a normal probability distribution, the function describing the normal curve is

$$f(x) = \frac{1}{\sqrt{2\pi}\sigma}\, e^{-1/2[(x-\mu)/\sigma]^2} \qquad (16.22)$$

where $\pi \doteq 3.14159$, $e \doteq 2.71828$, and $f(x)$ is the height of the normal curve corresponding to a given value of the random variable x.

FIGURE 16.5

$P(x)$

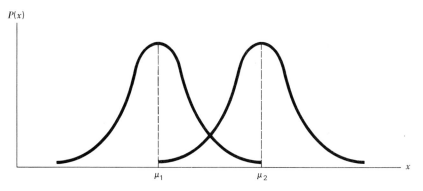

μ_1 μ_2 x

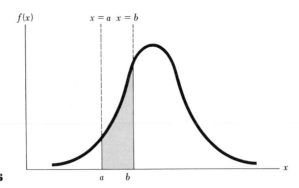

FIGURE 16.6

We rarely need to use Eq. (16.22). With continuous distributions the interest is in determining areas beneath the curve and between vertical lines passing through two points on the horizontal axis. Our reason for interest is that areas under the curve representing a probability distribution represent probabilities. If the total area under a normal curve is considered to equal 1, the probability that the random variable x will take on a value between a and b equals the area beneath the curve and bounded on the left and right by the vertical lines $x = a$ and $x = b$. This is illustrated in Fig. 16.6.

Consider a situation in which the scores on a standardized aptitude test have been found to be *normally distributed* with a mean of 70 and standard deviation of 7.5. Suppose we are interested in determining the probability that a student will score between 70 and 85 on the test. In order to determine this probability, we can take advantage of a very useful property of normal probability distributions. Any normal probability distribution with mean μ and standard deviation σ can be transformed into an equivalent *standard (unit) normal distribution* which has a mean equal to 0 and standard deviation equal to 1. The transformation redefines each value of the random variable x in terms of its distance from the mean, stated as a multiple of the standard deviation.

Figure 16.7 illustrates this transformation of x in terms of another variable z which equals the distance from the mean in multiples of the standard deviation. Note that z values to the right of the mean are positive, and those to the left of the mean are negative. A value of x which is one standard deviation to the right of the mean would be defined equiva-

FIGURE 16.7

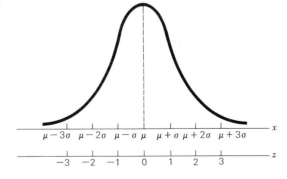

lently by a z value of 1. A point located three standard deviations to the left of the mean would be defined equivalently by a z value of -3.

Table 16.23 at the end of this section provides areas under the standard normal curve. Note that the areas given are areas under the curve between the mean and another point located z standard deviations from the mean. The normal curve is such that 50 percent of the area is to the left of the mean and 50 percent to the right. That is, there is a 50 percent chance that the value of the random variable x will be less than the mean and a 50 percent chance it will be greater than the mean. The symmetry of the normal curve suggests that Table 16.23 can be used to determine areas between the mean and another point when the second point is to the left *or* right of the mean. For instance, looking up a z value equal to 1 in Table 16.23 suggests that the area under the curve between $z = 0$ and $z = 1$ is 0.3413. *The same area occurs between $z = 0$ and $z = -1$.* Figure 16.8 illustrates these areas. Note also that we can make the statement that the area under the standard normal curve between $z = -1$ and $z = 1$ equals 0.6826.

Let's return to the original problem concerning the standardized aptitude test. Scores had been found to be normally distributed with a mean of 70 and standard deviation of 7.5. The problem was to determine the probability that a student selected at random will score between 70 and 85. To determine this probability, we must transform the original distribution into the standard normal distribution. In order to do this, equivalent z values must be identified for pertinent x values. The formula for transforming to equivalent z values is

$$z = \frac{x - \mu}{\sigma} \qquad (16.23)$$

The z value corresponding to the mean is always 0. Thus, in this case, the z value corresponding to an x of 70 is 0. The z value corresponding to an x value of 85 is

$$z = \frac{85 - 70}{7.5}$$

$$= \frac{15}{7.5}$$

$$= 2$$

FIGURE 16.8

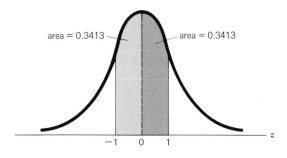

area = 0.3413   area = 0.3413

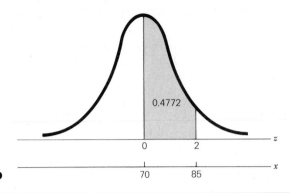

FIGURE 16.9

This means that a score of 85 is two standard deviations above (to the right of) the mean score of 70.

Thus, the probability that a student will score between 70 and 85 is equal to the area under the standard normal curve between $z = 0$ and $z = 2$. This area, illustrated in Fig. 16.9, is read directly from Table 16.23 as 0.4772. Therefore, the probability that a student will score between 70 and 85 equals .4772. Note in Fig. 16.9 that an equivalent x scale has been drawn below the z scale to show the corresponding value of x. This is not necessary, but it helps to remind us of the pertinent values for the random variable x.

Suppose we are interested in the probability that a student will score between 0 and 85 on the examination. This probability is equal to the probability that z will be less than 2 for the standard normal distribution. The probability is the area under the standard normal distribution, illustrated in Fig. 16.10. This area consists of the 50 percent to the left of the mean and the .4772 we identified previously, or

$$P(z \le 2) = P(z \le 0) + P(0 < z \le 2)$$
$$= .5000 + .4772 = .9772$$

FIGURE 16.10

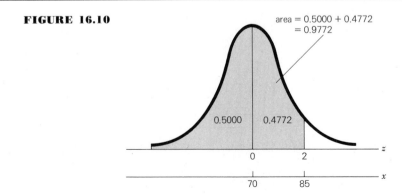

NOTE
In any problems requiring the identification of probabilities for a normally distributed variable, it is strongly advised that you make a rough sketch which identifies the equivalent area or areas under the standard normal curve.

A survey of per capita income indicated that the annual income for people in one state is normally distributed with a mean of $9,800 and a standard deviation of $1,600. If a person is selected at random, what is the probability that the person's annual income is (*a*) greater than $5,000, (*b*) greater than $12,200, (*c*) between $8,520 and $12,200, (*d*) between $11,400 and $13,000?

Example 16.22

(*a*) The z value corresponding to an income of $5,000 is

Solution

$$z = \frac{5,000 - 9,800}{1,600}$$

$$= \frac{-4,800}{1,600} = -3$$

From Fig. 16.11 we can conclude that the probability that a person's salary is greater than $5,000 is equal to the probability that z is greater than -3 for the standard normal distribution. From Table 16.23,

$$P(z > -3) = P(-3 < z \le 0) + P(z > 0)$$
$$= .49865 + .5000$$
$$= .99865$$

(*b*) The z value corresponding to an income of $12,200 is

$$z = \frac{12,200 - 9,800}{1,600}$$

$$= \frac{2,400}{1,600} = 1.5$$

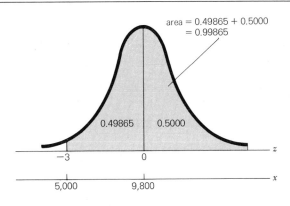

area = 0.49865 + 0.5000
= 0.99865

0.49865   0.5000

−3   0 z

5,000   9,800 x

FIGURE 16.11

From Fig. 16.12 we can conclude that the probability that a person's salary is greater than \$12,200 is equal to the probability that z is greater than 1.5. From Table 16.23 we can determine that $P(0 < z \le 1.5) = .4332$. Since

$$P(z > 0) = .5000$$
$$P(z > 1.5) = P(z > 0) - P(0 < z \le 1.5)$$
$$= .5000 - .4332$$
$$= .0668$$

(c) The z value corresponding to an income of \$8,520 is

$$z = \frac{8,520 - 9,800}{1,600}$$
$$= \frac{-1,280}{1,600}$$
$$= -.8$$

From Fig. 16.13, the probability that a person's salary is between \$8,520 and \$12,200 is equal to the probability that z is between $-.8$ and 1.5, or

$$P(-0.8 \le z \le 1.5) = P(-0.8 \le z < 0) + P(0 \le z \le 1.5)$$
$$= .2881 + .4332$$
$$= .7213$$

(d) The z value corresponding to an income of \$11,400 is

$$z = \frac{11,400 - 9,800}{1,600}$$
$$= \frac{1,600}{1,600} = 1$$

The z value corresponding to an income of \$13,000 is

$$z = \frac{13,000 - 9,800}{1,600}$$
$$= \frac{3,200}{1,600} = 2$$

FIGURE 16.12

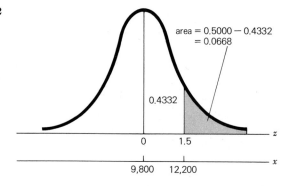

area = 0.5000 − 0.4332
= 0.0668

0.4332

0   1.5 z

9,800   12,200 x

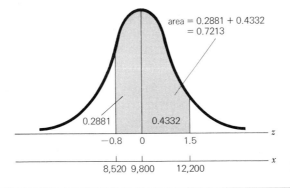

area = 0.2881 + 0.4332
= 0.7213

0.2881

0.4332

FIGURE 16.13

From Fig. 16.14, the probability that a person's salary is between $11,400 and $13,000 is equal to the probability that z is between 1 and 2. To determine this probability, we must find the area between $z = 0$ and $z = 2$ and subtract from this the area between $z = 0$ and $z = 1$. Or,

$$P(1 \leq z \leq 2) = P(0 \leq z \leq 2) - P(0 \leq z \leq 1)$$
$$= .4772 - .3413$$
$$= .1359$$

One point should be made regarding the use of Table 16.23. It was mentioned earlier that for continuous variables, the probability of occurrence of any specific value of the variable equals 0. That is, for any point a,

$$P(x = a) = 0$$

Thus, for any two constants $a < b$,

$$P(a \leq x \leq b) = P(a < x \leq b) = P(a \leq x < b) = P(a < x < b)$$

The practical implication of this is that the values in Table 16.23 represent the probabilities that z will assume values between two points z_1 and z_2 where the exact values of z_1 and z_2 may or may not be included. In Example 16.22a, the probabilities that a person's salary is greater than $5,000 or greater than or equal to $5,000 are both the same—.99865.

FIGURE 16.14

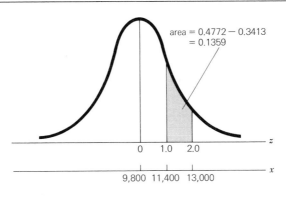

area = 0.4772 − 0.3413
= 0.1359

One final observation about normally distributed random variables is that of all the possible outcomes of the random variable x, approximately 68 percent are expected to occur within plus or minus one standard deviation from the mean (that is, $\mu \pm 1\sigma$), approximately 95 percent are expected to occur within plus or minus two standard deviations of the mean ($\mu \pm 2\sigma$), and about 99 percent within plus or minus three standard deviations of the mean ($\mu \pm 3\sigma$).

Integral Calculus and Probability (Optional)

A mathematical function which determines the probability of each possible outcome of an experiment is called a *probability density function* (*pdf*). Compared with probability distributions which display each outcome and its probability, density functions can be thought of as the mathematical functions used to compute the probability. If x is a continuous random variable, its density function $f(x)$ must satisfy the two conditions

1 $f(x) \geq 0$ for all x.

2 The area under the graph of $f(x) = 1$.

The first condition prohibits negative probabilities for any event while the second condition guarantees that the events are mutually exclusive and collectively exhaustive.

The probability that a random variable x assumes a value in the interval between a and b, where $a < b$, equals the area under the density function between $x = a$ and $x = b$. If you recall the use of the definite integral in determining areas under curves, the probability that x will assume a value between $x = a$ and $x = b$ equals $\int_a^b f(x)\, dx$.

The density function for normally distributed variables was presented in Eq. (16.22). Technically, if we wanted to determine the probability that a normally distributed variable x, having a mean μ and standard deviation σ, will assume a value between $x = a$ and $x = b$, $a < b$, we could determine the probability by integrating the density function, or

$$P(a \leq x \leq b) = \int_a^b \frac{1}{\sqrt{2\pi}\sigma} e^{-1/2[(x-\mu)/\sigma]^2}\, dx$$

Fortunately, the equivalent conversion to the standard normal distribution and the availability of tables such as Table 16.23 eliminate any need to perform what appears to be a cumbersome integration.

Example 16.23 Consider the probability density function for the random variable x

$$f(x) = \frac{2 + x}{30} \qquad 0 \leq x \leq 6$$

Determine the probability that x will assume a value between 2 and 5.

The density function and the area of interest are illustrated in Fig. **Solution**
16.15. The probability is computed as

$$P(2 \leq x \leq 5) = \int_{2}^{5} \frac{2 + x}{30} \, dx$$

$$= \frac{x}{15} + \frac{x^2}{60} \Big]_{2}^{5}$$

$$= \left(\frac{5}{15} + \frac{5^2}{60} \right) - \left(\frac{2}{15} + \frac{2^2}{60} \right)$$

$$= \frac{5}{15} + \frac{25}{60} - \frac{2}{15} - \frac{4}{60}$$

$$= \frac{20 + 25 - 8 - 4}{60}$$

$$= \frac{33}{60} = 0.55$$

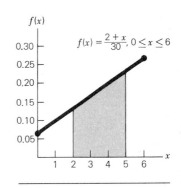

FIGURE 16.15

A 3-hour examination is given to all prospective salespeople of a na- **Example**
tional retail chain. The time x in hours required to complete the exami- **16.24**
nation has been found to be random with a density function

$$f(x) = \frac{-x^2 + 10x}{36} \qquad 0 \leq x \leq 3$$

Determine the probability that someone will complete the test in 1 hour
or less.

The density function and area of interest are shown in Fig. 16.16. The **Solution**
probability is computed as

$$P(0 \leq x \leq 1) = \int_{0}^{1} \frac{-x^2 + 10x}{36} \, dx$$

$$= \frac{-x^3}{108} + \frac{10x^2}{72} \Big]_{0}^{1}$$

$$= \frac{-(1)^3}{108} + \frac{10(1)^2}{72}$$

$$= \frac{-1}{108} + \frac{10}{72}$$

$$= -.009 + .139$$

$$= .13$$

FIGURE 16.16

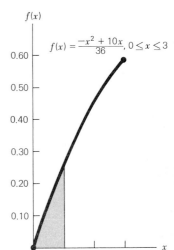

Follow-up Exercises

16.49 For the standard normal distribution determine
(a) $P(z > 1.0)$ (b) $P(z < 1.2)$
(c) $P(0.3 < z < 0.9)$ (d) $P(-1.1 \leq z \leq 1.7)$
16.50 For the standard normal distribution determine
(a) $P(z > -0.3)$ (b) $P(z < -0.6)$
(c) $P(-1.4 < z < -0.2)$ (d) $P(-0.6 \leq z \leq 2.4)$

16.51 Given a random variable x which is normally distributed with a mean of 12 and standard deviation of 2.2, determine
(a) $P(x \geq 10.9)$ (b) $P(x \leq 15.3)$
(c) $P(7.6 \leq x \leq 13.1)$ (d) $P(9.8 \leq x \leq 10.9)$

16.52 Given a random variable x which is normally distributed with a mean of 85 and standard deviation of 5, determine
(a) $P(x \geq 75)$ (b) $P(x < 72.5)$
(c) $P(70 \leq x \leq 77.5)$ (d) $P(80 < x < 92.5)$

16.53 The weights of newborn babies at a particular hospital have been observed to be normally distributed with a mean of 7.2 pounds and a standard deviation of 0.6 pounds. What is the probability that a baby born in this hospital will weigh more than 9 pounds?

16.54 The annual income of workers in one state is normally distributed with a mean of $10,500 and a standard deviation of $2,500. If a worker is chosen at random, what is the probability that the worker earns more than $15,000?

16.55 A manufacturer has conducted a study of the lifetime of a particular type of light bulb. The study concluded that the lifetime, measured in hours, is a random variable with a normal distribution. The mean lifetime is 900 hours with a standard deviation of 100 hours. What is the probability that a bulb selected at random would have a lifetime between 750 and 1,000 hours?

16.56 Grades on a national aptitude test have been found to be normally distributed with a mean of 75 and a standard deviation of 8. What is the probability that a student selected at random will score between 79 and 95?

16.57 In a large city the number of calls for police service during a 24-hour period seems to be random. The number of calls has been found to be normally distributed with a mean of 355 and a standard deviation of 50. What is the probability that for a randomly selected day the number of calls will be fewer than 325? More than 400?

16.58 The probability density function for a continuous random variable x is

$$f(x) = \frac{5 - x}{4.5} \qquad 2 \leq x \leq 5$$

What is the probability that the random variable will assume a value greater than 4?

16.59 The probability density function for a continuous random variable x is

$$f(x) = \frac{x^2 - 10x + 25}{39} \qquad 0 \leq x \leq 3$$

Determine the probability that the random variable will assume a value less than 2.

16.6   **SUMMARY**

The purpose of this chapter has been to provide an introduction to probability theory. After the special counting methods for permutations and combinations were introduced, considerable time was spent discussing

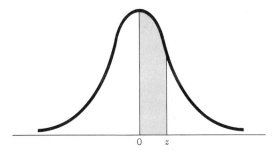

Table 16.23
Area Under the Standard Normal Curve

z	.00	.01	.02	.03	.04	.05	.06	.07	.08	.09
0.0	.0000	.0040	.0080	.0120	.0160	.0199	.0239	.0279	.0319	.0359
0.1	.0398	.0438	.0478	.0517	.0557	.0596	.0636	.0675	.0714	.0753
0.2	.0793	.0832	.0871	.0910	.0948	.0987	.1026	.1064	.1103	.1141
0.3	.1179	.1217	.1255	.1293	.1331	.1368	.1406	.1443	.1480	.1517
0.4	.1554	.1591	.1628	.1664	.1700	.1736	.1772	.1808	.1844	.1879
0.5	.1915	.1950	.1985	.2019	.2054	.2088	.2123	.2157	.2190	.2224
0.6	.2257	.2291	.2324	.2357	.2389	.2422	.2454	.2486	.2518	.2549
0.7	.2580	.2612	.2642	.2673	.2704	.2734	.2764	.2794	.2823	.2852
0.8	.2881	.2910	.2939	.2967	.2995	.3023	.3051	.3078	.3106	.3133
0.9	.3159	.3186	.3212	.3238	.3264	.3289	.3315	.3340	.3365	.3389
1.0	.3413	.3438	.3461	.3485	.3508	.3531	.3554	.3577	.3599	.3621
1.1	.3643	.3665	.3686	.3708	.3729	.3749	.3770	.3790	.3810	.3830
1.2	.3849	.3869	.3888	.3907	.3925	.3944	.3962	.3980	.3997	.4015
1.3	.4032	.4049	.4066	.4082	.4099	.4115	.4131	.4147	.4162	.4177
1.4	.4192	.4207	.4222	.4236	.4251	.4265	.4279	.4292	.4306	.4319
1.5	.4332	.4345	.4357	.4370	.4382	.4394	.4406	.4418	.4429	.4441
1.6	.4452	.4463	.4474	.4484	.4495	.4505	.4515	.4525	.4535	.4545
1.7	.4554	.4564	.4573	.4582	.4591	.4599	.4608	.4616	.4625	.4633
1.8	.4641	.4649	.4656	.4664	.4671	.4678	.4686	.4693	.4699	.4706
1.9	.4713	.4719	.4726	.4732	.4738	.4744	.4750	.4756	.4761	.4767
2.0	.4772	.4778	.4783	.4788	.4793	.4798	.4803	.4808	.4812	.4817
2.1	.4821	.4826	.4830	.4834	.4838	.4842	.4846	.4850	.4854	.4857
2.2	.4861	.4864	.4868	.4871	.4875	.4878	.4881	.4884	.4887	.4890
2.3	.4893	.4896	.4898	.4901	.4904	.4906	.4909	.4911	.4913	.4916
2.4	.4918	.4920	.4922	.4925	.4927	.4929	.4931	.4932	.4934	.4936
2.5	.4938	.4940	.4941	.4943	.4945	.4946	.4948	.4949	.4951	.4952
2.6	.4953	.4955	.4956	.4957	.4959	.4960	.4961	.4962	.4963	.4964
2.7	.4965	.4966	.4967	.4968	.4969	.4970	.4971	.4972	.4973	.4974
2.8	.4974	.4975	.4976	.4977	.4977	.4978	.4979	.4979	.4980	.4981
2.9	.4881	.4982	.4982	.4983	.4984	.4984	.4985	.4985	.4986	.4986
3.0	.49865	.4987	.4987	.4988	.4988	.4989	.4989	.4989	.4990	.4990

the nature of probability and different probability environments. This was followed by a discussion of some basic rules of probability and their application. Marginal, joint, and conditional probabilities were discussed for states of statistical independence and statistical dependence.

After the introduction of the basics of probability theory, the next section introduced random variables, probability distributions, and the concept of expected value. An important distinction in this section is made between discrete random variables and discrete probability distributions as opposed to continuous random variables and continuous probability distributions. The last topic in Sec. 16.3 illustrated the use of expected monetary value as a possible criterion for making decisions under uncertainty.

The remainder of the chapter discussed two of the more commonly used probability distributions, their characteristics, and applications. The two distributions were the binomial distribution, which is a discrete distribution, and the normal distribution, which is a continuous distribution. In addition to summarizing characteristics of continuous probability distributions, the final discussion of the chapter illustrates the relationship between integral calculus and the computation of probabilities for continuous distributions.

CHAPTER CHECKLIST

If you have read all the sections of this chapter, you should

_____ Understand the difference between a *permutation* and *combination* and be able to compute the number of permutations and combinations of a given size associated with a finite set of objects

_____ Understand what a *probability* is, the *relative frequency* concept of a probability, and the relationship between *odds* and probabilities

_____ Understand the meaning of and how to compute *marginal, joint,* and *conditional probabilities* under states of statistical *independence* and statistical *dependence*

_____ Be familiar with the notions of *discrete* and *continuous random variables*

_____ Understand the meaning of and how to compute the *mean* and *standard deviation* of a discrete random variable

_____ Be familiar with *expected monetary value* as a decision criterion

_____ Be familiar with the characteristics of *Bernoulli processes*

_____ Be able to compute probabilities associated with the *binomial distribution*

_____ Be familiar with the notion of *normally distributed* random variables and know how to compute probabilities related to such variables

_____ Understand the meaning of a *probability density function* and the use of integral calculus in computing probabilities relative to such a function

KEY TERMS AND CONCEPTS

permutation

combination

random process (experiment)

event

relative frequency

probability of an event

objective probability

subjective probability

odds

mutually exclusive events

collectively exhaustive events

statistical independence

statistical dependence

marginal probability

joint probability

conditional probability

probability tree

random variable (discrete
and continuous)

probability distribution
(discrete and continuous)

mean

standard deviation

expected monetary value

expected payoff (profit)

conditional profit table

Bernoulli process

binomial probability
distribution

normal probability distribution

standard (unit) normal
distribution

z value

probability density function

IMPORTANT FORMULAS

$$_nP_n = n! \tag{16.2}$$

$$_nP_r = n(n - 1)(n - 2) \cdots (n - r + 1) \tag{16.3}$$

$$_nP_r = \frac{n!}{(n - r)!} \tag{16.4}$$

$$_nC_r = \frac{n!}{r!(n - r)!} \tag{16.5}$$

$$0 \leq P(A) \leq 1 \tag{16.6}$$

$$P(\overline{A}) = 1 - P(A) \tag{16.7}$$

$$P(A \cup B) = P(A) + P(B) \quad \text{(mutually exclusive)} \tag{16.8}$$

$$P(E_1 \cup E_2 \cup \cdots \cup E_n) = P(E_1) + P(E_2) + \cdots + P(E_n)$$
$$\text{(mutually exclusive)} \tag{16.9}$$

$$P(A \cup B) = P(A) + P(B) - P(A \cap B) \tag{16.10}$$

$$P(A \cap B) = P(A)P(B) \quad \text{(independence)} \tag{16.11}$$

$$P(E_1 \cap E_2 \cap \cdots \cap E_n) = P(E_1)P(E_2) \cdots P(E_n)$$
$$\text{(independence)} \tag{16.12}$$

$$P(A|B) = P(A) \quad \text{(independence)} \tag{16.13}$$

$$P(A|B) = \frac{P(A \cap B)}{P(B)} \quad \text{(dependence)} \tag{16.14}$$

$$P(A \cap B) = P(B)P(A|B) \tag{16.15}$$

$$\mu = x_1p_1 + x_2p_2 + \cdots + x_np_n \tag{16.16}$$

$$\sigma = \sqrt{\sum_{j=1}^{n} (x_j - \mu)^2 p_j} \tag{16.18}$$

$$P(x, n) = {}_nC_x p^x q^{n-x} \quad \text{(binomial)} \tag{16.19}$$
$$\mu = np \quad \text{(binomial)} \tag{16.20}$$
$$\sigma = \sqrt{npq} \quad \text{(binomial)} \tag{16.21}$$

$$z = \frac{x - \mu}{\sigma} \quad \text{(normal)} \tag{16.23}$$

ADDITIONAL EXERCISES

Exercises 16.60 to 16.61 are related to Sec. 16.1.

16.60 How many different telephone numbers can be dialed (or pushed) with a three-digit area code and a seven-digit regional number?
16.61 An automobile dealer has eight different car models. The dealer can display only four in the showroom. How many different combinations of cars could the dealer select for the showroom?

Exercises 16.62 to 16.65 are related to Sec. 16.2.

16.62 Oddsmakers estimate the probability that a certain yacht will win a national championship at .10. They estimate that the yacht has a 25 percent chance of finishing second and a 15 percent chance of finishing third. What is the probability that the yacht will lose the championship? What is the probability that the yacht will finish third or worse?
16.63 A card is to be drawn at random from a well-shuffled deck of 52 cards. What is the probability that the card will be (a) a queen or jack, (b) an ace, a heart, or a card from a red suit?
16.64 The probability that a person admitted to a hospital emergency room will require hospitalization is .24. Two persons are admitted to the emergency room.
(a) What is the probability that neither will be hospitalized?
(b) What is the probability that both will be hospitalized?
(c) What is the probability that precisely one of the two will be hospitalized?
16.65 The probability that the price of a particular stock will increase during a business day is .30. If the nature of the change in price on any day is independent of what has happened on previous days, what is the probability that the price will (a) increase three days in a row, (b) remain the same or decrease three days in a row, (c) increase two days out of three?

Exercises 16.66 to 16.69 are related to Sec. 16.3.

16.66 Construct the discrete probability distribution which corresponds to the experiment of tossing a coin 3 times. Assume that $P(H) = .3$, and let the random variable x equal the number of heads in three tosses.
16.67 Compute the mean and standard deviation associated with the probability distribution in Table 16.24.

Table 16.24

x	$P(x)$
100	.20
200	.35
300	.25
400	.15
500	.05
	1.00

16.68 A product is purchased by a retailer for $40 and sold at a price of $60. Daily demand varies at random according to the distribution in Table 16.25. If an item is not sold on the first day, it can be salvaged for $20. The retailer wishes to determine the level to stock each day so as to maximize expected daily profit.
(a) Set up the conditional profit table.
(b) What stock decision results in the maximum expected daily profit?
(c) What is the maximum expected daily profit?
16.69 In Exercise 16.68, what is the expected profit with perfect information? How does it compare with the maximum expected profit without perfect information?

Exercises 16.70 to 16.73 are related to Sec. 16.4.

16.70 The election board in a particular state claims that 60 percent of the registered voters are Democrats. If a sample of six voters is selected at random from registration records, what is the probability that five or more will be Democrats?
16.71 Exactly 70 percent of the employees of a large chemical company belong to a union. If five employees are selected at random to serve on a salary review committee, what is the probability that the five will all be union members?
16.72 A manufacturing process produces defective parts randomly at a rate of 30 percent. If eight parts are selected at random, what is the probability the seven or more will be free of defects?
16.73 A Bernoulli process is characterized by a probability of success equal to .36. Determine the mean and standard deviation for this distribution if $n = 2,500$.

Exercises 16.74 to 16.77 are related to Sec. 16.5.

16.74 Given a random variable x which is normally distributed with a mean of 150 and standard deviation of 30, determine
(a) $P(x \leq 102)$ (b) $P(87 \leq x \leq 168)$
(c) $P(168 \leq x \leq 171)$
16.75 A survey of checking accounts revealed that the checking account balances are normally distributed with a mean of $180 and a standard deviation of $40. If an account is selected at random, what is the probability that the balance is (a) less than $100, (b) between $100 and $200, (c) more than $300?
16.76 The Environmental Protection Agency estimates that the average mileage for a particular model of a car is normally distributed with a mean of 20.4 miles per gallon and a standard deviation of 0.8. If one of these cars is selected at random, what is the probability that the average mileage will be (a) greater than 22 miles per gallon, (b) less than 18 miles per gallon?
16.77 The probability density function for a continuous random variable x is

$$f(x) = \frac{-x^3 + 80}{256} \qquad 0 \leq x \leq 4$$

What is the probability that the random variable will assume a value between 2 and 4?

Table 16.25

Daily Demand (x)	P(x)
100	.05
101	.40
102	.35
103	.15
104	.05

CHAPTER TEST

1 (*a*) What is the difference between the states of statistical independence and statistical dependence?

(*b*) What are the characteristics of a Bernoulli process?

2 A grocer has display space for three products. He has six products that he would like to display.

(*a*) How many different arrangements of three products can be made?

(*b*) How many different combinations of the six products could he put on display?

3 What is the probability of drawing three cards, without replacement, from a deck of cards and getting three kings?

4 An urn contains 18 red balls, 14 red-striped balls, 16 yellow balls, and 12 yellow-striped balls.

(*a*) Given that a ball selected from the urn is striped, what is the probability it is yellow?

(*b*) Given that a ball selected from the urn is not striped, what is the probability it is red?

5 A perishable product is purchased by a retailer for $3 per unit and is sold at a price of $5 per unit. Daily demand has been observed to be random with the following distribution. If an item is not sold on the first

Demand (*x*)	*P(x)*
6	.30
7	.25
8	.18
9	.15
10	.12
	1.00

day, the retailer must absorb the $3 cost as a loss. The retailer wishes to determine the number of units to stock each day so as to maximize expected daily profit.

(*a*) Set up the conditional profit table.

(*b*) What stock decision results in maximum expected daily profit?

(*c*) What is the maximum expected daily profit?

6 A fair coin is to be flipped 6 times. What is the probability of getting exactly four tails in the six flips?

7 A random variable x is normally distributed with a mean of 180 and a standard deviation of 40. Determine (*a*) $P(x \leq 172)$, (*b*) $P(192 \leq x \leq 204)$.

Table A.1
Exponential Functions

x	e^x	e^{-x}	x	e^x	e^{-x}	x	e^x	e^{-x}
0.00	1.0000	1.0000	0.49	1.6323	0.6126	0.98	2.6645	0.3753
0.01	1.0101	0.9900	0.50	1.6487	0.6065	0.99	2.6912	0.3715
0.02	1.0202	0.9801	0.51	1.6653	0.6004	1.00	2.7183	0.3678
0.03	1.0305	0.9704	0.52	1.6820	0.5945	1.1	3.0042	0.3329
0.04	1.0408	0.9607	0.53	1.6989	0.5886	1.2	3.3201	0.3012
0.05	1.0513	0.9512	0.54	1.7160	0.5827	1.3	3.6693	0.2725
0.06	1.0618	0.9417	0.55	1.7333	0.5769	1.4	4.0552	0.2466
0.07	1.0725	0.9323	0.56	1.7507	0.5712	1.5	4.4817	0.2231
0.08	1.0833	0.9231	0.57	1.7683	0.5655	1.6	4.9530	0.2019
0.09	1.0942	0.9139	0.58	1.7860	0.5598	1.7	5.4739	0.1827
0.10	1.1052	0.9048	0.59	1.8040	0.5543	1.8	6.0496	0.1653
0.11	1.1163	0.8958	0.60	1.8221	0.5488	1.9	6.6859	0.1496
0.12	1.1275	0.8869	0.61	1.8404	0.5433	2.0	7.3891	0.1353
0.13	1.1388	0.8780	0.62	1.8589	0.5379	2.1	8.1662	0.1225
0.14	1.1503	0.8693	0.63	1.8776	0.5325	2.2	9.0250	0.1108
0.15	1.1618	0.8607	0.64	1.8965	0.5272	2.3	9.9742	0.1003
0.16	1.1735	0.8521	0.65	1.9155	0.5220	2.4	11.023	0.0907
0.17	1.1853	0.8436	0.66	1.9348	0.5168	2.5	12.182	0.0821
0.18	1.1972	0.8352	0.67	1.9542	0.5117	2.6	13.464	0.0743
0.19	1.2092	0.8269	0.68	1.9739	0.5066	2.7	14.880	0.0672
0.20	1.2214	0.8187	0.69	1.9937	0.5015	2.8	16.445	0.0608
0.21	1.2337	0.8105	0.70	2.0138	0.4965	2.9	18.174	0.0550
0.22	1.2461	0.8025	0.71	2.0340	0.4916	3.0	20.086	0.0498
0.23	1.2586	0.7945	0.72	2.0544	0.4867	3.1	22.198	0.0450
0.24	1.2712	0.7866	0.73	2.0751	0.4819	3.2	24.533	0.0408
0.25	1.2840	0.7788	0.74	2.0959	0.4771	3.3	27.113	0.0369
0.26	1.2969	0.7710	0.75	2.1170	0.4723	3.4	29.964	0.0334
0.27	1.3100	0.7633	0.76	2.1383	0.4676	3.5	33.115	0.0302
0.28	1.3231	0.7557	0.77	2.1598	0.4630	3.6	36.598	0.0273
0.29	1.3364	0.7482	0.78	2.1815	0.4584	3.7	40.447	0.0247
0.30	1.3499	0.7408	0.79	2.2034	0.4538	3.8	44.701	0.0224
0.31	1.3634	0.7334	0.80	2.2255	0.4493	3.9	49.402	0.0202
0.32	1.3771	0.7261	0.81	2.2479	0.4448	4.0	54.598	0.0183
0.33	1.3910	0.7189	0.82	2.2705	0.4404	4.1	60.340	0.0166
0.34	1.4049	0.7117	0.83	2.2933	0.4360	4.2	66.686	0.0150
0.35	1.4191	0.7046	0.84	2.3164	0.4317	4.3	73.700	0.0136
0.36	1.4333	0.6976	0.85	2.3396	0.4274	4.4	81.451	0.0123
0.37	1.4477	0.6907	0.86	2.3632	0.4231	4.5	90.017	0.0111
0.38	1.4623	0.6838	0.87	2.3869	0.4189	4.6	99.484	0.0101
0.39	1.4770	0.6770	0.88	2.4109	0.4147	4.7	109.55	0.0091
0.40	1.4918	0.6703	0.89	2.4351	0.4106	4.8	121.51	0.0082
0.41	1.5068	0.6636	0.90	2.4596	0.4065	4.9	134.29	0.0074
0.42	1.5220	0.6570	0.91	2.4843	0.4025	5	148.41	0.0067
0.43	1.5373	0.6505	0.92	2.5093	0.3985	6	403.43	0.0025
0.44	1.5527	0.6440	0.93	2.5345	0.3945	7	1096.6	0.0009
0.45	1.5683	0.6376	0.94	2.5600	0.3906	8	2981.0	0.0003
0.46	1.5841	0.6312	0.95	2.5857	0.3867	9	8103.1	0.0001
0.47	1.6000	0.6250	0.96	2.6117	0.3828	10	22026.0	0.00005
0.48	1.6161	0.6187	0.97	2.6379	0.3790			

Table A.2
Natural Logarithms

x	$\ln x$	x	$\ln x$	x	$\ln x$
0.0	. . . . .	4.4	1.4816	8.8	2.1748
0.1	−2.3026	4.5	1.5041	8.9	2.1861
0.2	−1.6094	4.6	1.5261	9.0	2.1972
0.3	−1.2040	4.7	1.5476	9.1	2.2083
0.4	−0.9163	4.8	1.5686	9.2	2.2192
0.5	−0.6932	4.9	1.5892	9.3	2.2300
0.6	−0.5108	5.0	1.6094	9.4	2.2407
0.7	−0.3567	5.1	1.6292	9.5	2.2513
0.8	−0.2231	5.2	1.6487	9.6	2.2618
0.9	−0.1054	5.3	1.6677	9.7	2.2721
1.0	0.0000	5.4	1.6864	9.8	2.2824
1.1	0.0953	5.5	1.7047	9.9	2.2925
1.2	0.1823	5.6	1.7228	10	2.3026
1.3	0.2624	5.7	1.7405	11	2.3979
1.4	0.3365	5.8	1.7579	12	2.4849
1.5	0.4055	5.9	1.7750	13	2.5649
1.6	0.4700	6.0	1.7918	14	2.6391
1.7	0.5306	6.1	1.8083	15	2.7081
1.8	0.5878	6.2	1.8245	16	2.7726
1.9	0.6419	6.3	1.8405	17	2.8332
2.0	0.6931	6.4	1.8563	18	2.8904
2.1	0.7419	6.5	1.8718	19	2.9444
2.2	0.7885	6.6	1.8871	20	2.9957
2.3	0.8329	6.7	1.9021	25	3.2189
2.4	0.8755	6.8	1.9169	30	3.4012
2.5	0.9163	6.9	1.9315	35	3.5553
2.6	0.9555	7.0	1.9459	40	3.6889
2.7	0.9933	7.1	1.9601	45	3.8067
2.8	1.0296	7.2	1.9741	50	3.9120
2.9	1.0647	7.3	1.9879	55	4.0073
3.0	1.0986	7.4	2.0015	60	4.0943
3.1	1.1314	7.5	2.0149	65	4.1744
3.2	1.1632	7.6	2.0281	70	4.2485
3.3	1.1939	7.7	2.0412	75	4.3175
3.4	1.2238	7.8	2.0541	80	4.3820
3.5	1.2528	7.9	2.0669	85	4.4427
3.6	1.2809	8.0	2.0794	90	4.4998
3.7	1.3083	8.1	2.0919	95	4.5539
3.8	1.3350	8.2	2.1041	100	4.6052
3.9	1.3610	8.3	2.1163	200	5.2983
4.0	1.3863	8.4	2.1282	300	5.7037
4.1	1.4110	8.5	2.1401	400	5.9914
4.2	1.4351	8.6	2.1518	500	6.2146
4.3	1.4586	8.7	2.1633		

The Greek letter Σ (sigma) is the mathematical symbol which denotes the summation or addition operation. It provides a type of "shorthand" notation for representing addition. The expression

$$\sum_{j=l}^{u} f(j) \qquad\qquad (B.1)$$

is read "summation of $f(j)$ where j goes from l to u. To the right of Σ is the general function or expression being added. The letter j beneath Σ is the summation index. The summation index increments one unit at a time from a lower limit l to an upper limit u. For each value of j, $f(j)$ is evaluated and added to the other values of $f(j)$.

Suppose that we wanted to add the positive integers 1 through 10. One way of denoting this is by the expression

$$\sum_{j=1}^{10} j.$$

The longhand equivalent of this expression is

$$1 + 2 + 3 + 4 + 5 + 6 + 7 + 8 + 9 + 10$$

The following are other examples of summation notation.

$$\sum_{j=5}^{8} j^2 = (5)^2 + (6)^2 + (7)^2 + (8)^2 = 174$$

$$\sum_{i=1}^{4} (i^3 - 1) = [(1)^3 - 1] + [(2)^3 - 1] + [(3)^3 - 1] + [(4)^3 - 1] = 96$$

$$\sum_{i=1}^{3} (-3i) = (-3)(1) + (-3)(2) + (-3)(3) = -18$$

$$\sum_{j=1}^{5} x_j = x_1 + x_2 + x_3 + x_4 + x_5$$

Note that the name of the index is not restricted to j.

Summation notation can provide considerable efficiency in expressing the summation operation. It is a convenient way of representing systems of equations. And, it has particular value when the computer can be used to perform computations.

SELECTED BIBLIOGRAPHY

Bittinger, Marvin L.: *Calculus: A Modeling Approach*, Addison-Wesley, Reading, Mass., 1976.

Bowen, Earl K.: *Mathematics With Applications in Management and Economics*, 4th ed., Richard D. Irwin, Inc., Homewood, Ill., 1976.

Budnick, Frank S., Richard Mojena, and Thomas E. Vollmann: *Principles of Operations Research for Management*, Richard D. Irwin, Inc., Homewood, Ill., 1977.

Chiang, Alpha: *Fundamental Methods of Mathematical Economics*, 2d ed., McGraw-Hill Book Company, New York, 1974.

Childress, Robert L.: *Mathematics for Managerial Decisions*, Prentice-Hall, Inc., Englewood Cliffs, N.J., 1974.

Freund, John E.: *College Mathematics with Business Applications*, 2d ed., Prentice-Hall, Inc., Englewood Cliffs, N.J., 1975.

Goldstein, Larry J., David C. Lay, and David I. Schneider: *Calculus and Its Applications*, Prentice-Hall, Inc., Englewood Cliffs, N.J., 1977.

Graiwoig, Dennis E., Bruce Fielitz, James Robinson, and Dwight Tabor: *Mathematics: A Foundation for Decisions*, Addison-Wesley, Reading, Mass., 1976.

Haeussler, Ernest F., and Richard S. Paul: *Introductory Mathematical Analysis for Students of Business and Economics*, 2d ed., Reston Publishing Company, Inc., Reston, Va., 1976.

Hoffmann, Laurence D.: *Practical Calculus for the Social and Managerial Sciences*, McGraw-Hill Book Company, New York, 1975.

Kovacic, Michael L.: *Mathematics: Fundamentals for Managerial Decision-Making*, Prindle, Weber, and Schmidt, Boston, Mass., 1975.

Mizrahi, Abe, and Michael Sullivan: *Mathematics for Business and Social Sciences: An Applied Approach*, John Wiley and Sons, Inc., New York, 1976.

Theodore, Chris A.: *Applied Mathematics: An Introduction*, 3d ed., Richard D. Irwin, Inc., Homewood, Ill., 1976.

Thomas, George: *Calculus and Analytic Geometry*, 4th ed., Addison-Wesley, Reading, Mass., 1968.

Thompson, William W., Jr.: *Calculus with Applications in the Management and Social Sciences*, Prentice-Hall, Inc., Englewood Cliffs, N.J., 1977.

Weber, Jean E.: *Mathematical Analysis: Business and Economic Applications*, 3d ed., Harper and Row, New York, 1976.

Whipkey, K. L., and M. N. Whipkey: *The Power of Calculus*, John Wiley and Sons, Inc., New York, 1972.

Williams, Donald R.: *Modern Mathematics for Business Decision-Making*, Wadsworth Publishing Company, Inc., Belmont, Cal., 1974.

Chapter 0

1 -6; **3** -5; **5** 20; **7** -6; **9** $-a + b + c$; **11** 100; **13** 11; **15** 8;
17 5; **19** -11; **21** 3; **23** 0; **25** 21; **27** -1; **29** -15; **31** 5; **33** 1;
35 -30; **37** 28; **39** 7; **41** 25; **43** -24; **45** 54; **47** 8; **49** -4;
51 1; **53** 5^4; **55** $(3)^2(-2)^3$; **57** $(-x)^3$; **59** $a^2b^3c^2$; **61** $2^7 = 128$;
63 x^8; **65** x^5y^4; **67** x^6; **69** x^{14}; **71** a^{12}; **73** $27x^6$; **75** $1/a^4$; **77** 8;
79 x^2; **81** $\frac{1}{8}$; **83** 3; **85** 1; **87** yes, 0; **89** yes, 3; **91** yes, 6; **93** no;
95 $13x$; **97** $3x^2$; **99** $5y^3 + 2y^2 - 4y$; **101** $25x^3y^2 - 25xy^3$; **103** 0;
105 $-20x^3$; **107** $-24x^6$; **109** $5x^2 - 50x$; **111** $2a^3 - 4a^2 + 10a$;
113 $x^2 + x - 30$; **115** $4x^2 - 12x + 9$; **117** $x^2 - 16$; **119** $7x^4$;
121 $2a^3$; **123** $5a/bc$; **125** $2x^2y - xy + 4y$; **127** $-3xz^2 + 4y$;
129 $2a(x - 4a^2)$; **131** $2xy(2x^2 - 3y^2 + 4xy)$; **133** $3a(3a^2 - 5a - 9)$;
135 cannot; **137** $(p + 12)(p - 3)$; **139** $(r - 22)(r + 1)$; **141** cannot;
143 $(6m - 1)(m - 3)$; **145** $(2x + 1)(4x - 3)$; **147** $(x^2 + 9)(x + 3)(x - 3)$;
149 $(9x^2 + 25)(3x + 5)(3x - 5)$; **151** cannot; **153** $(1 + 2x)(1 - 2x + 4x^2)$; **155** $x^2(x - 2)(x + 1)$; **157** yes; **159** no; **161** yes; **163** $\frac{7}{3}$;
165 $\frac{1}{5}x^3$; **167** xy^3/z^2; **169** $\frac{120}{96}$; **171** $\dfrac{40x}{12x^2}$; **173** $\dfrac{20xy}{35xy}$; **175** $\frac{11}{30}$;
177 $\frac{1}{8}$; **179** $\dfrac{(x - 2)}{x^2}$; **181** $\dfrac{(x^2 + 7x)}{(x^2 - 4)}$; **183** $\dfrac{(10x^2 - 2)}{x^2}$;
185 $\dfrac{(3a^2 + 3a - 5)}{(a^2 + 2a + 1)}$; **187** -3; **189** $\dfrac{1}{3a^2b}$; **191** $\frac{7}{15}$; **193** $\dfrac{2a^3b^2}{3x^3}$;

195 $\dfrac{(x-4)}{(x^2-5x-4)}$; **197** $a^{17/6}$; **199** $x^{31/30}$; **201** $a^{5/4}$; **203** $-27x^2$;

205 $a^{4/3}$; **207** 25; **209** $-a$; **211** $-2x^2$; **213** $12x^3$; **215** $5\sqrt{7}$;

217 $7\sqrt{2}$; **219** $4\sqrt{x}-x\sqrt{x}$; **221** 4; **223** $\frac{8}{3}$; **225** $\dfrac{25x}{7y^2}$; **227** $\sqrt[3]{x^2}$;

229 $\sqrt[5]{(ab)^3}$; **231** $\dfrac{1}{\sqrt{x}}$; **233** $\frac{1}{2}$; **235** $(45x)^{1/2}$; **237** $x^{3/4}$; **239** $x^{5/3}$;

241 x^2; **243** 6; **245** 6; **247** -10; **249** -3; **251** 3.5; **253** ±6;

255 4, 1; **257** 5, -2; **259** none; **261** 4, $-\frac{1}{2}$; **262** $\frac{5}{4}$, $-\frac{3}{2}$

Chapter Test **1** -10; **2** 10; **3** 14; **4** -3; **5** $256x^8$; **6** 27;

7 m^{-3} or $\dfrac{1}{m^3}$; **8** $8a-9b-c$; **9** $2x^3$; **10** $3x^3y^3(2x-y+5x^2y^2)$;

11 $(x^2+\frac{1}{4})(x+\frac{1}{2})(x-\frac{1}{2})$; **12** $(x+9)(x-4)$; **13** $-\frac{1}{8}$; **14** $\dfrac{2ab}{5c^2}$; **15** $\dfrac{b^2}{c^2}$;

16 $\dfrac{2x}{(x+2)}$; **17** $a^{5/3}$; **18** $9\sqrt{3}$; **19** $\dfrac{3a^2b}{c^3}$; **20** $x^{3/5}$; **21** $\dfrac{1}{\sqrt[4]{x}}$;

22 none; **23** -4; **24** 3, 4; **25** none

Chapter 1

1 $A=\{a|a$ is a nonnegative even integer less than 21$\}$; **3** $V=\{v|v$ is a vowel$\}$; **5** $C=\{c|c=x^3$ where $x=1,2,3,$ or $4\}$; **7** $B=\{1,2,3,4\}$; **9** $B=\{-3\}$; **11** $A'=$ set of rational numbers; **13** $B'=\{2,4,6,8,9,10\}$; **15** $S=\{6,8,11,14\}$; **17** $A\subset\mathcal{U},B\subset\mathcal{U},C\subset\mathcal{U},A\subset C,B\subset C$; **21** $A=B$; **23** **a–c** $\{-1,-2,-3,-4,-5,-6,-7,-8,-9\}$ **d** $\{-1,-3,-5,-7,-9\}$ **e** ϕ **f** $\{-2,-4,-6,-8\}$; **25** **a** $\{-5,-4,-3,-2,-1,0,1,2,3,4,5\}$ **b** $\{2,4\}$ **c** $\{-4,-2,0,1,2,3,4,5\}$ **d** $\{1,2,3,4,5\}$; **31** **b** 125 **c** 25 **d** 575; **33** **b** 70, 130, 35 **c** 30 **d** 55 **e** 40 **f** 620; **35** **a** 0.15 **b** 0.02 **c** 0.03 **d** 0.04 **e** 0.30 **f** 0.33; **37** **a** $\{a|a=2^x$ where x is a positive integer less than 7$\}$ **b** $\{a|a=3^x$ where x is a positive integer less than 6$\}$ **c** $\{a|a=(-1)^x x^2$ where x is a positive integer less than 9$\}$ **d** $\{a|a=10^x$ where x is a positive integer less than 6$\}$; **41** $A\subset\mathcal{U},B\subset\mathcal{U},C\subset\mathcal{U},A\subset B$; **45** **a** $\{10\}$ **b** $\{1,2,4,5,6,8,9,10,15,17\}$ **c** $\{1,3,7,9,11,12,13,14,16,17,18,19\}$ **d** $\{1,2,3,4,6,7,8,9,10,11,12,13,14,16,17,18,19\}$; **49** **a** 0.08 **b** 0.10 **c** 0.10 **d** 0.14

EXERCISE 1.19

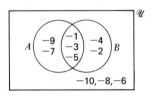

Chapter Test **1** $\{a|a=(10x)^2$ where x is a positive integer less than 5$\}$; **2** **b** ϕ **c** 0; **3** see figure; **4** **a** 410, **b** 200, **c** 35.

CHAP. 1 TEST: PROB. 2a

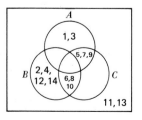

CHAP. 1 TEST: PROB. 3a

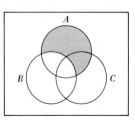

CHAP. 1 TEST: PROB. 3b

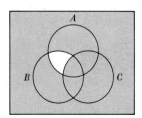

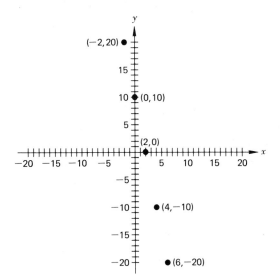

EXERCISE 2.19

Chapter 2

1 $\{(-4, 1), (-4, 3), (-4, 5), (-2, 1), (-2, 3), (-2, 5), (0, 1), (0, 3), (0, 5)\}$;
3 $\{(10, a), (10, b), (10, c), (10, d), (10, e), (20, a), (20, b), (20, c), (20, d),$
$(20, e)\}$; **5 a** $\{(1, -2), (1, 0), (1, 3), (4, -2), (4, 0), (4, 3)\}$; **7 a** $\{(-1, -4),$
$(-1, 4), (2, -4), (2, 4), (5, -4), (5, 4)\}$; **9 a** $\{(1, -3), (1, 3), (2, -3), (2, 3)\}$
b $\{(1, -3)\}, \{(1, 3)\}, \{(2, -3)\}, \{(2, 3)\}, \{(1, -3), (1, 3)\}, \{(1, -3), (2, -3)\},$
$\{(1, -3), (2, 3)\}, \{(1, 3), (2, -3)\}, \{(1, 3), (2, 3)\}, \{(2, -3), (2, 3)\}, \{(1, -3),$
$(1, 3), (2, -3)\}$ $\{(1, -3), (1, 3), (2, 3)\}, \{(1, -3), (2, -3), (2, 3)\}, \{(1, 3),$
$(2, -3), (2, 3)\}, \{(1, -3), (1, 3), (2, -3), (2, 3)\}, \varnothing$; **11** $(1, 1), (2, 0), (3, -1)$;
13 $(1, -1), (1, 0), (3, -1), (3, 0), (3, 1)$; **15 a** $D = \{-3, -1, 5, 20\}$
b $R = \{2\}$; **17** $\{(6, -6), (7, -7), (8, -8), \ldots\}$; **23** yes; **25 a** -5
b -25 **c** 15 **d** $10a + 10b - 5$; **27 a** 20 **b** 20 **c** 20 **d** 20; **29 a** 10
b 18 **c** 2 **d** $10 - 4a - 4b$; **31 a** 0 **b** 8 **c** 125; **33 a** 9 **b** 1600;
35 $x \neq 4$ or -4; **37** $x \leq 100$; **39** $x \geq 25$; **41 a** $c = 5x + 100,000$
b $200,000$, total cost of producing $20,000$ units **c** $0 \leq x \leq 50,000$;
43 a $2(x - 5)^2 + 5(x - 5) - 1 = 2x^2 - 15x + 24$ **b** 24 **c** 62; **45 a** $(50x$
$100)/(25x^2 - 100x + 99)$ **b** $-100/99$ **c** $100/99$; **57** a,b,d; **59** $\{(a, x),$
$(a, y), (a, z), (b, x), (b, y), (b, z), (c, x), (c, y), (c, z), (d, x), (d, y), (d, z), (e, x),$
$(e, y), (e, z), (f, x), (f, y), (f, z)\}$; **61** $(-2, -4), (-2, -2), (3, 5), (3, 10),$
$(-1, -4), (-1, -2), (4, 5), (4, 10)$; **63 a** F $= \{(-5, -64), (-3, -8),$
$(-1, 0)\}$ **b** D $= \{-5, -3, -1\}$ and R $= \{-64, -8, 0\}$; **67** not a function;
69 a 25 **b** 1 **c** $a^2 - 8a - 2ab + 8b + b^2 + 16$; **71 a** 4 **b** 0
c $(2a - b)^2 = 4a^2 - 4ab + b^2$; **73** $x \neq 0$ or 2; **75 a** $(-x^2 + 3)^3$ **b** 27
c 8

Chapter Test 2 2 a $\{(-2, 0), (-1, 3), (0, 4), (1, 3), (2, 0)\}$ **b** D $=$
$\{-2, -1, 0, 1, 2\}$ and R $= \{0, 3, 4\}$; **3** yes; **4 a** -10 **b** 115 **c** $(x + 1)^2 +$
$20(x + 1) - 10 = x^2 + 22x + 11$; **5** $x \leq 6$ but $x \neq 0$; **6** see figure;
7 $y = f(x) = \begin{cases} 5x \text{ when } 0 \leq x < 20 \\ 5x + 25 \text{ when } x \geq 20 \end{cases}$; **8 a** $\dfrac{(x^2 - 18x + 81)}{(x - 4)}$ **b** $-169/8$

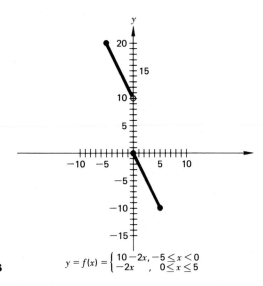

$$y = f(x) = \begin{cases} 10 - 2x, & -5 \le x < 0 \\ -2x, & 0 \le x \le 5 \end{cases}$$

Chapter 3

1 linear; **3** linear; **5** linear; **7** $S = \{(s, t) | -3s + 5t = -15\}$; **9 a** 6, 0, 90 **c** (15, 10) **d** no pairs **e** $x = 15$ whereas y can equal any value;

11 a (1, 1, 1) **b** (0, 0, 0); **13** $(-16.5, 0), (0, -5.5)$; **15** (6, 0), no y-intercept; **17** both at (0, 0); **25** the two equations are linear multiples of each other;

29 0; **31** 3, y increases 3 units for each unit that x increases; **33** $\dfrac{(d - b)}{(c - a)}$;

35 $y = \frac{50}{3} - 2x$, $m = -2$, $i = \frac{50}{3}$; **37** $y = 4$, $m = 0$, $i = 4$; **39** no slope intercept form, m undefined, no y intercept; **43 a** $m = \frac{5}{9}$, $i = -\frac{160}{9}$

b Celsius temperature increases by $\frac{5}{9}$ of a degree for each increase in temperature by 1 degree Fahrenheit; $0°F$ equals $-\frac{160}{9}$ °C **c** $F = \frac{9}{5}C + 32$, $m = \frac{9}{5}$

EXERCISE 3.19   **EXERCISE 3.23**

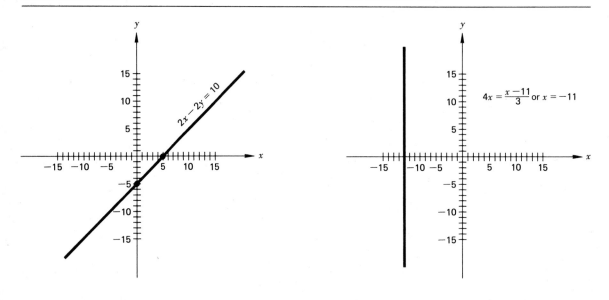

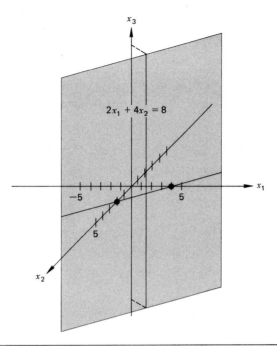

$2x_1 + 4x_2 = 8$

EXERCISE 3.65

$i = 32$, Fahrenheit temperature increases by $\frac{9}{5}$ of a degree for each increase in temperature by 1 degree Celsius, 0°C equals 32°F   **45** $y = -5x + 10$, $5x + y = 10$;   **47** no slope-intercept form, $x = 0$;   **49** $y = -2.5x - 2.5$, $2.5x + y = -2.5$;   **51** $y = 6$;   **53** no slope-intercept form, $x = 4$; **55** $y = c$;   **57** not colinear;   **59** $y = x - 2$;   **61** $F = \frac{9}{5}C + 32$; **63** $(0, 4, 0), (3, 4, 0), (3, 0, 0), (-6, 0, 0), (-6, 0, 6), (-6, -2, 6), (0, -2, 6)$, $(0, 0, 6), (0, -2, 0)$;   **65** $(4, 0, 0), (0, 2, 0)$, does not cross x_3 axis;   **67** see figure;   **69** plane is parallel to the axis corresponding to the missing variable;

EXERCISE 3.67

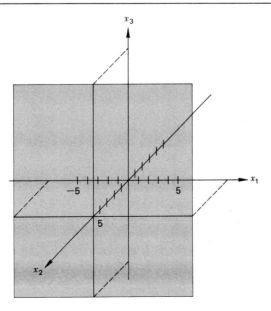

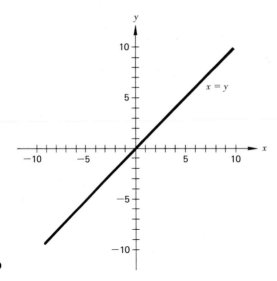

EXERCISE 3.89

71 $150x_1 + 100x_2 + 60x_3 + 70x_4 = 40,000$; **73** $2x_1 + 3x_2 + 5x_3 + 3.25x_4 + 50x_5 + 20x_6 = 500,000$; **75** $x_1 + x_2 + x_3 + x_4 + x_5 = 40$; **77** $x_1 + x_2 + x_3 + x_4 = 34,000$, where x_j = number of units shipped to wholesaler j **79** if x_j = number of acres of soybeans planted at farm j, $25x_1 + 23x_2 + 27x_3 = 500,000$ **81** no; **83** **a** $5x + 3y = 100$ **c** 20 **d** $P = \{(x, y)|5x + 3y = 100\}$; **85** both at $(0, 0)$; **87** $(-\frac{17}{3}, 0)$, $(0, \frac{17}{36})$; **93** $-\frac{1}{3}$; **95** $m_1 = -\frac{7}{5}$, $m_2 = -\frac{1}{2}$, first equation steeper; **97** $y = -x$, $m = -1$, $i = 0$; **99** $y = -\frac{5}{2}x + \frac{15}{2}$, $m = -\frac{5}{2}$, $i = \frac{15}{2}$; **101** $y = x - 5$, $x - y = 5$; **103** $y = -\frac{8}{3}x + 17$, $\frac{8}{3}x + y = 17$; **105** $y = 3x + 5$; **107** $(\frac{10}{3}, 0, 0)$, $(0, -10, 0)$, $(0, 0, \frac{5}{2})$; **109** **a** $20x_1 + 5x_2 + 8x_3 + 2x_4 = 20,000$ **b** $0 \leq x_1 \leq 1000$, $0 \leq x_2 \leq 4000$, $0 \leq x_3 \leq 2500$, $0 \leq x_4 \leq 10,000$; **111** $35,000x_1 + 20,000x_2 + 15,000x_3 + 9,000x_4 = 150,000$

EXERCISE 3.91

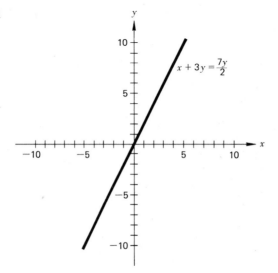

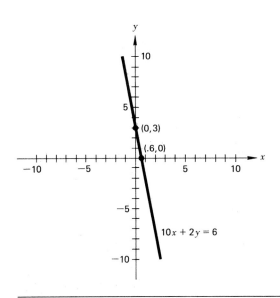

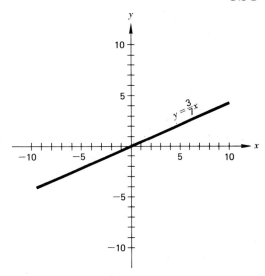

CHAP. 3 TEST: PROB. 2b   **CHAP. 3 TEST: PROB. 3c**

Chapter Test 1 a $3x_1 + 2.5x_2 = 500$ 2 a $(\frac{3}{5}, 0)$ and $(0, 3)$ b see figure; 3 a $y = \frac{3}{7}x$ b $\frac{3}{7}$ c see figure; 4 $m = -\frac{1}{2}$, $i = 12$; 5 $10,000p_1 + 2000p_2 + 1500p_3 + 8000p_4 = 500,000$; 6 $y = -\frac{1}{3}x$ or $x + 3y = 0$

Chapter 4

1 unique; 3 infinite; 5 no solution; 7 infinite; 17 $x = 4$, $y = -3$; 19 no solution; 21 infinite number of solutions; 23 infinite number of so-

EXERCISE 4.9   **EXERCISE 4.11**

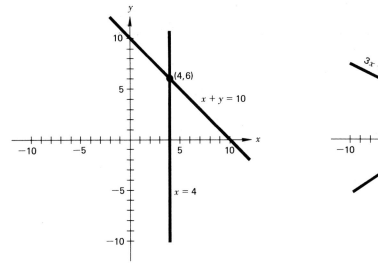

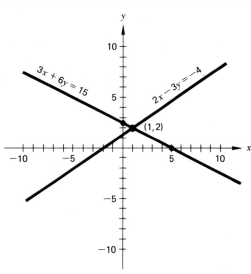

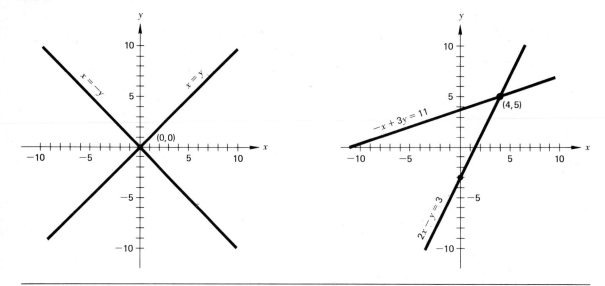

lutions; **25** no solution; **27** no solution; **29** no solution; **31** $x_1 = 1$, $x_2 = 0$, $x_3 = 1$; **33** no solution; **35** $x_1 = 2$, $x_2 = 2$, $x_3 = 5$; **37** $x_1 = 5$, $x_2 = -5$, $x_3 = 10$; **39 a** (5, 7.5, 7.5) **b** (−25, 0, 45) **c** (15, 10, −5) **d** (−25, 0, 45); **43** infinite number of solutions; **45** infinite number of solutions; **47** no solution; **49** $x_1 = 5$, $x_2 = 2$, $x_3 = 3$; **51** two intersecting planes which (according to the result of Example 4.10) have a line of common points; **53** $x_1 = -2$, $x_2 = -6$; **55** $x_1 = 1$, $x_2 = 7$; **57** $x_1 = 8$, $x_2 = 4$; **59** $x_1 = 1$, $x_2 = -1$, $x_3 = 0$; **61** $x_1 = 3$, $x_2 = 5$, $x_3 = -4$; **67** unique; **69** unique; **73** $x = 6$, $y = 2$; **75** $x = 42$, $y = -52$; **77** no solution; **79** $x_1 = 3$, $x_2 = 4$, $x_3 = 7$; **81** $x_1 = 0$, $x_2 = 0$, $x_3 = 7$; **83** infinite number of solutions; **85** $x_1 = 3$, $x_2 = 4$, $x_3 = 2$; **87** no graphical representation possible; **89** $x_1 = 4$, $x_2 = 1$; **91** infinite number

Chapter Test **1** see figure; **2** no solution; **3** $x = 2$, $y = 3$, $z = 1$; **4** no solution

Chapter 5

1 $y = a_1x_1 + a_2x_2 + a_3x_3 + a_4x_4 + b$;

3 $y = f(x) = \begin{cases} 5x_1 + 3x_2 + 25 \text{ when } x_1 + x_2 \le 30 \\ 5x_1 + 3x_2 + 1.5(x_1 + x_2 - 30) + 25 \text{ or} \\ 6.5x_1 + 4.5x_2 - 20 \text{ when } x_1 + x_2 > 30 \end{cases}$

5 a $R = 75x_1 + 90x_2 + 110x_3$ **b** $C = 50x_1 + 70x_2 + 80x_3 + 100,000$ **c** $P = R - C = 25x_1 + 20x_2 + 30x_3 - 100,000$ **d** $1,500,000;

7 $V = 50,000 - 6250t$; **9 a** yes **b** $V = 5,500,000 - 550,000t$ **c** 10 years; **11 a** $c = 800 - 4.5x$, where x = number of patrol cars and c = number of serious crimes per week **b** $0 \le x \le 120$ **c** reduces number of serious crimes per week by 4.5; **13 a** $q = 235,000 - 4000p$ **b** $43.75 **c** for every dollar increase in price, demand decreases by 4000 units; **15 a** $q = $

$6000p$ **b** \$8.33 **c** for every dollar increase in market price, supply will increase by 6000 units; **17 a** $g = 2.42 + .06t$ **b** $t = 9.67$ or sometime between 1982 and 1983 **c** 2.84 **d** cumulative grade point average increases .06 per year; **19 a** 12,500 units **b** \$1,875,000 **c** $-$\$10,000 (loss); **21 a** 5000 **b** 9000; **23 a** \$4.00 **b** \$7.20; **25 a** 40 min **b** $R =$ \$3,000,000, $C =$ \$2,950,000, $P =$ \$50,000; **27 a** \$.244 **b** \$.264; **29** p* = \$20, q* = 70,000 units; **31** p* = \$192.86, q* = 7857; **33** $y = -4x + 14$; **35** $y = x^2 + 2x + 5$; **37** $x_1 = 3, x_2 = 2, x_3 = 4$; **39** $x_1 = 25,000, x_2 = 25,000, x_3 = 10,000$; **41 a** $R = 10x_1 + 15x_2 + 8.5x_3$ **b** $C = 7.5x_1 + 10.5x_2 + 6x_3 + 50,000$ **c** $P = R - C = 2.5x_1 + 4.5x_2 + 2.5x_3 - 50,000$ **d** \$120,000; **43 a** $R = 25.6 - .25t$ **b** births per thousand of population are decreasing by .25 per year **c** 21.6 **d** $0 \le t \le 102.4$; **45 a** $q = 60,000p - 150,000$ **b** \$4.167 **c** quantity supplied will increase by 60,000 units for every increase in market price by \$1 **d** 2.5 (price must be greater than \$2.50 if any quantities are to be supplied); **47 a** 36,000 **b** $-$\$15,000; **49 a** \$1.25 **b** \$4.375; **51** p* = 400, q* = 20,000; **53** $y = 2x^2$

Chapter Test 1 **a** $P = 15x - 75,000$ **b** 15,000; **2 a** \$75,000 **b** \$7500 **c** 10 years; **3 a** 80 **b** 56; **4** p* = 100, q* = 35,000; **5** $6x_1 + 2x_2 + 2x_3 = 80, 7x_1 + 4x_2 + x_3 = 60, 5x_1 + 5x_2 + 3x_3 = 100$

Chapter 6

1 $x \ge -10$; **3** no solution; **5** $x \le 4$; **7** $x \ge -6$; **9** $-36 \le x \le -4$; **11** no solution; **13 a** $x \le 40 - 4y$ **b** $x \le 20$ **c** $y \le 10 - x/4$ **d** $y \le 20$; **29** $2x_1 + 4x_2 \le 40, 3x_1 + 2x_2 \le 36, 1.5x_1 + 3x_2 \le 30, x_1 \ge 0, x_2 \ge 0$, (see graph);

EXERCISE 6.15

EXERCISE 6.21

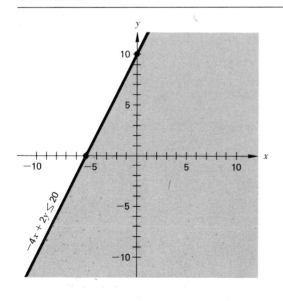

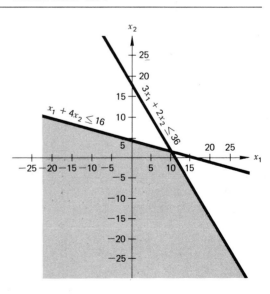

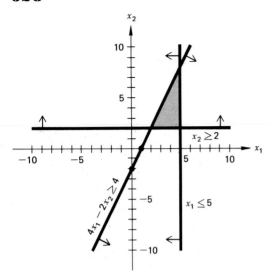

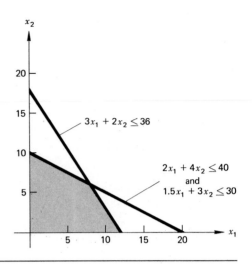

EXERCISE 6.25

EXERCISE 6.29

31 minimize

$$z = .12x_1 + .15x_2$$

subject to

$$2x_1 + 3x_2 \geq 18$$
$$4x_1 + 2x_2 \geq 22$$
$$x_1, x_2 \geq 0$$

33 maximize

$$z = 9x_1 + 20x_2 + 22x_3$$

subject to

$$3.5x_1 + 4x_2 + 2x_3 \leq 120$$
$$2x_2 + 2x_3 \leq 100$$
$$4x_1 + x_2 \leq 80$$
$$2x_1 + 3x_2 + 6x_3 \leq 150$$
$$5.5x_1 + 4x_2 + 3.5x_3 \leq 250$$
$$x_1, x_2, x_3 \geq 0$$

35 minimize

$$z = 100x_{11} + 250x_{12} + 300x_{13} + 150x_{14} +$$
$$400x_{21} + 75x_{22} + 100x_{23} + 200x_{24} +$$
$$300x_{31} + 100x_{32} + 50x_{33} + 400x_{34}$$

subject to

$$x_{11} + x_{12} + x_{13} + x_{14} \leq 150$$
$$x_{21} + x_{22} + x_{23} + x_{24} \leq 125$$
$$x_{31} + x_{32} + x_{33} + x_{34} \leq 180$$
$$x_{11} + x_{21} + x_{31} = 40$$
$$x_{12} + x_{22} + x_{32} = 80$$
$$x_{13} + x_{23} + x_{33} = 90$$
$$x_{14} + x_{24} + x_{34} = 150$$
$$x_{ij} \geq 0 \text{ for all } i \text{ and } j.$$

37 $z = 200$, $x_1 = 40$, $x_2 = 0$; **39** $z = 30$, $x_1 = 15$, $x_2 = 0$; **41** $z = 27$, $x_1 = 3$, $x_2 = 4$; **43** $z = 85$, $x_1 = 15$, $x_2 = 10$, both departments at 100 percent of capacity; **45** $z = 24$ at $(4, 0)$ and $(2, 3)$; **47** $z = 40$ at $(1, 4)$ and $(\frac{4}{3}, \frac{8}{3})$; **51** $x =$ any real number; **53** $-7 \leq x \leq 16$; **57** $x \leq \dfrac{15}{7} - \dfrac{3y}{7}$, $x \leq 3$;

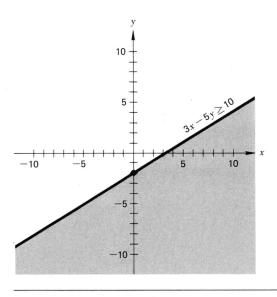

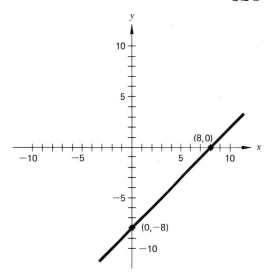

EXERCISE 6.55

EXERCISE 6.59

63 minimize $\qquad z = 540x_1 + 744x_2$

subject to $\qquad 200x_1 + 400x_2 \leq 20{,}000$
$100x_1 + 120x_2 \leq 10{,}000$
$5x_1 + 8x_2 \leq 400$
$x_1 \geq 10$
$x_1 + x_2 \geq 35$
$x_1, x_2 \geq 0$

65 $z = 20$, $x_1 = \frac{20}{7}$, $x_2 = \frac{20}{7}$; **67** $z = 20$, $x_1 = \frac{20}{7}$, $x_2 = \frac{20}{7}$; **69** $z = 2500$, $x_1 = 0$, $x_2 = 50$

EXERCISE 6.61

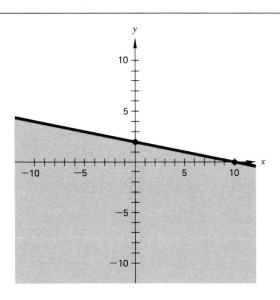

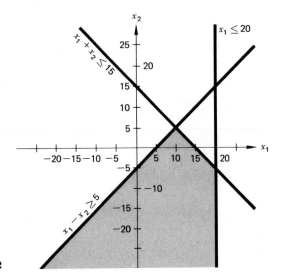

CHAP. 6 TEST: PROB. 2

Chapter Test 1 a $x \leq 3.5$, b $-\frac{7}{4} \leq x \leq 9.3$; 2 see figure;
3 maximize $\qquad z = 20A + 10B + 50C + 25D + 2E$

subject to
$$A \geq 20$$
$$B \geq 10$$
$$A + B + C + D + E \leq 75$$
$$C - E = 0$$
$$A, B, C, D, E \geq 0$$

4 $z = 16, x_1 = 4, x_2 = 8$

Chapter 7

1
$$x_1 + x_2 + x_3 + S_1 = 100$$
$$2x_1 - x_3 + S_2 = 25$$
$$x_2 + S_3 = 20$$
$$x_3 + S_4 = 50$$
$$x_1, x_2, x_3, S_1, S_2, S_3, S_4 \geq 0$$

3 a $5x_1 + 4x_2 + S_1 = 48$ b $x_1 = 0, x_2 = 0, S_1 = 48, S_2 = 26*$
$\quad 2x_1 + 5x_2 + S_2 = 26 \qquad x_1 = 0, S_1 = 0, x_2 = 12, S_2 = -34$
$\quad x_1, x_2, S_1, S_2 \geq 0 \qquad x_1 = 0, S_2 = 0, x_2 = 5.2, S_1 = 27.2*$
$\qquad\qquad\qquad\qquad\qquad x_2 = 0, S_1 = 0, x_1 = 9.6, S_2 = 6.8*$
$\qquad\qquad\qquad\qquad\qquad x_2 = 0, S_2 = 0, x_1 = 13, S_1 = -17$
$\qquad\qquad\qquad\qquad\qquad S_1 = 0, S_2 = 0, x_1 = 8, x_2 = 2*$

c * solutions in part b
d $x_1 = 9.6, S_2 = 6.8, x_2 = S_1 = 0, z = 134.4$; 5 $x_1 = 40, x_2 = 10, z = 180$;
7 $x_1 = 20, x_2 = 40, S_1 = 90, z = 680$; 9 $x_1 = 27.5, x_2 = 30, x_3 = 40$,
$z = 525$; 11 The corresponding basic variable *increases* in value as quantities of the incoming variable are introduced;
13
$$x_1 + x_2 + x_3 - E_1 + A_1 = 25$$
$$6x_1 - 2x_2 + A_2 = 20$$
$$x_1 + 4x_2 + 3x_3 + S_3 = 100$$
$$x_1, x_2, x_3, E_1, A_1, A_2, S_3 \geq 0$$

15 $x_1 = 10, S_2 = 10, E_1 = 20, z = 30;$ **17** $x_1 = 45, x_2 = 52.5, z = 697.5;$
19 $x_3 = 40, S_1 = 60, z = 240;$ **21** $x_2 = 25, x_3 = 125, S_1 = 850, z = 925;$
23 $x_2 = 40, E_1 = 120, z = 160;$

Chapter Test **1** $4x_1 - 2x_2 + x_3 + S_1 = 25$
$$-x_1 - 3x_2 + S_2 = 10$$
$$-2x_1 - 3x_3 + A_3 = 20$$

2 $x_1 = 4, x_2 = 8, z = 272;$
b A_2 **c** x_1
3 **a**

Basic Variables	z	x_1	x_2	E_1	A_1	A_2	b_i	Row no.
	1	$3M - 5$	-4	$-M$	0	0	$25M$	(0)
A_1	0	1	1	-1	1	0	10	(1)
A_2	0	2	-1	0	0	1	15	(2)

Chapter 8

1 $\begin{pmatrix} 3 \\ -4 \\ 2 \end{pmatrix}$; **3** $(6 \quad 8 \quad -7)$; **5** $\begin{pmatrix} 1 & 0 & 0 \\ 0 & 1 & 0 \\ 0 & 0 & 1 \end{pmatrix}$ **7** $\begin{pmatrix} 3 & 6 \\ -4 & 2 \\ 0 & 6 \end{pmatrix}$ **9** $\begin{pmatrix} 0 & 5 \\ 8 & -5 \end{pmatrix}$;

11 $\begin{pmatrix} -3 & 5 & 3 \\ 2 & -1 & -6 \\ 3 & 4 & 5 \end{pmatrix}$ **13** $\begin{pmatrix} -10 & 5 \\ 8 & -10 \end{pmatrix}$ **15** $\begin{pmatrix} ka_{11} & ka_{12} \\ ka_{21} & ka_{22} \end{pmatrix}$;

17 0; **19** 1; **21** $\begin{pmatrix} -11 & 2 \\ 11 & 4 \end{pmatrix}$; **23** $\begin{pmatrix} 2 & 6 & 4 \\ 1 & 0 & 1 \\ 0 & 0 & 2 \end{pmatrix}$; **25** $(17 \quad 16 \quad 27)$;

27 $\begin{pmatrix} -4 & 8 \\ 2 & -4 \end{pmatrix}$; **29** $\begin{pmatrix} ax_1 + bx_2 \\ cx_1 + dx_2 \end{pmatrix}$; **31** yes;

33 $\begin{pmatrix} 2 & -1 \\ 3 & -4 \end{pmatrix}\begin{pmatrix} x_1 \\ x_2 \end{pmatrix} = \begin{pmatrix} 10 \\ 25 \end{pmatrix}$; **35** $\begin{pmatrix} 1 & 1 & 1 \\ 1 & -1 & 0 \\ 2 & 0 & 1 \end{pmatrix}\begin{pmatrix} x_1 \\ x_2 \\ x_3 \end{pmatrix} = \begin{pmatrix} 15 \\ 4 \\ 14 \end{pmatrix}$;

37 $\begin{matrix} x_1 = 10 \\ x_2 = 5 \\ x_3 = -5 \end{matrix}$ **39** $\begin{matrix} 2x_1 - 3x_2 = 10 \\ 4x_1 \quad\quad = 18 \end{matrix}$

41 $ax_1 + bx_2 + cx_3 = j$
$dx_1 + ex_2 + fx_3 = k$
$gx_1 + hx_2 + ix_3 = l$

43 15; **45** 0; **47** -34; **49** $\begin{pmatrix} 6 & 2 \\ -5 & 3 \end{pmatrix}$ **51** $\begin{pmatrix} 6 & 0 & -12 \\ -7 & 0 & 14 \\ -3 & 0 & 6 \end{pmatrix}$

53 28; **55** 0; **57** -135; **59** $\begin{pmatrix} 3 & -1 \\ 2 & -1 \end{pmatrix}$ **61** no inverse **63** $\begin{pmatrix} 1 & 0 \\ 0 & 1 \end{pmatrix}$

65 $\frac{1}{8}\begin{pmatrix} -3 & 6 & 1 \\ 3 & 2 & -1 \\ -1 & -6 & 3 \end{pmatrix}$ **67** $\begin{pmatrix} 5 & -7 \\ -2 & 3 \end{pmatrix}$; **69** no inverse;

71 $x_1 = 2, x_2 = 3;$ **73** $x_1 = 10, x_2 = 5;$ **75** $x_1 = 20, x_2 = 10, x_3 = 30;$
77 either no solution or infinite number; **79** $x_1 = 1, x_2 = 5, x_3 = 0;$

81 $\begin{pmatrix} 3 \\ -8 \\ 9 \\ 0 \\ 14 \end{pmatrix}$

83 $\begin{pmatrix} 0 & 2 & 1 & 6 \\ 1 & 3 & 0 & 7 \\ 0 & 4 & 0 & 8 \\ 1 & 5 & 1 & 9 \end{pmatrix}$ **85** $\begin{pmatrix} 24 \\ 72 \\ 39 \end{pmatrix}$ **87** $\begin{pmatrix} 5.2 & 26.5 \\ 45.5 & 2.0 \\ 22.5 & 49.0 \end{pmatrix}$ **89** 182;

91 $\begin{pmatrix} 7 & 8 \\ 9 & 10 \end{pmatrix}$ **93** cannot be done; **95** $\begin{pmatrix} 8 & 14 \\ 8 & 11.5 \\ 11 & 13.5 \end{pmatrix}$

97 $\begin{pmatrix} 40 & 35 \\ 5 & 10 \end{pmatrix}\begin{pmatrix} x_1 \\ x_2 \end{pmatrix} = \begin{pmatrix} 100 \\ 15 \end{pmatrix}$ **99** $\begin{matrix} 8x_1 + 7x_2 + 6x_3 = 5 \\ 5x_1 + 4x_2 + 3x_3 = 7 \end{matrix}$ **101** 23;

103 none exists; **105** $\begin{pmatrix} 0 & 0 & 0 \\ 0 & 0 & 0 \\ 0 & 0 & 0 \end{pmatrix}$ **107** 0; **109** -118;

111 $\begin{pmatrix} -\frac{3}{8} & \frac{1}{8} \\ 1 & 0 \end{pmatrix}$ **113** $\frac{1}{182}\begin{pmatrix} -23 & 36 & 19 \\ 37 & -50 & 9 \\ -13 & 52 & -13 \end{pmatrix}$ **115** $-\frac{1}{6}\begin{pmatrix} 13 & -10 \\ -11 & 8 \end{pmatrix}$

117 $x_1 = 0, x_2 = 4$; **119** $x_1 = 1, x_2 = -1, x_3 = 1$; **121** $x_1 = -2, x_2 = 2$;

123 $C^t A^t = \begin{pmatrix} 3250 \\ 2250 \\ 3625 \\ 875 \end{pmatrix} \begin{matrix} A \\ B \\ C \\ D \end{matrix}$

125 **a** $(500 \quad 1,000 \quad 400)\begin{pmatrix} 2 & 4 & 5 & 5 \\ 3 & 2 & 3 & 8 \\ 1 & 3 & 5 & 4 \end{pmatrix} = (4,400 \quad 5,200 \quad 7,500 \quad 12,100)$

b $(4,400 \quad 5,200 \quad 7,500 \quad 12,100)\begin{pmatrix} \$2.00 \\ \$3.00 \\ \$1.50 \\ \$5.00 \end{pmatrix} = \$96,150$

Chapter Test

1 $\begin{pmatrix} 1 & 6 \\ -3 & -2 \\ 0 & 4 \\ 5 & 9 \end{pmatrix}$ **2** $ae + bf + cg + dh$;

3 **a** not possible **b** $\begin{pmatrix} -11 & -22 \\ 2 & -1 \\ 26 & 9 \end{pmatrix}$ **c** not possible;

4 $\begin{pmatrix} 1 & 0 & 0 & -1 \\ 0 & 1 & 1 & 0 \\ 0 & 0 & 1 & 1 \\ 0 & 0 & 0 & 1 \end{pmatrix}\begin{pmatrix} x_1 \\ x_2 \\ x_3 \\ x_4 \end{pmatrix} = \begin{pmatrix} 20 \\ 15 \\ 18 \\ 9 \end{pmatrix}$ **5** -30; **6** no inverse;

7 $\begin{matrix} 3x_1 + 7x_2 = 15 \\ 2x_1 + 5x_2 = 11 \end{matrix}$

Chapter 9

1 $4500; **3** $3000, $60,000; **5** *Period*

Period	*P*	*I*	*S*
1	$5000.00	$200.00	$5200.00
5	5200.00	208.00	5408.00
3	5408.00	216.32	5624.32
4	5624.32	224.97	5849.29

7 a $5858.30 **b** quarterly by $9.00; **9** $738.73, $238.73;
11 $1,228,957.50, $478,957.50; **13 a** $1.79, $.79 **b** $1.81, $.81
c $1.82, $.82; **15** 58,640; **17** $8248.37; **19** $6590.90, $3409.10;
21 $67,297, $32,703; **23** 23 semiannual periods; **25 a** 8.16%,
b 8.243%; **27** between 5% and 6% annually; **29 a** $126,498.06,
b $76,498.06; **31 a** $12,655.19 **b** $5455.19 **33 a** $79,084.74
b $80,611.11 **c** $81,669.66; **35** $1,010.30, $1917.60; **37** $872.30,
$1277.00; **39** $31,958.38; **41** $26,015.86; **43 a** $127,833.50
b $122,166.50; **45** $14,902; **47** $41,932.50; **49 a** $166.05 **b** $977.80;
51 $251.76, $75,528.00, $45.528.00; **53** $441.86, $106,046.40, $56,046.40;
55 $20.85, $6255.00 **57** $32.40, $7776.00; **59** $42,108.48 **61** 16,422.72;
63 $19.80; **65** approximately 6 years; **67** approximately 6%;
69 a 6.09% **b** 6.136%; **71** $76,633.95, $16,633.95; **73** $552.35, $581.20;
75 8 years; **77** $12,471.33; **79** $26,440; **81** 15; **83** $328.86,
$98,658.00, $58,658.00; **85** $47,664.67.

Chapter Test 1 $37,459.60; **2** $47,629.80; **3 a** $135,669.72
b $35,669.72; **4** $1590, $4100; **5** $3147.50; **6** 8.243%; **7** $359.89 vs.
$321.85, or $38.04.

Chapter 10

1 not quadratic; **3** not quadratic; **5** $a = \frac{1}{3}$, $b = 0$, $c = 0$, **7** $a = 40$,
$b = -6$; $c = 0$; **9** concave down, y-int. at $(0, 0)$, x-int. at $(0, 0)$, vertex at
$(0, 0)$; **11** concave up, y-int. at $(0, 2)$, no x-int, vertex at $(\frac{2}{3}, \frac{2}{3})$; **13** concave

EXERCISE 10.9   **EXERCISE 10.11**

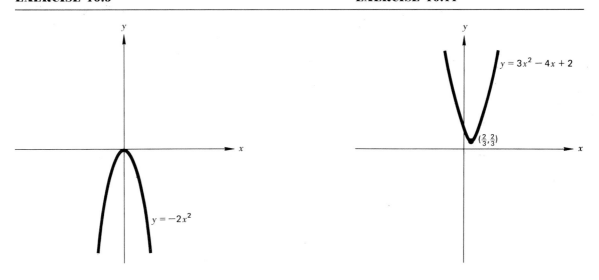

$y = -2x^2$

$y = 3x^2 - 4x + 2$

$(\frac{2}{3}, \frac{2}{3})$

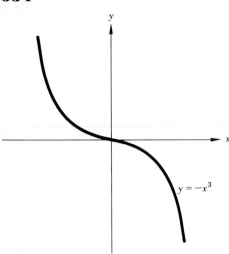

EXERCISE 10.19

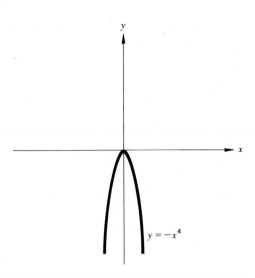

EXERCISE 10.21

down, y-int. at $(0, -10)$, no x-int, vertex at $(0, -10)$; **17** $y = x^2 + 4x + 1$;
19 3; **21** 4; **23** 5; **25** 4; **27** $R = g(p) = 4500p - 2.5p^2$, down, y-int.
at $(0, 0)$, $g(20) = \$89,000$; **29** $R = 1800q - .4q^2$; **31** **a** $q_s = 2p^2 - 5000$
c $p = 50$ **d** 7800; **33** $q_d = 4p^2 - 400p + 10,000$, 400; **35** $p = 33.45$,
$q = 1094.5$; **37** horizontal line, $y = a$; **43** **a** $\$146,932$ **b** $\$148,024$
c $\$148,594$ **d** $\$149,180$; **45** **a** $P = 5000(1 + .07)^{-10}$ **b** $\$2541.70$;
47 $t = 15.4$ or during 1986, $t = 9.11$ or during 1979; **49** **a** $\$48,596.40$
b $\$88,545.60$; **51** **a** $\$100,000$ **b** $\$60,650, \$36,780$; **53** **a** 2.96%,
25.92%, 45.12%; **55** **a** $2^6 = 64$ **b** $3^5 = 243$ **c** $0.5^{-1} = 2$ **d** $4^1 = 4$
e $10^{-2} = .01$; **59** $a = 3, b = -8, c = 9$; **61** $a = 5/4, b = 0, c = 0$;
63 not quadratic; **65** concave up, y-int. at $(0, 0)$, x-int. at $(0, 0)$ and $(4, 0)$,
vertex at $(2, -1)$; **67** concave up, y-int. at $(0, 16)$, x-int. at $(4, 0)$; vertex at

EXERCISE 10.23

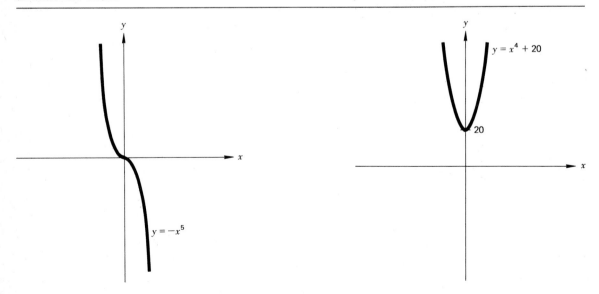

EXERCISE 10.25

(4, 0); **69** functions intersect at (2.36, 3.0) and (.63, 3.0); **71** **a** $R = g(p) = 120,000p - 3p^2$ **b** down **c** y-int. at (0, 0), x-int at (0, 0) and (40,000, 0) **d** $p = \$20,000$ **e** $\$1,200,000,000$; **73** $p = \$62.50$, $q = \$1,406,250$; **75** **a** no **b** yes **c** yes **d** yes; **79** \$91,105, \$41,105; **81** 491.92 million; **83** 1982 ($t = 6.83$); **85** 159.07 crimes per day, 110.14 crimes per day; **87** **a** $\log_3 243 = 5$ **b** $\log 100,000 = 5$ **c** $\log_6 216 = 3$; **89** **a** 4.3175 **b** 6.9077 **c** 8.5172 **d** 6.8024.

Chapter Test **1** **a** up **b** (0, 25) **c** (−5, 0) **d** (−5, 0) **e** see sketch; **2** $R = 400,000p - 30p^2$;

3 $400a + 20b + c = 400$
$625a + 25b + c = 850$
$900a + 30b + c = 1400$

4 82.1; **5** \$40,552, \$30,552; **6** $\log_4 65536 = 8$.

Chapter 11

1 50; **3** 5; **5** no limit; **7** 14; **9** −5; **11** 0; **13** no limit; **15** 0; **17** $13\frac{3}{4}$; **19** $-\frac{11}{3}$; **21** 18; **23** 250; **25** −4; **27** 13; **29** $b^2 + 2b + 1$; **31** 1; **33** none; **35** none; **37** $x = 3$; **39** none; **41** $x = 3, \frac{3}{2}$; **43** $x = 0, 3, -3$; **45** 6; **47** 4; **49** \$2.733 million/year, \$2.5 million/year, \$2.3 million/year, \$2.85 million/year; **51** 1.1 billion ft^3/year, .933 billion ft^3/year, 1.35 billion ft^3/year; **53** **a** $2x + \Delta x - 4$ **b** 0; **55** **a** 10 **b** 10; **57** **a** $3x^2 + 3x\Delta x + \Delta x^2$ **b** 13; **59** **a** $-\dfrac{1}{x(x + \Delta x)}$ **b** $-\frac{1}{3}$;

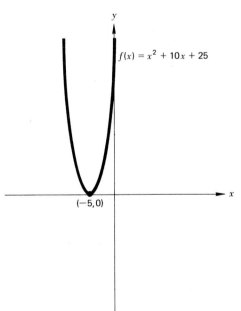

CHAP. 10 TEST: PROB. 1

$f(x) = x^2 + 10x + 25$

(−5,0)

61 a 3 **b** 3, 3; **63 a** $-2x$ **b** 2, -4; **65 a** $10x$ **b** $-10, 20$;

67 a $-\dfrac{1}{x^2}$ **b** $-1, -\frac{1}{4}$; **69 a** $-6x^2$ **b** $-6, -24$; **71** $-3, -15$,

$x = \frac{1}{4}$; **73** 25, 25, no points of zero slope; **75** 0, 9, $x = 0$ and $x = 2$; **79** 0;

81 $-3/2$; **83** $-8x$; **85** $\dfrac{5x^{2/3}}{3}$; **87** $-40/x^6$; **89** $9x^2 + 20x - 3$;

91 $-12x^3 + 36x^2 - 24x - 27$; **93** $\dfrac{10 + 4x^2}{(5 - 2x^2)^2}$;

95 $\dfrac{(2x^7 - 14x)(14x) - 7x^2(14x^6 - 14)}{(2x^7 - 14x)^2}$; **97** $6(2x - 5)^2$; **99** $\frac{1}{2}(x^5 - 5)^{-1/2}(5x^4)$;

101 $-6x(x^2 - 9)^{-4}$; **103** $3x^2e^{x^3}$; **105** $10e^x + 10xe^x$;

107 $\dfrac{8x - 2}{4x^2 - 2x + 9}$; **109** $2ax + b$; **111** 0; **113** ae^{ax+b}; **115 a** 4

b none; **117 a** -3 **b** $x = \pm2$; **119 a** $2a + b$ **b** $x = -b/2a$;
121 a 21(100) ft/s **b** 75(100) ft/s, 1200(100) ft/s; **123 a** 48 ft/s
b 32 ft/s **c** 128 ft/s; **125 a** \$550,700 **b** \$17,972/day; **127 a** $f''(x) = 0$
b $f'(1) = 0, f''(1) = 0$; **129 a** $f''(x) = -6$ **b** $f'(1) = -6, f''(1) = -6$;
131 a $f''(x) = 6x$ **b** $f'(1) = 3, f''(1) = 6$; **133 a** $f''(x) = 20x^3$
b $f'(1) = 5, f''(1) = 20$; **135 a** $f''(x) = e^x$ **b** $f'(1) = e, f''(1) = e$
137 a 160 ft/s **b** 32 ft/sec²; **139** $f'(x) = -12x^2, f''(x) = -24x, f'''(x) =$
$-24, f^{IV}(x) = 0$; **141** $f'(x) = 6x^5, f''(x) = 30x^4, f'''(x) = 120x^3, f^{IV}(x) =$
$360x^2, f^V(x) = 720x, f^{VI}(x) = 720, f^{VII}(x) = 0$; **143** $f'(x) = 2ax + b, f''(x) =$
$2a, f'''(x) = 0$, **145** $8x$; **147** 0; **149** $2x^5 + 8x^2$; **151** $8x^3 - 14x$;

153 $4(x + 3)^3 - 12(x + 3)^2 + 6$; **155** $\dfrac{1}{3x^2 - 6x + 5}$, $x = $ real;

157 $\dfrac{1}{12x - 5}$, $x \neq \frac{5}{12}$; **159** $\dfrac{1}{m}$; **161** $\dfrac{1}{(-6y + 2)}$; **163** -11; **165** 7;

167 0; **169** no limiting value; **171** none; **173** $x = 0, x = 6$;

175 none; **177** $x = \dfrac{-b \pm \sqrt{-b^2 - 4ac}}{2a}$; **179** 16; **181 a** 0 **b** 0;

183 a $4x + 2\Delta x - 1$ **b** 5; **185 a** $3x^2 + 3x\Delta x + \Delta x^2$ **b** 7;

187 a a **b** a; **189 a** 0 **b** 0 **c** all x; **191 a** $\dfrac{1}{x^2}$ **b** $\frac{1}{4}$ **c** none

193 a a **b** a **c** all x when $a = 0$, none when $a \neq 0$; **195** $\dfrac{1}{x}$

197 $5x^2 + 4x$; **199** $\dfrac{7x^{5/2}}{2}$; **201** $\frac{3}{2}x^{1/2}$; **203** $4x^3 - 30x^2 + 46x - 14$;

205 $(-2x)(x + 3)^4 + 4(x + 3)^3(9 - x^2)$; **207** $5e^{5x-10}$; **209** $3e^x(e^x + 12)^2$;

211 $\dfrac{(2ax + b)}{(ax^2 + bx + c)}$; **213** $(x^4 + 8) + (5x^4 + 8)lnx$; **215 a** -6 **b** $x = 5$;
217 a 8664 **b** $x = -\frac{3}{8}$; **219 a** $3\sqrt{12}/2$ **b** $x = -10$; **221 a** $16e^6$,
b $x = 0$; **223 a** $2/x^3$ **b** $-1, 2$; **225 a** $e^x + e^{-x}$ **b** $e - e^{-1}, e + e^{-1}$;
227 a 0 **b** 1, 0; **229** $f'(x) = 12x^5 - 20x^4 + 4x, f''(x) = 60x^4 -$
$80x^3 + 4, f'''(x) = 240x^3 - 240x^2, f^{IV}(x) = 720x^2 - 480x, f^V(x) = 1440x -$
$480, f^{VI}(x) = 1440, f^{VII}(x) = 0$, **231** $f'(x) = -20x^3 + 9x^2 - 4x, f''(x) =$
$-60x^2 + 18x - 4, f'''(x) = -120x + 18, f^{IV}(x) = -120, f^V(x) = 0$, **233** $9x^8$;

235 $\frac{1}{2}\left(\dfrac{1}{x^2} + \dfrac{3}{x}\right)^{-1/2}\left(-\dfrac{2}{x^3} - \dfrac{3}{x^2}\right)$; **237** $32x + 72$; **239** $2y - 5$;

241 $\frac{1}{2}(2y^2 - 3y + 2)^{-1/2}(4y - 3)$, not defined when $2y^2 - 3y + 2 \leq 0$;

243 $\dfrac{1}{(6x^2 + 8x - \frac{3}{2})}$, $x = \frac{1}{6}, x = -1.5$.

Chapter Test **1 a** 5 **b** 2; **2** none; **3** $-6x + 1$;
4 a $-8x^{-7/5}/5$ **b** $8x^7 - 28x^3 - 2x$ **c** $\dfrac{(x^3 + 5)(-2x) - (12 - x^2)(3x^2)}{(x^3 + 5)^2} =$
$\dfrac{x^4 - 36x^2 - 10x}{(x^3 + 5)^2}$ **d** $4(e^{x^2} - x^5)^3(2xe^{x^2} - 5x^4)$ **e** $(8x) \ln (x^3) + \left(\dfrac{3}{x}\right)(4x^2 - 5)$
$= 8x \ln x^3 + 12x - 15/x$; **5** $x = 1$; **6** $f'(x) = x^2 - 4x + 5, f''(x) = 2x - 4$,
$f'''(x) = 2, f^{\text{IV}}(x) = 0$; **7** $8x(x^2 - 15)^3 - 4x$; **8** $\frac{1}{10}$

Chapter 12

1 a decreasing **b** none **c** all x, none; **3 a** neither **b** $x > 1$
c $x < 1$ **d** $x = 1$; **5 a** increasing **b** $x \neq 0$ **c** none, $x = 0$; **7 a** increasing **b** $x > 0$ **c** $x < 0$ **d** $x = 0$; **9 a** increasing **b** $x \neq 0$,
c none **d** $x = 0$; **11** up, up; **13** up, down; **15** down, up; **17** up, up;
19 up, up; **21** up, up; **23** $x = 0$; **25** $x = \frac{1}{6}$; **27** $x = -1, 1, 0$;
29 none; **31** $x = \pm.71$; **33** $x = 4$, relative max., $f(4) = 58$; **35** $x = 0$,
stationary infl. point, $f(0) = 0$; **37** relative min. at $x = 3, f(3) = -13.5$, relative max. at $x = -2, f(-2) = 7\frac{1}{3}$; **39** relative max. at $x = 0, f(0) = 10$,
relative min. at $x = 4, f(4) = -54$, relative min at $x = -4, f(-4) = -54$;
41 stat. infl. point at $x = 0, f(0) = 0$, relative min. at $x = 4, f(4) = -72.53$,
relative max. at $x = -1, f(-1) = \frac{23}{60}$; **43** stat. infl. point at $x = \frac{5}{2}, f(\frac{5}{2}) = 0$;
45 relative min. at $x = 0, f(0) = 1$; **47** relative min at $x = 0, f(0) = 0$;
49 relative max. at $x = 34.5, f(34.5) = 767.5$; **55** min. at $x = 10$,
$f(10) = -350$, max. at $x = \frac{3}{4}, f(\frac{3}{4}) = -7\frac{3}{4}$; **57** min. at $x = 5, f(5) = 72.25$,
max. at $x = 10, f(10) = 2116$; **59** min. at $x = 6, f(6) = -1082.8$, max. at
$x = 0, f(0) = -10$; **61** min. at $x = 0, f(0) = 0$, max. at $x = -5$,
$f(-5) = 7291.67$; **63** min. at $x = 30, f(30) = -401.2$, max. at $x = 10$,
$f(10) = -331.3$; **71 a** all x if $m > 0$ **b** all x if $m < 0$ **c** all x if $m = 0$;
73 a $x > \frac{5}{2}$ **b** $x < \frac{5}{2}, x = \frac{5}{2}$; **75 a** $x > 0$ if $a > 0$ and $x < 0$ if $a < 0$

EXERCISE 12.65　　　　　　　　　　　　**EXERCISE 12.67**

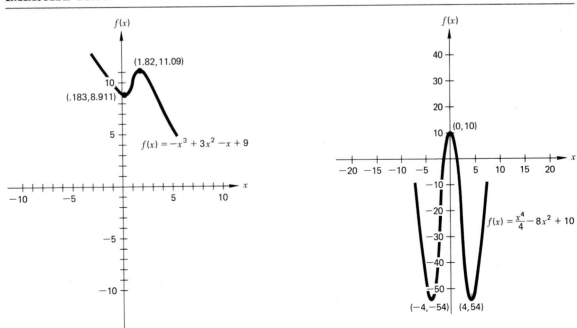

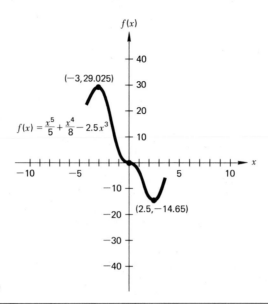

$$f(x) = \frac{x^5}{5} + \frac{x^4}{8} - 2.5x^3$$

(−3, 29.025)

(2.5, −14.65)

EXERCISE 12.69

b $x < 0$ if $a > 0$ and $x > 0$ if $a < 0$ **c** $x = 0$;   **77** up at $x = -1$ and $x = 0$;   **79** down at $x = -1$ and up at $x = 0$;   **81** down at $x = -1$, $f''(0)$ doesn't reveal concavity;   **83** down at $x = -1$ and $x = 0$;   **85** $(2, \frac{19}{3})$;   **87** none;   **89** $(0, 0)$, $(\frac{1}{3}, -\frac{1}{729})$;   **91** none;   **93** relative min. at $(\frac{5}{4}, -\frac{1}{8})$;   **95** relative min. at $(0, 0)$;   **97** relative max. at $(0, 4)$, relative min. at $(\frac{4}{3}, \frac{76}{27})$;   **99** relative min. at $(1, -\frac{1}{3})$, relative max. at $(-\frac{1}{5}, \frac{7}{9375})$, stat. infl. point at

EXERCISE 12.111   **EXERCISE 12.113**

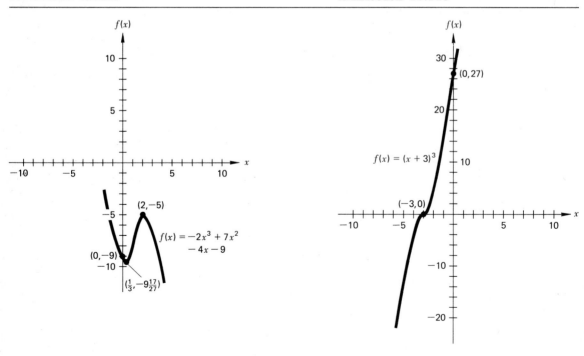

(2, −5)

$$f(x) = -2x^3 + 7x^2 - 4x - 9$$

(0, −9)

$(\frac{1}{3}, -9\frac{17}{27})$

(0, 27)

$$f(x) = (x + 3)^3$$

(−3, 0)

(0, 0); **101** none; **103** none; **105** max. at $(-1, 22)$, min. at $(1, 12)$; **107** max. at $(0, 0)$, min. at $(-2, -120\frac{4}{5})$; **109** max. at $(-1, 7.5)$, min. at $(-2, 4)$;

Chapter Test **1** $x < 4$; **2** see figure; **3** min. at $(7, -129\frac{2}{3})$, max. at $(-3, 37)$; **4** $x = \pm\sqrt{2}$; **5** max. at $(1, 1\frac{1}{6})$, min. at $(-1, -2\frac{1}{6})$; **6** see figure.

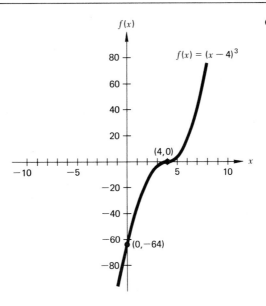

CHAP. 12 TEST: PROB. 2

Chapter 13

1 **a** \$17.50 **b** \$7,656.25; **3** **a** \$1.25 **b** \$2500 **c** 2000; **5** **a** 30 **b** \$900,600; **7** **a** 1000 **b** \$2,000,240; **9** **a** 1414.2 **b** \$5282.84 **c** \$7,470,935.70; **11** **a** \$7.85 **b** \$2,831,125; **13** **a** 50,000 **b** \$400 **c** \$7,300,000; **15** $R = 80q - .008q^2$, $q = 5000$, $R = \$2000$, $p = 40$; **17** **a** $q = 362.5$ **b** \$26,181.25; **19** **a** $q = 80,000$ **b** \$31,000,000; **21** **a** $q = 50,000$ **b** \$400 **c** 7,300,000; **23** $x = 100$, $y = 50$, A = 5000; **25** $x = 300$, $y = 200$, A = 60,000; **27** **a** 55 **b** \$450,000, 66.7%; **29** $t = 5$ days, \$41.075 million; **31** **a** 1000 hours **b** \$800 **c** \$200,000; **33** **a** 500 hundreds **b** \$1785.40 **c** \$89,270,000; **35** **a** 250 **b** \$919.5 thousands or \$919,500; **37** **a** $R = 100,000p - 12.5p^2$ **b** $p = \$4000$ **c** 50,000 units; **39** **a** $p = 300 - 2.5x$ **b** $0 \le x \le 120$ **c** $R = (100 + x)(300 - 2.5x)$ **d** 10 **e** \$30,250, **f** \$275.; **41** **a** 25,000 units **b** \$1100 **c** \$27,500,000; **43** **a** $P = -.1x^2 + 200x - 150$ **b** 1000 units **c** \$250,000 **d** \$150,150; **45** 10,000 by 10,000, 100,000,000 sq.ft.; **47** **a** $x = 86.6$, $y = 115.47$ **b** 146.6 by 195.47 **c** 28,655.9 ft²; **49** $\sqrt{40}$ and $\sqrt{40}$ or 6.32 and 6.32, sum equals 12.64; **51** $x = 33\frac{1}{3}$.

Chapter Test **1** $R = 50,000p - 7.5p^2$; **2** **a** $P = -5x^2 + 350x - 5000$ **b** $x = 35$ hundreds **c** \$1125 hundreds; **3** **a** 316.23' by 316.23' **b** \$12,649.20; **4** **a** $q = 200$ **b** \$50,200; **5** $N = 1,500,000 (1 - e^{-.06x}) - 5000x$.

CHAP. 12 TEST: PROB. 6

$f(x)$

$f(x) = (x - 4)^3$

80

60

40

20

(4, 0)

−10   −5   5   10 x

−20

−40

−60   (0, −64)

−80

Chapter 14

7 $f_x = -10x - 2y, f_y = 8y - 2x$; **9** $f_x = 20x^3 - 9yx^2 + 2y^2, f_y = -3x^3 + 4xy - 3y^2$; **11** $f_x = 8x(x^2 - 2y^2)^3, f_y = -16y(x^2 - 2y^2)^3$; **13** $f_x = e^{x+y}$, $f_y = e^{x+y}$; **15** $f_x = \dfrac{2x}{y^3}$, $f_y = -\dfrac{3x^2}{y^4}$; **17** $f_{xx} = 30y^2x, f_{yy} = 10x^3, f_{xy} = f_{yx} = 30x^2y$; **19** $f_{xx} = 6x/y^2, f_{yy} = \dfrac{6x^3}{y^4}, f_{xy} = f_{yx} = -\dfrac{6x^2}{y^3}$; **21** $f_{xx} = -\dfrac{1}{x^2}, f_{yy} = -\dfrac{1}{y^2}, f_{xy} = f_{yx} = 0$; **23** $f_{xx} = 960y^2x, f_{yy} = 320x^3 - 2x, f_{xy} = f_{yx} = 960x^2y - 2y$; **25 a** 0, **b** 8000, **c** actual = 8720, **d** -8000 est., -8930 actual; **27** $x = \frac{1}{2}, y = \frac{1}{2}$, min, $f(\frac{1}{2}, \frac{1}{2}) = -\frac{3}{4}$; **29** $x = 6, y = 10$, max, $f(6, 10) = 308$; **31** $x = 2, y = 1$, saddle pt., $f(2, 1) = 5$; **33** $x = 2, y = 3$, saddle pt., $f(2, 3) = -4$; **35** $x = \frac{1}{2}, y = -2$, min., $f(\frac{1}{2}, -2) = -44.5$; **37** $x = 16, y = 0$, max, $f(16, 0) = 2148$; $x = 0, y = 0$, saddle pt., $f(0, 0) = 100$; **39** $x = 0, y = 0$, saddle pt., $f(0, 0) = 0$; $x = 0, y = 4$, saddle pt., $f(0, 4) = 0$; $x = -2, y = 2$, min., $f(-2, 2) = -4$; **41 a** $x = 500, y = 0$, **b** \$2,500,000; **43** $x = 10, y = 6\frac{2}{3}$; **45** $x = 6\frac{2}{3}, y = 3\frac{1}{3}$; **47** $f_x = 16x^3y^4$, $f_y = 16x^4y^3$; **49** $f_x = 6xy + y^2, f_y = 3x^2 + 2xy - 2$; **51** $f_x = 2x^3 + 15x^2y^3 + 4xy + 4y, f_y = 15x^3y^2 + 2x^2 + 4x$; **53** $f_x = 3x^3\left(\dfrac{x^4}{4} - \dfrac{2y^5}{5}\right)^2, f_y = -6y^4\left(\dfrac{x^4}{4} - \dfrac{2y^5}{5}\right)^2$; **55** $f_x = e^x + e^{x+y}, f_y = e^{x+y}$; **57** $f_{xx} = 2y^4x^3, f_{yy} = \frac{6}{5}x^5y^2, f_{xy} = f_{yx} = 2x^4y^3$; **59** $f_{xx} = \dfrac{4}{y^2 + 2}, f_{yy} = \dfrac{4x^2(3y^2 - 2)}{(y^2 + 2)^3}, f_{xy} = f_{yx} = -\dfrac{8xy}{(y^2 + 2)^2}$; **61** $f_{xx} = 2\ln y, f_{yy} = -\dfrac{x^2}{y^2}, f_{xy} = f_{yx} = \dfrac{2x}{y}$; **63** $x = -2, y = -1$, min, $f(-2, -1) = -3$; **65** $x = -3, y = -8$, min, $f(-3, -8) = -43$; **67** $x = 0, y = 0$, saddle pt., $f(0, 0) = 15$; $x = -7, y = -14$, max, $f(-7, -14) = 186.5$; **69** $x = \frac{1}{2}, y = -\frac{1}{2}$, saddle pt., $f(\frac{1}{2}, -\frac{1}{2}) = \frac{3}{4}$; **71** $y = -5x + 7.5$

Chapter Test **1** instantaneous rate of change in $f(x, y)$ given that y is held constant, general tangent slope expression for family of traces parallel to the xz plane; **2** Geometric representation of $f(x, y)$ with one variable held constant; **3** $f_x = 15x^2 + 10xy, f_y = -8y + 5x^2$; **4** $f_{xx} = 80x^3 + 36x - 6y^2, f_{yy} = -6x^2, f_{xy} = f_{yx} = -12xy$; **5 a** $x = 1, y = 3.5$, min **b** -20.75; **6** 200 acres of soybeans, 100 acres of corn, \$200,000.

Chapter 15

1 $2.5x + C$; **3** $-\dfrac{3x^2}{2} + C$; **5** $\dfrac{x^3}{3} + C$; **7** $\dfrac{x^3}{6} + \dfrac{5x^2}{2} - 2x + C$; **9** $f(x) = 7.5x + 2.5$; **11** $f(x) = -\dfrac{x^2}{4} + 10$; **13** $f(x) = -\dfrac{x^3}{3} + x^2 + 12$; **15** $R = 40,000x - x^2$; **17** $P = -x^2 + 500x - 5000$; **19** $-50x + C$; **21** $\dfrac{x^2}{8} + C$; **23** $10x - 3x^2 + C$; **25** $\dfrac{x^5}{5} + C$; **27** $15x^{1/3} + C$; **29** $x + C$; **31** $\dfrac{ax^3}{3} + \dfrac{bx^2}{2} + cx + C$; **33** $\dfrac{(x^2 - 5)^4}{4} + C$; **35** $2\sqrt{2x^2 - 5} + C$; **37** $\frac{1}{40}(4x^4 -$

$16x)^{5/2} + C$; **39** $\left(\dfrac{x^2}{6} - 20\right)^6 /2 + C$; **41** $\dfrac{e^{5x}}{5} + C$; **43** $(\tfrac{1}{4})e^{2x^2-4x} + C$;

45 $\tfrac{1}{3} \ln (x^3 - 3x) + C$; **47** $\left(\dfrac{1}{m}\right) \ln (mx + b) + C$; **49** 7; **51** 50;

53 20.34; **55** $10\tfrac{2}{3}$; **57** -38; **59** $e^3 - 1$; **61** $\ln (2)$; **63** $\dfrac{8a}{3} + 2b + 2c$;

65 $\tfrac{875}{3}$; **67** 42; **69** 1248; **71** 54; **73 a** $\displaystyle\int_o^b g(x)\, dx - \int_a^b f(x)\, dx$

b $\displaystyle\int_o^a f(x)\, dx$ **c** $\displaystyle\int_a^b f(x)\, dx + \int_b^c g(x)\, dx$; **75** 24; **77 a** \$1900

b \$875; **79 b** 9 days **c** \$53,550 **d** \$24,300; **81 a** 195,200 **b** 9.4 hours; **83 b** $p = 5, q = 75$ **c** \$166.67; **85** approximately 4 days (4.02); **87 a** 4.234 billion tons/year **b** 29.79 billion tons; **89 a** 7 h/unit

b 68.026 h **d** min. of 5 h/unit; **91** $-xe^{-x} - e^{-x} + C$; **93** $\dfrac{3x(x + 1)^{4/3}}{4} -$

$\dfrac{9(x + 1)^{7/3}}{28} + C$; **95** $x^6/2 + C$; **97** $\left(\dfrac{x^2}{2} + 4x\right) \ln x - \dfrac{x^2}{4} - 4x + C$;

99 $\dfrac{x(x + 2)^5}{5} - \dfrac{(x + 2)^6}{30} + C$; **101** $2x(x - 3)^{1/2} - \tfrac{4}{3}(x - 3)^{3/2} + C$;

103 $\dfrac{-\ln x}{x} - \dfrac{1}{x} + C$; **105** $3x + C$; **107** $\dfrac{x^2}{4} + 2x + C$; **109** $\dfrac{5x^3}{3} +$

$\dfrac{x^2}{2} + 7x + C$; **111** $f(x) = 8x + 4$; **113** $f(x) = -\dfrac{x^4}{3} + \dfrac{x^3}{3} + x^2 + x + 1$;

115 $-12x + C$; **117** $-\dfrac{x^2}{2} + x + C$; **119** $\dfrac{x^2}{4} + 7x + C$; **121** $\dfrac{x^5}{25} +$

$\dfrac{3x^4}{4} - 5x + C$; **123** $(x + 3)^5/5 + C$; **125** $\dfrac{ax^5}{5} + \dfrac{bx^4}{4} + \dfrac{cx^3}{3} + \dfrac{dx^2}{2} +$

$ex + C$; **127** $\tfrac{4}{3}x^{3/4} + C$; **129** $\dfrac{x^3}{3} + 3e^x + 2x + C$; **131** $\dfrac{(x^2 + 1)^2}{2} + C$;

133 $\tfrac{1}{6}(2x^3 - x^2)^3 + C$; **135** $-\dfrac{1}{x^2} + \dfrac{1}{x} + C$; **137** $(\tfrac{1}{8})e^{8x} + 2x + C$;

139 $-\dfrac{1}{4(x^2 + 4)^2} + C$; **141** $44\tfrac{2}{3}$; **143** 1; **145** -2; **147** $1 - \dfrac{1}{e^{27}}$;

149 $\ln 20 - \ln 5$; **151** $\dfrac{(e^{23} - e^{-1})}{6}$; **153** $\tfrac{5}{3}$; **155** $\tfrac{1}{4}$; **157** 319.455 bil-

lion barrels; **159 a** 137,200 units/year **b** 1,294,833.2;

161 $\left(\dfrac{x^2}{2} + 4x\right) \ln x - \dfrac{x^2}{4} - 4x + C$; **163** $-e^{-x} - e^{-x}(x + 5) + C$.

Chapter Test **1** $f(x) = x^4 - x^2 - 10x - 450$; **2 a** $-3/2x^{2/3} + C$
b $\dfrac{(x^4 - 10)^8}{32} + C$ **c** $-\tfrac{1}{10}e^{-10x} + C$; **3** 4/3; **4 a** see figure **b** 26 2/3;
5 a \$248/year **b** \$432.

Chapter 16

1 120; **3** 30,240; **5** 120; **7** $8! = 40,320$; **9** 15; **11** $10 \cdot 9 \cdot 8 = 720$;
13 a 0.6 **b** 0.4 **c** 0.025 **d** .15; **15** 0.714, 2 to 5; **17 a** 0.80
b 0.75 **c** 0.55; **19 a** 0.35 **b** 0.50 **c** 0.65; **21 a** 0.8464 **b** 0.005888

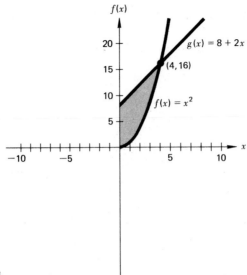

CHAP. 15 TEST: PROB. 4a

c 0.659; **23** 0.288; **25 a** 0.19 **b** 0.3 **c** 0.625 **d** 0.267 **e** 0.056;
29 a 2.3 **b** 1.45 **c** 0.40; **31** $1.00; **33 b** stock 11 **c** $84.00;
35 stock 23 units; exp. payoff = $66.00; **37** a, c, and g are variables in a
Bernoulli process; **39** $\frac{5}{324}$, $\frac{625}{1296}$; **41** P($x = 0$) = 0.0000003125, P($x = 1$) =
0.0000296875, P($x = 2$) = 0.0011281250, P($x = 3$) = 0.0214343750,
P($x = 4$) = 0.2036265625, P($x = 5$) = 0.7737809375; **43** 0.1718;
45 .10737418, 0.205065; **47** $\mu = 2$, $\sigma = 1.265$; **49 a** 0.1587 **b** 0.8849
c 0.198 **d** 0.8197; **51 a** 0.6915 **b** 0.9332 **c** 0.6687 **d** 0.1498;
53 0.00135; **55** 0.7745; **57** 0.2743, 0.1841; **59** 0.838; **61** 70;
63 a $\frac{8}{52}$ **b** $\frac{28}{52}$; **65 a** 0.027 **b** 0.343 **c** 0.189; **67** $\mu = 250$,
$\sigma = 111.80$; **69** $2035, $15 higher; **71** 16807; **73** $\mu = 900$, $\sigma = 24$;
75 a 0.0228 **b** 0.6687 **c** 0.00135; **77** $\frac{100}{256} = 0.391$

Chapter Test **2 a** 120 **b** 20; **3** $\frac{24}{132,600}$; **4 a** $\frac{12}{26}$ **b** $\frac{18}{34}$; **5 a**

Stock Action

		6	7	8	9	10
	6	12	9	6	3	0
	7	12	14	11	8	5
Demand	8	12	14	16	13	10
	9	12	14	16	18	15
	10	12	14	16	18	20

b stock 7 **c** $12.50; **6** 0.234375; **7 a** 0.4207 **b** 0.1078

INDEX